January 18, 1999

What do I consider my most important Contributions?

- That I early on—almost sixty years ago—realized that MANAGEMENT has become the constitutive organ and function of the <u>Society of Organizations</u> ;

- That MANAGEMENT is not "Business Management- though it first attained attention in business- but the governing organ of ALL institutions of Modern Society;

- That I established the study of MANAGEMENT as a DISCIPLINE in its own right;

and

- That I focused this discipline on People and Power; on Values; Structure and Constitution; AND ABOVE ALL ON RESPONSIBILITIES- that is focused the <u>Discipline of Management</u> on Management as a truly LIBERAL ART.

Peter F. Drucker

我认为我最重要的贡献是什么？

- 早在60年前，我就认识到管理已经成为组织社会的基本器官和功能；

- 管理不仅是"企业管理"，而且是所有现代社会机构的管理器官，尽管管理一开始就将注意力放在企业上；

- 我创建了管理这门学科；

- 我围绕着人与权力、价值观、结构和方式来研究这一学科，尤其是围绕着责任。管理学科是把管理当作一门真正的综合艺术。

彼得·德鲁克
1999年1月18日

注： 资料原件打印在德鲁克先生的私人信笺上，并有德鲁克先生亲笔签名，现藏于美国德鲁克档案馆。为纪念德鲁克先生，本书特收录这一珍贵资料。本资料由德鲁克管理学专家那国毅教授提供。

彼得·德鲁克和妻子多丽丝·德鲁克

德鲁克妻子多丽丝寄语中国读者

在此谨向广大的中国读者致以我诚挚的问候。本书深入介绍了德鲁克在管理领域方面的多种理念和见解。我相信他的管理思想得以在中国广泛应用，将有赖出版及持续的教育工作，令更多人受惠于他的馈赠。

盼望本书可以激发各位对构建一个令人憧憬的美好社会的希望，并推动大家在这一过程中积极发挥领导作用，他的在天之灵定会备感欣慰。

Doris Drucker

本页照片和多丽丝寄语原文与亲笔签名由彼得·德鲁克管理学院提供

创新与企业家精神

中英文双语版

INNOVATION AND ENTREPRENEURSHIP PRACTICE AND PRINCIPLES

[美] 彼得·德鲁克 著

魏江
陈侠飞 译

机械工业出版社
China Machine Press

图书在版编目（CIP）数据

创新与企业家精神（中英文双语版）/（美）彼得·德鲁克（Peter F. Drucker）著；
魏江，陈侠飞译. -- 北京：机械工业出版社，2021.6
书名原文：Innovation and Entrepreneurship: Practice and Principles
ISBN 978-7-111-68197-7

I. ①创… II. ①彼… ②魏… ③陈… III. ①企业管理 - 汉、英 IV. ①F272

中国版本图书馆 CIP 数据核字（2021）第 093443 号

本书版权登记号：图字 01-2006-4270

本书两面插页所用资料由彼得·德鲁克管理学院和那国毅教授提供。封面中签名摘自德鲁克先生为彼得·德鲁克管理学院的题词。

创新与企业家精神（中英文双语版）

出版发行：机械工业出版社（北京市西城区百万庄大街 22 号 邮政编码：100037）

责任编辑：赵陈碑　　　　　　　　　　　　　　责任校对：殷　虹

印　　刷：北京诚信伟业印刷有限公司　　　　　版　　次：2021 年 6 月第 1 版第 1 次印刷

开　　本：170mm×230mm　1/16　　　　　　　印　　张：34.5

书　　号：ISBN 978-7-111-68197-7　　　　　　定　　价：109.00 元

客服电话：（010）88361066　88379833　68326294　　投稿热线：（010）88379007
华章网站：www.hzbook.com　　　　　　　　　　　读者信箱：hzjg@hzbook.com

本书法律顾问：北京大成律师事务所　韩光/邹晓东

　　如果您喜欢彼得·德鲁克（Peter F. Drucker）或者他的书籍，那么请您尊重德鲁克。不要购买盗版图书，以及以德鲁克名义编纂的伪书。

| 目　录 |

创新需转化为行动及结果

2002 年，英国《经济学人》曾宣告说"偶像的黄昏"来了，它是对的，从此许多人也认为我们不再需要偶像。但是，四年之后，我们强烈地发现，我们还是需要偶像，需要具有超凡能力的新的商业领袖。正当我们无法界定所需要的新的商业领袖具有什么样的特质之时，彼得·德鲁克先生 1985 年写就的《创新与企业家精神》给了我们一个很好的视角，让我们能够寻求真正意义上的新的商业领袖。

在商业史上，拥有远见的企业家早已提出过零星的创新性思维，甚至我们可以这样认为，经济繁荣与社会发展正是企业家创新性思维转化为行动的结果，正如德鲁克先生书中所言：本书认为在过去的 10～15 年间，在美国出现的真正的企业家经济是现代经济和社会史上最具深远意义和最鼓舞人心的事件。这种现象本身引发了德鲁克先生的思考：什么是创新与企业家精神？何时以及为什么进行创新与企业家精神的实践？

事实上，商业本身已经进入了一个自我探索、理论和实践结合的领域，德鲁克先生提出创新和企业家精神是为了探讨人们的行动和行为。在过去的几十年中，复杂的理论、严谨的分析不断启发人们对这一问题的辩论和研究，与人们一样，德鲁克先生坚信创新与企业家精神的重要性，以此为前提，他更注重于创新与企业家精神的实践。事实上，他将创新与企业家精神视为企业高层管理者的工作重点的一部分。这是德鲁克先生的着眼点。

创新是实践的创新。德鲁克先生在本书中告诉人们："创新是一门有目的的学科。"所以在本书中，他首先向读者展示了企业家应该在哪里以及如何寻找创新机遇，随后又探讨了将创意发展成为可行的事业或服务所需注意的原则和禁忌。在这部分的分析中，德鲁克先生认为：创新是企业家特有的工具。他们凭借创新，将变化看作开创另一个企业或服务的机遇。创新可以成为一门学科，供人学习和实践。企业家必须有目的地寻找创新机会源，寻找能够预示成功创新机会的变化和征兆。他们还应该了解成功创新的原理，并加以应用。我想到一个例子：孟加拉国经济学家尤努斯，他创造性缔造的"微贷"事业正在以成功的商业运作在全世界范围内消灭贫困。2006 年，尤努斯的项目已经遍及 100 个国家，累计为 400 万穷人放贷 53 亿美元。2004 年，尤努斯甚至向 26 000 位乞丐放贷，每人 9 美元，这笔钱可以让一个乞丐开始贩卖糖果等小生意，而不是沿街乞讨。2005 年，尤努斯被评为 1979 年以来全球最具影响力的 25 位经济领袖之一。尤努斯的创新实践正是德鲁克先生理论的一个全新例证。

企业家精神是创新实践的精神。如何成功地培育出企业家精神，是德鲁克先生重点讨论的第二个问题。德鲁克先生从现有企业、公共服务机构以及新创企业三个方面来讨论企业家管理。这三类组织也正好涵盖了目前我们能够理解的所有组织机构的特性，现有企业会更多地从商业角度出发，注重那些与企业息息相关的社会问题，对于社会问题的长期关注，可能会从根本上重新定义"公司"的根本目的。公共服务机构更多是从社会问题本身出发，将企业的管理技能运用到社会目标的实现上，它们通常具有更强大的道德力量。

最后是新创企业。一如其在所有主要的企业家时期所表现的一样，新创企业将继续成为创新的主要载体。托马斯·爱迪生说过："如果所有人都能真正做到力所能及的事情，结果会使我们自己震惊。"

企业家战略是创新市场的战略。如何成功地将一项创新引入市场是企业家战略的核心。德鲁克先生告诫我们：创新是否成功不在于它是否新颖、巧妙或具有科学内涵，而在于它是否能够赢得市场。不具有创新市场的能力就会被远远地抛在后面，这是人们的共识。但问题的关键不在于是否理解，而在于别人已经开始运用全新商业理念的时候，我们却处于被动的状态，因此在判断是否具有创新能力时，我们需要看到的是用什么样的方式进入市场。

德鲁克先生在本书结论部分中探讨了创业型社会的问题，虽然他是从福利社会的困境出发，提出创业型社会的概念，但结论如何并不重要，重要的是德鲁克先生明确了创新在各个领域中的作用，只有发挥创新的功效，才有社会的发展。

这是一本基于创新但又强调行动的书，这一点正是本书最为精华的地方。如果创新停留在观念、思想和制度上，如果创新没有转化为行动和结果，就没有任何价值和意义。而企业家的本质就是实践，所以，我们需要静下来，评判一下我们与德鲁克先生所倡导的有着多大差距，或者我们可以对照德鲁克先生的观点想一想：我们是否做到了让创新转化为行动及结果？如果好好地深读这本书，我们一定能够做到这一点，进而成为真正意义上的商业领袖。

陈春花

北京大学王宽诚讲席教授、国家发展研究院 BiMBA 商学院院长、

华南理工大学工商管理学院教授、新华都商学院理事长、

新加坡国立大学商学院客座教授

本来我认为在德鲁克先生的众多著作中,《创新与企业家精神》是我唯一有资格写序的一本书,因为在过去十多年里我不仅读过很多遍,而且以此为教材,培训过几班职业经理人。但这次重读时我才发现,事情并非我原以为的那么简单。对有关主题该说的话德鲁克在书中几乎都写了,我当然不可能比他写得更好,而且从"序言""引言"直至"结论",全书结构严谨,没有给另一篇序言留下任何机会。所以这里我写的并不是序言,而是一篇读后感,如果按我的意见,我宁可它出现在书末而不是书首,仅供读完全书仍有耐心的读者参阅。

什么是"创新"

"创新"这个字眼在今天很流行,也很时髦,许多机构都把它当作口号,甚至写进自己的宣言,但是对它的理解却是千差万别的。首先,把"创新"与聪明的创意或发明混为一谈;其次,一提到它就意会到科技方面;最后,很多人认为凡开创一项新生意或者新事业就是创新。

德鲁克深刻地指出,"创新"与上述误解的区别在于是否为客户创造出新的价值。什么是价值?价值并不是价格。价值是客户得到的,价格是客户付出的。做企业的，推出一项新产品、新服务或新流程，要满足客户未被满足的需求或潜在的需求，创造出新的客户满意。客户有新的所得，才会从不买到买、从买得少到买得多，或者愿意付出比过去更高的价格。这反映在企业的收入和利润上，就是创造了新的财富。同样，非营利机构的创新也要让服务对象有新的满意度，从而愿意接受你的服务；政府的政策创新或体制改革也要产生让人民可以感受得到的新便利或保障。虽然很多"创新"与科技有关，但是科技含量很低甚至"零科技"的社会创新，不但机会更多，而且效益更大。一家新公司如果只是以同等价格提供市面上已有的产品或服务并不算创新，因为它只是对别人已经创造出来的客户群进行瓜分，并没有创造新客户，这样的新公司注定会在市场萎缩的时候被"边缘化"。

创新是可以学会的

在德鲁克的笔下，无论政治、经济、科技、文化，无论是历史悠久的大企业还是新开办的小企业，无论是企业界还是非营利机构和政府组织，处处都有创新的机会，人人都可以成为企业家。他认为创新是组织的一项基本功能，是管理者的一项重要职责，它是有规律可循的实务工作。创新并不需要天才，但需要训练；不需要灵光乍现，但需要遵守"纪律"（创新的原则和条件）。因此，创新是可以作为一门学科去传授和学习的，只要照书中所总结的规则去操作，就可以学会如何成功地创新。这打破了以往创新给人的神秘感。但是，在大家同样都认真阅读了本书，或者上过同一个创新课程之后，为什么总是只有为数不多的人实行了创新呢？

养成正确的心态

德鲁克的回答是：首先，必须不惧怕任何变化，不对外部和内部的改变产生反感。企业家总是把变化当作正常的、健康的事物，张开双臂去欢迎它，并主动从中寻找创新的机会。仅仅懂得创新的原理和规则是不够的，必须养成这样的心态。工作和生活中经常会出现不协调、不一致的现象，成功或失败、灾难或惊喜，处在一个大的经济和社会转型时期更是这样。身处其中的人，是抱怨它，力图保留原来的生活方式和工作方式，还是把它当作契机，观察它、理解它、利用它？在书中德鲁克把"系统地放弃"列为一个组织实行创业管理的头等重要的制度，具有警示的作用。因为是否能执行这一制度，是对每一个管理者，尤其是首席执行官的严峻考验。

我曾在几年前应邀为一家大型海洋渔业公司做"领导变革"的培训，这家企业的总经理是一位很有魄力的成功企业家，他很重视这次培训，召集了全公司中层以上的管理者五六十人参加。在讨论到公司目前的各项业务到底有哪些应该放弃时，有人大胆地提出，鉴于世界性的外部环境的变化，最应该放弃的正是目前公司的核心业务之一传统的远洋捕捞业务。这引起了与会者的一场激辩。培训结束后我和这位总经理促膝长谈，他认为开展渔产品深加工和营销方面的创新项目都是可行的，但若放弃远洋捕捞，公司的上百条渔轮、上万名从事远洋捕捞的员工怎么办？而且这样一来，他的企业也就不是一家"海洋渔业公司"了。以后三年，这位总经理为了挽救远洋捕捞，把公司最好的人才包括他本人的大量精力都投放在那上面，又贷款购置技术装备更先进的新船，但公司绩效却每况愈下。最近我听说，该公司所属的集团总部已做出决定，对公司进行重组或出售，而在公司内部，总经理把这两年的亏损归罪于"油价高涨"。

在这个实例中，我们可以看到一位对企业、对员工很有责任心和做出很大承诺的领导人，但是他错误地把这一承诺当成了对现有业务和现有商业模式的承诺。套用一句成语，这是一种"妇人之仁"，最后的结果表明，他的决策无论对员工、对企业其实都是不负责任的。

著名的投资大师沃伦·巴菲特在他的经验之谈中，曾经检讨了自己过迟退出纺织业的类似错误，他把使人们本能地恐惧和抗拒改变的影响力，称之为"强制性力量"，他本人是花了超过十年时间，付出了重大代价，才学会如何摆脱这种"强制性力量"。可见对任何管理者来说，养成一个企业家的正确心态，都是知易行难的。但是这个基本的心态转变问题，对创新者来说，却又是不能不重视、不能不解决的。

使组织成为"企业家"

历史上有很多杰出的企业家（或创业者），一手创办了生机勃勃的企业王国，他们成功了。但是在第一代企业家离开之后，企业却走向平淡无奇，甚至衰败。反观像宝洁、3M 这样的公司，尽管历史悠久，却一直推陈出新，引领行业发展的方向。究其原因，是它们并不依赖一两个单打独斗的个人企业家，而是经年累月在组织内部建立起一套创新管理机制，德鲁克称之为"创业管理"，他又把宝洁、3M 这类公司称为"创业型企业"或者"企业家型企业"。本书的第二部分集中阐述了"创业管理"独特的政策、措施、组织结构、人事安排和财务预算。德鲁克在这部分中所讲的"管理"，在流行的管理教科书或商学院的 MBA 课程中是见不到的。市面上一些畅销的管理书籍，包括某些"大师"的著作偶有涉及对创新或创业活动的管理，至多也是东一点西一片，不像 20 多年前德鲁克这本书阐述得那么精辟和系统。作为一位高层管理者，尤其是第一代白手起家的成功企业家，如果我们能认识这套"创业管理"工具的价值，肯运用它们去把自己的组织打造成一个"创业型企业"，那么即使有一天我们不在了，组织仍然可以自动持续创新，成为时下人们所推崇的"永续经营"的企业。

创新与经济发展和社会发展

创新固然可以令一个企业成功并赢得财富，但是它的意义不仅限于此。在本书"引言"中，德鲁克剖析了创新及企业家是如何有效地创造了就业机会，也创造了 GDP，从而打破了苏联著名经济学家康德拉季耶夫的"经济发展过程必然出现周期性的经济危机"的论断。在德鲁克看来，是成千上万企业家的创新活动避免了经济大衰退，而不是美国联邦储备局或者任何一国的政府。所以，创新是唯一能造就一个持续和健康发展的经济（使经济不在发展过程中"休克"）的工具。

在本书的"结论"中，德鲁克把创新引申到他一生最关注的主题——社会的健康发展上。凡深入阅读过德鲁克著作的人都知道，他一贯把推动一个国家、一个社会进步，同时又避免使用破坏性手段的希望，寄托在千千万万个有效运转的组织和它们的领导人身上，这些组织其实也包括了政府机构。

在"结论"中，他具体地提出了政府机构如何扮演"企业家"的角色，以及进行哪些方面的政策创新的建议。他的建议无疑切中要害。但是这最后的"结论"最重大的意义，并不是这些具体的建议，而是他关于"我们需要的是一个创业型社会"的论断。走笔至此，我不得不引述他以下的精彩论述，虽然是重复："首先，创新与企业家精神并非对现有事物'连根拔除'，而是'循序渐进'地推出新产品，随后制定一项新策略，进而改善公共服务。其次，它们并不是事先计划好的，而是专注于机会和需求。最后，它们是试探性的。如果不能实现预期，它们就会消失。换句话说，它们是务实的而非武断的，是谦虚的而非浮夸的。创新与企业家精神可以使社会、经济、产业、公共服务或企业保持灵活性，并自我更新。无须通过流血、内战、集中营和经济危机的方式，创新与企业家精神就可以在有目的、有方向、可控的情况下，实现杰斐逊希望通过革命达到的目标。"社会变革方面的创新"不会随'暴风雨'降临，而是如微风般悄然而至"。请注意，德鲁克在这里是把通过强权、战争、暴力、群众运动和"革命"（20 世纪最时髦的词）这类试图一次性简单化解决社会问题的方式，作为创新的对立面明确地予以否定的。

关于"自主创新"

中国在过去几十年的改革开放中，经济得到了长足发展，随着全球化和加入 WTO，中国也面临着越来越激烈的竞争。有鉴于此，政府提出"自主创新"的口号，希望中国的企业不再停留在引进和模仿国外的先进产品和技术上，中国的企业要以自己独创的科技产品，成为世界范围内某些行业和领域中的领导者和标准制定者。其用心是良好的，但这种提法却值得商榷。

首先，创新从其本质而言都是自主的。创新者或者说企业家都是一些独立自主、不等待高层指令的人，他们因为接触具体事件，随机而发才能捕捉到创新的机会，按照指令和"规划"去创新而能取得成果者稀少，即使取得所谓的"成果"，所投入的资源也将是惊人的浪费。在书中德鲁克批评了法国、德国和英国向"高科技创业"倾斜的国策，说这是对创新（包括科技创新）的一种误解（我猜这也是为什么相对于美国，欧洲反而没有出现创业型经济的原因）。他举了法国投入巨资研发协和式飞机的例子，这种所谓"创新"其实只是追求表面风光的虚荣，其结果并没有产生商业用途，也没有增加就业机会，反而带来大笔财政赤字。

其次，创新必须把力量放在自己的长处上。在这一点上日本曾经做出很好的示范。日本在 20 世纪后半叶崛起为世界第二大工业强国，并没有走高科技自主创新的道路，相反它的策略是"创造性模仿"或"创业柔道"。日本在科技方面没有多少原创，而是在别人尤其是美国人的原创上加以改进，然后通过市场创新去打败原创者，从书中德鲁克所举的索尼和精工的例子即可见一斑。

我在前边已经提到，德鲁克一贯强调，没有科技含量的社会创新或市场创新比起科技创新，不但更容易发现机会，而且工作周期更短、效益更大；而基于新知识，尤其是高科技方面的创新，时间跨度大、风险高、成功概率小。不错，高科技创新一旦成功可以名利双收，但是既然我们只为追求实效，就不应该刻意规划，也不应该引导国家和企业界把资源倾斜到"自主（科技）创新"这一方面。如果政府要引导，更重要的倒是出台一些政策，去鼓励形成一个中国的"创业型经济"——诚如德鲁克所言：没有刀（创业型经济），哪有刀刃（高科技创新）？

永不枯竭的创新动力

和许多人想象的相反，创新并不是有趣的、风光的事，而是艰苦的、枯燥的、令人沮丧的工作。所以，经常会有人问到这个问题：那些企业家（包括作为组织的"企业家"——创业型企业）为什么会热衷于创新？特别是在他们已经功成名就之后，为什么还会一再地推陈出新？

很可惜在本书中，德鲁克对这个问题着墨不多。但在第2章中仍有一句话透露出他的看法："不论出于何种动机，如金钱、权力、好奇心，或名誉及他人的认可，成功的企业家总是希望能够创造价值、做出贡献。"在第11章中他又写道："……创新也需要'性情相投'。若非真正热爱，企业很难有优异的表现……对创新者而言，这个创新机会必须是重要的、有意义的。否则，他们很难持续投入到成功创新所必需的艰苦且困难重重的工作中。"

上述见解不仅是德鲁克对他人的观察所得，也是他本人的切身体验。

20世纪最伟大的创新之一是现代管理学的诞生，而创新者正是德鲁克。从20世纪40年代初到2005年年末去世，他为此持之以恒地工作了65年。他通过写作、做咨询顾问以及教学去研究和推广管理学不辍，而他最擅长，也最主要的工作是写作。2001年夏天他92岁时动过切除癌细胞的手术，这之后在最后的岁月里，他还写作和出版了《下一个社会的管理》和《功能社会》这两部重要著作，并和他的同事合作，编辑了《德鲁克日志》和《卓有成效管理者的实践》。在他去世前三个星期，那段时间他已是昏睡多于清醒，在最后一次醒来后，他对太太多丽丝说了一句心有不甘的话："看来我是再也不能写了……"之后就陷入了永久的昏迷。在他去世后，一次多丽丝和我以及几位同事谈及他的生平往事，令我联想到他在自己的回忆录《旁观者》中流露出的对人类和社会环境的忧患、热忱和关怀。最后多丽丝说了一句话作为对他一生的概括："彼得永远在写，他热爱写作，**但他从不为了使自己重要而写。**"

这是所有伟大的创新者或企业家的真实写照。为名、为利、为权、为自己，这些人类的欲望固然可以激发一时的创业热情，但不能持久，在他们达到预期的目标后，往往会停顿下来。许多企业家成功之后转入"守业"就是这个原因。但是如果你有一个远大的目标是超越个人和组织的需求，在个人和组织以外，即使穷个人一生的精力、组织的全部资源也无法真正达成时，你就会获得永不枯竭的创新动力，这种动力会推动你去做不足为外人道的艰苦工作。我曾参加过一次德鲁克基金会组织的圆桌会议，席间有人问德鲁克："如果要你用一句话描述一下企业家的特征，你会说什么？"德鲁克答道："企业家就是那些愿意过不舒服的日子，或者说不愿意过舒服日子的人。"我想他不会反对我为他补充一句："为了一个值得他们那样去做的目标。"

小结

关于"创新和企业家精神"的话题如果继续展开，会涉及德鲁克数十部著作中的多数重要观点——而本来它们之间就存在着内在关联，不论从现实还是从逻辑角度来看。例如，创新需要"分权自治"，只有"分权自治"才能释放出组织中每一个部门、每一个分支的创新活力；创新同样需要"目标管理与自我控制"，个人只有在他本人参与制定和认同的目标下，自主地做出决定，运用所长，采取行动，并憧憬和一步一步地看到预期结果的出现，他才会享受工作，得到乐趣——或者说以苦为乐。本文围绕的是创新的主题，但是如果它能引起读者对德鲁克著作的进一步学习、探讨和应用，那将是我最大的荣幸。

邵明路

彼得·德鲁克管理学院创办人

堪称史上最为经典的"创新实务与创业策略"

有目的的创新、创业策略及创业管理三者同等重要，三者综合，就组成了《创新与企业家精神》一书的经典内涵和实务。这是史上罕见的将"创新与企业家精神"系统化的伟大作品。

中国是一个极为典型的"创业型社会"，紧接着必须迈入"管理型社会"，为此，将面临"管理能力"的极大挑战，更遭遇"知识工作者"个人与总体生产力的严峻考验。但这与德鲁克所指出的主张有些不同，因为他认为全球经济已由"管理型经济体系"彻底转变为"创业型经济体系"了。可是就本质来讲，所面对的挑战和考验并没有什么不同，只是顺序上不同而已。

德鲁克所主张的"创新"，其实指的是"集体的创新"，而不是"个别的创意"，是产业的变革与社会的重大改变，它是社会性和经济性的用语，而不是科技性和技术性的名词。"创新"是创业家或企业家的特殊工具，他们凭借创新，将变革当作开创另一事业或服务的大好机会。"创新"是可以加以训练、可以学习和可以实地运营的。然而创业家或企业家必须有目的地寻找"创新"的来源、发现变革以及成功创新机会的征兆。他们也必须了解成功创新的原则，并加以运用。

《创新与企业家精神》一书不仅是实务的综合，更是企业经营成功的范本。该书有目的、有条理、有系统地将上百个成功的实务案例，通过动态系统的思考和剖析，呈现了极具启发性与参考性的价值。不仅对高科技企业适用，对一般企业甚至于农业专业化、现代化、精致化、休闲化来说，都是值得一读再读的经典作品。因为他指出一个"可能的最好方式"可以创造一个既和谐又繁荣的社会。

德鲁克对创新的分类有三：①产品的创新——产品或服务的创新；②管理的创新——制造产品与服务，并且将它们上市销售所需要的各种技能与活动的创新；③社会的创新——市场、消费者行为和价值的创新。

分别举例说明：发明多达1900多种不同的电力与照明周边产品的发明大王爱迪生，其实并非唯一发明电灯泡的人，有一位英国物理学家斯旺，与爱迪生同时发明了电灯泡。就技术来说，斯旺的电灯泡比爱迪生的要好，于是爱迪生买下了斯旺的专利特许权，并将其应用在自己的灯泡工厂里。但是，爱迪生不仅详细思考技术上的要求，还思考了他的关注重点，甚至在开始进行玻璃外壳、真空状态、发热纤维板等技术性工作之前，他就已经决定了一个"系统"，他的电灯泡是为了适应电力公司使用而设计的。他甚至已经安排好融资，安排好供电给电灯泡客户的接线专利，也安排好配销系统。斯旺是一名科学家，他只是发明了一个产品。然而，爱迪生却创造了一个产业。因此，爱迪生能够销售并安装电力设备，而斯旺却还在那边苦思，试图找出可能会对他的科学成就感兴趣的人。

然而爱迪生不肯就此罢手，他渴望成为一位成功的商人和大公司的老板。他应该能获得成功，因为他是一位极佳的事业规划者。他确实知道电力公司必然采用他所发明的电灯泡，也确实知道如何为他的新事业筹集所需的资金。当他推出产品后，立即获得成功，而且需求源源而来。但是，爱迪生仍然维持其创业家的身份，或者应该这样说，他以为"管理"就是当老板。为此，他拒绝建立高层经营团队。因此，当公司步入中型规模之后，他所拥有的四五家公司都遭遇惨重的失败。最后这些公司只好逼退爱迪生，代之以专业管理人才，才挽救了公司。而这些公司后来组建成为现在大名鼎鼎的通用电气公司。

总的来说，爱迪生发明了电灯泡产品，让世界因此光明了。爱迪生建立了一套系统产业，服务了全世界。为此，爱迪生创新了产品与服务，是一个典型的成功案例。就创业策略来说，他也做到了，只不过在创业管理上，他彻底失败。

因为新事业的创业管理需要具备四个要件：①需要以市场为重心；②需要一个前瞻性的财务计划，特别是现金流量和未来资金需求的规划；③建立一个最高管理团队；④创始事业的创业家必须设定自己的角色、工作范围，以及工作、角色的关系（爱迪生即败在后两项）。

更重要的是创业管理需制定"政策"与"实务"：①企业必须接受创新，并视改变为机会，而非威胁；②企业必须通过有系统的衡量尺度，同时必须培养有系统的学习能力，以改善公司现有的成就；③创业管理必须明确制定出企业结构、任用与管理、津贴、激励及奖励等实施办法；④在创业管理中，存在若干禁忌，即不该做的事。

全球已拥有三万多家分店的成功快餐连锁集团——麦当劳，连三岁的小婴儿看到拱形 M 字母都会发自内心地露出喜爱的微笑，这足以证明它的成功是无处不在的。

然而，这故事要从麦当劳的创始人雷·克罗克说起：起初他推销奶昔制造机给汉堡贩卖店，他注意到其中有一个客户——一家位于加州小镇的汉堡店，购买数倍于其店址与规模正常需要的机器。他对这种现象加以调研，发现有个老年人通过将快餐作业加以系统化创新，改变了快餐业的运营方式。于是，克罗克买下了他的设备，并基于原始拥有者的意外成功，将它建构成一个如今数百亿美元级的大企业。

麦当劳所展现出来的就是"创业精神"或"企业家精神"。确切地说，麦当劳并没有发明任何新东西，任何一家美国的高级餐厅老早就开始供应它的最终产品了。但是，通过应用"管理的概念和技术"（思考顾客所重视的价值），使产品标准化、规格化，设计流程与操作工具，以及分析工作流程与结果并设定标准，并依据该标准培训员工，麦当劳不但大幅提高了"资源的产出"，而且开创了一个新市场和新顾客阶层，这就是创业精神，也是企业家精神的精髓所在。

克罗克直到八十多岁过世，一直担任该公司的董事长。但是他建立了一个最高的管理团队，使它经营公司的全盘业务，同时还任命自己为公司的"营销良心"。一直到去世前，他每周访问两三家麦当劳连锁店，检查它们的产品品质、清洁卫生程度以及服务是否亲切友善。更重要的是，他观察来到店里的顾客，和他们交谈，并倾听他们的意见。这使得公司能做出必要的改变，并维持它在快餐界的领导地位。

迪士尼公司的迪斯尼与麦当劳的克罗克，都是受人尊敬的企业创始人。他们都有丰富的想象力以及自我驱策力，并富于创造力、创业精神（或企业家精神）与创新的思想。他们积极参与公司的例行性业务，并负起公司的创业责任。他们都依赖本人的"创业家性格"，而并未将企业家精神根植于明确的政策与实务当中。两人辞世后没有几年，他们的公司就变得懒散、缅怀过去、胆小且较保守。

至于那些建立创业管理的企业——GE、宝洁、强生——尽管CEO屡经更替，经济环境屡遭变迁，10年、20年、30年……过去了，它们仍然拥有创新与创业的领导地位。

为此，培养接班人制度与维持不断的创新和企业家精神，才是永续经营之道。建立创业管理的企业创新，乃属于"管理的创新"，是值得企业界认真学习的。

再来看看社会的创新。在19世纪早期，美国的农民事实上没有什么购买力，没有能力购买农业机械。当时，虽然市场上已经出现许多收割机器，但不论农民多么渴望获得它们，却没有钱购买。后来，收割机的发明者之一麦考密克发明了"分期付款"制度，这种方式使得农民能够以未来的收入购买收割机，不必靠过去的储蓄。于是，突然之间，农民就有了购买农业机械的"购买力"了。

麦考密克是第一位清楚地将"营销"看作企业特有核心功能的人，他认为管理的特殊任务在于"创造顾客"。史书往往只提到麦考密克发明了收割机，其实他也发明了现代营销的基本工具，如市场研究与市场分析、定位的观念、现代定价政策、以服务作为商品的推销员、为客户提供零件与服务、分期付款的观念。他是真正的企业管理之父（德鲁克则是管理学教父），而且早在 1850 年之前，他就已达成上述成就。但直到 50 年后，美国人才普遍效仿他的榜样。"分期付款"是市场、消费者行为和价值的创新，这说明麦考密克做了"社会的创新"。

"创新"是指系统化创新，德鲁克具有创见地提出了创新的"七大机会源"，前四项来源存在于企业内部（或组织内部），后三项则发生于企业或产业外部的改变：①意外事件——意外的成功、意外的失败；②不协调事件——实际状况与预期状况之间不一致；③基于流程需求的创新；④产业和市场结构上的改变；⑤人口统计数据；⑥认知、情绪以及意义上的改变；⑦新知识——包括科学与非科学的。

这七个创新机会源的界线相当模糊，而且彼此之间有相当大的重叠部分。它们可以被比拟为位于同一个建筑物不同方位的七扇窗户，每扇窗户所显现的某些景色，都可以从附近的窗户窥见，但是，每一扇窗户的中心部位所呈现的景观却互不相同。

德鲁克举出了许多实例，为了使自己容易理解与应用，可以对照自己的企业属性、特性及核心能力，予以反复思考、追根究底，即可掌握个中秘诀，且善加利用，必大有斩获。

所谓"企业家战略"也是德鲁克的创见之一。企业家战略相当重要，而且与众不同，分别有"孤注一掷、攻其软肋、生态利基、改变价值和特征"。

"创新、创业策略及创业管理"才是迈向创业型或企业家型社会的真正根源，正因为如此，"创新"——这是这本书的主题——是一种有组织的、系统的、理性的工作。明确地说，创新者所见所闻必须依据严谨的逻辑分析，凭直觉行事是不够的。

事实上，若根据直觉就意味着根据"我的直觉"，不会有什么好处，因为那通常代表"我希望它怎样"，而非"我认识到什么"。但是分析本身——需要进行测试、试验和评估，必须严格地奠基于对改变、对机会、对新的现况，以及对大部分人仍然相信的现象与实际现象之间不一致的认知。这需要人们有这样的态度："我所知的仍不足以进行分析，但我将会发掘足够的资料、信息，我会走出象牙塔，四处看看，问一些问题，并聆听他人的意见。"这是1925年通用汽车公司总裁斯隆所惯用的调研方式，今天，也成了海尔集团张瑞敏的方式。

詹文明

远流管理咨询公司大中华区 CEO 首席顾问

我们该需要怎样的创新

魏江院长新译的《创新与企业家精神》就要付梓出版了，我十分高兴，一则我对德鲁克这本书情有独钟，曾多次介绍和讲解书中的观点，二则魏江和我同在浙江大学管理学院执教，不过他是院长，我是兼职教授，我对他的探索和治学精神十分敬佩。浙大管理学院20多年前就开始引入创新概念并进入深入研究，魏江教授又是研究创新的核心学者，以他对创新的理解，由他重译《创新与企业家精神》一定会带来不少新意，也会更加逼近德鲁克先生的真实见解。所以当机械工业出版社华章公司找到我，希望我为此书写一段100字的推荐语时，我很愿意自告奋勇写篇序，说说我的想法，同时也推荐一下这本书。

德鲁克先生是管理大师中的大师，是他把管理真正确立为一门学科的。而在1985年，他却笔锋一转，出版了《创新与企业家精神》这本书，这是很耐人寻味的事情。我常在读他这本书时陷入迷思，我在想，德鲁克当时一定是想把创新也发展成一门学科吧。这再也无法向他本人求证了，但我还是不禁对书的立意、观点、结构遐想不止。而让人欣慰的是，今天中国各大学校大都设立了创新创业学院，我想德鲁克先生在天之灵一定十分欣慰。

这本书从英文版出版至今已 36 年，但如果我们认真去读，仍会觉得许多观点就像针对发生在昨天的事情，它们历久弥新，让人不由心生感慨，大师毕竟是大师。

德鲁克先生研究创新和企业家精神是奔着问题来的，他首先从美国的经济发展入手。著名的康德拉季耶夫周期理论，也就是经济长周期理论，讲到每 50 年一个周期，战后 1945～1965 年西方经济经历了快速发展，而 1965 年后，欧洲出现了衰退，但美国却反其道而行之，1965～1985 年出现了惊人的繁荣。德鲁克发现，出现这一变化的根本原因正是美国用创新经济取代了管制经济。而纵观我国改革开放后的经济发展，1992 年邓小平南方谈话正式确立了我国社会主义市场经济，1992～2012 年这 20 年间，我国经济以两位数的速度飞速增长。从 2012 年开始，中国经济进入了新常态，而化解经济下行压力的办法就是中央提出的"大众创业，万众创新"。这一点既让人想到中美经济发展的相似性，也让人想到德鲁克先生论述的创新经济的穿透性。

德鲁克先生对创新有很多独特的观点。比如，他认为创新要有目的地进行，不能盲目，有目的地创新可以降低 90% 的风险；再比如，他认为创新不仅是高科技，中科技、低科技、零科技也都可以创新，在美国，高科技对社会的贡献率只有 1/4，他认为商业模式创新大都是零科技，但创造了财富和价值；还比如，他认为企业不能只重视创新，如果没有好的管理，创新也会毁于一旦。他举了当年爱迪生的例子，爱迪生是个大发明家，也很会讲故事吸引基金投资者，但爱迪生认为企业就是"技术 + 资本"，他不相信管理，不聘请职业经理人，结果他开办的 7 家企业全都经营不善，最后他本人也被基金投资者赶出了公司。即使到了今天，我们重温德鲁克先生的这些创新思想，而后开始有目的的、有效的、高质量的创新，对我们而言，这不也是一剂良药吗？

德鲁克先生在这本书中对企业家和企业家精神的论述也让人醍醐灌顶。他认为企业家是创新并创造了财富的人，和熊彼特认为的冒险是企业家精神不同，他认为企业家应具备规避风险的能力，他认为企业家最大的长处是发现机遇而不是冒险。我常想这个问题，熊彼特提出企业家精神是创新精神和冒险精神，这是他在 1912 年《经济发展理论》中提出的，当时是工业早期，是个机会时代，但德鲁克写《创新与企业家精神》是在 1985 年，已经是工业成熟时代，创新成本已大大提高，所以如果再把冒险作为企业家的选项必然会增加失败的概率。同样，回首我国改革开放 40 多年历史，改革开放初期机会遍地，有一定胆商、敢冒险的人就容易成功，而 40 多年后的今天，如果没有科学的态度，只靠拼运气必然会失败。

关于企业家精神，德鲁克认为企业家和企业大小无关，和企业所有制无关，他认为许多公共部门的人，甚至公职人员也具备企业家精神。当然，这可能是和 Entrepreneur 这个词翻译成的中文用语有关，原意是创业者，我们翻译成了企业家，但企业家这个词可能更好地反映创新创业与创造财富的过程和特征。也因此，不必拘泥于这些翻译用词，只要能说明问题的就是好翻译和好名词。故而，我们提出，社会上不仅有民营企业家，也有国有企业家，因为国有企业家也具有创新精神并创造了财富。德鲁克先生提出的企业家精神不只企业家拥有，整个社会所有人都应该学习企业家精神、弘扬企业家精神，这也正是德鲁克先生所倡导的。

德鲁克先生在这本书的结尾还对我们提出了忠告，他说人们都向往高福利社会，他认为如果没有人创造财富，高福利只能是空中楼阁，只有建设创业型社会，才能创造大量财富，支持福利社会。他的忠告不幸言中，2012 年在欧洲爆发的主权债务危机恰恰就是从摇篮到坟墓的高福利社会带来的。在我国也存在是做大饼还是分好饼的争论，其实，创业型社会是一个做大饼的社会，是一个创造财富的社会，效率带动公平，应是我们的选择。我国有 1.43 亿个市场主体，有海量的企业家，既有顶天立地的大企业家，也有铺天盖地的小企业家，这是多么磅礴的力量，这也是我们伟大中华民族复兴的力量所在。

我国正进入一个创业型社会，也正在用创新型经济推动高质量发展。他山之石，可以攻玉，在这个时刻，我们重温德鲁克这本《创新与企业家精神》，并结合我们今天的鲜活的创新实践，有着重要的和特殊的意义。

有一年，我在浙大的一个沙龙上谈到创新的有效性时，魏江教授反问我："如果创新都要保证成功和赚钱，那创新者的压力不就太大了吗？"他是对的，这也反映出了浙大学者们的创新意识。由于我做企业 40 年，看到了太多创新的失败，也看到了太多盲目创新带来的损失，企业受效益的严格约束，不赚钱就顷刻倒闭，所以，我这么多年越做越胆小，常是战战兢兢地经营，如临深渊，如履薄冰。以学者而言，魏江教授是希望企业家的创新再果敢一些；以企业家而言，创新时常有所顾忌，思前想后，有时还囊中羞涩。这正是那种"不创新等死，创新找死"的两难，幸好有德鲁克先生为我们破解了这个创新的怪圈。

再次希望大家认真阅读此书，也希望魏江教授推出更多经管精品。

宋志平

中国上市公司协会会长、中国企业改革与发展研究会会长

"在快与变之中，在速生与速朽之间，那旋转的万花筒，有一个坚定稳固的内核，它经历时间的淬炼，依然散发出不变的灼灼光芒。"⊖在管理学界，彼得·德鲁克的著作无疑是当之无愧的"内核"。德鲁克深信，管理不应局限于理论和学术研究，更重要的是，要为社会和企业解决实际问题。正因为如此，德鲁克终其一生都在坚持咨询工作，深入企业实践活动，而这一切增强了他对事物的洞察力，并内化为其管理学思想的源泉。正如德鲁克所言，旁观者"犹如在剧院中坐镇的消防队员，能见人所不能见者，注意到演员或观众看不到的地方"。同样，作为管理的旁观者，德鲁克能够把握时代的命脉，从不同的角度来审视企业和社会的发展，一窥究竟。时至今日，德鲁克的著作依然备受推崇，不仅能帮助人们了解现代管理理论和实践，也能为企业家答疑解惑。

值此百年未有之大变局之际，人工智能、数字技术、虚拟现实、区块链系统等的蓬勃发展，深刻影响着产业发展和国际产业分工，也为企业家重塑创新驱动的发展战略路径提供了绝佳机会。透过这些"乱

⊖ 南方周末编辑部. 在巨变的时代相依前行 [N]. 南方周末，2016-01-01.

花渐欲迷人眼"的技术情境，回归管理理论的本源和管理实践的真谛，发现管理的基本逻辑其实是相对稳定的。技术一方面驱动管理理论和实践演化，另一方面驱使我们冷静看待管理实践的背后规律，让我们越来越发现管理的科学成分是长青的。正是基于这样的判断，我才来翻译《创新与企业家精神》一书。不管是德鲁克时代还是数字时代，企业创新精神、企业家精神其实没有根本性的变化，相信这部书的再次翻译出版，能够让我们从似是而非的管理窘境中，识别出最真实的管理问题。

感谢机械工业出版社的邀请，让我们得以有机会重新翻译《创新与企业家精神》这一经典之作。在翻译过程中，我们最大程度去忠于原著本意，再结合中文阅读习惯，尽量以简单明了的方式传达作者的思想，力求其易解。为帮助读者理解，在此对书中的几个关键词的翻译进行说明。几经斟酌，结合语境及词语的内涵，我们将 entrepreneur 译作"企业家"，entrepreneurship 译作"企业家精神"，entrepreneurial economy 译作"创业型经济"，entrepreneurial society 译作"创业型社会"，entrepreneurial management 译作"创业管理"，entrepreneurial practices 译作"创业实践"，entrepreneurial strategy 译作"创业战略"。[⊖]

德鲁克从 20 世纪 50 年代开始对创新和企业家精神进行研究，历经几十年的观察和实践，于 1985 年出版了《创新与企业家精神》。该书遵循德鲁克的一贯思想，坚持倡导实践的重要性，以翔实的案例、直指人心的故事，引领人们去感悟"企业家精神是一种实践"。当美国经济转向创

⊖ "entrepreneur"源于古法语"entreprendre"（12 世纪），意思是"介入（entre-）和接手（prendre）"的人。15 世纪，"entreprendre"传入英国。15 世纪后期，它具有"冒险的性格、乐于接受挑战、大胆的精神"的意思。到 1852 年，"entrepreneur"演变为同时含有企业管理者的意思。企，就是"立"；创，就是"创立"。从这个角度看，创业和企业也有一定的关系。以企业为事业的人，大多具有开创精神。作为企业的管理者，如果没有这样的精神，企业也不会长久，管理者也难称为企业家。所以，本书沿用"企业家精神"和"企业家"的译法。对于"创业管理""创业型经济"等，则是企业家精神在当今世界的最突出的表现。——译者注

业型经济时，一种"新技术"即"创业管理"成为美国就业现象的最好解释。在书中，德鲁克用生动的案例，打破人们固有的认知，给人以启发与思考。他告诉我们企业家精神并非难以捉摸，并非高风险，而是一项有目的的、系统的工作；企业家精神的具体体现是创新，并有七个创新机会源；企业家精神的实践应遵循一定的原则，有一些策略，也有一些禁忌；实践企业家精神也要求在市场中开展创业战略。最后，他告诉我们如何将挑战化为机会，在创业型社会中开展创新与企业家精神的实践。

历史车轮滚滚向前，时代潮流浩浩荡荡。面对新的挑战和机遇，我们又该如何把握？翻开这本书，细细品味，相信它会给你带来耳目一新的感觉。最后，限于译者水平和阅历，书中必定存在疏漏之处，敬请各位读者批评指正。

魏江

2020 年秋于启真湖畔

本书将创新与企业家精神视为一种实践和一门学科。它并没有提到企业家的心理和品格特质，而是探讨他们的活动和行为。本书列举了很多例子，这些例子旨在阐释某个观点、规则或警示，而非讲述成功故事。因此，相比于此前已经出版或发表的关于创新与企业家精神的书籍和文章，本书在写作意图和写作手法上都有所不同。同其他出版物一样，本书也强调创新与企业家精神的重要性。但本书关注的是近代经济社会史中最振奋人心的事件，即美国在过去10~15年里出现的创业型经济。当下许多讨论认为企业家精神是一种略带神秘色彩的东西，将其视为天赋、才干、灵感或"灵光乍现"（flash of genius）。而本书认为创新与企业家精神是一项能够加以组织（并必须加以组织）的有目的的任务，也是一项系统工作。事实上，它是管理者工作的一部分。

本书具有很强的实用性，但并非为了教人们"如何做"。通过对"策略和决策""机会和风险""结构和战略""人事、报酬和激励"的分析，本书讨论了"什么是创新与企业家精神""何时开展创新与企业家精神"，以及"为什么开展创新与企业家精神"。

本书主要包括三个主题：创新实践、企业家精神实践和创业战略。

每个主题是创新与企业家精神的一个"方面",而非一个阶段。

第一部分是创新实践,指出创新是一门有目的的学科。首先,它阐释了企业家从何处以及如何寻找创新机会。随后,它进一步探讨了人们在将创意转化为可行的业务和服务的过程中,应遵循的行为原则与不能触碰的禁忌。

第二部分是企业家精神实践,重点关注机构,即创新的载体。它从现有企业、公共服务机构、新创企业三个方面来讨论创业管理。什么样的策略和实践有助于机构(无论是企业还是公共服务机构)成为成功的企业家?为培育企业家精神,应该如何组织和配备人员?会有哪些干扰、障碍、陷阱以及常见错误?最后,本部分就企业家的角色和决策进行探讨。

第三部分是创业战略,主要讨论如何将创新成功地推向市场。创新的检验标准并不是它的新颖性、科技含量或者巧妙性,而是要赢得市场。

本书的引言将创新与企业家精神同经济相联系,结论则将它们与社会相联系。引言、三个主题和结论构成了整本书。

企业家精神既非科学也非艺术,而是一种实践。当然,它具有一定的知识基础,本书将系统地呈现这一知识基础。正如医学、工程学等其他实践知识一样,企业家精神的知识只是达到目的的一种手段。实践知识的内容主要由目的,也就是实践本身来界定。因此,本书是基于多年的实践经验总结而成的。

30 年前,也就是 20 世纪 50 年代,我开始研究创新与企业家精神。当时有两年的时间,在纽约大学商学院我所领导的研究小组每周一次的晚间研讨会上,都会对创新与企业家精神进行长时间的探讨。这个小组的一些成员刚刚开始创业,大都很成功;还有一些成员在现有机构中担任中层管理者,这些机构大都规模庞大,包括两家大医院、IBM、通用电气公司、一两家大银行、一家证券经纪公司、几家杂志和书籍出版商、几家制药公司、一家全球性慈善组织、纽约天主教大主教管辖区以及长老会，等等。

在连续两年中，研讨会成员在他们的工作中对讨论出的概念和想法加以检验。在随后长达20多年的咨询生涯中，我进一步对这些概念和想法加以检验、确认、精炼和修正。我的咨询工作同样也涉及各种机构，一些是企业，如制药和计算机等高科技公司、灾害保险等非科技公司、美国和欧洲的全球性银行、个人公司、区域性建材批发商以及日本的跨国公司等；还有一些是非营利组织，如工会组织、主要社区组织（如美国女童子军、国际救援与发展合作组织）、医院、大学、研究实验室和不同的宗教组织。

本书浓缩了多年的观察、研究和实践，所以我运用大量"微案例"从正反两方面来阐释策略和实践。书中提到名称的机构都不是我的客户（如IBM），这些机构的案例要么是公开报道的，要么是机构本身披露的。我的所有管理书籍都不会公布与我有业务往来的机构的名称。本书所选取的案例都是真实案例，讨论的企业也是现实存在的企业。

直到最近几年，管理学者才开始关注创新与企业家精神。早在几十年前，我的管理类书籍就开始探讨这方面的问题。本书首次全面系统地对此加以阐述。我确信本书是这一重要课题的开端而非结束，并衷心希望这一开创性作品能为广大读者所接受。

彼得·德鲁克

1984年圣诞节于加州克莱蒙特

创业型经济

I

20 世纪 70 年代中期以来，"经济零增长""美国去工业化"及长期的"康德拉季耶夫经济停滞"等口号广为流传，被视为真理。但是，事实和数据表明这些口号纯属谬论。这一时期，美国经济形势出现了从管理型经济向创业型经济转变的重大变化。

1965—1985 年这 20 年间，16 岁以上的美国人口（按照美国统计标准，这些人属于劳动力范畴）增长 2/5，从 1.29 亿人上升到 1.8 亿人。同期美国就业人口增长 1/2，从 0.71 亿人上升到 1.06 亿人。这一阶段的第二个 10 年（1974—1984 年）中，劳动力增长最快。这段时间，美国经济创造的就业岗位增加了 2400 万个。

无论从百分比还是绝对数字来看，美国在这 20 年创造的就业岗位比其他任何和平时期都多。但自 1973 年深秋的石油危机之后的 10 年，美国社会动荡不安，依次经历了能源危机、"烟囱工业"几近崩溃和两次相当严重的经济衰退。

美国的经济发展极其独特，其他国家都未曾发生过类似情况。1970—1984年，西欧实际上失去了三四百万个就业岗位。1970年，西欧的就业岗位比美国多2000万个；但到了1984年，它却比美国少了近1000万个。在就业岗位创造方面，日本也远不如美国。1970—1982年的12年间，日本的就业岗位只增长了10%，还不到美国同期增长率的一半。

美国就业岗位在20世纪70年代和80年代初的增长状况，与25年前专家的预测背道而驰。那时大多数劳动力分析专家预测，即便以最快速度发展，美国经济也无法在70年代与80年代初为达到就业年龄的男子提供足够的就业岗位。这些适龄劳动力出生于1949年和1950年，是"婴儿潮"的第一梯队。事实上，美国提供的就业岗位是预期需求量的两倍。70年代中期，许多已婚女性纷纷涌入劳动力市场，这在1970年是无法想象的。这就导致了80年代中期的今天，每2个有孩子的已婚女性中就有1个参加工作；而在1970年，每5个中才有1个。美国经济为这些女性都提供了就业岗位，而且大多数岗位都优于过去女性所从事的工作。

众所周知，20世纪70年代和80年代初是美国的"零增长"时期，经济陷入停滞和衰退，也是美国"去工业化"时期。之所以这样认为，是因为人们的关注点依然在第二次世界大战（简称二战）之后25年这段时期（大约结束于1970年）内快速发展的领域。

早些年，美国经济发展的动力主要来自越来越大的机构，包括《财富》500强、联邦政府、州政府及当地政府，大型学校和超大型大学，学生人数为6000及以上的大型高中，成长型的大医院。战后25年的美国新增就业岗位，实际上都是由这些机构创造的。这期间出现的经济衰退，包括就业岗位减少和失业现象，主要发生在小型机构中，当然主要是在小企业中。

自20世纪60年代末以来，美国就业领域出现全新的变化。在过去的

20 年，先前就业领域的工作机会不断减少。自 1970 年以来，《财富》500 强企业的固定岗位逐年减少（不考虑经济衰退引起的失业）。起初缓慢减少，到 1977 年或 1978 年，开始大幅削减。到 1984 年，《财富》500 强企业至少削减了 400 万～600 万个就业岗位。美国政府机构的雇员，也比 10 年或 15 年前要少。由于 60 年代初的生育率骤降，入学人数减少，教师岗位也随之减少。到 1980 年，美国大学发展停滞，工作机会减少。80 年代初，甚至连医院的雇员数量也停止增长。换句话说，为了弥补传统机构所失去的至少 500 万固定岗位的需求，我们创造了至少 4000 万个就业岗位，而非 3500 万个。这些新的就业岗位都是由中小型机构创造的，大都是 20 年前还不存在的中小型企业。据《经济学人》报道，现在美国每年新增的初创企业高达 60 万家，约是 20 世纪五六十年代繁荣时期的 7 倍。

II

美国为什么会出现这种情况呢？很多人会立刻联想到"高科技"。事实并非如此简单。1965 年以来创造的 4000 多万个就业岗位中，高技术领域所贡献的不过 500 万～600 万个。高技术领域所创造的就业岗位最多只能弥补"烟囱工业"所失去的，其余的就业岗位则是由其他领域创造的。即便给"高科技"下一个最广泛的定义，每 100 家新创企业中，也只有一两家称得上是"高科技"。

我们正处于重大技术变革的初始阶段，其影响之大远远超过"未来学家"的设想，甚至连《大趋势》（Megatrends）和《未来的冲击》（Future Shock）中的描述都无可比拟。第二次世界大战之后，历经 300 年的技术发展告一段落。在这 300 年里，技术模式或模型无外乎是一种机械模式，也就是太阳等恒星内部进行的各种反应模式。1680 年左右，当时原本籍籍无名的法国物理学家丹尼斯·巴本（Denis Papin）发明了第一台蒸汽机，揭开了这一时代科技发展的序幕。直到我们在核爆炸中再现恒星内部的核反应，这一时代才终结。由于技术在机械过程中的作用，这300年间的技术进步意味着更快的速度、更高的温度、更强的压力。第二次世界大战之后，技术模式转变为生物过程模式，主要研究有机体内部的反应。在有机体内部，过程主要围绕信息来组织，而非围绕物理学家所阐述的能量来组织。

无论是以计算机还是电信、工厂里的机器人还是办公自动化、生物遗传学还是生物工程的形式呈现，高科技的重要性都不可估量。高科技令人振奋、夺人眼球。它创造了创新和企业家精神的愿景，并为人接受。由于高科技的神秘色彩，许多受过良好训练的年轻人更愿意去不知名的小企业，而非银行巨头或世界级电气设备制造商。虽然对这些年轻人而言，绝大多数所工作的企业的技术平淡无奇而又枯燥乏味。此外，高科技也推动了美国资本市场的重大转变。20世纪60年代初，风险资本还不足以满足市场需求，到80年代中期就达到盈余状态。因此，高科技就是逻辑学家所称的"认识根据"（ratio cognoscendi）。它是我们感知和理解现象的根据，而非仅仅只是解释现象。

从数量上看，如前所述，高科技所创造的就业岗位不到总数的1/8。从就业岗位来讲，在不久的将来，高科技的表现不会有所改善。从现在（1984年）到2000年，在美国经济创造的就业岗位中，高科技所占的比例不会超过1/6。如果真如大多数人所认为的，高科技是美国经济中的创业领域，那么美国经济真的会"零增长"，并陷入"康德拉季耶夫波"中的停滞状态。

20世纪30年代中期，俄国经济学家尼古拉·康德拉季耶夫（Nikolai Kondratieff）用其计量模型预测苏联的农业集体化将导致农场产量急剧下降。事实证明，这一预测完全正确。"康德拉季耶夫周期"理论基于技术的内在动态，提出50年为一个经济周期。康德拉季耶夫断言，技术每隔50年会到达顶峰。在康德拉季耶夫经济周期的连续20年中，持续的技术进步会使成长型行业发展良好。但是，这些行业看起来像创纪录的利润只是因为发展停滞的产业不需要的资本回笼而已。这种发展态势不会超过 20 年，随后经济会突然陷入危机之中。这种危机出现之前，通常会有某种恐慌作为预兆。接下来就是长达 20 年的经济停滞（stagnation），新兴技术无法创造充足的就业岗位使经济自行复苏。对于这种境况，所有人都无能为力，政府尤其如此。[⊖]

第二次世界大战之后，促使长期经济扩张的产业，如汽车、钢铁、橡胶、电气设备、消费电子品、电话还有石油[⊜]，完全符合康德拉季耶夫周期理论。从技术层面来看，这些产业可以追溯到 19 世纪的最后 25 年，或者稍近一点，可以追溯到第一次世界大战（简称一战）之前。自 20 世纪 20 年代以来，无论从技术还是经营理念上，这些产业都没有重大突破。第二次世界大战后，当经济开始增长时，它们已经是成熟产业了。只需投入少许资本，这些产业就能扩张并创造新的就业岗位。这也解释了为何在工资和福利飞涨的情况下，它们依旧能获得高额利润。但是，正如康德拉季耶夫的预测，这些信号就像肺病患者红润的脸颊，只是经济强健的假象而已。事实上，这些产业内部已经开始衰败。它们并非陷入停滞或缓慢衰退，而是在 1973 年和 1979 年的"石油危机"（oil shocks）之后迅速崩溃。短短几年，它们从利润创新高到濒临破产。很快形势完全明朗，这些产业即便能够复苏也很难在短时间恢复到先前的雇佣水平。

高科技产业也符合康德拉季耶夫周期理论。正如康德拉季耶夫所预测的那样，迄今为止，高科技产业创造的就业岗位不足以抵消旧产业失去的就业岗位。所有预测都表明，在未来相当长的时间内——至少在本世纪（20世

⊖　美籍奥地利经济学家约瑟夫·熊彼特（Joseph Schumpeter）的不朽巨著《商业周期》（*Business Cycles*）（1939）一书，将康德拉季耶夫周期曲线传播到西方。如今，麻省理工学院的科学家杰伊·福里斯特（Jay Forrester）是康德拉季耶夫周期理论最著名、最严谨和最权威的信徒，也是"长期经济停滞"理论的最严肃和最博学的倡导者。

⊜　与普遍看法相反，石油业是第一个进入衰退阶段的。事实上，1950 年左右，石油业就不再发展了。自此，不管是制造业、交通业、取暖业还是空调业，产出每增加一单位所需的石油增量一直在下降，起初较缓慢，在 1973 年以后，下滑迅速加快。

纪）最后十几年——高科技产业提供就业岗位的情形不会有所改善。举例来说，虽然计算机行业迅猛发展，但数据加工和信息处理（包括软硬件的设计与工程、生产、销售和服务等）在20世纪80年代末和90年代初创造的就业岗位无法弥补钢铁业和汽车业同期（几乎确定）将失去的就业岗位。

然而，康德拉季耶夫周期理论无法解释美国经济创造的4000万个就业岗位。迄今为止，西欧的发展一直遵循康德拉季耶夫模式，但美国并非如此，日本可能也非如此。美国发生的某些事件，抵消了康德拉季耶夫"技术长波"的影响，而且与经济长期停滞理论并不相符。

美国并非仅仅延长了康德拉季耶夫周期。在接下来的20年里，美国所需要的就业岗位将远少于过去20年的需求，经济发展对工作的依赖程度也会降低。到20世纪末，确切地说到2010年，美国新增劳动力会比1965—1980年期间少1/3。这是因为"婴儿潮"时期出生的婴儿到1965—1980年长大成人，而1960—1961年"生育低潮"时期的出生率比"婴儿潮"时期低30%。此外，目前50岁以下参加工作的女性人数与男性持平。从现在起，职业女性数目也会受到人口自然增长的限制，也就是说，女性就业人数也会减少30%左右。

对于"烟囱工业"的发展趋势，即便康德拉季耶夫周期理论不是目前最合理的解释，我们也应将其视为严谨的假设。考虑到高科技产业无法抵消昔日成长型产业的停滞效应，我们应该再次重视康德拉季耶夫理论。作为愿景的开拓者和带头人，高科技产业发挥着重大的实质性作用。就数量而言，高科技产业代表着明天而非今天，尤其是作为提供就业岗位的产业。它们将造就未来而非造就现在。

虽然康德拉季耶夫理论能够解释美国经济行为并预测其发展方向，但它依然遭到质疑。因为这个理论无法解释"康德拉季耶夫长期停滞期"美国经济中创造的4000万个就业岗位。

我并不是指不存在经济问题或危机。恰恰相反。20世纪即将结束的这

25 年中，经济的技术基础发生了重大转变，这将带来经济、社会和政治中的诸多问题。我们也在经历重大的政治危机。这一危机的根源在于，20 世纪的伟大成功——福利国家（它带有无法控制或看起来无法控制的巨额通胀赤字）。国际经济风险加大，巴西、墨西哥等快速工业化国家在经济腾飞和灾难性崩溃之间徘徊。这可能会导致 1930 年的经济大萧条再次在全球出现，持续时间也许更久。此外，还有一个令人恐惧的忧虑，失控的军备竞赛。不过，对于康德拉季耶夫经济停滞现象，美国至少可以将其视为幻象而非事实。因为，美国出现了全新的创业型经济。

现在去判断创业型经济到底只是美国现象还是同时存在于其他发达国家，还显得为时过早。我们有充分的理由相信，创业型经济正以其特有的模式在日本显现。不过，至今尚未确定创业型经济能否在西欧出现。从人口统计特征来看，西欧的发展滞后于美国 10～15 年。西欧的"婴儿潮"和"生育低潮"都比美国要晚。西欧延长学校教育年限的策略也比美国或日本晚了10 年左右，而英国尚未启动这项举措。如果（事实上，极有可能）人口因素是美国创业型经济出现的原因之一，那么可以预测，到 1990 年或 1995 年，欧洲会出现类似的发展。当然，这纯属猜测。迄今为止，创业型经济只是美国的特有现象。

Ⅲ

这些新的就业岗位从何而来？答案是任何地方。换句话说，其来源并不唯一。

自 1982 年以来，波士顿一家名叫 *Inc.* 的杂志社每年都会对 100 家快速增长、创立时间在 5～15 年的美国上市公司进行排名。由于仅限于上市公司，这个排行榜的排名明显偏向高科技企业。高科技企业备受推崇，易于找到证券承销商，在股市中募集资金，在证券交易所或柜台交易股票。其他新创企业必须经过多年努力，必须 5 年以上都盈利，才能上市。即便如此，每年这个 100 强排行榜中，只有 1/4 是高科技企业，其余 3/4 大都是"低科技"企业。

例如，1982 年的排行榜上有 5 家连锁餐厅、2 家女装制造商、20 家医疗保健服务机构，而只有 20～30 家高科技企业。虽然 1982 年的美国报纸频频悲叹"美国去工业化"，但排行榜中制造业企业占 1/2，服务业企业仅占 1/3。虽然 1982 年有文章称，美国北部霜冻地带的经济衰竭，阳光地带可能是唯一的增长区域，但是排行榜中阳光地带的企业仅占 1/3。从排行榜来看，纽约、加利福尼亚和得克萨斯的企业所占比例相同。据推测，宾夕法尼亚、新泽西和马萨诸塞的经济濒临绝境。事实上，排行榜中这 3 个州的企业同纽约、加利福尼亚和得克萨斯 3 个州的一样多。甚至连冰雪天堂明尼苏达，也有 7 家企业榜上有名。在行业和地理分布上，1983 年和 1984 年的排行榜也是如此。

1983 年，*Inc.* 又推出了一个 500 强企业排行榜，包括 500 家新近成立、快速发展的私营企业（非上市企业）。排名前两位的是太平洋沿岸西北地区的一家建筑承包商（当年建筑业空前不景气）和加利福尼亚的一家家用健身设备制造商。

针对风险投资家的调查结果，也遵循同样的模式。在风险投资家的投资组合中，高科技企业并不起眼。一位非常成功的风险投资家的投资组合中包括几家高科技企业：一家新成立的计算机软件制造商、一家医药技术的新创企业，等等。但是 1981—1983 年间，该投资组合中营收和利润增速第一的是一家平淡无奇、毫无科技含量的理发连锁店。紧随其后的依次是一家牙医诊所连锁店、一家手工工具制造商和一家向小企业出租机器的金融企业。

据我所知，1979—1984 年间的众多企业中，创造最多就业岗位的、营收和利润增长最快的企业是一家金融服务企业。这家企业在 5 年时间里创造 2000 个就业岗位，且大多数岗位的待遇极其优厚。虽然它是纽约证券交易所的成员，但股票交易业务只占营业额的 1/8。其他业务是年金、免税债券、货币市场基金和公募基金、抵押信托保证、避税项目合作，以及为该企业所称的"明智投资者"提供大量类似的投资项目。它指的"明智投资者"包括小镇和郊区并非极其富有的专业人士、小商人或农场主，他们希望能将多余的资金储存起来。这类人是现实主义者，并不奢望通过投资致富。

　　我能找到的最能揭示美国经济增长点的资料，是一项针对 100 家快速成长的中等规模成长型企业（营业收入为 0.25 亿～10 亿美元）的研究。这项研究是美国商业联合会（American Business Conference）委托麦肯锡咨询公司的两位高级合伙人于 1981—1983 年开展完成的。[○]

　　无论在销售收入还是利润上，这些中等规模企业的增长速度都是《财富》美国 500 强企业的 3 倍。自 1970 年以来，美国 500 强企业的就业岗位不断流失；而在 1970—1983 年，这些中等规模成长型企业就业岗位的增速是整个美国经济的 3 倍。即便在 1981—1982 年的经济萧条期，美国产业的就业岗位减少了 2%，而这 100 家企业的雇佣水平也增加了 1%。这些企业遍及美国各经济领域。当然，一些高科技企业也包括在内。此外，也有一些金融服务企业，如纽约帝杰证券公司（Donaldson, Lufkin & Jenrette）。这 100 家企业中，表现最突出的是一家生产和销售起居室家具的公司，第二是一家生产和销售甜甜圈的公司，第三是一家精品瓷器公司，第四是一家书写用品公司，第五是一家家用涂料公司，第六是一家从印刷出版当地报纸拓展到提供消费者市场营销服务的公司，第七是一家为纺织厂生产纱线的公司，等等。尽管"每个人都知道"美国经济中只有服务业是增长的，但超过一半的中等规模成长型企业属于制造业。

　　更令人费解的是，在过去 10～15 年，美国经济的增长领域包括很多且

　　○　该文章名为《美国中等规模成长型企业给我们的启示》，由理查德·卡夫诺（Richard Cavenaugh）和小唐纳德·克利福德（Donald Clifford, Jr.）于 1983 年秋发表在《麦肯锡季刊》(*McKinsey Quarterly*）上。

不断增加的"通常不被视为企业"的机构。这些都是非政府组织，而且很多正在转变为营利性企业。这些机构中，最为常见的当属医疗保健领域。这段时期，传统的美国社区医院陷入困境。但也有很多连锁医院快速发展且欣欣向荣，包括营利性医院和日益增多的非营利性医院。一些"独立的"医疗机构发展更为快速，如临终关怀中心、医疗与诊断实验室、独立外科中心、独立妇产院、"免预约"精神诊所，或者老年诊断和治疗中心。

如今，几乎所有的美国社区学校都日趋衰落。尽管 20 世纪 60 年代的"生育低潮"导致学龄儿童大量减少，一种全新的非营利性私立学校却在繁荣发展。1980 年左右，在我居住的加州小城里，几个母亲为照顾自己的孩子成立了一家社区托儿所。到 1984 年，这家托儿所已经成为一所学校，拥有 200 名即将就读 4 年级的学生。此外，当地浸礼会教徒几年前创办的一所教会学校，正准备接管克莱蒙特的一所初级中学（这所中学创办于 15 年前，在过去 5 年里因为一直没有生源而空了下来）。不过，各种成人教育项目都在加快发展，无论是针对中层经理的行政管理项目，还是针对医生、工程师、律师和理疗学家等的进修项目。即便在 1982—1983 年的经济萧条期，这些项目也只是暂时受挫而已。

另一个显现出企业家精神的重要领域是新兴的公私合营的"第四部门"。这一领域由政府部门（州政府或市政府）出资并确定绩效标准，然后将消防、垃圾回收或公共汽车运输等服务以公开招标方式委托给私营部门。这种方式能够以较低的成本获得更好的服务。自 1975 年海伦·布萨里斯（Helen Boosalis）首次当选为内布拉斯加州林肯市市长以来，林肯市一直是这一领域的开拓者。100 年前，同样在林肯市，平民党人和威廉·詹宁斯·布莱恩（William Jennings Bryan）首次引领我们走上公用事业的市政所有权之路。得克萨斯州也是公私合营方面的先行者，圣安东尼奥市和休斯敦市就是很好的例子。明尼阿波利斯市的明尼苏达大学休伯特·汉弗莱学院的表现尤为突出。同样地，位于该市的一家领先计算机制造商，控制数据公司（Control

Data Corporation）在教育，甚至是罪犯管理和改造方面与政府建立了良好的公私合营关系。考虑到公众不愿为日益衰落的邮政服务支付更多的补贴和费用，从长期来看，能够拯救这项服务的唯一办法就是通过竞标选择"第四部门"以获取一流服务。否则，10年后，邮政服务将消失无踪。

IV

除了快速增长和违背康德拉季耶夫经济停滞理论之外，这些成长型机构还有什么共同之处呢？事实上，它们都是"新技术"的代表，都以全新的方式将知识应用到人类工作中，而这才是"技术"的定义。这种"新技术"不是电子学、遗传学或者新材料技术，而是创业管理。

只要弄清了这一点，美国经济在过去20年，尤其最近10年就业岗位的惊人增长就不难解释了。这种"新技术"甚至可以与康德拉季耶夫理论相调和。美国正在经历一种所谓的"非典型康德拉季耶夫经济周期"。从某种程度上讲，日本也是如此。

自约瑟夫·熊彼特于1939年首次指出以来，我们就意识到，从1873年到第一次世界大战之间的近50年，美国和德国的实际发展状况与康德拉季耶夫周期理论并不相符。第一个康德拉季耶夫周期开始于铁路发展热潮，结束于1873年维也纳的股市崩盘。那次股市崩盘对全球股票市场造成了沉重的打击，进而引发经济大萧条。之后，英国和法国的工业发展都陷入漫长的停滞期。当时钢铁、化工、电气设备、电话以及最后出现的汽车业等新兴技术产业所创造的就业岗位都不足以弥补铁路建设、煤矿开采及纺织业等传统产业停滞所引发的失业。

但是，这种情况并未出现在美国和德国。而且尽管维也纳股市崩溃导致奥地利政治局势动荡不安且尚未恢复，但奥地利也未出现经济停滞现象。起初，这几个国家的经济也备受打击。但5年后，它们摆脱困境，重新腾飞。就"技术"而言，这些国家与深受经济停滞之苦的英国和法国并无区别。企业家是唯一能够解释这种经济行为差异的因素。比如，在1870—1914年期间，德国最重要的经济事件就是综合银行的成立。首个综合银行是由乔治·西门子（Georg Siemens）于1870年创办的德意志银行（Deutsche Bank）[⊖]。德意志银行的使命是发现并投资创业者（创业型企业），对他们（它们）进行有组织有纪律的管理。在美国经济史中，诸如纽约的 J. P. 摩根公司（J. P. Morgan）[⊜]之类的创业型银行也扮演着同样的角色。

如今，类似的情况再次出现在美国，或多或少也可能出现在日本。

事实上，高科技并不属于"创业管理"这一"新技术"。硅谷的高科技企业家依旧推崇19世纪的管理模式。他们深信本杰明·富兰克林（Benjamin Franklin）的名言："如果你发明出一个更好的捕鼠器，你的门槛将被踏破。"可是，他们未曾想过去问："更好的"捕鼠器究竟是什么样的？为谁所用？

当然也有例外。很多高科技企业了解如何管理创新与企业家精神。19世纪就有这样的例外事件。德国人维尔纳·西门子（Werner Siemens）创办了一家至今仍以他的名字命名的公司（即西门子公司）。美国人乔治·威斯汀豪斯（George Westinghouse）不仅是伟大的发明家，还是成功的企业家，有两家公司至今仍以他的名字命名，一家是运输业的领先者（即西屋公司），另一家是电气设备业的主力（即西屋电气公司）。

但是，对于"高科技"企业家而言，他们的原型似乎依然是托马斯·爱迪生（Thomas Edison）。爱迪生是19世纪最伟大的发明家。他将发明转变为一门学科，也就是我们现在所称的"研究"。但是，他真正的志向是创办企业，并成为商界大亨。然而，他对企业管理一窍不通，最终为了挽救企业不得不让位他人。如今，很多企业（即便不是大多数）仍然以爱迪生的方式

⊖ 乔治·西门子（又译作格奥尔格·西门子）和综合银行的故事，详见第9章。
⊜ 2000年J. P. 摩根公司与其他公司合并成立摩根大通。

管理企业。确切地说，这些企业管理不善。

这就解释了为什么这些高科技企业依然遵循传统模式。这种模式起初令人振奋，接着快速扩张，然后突然崩溃，在 5 年内经历"麻雀变凤凰，再变回麻雀"的转变。大部分硅谷企业以及大部分高科技生物企业，仍然是发明家而非创新者，是投机者而非创业者。这在一定程度上也解释了为何高科技产业突破不了康德拉季耶夫周期的预测，并且无法创造足够的就业岗位使经济复苏。

但是，有系统、有目的、以企业家精神管理的"低科技"机构却能做到这点。

V

在所有重要的现代经济学家中，只有熊彼特关注企业家及其对经济的影响。每个经济学家都知道企业家的重要性和影响力。但是，经济学家认为企业家精神是"超经济的"（meta-economic）。它深刻影响并塑造经济，但并非经济的一部分。对经济学家来说，技术同样如此。至于企业家精神为何会出现以及为何局限于某个国家或某种文化中，经济学家对此没有做出任何解释。企业家精神曾出现在 19 世纪末，如今似乎再次出现。的确，企业家精神为何有效的原因也许并不属于经济范畴。这可能源于价值观、认知和态度的变化，也可能是人口统计特征的变化、机构（如 1870 年左右美国和德国的创业型银行）和教育的变化。

在过去 20～25 年间，相当多美国青年的态度、价值观和志向确实都发生了转变。显然，关注于 20 世纪 60 年代末美国青年的观察者并没有预测到这种变化。突然之间，很多人开始长年拼命工作，追求高风险而非贪图大公司的安稳。这该如何解释呢？那些享乐主义者、追求地位者、附庸者、墨守成规者到哪儿去了呢？ 15 年前我们所知的那些不在乎功名利禄，只求美国重回怡然自得状态（如果回不到田园绿色）的青年，又去哪儿了呢？不管怎样解释，这都不同于过去 30 年里预言家的设想，如大卫·里斯曼（David Riesman）的《孤独的人群》（*The Lonely Crowd*）、威廉·H. 怀特（William H. Whyte）的《组织人》（*The Organization Man*）、查尔斯·赖克（Charles Reich）的《绿化美国》（*The Greening of America*）以及赫伯特·马库塞（Herbert Marcuse）等对青年一代的预想。的确，创业型经济的出现不仅仅是经济和技术事件，还是文化和心理事件。不管原因何在，其都最终影响到整个经济领域。

这种态度、价值观以及最终行为的深刻变化来源于一种"技术"。我们称之为管理。正是管理的新应用催生了美国创业型经济的出现，主要表现为：

- 应用于新创企业，无论其是否为商业企业。然而直到现在，大多数人仍然认为管理只适用于已有企业。
- 应用于小规模企业。仅仅几年前，大多数人还断定管理只适用于大规模企业。
- 应用于非商业性机构，如医疗保健、教育机构。大多数人遇到"管理"这个词，想到的仍是"商业"。
- 应用于根本不被视为"企业"的单位，如当地餐馆。
- 最重要的是，应用于系统的创新。这是为满足人类需求，去寻找并利用新机会。

作为一种"有用的知识"、一种技术，管理与当今高科技产业的其他基本知识（如电子学、固态物理学、遗传学以及免疫学）出现在同一时期。管理起源于第一次世界大战左右，发展于 20 世纪 20 年代中期，作为同工程和医学一样的"有用的知识"，管理也是从实践中发展而来，最后成为一门学科。20 世纪 30 年代末，美国有几家大型企业（主要是商业企业）开始运用管理实践，如杜邦公司（DuPont Company）、通用汽车公司（General Motors）、大型零售商西尔斯百货（Sears, Roebuck）。在大西洋彼岸，有德国西门子公司和英国玛莎百货公司（Marks and Spencer）。管理成为一门学科，是在第二次世界大战期间及之后。⊖

大约从 1955 年开始，发达国家经历了一股"管理热潮"⊜。大约 40 年前，我们所称为"管理"的这一社会技术，首次出现在大众（包括管理者本人）视野中。此后，管理迅速发展成为一门学科，而非少数独立信仰者的随意实践。这 40 年来，与同时期的"科学突破"一样，管理具有重要的影响力，甚至比科学突破更为重要。第二次世界大战后，发达国家都变为"组织社会"，而管理也许并不是唯一因素，或甚至不是重要因素。如今，发达国家中的大多数人，尤其是绝大多数接受过教育的人，都在组织中工作，包括老板自己。企业的老板日益趋向于变成"职业经理人"，身份是雇员而非企业所有者。无法肯定管理是不是唯一因素，是不是重要因素。但可以肯定的是，如果管理没有成为一门系统的学科，发达国家就不会出现目前的社会现状："组织社会"和"员工社会"。

对于管理，尤其是对知识工作者的管理，我们还有很多东西需要学习。不过在某种程度上，管理的基本原理已经为人所知。40 年前，大部分人甚至是大公司的高层管理者都没有意识到他们所做的管理工作。如今，管理已是司空见惯。

但总的来说，人们至今仍然认为管理仅仅适用于商业企业，而且是大企业。20 世纪 70 年代初，美国管理协会邀请小企业负责人参加"高管培训项目"，得到的回复大都是："管理？那是针对大企业的，与我无关。"直到1970 年或 1975 年，美国医院管理者还依然排斥任何带有"管理"标签的事

⊖ 首次将管理作为一种系统知识，即一门学科，是我最初的两本著作：《公司的概念》（1946年，研究的是通用汽车公司）以及《管理的实践》（1954 年）。

⊜ 如今，中国也出现了这股管理热潮。

物。他们声称："我们是医务人员，不是企业员工。"（在大学里，尽管教职工会抱怨他们所在的机构如何"管理不当"，但他们的看法与医务人员是一致的。）自第二次世界大战结束到1970年这段时间，"进步"意味着创办更大规模的机构。

这25年来，企业、工会、医院、学校、大学等社会各领域都倾向于创建更大规模的组织，原因是多样的。最主要的因素肯定是，人们相信能够管理好大型机构却不知如何管理小型机构。当初美国创办大型综合高中的热潮与这个观念有很大关系。人们声称："教育需要专业化管理，而这只有在大型机构才能发挥效用。"

最近10或15年里，这种趋势才得以逆转。事实上，美国现在的趋势是"去机构化"，而非"去工业化"。自20世纪30年代以来的近50年里，美国和西欧普遍认为身体不适者最好去医院，重症患者尤其如此。医生和病人持有同样的观念："病人来医院越早，医生对他们的疗护越好。"最近几年，这种观念也在转变。现在，我们愈加相信病人远离医院的时间越长越好，越早出院越好。当然，这种转变与医疗保健或管理毫不相干。它只是一种逆反心理（无论是长久的或短暂的），是对崇拜集中化、计划和政府等的反叛情绪。这里所说的这种崇拜现象始于20世纪二三十年代，在60年代肯尼迪和约翰逊执政期间到达顶峰。然而，如果我们没有能力和信心管理好小型机构以及医院等非商业机构，那么就无法保障医疗保健领域的"去机构化"。

总体而言，相比于"管理良好"的大型组织，小型创业组织对于管理的需求更为迫切，管理所产生的影响也更大。最重要的是，无论对新的创业型企业还是对"管理良好"的持续存在的企业来说，我们现在所正学习的管理都发挥着重要作用。

举个具体的例子。早在19世纪，美国就出现了汉堡店。第二次世界大战之后，汉堡店已风靡城市街头。而麦当劳汉堡连锁店将管理应用到原本一直是毫无规划的夫妻店中，成为一个近25年来广为流传的成功故事。首先，麦当劳设计了终端产品；然后它重新设计整个制作流程；接着，它重新设计或发明了制作工具，这样使得每块肉、每片洋葱、每块面包、每根炸薯条都是一样的，进而形成一个可以精准控制的全自动化制作流程；最后，麦当劳将客户"价值"定义为产品的品质和可预知性，快速便捷的供餐服务、绝对干净以及亲切友好，并基于此制定标准和培训员工，根据标准确定员工收入。

这些举措就是管理，而且是相当先进的管理。

管理是使美国经济迈向创业型经济的新技术，而非某种新科学或新发明。它也将促使美国走向创业型社会。事实上，在美国等发达国家，相比于商业和经济领域，社会创新在教育、医疗保健、政府和政治领域中具有更加广阔的发展空间。再次强调，社会中极其需要的企业家精神要求将管理的基本概念、基本技术应用于新问题和新机会。

这意味着，我们必须将30年前为管理发展所做出的努力投入到创新与企业家精神中，那就是：制定原则、注重实践、创立学科。

1

第一部分

创新实践

INNOVATION AND ENTREPRENEURSHIP
PRACTICE AND PRINCIPLES

创新是企业家的特有工具。凭借创新，企业家可以将变化视为开创新业务或新服务的机会。创新可以成为一门学科，能够加以学习和实践。企业家必须有目的地搜寻创新源、能够预示成功创新的变化和征兆。此外，他们需要了解成功创新的基本原则，并加以利用。

系统的企业家精神

I

1800 年左右，法国经济学家萨伊（J. B. Say）曾说："企业家的作用在于将资源从生产率和产出效率较低的领域转移到较高的领域。"但是，他并没有告诉我们企业家是谁。自从 200 多年前萨伊提出企业家这个词，企业家和企业家精神的定义完全令人混乱不清。

例如，在美国，企业家通常被定义为成立新创企业的人。最近盛行于美国商学院的"企业家精神"课程，就是从 30 年前的"如何创业"课程发展而来的。在许多方面，两者并无显著差异。

但是，并非所有新开办企业都具有创业性行为，或具有企业家精神。

一对夫妇在美国某市郊区开了一家熟食店或墨西哥餐馆，他们的确承担一定的风险。但是，他们是企业家吗？他们所做的事情是已被无数次重复过的老套路而已。他们把赌注压在该地区外出就餐的人口会日渐增多之上，但并未创造出新的诉求或消费需求。从这一点来看，即使他们开办了新店，也不能称之为企业家。

然而，麦当劳所表现出来的则是企业家精神。的确，麦当劳并没有发明任何新东西，任何一家不错的美国餐厅都能制作它的餐品。但是，通过应用管理概念和技巧，即研究顾客所注重的价值，实现产品标准化，设计烹制流程和工具，基于工作分析设定标准，并根据标准培训员工，麦当劳不仅大幅提高了资源的产出效率，而且开发了新市场和新客户。这就是企业家精神。

几年前，美国中西部一对夫妇创办的一家欣欣向荣的铸造厂也是企业家精神的体现。该铸造厂对铸铁进行热处理，以达到高性能规格。例如，它制造大型推土机所用的车轴，这种推土机主要用于阿拉斯加天然气管道的建设。虽然这种生产作业所需的技术背景广为人知，这家公司所做的工作也基本都有人做过，但是，其不同之处在于：第一，它将技术信息系统化。这样可以将性能规格输入计算机，立即打印出所需的方案。第二，它将工序系统化。一般来说，尺寸相同、金属成分相同、质量相同、性能规格相同的铸件订单数不会超过 6 件，但是，通过计算机来控制设备并自动调节加热炉，该厂能以流水线式而非批量式生产铸件。

先前这类精密铸件的次品率高达 30%～40%，而这家铸造厂的产品合格率却高达 90% 以上。虽然该厂要支付美国工会所规定的员工工资和福利，但与行业中价格最低的竞争者（一家韩国造船厂）相比，其成本仅为后者的 2/3，甚至更低。可见，这家工厂之所以是创业型企业，并非因为它是一家全新的小企业，而在于它创造出一种独具特色的铸铁工艺，且市场对这种铸铁的需求已经大到足以创造出一个利基市场。此外，还在于它将技术，特别是计算机技术应用到传统工艺中，将这种工艺转化成一套科学流程。

无可否认，所有的新的小企业有很多共同点。但是，这些企业若要成为创业型企业，除了小和新以外，还必须具备其他特性。事实上，在新企业中，只有小部分属于创业型企业。这些创业型企业创造出了与众不同的东西，改变或转换了价值。

并非只有新的小企业才能成为创业型企业。事实上，许多大型的尤其是历史悠久的企业也具有企业家精神，比如全球最大的企业之一，具有 100 多年历史的通用电气公司。长久以来，通用电气公司善于从零开始建立创业型业务，进而将其发展成具有相当规模的企业。通用电气公司并未将企业家精神局限于制造业中，它的融资机构通用电气信贷公司（G. E. Credit Corporation）曾经掀起一场大变革，改变了美国的金融体系，而且这场革命正迅速扩展到全美国和西欧。20 世纪 60 年代，当通用电气信贷公司发现可以将商业票据用于金融业时，它便绕过了金融界的"马其诺防线"，打破了传统银行对商业信贷的垄断。

近 50 年来，英国的大型零售商玛莎百货的表现可能比西欧任何一家企业更具有企业家精神和创新性。玛莎百货对英国经济甚至社会产生了巨大影响。这可能比英国国内任何一个变革推动者，甚至比政府或法律的影响还要大。

不过再次要说的是，通用电气公司和玛莎百货与其他完全没有企业家精神已成立的大型企业有许多共同之处。通用电气公司和玛莎百货之所以具有企业家精神，并不是因为它们的规模或发展，而是因为其他特性。

此外，企业家精神并非局限于经济组织/经济机构。

关于"企业家精神的发展史"，没有比现代大学尤其是美国现代大学的创建和发展史更好的教材了。众所周知，现代大学是德国外交官、公务员威廉·冯·洪堡（Wilhelm von Humboldt）发明的。1809 年，洪堡构思并创办了柏林大学。当时他的目标非常明确：一是让德国人取代法国人，获得学术和科学的领导地位；二是吸收法国大革命所释放出的能量，并用来对抗法国人，特别是拿破仑。60 年以后，即 1870 年左右，当德国的大学的声望如日中天时，洪堡将大学视为变革推动者的想法越过大西洋，为美国人所采纳。美国南北战争结束时，在殖民时期创办的旧式"学院"因过于陈旧而逐渐衰落。1870 年，美国的学院学生人数还不到 1830 年的一半，但这段时间的人口几乎已增至 3 倍。接下来的 30 年里，一大批优秀的美国大学校长创办了新型美国大学[⊖]，新型大学既新颖又美国化。第一次世界大战后，凭借新型大学，美国获得了学术和研究领域的世界领导地位。这如同一个世纪之前，洪堡创办的柏林大学使德国成为世界上学术和研究领域的领导者一样。

第二次世界大战以后，美国学术界的新一代创业者再度创新，创办了一批私立、都市化的新型大学：纽约地区有佩斯大学、菲尔莱－狄更斯大学和纽约理工学院；波士顿有东北大学；西海岸有圣塔克拉拉大学和金门大学，等等。这些大学构成了近 30 年来美国高等教育的主要增长点。在课程设置上，大多数新式学校似乎与历史悠久的学校并无差异。但是，新式大学是针对一个新的市场而精心设计的。它们招收的是有工作经历的人，而非高中应届毕业生；是整天往返于大学和住处之间的大城市学生，而非每周五天、朝九晚五上课的住校学生；是那些具有多样化背景的学生，而非传统的高中毕业生。它们因市场的重大转变而出现，这个转变就是大学文凭的地位从精英阶层转变为中产阶层。此外，"上大学"的意义也发生了重大转变。这些大学就代表了企业家精神。

同样，根据医院的发展史也可以写一些关于企业家精神的案例。18 世纪末，爱丁堡和维也纳出现了现代医院。到了 19 世纪，美国出现了各种形式的社区医院。20 世纪初，开始出现大型专业化中心，如梅奥诊所（Mayo Clinic）和门宁格基金会（Menninger Foundation）都是这个时期的产物。第二次世界大战之后，又出现了医疗保健中心。如今，新一代的创业者又致力于将医院改变成专业化的治疗中心，包括流动的外科诊所、独立的妇产中心和心理治疗中心。与传统医院不同，它们的工作重点不再是对病人的护理，而是专注于病人的特殊需求。

⊖　详见彼得·德鲁克，《管理：使命、责任、实践》(New York: Harper & Row,1973)，150-152。

此外，并非所有的非商业性服务机构都具有企业家精神，可能相差甚远。少数具有企业家精神的服务机构，不仅具有传统服务机构的所有特征、所有问题以及所有识别性标志[⊖]，还具备一些独特的因素，因而使这些服务机构具备了企业家精神。

虽然英语国家的人将企业家精神等同于新创企业，但德国人将它与权力和产权等同起来，更令人费解。德语的 unternehmer（企业家）就是 entrepreneur 的德译词，主要是指那些拥有并自主经营企业的人（英文为 owner-manager）。这个词主要用于将拥有企业的老板、职业经理人和雇员相区分。

但是，人们建立系统的企业家精神的最初目的并非着眼于产权。1857 年，法国的皮埃尔兄弟（Brothers Pereire）成立了创业型银行，即工业信贷银行（Crédit Mobilier）。1870 年，这种做法跨越莱茵河，在德国人乔治·西门子建立的德意志银行中进一步发展和完善。同一时期，年轻的摩根也将这种做法引到了大西洋彼岸的纽约。作为创业型银行家，其任务就是将资金分配到高生产率、高产出效率的领域。早期的银行家已经变成了企业所有者，如罗斯柴尔德家族。他们都是动用自己的资金修建铁路。创业型银行家与之截然不同，他们不想成为所有者。这些银行家为筹建企业而融资，并通过向公众出售股票来赚钱。然后，他们再向公众募集资金进行下一次投资。虽然企业家需要资本开展经济活动和大多数非经济活动，但他们并不是资本家，也不是投资者。他们需要承担风险，但这是任何从事经济活动的人都要面临的事情。经济活动的本质在于以现有的资源实现未来期望，意味着不确定性和风险。企业家也不一定是雇主，但他可以是，也往往是一个雇员或一个单打独斗的人。

无论对个人还是对机构而言，企业家精神都是一种独特的特性，但它并不是人格特征。30 年来，我见过许多个性不同、气质迥异的人在各种创业挑

⊖ 详见《管理：使命、责任、实践》中"服务机构中的绩效"和"服务机构中的企业家精神"部分。

战中表现出色。诚然，追求确定性的人往往不能成为优秀的企业家。其实，这些人在其他领域中也不会有上佳表现。例如政界要员、部队指挥官或远洋轮船船长，这些人不可避免要制定决策，然而决策的实质就是不确定性。

任何敢于直面决策的人都能学习成为企业家，并表现出企业家精神。因此，企业家精神是一种行为，而不是人格特征。它基于观念和理论，而非直觉。

II

一切实践都建立在理论之上，即使实践者本人并未意识到这一点。企业家精神以经济和社会理论为基础。该理论视变化为常态。它认为，在社会中，尤其在经济中，人们最主要的任务是创新，而非优化现存事物。这就是200多年前萨伊提出企业家一词时所表达的含义。它原本是用来作为一种对现实不满的宣告，即企业家颠覆现状，推陈出新。正如熊彼特所阐明的，企业家的工作就是创造性破坏。

萨伊是亚当·斯密（Adam Smith）的一个仰慕者。他将斯密的《国富论》（1776）翻译成法文，终生不倦地宣扬斯密的思想和策略。但是，他本人对经济思想的贡献——企业家和企业家精神的概念，却与古典经济学的理论背道而驰。古典经济学注重优化现有事物，这与目前经济理论的主流思想包括凯恩斯主义、弗里德曼货币学派的理论、供给学派经济理论是一致的。它注重发挥现有资源的最大效用，并力求实现均衡。由于它无法解释企业家这一现象，因此将企业家归为外部力量，与气候和天气、政府和政治、瘟疫和战争以及科技等划为一类。当然，传统经济学家无论属于何种学派或何种主义，并不否认这些外部力量的存在及其重要性。但是，这些外部力量并非他们所研究的，不能以他们的模型、方程式或预测加以解释与说明。

约瑟夫·熊彼特是首个回归萨伊观点的主流经济学家。在1911年出版的经典之作《经济发展理论》中，熊彼特与传统经济学决裂。他的这一举动远比 20 年后凯恩斯的行为更激进。他主张由创新的企业家引起的动态失衡，而非均衡和最优化，这是健康经济的常态，也是经济理论与实践的精髓。

萨伊重点关注经济领域，但是他的定义只强调资源的经济特性。事实上，这些资源并非用于传统的经济范畴。教育通常不被认为是经济的，虽然没有人知道应采用何种标准来评判教育产出，但经济标准是不适用的。然而教育资源一定是经济资源。事实上，它们与用于具有明确经济目的的活动（如生产商品肥皂）的资源是相同的。用于人类社会活动的资源都是相同的经济资源，例如资本（即用当前消费换取未来期望的资源）、物质资源（无论是土地、玉米种子、铜、教室，还是病床）、劳动力、管理和时间等。因此，尽管企业家精神一词源于经济层面，但它并非局限于经济范畴。除了那些被称为"存在主义"和"社交"的行为外，它适用于人类的所有行为。我们目前得知，无论在哪个领域，企业家精神的差异都微乎其微。教育领域和医疗保健领域都是有丰硕创业成果的领域，这两个领域的创业者与企业或工会中的创业者做同样的事情、用同样的工具、面临同样的问题。

企业家将变化视为健康的标准。通常，企业家并不引发变化。但他们总是**积极寻找变化和回应变化，将其视为机会并加以利用**，这也是企业家与企业家精神的定义。

Ⅲ

人们普遍认为，企业家精神充满风险。的确，在那些引人注目的创新领域诸如微型计算机或生物遗传等高科技领域中，创业的失败率非常高，成功甚至幸存的概率相当低。

原因何在？从定义来看，企业家将资源从低生产率和低产出效率的领域转移到高生产率和高产出效率的领域。这必然存在失败的风险。但是，只要略有成就，其回报足以弥补这一过程中的风险。因此，创业风险应该低于实现资源最优配置所面临的风险。事实上，当创新是正确的并有利可图时，也就是创新机会已经存在时，没有比实现资源最优配置更有风险的了。从理论上讲，企业家精神的风险应该最低而非最高。

事实上，许多创业型组织的高成功率足以推翻创新与企业家精神的高风险性的普遍看法。

例如，美国贝尔电话公司（Bell Telephone System）的创新部门是贝尔实验室。从 1911 年设计的第一个自动交换台，到 1980 年设计出的光纤电缆，其中还包括晶体管和半导体的发明，以及关于计算机的理论和工程工作，在这 70 多年的时间里，贝尔实验室创造了一个又一个成功。贝尔实验室创造的这些纪录表明，即使在高科技领域，创新和企业家精神也可能是低风险的。

IBM 处于快速发展的高科技领域计算机行业中，虽然与电力和电子行业的资深企业竞争，但迄今为止，尚未遇到重大挫败。英国玛莎百货公司是全球主要零售商中最具企业家精神的大公司，虽然是处于普通行业中，但从未有过败绩。宝洁公司（Procter & Gamble）是全球最大的消费品制造商，同样拥有近乎完美的成功创新的纪录。3M 公司是位于明尼苏达州圣保罗市的"中等技术水平"公司，在过去的 60 年中，创立了近 100 个新创业务和全新的主要产品生产线，其中 4/5 均取得了成功。这只是一小部分创业者 / 创业型企业低风险从事创新活动的例子。当然，以低风险从事创业活动的成功个案太多了，绝然不是纯属侥幸、天公作美、意外事件，或仅仅因为运气而已。

此外，还有很多个体创业者成立新创企业并有很高的成功率，这也足以反驳企业家精神具有高风险性的论调。

企业家精神之所以具有风险，主要是因为在所谓的创业者中，只有少数人知道自己在做什么。创业者，尤其是高科技领域的创业者，缺乏方法论，违背众所周知的基本原则。确切地说（第 9 章将会讨论到），从本质而言，相比于基于经济理论和市场结构的创新、基于人口统计特征的创新，甚至基于看似虚无缥缈的认知和态度如世界观的创新，高科技领域的企业家精神和创新更加困难、风险更大。但是，高科技领域的企业家精神并非一定具有高风险性，贝尔实验室和 IBM 已经证实了这一点。然而，它必须是系统的，也必须加以管理。最重要的是，它应该以有目的的创新为基础。

有目的的创新和七个创新机会源

　　企业家从事创新活动，创新是企业家精神的具体体现。创新活动能够赋予资源以新的能力，进而创造财富。事实上，创新活动本身就能创造资源。只有当人类发现自然界中某种物质的用途，并赋予它经济价值时，资源才得以称为资源。在此之前，植物只是杂草，矿物只是岩石而已。不到 100 年前，从地下渗出的石油以及铝土矿（铝的生产原料）都还不是资源。由于它们会导致土壤贫瘠，人们将它们视为有害物质。青霉菌也曾被认为是有害物质，而不是资源。当时，细菌学家在培养细菌时，必须竭尽全力保护培养基以免被青霉菌污染。到了 20 世纪 20 年代，英国医生亚历山大·弗莱明（Alexander Fleming）发现，这种"有害细菌"正是细菌学家苦苦寻找的细菌杀手。自此之后，青霉菌才成为一种有价值的资源。

　　在社会和经济领域，情况同样如此。在经济领域中，"购买力"是最重要的资源，而它却是由具有创新精神的企业家所提出的。

　　19 世纪初期，美国农民的购买力水平很低，因此无法购买农业机械。

虽然市场上有各种收割机，农民也很需要这种机械，但是他们无力购买。于是，收割机的发明者之一，赛勒斯·麦考密克（Cyrus McCormick）提出了以分期付款方式购买。这样，农民可以用未来的收入来购买收割机，而不是仅仅依靠过去的积蓄。忽然之间，农民就拥有了购买农业机械的能力（购买力）。

同样地，凡是能够改变现有资源的财富创造潜力的事物，都能被称为创新。

将卡车车身（车厢）从轮子上卸下来，再将其放置于货运轮船上，这一想法并没有什么新技术。集装箱这一创新并不是源于技术，而是源于一种新的认知，即将货轮视为一种"货箱容器"而不是一艘"船"。这意味着，真正重要的事情是，尽可能地缩短货轮在港口停泊的时间。这项看似普通的创新，却使远洋货船的运载能力大概提高了 4 倍，可能也因此拯救了船舶运输业。如果没有这项创新，在过去 40 年里，世界贸易很难获得如此巨大的发展。想想在那 40 年内，所有主要的经济活动可是都实现了有史以来最快的发展。

真正使普及教育成为可能的，不是对教育价值的广泛承诺，也不是教师在教育学院受到的系统培训或某个教育理论，而是一项不起眼的创新：教科书。教科书很可能是捷克[⊖]伟大的教育改革家约翰·阿莫斯·科梅纽斯（Johann Amos Comenius）的发明。17 世纪中期，科梅纽斯设计并使用了第一套拉丁文入门教材。如果没有教科书，即便是非常优秀的老师，一次也只能教授一两个学生。有了教科书，即便是普通的老师，一次也可以给三四十个学生传授知识。

上述事例表明，创新并非一定与技术相关，甚至不必是创造一个"实

⊖ 1620 年，波西米亚（日耳曼语对捷克的称呼）战败，此后由奥地利哈布斯堡王朝统治；1867 年后，捷克处于奥匈帝国统治之下；1918 年，奥匈帝国解体后，捷克和斯洛伐克联合，成立捷克斯洛伐克共和国；在经历了第二次世界大战以及多次社会、政治动荡之后，多次更名，于 1993 年起成为捷克和斯洛伐克两个国家。

物"。就影响力而言，很少有技术创新能与报纸、保险之类的社会创新相提并论。分期付款购买方式完全改变了经济。任何地方只要引入分期付款购买方式，不管当地生产力水平如何，都能使经济由供给驱动型变为需求驱动型。起源于18世纪欧洲启蒙运动时期的社会创新，现代医院对医疗保健的影响，远远大于其他医学上的进步。管理作为"有用的知识"，首次使具有不同技能和知识的人在一个组织里工作，这是20世纪的创新。它将现代社会转变为一个我们过去的政治理论和社会理论中都没有的崭新体系：一个有组织的社会。

经济史书籍中提到，奥古斯特·博尔西希（August Borsig）是德国制造蒸汽机车的第一人。博尔西希在开展这项创新时，遭到了同业工会、教师和政府官员的强烈反对。直到今天，这项创新仍然是德国工厂的组织系统以及德国工业实力的基础。博尔西希还提出师傅（Meister，即能够自主运营工厂的受人敬重的高技能人才）的概念；还有学徒制（Lehrling System），该项制度实现了在职训练（Lehre）与课堂教学（Ausbildung）的有机结合。1513年，马基雅维利（Machiavelli）出版的《君主论》一书中提出的"现代政府"，以及其思想的早期追随者让·博丹（Jean Bodin）60年后主张的"现代民族国家"，这两项密切相关的社会创新显然比大多数技术创新的影响更为深远。

一个非常有意思的社会创新及其重要性的例子，出现在现代日本。

自1867年向现代世界开放门户以来，日本在20世纪七八十年代一跃成为超级经济强国和国际市场中强有力的竞争对手，但它却一直受到西方人士的轻视。出现这种现象的根源在于"创新必须与实物相关并以科技为基础"的盛行观念。无论西方人还是日本国内的一些人，都将日本视为模仿者，而非创新者。总体而言，日本人并没有取得令人瞩目的技术创新或科学创新，他们的成功源于社会创新。

自1867年开始实行明治维新以来，日本人极不情愿地向世界敞开了国门。此举完全是为了避免重蹈印度的覆辙。当时，印度遭受西方国家征服、殖民和西化。日本的基本目标则是，以纯粹"柔道"的方式，运用西方的武器将西方人"抵御"在国门之外，以保持日本的独立。

这表明社会创新远比蒸汽机车或电报更重要。而且，从学校、大学、行政机关、银行以及劳资关系等机构的发展来看，相比于制造机车或者发明电报，开展社会创新更为困难。一列从伦敦开到利物浦的火车，无须加以调整或改变就可以用来从东京开到大阪。但是，日本的社会体制纯粹是"日本独有的"，当然也是"现代化的"。因此，日本人需要推动社会体制变化以适应具有高技术特征的"西化的"经济体系。人们能够以较低成本从国外引进技术，这并不会有太大的文化冲突风险。与之相反，体制则必须依赖深厚的文化根基才能发展。100 年前，经过再三考虑，日本人决定集中资源全力发展社会创新，而通过模仿、引进和改造来进行技术创新，最后取得了惊人的成就。事实上，即使现在，这一政策依然是日本最好的选择。如同在第 17 章中将要谈到的，人们有时开玩笑似的称之为创造性模仿，其实是一种备受推崇、非常有效的创业战略。

尽管当下日本人必须学会自主创新，而不是简单地模仿、引进和改造其他国家的人的技术，为慎重起见，我们还是不应低估他们的能力。科学研究本身就是离社会创新最近的一种形式。历史表明，只要形势需要，日本总能表现出这种强大的社会创新能力。最重要的是，它已经向社会展示了其运用创业战略的超凡能力。

由此得知，"创新"是一个经济术语或者社会术语，而非技术术语。借用萨伊对企业家精神的定义，我们可以将其定义为："创新就是改变资源的收益率。"或者按照现代经济学家的习惯，从需求角度而非从供给角度将其定义为："创新就是改变消费者从资源中获取的价值和满意度。"

我认为，不能根据理论模型来判断哪种定义更为合适，而应视具体情况而定。钢铁厂从一体化的综合炼钢厂到迷你钢铁厂（微型钢铁厂）的转变，从供给角度进行分析最为合适。这种迷你钢铁厂以钢屑而非铁矿石为原材料，最终产品不是需要再加工的粗钢，而是钢梁或钢杆。这种转变使成本大大降低，但并没有改变最终产品、最终用途及客户。同样地，我们可以从供给角度分析集装箱的出现。虽然录音带或录像带的技术含量可能比钢铁更高（至少与之持平），但采用消费者价值和满意度对其创新加以分析，则更为合适。此外，20 世纪 20 年代由亨利·卢斯（Henry Luce）创办的《时代》《生活》和《财富》等杂志，以及 20 世纪 70 年代末和 80 年代初出现的货币市场基金等，这些社会创新也应从需求的角度加以分析。

然而，迄今为止，我们尚未发展出一种创新理论。但是我们已经能够阐述一个人何时、何地、如何系统地发现创新机会，以及如何判断成功的概率和失败的风险。尽管相当粗略，但是我们的知识已经足以发展出创新实践。

19 世纪最伟大的成就之一是"发明的发明"。对科技史学家而言，这已是老生常谈。大约在 1880 年以前，发明带有浓厚的神秘色彩。19 世纪早期的书籍总是提到"灵光乍现"。发明家被认为是既浪漫又荒谬的人物，把自己关在在孤寂的阁楼里摆弄捣鼓。1914 年第一次世界大战爆发时，发明已逐渐变成了研究，变成了一种系统的、有目的的活动。无论在目标还是在可获得的成果方面，这种活动都可以进行有高度可预见性的策划和组织。

对创新而言，情况同样如此。如今，企业家应该学习如何进行系统的创新实践。

成功的企业家不会坐等"缪斯之吻"而获得灵感，他们通常勤奋实干。他们并非想要惊天动地的成就，诸如那些能够引起产业变革、高达上亿元的业务或能够一夜暴富的创新。而那些急于成就一番大事业的创业者注定会做错事、走错路，导致创业失败。一个看似伟大的创新，可能除了技艺之外，别无其他。而一个看似寻常的创新，比如麦当劳的创新活动，反而可能成就一番惊人且具有高利润的事业。这一道理同样也适用于非商业领域和公共服务领域的创新。

不论出于何种动机，如金钱、权力、好奇心，或名誉及他人的认可，成功的企业家总是希望能够创造价值、做出贡献。他们目标远大，并不满足于对现有事物的改进或者修正，而是试图创造出全新的、独特的价值和满足感。他们尝试将物质转化成资源，并以一种新型的更高生产力的方式对现有资源进行整合。

正是变化总能为独特的新生事物的产生提供机会。因此，**系统的创新存在于有目的地、有组织地对变化的寻找之中，存在于对这些变化所催生的经济或社会创新机会的分析之中。**

通常来说，这些变化已经产生或者正在发生。绝大多数成功的创新都是基于变化而实现的。诚然，有些创新本身就蕴含着重大变化，例如莱特兄弟发明的飞机。但这些是特例，而且是不同寻常的特例。成功的创新大都很普通，仅仅是利用了变化而已。因此，创新学科，也就是企业家精神的基础，是一种诊断式学科，即系统地审查能够带来创业机会的变化的领域。

具体而言，系统的创新就是关注七个创新机会源。

前四个创新机会源存在于机构内部（不论是商业机构还是公共服务机构），或是存在于产业或服务业内部。因此，通常只有产业或者服务业内部的人才能察觉到这种创新。这些创新都有一些表征，已经发生变化或者稍加努力就能产生变化。这四个创新机会源是：

- 意外事件——意外的成功、意外的失败、意外的外部事件。
- 不协调事件——与假定或者推测不一致的事件。
- 基于流程需求的创新。
- 产业结构和市场结构的变化。

第二组创新机会源有三个，指的是存在于企业或产业之外的变化：

- 人口统计特征（人口变化）。

- 认知、情绪及意义上的变化。

- 新知识，包括科学和非科学知识。

这七个创新机会源的界限模糊，且存在很大的重叠部分。好比同一建筑物上不同侧面的七扇窗户，透过某扇窗户可以看到相邻窗户所展现的景致。但是，透过特定窗户的中心所看到的景致是截然不同的。

考虑到每一创新机会源都有其独特性，我们应分别对这七个来源加以分析。从本质上讲，没有一个机会源比其他机会源更重要或更有生产力。重大创新可能来自对变化表征的分析（如产品或价格的微小变化所引起的意外成功），也同样可能来自重大突破性知识的广泛应用。

这些创新机会源是按照可靠性和可预见性的高低依次讨论，而非随意排序。与大众所认知的不同，新知识（特别是新科学知识），并非成功创新的最可靠或最可预见的来源。虽然基于科学的创新是可见的、迷人的、重要的，但实际上是最不可靠的、最不可预见的。相反，对诸如意外成功或意外失败等潜在变化的表征的一般性分析，其风险性和不确定性则相当低。通常情况下，由意外事件所引起的创新，从新企业的创立到产生结果（要么成功要么失败），历程最短。

创新机会源一：意外事件

I

意外的成功

在所有创新机会源中，没有哪种来源能比意外的成功创造更多的创新机会了。而且，意外的成功引起创新机会的风险更小，过程也更顺畅。但是，意外的成功往往遭到忽视。更为糟糕的是，管理者还往往将其拒之门外。

下面举个例子。

30 多年前，纽约最大的百货公司梅西百货公司的董事长罗兰·哈斯·梅西（R. H. Macy）告诉我："我们不知道如何才能降低家电的销售势头。"

"为什么要降低这种销售势头呢？"我疑惑道，"难道这项业务赔钱了吗？"

"恰恰相反，"这位董事长答道，"家电的利润率高于时装，而且没有退货，也没有出现小偷小摸现象。"

"是不是这些家电客户挤走了时装客户呢？"我问道。

"哦，不是。"他答道。"以前，我们主要向购买时装的客户推销家电产品，现在反过来向购买家电的客户推销时装。但是，"他继续说道，"像我们这种商店，时装的销售额达到 70% 才算是常态。现在，家电产品增长过快，占到销售额的 3/5，这太反常了。我们尝试过各种方法使时装销售恢复到正常比例，但成效甚微。目前唯一的办法就是降低家电的销量，使其回到应该的正常销售水平。"

这番对话之后的近 20 年内，纽约梅西百货公司的发展每况愈下。关于梅西百货公司无法利用其在纽约市场中的主导地位的原因，众说不一，比如有市中心的衰落、规模过大导致不经济，等等。1970 年，梅西百货公司更换了管理层，转变了经营重心，认可了家电对销售收入的贡献。尽管市中心依然衰落，人力成本依然高昂，规模依然庞大，但梅西百货公司却实现了再度繁荣。

在梅西百货公司拒绝意外成功的同时，纽约另一家零售商店布鲁明戴尔百货（Bloomingdale's）对同样的意外成功加以利用，因此跃升为纽约市场第二。在此之前，布鲁明戴尔百货最好也就只能排在第四位。相比于梅西百货公司，布鲁明戴尔百货更是一家以时装销售为主的公司。但是，20 世纪 50 年代早期，当家电产品的销售逐渐攀升时，布鲁明戴尔百货把握住了这个机会。它察觉到某种意料之外的事件正在发生，并加以分析。随后，它调整了家庭用品部，并将其在市场中重新定位；同时调整时装、服饰的销售重心，以获取新客户。电器销售量的剧增也只是这一新客户群体出现的一个表征。虽然在纽约市场中，梅西百货的销量仍占据首位，但布鲁明戴尔百货已经赢得"聪明的纽约商店"的头衔。而 30 年前那些为这一头衔角逐的商店——1950 年的时装先驱比如贝斯特（Best），以及昔日排行数一数二的那些百货商店，如今在排行榜上早已消失无踪（更多例子，详见第 15 章）。

梅西百货公司可能被认为是极端案例。这个案例中唯一的不寻常之处是，公司董事长对自己的所作所为了然于胸。然而，大多数管理者对自己的愚蠢行为浑然不知，却也按照梅西百货公司的处理方式行事。让管理者接受意外成功并非易事。它需要决心、具体策略、直面现实的意愿，以及足够的谦逊（来说"我们错了"）。

管理者难以接受意外成功的原因之一是，人们往往认为，凡是能够长时间持续存在的事物一定是正常的、永恒的。因此，那些违背人们认定的自然法则的事物，通常被视为是不合理的、不健康的，而且是反常现象。

这也解释了 1970 年左右美国一家大钢铁公司为什么拒绝实行迷你钢铁厂[⊖]模式。管理者知道，他们的钢铁厂很快就会惨遭淘汰，必须投入数十亿美元才能使其现代化。他们知道自己根本无法获取必要的资金。在这种情况下，只有小而新的迷你钢铁厂才是解决之道。

几乎是偶然，该公司收购了一个迷你钢铁厂。不久以后，这个迷你钢铁厂就开始迅速发展，创造现金流，并获得利润。一些年轻员工建议，用手头的资金再收购几家迷你钢铁厂并新建一些迷你钢铁厂。这样几年之内，凭借高技术含量、低人工成本和清晰的市场前景，这些迷你钢铁厂就能为公司带来数百万吨的钢产量。然而，高层管理者愤怒地否决了这项提议。随后的几年内，参与这项提议的人员陆续被解雇。高层管理者声称："一体化炼钢工序是唯一正确的工序，其他东西都是骗人的把戏，是一时的狂热，是不健康现象，根本不会持久。"毋庸讳言，十年后美国钢铁产业中，依然能够健康发展且相当繁荣的只有迷你钢铁厂。

对一个用尽毕生精力来完善一体化炼钢工序的人、一个以大型钢铁厂为家的人、一个可能是钢铁工人后代的人（很多美国钢铁公司的高管都是如此）而言，除了大型钢铁厂之外，其他事物都是诡异和陌生的，甚至是一种威胁。在这种"敌对"状态之下，要找到最佳发展机会的确需要付出努力。

⊖ 关于迷你钢铁厂，详见第 4 章。

无论规模是大还是小，是公共服务机构还是企业，大多数组织中的高管人员，通常都是从某一职能或某一领域成长而来。对他们而言，只有这些职能或领域才能使他们感到舒心。例如，我在和董事长梅西交流时得知，梅西百货公司的高管人员，除了一位人事副总之外，起初都是时装采购者，最终也是在服装业中成就自己的事业的。对这些人而言，家电产品与他们不大相关。

意外成功有时令人感到尴尬。设想一下，一家公司全心全意地改进和完善一项旧产品。这项旧产品是该公司多年以来的旗舰产品，代表着公司的品质。与此同时，公司不得不对另一项陈旧过时且质量低劣的产品进行改进，人人都觉得这项改进毫无意义。之所以这样做，只是因为公司某个销售领导人的游说，或因为某个客户无法拒绝的要求。但是，没有人认为这项产品能够大卖，甚至根本没人愿意推销它。结果这个不被看好的产品却轻松地赢得市场，其销售额甚至达到了那个备受期望的产品的预期销量水平。不足为奇，每个人都感到吃惊，并将这一成功视为"鸠占鹊巢"（这个词我已经听过多次）。人们的反应可能与梅西百货公司的董事长看到家电的表现超过其钟爱的服装一样。毕竟他将全部的工作和毕生精力都倾注于时装之上。

对管理者的判断力而言，意外成功是一种挑战。那家大型钢铁厂的董事长在否决迷你钢铁厂的提议时曾说："如果迷你钢铁厂是一个机会，我们自己肯定会看得出来。"管理者的确是凭借判断力来获取薪酬，但这并非意味着他们的判断不会出错。事实上，企业聘用管理者时，也希望他们能够意识到并承认错误，尤其是当承认错误能够为公司打开新机会时。但是，这并不常见。

瑞士有一家制药公司，虽然从未自主研发过一种兽药，如今却在兽药制造领域占据世界领先地位。究其原因，是研制这些药物的制药厂或制药公司当时拒绝将药物供应给兽医市场。这些药物，主要是抗生素，起初是为了治疗人类疾病而研发的。当兽医们发现这些药物对动物疗效显著并下单订购时，制药厂却大为不快。一些制药厂拒绝向兽医供货，还有一些制药厂不愿为动物重新调配药方或更换药物包装，等等。1953 年左右，一家领先的制药厂的药品主管还抗议将新抗生素用于动物治疗，认为这是滥用药品的行为。因此，当瑞士人与这几家制药厂接洽时，毫不费力地以低廉价格获取了这些药物的使用许可。一些制药厂也为能够摆脱这种意外成功带来的尴尬感到欣慰。

之后，人类用药的价格压力越来越大，并且受到监管局的严格管制。这使兽药成为医药行业中最为盈利的领域。但是，早期研发兽药的制药厂并没有从中获利。

通常情况下，意外成功根本不会被人们看到。人们没有注意到它，更不会对它加以利用。无法避免的是，竞争对手往往会抓住机会，获得回报。

一家领先的医疗设备供应商引进了一条全新的生产线，用于生产生物和临床实验仪器。新产品反响很好。很快，工业界和大学实验室也纷纷下单订购。但是，该医疗设备供应商事先不知道这种情况，也没有对此加以注意。除了预期客户之外，这家公司的新产品还意外地吸引了其他更多更好的客户。但是该公司并未因此派销售人员去拜访这些新客户，也没有提供相应的服务支持。5～8 年后，另外一家公司占领了这些新市场。由于这些市场具有足够大的交易量，很快新进入者以比在位者更低的价格和更优的服务进入了医院市场。

对意外成功缺乏认知的原因之一，在于现有报告体系并未对其加以汇报，更不用说引起管理者的注意了。

实际上，任何一家公司包括公共服务机构都有月度或季度报告。报告的第一页通常是绩效低于预期的领域，主要是存在的问题。在管理层和董事会的月度会议上，每个人只关注不足之处，而不会去注意业绩表现异常突出的地方。另外，如果意外成功表现在质上而不是量上，比如上文提到的医疗设备重新开拓了一个市场，数字通常无法显示出这种意外成功。

　　要利用意外成功所带来的创新机会，我们必须要加以分析。意外成功只是一个表征，但它表示什么呢？人们对现象的分析，往往会受自身认知、知识水平和理解力所限。以上面讲的制药厂为例，它们拒绝接受其药品在动物医疗市场的意外成功。这表明它们不了解全球牲畜市场的巨大和重要性，没有看到第二次世界大战之后全球对动物蛋白质的巨大需求，也不知道全球农民、牧民的知识、经验和管理能力的巨大变化。

　　梅西百货公司在家电产品上的意外成功，表明大批消费者的行为、期望和价值观发生了根本转变。布鲁明戴尔百货清晰地认识到了这一点。第二次世界大战之前，美国百货商店的消费者主要是按照社会经济地位即收入阶层而购物的。第二次世界大战之后，消费市场逐渐按照我们所称的生活方式来划分。布鲁明戴尔百货是第一家，尤其是美国东海岸的第一家，意识到这种现象并对其加以利用，进而创建全新零售形象的百货商店。

　　为医院设计的实验仪器却在工业和大学实验室获得意外成功，表明科学仪器用户之间的差异消失。过去近一个世纪里，这种差异产生了截然不同的市场，不同的用途、规格和期望。这一现象不仅仅表明某个产品具有出乎意料的用途，还表明该公司在医院市场所享有的特定市场利基的终结，然而它却没有意识到这一点。在三四十年的时间里，该公司一直将自己成功地定义为医院实验仪器的设计者、制造者和经销者。最终还是不得不将自己重新定义为实验仪器的制造者，并在原先领域之外发展新的设计、制造、分销和服务能力。然而，等一切就绪，它已经失去了大部分市场。

　　由此可见，意外成功不仅仅是创新机会，同时还需要有所创新。它迫使我们自问，就公司的经营业务而言，哪些基本变化比较适合呢？就技术而言呢？就市场而言呢？如果能够慎重对待这些问题，那么意外成功可能会带来回报最高、风险最小的创新机会。

　　世界上最大的两家企业，全球最大的化工企业杜邦公司和计算机行业的巨头 IBM 都将其卓越成就归功于把意外成功视为创新机会，并积极加以利用。

在长达 130 年的时间里，杜邦公司的业务聚焦于军火和炸药领域。20 世纪 20 年代中期，它开始将研发力量拓展到其他领域，其中之一是全新高分子化学。第一次世界大战期间，德国在高分子化学领域一直居于领先地位。持续几年后，杜邦公司的该项研究毫无进展。1928 年，一位研究助理因忘记关掉炉火，导致炉火烧了整整一个周末。到星期一早晨，公司有机化学部的负责人华莱士·H. 卡罗瑟斯（Wallace H. Carothers）发现，壶里的东西已经凝结成纤维。随后又过了 10 年，杜邦公司才找到研制尼龙的方法。这个故事的关键在于，很早之前，德国大型化学公司的实验室里也多次发生过同样的意外。那时，德国人正在寻找聚合纤维，他们本可以早于杜邦公司 10 年研制出尼龙，并获得全球化工领域的领导地位。但是，由于德国人没有预料到这项实验并忽略了这一实验结果，倒掉了意外产生的纤维，随后又重新开始。

IBM 的发展史同样表明，企业对意外成功加以重视能够带来一定的好处。IBM 之所以能够成就今日的辉煌，很大程度上是由于不止一次利用了意外成功。20 世纪 30 年代初，IBM 面临倒闭。它将全部资金用于设计第一台银行专用的电动机械记账机。但是在 30 年代初的大萧条时期，美国银行并不想购买任何新设备。即便那时，IBM 也不曾实行减员策略，而是继续生产这种机器，并将成品囤放在仓库里。

就在 IBM 处于低谷时，故事发生了。一天，IBM 的创始人托马斯·沃森（Thomas Watson）参加一个晚宴，他旁边坐着一位女士。当这位女士得知他的名字时，她问道："你就是 IBM 的沃森先生？你的销售经理为何不愿向我展示你们的机器呢？""一位女士要记账机做什么？"老沃森有点疑惑。当她告诉老沃森自己是纽约公共图书馆馆长时，他仍旧迷惑不解。这也说明老沃森从未去过公共图书馆。第二天早上，图书馆刚开门，他就出现在了那里。

当时，图书馆拥有数目可观的政府拨款。两个小时后，当沃森走出图书馆时，他手中拿着一份足够支付下个月工资的订单。后来每次谈及此事，他都会笑着补充一句："我当场提出一项新要求，先交款，后送货。"

15年后，IBM研制出一台早期计算机。与其他早期的美国计算机一样，IBM的计算机是专为科学研究而设计的。事实上，IBM之所以会进入计算机行业，很大程度上源于老沃森对天文学的浓厚兴趣。当IBM的计算机首次亮相在麦迪逊大街的IBM展览窗时，大批人群争相围观。通过编程设计，这台计算机能够计算月亮过去、现在、未来的所有状态。

但是随后，企业开始购买这项"科技奇迹"用于处理一般性事物，比如工资结算。当时尤尼瓦克公司（Univac）拥有最先进、最适用于商业用途的计算机，但它却不愿供货给企业，生怕贬低了自己的科技奇迹。虽然IBM对企业界的计算机需求同样感到惊讶，但是它对这一现象立即做出回应。考虑到自己的计算机设计并不特别适用于会计工作，IBM使用了竞争对手尤尼瓦克公司的产品设计。于是，短短4年之内，IBM就获得了计算机市场的领导地位。虽然在技术层面上，IBM的计算机在随后的10年里依然比不上尤尼瓦克公司生产的计算机。IBM非常乐意站在企业的立场上，满足企业的业务需求，比如为企业培训编程人员。

同样地，日本龙头电器公司，松下电器（以品牌Panasonic和National闻名于世）也将其崛起归功于对意外成功的利用。

20世纪50年代初期，松下电器还是一家不起眼的小公司，各方面都远远落后于历史悠久且实力雄厚的行业巨头，如东芝、日立。正如同时期其他日本家电厂商一样，松下公司知道电视在日本难以迅速发展。1954年或1955年，东芝公司总裁在纽约的一次会议上说道："日本还很穷，无力购买电视之类的奢侈品。"但松下公司相当聪明，它认为日本农民显然不觉得自己太穷而买不起电视机。这些农民所了解的是电视机为他们打开了外面的世界。即便暂时无力购买，无论如何他们都是愿意购买电视机的。当时，东芝和日立生产的电视机质量比较好，它们只将这些电视机放在东京的银座和大城市的百货公司展示。在这些高雅的地方，农民显然不太受欢迎。然而，松下却来到农村，挨家挨户地推销电视机。在当时的日本，除了是卖棉布裤或围裙，根本没有人用这种方式推销较贵重的产品。

当然，仅仅靠意外事件是远远不够的，苦等邻座的女士对一个濒临失败的产品表现出意外的兴趣（IBM 的故事），也不是办法。因此，必须要有组织地寻找意外成功。

首先，要确保意外成功能够引来人们的关注。应该以特写的形式将它刊载于管理者接触和研究的信息册子中（如何做到这一点，详见第 13 章）。

管理者必须带着问题来看待每一次的意外成功。这些问题包括：①如果对它加以利用，对我们有什么意义？②它会将我们引领到何处？③如何才能将它转换成机会？④如何着手进行？这意味着，首先，管理者要安排具体时间来讨论意外成功；其次，要委派相关人员研究意外成功，以及如何对它加以利用。

管理者还要了解意外成功对管理者的要求。举一个具体的例子来说明这点。

20 世纪 50 年代初，美国东海岸一所著名大学为成年人开设继续教育的夜校项目，计划为拥有高中学历的成年人讲授正规大学课程，并向他们颁发大学学位。

没有一个教职工真正认可这个项目。开设这个项目的唯一原因是参加第二次世界大战的退伍军人中，有一部分人没有获得大学学位就被迫去工作了。这些人吵嚷着希望有机会完成未完成的学分。令人吃惊的是，很多满足要求的人都来申请该项目，这个夜校项目取得了巨大的成功。事实上，参加这个项目的学生比普通在校生的表现更为出色。这一现象反而使学校陷入尴尬境地。如果利用这个意外成功，学校必须要配备一流的师资队伍。但这样会削弱学校的主要项目，至少会分散学校的注意力而不能专注于培养在校生的使命。另一个方案就是停办这个新项目。这两种方案都是负责任的决策。然而，学校却选用低薪的临时教职工，大多是正在攻读更高学位的助教来担任该项目的教员。结果，这种做法在几年内就摧毁了这个项目。更为糟糕的是，学校的声誉也受到了严重损害。

意外的成功是一种机会，但它也有一定的要求。它要求人们慎重地对待它；它要求配备最优秀的、最有能力的人员，而不是随意抽调人员；它要求管理者给予与机会相匹配的关注和支持。总而言之，机会需慎重考虑。

II

意外的失败

不同于成功，失败是无法拒绝的，而且很难被忽视。人们很少会将失败视为机会的表征。当然，很多失败不过是错误、贪婪、愚昧、盲目追风或者设计和执行不力的结果。但是，如果在仔细规划、精心设计并审慎执行之后，仍然失败，那么这种失败常常预示着根本性变化，随之而来的还有机会。

也许是产品或服务的设计或者营销策略所依据的前提假设，与现实情况不符；也许是客户价值和客户认知发生了转变，即便购买同一种东西，他们的实际购买价值截然不同；也许是原来的同一市场或同一终端用途，现在细分成两个或者更多，而且具有各不相同的需求；诸如此类的变化都是创新机会。

大约 60 年前，刚刚高中毕业的我在职业生涯初期经历了第一次意外的失败。我的第一份工作是在一家老牌出口公司当实习生。100 多年来，这家公司一直向英属印度出口五金产品。多年来，这家公司的畅销产品一直是一种便宜的挂锁。每个公司都能出口一整船这样的挂锁。这种挂锁很容易被损坏，用一枚别针就能轻易地打开它。20 世纪 20 年代，随着印度人收入的增长，这种挂锁的销量反而急剧下降。我的老板于是采取了显而易见的行动，重新设计挂锁使它更牢靠，也就是提高挂锁的质量。这种改变所增加的成本微不足道，但挂锁的质量大为提升。然而，改良后的挂锁依然滞销。四年后，这家公司停业清算，其破产的首要原因是挂锁业务在印度市场的失利。

在出口印度的业务领域，曾有一家规模很小的公司是我所在公司的竞争对手。这家小公司的规模不到我所在公司的 1/10，当时几乎难以继续生存，但这家小公司意识到，这个意外的失败其实是根本变化的一个表征。据我所知，对居住在乡村的大多数印度人而言，挂锁是一种神秘的象征，目前仍然如此。从来没有小偷胆敢开启这种锁。因此，钥匙从未派上用场，反而常常丢失。如此一来，拥有一把没有钥匙就很难打开的锁，就像我老板花费极少成本改良的那种锁，实在是一种灾难而不是福利。

但是，居住在城市里的中产阶级需要真正的锁。他们虽然人数不多，但在迅速增长。由于不够牢靠而难以满足他们的需求，老式挂锁逐渐失去了客户和市场。即便重新设计改良后的挂锁，对他们而言，仍然不太适用。

老板的竞争对手于是将挂锁细分为两类不同的产品。一种没有锁头和钥匙，仅仅是一个简单的拉栓，其售价是老式挂锁的 1/3，利润却是后者的两倍。另外一种非常牢固，配有三把钥匙，其售价是老式挂锁的两倍，利润也远远大于后者。这两种产品很快就在市场中大受欢迎。短短两年，这个竞争对手就一跃成为向印度出口五金产品最大的欧洲公司。它维持这一地位长达十年之久，直到第二次世界大战爆发终止了欧洲对印度的出口。

人们可能会说，这只是陈年旧事罢了。当然，在当今计算机时代，市场调查和 MBA 商学院普及的时代，人们会愈加"成熟"。

但是，下面这个半个世纪之后发生在成熟行业的案例，给了我们同样的启示。

1973—1974 年，当第一批婴儿潮人群到 20 多岁时，即到成家立业购置房子时，经济出现大衰退。通货膨胀严重，尤其是房价，比其他任何东西上涨得都快。与此同时，房屋抵押贷款的利率也在飙升。美国建筑商开始设计并提供所谓的基础房屋。这种房屋比标准房屋要小，设计简单，价格便宜。

虽然这种基础房屋具有这样的价值，价格在首次购房者的财力范围之内，但它还是惨遭失败。建筑商试图通过降低贷款利率、延长贷款期限以及大幅降低价格来挽回败局，但没有任何起色。

同一般商人遭遇意外失败时一样，大多数建筑商将失败归咎于不明智的客户。然而，一家很小的建筑商决定出去看看，到底是什么情况。他发现美国年轻夫妇对第一栋房子的要求已经有所变化。与他们的祖父母辈不同，对他们而言，第一栋房屋不再代表家庭的永久住房（一个用于度过余生至少相当长时间的房屋）。20 世纪 70 年代，年轻夫妇在购买第一栋房子时，所购买的不是一种而是两种不同的价值取向。他们先买下一个栖身之所，以度过短暂时光。同时也购买了一个选择权，几年之后，在一个更好的社区、拥有优质教育的地方，购买一个大而豪华的真正住房。依靠投入到第一栋房子上的资产净值，他们才能支付价格昂贵的永久住房的首期付款。虽然有能力购买基础房屋，但这些年轻人清楚地知道，这些基础房屋并非他们和同时代人的理想住房。他们担心这些基础房屋很难卖到一个好价钱，这完全合乎情理。所以，基础房屋不仅不能帮助他们获得将来购置真正房屋的选择权，反而会阻碍他们实现愿望。

总的来说，20 世纪 50 年代的年轻夫妇大都认为自己是工人阶级。在西方，刚刚结束学徒生涯，获得第一份正式工作的工人阶级，并不奢望自己的收入和生活水平能够得到显著改善。除了日本之外，对西方国家的工人阶级而言，资历而非更高的工资意味着更大的工作保障。按一般惯例，中产阶级家庭的一家之主在 45 岁或 48 岁之前，收入都会稳步提高。1950—1975 年，美国年轻人的现实状况及自我印象，包括教育、期望和工作，都从工人阶级转变为中产阶级。伴随这一变化的，是年轻人第一个家的意义及相关价值的巨大转变。

只要花费几个周末的时间去倾听潜在购买者的想法，就能了解这一点。成功的创新也就很容易产生了。无需对房子进行大的改动，只需重新设计厨房使它更加宽敞。除此之外，同其他建筑商没有销路的基础房屋相比，这种房屋相差无几。但是，这种房屋并不是以"你的房屋"的方式推出，而是以"你的第一栋住房"和"构筑你理想住房的基石"的方式出售。确切地说，这意味着展现在年轻夫妇面前的，不仅仅是一栋基础房屋，还有这栋房子未来扩建的模式，如增加一个卫生间、一两个或更多卧室，或地下室。事实上，该建筑商已经获得了必要的城建许可证，以便能够将基础房屋改建成永久住房。此外，建筑商还向年轻夫妇承诺，给予第一栋住房一个固定的出让价格，折价到他们在 5～7 年之内向该公司购买第二栋更大的永久性住房中。"这样做没有任何风险，"该公司解释道，"毕竟人口统计特征表明，到 20 世纪八九十年代，这段时间正好是 1961 年生育低谷期出生的婴儿长到 25 岁，开始成家立业之时。市场对第一栋住房的需求会稳步上升。"

这家建筑商将失败转化为创新机会之前，其业务仅限于一个大都市内，而且市场份额很小。五年之后，这家公司的业务扩展到 7 个大都市，并且在每个城市都占据数一数二的市场份额。1981—1982 年，建筑业处于严重的衰退期，有些美国建筑商在一个季度里一栋房子都卖不出去。即便在如此萧条的时期，这家创新建筑商的销量仍在增长。"其中一个理由是"，公司创始人解释道，"当我决定向首次购房者提供房屋转售价格保证时，未曾料想到，这竟然使我们不断地获得建造良好且相当新的房子。只需对这些房子稍加整修，我们就可以将它们转售给下一批首次购房者，并获得相当可观的利润。"

面对意外的失败时，高层管理者，尤其是大型组织中的高层管理者，往往会倾向于做较多的研究和分析。但是，正如挂锁和基础房屋的例子所示，这种反应是错误的。当遭遇意外的失败时，你需要走出去，四处察看并仔细倾听。失败应该被视为创新机会的表征，并得到认真对待。

同从客户的角度出发一样，从供应商的角度观察意外事件同样重要。举个例子来说，麦当劳的创立就是因为其创始人雷·克罗克（Ray Kroc）留意到他的一个客户的成功。当时，克罗克正在向汉堡包店推销冰激凌机。他发现加州某偏远小镇一个汉堡包店的经营者购买了几倍于同样规模的店铺所需的冰激凌机。调查之后，他发现这位老人将快餐业务加以系统化并重新定义了快餐的经营模式。于是，克罗克买下了他的快餐店，并在先前意外成功的基础上，将该快餐店发展成为数十亿美元的企业。

同样地，竞争对手的意外成功或者意外失败也很重要。任何情况下，人们都应该将这些事件看作创新机会的表征，并慎重对待。对于意外事件，不仅仅要加以分析，还要走出去全面调查。

创新，即这本书的主题，是一种有组织的、系统的、理性化的工作。但它不仅仅是概念化的，也是感知性的。诚然，创新者的所见所闻必须要经过严格的逻辑分析，而不能仅仅凭借直觉。事实上，如果直觉就是"我觉得"，那直觉就变得毫无益处了。通常情况下，那只不过是"我希望它怎样"的另一种说法，而不是"我认识到它怎样"。虽然分析是严谨的，需要进行测试、试验和评估，但这些分析必须建立在对变化、机遇和新情况的认知上，还需要敏锐地察觉到人们所确信的情况和实际情况之间不协调的地方。这需要人们意识到："我所知道的不足以去进行分析，但我会进一步去发现。我应该走出去，四处观察，提出问题并用心倾听。"

意外事件能使我们超越预设观念、假设及先前的必然之事，因此它是创新的不竭源泉。

事实上，企业家并非一定要弄清楚现实情况为何会发生变化。在上述两个案例中，我们很容易就能了解发生了什么以及事情发生的原因。通常情况下，我们虽然知道所发生的事情，但无法对它加以解释。这种情况下，我们仍然能进行成功的创新。

下面我讲一个例子。

1957 年，福特汽车公司推出一款新型汽车艾德赛尔（Edsel）却惨遭失败，这是美国家喻户晓的故事。在艾德赛尔惨败之后出生的人也听说过这个故事，至少在美国是这样的。人们普遍将艾德赛尔的推出视为一种轻率的赌博行为，这种看法完全是错误的。

很少有产品能够像艾德赛尔那样精心地设计、审慎地推出并巧妙地营销。艾德赛尔的推出原本是美国商业史上最详细的战略规划中的最后一步。经过长达十年的努力，第二次世界大战后，福特汽车公司从濒临破产转变为汽车行业中一个强有力的竞争者，在美国市场中位居第二。几年之后，在迅速发展的欧洲市场中，成为争夺霸主地位的有力角逐者。

1957 年，在美国四大汽车市场的三大市场中，福特已经成功地重新树立了自己强有力的竞争地位。在标准汽车市场中，它的品牌有福特（Ford）；在中低端汽车市场中，有水星（Mercury）；在高端汽车市场中，有大陆（Continental）。为了打入最后一个市场，即中高端市场，福特公司专门设计了艾德赛尔。在中高端市场中，有福特公司的头号劲敌通用汽车生产的别克（Buick）和奥尔兹莫比尔（Oldsmobile）。第二次世界大战后，中高端市场成为汽车市场中发展最快的领域。当时位列第三的汽车公司克莱斯勒（Chrysler）尚未进入这一领域，市场向福特公司敞开了大门。

福特公司全力地规划和设计艾德赛尔。在艾德赛尔的设计中，融入了市场调研所获得的最新信息、客户对汽车外观和款式的偏好信息以及高标准的质量控制。

但是，艾德赛尔一经面市就彻底失败了。

福特公司对这次失败的反应，令人深思。它并没有归咎于不理智的消费者。福特公司认为一定存在某些事情，与汽车从业者对消费者行为的假设不相符合。而长久以来，他们一直把这些假设视为不可置疑的真理。

福特公司的人员决定走出办公室，对失败进行调查。这是继阿尔弗雷德·斯隆（Alfred P. Sloan）之后，美国汽车史上一项真正的创举。20 世纪 20 年代，按照社会经济地位，斯隆将美国汽车市场划分为低端、中低端、中高端和高端四个细分市场，并在此基础上创办了通用汽车公司。当福特公司的人员走出去后，发现这种划分方式正被另一种方式快速取代（至少是同时存在）。这种新的划分方式，就是我们所称的生活方式划分法。于是，在艾德赛尔失败后不久，福特推出了雷鸟（Thunderbird），它是自 1908 年亨利·福特（Henry Ford, Sr.）推出 T 型轿车以来最成功的美国汽车。雷鸟使福特公司凭借自身实力再度成为主要汽车制造商，而不再是通用汽车的追随者或模仿者。

时至今日，我们仍然不清楚引起这种变化的根本原因。经常被用来解释变化出现的事件，如战后婴儿潮所引起的人口结构重心向青少年转移、高等教育的迅速普及以及性观念的转变等，都在这个变化之后。同时，我们并不能理解生活方式的真正含义。迄今为止，所有试图对其加以解释的尝试都是徒劳。我们所知道的只是发生了某些事情。

但是，这足以将意外事件（无论是成功还是失败），转化为有效且有目的的创新机会。

III

意外的外部事件

到目前为止，我们所讨论的意外成功和意外失败都发生在企业或者行业内部。但是那些没有记录在管理者用以掌管其机构的信息和数字资料中的外部事件，同样重要。事实上，往往应该说它们更为重要。

下面列举了一些典型的意外的外部事件。对这些外部事件的利用也是成功创新的重大机会。

其中之一与 IBM 和个人计算机有关。

不管 IBM 的管理人员和工程师的想法多么不同，在 20 世纪 70 年代之后，他们对一件事的看法几乎完全一致。这个看法就是，未来是属于具有更大内存和更快计算能力的集成大型计算机的。而其他产品不是更加昂贵，就是令人混淆不清，或者运行能力有限。关于这一点，IBM 的任何一位工程师都能充分证明。于是，IBM 集中全部力量和资源以保持其在大型计算机市场上的领导地位。

1975 年或 1976 年左右，令人惊奇的是，10 岁和 11 岁的小孩竟然玩起了电脑游戏。他们的父亲则想要一台自己的办公电脑或个人电脑，即一台分开的、独立的小型机器，其容量即便比最小的主机还小也无所谓。IBM 预料的不好的事情最终还是发生了。这些独立的机器比插入式终端的成本高出好几倍，而且容量减小了很多。这种机器及其程序如雨后春笋般涌现，彼此之间很难兼容。计算机市场开始陷入混乱状态，基本的服务和维修也跟不上。但是，这并没有影响到消费者的购买欲望。与之相反，1979—1984 年这短短 5 年内，在美国计算机市场中，个人电脑市场的年销售额是大型计算机市场 30 年销售额的总和，即 150 亿～160 亿美元。

IBM 完全可能忽略了这一发展趋势。然而，早在 1977 年，当全球个人电脑的销售额还不到 2 亿美元，大型计算机的销售额还是 70 亿美元时，IBM 就成立了彼此竞争的任务攻关小组来研发个人电脑。1980 年，IBM 生产出个人电脑，恰好赶上了个人电脑市场的蓬勃发展期。3 年之后，即 1983 年，如同在大型计算机领域中一样，IBM 占领了个人电脑领域的世界领导地位。同年，IBM 还推出了微型家用电脑，被称为"花生"（Peanut）。

每当与 IBM 人员讨论起这段经历时，我都会问同样的问题："既然当时 IBM 的每一个人都确信这种事情不可能发生而且毫无意义，那是什么使你们将这种变化视为机会呢？"我得到的回复总是一样的："就是因为我们认为这种事情不可能发生并且毫无意义，所以这种变化令我们震惊。我们意识到，先前所做的假设以及确定的事情全被否定了。因此，我们必须走出去，重新组织自己，充分利用我们认为不会发生却真实存在的变化。"

第二个案例较为平淡。虽然缺乏迷人之处，但同样具有启发性。

在美国，由于免费的公共图书馆随处都是，人们没有购书的习惯。20世纪50年代初，电视机出现了。越来越多的美国人把时间花费在电视机前，特别是正处于重要读书阶段的高中生和大学生。当时，所有人都认为书籍的销量将大幅下滑。于是出版商们开始盲目地转向高科技媒体，如教学片或者电脑程序，但大都以失败告终。然而，自电视机出现以来，书籍的销量非但没有暴跌，反而大幅增长。其增幅比人们对其他指标，如家庭收入、处于最佳读书阶段的人数、拥有较高学位的人数，所预测的增长速度高好几倍。

关于为什么这种情况会出现，我们不得而知。事实上，没人真正了解究竟发生了什么。与从前一样，在典型的美国家庭里，藏书量同样少。那么，这些书都到哪里去了呢？虽然我们无法回答这个问题，但这并不改变图书销量日益增加的事实。

当然，所有出版商和书店都知道图书的销量与日俱增。但反而是一些大型零售商，如明尼阿波利斯和洛杉矶的一些百货公司利用了这起意外事件。这些零售业的人以前并未涉足过图书领域，不过他们了解零售业。他们建立了与美国早期书店截然不同的连锁书店。从本质上而言，这些书店都是超市。他们并不把书籍视为文学作品，而将其视为大众商品。此外，他们专营畅销书，以确保每单位的货架能产生最大的销售额。这些连锁书店通常位于租金昂贵、客流量较大的购物中心，而一般从事图书生意的人认为，书店应该位于租金低廉、最好离大学较近的地方。传统的书商通常书卷气十足，也喜欢雇用一些爱书人士。新式连锁书店的经理们则都是化妆品推销员出身。他们之间流传着一则笑话：任何一个除了看书的标价还想看书的内容的人，都不是一个有希望的、合格的推销员。

10年来，这些新式连锁书店成为美国零售业中最为成功、发展最快的领域，同时也是美国发展最快的新兴行业。

上述案例都代表着真正的创新，但都不能代表多元化。

IBM 自始至终都在计算机行业中。连锁书店是由一直在零售业、购物中心或时装店的人所经营。

成功地利用意外的外部事件的一个前提是，意外事件必须与所在行业的知识和技巧相吻合。许多没有零售业知识的公司，甚至是大公司，贸然进入书籍市场或大众商品市场，都无一例外地失败了。

尤为重要的是，意外的外部事件只是一种将已有专业知识重新应用的机会，这种应用并不能改变我们经营业务的本质。与其说它是多元化，不如说是一种扩展。然而，正如上述案例所示，它也要求我们在产品、服务以及分销渠道等方面进行创新。

这些案例的第二个特点是，它们都是大公司的例子。同许多管理书籍一样，本书列举的大都是大公司的案例。一般而言，大公司的案例更容易获得，是在出版物上唯一能找到的资料，也是在报刊或杂志的商业版上唯一能公开讨论的案例。小公司的案例通常不易获得，而且很难在不泄露商业机密的情况下加以讨论。

利用意外的外部事件似乎特别适用于现有的企业，尤其是具有一定规模的企业。据我所知，能够成功利用意外的外部事件的小企业少之又少。参加我的创新与企业家精神研讨班的学生，也深有同感。可能只是一种巧合，也可能是因为大企业更能看到经济发展的大趋势。

美国的大型零售商习惯看数据，这些数据能够显示消费者的消费目标和消费方式。大型零售商能够清楚地了解购物中心的位置有哪些以及如何得到一个好位置。而小企业是否能像 IBM 那样，派遣四组由一流设计人员和工程师组成的攻关小组来开发新产品呢？处于快速发展行业里的小型高科技公司，在现有业务上都感到人手不足，更何况是开发新产品了。

　　对大型企业而言，意外的外部事件也许是机会最大而风险最小的创新领域，也许是特别适于现有大型企业进行创新的领域，也许是专业知识最具影响力且迅速调动大量资源的能力具有重大意义的领域。

　　但是，正如这些例子所示，创业时间久、规模大不能保证企业能够察觉到意外事件并成功地加以利用。IBM 的美国竞争对手都是销售额高达数十亿美元的大企业，它们都忙于与 IBM 竞争，却没有一家企业开发个人电脑。美国的旧式大型连锁书店，如纽约的布伦塔诺（Brentano's），也没有利用新的图书市场。

　　换言之，机会就在眼前。重大机会经常会出现。机会一旦出现，就能带来广阔的前景，尤其对大企业而言。但是，这些机会所需要的并非只是运气或直觉。企业要积极寻求创新，并加以组织和管理，以便抢占先机。

创新机会源二：不协调事件

不协调是指现状与预期之间的差距，或者现状与假定之间的不符。我们也许不能了解它产生的原因，而且事实上，我们并不了解它。但是，不协调仍然是创新机会的一个表征。用地质学家的术语来说，它表示存在一个断层（fault），这种断层能提供创新机会。不协调能够引起不稳定，只需稍加努力就能使这种不稳定产生巨大变化，并导致经济结构和社会结构的重新调整。通常情况下，管理人员收到以及研究的数据和报告并不能显现出不协调事件。这些不协调事件是定性而非定量的。

同意外成功或意外失败一样，不协调事件也是变化的表征，无论这种变化是已经发生的还是将能够发生的。而且，就像存在于意外事件之中的变化一样，不协调事件之中的变化也通常发生在产业、市场或者流程内。因此，对接近或者处于该产业、市场或流程的人来说，不协调事件很容易被察觉，因为就在他们眼前。但是业内人士往往将不协调事件视为理所当然而忽略它们。他们会说，"事情一直是这样的"，即使一直极可能只是最近而已。

不协调事件有以下几种情形：

- 产业（或公共服务领域）的经济现状之间的不协调。
- 产业（或公共服务领域）的现实与假设之间的不协调。
- 产业（或公共服务领域）的努力与客户价值和期望之间的不协调。
- 流程的节奏或逻辑的内部不协调。

I

经济现状之间的不协调

如果某个产品或服务的需求稳步增长，那么其经济效益也应该稳步提高。在一个需求稳步增长的产业里，盈利是顺其自然的事情。如果这样的产业不能盈利，则说明经济现状之间存在着不协调。

一般而言，这种不协调都是宏观现象，发生在整个产业或整个服务部门内。不协调之中孕育着重大的创新机会，这种机会通常只适用于高度专业的小型新创企业。在现有企业和供应商意识到危险的新竞争对手的存在之前，利用这种不协调的创新者往往有较长时间不受干扰。因为前者忙于弥补不断增长的需求与滞后的效益之间的差距，无暇顾及其他公司正在做不同的事情。而这些不同的事情能够使其他公司利用不断增长的需求，有所作为。

有时，我们能够理解究竟发生了什么，但有时，我们无法弄清楚为什么需求增长了却并没有带来效益提升。创新者不必非要弄清楚为什么事情没有按照预定的模式发展，而是要提出下述问题："如何才能利用这种不协调？如何将它转化为机会？我们能做些什么？"经济现状之间的不协调是需要采取行动的一个信号。有时候，尽管问题本身相当模糊，所需要采取的行动却很明朗；而有时候，虽然我们完全理解问题，却不知该如何行动。

"迷你钢铁厂"就是一个很好的例子，它成功地利用了不协调进行创新。

自第一次世界大战之后 50 多年来，发达国家的大型综合钢铁厂只有在战争时期才出现过辉煌。在和平年代，尽管钢铁的需求量稳步上升，至少在 1973 年以前如此，这些工厂的表现却一直不尽如人意。

出现这种不协调的原因，早已众所周知。为了满足对钢铁的额外需求小幅度提升产量，大型钢铁厂不得不进行巨额投资并大幅扩充产能。但如果扩建现有钢铁厂的规模，在相当长的一段时间内，钢铁厂的利用率都会偏低，直到需求水平达到新的产能水平为止。然而，除了战争时期，钢铁在其他时期的需求量总是少量地、缓慢地增加。但是如果面对增长的需求却不进行扩产，就意味着永远失去了市场份额。没有哪家公司敢冒这种风险。因此，整个产业只能在短暂的几年内有利可图，即从每家公司开始扩建新产能，到这些新产能实现满负荷运转的几年。

多年以来，人们都认识到 19 世纪 70 年代发明的炼钢工艺并不经济。这种炼钢工艺试图挑战物理定律，这意味着它违反了经济学准则。在物理学中，除了克服重力和惯性，没有比制温更费劲的事了，无论是制热还是制冷。而综合炼钢工艺要求有四次相当高的温度，而且每次还要通过淬火降温。此外，在这个过程中，有大量的沉重的灼热物质（炼钢流程中的中间品）被高高举起，并移动相当长的距离。

众所周知，工艺中的创新如果能够减少这些固有的不足，将会使成本大幅下降。这正是迷你钢铁厂所做的事情。迷你钢铁厂并非什么小型工厂，其最低经济规模能产生大约 1 亿美元的销售额。但是，这只是综合钢铁厂最小经济规模的 1/10～1/6。因此，通过创建迷你钢铁厂来满足市场上额外的钢铁需求，是非常经济的。迷你钢铁厂在整个炼钢过程中，只产生一次高温且不必淬火，而是将温度用到接下来的工艺中。它的原材料是钢屑而非铁矿石，只集中生产一种最终产品，比如钢板、钢梁或钢杆。综合钢铁厂是高度劳动密集型企业，而迷你钢铁厂是自动化控制的，它的炼钢工艺成本还不到传统炼钢工艺的一半。

虽然遭到政府、工会以及综合钢铁厂的不断阻挠，迷你钢铁厂依然顽强地稳步发展。预计到 2000 年左右，美国使用的钢材中，一半或者更多将来自迷你钢铁厂，而大型钢铁厂将不可逆转地走向衰败。

还有一个不得不说且相当重要的案例。在造纸业中，需求与制造工艺的经济现状之间，同样存在着这种不协调现象。只有在这个案例中，我们不知道如何将其转化为创新机会。

虽然发达国家和大多数发展中国家政府都在持续不断地努力提高纸张的需求量，这也许是各国政府唯一一致的目标，但造纸业的表现仍然欠佳。造纸业通常是持续 3 年获得空前利润，接着必是长达 5 年的生产过剩和亏损状态。迄今为止，我们还找不出类似于迷你钢铁厂的方案来解决造纸业的问题。八九十年以前，我们已经知道木质纤维是一种单体。也许有人会说，寻找一种塑化剂将它转化成聚合体，这并不困难。这种创新能使造纸业从原先低效率、高浪费的机械工艺转变成高效率的化学工艺。事实上，大约在 100 年前，人们就用这种方法成功地从木浆中提炼出纺织纤维，比如人造丝的制造过程可追溯到 19 世纪 80 年代。尽管人们在造纸研究中已经投入了大量资金，但目前仍未发现用化学工艺造纸的新技术。

上述案例表明，在不协调事件中，创新的解决方案应该能够被清楚地界定，应该能够依靠现有的已知的技术和可用资源而实现。当然，它同样需要艰苦的研发工作。如果它还需要大量的研究和新的知识，那么就尚未成熟，难以被企业家应用。成功利用经济现状之间的不协调而进行的创新，必须是简单而非复杂的，必须是清晰而非浮夸的。

同样地，公共服务领域也存在着经济现状不协调状况。

发达国家的医疗保健提供了一个很好的示例。就在最近的 1929 年，医疗保健在发达国家的支出只占很小的比例，还不到国民生产总值或消费者支出的 1%。半个世纪之后的今天，医疗保健尤其是医院，在国民生产总值中所占比例已高达 7%～11%。但是，医疗保健的经济绩效非但没有提高反而降低了。成本的增长远远快于业务的增长，前者可能是后者增长速度的三四倍。在接下来的 30 年中，随着老年人口的稳步增长，发达国家的医疗保健需求也会持续增长。由于成本与人口的年龄结构紧密相关，成本也会随之增加。

我们并不了解这一现象⊖。但是，英国和美国已经出现了简单的、针对具体目标的成功创新。由于英美两国的体制机制存在很大的差异，这些创新也完全不同。它们都利用了自己国家体制的薄弱环节，并将其转化为机会。

英国的激进式创新是私人健康保险。目前私人健康保险在英国是发展最快、备受推崇的员工福利。这个福利让投保人无须排队就能接受专家的诊疗，即便是进行选择性外科手术⊖。英国的制度原先是通过分流来降低医疗保健成本。这种方法是先做紧急治疗，即常规疾病和危及生命的疾病，而延迟其他疾病特别是选择性外科手术的治疗。有些选择性外科手术已经等候 1 年多了，如治疗因关节炎而受损的髋关节。私人健康保险则可以使投保人立即接受治疗。

不同于英国，美国不计成本地满足各类医疗保健需求，结果导致医院成本急剧增长。这种现象产生了一个创新机会，剥离。将医院不需要的高成本医疗设备，如人体扫描仪、治疗癌症的钴 X- 射线、高配置的自动化医疗实验室或生理康复治疗等业务剥离出来，成立独立的机构。这些创新机构小而专业，比如，为母亲和新生儿提供旅馆设施的独立妇产中心、为开展无须住院和术后护理的外科手术的流动外科手术中心、心理诊断和咨询中心、类似性质的老年中心，等等。

⊖ 1984 年 4 月 29 日发表在《经济学人》的一篇文章，是迄今对医疗保健问题最好的论述，也是唯一超越国家来审视医疗保健的文章。

⊖ 有些疾病必须进行手术，或者说，有些手术必须要做，不进行手术，疾病无法改善，但也不会"危及生命"，例如白内障、髋关节移植手术以及一般意义上的整形外科手术，或者是子宫下垂等疾病。

这些新机构并没有取代医院。实际上，它们推动了美国医院去承担英国赋予医院的角色，即治疗急诊病人和危及生命的疾病以及提供悉心护理的场所。同英国一样，这些创新主要出现在以盈利为目的的医院里。在这个例子中，不断增长的医疗保健需求与不断下降的医疗保健绩效这两种经济现状之间的不协调，转化成了创新机会。

这些绝佳案例都来自重点行业和公共服务机构。正是如此，我们才能够接近、察看并理解它们。最重要的是，这些例子表明了为什么经济现状之间的不协调能够产生如此巨大的创新机会。在这些行业或公共服务机构工作的人们，对这些根本缺陷都了然于胸。但是整天忙于修修补补和救急填坑之类的工作，他们不得不忽视这些缺陷。如此一来，他们就无法认真对待新生事物，更不会与它开展竞争。一般而言，只有当新生事物成长到足以侵犯他们所在的行业或者服务时，他们才会加以注意。到那时，一切都无法逆转。而创新者也拥有了自己的一席之地。

II

现实与假设之间存在的不协调

无论何时，如果工业或者服务业中的人错误地理解现实并做出错误的假设，他们就会朝着错误的方向努力。他们将精力投入到不会有结果的领域。这样现实和行为之间就产生了不协调。任何人如果能有所察觉并加以利用，这种不协调就会提供成功的创新机会。

举一个简单的例子来说明，昔日世界贸易的运输工具通常为远洋货轮。

早在35年前，即20世纪50年代初，人们就认为远洋货轮将会消失。除了用来运输大宗货物之外，远洋货轮将被航空运输取代。当时，海上货运的成本快速上升。由于港口往往拥挤不堪，货轮运送货物所花费的时间大大增加。除此之外，当轮船尚未停靠到码头时，随着堆积货物越来越多，偷盗现象也越来越多。

多年来，航运业一直将精力投入到错误的领域，是导致这种混乱局面的根源。航运业专注于船只在海上及各港口间运输的经济性。因此，它努力设计并制造速度更快的轮船，还有需要更少燃料和船员的轮船。

然而，轮船是资本设备，资本设备的最大成本在于闲置成本。设备一旦闲置，就无法赚钱但仍要支付利息。当然航运业的人都知道，轮船的主要花费是对轮船投资的利息。但是，业界依旧将重心放在已经相当低的花费上，也就是轮船在海上和运输航程的费用。

只需将装货和装船两个步骤分开，就能解决这个问题。陆地上的空间足够大，可以在轮船进入港口之前先在陆地上完成装货。这样等轮船进入港口之后，将预先装好的货物装卸到轮船上就可以了。换句话说，要重点解决轮船的闲置成本而不是运输成本。滚装船和集装箱船则是这一问题的解决办法。

这个看似简单的创新竟然产生了惊人的效果。过去 30 年来，轮船货运量提高了 5 倍，成本却下降了 60%。多数情况下，轮船在港口停留的时间下降了 60%，港口的拥挤和盗窃现象也大幅减少。

认知与现实之间的不协调，通常是显而易见的。如果努力专注地工作反而使情况恶化，正如更快的船只会造成港口的严重拥堵和更长的货运时间，这很可能是努力的方向错了。只要将精力转换到会产生结果的领域，就可能会快速获得高额回报。

在极少的情况下，认知与现实之间的不协调需要伟大的创新。将装货从装运作业中剥离出来，只是对铁路和卡车运输中的方法加以改进应用到远洋运输业而已。

认知与现实之间的不一致，通常是整个工业或者服务业的特点。解决方案应该小而简单，专注且具体。

Ⅲ

认知与实际的客户价值和期望之间的不协调

在第 3 章中，我提到了日本电视机的案例，并将其作为意外成功的一个例子。它也是认知与实际的客户价值和期望之间不协调的很好的例子。美国和欧洲的穷人早已表示电视机能够满足他们的期望，这些期望与经济状况无关。这比日本的一位实业家向美国人发表"日本穷人根本买不起电视机，也不会购买它"这番言论还要早。但是，这位聪明的日本人无法理解一个事实，即对客户而言，尤其是贫穷的客户，电视机不只是一件产品，电视机代表了走向新世界甚至新生活的通道。

1956 年，赫鲁晓夫访问美国时说："俄罗斯人不想拥有自己的汽车，便宜的出租车更为合适。"可见，赫鲁晓夫也无法理解汽车不只是一件产品这一事实。任何一个青少年都知道，四轮汽车不仅仅是交通工具，还是自由、流动、权利和浪漫的象征。赫鲁晓夫的错误认知创造了一个最为疯狂的创业机会：俄罗斯的汽车的短缺创造了一个最大且最有活力的黑车市场。

有人会说，这些例子过于宏大，对商人和医院、大学或贸易协会的管理人员的启示不大。但其实这些例子都是普遍存在的现象。下面是一个不同的例子，同样宏大，但很有实践意义。

过去几年，美国成长最快的金融机构之一是位于中西部城市的郊区而不是位于纽约的一家证券公司。如今，这家证券公司在美国已经有 2000 个分支机构。它认为自己的成功来自对某种不协调事件的利用。

那些大型的金融机构，如美林（Merrill Lynches）、添惠（Dean Witters）以及哈顿（E. F. Huttons），认为它们与客户的观念一致。在这些大型金融机构看来，人们投资的目的就是赚钱，这即便不是真理也是显而易见的事情。这是纽约证券交易所成员的动机所在，也决定了它们所称的成功。但是，这个假设只适用于一部分投资者而非大多数人。大多数人并非金融人员。通过投资挣钱需要投入大量的时间和精力，还要具备充足的金融知识，然而，当地的专业人士、小商人以及富裕农民既没有时间也没有足够的相关知识。他们通常忙于赚钱，无暇管理资金。

这家中西部的证券公司正是利用了这种不协调。表面看来，它与其他证券公司别无二致。它也是纽约证券交易所的成员，但是只有很少一部分股票交易业务，大约 1/8。它避开华尔街上大型交易所极力推崇的项目，如期权、商品期货等，而去吸引它所认为的明智投资者。它并不向客户承诺会赚大钱，这也是美国金融服务机构的一大创新。它甚至不想要做大买卖的客户。它青睐的客户是那些收入超过支出的人，如成功的专业人士、富裕的农民和小镇的商人。之所以选择这些客户，主要是因为这些人消费适度而非收入较高。它主要满足了这些人储存金钱的心理需求。这家证券公司出售的是保证资金不贬值的机会，主要投资债券和股票，还有递延年金、避税项目合作、房地产信托等。该公司提供了一项不同的产品"平静心灵"（对应上文说的心理需求），这是华尔街券商从未出售过的产品。这代表着明智的投资者真正的投资价值。

华尔街的大型券商甚至无法相信这种客户的存在，这些客户的出现否决了他们一直深信不疑、视为真理的事情。如今，这家成功的公司被广泛报道。在每个成长的大型证券交易公司榜单上，都有它的名字。但是，那些大型证券公司的高管人员并未把这家公司当作竞争者，更不用说认可它的成功了。

现实与认知的不协调的背后，往往存在知识的傲慢、知识的僵硬和教条主义。那位日本实业家如此断言："是我而不是他们了解日本穷人买得起什么。"这也解释了创新者为什么能够更容易利用不协调：他们不受干扰并埋头于工作。

在所有不协调事件中，现实与认知的不协调最为常见。制造商和供应商对顾客的真实需求往往存在误解。他们总把生产者的价值与顾客的价值等同起来。的确，如果想成功做一件事情，必须相信这件事情并认真去执行。化妆品制造商必须相信自己的产品，否则这些产品就变成了伪劣产品，将很快失去客户。医院经营者必须相信医疗保健的重要性，否则医疗质量和护理水平将迅速下降。然而，没有一个顾客认为他的需求等同于制造商或供应商的供给。两者在价值和期望上，总是会存在差异的。

对于这种差异，制造商和供应商总是抱怨顾客的不理智或者不愿为高品质买单。只要听到这种抱怨，我们就有理由相信，制造商或供应商与顾客在价值和期望上存在不协调。此时，我们有足够的理由去寻找一种具体的、成功率极高的创新机会。

VI

流程的节奏或逻辑的内部不协调

大约 25 年前，也就是 20 世纪 50 年代末，一家制药公司的一名推销员决定自主创业。他开始在医疗操作流程中寻找不协调之处并很快就找到了。在外科手术中，老年白内障手术最为常见。多年来，该手术步骤已经十分精细化、程序化和仪器化，整个手术操作过程完全可控、节奏完美。但是，这个手术仍然存在一点不完善、不协调之处。在手术的某个阶段，眼科医生必须切断病人的眼部韧带，栓紧血管，这可能导致出血使眼睛受损。虽然这一步骤的成功率大于 99%，完成这一步骤也不困难，但是它会干扰眼科医生。这会改变医生的操作节奏，并引起他们的担忧。任何一位眼科医生，不管做过多少次手术，在这一环节都会感到些许恐惧。

制药公司的这名推销员威廉·科纳（William Connor），稍做研究就发现 19 世纪 90 年代分离出的一种酶能够迅速溶解那个特殊的韧带。只是在当时，没有人能使这种酶长期保存。即便在冷冻状态下，也存放不了几个小时。而 1890 年之后，储存技术才开始有些发展。短短的几个月内，通过反复试验，科纳发现了一种可以长期储存酶又不丧失其活性的储存方法。随后，科纳的专利化合物在短短几年内就被全球的眼科医生采用。20 年后，一家跨国公司高价收购了科纳创办的爱尔康公司（Alcon Laboratories）。

下面还有一个很好的例子。

斯科特公司（O. M. Scott & Co）是美国草坪护理产品制造商的领导者，其产品包括草籽、肥料和杀虫剂等。该公司目前是一家大型公司 ITT 的子公司。当还是一家独立小公司时，斯科特公司就与超出其规模几倍的公司展开竞争，从希尔斯公司（Sears, Roebuck and Co）到陶氏化学公司（Dow Chemicals），并占领领导地位。斯科特公司的产品很好，那些竞争对手同样也很好。它之所以能够获胜，主要在于一种被称为"撒布机"的简单轻便的独轮车。这种独轮车上的一些小孔能使斯科特的产品适量地、均匀地撒播。草坪护理产品一向被宣称是科学的经过大量实验合成的。在一定的土壤条件和温度下应撒播多少草坪护理产品，所有公司都会对这一点给出详细说明。它们都在向消费者传递一个信息：草坪种植即便不是一项科学作业，也是一项精细的、需要控制的作业。但在斯科特公司推出撒布机之前，没有一家厂商提供工具帮助客户控制作业流程。这就使得整个流程逻辑内部就存在某种不协调，令客户失望和沮丧。

这种流程内部不协调的识别是否依赖直觉和意外事件呢？能否对它加以组织或系统化呢？

正是通过向外科医生询问他们工作中不甚如意的地方，威廉·科纳才开始进行创新。正是斯科特公司经常向批发商和客户了解现有产品的不足之处，才得以从一家当地种子零售商发展成为一家具有相当规模的全国性公司，随后，它开始围绕着"撒布机"设计自己的产品线。

流程内部的不协调，无论在节奏还是逻辑上，都并非难以捉摸。产品的使用者总能意识到这种不协调。每位眼科医生都很清楚自己在切割眼部韧带时的不协调，并经常谈论这个问题。同样地，每个五金店的员工都知道草坪护理顾客的困扰，也经常谈论它。但是真正缺少的是，愿意倾听、愿意认真对待挂在嘴边的信念，即"产品或服务的目的是满足顾客需求"。如果人们接受这个信念，并付诸实践，那么利用这种不协调所产生的创新机会，将会变得容易而高效。

但是，这里存在一个严格的限制条件，就是通常只有特定工业或者服务业内部人员才能发现这种不一致，而外部人士很难发现、理解并加以利用。

创新机会源三：流程需求

前面章节的主题都是"机会是创新的来源"，但是，正如一句古谚所言，"需求乃发明之母"，所以，本章把需求看作创新的一个来源，并且实际上把它视为一个重要的创新机会。

我们所要讨论的作为创新机会源之一的需求，是一种具体的需求，我称之为"流程需求"。这种需求既不模糊也非笼统，相当具体。就像意外事件或不协调事件，它也存在于商业、工业或者服务业内部。一些基于流程需求的创新利用了不协调事件及人口统计特征。不同于其他创新源，流程需求并非源于环境中的事件，无论是内部环境还是外部环境。它基于有待完成的工作而出现。它以任务为中心，而非以环境为中心。它完善现有流程，替换薄弱环节，用新知识重新设计旧流程。它有时通过补齐缺失环节，使某个流程成为可能。

基于流程需求的创新中，组织中的每个人都知道需求的存在。但是，人们常常对它无动于衷。而一旦出现创新，人们立即把创新视为"显而易见之事"，并很快当作"标准"。

我们在第 4 章中曾提到一个案例。威廉·科纳实现了将白内障手术中分解韧带的酶，从一个书本中的名词概念转变为手术必需的产品。白内障手术的流程由来已久。能够完善该流程的酶几十年来也早已为人所知。这里的创新仅仅是使酶在冷冻状态下保持活力的储存方式。当这一流程需求得以满足后，眼科医生无法想象如果没有科纳的产品会是怎样的情形。

在基于流程需求的创新中，很少有创新像上述的例子那样聚焦，一旦发现需求立即能找到解决方案。但是大多数（如果不是全部）基于流程需求的创新本质上都有一些共性。

下面是另一个基于流程需求进行创新的案例。

1885 年，奥特马尔·默根特勒（Ottmar Mergenthaler）发明了用于排版的莱诺铸排机。在此之前的几十年里，随着识字人口的增长和交通、通信的发展，各种印刷品（杂志、报纸和书籍）都呈指数增长，印刷流程的其他要素均已得到改善。例如，当时已经有高速印刷机和高速造纸机。然而，在古腾堡（Gutenberg）所在的时代及其之前 400 多年里，排字这一工序一直没有变化。排字是一项耗时耗力的昂贵手工作业，需要高超的技艺和多年的学习训练。同科纳一样，默根特勒首先界定需求，包括一个可以自动从字母库里挑选正确字母的键盘；一个可以拼组字母并将它们排成一条线的机械装置；以及一个将字母准确放回容器以供将来使用的机械装置，这也是最为困难的一个部分。以上每一部分都需要多年的努力和足够的才能，但并不需要新知识，更别说需要新科技了。尽管遭到了老排字工的激烈反对，但是在不到五年的时间里，默根特勒的莱诺铸排机就成为行业标准。

上述两个案例中，科纳的酶和默根特勒的莱诺铸排机，流程需求都是基于流程中的不协调而产生的。此外，人口统计特征也是流程需求的重要来源，也是流程创新的机会所在。

1909 年左右，贝尔电话公司的一名统计员绘制了两条从那之后 15 年的预测发展曲线：一条是美国人口的增长曲线，另一条是日益增长的电话量所需要的中心局接线员数量的增长曲线。这两条曲线表明，如果继续人工接线服务，到 1925 年或 1930 年，17～60 岁的美国妇女都要从事接线员工作。两年以后，贝尔电话公司的工程师设计出第一台自动交换机，并投入使用。

现在，人口统计特征带来的流程需求还引发了机器人的研究热潮。人们早已熟知机器人的相关知识，但在工业化国家，尤其是日本和美国，直到生育低潮的影响显现在主要制造商面前，他们才意识到机器取代半熟练装配工人的必要性。日本在机器人领域的领先地位，并非在于技术优势。他们的技术大多是由美国引进的。其主要原因是，日本的生育低潮比美国早四五年，比德国早十年左右。日本用了十年时间意识到劳动力短缺的问题，这与德国和美国所用的时间一样。但是，日本比美国更早启动机器人的研究，而在我写下这几句话的时候，德国的十年尚未结束。

默根特勒的莱诺铸排机在很大程度上也是人口压力的结果。随着印刷品需求的激增，需经 6～8 年学徒训练的排版工人大量紧缺，而且排版工的薪酬飞涨。印刷商开始意识到这个薄弱环节，很乐意花费大价钱购买一台机器并用一名半熟练机器操作员替代五名高薪技术工人。

不协调事件和人口统计特征可能是流程需求最常见的来源。还有一种难度更大、风险更高，也更重要的来源。这一来源就是所谓的项目研究，与传统的纯科学研究相对应。事实上，确实存在一种薄弱环节，它能够加以界定，而且清晰可见，并能引起人们的强烈感受。只有获得大量的新知识，才能满足这种流程需求。

很少有发明能比摄影更快地取得成功。自摄影发明以来短短 20 年里，就在全世界迅速流行。也是 20 年左右的时间，每个国家都出现了伟大的摄影师。如马修·布雷迪（Mathew Brady）的美国内战的作品，至今无人超越。到 1860 年，每位新娘都会拍照留念。日本在明治维新之前首次引进的西方技术是摄影技术，而当时的日本可是极度排斥外国人和外国思想的。

1870 年，业余摄影师纷纷出现。但对他们而言，当时的技术水平使摄影显得异常困难。摄影需要的一种重且易碎的玻璃板，必须要极其小心地随身携带。另外，还需要一台笨重的照相机，而且拍照之前要长时间的准备、精心的布置，等等。这些困难是众所周知的。当时的摄影杂志，也是首批发行的专业性大众杂志，充斥着对这种极其困难的拍照的抱怨，也提出了很多改进建议。但是，1870 年的科学技术水平并不能解决这些问题。

但是，到 19 世纪 80 年代中期，新知识出现了。柯达公司的创始人乔治·伊士曼（George Eastman）发明了可以替代厚重玻璃板的超轻薄纤维胶片。这种胶卷无须小心操作，一般不会损坏。基于这种胶卷，伊士曼还设计了一款轻便的照相机。10 年内，柯达占领了世界摄影市场上的领导地位，并维持至今。

将流程从可能转化为现实，往往需要项目研究。当然，人们必须能够感知需求并清晰识别需求什么，接下来去创造新知识。爱迪生就是基于流程需求进行创新的典型创新者（详见第 9 章）。20 多年来，人人都知道将会出现电气行业。在电气行业出现前的五六年里，情况愈发清晰，缺失环节是电灯泡。没有电灯泡，就不可能有电气行业。爱迪生明确了使潜在的电气行业成为现实的新知识，然后开展研究工作，并在两年内发明了电灯泡。

将可能变为现实的项目研究，已经成为一流工业研究实验室的主要方法。同样地，它也是国防、农业、医药、环境保护等研究的主要方法。

项目研究听起来宏大。对很多人来说，它意味着把人送上月球或是研发小儿麻痹症疫苗之类的项目。但实际上，项目研究最成功的应用是在小而具体的项目上，越小越专注越好。最好的例子，也许是基于流程需求创新的最佳案例，正是一个非常小的项目。这个项目就是使日本的汽车事故减少了近 2/3 的公路反射镜项目。

1965 年，除了大城市之外，日本的其他地区基本没有铺设公路。整个国家却迅速进入了汽车时代，因此日本政府开始疯狂地铺设公路。现在，汽车可以并且确实在公路上高速行驶了。但是，公路还是按照 10 世纪的牛车宽度铺设的。这种老式道路只能勉强允许两辆车同时通过，而且处处都是死角和隐蔽的入口。每隔几公里，就有多条道路从不同角度相交，形成交叉路口。因此，交通事故发生率以惊人的速度攀升，尤其是夜间事故率。新闻、广播和电视媒体以及议会的反对党很快开始大声疾呼，要求政府有所作为。但是重新修建公路是不可能的，因为那至少需要 20 年的时间。与以往相同类型活动一样，倡导小心驾驶的公众宣传活动，也毫无效用。

日本的一个年轻人岩佐多闻抓住了这个危机，把它当作创新机会。他重新设计了传统的公路反射镜，使这块玻璃片可以加以调整，进而能反射来自任何方向的汽车的车前灯。政府随即大量安装这种反射镜，事故发生率大大降低。

再举一个例子。

第一次世界大战催生了美国大众对国内外新闻的兴趣。每个人都注意到了这一点。事实上，战后初期，报社和杂志社就如何满足这种需求进行了广泛的探讨。地方报纸是无法胜任这项工作的。《纽约时报》等几家大型出版商也进行过这方面的尝试，但都没有成功。后来，亨利·卢斯确定了流程需求以及如何满足这一需要。这种出版物不能是地方性出版物，必须是国家级出版物，否则很难吸引足够多的读者和广告商。除此之外，这种出版物不能每日一期，因为难以有足够多的趣闻来吸引读者。这些要求大体明确了出版物的风格。作为全球第一本新闻性杂志，《时代》一经面世，就大获成功。

这些案例，尤其是岩佐的故事，表明基于流程需求的成功创新要具备五种基本要素：

• 一个独立的流程。

- 一个薄弱或缺失的环节。

- 一个明确的目标。

- 可以清晰界定的解决方案。

- 认可更好方式的存在性，即具有较高的可接受性。

但需要特别注意的是：

1. 需求必须能够被清楚理解。仅仅感知到需求是远远不够的，否则，将无法明确解决方案的要求。

例如，几百年来，数学一直是学校里较难的一门学科。只有很少一部分学生，不超过 1/5，学习数学没有什么困难而且还相当轻松。然而其他学生从未真正学会过它（的确，学生可以通过做大量练习题来通过数学考试）。日本人极为重视这门学科，也确实都是这么去做的。但这并不意味着，日本的孩子都学会了数学。他们只是学会了如何通过考试，随即就把数学全忘了。十年后，当他们快 30 岁时，他们数学考试的表现同西方人一样差。然而，每个时代都会有天才教师，他们能教毫无天赋的学生学好数学，至少能够让学生有很大进步。但是，没有人能够复制这种教师的做法。人们切实感受到了这种需求，但是却不能理解这个问题。是孩子缺乏天赋？是我们教育方法不对？还是心理和情感问题？没有人知道答案。对这个问题没有透彻的理解，我们就无法找到解决方案。

2. 我们可能了解流程，但仍缺乏解决问题的知识。第 4 章提及的造纸业中存在人人皆知的明显不协调，即要找到一种比当时的造纸流程更少浪费、更加经济的造纸流程。一个世纪以来，许多有能力的人都曾努力去解决这个问题。我们清楚地知道需求是木质素的聚合物。我们已经有很多类似的分子聚合物，因此它应该容易获得。尽管 100 年来，受过良好训练的人们为此辛勤工作，但仍然缺乏所需的知识。我们只能说一句："让我们再试点别的材料吧。"

3. 解决方案必须符合人们的做事方式，并且人们愿意去做。 业余摄影师对早期摄影流程的复杂技术并没有心理预期。他们只想要尽可能简单地得到一张不错的照片。因此，他们很乐意能有一个只需要较少操作和技能的摄影流程。同样地，眼科医生感兴趣的只是一个精细的、合理的和不出血的治疗流程，因此能提供这种效用的酶就可以满足他们的期望和价值。

但是，下面还有一个的例子。它是基于明确且实际流程需求的创新，但不符合人们的做事方式，因此尚未得到认可。

多年以来，许多专业人士（如律师、会计师、工程师、医生）所需要信息的增长量已远远超过他们的搜寻能力。这些专业人员一直抱怨，他们不得不花费更多时间在法律图书馆、手册、教科书以及活页信息摘要上，来查询所需要的信息。因此有人认为做一种能提供这些信息的"数据库"能立即取得成功。通过电脑程序和显示器终端，这种数据库能够直接向专业人员提供信息：为律师提供法院判决信息，为会计师提供税收政策，为医生提供药物及其药性信息。但是这些服务却很难吸引到客户，以致连收支平衡都无法实现。现实生活中，为律师提供服务的律商联讯集团，用了数十年的时间并投入了巨额资金才获得客户。造成这种状况的根源可能是，数据库使得信息获取变得过于简单了。专业人士为之自豪的资本是他们的记忆力，也就是能够牢记所需要的信息或者找到这些信息的能力。"你必须记住你所需要的法院裁决信息，并清楚地知道如何获取这些信息。"这依然是新人律师从资深律师那里得到的忠告。尽管数据库对专业人士的工作有很大帮助，大大节省了工作时间和金钱，却违背了他们的价值观。曾经一位著名医生的病人问他，为什么不使用能够帮助他核查诊断并选择特定病例最佳疗法的信息服务？这位医生答道："如果信息服务能够用来检查和诊断，那还要我做什么？"

人们可以系统地寻找基于流程需求的创新机会。正是采取了这种方法，爱迪生在电子学和电力学领域做出了卓越的贡献。当时还是耶鲁大学的一名在读生的卢斯采用了同样的方法，科纳也不例外。事实上，这一创新机会源本身也适用于系统的研究和分析。

一旦找到某种流程需求，必须根据上述五个基本要素准则检验。最后，还要看它是否符合三个限制条件：我们理解需求是什么吗？我们拥有解决问题的知识，或者最新技术可以解决这个问题吗？这一解决方案是否符合目标用户的习惯和价值？

创新机会源四：产业结构和市场结构

有时候，产业结构和市场结构会持续很多年，看起来完全稳定。例如，一个世纪以来，世界制铝业的领导者一直是位于匹兹堡的美国铝业公司（Aluminum Company of America）及其加拿大蒙特利尔的子公司。美国铝业公司拥有原始专利权。自 20 世纪 20 年代以来，世界烟草业只增加了一个重要新成员南非伦勃朗集团（The South African Rembrandt）。整整一个世纪里，只有两家企业成为世界领先的电器制造公司：荷兰飞利浦（Philips）和日本日立（Hitachi）。自 20 世纪 20 年代初期西尔斯公司从邮购业进入零售业起，到 60 年代中期历史久远的连锁折扣店克雷斯吉公司（Kresge）创办了凯马特（K-Mat）折扣商店止，在这 40 年里，美国的零售连锁店没有重要的新成员出现。产业结构和市场结构显得如此坚不可摧，业内人士因此认为它们是注定的，是自然规律，而且必然一直延续。

实际上，市场结构和产业结构相当脆弱，一个小小的干扰就能使它们迅速瓦解。一旦出现这种情况，产业内的成员都要采取应对措施。因循守旧注定会给企业带来灾难，甚至会使企业走向灭亡。不采取应对措施，企业至少会失去领导地位，一旦跌下神坛，就很难重登宝座。但是，市场结构和产业结构的变化也是一个重要的创新机会。

产业结构的变化要求产业内部成员都要发挥企业家精神。每个人都要自问："我们的业务是什么？"当然，不同的人会给出不同的答案。重要的是这些答案都是全新的。

I

汽车的故事

20世纪初，汽车业迅速发展，汽车市场发生了彻底的改变。针对这种变化，人们采取了四种应对策略，最终都取得了成功。1900年左右，早期汽车业主要为富人提供汽车这一奢侈品。当时汽车销量每三年翻一番，早已超出上层人士这一狭窄市场。然而，当时的汽车公司依旧专注于满足上层人士的需求。

针对这种现象，创办于1904的英国劳斯莱斯公司（Rolls-Royce）采取了应对措施。公司创始人意识到，汽车正快速增长并势必走向大众化。于是他们决定生产并销售具有贵族气质的汽车，这也是公司早期创业计划书里的设想。他们特意采用早已过时的制造方法，即每一辆车由一个熟练工人独自手工制造并完成装配。他们做出承诺，保证车子永不磨损。他们还规定，只有接受过劳斯莱斯培训的专业司机才能驾驶这款汽车。他们严格限制目标客户群体，比较偏好那些有尊贵头衔的人。劳斯莱斯汽车的价格高昂，与小游艇的价格不相上下，相当于一个熟练工人或者富裕商人年收入的40倍。这也确保了一般的平民根本无力购买。

几年后，底特律的年轻人亨利·福特也注意到了这一市场结构的变化：

美国汽车不再只是富人的玩物。他决定设计一种可以批量生产，由半熟练工人装配的汽车。这种汽车可以由车主本人驾驶和修理。但是，1908 年推出的 T 型汽车并非传说中的那样便宜。它的价格比世界上薪金最高的工人，也就是美国熟练工人的年收入还要略高。目前，美国市场上最便宜的汽车价格仅为非技术性装配工人一年收入和福利的 1/10。不过在当时，T 型汽车的价格是之前市场中最便宜的汽车的 1/5，而且更易于驾驶和保养。

另一个美国人威廉·杜兰特（William Crapo Durant），从市场结构的变化中看到了成立专业管理型大型汽车公司的机会。他预计一个全方位市场将会出现，并试图满足不同细分市场的汽车需求。1905 年，杜兰特创办了通用汽车公司，开始收购当时的汽车公司，并将它们整合为一家大型的现代化企业。

在此之前的 1899 年，年轻的意大利人乔瓦尼·阿涅利（Giovanni Agnelli）认为汽车将会成为军需用品，尤其是作为军官的指挥车。因此，他在都灵创立了菲亚特汽车公司（Fabbrica Italiana Automobili Torino，FIAT）。短短几年，该公司就成为意大利、俄国和奥匈帝国军队指挥车的主要供应商。

1960—1980 年，全球汽车业的市场结构再次发生变化。第一次世界大战之后的 40 年里，各国的汽车市场由本国的汽车厂商主导。在意大利的公路上和停车场内，汽车大都是菲亚特，还有小部分是阿尔法·罗密欧（Alfa-Romeo）和蓝旗亚（Lancia）；而在意大利之外的国家，人们就很难看到这些品牌的汽车了；在法国，有雷诺（Renault）、标致（Peugeot）和雪铁龙（Citroen）汽车；在德国，有梅赛德斯（Mercedes）、欧宝（Opels）和德国福特汽车；在美国，到处都是通用、福特和克莱斯勒汽车。然而到 1960 年左右，汽车业突然成了全球性产业。

对此，不同公司的反应截然不同。当时的日本（仍然相当封闭并且几乎没有出口过汽车），决定成为世界级汽车出口国。20 世纪 60 年代末，日本进入美国市场的首次尝试遭遇惨败。随后，他们重新部署，再三考虑出口策略，重新设计用以出口美国的汽车。这种汽车具有美式汽车特点，如美式设计风格、美式舒适度和美式性能，同时又兼具日式汽车特点，如车身较小、耗油量更低、质量控制更为严格，以及最重要的客户服务更为完善。在1979 年的石油危机时期，日本抓住了这一机会并大获成功。与此同时，福特公司也决定进入欧洲市场以走向全球化。十年后，即 20 世纪 70 年代，福特成为欧洲汽车市场中头把交椅的有力竞争者。

菲亚特汽车公司决定成为一家欧洲公司，而不仅仅是一家意大利公司。在保持其在意大利汽车市场主导地位的同时，菲亚特计划进入其他主要的欧洲国家，并在这些国家的汽车市场占据第二的位置。通用汽车公司也是起初决定坚守美国市场，并保持美国汽车市场 50% 的份额，进而获得北美汽车市场利润总额的 70%。这一计划获得了成功。十年后，到了 70 年代中期，通用改变了想法，决定同福特和菲亚特竞争欧洲市场的领导地位，并再次获得了成功。1983—1984 年，通用公司最终决定成为一家真正的全球化公司，并和一些日本公司开展合作，起初是两家规模较小的公司，后来是丰田。德国的梅赛德斯公司采取了另外一种全球化战略。它专注于全球市场中的几个细分市场，包括豪华轿车、出租车和公共汽车。

所有的战略都获得了成功。的确，我们无法评判哪种战略更好。但是，那些拒绝改变、拒绝接受变化的公司，最后境况都很糟糕。如果它们幸运地活下来，也仅仅是由于政府不愿坐视其倒闭。

克莱斯勒就是一个例子。公司内部人士都清楚所发生的变化，业界人士也都知道，但他们没有采取任何行动。考虑到美国当时仍然是世界上最大的汽车市场，克莱斯勒可以选择美国本土化战略，集中资源巩固其在美国市场的地位。它也可以与某家强大的欧洲公司合并，力争在全球最重要的汽车市场——欧洲市场和美国市场中占据第三把交椅。众所周知，梅赛德斯公司曾对此表现出极大的兴趣，但是克莱斯勒却并不来电。与之相反，克莱斯勒把资源一点点地浪费在表面功夫上。它收购了一些在欧洲市场遭遇挫败的公司，以营造跨国公司的形象。这种做法非但没有增强克莱斯勒的实力，反而耗尽资源，致使无法在美国市场投资。1979 年石油危机之后，克莱斯勒在欧洲市场和美国市场几乎没有了什么份额，最后依靠美国政府才得以存活。

与克莱斯勒一样，英国利兰汽车公司（Leyland）也经历了相似的境遇。利兰曾是英国最大的汽车公司，也是欧洲汽车市场领导地位的有力竞争者。法国标致汽车公司的情况同样如此。这两家公司都不愿做出必要的决策，结果迅速失去了市场地位和盈利能力。目前这三家公司，克莱斯勒、利兰和标致，都处于汽车市场的边缘位置。

那些小公司的案例更加有趣，也更加重要。全球市场中的汽车制造商，无论规模是大还是小，都不得不做出行动，否则就面临永久的衰败。然而，三家小型的边缘公司从中看到了重大的创新机会。这三家小公司是沃尔沃（Volvo）、宝马（BMW）和保时捷（Porsche）。

1960 年左右，汽车市场突然变化。知情人士断言，在即将开始的大淘汰中，这三家公司将会消失。然而这三家公司表现出色，创造了自己的利基市场并成为其中的领导者。它们之所以取得如此成就，全在于采用了创新战略。这种创新战略使它们转型到不同的业务中。1965 年，沃尔沃公司只是一家挣扎在收支平衡边缘的小公司。在关键的几年里，它出现严重亏损，后来开始重新寻找定位。它在全球尤其美国，将自己打造为"明智型"汽车的世界级经销商。这种汽车并非豪华，价格不低，也不能引领潮流。但是它很牢靠，气质非凡，更能彰显价值。沃尔沃将自己定位为专业人士用车的提供者。专业人士通常无须通过所驾驶的汽车来展示自己的成功，他们更加重视因明智决策而为人所知。

1960 年的宝马公司同样处于亏损边缘，后来也获得了成功，尤其在意大利和法国。它将自己定位为年轻人用车的提供者，这些人主要包括在工作或者职业中已经取得成功，但仍然希望被视为年轻人的人；或者想要展示自己的不同，并愿意为此买单的人。宝马毫无疑问是属于富人的高档汽车，但它对那些希望看似平凡的富人具有更大的吸引力。奔驰和凯迪拉克主要适用于企业或者国家领导，而宝马则将自己定位为"终极驾驶机器"并加以推广。

保时捷，起初是大众汽车的一个特别款式，把自己重新定位为跑车。它的目标客户是将汽车视为寻求刺激的工具而不仅仅是交通工具的人群。

然而，那些没有进行创新也没有显示出独特性，在变化的汽车业中因循守旧的企业，处境堪忧。比如，英国标志性汽车品牌 MG，30 年前就已经有今日的保时捷的地位。MG 的跑车曾闻名于世，现在却不见踪影。雪铁龙，又在何方呢？30 年前，雪铁龙拥有雄厚的创新基础、牢靠的车身以及中等的可靠性，其定位应该是当下沃尔沃汽车所在的细分市场。然而，它并没有深入思考自身业务并开展创新，导致品牌和战略的缺失。

II

机会

产业结构的变化提供了极好的机会。对于行外人，这些机会是可见的、可预测的。业内人士通常将这些变化视为威胁。因此行外人可以迅速开展创新，风险很小。这种创新往往会成为某一重要行业或领域的关键要素。

下面是一些例子。

20 世纪 50 年代末，三个年轻人偶然相遇在纽约。他们都在金融业工作，主要是华尔街的金融公司。他们有一个共同的看法：自 20 年前的大萧条以来，一直未变的证券业可能会经历快速的结构转变。他们相信这种变化将创造新的机会，于是对金融业和金融市场进行系统的研究，希望能发现适合于资金有限又没有社会关系的新进入者的创业机会。1959 年，他们创立了一家新公司，帝杰证券（Donaldson, Lufkin & Jenrette）。五年后，这家公司成为华尔街上的重要力量。

这三位年轻人发现，新的客户，即养老基金管理者正在出现。这些客户不需要任何难以提供的东西，而需要一些不同的东西，只不过那时还没有提供这种服务的公司。于是，唐纳森（Donaldson）、拉夫金（Lufkin）和詹雷特（Jenrette）这三个年轻人成立了这家经纪公司，专注于为这些客户提供所需的服务。

与此同时，证券业的另一位年轻人也意识到证券业正在发生动荡的结构变化，这提供了创办不同证券公司的机会。他发现的机会就是前文提到的明智投资者。他抓住了这个机会并创办了如今规模庞大且发展迅速的公司。

20 世纪 60 年代早中期，美国医疗保健业开始发生快速的结构变化。当时在中西部一家大型医院做基层管理者的三个年轻人（最大的不到 30 岁），认为这为他们提供了自主创业的机会。他们断定，医院对家政服务方面，如厨房服务、洗衣服务、维修服务等的专业技能需求将会大大增加。他们将要做的事情系统化并与医院签订合同。他们的公司派遣专业人员提供这些服务，费用只相当于医院自主料理这些服务的花费的一小部分。20 年后，这家公司提供了价值高达 10 亿美元的服务。

最后一个例子是美国长途电话市场中的折扣运营商，如 MCI 公司和斯普林特公司（Sprint）。它们都是纯粹的行外企业，斯普林特起初是一家名叫南太平洋的铁路公司。这些行外企业开始挖掘贝尔系统（Bell Systems）中的不足之处。它们发现长途电话服务的定价结构问题。直到第二次世界大战，长途电话仍是一种奢侈品，仅限于政府和大型企业（或者家人去世之类的紧急事件中）使用。第二次世界大战之后，长途电话开始普及。的确，它成为电信业中的增长业务。但是在各州控制电话费率的监管机构的压力下，贝尔系统仍然将长途电话视为奢侈品，定价远远高于成本，并将所得利润用于补贴市内电话业务。为了增加长途电话的吸引力，贝尔系统给予长途电话的大客户较大折扣。

1970年，长途电话的收入很快赶上并超过市内电话的收入。但是，先前的价格结构依旧保持不变。这恰恰是新进入者的机会所在。他们以折扣价格签订批量服务，然后以零售方式卖给小客户并与之共享折扣。这为他们带来巨大利润，也使客户能以较低价格使用长途电话服务。10年后，也就是20世纪80年代初，长途折扣运营商处理的电话比它们成立初期整个贝尔系统处理的电话还要多。

如果不是因为存在一个事实，这些例子只会是奇闻逸事罢了。这个事实就是：每个创新者都知道行业内存在一个重大的创新机会。他们同时确信创新会以极小的风险获得成功。他们为何如此确信呢？

III

产业结构何时变化

下面四个指标能够近乎确定地、清楚地表明产业结构即将发生变化。

1. **最可靠也最易于发现的指标是产业的快速增长。**这实际上也是上述例子（包括汽车业的例子）的共同点。如果一个产业的增长速度远远超过经济或者人口的增长速度（至少是翻番增长），我们可以推断其产业结构极有可能发生巨大变化。目前的运营方式依然很成功，因此没有人想要做出改变。这些运营方式会逐渐变得不合时宜。但是，雪铁龙和贝尔系统的人都不愿意接受这一事实。这也解释了为什么一些新进入者、行外人或者起初微不足道的人能够在成功企业已占据的市场中战胜它们。

2. **当一个产业翻番增长时，它对市场的感知方式和服务方式可能不再**适用。特别是，传统领导者界定和划分市场的方式不再能反映现实而只能反映历史。同时，报告和数字也只代表传统市场观念。这就是两个不同的创新者，帝杰公司和中西部明智投资者的经纪公司都能取得成功的原因。它们每个都找到了现有金融服务机构既没有感知到，也没有提供充分服务的细分市场：养老基金比较新颖，而"明智投资者"不属于华尔街固有的客户群体。

医院管理的例子同样说明了，经历了一段快速发展之后，传统的综合医院已不足以满足需求。第二次世界大战之后，医院里的医护人员大大增加了。这些医院专职人员包括放射科、病理学、医学实验室以及各种治疗学家，等等。而第二次世界大战之前，医院里根本没有这些职业。医院管理也成了一项专业化的工作。传统的家政管理服务曾是早期医院的主要业务，现在成了医院管理者头疼的问题。医院职工尤其是低收入人群成立工会之后，医院管理工作变得更为棘手。

前面第 3 章中提到的连锁书店，也是由于快速发展引起结构变化的例子。出版商和传统美国书店都没有意识到新客户（新购物者）正与老客户（传统读者）一同出现。因为没有意识到新客户群体的出现，所以从未尝试为他们提供服务。

产业如果增长过快，可能会出现自满现象并采用"撇脂定价"策略。这也是贝尔系统针对长途电话采用的策略。这种做法产生的唯一后果就是导致竞争（详见第 17 章）。

美国的艺术领域中也有同样的例子。第二次世界大战之前，博物馆被视为上层人士的专属场所；第二次世界大战之后，参观博物馆成为中产阶级的习惯；各个城市开始建立博物馆。第二次世界大战之前，艺术品收藏只是极少数有钱人的喜好；第二次世界大战之后，艺术品收藏变得流行起来，成千上万的人开始收集艺术品，包括一些资源有限的人。

博物馆的一位年轻工作人员从中看到了创新机会。他在保险业发现机会，这是他未曾想过甚至未曾听过的领域。他成为一名专注于艺术的保险经纪人，为博物馆和收藏家投保。由于他的艺术专长，一些不愿意为艺术收藏品作保的保险公司开始愿意承担这种风险，而且保费比先前低70%。如今，这位年轻人拥有了一家大型保险经纪公司。

3. 独立技术的整合，也会导致产业结构突然变化。

一个例子就是用户交换机（PBX），主要是用于办公场所和其他大型电话客户的电话总机。在美国，用户交换机的相关科技工作基本都是在贝尔实验室开展的。贝尔实验室研究了贝尔系统。该项研究的主要受益者却是诸如罗尔姆公司（ROLM Corporation）之类的新进入者。新型用户交换机由电话技术和电脑技术这两种不同的技术结合而成。因此，用户交换机可以看成应用电脑技术的电信设备，也可以看成应用电信技术的电脑。从技术层面讲，贝尔系统完全能处理这个问题。事实上，贝尔系统一直是计算机先驱。然而，从市场和用户的角度来看，贝尔系统将电脑技术和电话技术视为完全独立且不同的事物。虽然它设计并引进了电脑型的用户交换机，但并未加以推广。结果，新进入者成为这一市场中的主要竞争者。由四位年轻工程师创立的罗尔姆公司，起初是为了研究用于战斗机的小型计算机，却误打误撞地进入了电话业务。尽管贝尔系统在技术上仍然占据领导地位，但其市场占有率不超过1/3。

4. 产业运营方式的快速变化，说明产业结构变化的时机已经成熟。

30年前，美国绝大多数医生都是独立行医。到1980年，只有60%的医生独立行医。现在40%的医生（其中75%是年轻医生）采取团体行医方式，即合伙行医或者成为医疗保健机构或者医院的雇员。早在1970年左右，一些人就看到正在发生的变化并意识到创新机会。一家服务公司应运而生。这家公司为医生团体设计办公室，为他们建议合适的设备仪器，帮助他们管理团队或者培训管理者。

如果某个产业或市场由一个或少数几个大型制造商或供应商主导，那么其产业结构变化引起的创新机会更易把握。即便没有实现真正的垄断，这些大型制造商或供应商多年来一直很成功且无可匹敌，难免会狂妄自大。一开始，它们认为新进入者只是业余性的，无足轻重而不予理会。随着新进入者所占市场份额越来越大，它们才发现已经很难反击了。大概历经十年，贝尔系统对长途运营折扣商和 PBX 制造商才给出反应。

当非阿司匹林类药品泰诺（Tylenol）和戴特尔（Datril）出现时，美国阿司匹林类药品制造商同样反应迟缓（详见第 17 章）。产业的快速发展使创新者从即将发生变化的产业结构中捕捉到创新机会。无可置疑，现有的少数几家阿司匹林类药品制造商也在生产并销售非阿司匹林类药品。毕竟，阿司匹林类药品的不良反应和禁忌早已广为人知。医学文献里对这一点也作了全面论述。但是，在非阿司匹林类药品面世后的 5～8 年内，新进入者一直独占市场。

同样地，在创新者拿走越来越多的高利润业务的同时，美国邮局（United States Postal Service）持续多年毫无回应。先是美国联合包裹运送服务公司（United Parcel Service，UPS）拿走了普通包裹运输业务。随后，埃默里航空运输公司（Emery Air Freight）和联邦快递（Federal Express）分别拿走了更高利润的加急件、高价值物品和信件业务。美国邮政之所以如此不堪一击，主要在于其本身的快速增长。业务量的迅速增长使它忽视了细分领域，这却为创新者提供了机会。

当市场结构和产业结构变化时，行业领导者（无论是制造商还是供应商），往往会忽视增长最快的细分市场。它们依旧坚守很快就会机能失调而过时的实践方式。新生增长机会很少会与业界一贯的接触市场、界定市场以及为市场而自我组织的方式一致。因此，产业内的新生创新者可以不受干扰地发展。因为在一段时间内，特定领域的旧业务或旧服务通常用老方法为市场提供产品、服务，并表现良好。它们很少留意新的挑战，或者不以为然，甚至直接无视。

有一个重要提醒：在产业结构和市场结构这一领域，创新必须保持简单性原则。复杂的创新往往行不通。这里有一个例子，是我所知的最明智的企业战略，但损失也最为惨重。

1960年左右，大众汽车发动了一场变革，要将汽车业转变成全球性市场。自40年前福特汽车公司推出T型车以来，大众汽车公司的甲壳虫（Beetle）成为第一辆真正意义的国际汽车。同在德国一样，甲壳虫在美国也随处可见；在坦噶尼喀和所罗门群岛同样声名远扬。但是由于过于聪明，大众汽车错失了自己创造的机会。

在进入全球市场十年之后的1970年，甲壳虫在欧洲就过时了；在它的第二市场美国，销量却表现良好；在它的第三市场巴西，增长势头明显。显而易见，是时候实施全新的战略了。

大众汽车的首席执行官提议德国工厂全部投入甲壳虫后继车型的生产，新款车将在美国市场销售。美国市场对甲壳虫的持续需求全由大众汽车巴西分公司提供。这样，巴西分公司就具有足够的销量来扩大企业规模，同时也可以使甲壳虫在巴西市场获得另一个十年领导地位。为确保美国客户能享受到"德国品质"（也是甲壳虫的亮点之一），甲壳虫的关键部件如引擎、变速箱等，仍然由德国制造，最后在美国组装成车。

这是第一个真正的全球化战略。在不同国家生产不同的零配件，并根据不同的市场需求在不同地方组装。如果这个战略行得通，它将不仅是一个正确的战略，也将是一个高度创新的战略。但是，由于德国工会的反对，它最终未能实施。他们反对说："在美国组装甲壳虫就意味着德国的就业机会减少……我们绝不能容忍这种行为。"此外，尽管关键部件仍由德国制造，美国经销商对"巴西制造"的汽车依旧心存疑虑（巴西分公司的名字可能会引起误会）。最后，大众汽车不得不放弃这个完美的计划。

后来，大众失去了它的第二市场美国。由伊朗革命引发的第二次石油危机，使得小型汽车风靡一时。大众汽车原本可以占领小型车市场，而不是被日本抢占走，但德国当时没有产品来满足小型车市场。几年后，巴西陷入严重的经济危机，汽车销量大幅下降。大众汽车的巴西分公司陷入危机，20世纪 70 年代的扩增产能也没有了外销客户。

　　大众汽车这一明智战略的失败，致使企业的未来发展危机重重。它失败的具体原因是次要的。这个案例的主要启示是，聪明的创新战略往往会失败，尤其当它旨在利用产业结构变化产生的机会时。只有简单的、明确的战略才会成功。

创新机会源五：人口统计特征

到目前为止，从第 3 章到第 6 章，我们讨论的创新机会源包括：意外事件、不协调事件、流程需求、产业结构和市场结构。这些来源都体现在企业、产业或市场内部。它们可能是经济、社会或知识等外部变化的表征，但都是从内部展现出来的。

其他创新机会源包括：

- 人口统计特征。
- 认知、情绪及意义的变化。
- 新知识。

这些来源都是外部的。它们是社会、哲学、政治和知识环境的变化。

I

在所有外部变化中，人口统计特征最为明显。人口统计特征是指人口数量、人口规模、年龄结构、人口构成、就业情况、教育状况和收入水平。人口统计特征非常清晰，并且最容易产生可以预见的后果。

同时，人口统计特征有着已知且基本确定的时间。比如，即便此时并非全部生活在美国，2000 年将成为美国劳动力的人现在也都已出生。15 年后的许多美国工人现在可能是墨西哥某印第安村落里的孩子。发达国家中，在2030 年将达到退休年龄的人现在已经在劳动大军中。大多数情况下，他们会在自己的行业领域中工作，直到退休或者死亡。目前 20 岁出头的人所接受的教育水平，将在很大程度上决定他们今后 40 年的职业道路。

人口统计特征极大地影响购买对象、购买人群以及购买数量。比如，美国青少年一年会购买许多双便宜的鞋子，他们是为了时尚而非耐用性，而且他们的经济能力有限。十年后，这群人一年将只购买几双鞋子（仅仅是他们17 岁时所购买的 1/6），他们首先为了舒适性和耐用性，其次才是时尚。发达国家中那些六七十岁也就是刚刚退休的人，通常是旅游市场和度假市场的主力军。十年后，同样的人群将会是退休社区、养老院和昂贵医疗护理的客户。双职工家庭有更多的金钱和较少的时间，并以这两个要素为基础进行消费。那些年轻时接受学校教育，尤其是专业和技术教育的人，10～20 年后会成为高等职业教育的客户。

接受过学校教育的人主要是知识工作者。1955 年后，由于婴儿死亡率的下降，第三世界国家的年轻人数量激增。这些大量过剩的年轻人通常只被培训为非熟练工或半熟练工人。即便没有那些低收入国家的竞争，西方国家或者日本等工业发达的国家也必将会推行自动化。仅仅是人口统计特征，出生率的下降和教育普及的结合，就能几近确定这样一个事实：到 2010 年，发达国家中传统蓝领工人的数量将仅为 1970 年的 1/3 或者更少（哪怕自动化可能使制造业生产量达到 1970 年的三四倍）。

一切如此明显，以致人们认为根本无需强调人口统计特征的重要性。的确，商人、经济学家和政客高度认可人口趋势、人口流动和人口动态的重要性。但是，他们认为在日常决策中无须特别关注人口统计特征。人口变化如此缓慢，需要相当长的时间，因此没什么实际意义（无论这些人口变化是出生率或者死亡率的变化、教育水平的变化、劳动力构成和参与的变化，还是人口位置或流动的变化）。只有诸如14世纪发生在欧洲的黑死病之类的巨大人口灾难才会很快对社会和经济产生影响。但其他方面，人口变化是长期性变化，只会引起历史学家和统计学家，而非商人或者管理者的头趣。

这必是一个危险的错误认识。19世纪的移民大潮，人口从欧洲迁移到南美、北美、澳大利亚和新西兰，极大地改变了世界经济和政治地理。这种变化远远超出人们的认知。这次移民大潮催生了大量的创业机会。几个世纪以来，一直基于欧洲政治和军事战略的地理政治观念也变得不合时宜。这一切仅仅发生在50年内（从19世纪60年代中期到1914年）。任何忽视这些变化的人，很快就被时代抛弃。

举个例子，在1860年之前，罗斯柴尔德家族（the House of Rothschild）一直是世界金融市场的主导力量。由于它没有意识到这次移民潮的意义，认为只有底层人民才会离开欧洲，而最终没落。到1870年，罗斯柴尔德家族的地位变得无足轻重。他们仅仅是有钱人而已。J. P. 摩根（J.P. Morgan）取代罗斯柴尔德家族成为金融市场的领导者。他之所以取得如此成就，全在于他对移民潮的警觉和重视。他充分利用这次移民潮机会，在纽约而非欧洲建立全球性银行，为美国工业融资，而工业又同时促进劳动力移民。仅仅过了30年时间，也就是1830~1860年，西欧和美国东部以农业为主的乡村社会就转变为工业化城市。

更早时期，人口统计特征的变化同样迅速、突然，具有巨大的影响力。"人口统计特征在过去变化缓慢"这一观念纯粹是谬误。从历史上看，人口在较长一段时间内保持不变只是例外而非常态。⊖

⊖ 这方面的法国文明史学家的作品最具权威性。

在 20 世纪，忽视人口统计特征的行为愚蠢至极。人口本质上极不稳定，会突然发生变化，这必须是我们这个时代的基本假定。无论商人还是政客在制定决策时，都应把这一假定当作首要条件来分析。比如，在当下的国内和国际政治中，最重要的挑战有两点：一是发达国家内的老龄化，二是发展中国家内的年轻人过剩。无论出于何种原因，20 世纪的发达国家和发展中国家都容易发生激烈的人口变化。这些变化通常发生得毫无征兆。

1938 年，美国总统富兰克林·罗斯福（Franklin D. Roosevelt）将最有名的人口专家召集在一起。他们一致预测，美国人口将在 1943 年或 1944 年达到 1.4 亿的峰值，随后缓慢下降。加上小部分的移民，现在（1984 年）美国人口为 2.4 亿。因为 1949 年，在美国毫无征兆地出现了婴儿潮。随后 12 年里，还出现了数量空前的大家庭。1960 年，美国又突然迎来了生育低潮，产生了同样数量空前的小家庭。1938 年的人口统计学家并非无能之辈或愚蠢之人，只是因为当时婴儿潮的出现过于突然。

20 年后，美国另一位总统约翰·肯尼迪（John F. Kennedy）也组织一群知名专家来推出针对拉美的援助和发展计划项目，即"争取进步联盟"（Alliance for Progress）。1961 年，没有一个专家预料到婴儿死亡率的大幅下降，而这彻底改变了 15 年后拉美的社会和经济发展。这些专家毫无保留地认为拉美只是偏远乡村地区而已。同样地，他们也并非无能之辈或者愚蠢之人。只是当时，拉美的婴儿死亡率下降趋势尚未显现，城镇化也毫无迹象。

1972—1973 年，美国资深劳动力分析师断定，与多年来一样，美国女性劳动者数量将会持续下降。当婴儿潮一代以创纪录的人数进入劳动力市场时，分析师们担心没有足够的工作来满足年轻男性的需求。虽然事后证明，这种担心毫无必要。人们认为女性不需要工作，因此没有人考虑女性的工作岗位将从何而来。10 年后，美国 50 岁以下的女性参加工作的占 64%，创下纪录新高。这些参加工作的女性，在结婚与否、是否有孩子方面基本无差异。

这些转变不仅出人意料，而且令人难以琢磨。现在回想起来，第三世界国家婴儿死亡率的下降是可以加以解释的。它是旧技术（公共健康护理、厕所设在水源的下游、接种疫苗、安装窗纱）与新技术（抗生素、诸如DDT的杀虫剂）结合的结果。然而，这种变化不可预测。美国婴儿潮或生育低潮的原因何在呢？美国女性参加工作的原因呢？同样地，滞后美国几年的欧洲女性呢？拉美城市陷入贫困，这一现象又该如何解释呢？

20世纪的人口变化本质上可能无法预测，但产生影响之前通常会有很长一段时间间隔。这段时间间隔是可以加以推测的。新生儿需要5年才能进入幼儿园，需要教室、操场和老师；需要15年，才能成为重要的消费者；需要19～20年，才能长大成人、参加工作。拉美的人口死亡率下降后，人口很快开始大幅增长。但是，这些存活的婴儿在五六年后没有成为幼儿园学生。再十五六年后，长大的青少年也没有去找工作。而将教育成果转化为劳动力和劳动技能，则至少需要10年，往往是15年。

对企业家而言，人口统计特征是一个绝好的机会。决策制定者，无论是商人、公共服务人员还是政府决策制定者，往往会忽视这一机会。他们依旧断定人口统计特征不会发生变化，至少不会快速变化。事实上，他们甚至对最明显的人口变化都不予理会。下面是几个典型的案例。

1970年，美国学校学生数量明显比20世纪60年代时低了25%～30%。之后的10年或15年内，这一现象应该不会改变。毕竟1970年进入幼儿园的孩子，至少要在1965年前出生。当时生育低潮已成既定事实，根本无法逆转。但是，美国学校断然不接受这一事实。他们认为学龄儿童的数量将逐年增加，这是自然规律。因此，他们加大力度招收学生。这导致几年后大量毕业生失业、教师薪资下降压力大，许多学校被迫倒闭。

这里有我亲身经历的两个例子。1957年时，我预测25年以后，也就是20世纪70年代中期，美国大学生会达到1000万～1200万。这个数字只是将两个已经发生的人口事件简单相加得出来的。这两个人口事件是出生人口数量的增加和上大学青少年的比率提升。毫无疑问，这个预测完全正确。但实际上，知名大学都对此报以嘘声。20 年后，也就是 1976 年，通过分析年龄数据，我推测美国退休年龄将在 10 年内提高到 70 岁甚至直接废除。这一变化来得更快，一年后，即 1977 年，加州废除了强制退休制；两年后，即 1978 年，美国其他地区废除了 70 岁之前退休的规定。而使这一预测确定无疑的人口数字其实早已是众所周知的事情（出版物上就有）。但是大部分所谓的专家，包括政府经济学家、工会经济学家、企业经济学家和统计学家，都认为这一说法荒谬无比。他们众口一词："它永远不会发生。"实际上，工会当时还提议将法定退休年龄降低到 60 岁或更低。

专家们不愿意或不能接受与理所当然的事物不一致的人口现状，这恰恰为企业家提供了机会。时间间隔是确定可知的，事件也已经发生。但是没人接受这一事实，更不会将它视为机会。那些拒绝传统观念而接受事实的人，他们实际上是积极寻找事实的人，他们能够在相当长时间内专注于创新。一般情况下，只有在人口结构将被新的人口变化和新的人口现状所取代时，竞争者才会接受这一事实。

II

下面是几个成功利用人口变化的案例。

大部分美国大型学校都认为我的预测，即到 1970 年大学生将达到 1000 万～1200 万是荒谬的。但是一些具有企业家精神的大学认真对待这件事，如纽约的佩斯大学（Pace University）和旧金山的金门大学（Golden Gate University）。起初它们也持怀疑态度，它们经过认真思考意识到该预测的可靠性，事实上这是唯一合理的预测。于是它们为这些新增学生做入学准备。而传统大学，尤其是享有声望的大学，却毫无准备。结果 20 年后，那些做了充足准备的学校获得了生源。当生育低潮引致的全国入学人数下降时，这些学校的学生依然增长。

梅尔维尔公司（Melville）当时还是一家不知名的美国小型零售鞋店，接受了婴儿潮这一事实。1960年初，在婴儿潮一代步入青少年之际，梅尔维尔公司转向这个新市场。它为青少年创立与众不同的新型鞋店，并重新设计鞋子款式。它针对十六七岁的青少年进行宣传和推广。除鞋类外，它还将业务拓展到青少年服装上。结果，梅尔维尔公司成为美国增长速度最快、盈利能力最强的零售商。10年后，其他零售商才弄清楚现状开始迎合青少年的需求。而此时，人口结构的重心开始从青少年转向20～25岁的青年了。梅尔维尔也已将重心转移到新的主导人群上。

1961年，肯尼迪总统为"争取进步联盟"计划项目召集的研究拉美的学者，并没有看到拉美的城镇化趋势。美国一家零售连锁店西尔斯百货（Sears），在几年前就预见了这一现象。西尔斯百货并非通过研究统计，而是通过走访墨西哥城、利马、圣保罗和波哥大等城市的客户，做出这一预测的。20世纪50年代中期，西尔斯百货开始在拉美的大城市建立美式商店，这主要是为新兴城市的中产阶级设计的。这些人并不富裕，是货币经济体系的一部分并且曾渴望中产阶级的生活。短短几年内，西尔斯百货成为拉美的领先零售商。

这里还有两个利用人口统计特征建设高效人才队伍的案例。纽约花旗银行（Citibank）的扩张很大程度上是由于其很早就意识到受过高等教育、雄心勃勃的年轻女性将进入劳动力市场。1980年，大部分美国大型公司将这些女性视为麻烦，许多公司现在依然如此。在众多大型公司中，花旗银行几乎是唯一从中看到机会的公司。20世纪70年代，花旗银行大力招收女职员，对她们进行培训并作为信贷人员派遣到全国各地。这些雄心勃勃的年轻女性在很大程度上使花旗银行成为全国的领先银行，也使之成为首个真正意义上的全国性银行。同时，一些储蓄和信贷协会（这并不是一个因为创新或冒险而闻名的行业）意识到早期因为年幼的孩子辞职的年长的已婚女性，作为长期兼职人员再次参加工作时会有优异的表现。众所周知，兼职工作是暂时性的；曾经离开劳动力市场的女性也不会再次返回。在早期，这两条都是完全合乎情理的规则。但是，人口统计特征使它们变得不合时宜。储蓄和信贷协会之所以接受这个事实，同样并非因为统计数据，而是走出去观察的结果。对这一事实的接受，使它们建设了一支极其忠诚、高效的人才队伍。她们在加州表现尤为突出。

地中海俱乐部（Club Mediterranée）在旅游和度假业务上的成功，也是由于利用了人口变化。当时在欧洲和美国，出现了一群年轻人。这些年轻人很富有并接受了良好的教育，而他们的父辈都还是工人阶级。他们还不怎么自我肯定，并缺乏对旅游的自信心。他们渴望有人能安排他们的假期、旅行和娱乐，但并不想与他们的工人阶级父母或者年长的中产阶级同行。因此，一种新颖独特的年轻人旅游方式正好符合他们的需求。

Ⅲ

人口变化的分析从人口数字开始。但是，人口数字的绝对值毫无意义。比如，相比之下，年龄分布更加重要。20 世纪 60 年代，许多发达国家的人口数量攀升（英国的婴儿潮持续期比较短，是个例外），这是很重要的数字。20 世纪八九十年代，年轻人数量将会下降，中年人（40 岁以下）数量将稳步上升，老年人（70 岁以上）数量将会迅速增长。这些变化提供什么机会呢？不同的年龄群体在价值观、期望、需求和欲望上有什么区别呢？

传统大学的学生数量不会增长了。人们最大的期望就是这个数字不会下降。另外，继续深造的十八九岁中学生在增加，抵消了总人数的下降。但是，随着较早获得大学学位的三四十岁的人口增加，将会有一大批接受过高等教育希望接受高级职业培训和再培训的人群，如医生、律师、建筑师、工程师、管理人员和教师。这些人寻求什么？他们需要什么？他们如何买单？

传统大学如何才能吸引和满足如此不同的学生？最后，这些年长人口的欲望、需求、价值观是什么？是否真的存在这样一个平均年龄较大的人群？是否存在几个拥有不同期望、需求、价值观和满意度的人群呢？

人口重心的变化是年龄分布中最重要一点，也最有预测价值。人口重心指在任何时间内人口规模最大且增长最快的年龄群体。

美国总统艾森豪威尔（Eisenhower）卸任之际，即20世纪50年代末，美国人口重心的年龄达到历史最高值。但是，短短几年内就发生了剧烈的转变。受婴儿潮的影响，1965年，人口重心的年龄下降到十六七岁，是共和国早期以来的最低点。可以推测，人们的心理和价值观将会发生重大变化。事实上，那些重视人口统计特征并研究人口数字的人确实是如此预测的。60年代的青年反叛运动，主要是由于人们将关注点转移到典型青少年行为上。而在早些年，人口重心的年龄在二三十岁时，各个年龄段的人都很保守，青少年行为也被视为没什么大不了。但是到60年代时，青少年行为突然变成有代表性的行为了。

但是，当人们都在谈论价值观的转变和年轻化的美国时，年龄重心又剧烈地转变回来了。1969年，生育低潮的影响开始显现而不只是体现在统计数字上。1974年或者说1975年，是十六七岁的青少年构成人口重心的最后一年。自此之后，重心快速上升。20世纪80年代，人口重心年龄又回到最高值20岁。这种重心的转变，将会引起典型行为的变化。当然，青少年的行为实际上并未改变。人们再次将此视为青少年的正常行为，而不是上升到社会价值观和社会行为层面。因此可以近乎肯定地预测，到20世纪70年代中期，大学校园里将不再有激进分子和叛逆者，学生们将重点关注成绩和工作。事实上，确实有人这样预测。此外，1968年的辍学学生中，绝大多数在10年后将是积极努力的专业人士，主要关心事业、晋升、税收减免以及股票期权等。

按照教育水平进行人口分类，同样重要。就某些目的而言，如销售百科全书、职业进修以及假期旅行等，这种分类的意义更加深远。此外，还有按照劳动力参与和职业进行分类。最后，还可以按照收入分布分类，尤其是可支配收入的分布。举个例子：双职工的家庭储蓄会有什么不同？

实际上，我们可以找到大部分答案（它们是进行市场研究的材料）。而我们只需积极地提出问题。

仅仅依赖统计数字是远远不够的。确切地说，统计数字只是起点。它让梅尔维尔公司思考青少年的剧增给时装零售商带来的商机。同样，它也使西尔斯的高管开始重视拉美这一潜在市场。但是这些公司的管理者（还包括纽约佩斯大学和旧金山金门大学的管理者），必须要进行实地考察并广泛收集意见。

下面详述一下西尔斯百货进入拉美市场的过程。20 世纪 50 年代初，西尔斯百货的董事长罗伯特·伍德（Robert E. Wood）得知，到 1975 年，墨西哥城和圣保罗的增长将超过美国所有城市。他对此满怀兴趣，于是亲自走访拉美的主要城市，包括墨西哥城、瓜达拉哈拉、波哥大、利马、圣地亚哥、里约热内卢以及圣保罗。他在每个城市考察驻留一周，四处走动，观察商店，研究当地的交通方式。这样，它深入了解了目标客户群、商店风格、商店位置以及商店内的货物。

同样地，在建立第一个度假胜地之前，地中海俱乐部创始人对包办旅行的客户进行深入分析，与他们交谈并倾听他们的想法。梅尔维尔连锁店的两个年轻人同样花费数周乃至数月的时间在购物广场，观察顾客、倾听顾客并探索他们的价值观。他们研究年轻人的购物方式和购物环境，比如，少男少女们是喜欢在同一家商店购物，还是在不同商店购物呢？最终，梅尔维尔鞋店从一个老式的、毫无特色的众多连锁鞋店转变为美国发展最快的流行时装零售店。

因此，对那些真正想要进行实地考察并听取他人意见的人来说，人口统计特征变化是一个高效可靠的创新机会。

创新机会源六：认知变化

I

"杯子是半满的"

从数学的角度来看，"杯子是半满的"与"杯子是半空的"毫无差异。但这两种陈述方式所表达的意义完全不同，产生的影响也完全不同。如果一般认知从将杯子看成"半满的"转变为看成"半空的"，那么就会有很多创新机会。

这里有一些例子阐述认知的变化及其在商业、政治、教育或其他领域产生的创新机会。

1. **事实表明，20 世纪 60 年代初之后的 20 年里，美国医疗保健获得了空前的进步和改善。**无论从新生儿死亡率或老年人存活率，还是从肺癌之外的癌症发病率或癌症治愈率来看，人们身体机能的所有指标都飞快改善。但整个国家却陷入了集体恐慌。美国人从未如此关心健康，也从未如此害怕。突然之间，仿佛一切东西都能引发癌症、退行性心脏病或记忆力衰退。这种情况下，杯子明显是"半空的"。我们看到的并非身体机能的巨大改善，而是依然不能永生以及在实现永生方面毫无进展。事实上，如果美国人的健康状况在过去 20 年里真的有所恶化，那也是由于人们对健康和体能的过度关心，以及被日渐衰老、身材走形、长期疾病等困扰而引起的。25 年前，国民健康的小小进步都被视为巨大的前进，而如今，即便是重大的进步，人们也依然无动于衷。

无论这种认知变化产生的根源是什么，它都催生了大量的创新机会。比如，它创造了一个新型医疗保健杂志市场。其中一本杂志《美国健康》（*American Health*），在两年内发行量就达到了 100 万份。利用人们对传统食物会造成无法挽回损害的恐惧，一大批创新企业出现了。位于科罗拉多州博尔德市的诗尚草本公司（Celestial Seasonings），是由一名花童创立的。20 世纪 60 年代末，花童们上山采摘药草、香草，包装好拿到街上销售。15 年后，诗尚草本的年销售收入达到数亿美元，后来被一家大型食品加工商以 2000 多万美元收购。此外，保健食品商店也获得了相当可观的利润。慢跑器械也成了一项大生意。1983 年，美国发展最快的新创企业是一家生产室内运动器械的企业。

2. 传统上，人们的饮食方式在很大程度上取决于收入水平和所处的阶级。普通人"吃饭"，富人则是"品味"。过去 20 年里，这种认知发生了变化。如今人们同样都是"吃饭"和"品味"。一种趋势是以尽可能简单便捷的方式来摄取必需食物，如方便食品、冷冻快餐、麦当劳的汉堡或肯德基的炸鸡等。同样他们这个人群也是美食家。美食节目获得很高的收视率，得到人们的广泛好评。美食书成为大众市场的畅销书。许多新的美食连锁店纷纷开张。传统超市也开设了美食专柜，尽管超市 90% 的食品是速食食品，但多数情况下，相比于速食食品，美食专柜的食品利润更高。这种新认知不仅仅出现在美国。最近，德国一位年轻女医生告诉我："一周内，我们有 6 天在糊口，有 1 天则在享受美食。"而在不久之前，可是普通人一周 7 天都在糊口，而精英人士、富人和贵族 7 天都在品味美食。

3. 1960 年左右，在艾森豪威尔即将卸任总统一职而肯尼迪将要接任之际，如果有人能够预测美国黑人在接下来 10～15 年取得的进步，那么即便不被认为疯了也会被当作不切实际的幻想家。即便对美国黑人状况改善的预测水平是日后实际水平的一半，在那时也会被认为过分乐观。有史以来，从未有过一个群体的社会地位在如此短的时间内得到如此大的改善。在那时，接受高中以上高等教育的黑人仅是白人的 1/5 左右。到 20 世纪 70 年代初，这个比例已经赶上了白人，甚至比部分白人群体还要高。在就业、收入，特别是进入专业技术岗位和管理职位方面，也取得了同样的进步。在 12～15 年之前，具有超前眼光的人都会认为美国黑人问题已经解决了，至少已经取得很大的进步。

但在大部分美国黑人看来，20 世纪 80 年代的今天不是"半满的"而是"半空的"。对相当多的黑人而言，挫败、愤怒以及疏离等情绪加强了而非缓解了。他们并未看到 2/3 的黑人无论在经济地位还是社会地位上都已经进入美国中产阶级行列，反而过于强调 1/3 的黑人在状况改善上毫无进展。他们看到的不是取得的进步，而是尚未完成的工作。在他们看来，这些有待完成的事情进展很慢而且相当费劲。美国黑人的旧时盟友白人自由主义者，包括工会、犹太人以及学术机构，看到的是黑人取得的进步，认为杯子是"半满的"。这种认知的不一致导致黑人与白人自由主义者之间产生分歧，这使黑人更加确信杯子是"半空的"。

但是，白人自由主义者认为黑人不再是被剥削的，不应继续享受诸如反歧视之类的特殊待遇，也不再需要特别补助以及就业和升职方面的优先权，等等。这种状况成就了全新的黑人领袖杰西·杰克逊牧师（Jesse Jackson）。在将近 100 年的历史中，从世纪之交的布克·华盛顿（Booker T.

Washington），到罗斯福新政时期的沃尔特·怀特（Walter White），再到约翰·肯尼迪（John Kennedy）和林登·约翰逊（Lyndon Johnson）总统时期的马丁·路德·金（Martin Luther King, Jr.），黑人只有证明自己能够得到白人自由主义者的支持才能成为黑人领袖。这是获取足够政治支持为黑人谋取重要福利的唯一方式。然而，认知的变化使美国黑人和他们旧时的盟友及战友白人自由主义者产生了分歧。杰西·杰克逊将此视为一个创新机会，通过声讨甚至攻击白人自由主义者，成为一个全新类型的黑人领袖。在过去，杰克逊的这种反自由主义、反工会、反犹太人的行为，就是政治家自毁前程。但在 1984 年，这却使杰克逊在短短几周内成为无可置疑的美国黑人领袖。

4. 当下的美国女权主义者将 20 世纪三四十年代视为至暗时刻，因为当时女性的社会角色被否定。事实上，没有比这更荒谬的看法了。三四十年代，众多女性闪耀美国。美国第一夫人埃莉诺·罗斯福（Eleanor Roosevelt）是良知、原则和慈悲的代言。在美国，没有一个男人在社会中发挥的作用能与之媲美。埃莉诺的挚友弗朗西丝·帕金斯（Frances Perkins）是第一位作为劳工部部长进入美国内阁的女性。她也是罗斯福总统内阁成员中最具实力、最有影响力的成员。安娜·罗森伯格（Anna Rosenberg）是第一位在大型公司担任高级管理者的女性。她是当时美国最大的零售商店梅西百货公司的人事副总裁。后来朝鲜战争期间，她担任主管人事的助理国防部长，成为将军们的"老板"。许多杰出女强人在大学担任校长，而且个个是全国知名人物。著名剧作家克莱尔·布思·卢斯（Clare Boothe Luce）和莉莲·赫尔曼（Lillian Hellman）都是女性。克莱尔后来成为政界名人，担任康涅狄格州的国会议员和驻意大利大使。当时最受关注的医学进步也是女性的工作成就。海伦·陶西格（Helen Taussig）成功完成第一例心脏外科手术，"蓝婴"（blue baby）手术。它拯救了世界上无数孩子，开创了外科手术的新时代并直接促成心脏移植和心脏搭桥手术的出现。还有第一位将歌声传递到千家万户的黑人女歌星玛丽安·安德森（Marian Anderson），触动无数美国人的心灵。

在黑人中，只有25年后的马丁·路德·金取得的成就能与她相提并论。这份名单将一直延续下去。

这些女性意识到自己的成就、卓越表现以及发挥的重要作用并为之自豪。但是，她们并不将自己看作榜样。她们仅仅把自己当作独立的个体，而非女性。她们认为自己是例外的，不具有代表性。

这种变化为何会出现以及是如何出现的，这个问题留待历史学家解释。但是当1970年左右发生这种变化时，对女权主义者而言，这些伟大女性变得无足轻重了。而现在，女性如果不参加工作或者不在传统认为的男性职位上工作，那这个女性会被视为例外，缺乏代表性。

一些企业，尤其是花旗银行（详见第7章），将这个变化视为机会。但那些女性一直能担任专业人士和管理者的行业，如百货公司、广告公司、杂志或书籍出版商，却没有注意到这种变化。事实上，这些雇用女性担任专业人士和管理者的传统公司，目前重要岗位上的女性比三四十年前还少。相比之下，花旗银行之前基本都是男职员，这也许是它能意识到机会的原因之一。女性自我认知的变化，使花旗银行看到了重大机会。花旗银行开始大力招收并留住极为能干、雄心勃勃并具有拼搏精神的女性。它根本无须担心会引起传统的雇用女性的公司的竞争。正如我们所看到的，利用了这种认知变化，创新者往往在很长一段时间成为这个创新领域的唯一。

5. 20世纪50年代初的一个更早的例子，同样也利用了认知的变化。1950年左右，无论收入和职位如何，绝大多数美国人都认为自己是中产阶级。显然，美国人已经改变了对自身社会地位的认知。但这种改变有什么意义呢？一个名叫威廉·本顿（William Benton）的广告经理（后来担任康涅狄格州的参议员），走出去询问人们怎么看待"中产阶级"的意义。他得到的回复完全一致：相比于工人阶级，中产阶级意味着他们的孩子在学校的优异表现有助于实现良好的未来发展。本顿于是买下大英百科全书出版公司并开始兜售大英百科全书。他主要通过高中老师向家庭中第一代孩子正上高中的父母推销。"如果你想成为中产阶级，"本顿说道，"那么你的孩子必须有一套百科全书，从而在学校有良好表现。"三年内，本顿使这家濒临破产的公司重获新生。十年后，这家公司用同样的理由在日本采取同样的策略，同样获得了成功。

6. 意外的成功或意外的失败往往是认知和意义变化的表征。第 3 章阐述了"雷鸟"如何从"艾德赛尔"的溃败中获得成功。当福特公司分析"艾德赛尔"失败的原因时，发现是由认知变化引起的。稍早几年，汽车市场按照收入群体划分，现在已经按照生活方式划分了。

当认知变化出现时，事实本身并未改变。但是，事实的意义发生了变化。从"杯子是半满的"，到"杯子是半空的"，意义发生了变化。从将自己视为工人阶级并认为人的地位生来注定，到将自己视为中产阶级并认为社会地位及经济机会可以通过努力改变，意义也发生了变化。这种变化出现得十分迅速。不到十年，大多数美国人从将自己视为工人阶级转向视为中产阶级。

经济状况未必能指示这些变化。事实上，它们之间可能毫无关联。就收入分配而言，相比于美国，英国更为平等。仅仅从收入来看，尽管至少 2/3 英国人的收入超过工人阶级的标准，将近一半人的收入超过中低产阶级的标准，但是 70% 的英国人仍将自己视为工人阶级。因此，心态而非事实决定杯子是"半满的"还是"半空的"。它是由被称为"存在主义"的经历带来的。美国黑人认为"杯子是半空的"，这与过去几百年来未曾治愈的伤痛以及当下美国的状况有关。大部分英国人将自己视为工人阶级，很大程度上是 19 世纪的教派斗争引起的。相比于健康统计数据，美国的疑病症更体现了美国人的价值观（如崇尚年轻等）。

社会学家或经济学家能否解释认知现象无关紧要。认知依然是事实，通常无法量化，或者当它能够量化时，已经无法产生创新机会了。但它不是外来的或难以理解的。它是具体的，可以加以界定和检验，最重要的是可以加以利用。

II

时机问题

高管和管理人员都承认基于认知创新的效力，但他们往往认为它不切实际而回避它。他们认为基于认知的创新者是怪异的，或简直就是个疯子。大英百科全书、福特汽车的雷鸟以及诗尚草本公司，一点都不怪异。的确，任何领域成功的创新者大都离他们创新的领域很近。唯一使他们与众不同的是，他们对机会的警觉性。

当今最出色的美食烹饪杂志是由一位年轻人创办的。起初他是一家航空杂志社的饮食专栏编辑。当在同一份星期日报纸上看到三则相互矛盾的消息后，他就开始留意认知变化了。第一则称，在美国诸如速冻食品、冷冻快餐和肯德基炸鸡之类的速食食品，占据所有消耗的食品一半以上。而且几年内这一比例将上升至3/4。第二则称，美食烹饪节目备受观众推崇。第三则称，平装本（也是大众版本）的美食烹饪书位居畅销书排行榜的首位。这些明显的矛盾之处使他思忖：这到底是怎么一回事？一年后，他创办了一家完全不同的美食杂志。

花旗银行的校园招聘人员汇报说无法完成公司的指示，即招聘在金融和营销领域表现最优异的商学院男生。他们还汇报，这些领域最优秀的学生中女性比例越来越高（花旗银行开始意识到女性加入劳动大军所产生的机会）。当时其他许多公司（包括一些银行）的校园招聘人员也向公司管理者汇报了这一事实。但是，大多数公司敦促他们："尽更大的努力去引进最优秀的男性人才。"花旗银行的高层管理者将这个变化视为机会并付诸行动。

这些例子表明基于认知的创新存在一个关键问题：时机。如果福特公司在艾德赛尔惨败之后，推迟一年才采取行动，"生活方式"这一市场可能就会被通用汽车公司的庞蒂克（Pontiac）占领。如果花旗银行不是最先雇用女性 MBA 的公司，那么它也不会成为雄心勃勃的立志成就事业的优秀年轻女性的最佳选择了。

时机尚未成熟就利用认知变化，没有比这更危险的了。许多现象看似是认知的变化，其实只是一时的狂热而已。它们往往一两年就消失无踪。人们往往无法区分一时的狂热和真正的变化。孩子玩电脑游戏的行为是一时的狂热。然而，诸如雅达利（Atari）等公司将它视为认知变化并加以利用。这种现象只持续了一两年，这些公司因此也备受打击。孩子的父亲们对家用电脑的兴趣则才是真正的变化。认知的变化所产生的影响几乎难以预测。法国、日本、德国和美国的学生运动就是一个很好的例子。20 世纪 60 年代末，每个人都断定这场运动会产生持久而深刻的影响。但是，结果究竟如何呢？就大学而言，这场学生运动似乎没有产生任何持久的影响。但谁会料到，1968 年的这群反叛学生 15 年后竟然会成为雅皮士（Yuppies）？ 1984 年美国总统初选时，参议员哈特（Hart）还极力争取他们的支持。他们是极端唯物主义者，也是工作意识强、为升迁而时刻准备的积极向上的年轻专业人士。相比于过去，如今退学人数大大减少，唯一的不同是媒体对他们的关注。同性恋成为人们关注的焦点，这能够用学生运动解释吗？很显然，1968 年观察研究这些学生以及事件的观察者和学者，根本无法预测到这些结果。

但是，时机仍然十分重要。在利用认知的变化时，创造性模仿（详见第 17 章）不起作用。创新者必须占据先机。考虑到认知的变化是一时的狂热还是永久的变化是很难确定的，这种变化产生的影响也难以确定，因此基于认知的创新起初应当是小而具体的。

创新机会源七：新知识

基于知识的创新是企业家精神的"超级明星"。它备受瞩目又能创造财富。基于知识的创新就是人们通常所谈论的创新。并非所有基于知识的创新都很重要，有些的确微不足道。在创造历史的创新中，基于知识的创新位居前列。知识并非都是科学的或是技术的。基于知识的社会创新同样重要，甚至更为重要。

在时间跨度、失败率、可预测性、对企业家的挑战等基本特征上，基于知识的创新与其他类型的创新有所不同。正如大多数"超级明星"，基于知识的创新变幻无常，难以把握。

I

基于知识的创新的特征

在所有创新中，基于知识的创新的前导时间最长。首先，从知识的产生到成为可应用的技术，需要很长的时间；而且新技术转化为市场中的产品、工艺或服务，也需要很长的时间。

1970—1910 年，生化学家保罗·埃利希（Paul Ehrlich）提出了化学疗法，一种利用化合物控制细菌和微生物的理论。他还首次研发出用于治疗梅毒的抗菌药阿斯凡纳明。但直到 25 年后，即 1936 年，应用埃利希化学疗法研发的磺胺类药物（这种药物能控制多种细菌性疾病）才进入市场。

1897 年，鲁道夫·迪赛尔（Rudolph Diesel）发明了以他的名字命名的柴油发动机。人们立即意识到这是一项重要的创新。过了很多年，这项创新都没有应用到实践中。直到 1935 年，美国人查尔斯·凯特林（Charles Kettering）对迪赛尔发动机进行全新的设计，使这种推进装置能够适用于各种船只、火车、卡车、公共汽车和小客车。

各种知识的组合才使计算机得以成为可能。最早是二级制的出现，这种数学理论可以追溯到 17 世纪，只用 0 和 1 就可以表示所有数字。19 世纪上半期，查尔斯·巴比奇（Charles Babbage）将二进制应用到计算机器中。1890 年，赫尔曼·霍列瑞斯（Hermann Hollerith）发明了穿孔卡，它起源于 19 世纪初法国人雅卡尔（J-M. Jacquard）的发明。穿孔卡能将数字转化为指令。1906 年，美国人李·德福雷斯特（Lee de Forest）发明了三极管，因此开启电子计算机时代。随后 1910—1913 年间，伯特兰·罗素（Bertrand Russell）与艾尔弗雷德·诺思·怀特黑德（Alfred North Whitehead）在他们的著作《数学原理》（*Principia Mathematica*）中首次提出符号逻辑，这使人们可以用数字表示所有逻辑概念。最后，第一次世界大战期间主要用于高射炮射击的编程和反馈概念得到发展。换句话说，1918 年，发明计算机所需要的知识都准备就绪。直到 1946 年，世界上第一台能够运转的计算机才出现。

1951 年，福特汽车公司一位生产主管提出"自动化"一词，并详细描述了自动化所需要的整个生产工艺。之后的 25 年，机器人和自动化被广泛提及，但在很长一段时间内没有任何进展。直到 1978 年，日本的日立和丰田才在工厂中引进机器人。20 世纪 80 年代初，通用电气公司在宾夕法尼亚州的伊利（Erie）建立自动化汽车厂，随后通用汽车公司开启了发动机和汽车配件的自动化生产。1985 年初，大众汽车公司也开始使用几乎完全自动化的最后装配车间（Hall 54）。

自称是几何学家的巴克敏斯特·富勒（Buckminster Fuller），也是数学家和哲学家，将数学中的拓扑学应用于他称为 Dymaxion 的一栋房子的设计。之所以如此命名，是因为他喜欢这个词的发音。Dymaxion 房子能够以尽可能小的表面积提供尽可能大的生活空间（因此是一种圆形房子）。因此，这种房屋具有最好的隔音、取暖和制冷效果，同时还具有卓越的音响效果。建筑这种房屋只需用轻型材料和数量最小化的支撑物，不需要地基就足以承受地震或狂风。1940 年左右，富勒在新英格兰的一所面积不大的学院校园里建造了一栋 Dymaxion 房子，至今依然耸立。也许美国人不喜欢圆形房子，很少人建筑这种房子。1965 年左右，南极和北极开始出现这种房子。因为在那些地区，传统建筑昂贵却不实用而且难以修建。自此之后，Dymaxion 结构被广泛用于礼堂、音乐厅、运动场等大型建筑中。

只有重大的外部危机才能缩短基于知识的创新所需的前导时间。德福雷斯特于 1906 年发明的三极管，原本确实可以立即用来生产收音机。如果不是第一次世界大战迫使各国政府尤其是美国政府推动无线传输的发展，那么可能到 20 世纪 30 年代左右收音机才会问世。战场上的有线电话很不可靠，无线电报仅仅限于传输摩尔斯代码。因此 20 世纪 20 年代初，仅仅在相关知识出现之后 15 年，收音机就出现在市场中。

如果不是第二次世界大战，青霉素可能要到 20 世纪 50 年代左右才会出现。20 世纪 20 年代中期，弗莱明就发现了能够杀死细菌的青霉素。10 年后，英国生化学家霍华德·弗洛里（Howard Florey）开始研究这种青霉素。第二次世界大战使青霉素能够更快地进入市场。因为需要能有效抑制感染的药物，英国政府大力支持弗洛里的研究。不论在何处战斗，英国士兵都能当作试药者。同样，如果不是第二次世界大战，计算机很可能要等到贝尔实验室的物理学家 1947 年发明晶体管之后才会问世。第二次世界大战时美国政府投入大量人力和财力推动了计算机的研究。

并非只有基于科学知识和技术知识的创新需要较长的前导时间，那些基于非科学知识和非技术知识的创新，同样如此。

拿破仑战争之后，圣西门伯爵（Saint-Simon）提出了创业型银行理论，即有目的地利用资本创造经济利益。在此之前，银行家只是放债者，依据担保向人们发放贷款，比如君主征税权。圣西门伯爵所言的银行家做的是"投资"，也就是产生新财富的创造能力。在他的时代，圣西门伯爵具有非凡影响力。1826 年去世后，他的思想和理论备受推崇。然而直到 1852 年，他的两个门徒皮埃尔兄弟（Jacob and Isaac Pereire）才成立第一家创业型银行工业信贷银行（Credit Mobilier），并提出我们现在所称的金融资本主义。

第一次世界大战之后，我们现在所说的管理需要的许多要素都已具备。事实上，早在 1923 年，赫伯特·胡佛（Herbert Hoover，不久就成为美国总统）和捷克斯洛伐克创立者、首任总统托马斯·马萨里克（Thomas Masaryk）在布拉格召开了首届国际管理会议。与此同时，全球有几家大公司，特别是美国的杜邦公司和通用汽车公司，开始用新的管理概念重组公司。之后几十年里，一些"真正的信徒"，尤其是英国人林德尔·厄威克（Lyndall Urwick），开始撰写管理类书籍。厄威克创办了第一家管理咨询公司，这家公司至今仍以他的名字命名。但直到我的两本著作《公司的概念》（1946 年）和《管理的实践》（1954 年）出版后，管理学才成为一门为世界管理者所了解的学科。在那之前，"管理"的学者或实践者都只关注某个领域，如厄威克关注组织管理，其他人关注人事管理。我的书籍将管理进行编纂、组织，并使之系统化。几年内，管理学就成了全世界的一股强劲力量。

如今，学习理论也经历着同样的前导时间。1890 年左右，德国人威廉·冯特（Wilhelm Wundt）和美国人威廉·詹姆士（William James）开启了针对学习的科学研究。第二次世界大战之后，哈佛大学的两位美国人伯尔赫斯·弗雷德里克·斯金纳（B. F. Skinner）和杰罗姆·布鲁纳（Jerome Bruner）提出基本学习理论并加以验证。斯金纳专注于行为，布鲁纳则专注于认知。但直到现在，学习理论才开始成为学校里的一个要素。基于学习理论而非世代相传的教导来开办学校的时机也许已经到来。

也就是说，从知识到可应用的技术，再到被市场接受，这个前导时间为25～35 年。

有史以来，这一规律基本上没有发生过变化。人们普遍认为，如今科技发现向技术、产品和工艺的转化，比以往要快。这很大程度上只是幻觉而已。1250 年左右，圣芳济教会的一名修道士英国人罗杰·培根（Roger Bacon）认为眼镜可以矫正眼睛的屈光缺陷。这一观点与人们的认知不相符合，而且中世纪不容置疑的医学权威最伟大的医学家伽林（Galen）已经"确定地证明"了它的不可实现。培根生活和工作的地方在处于文明世界边缘的英国约克郡北部的偏远地区。然而 30 年后，阿维尼翁的教皇宫殿中有一幅戴着眼镜的红衣主教的壁画，这幅壁画现在仍在那里。又过了 10 年，描绘开罗苏丹皇宫的微型画中，几位年纪大的朝臣也戴着眼镜。早在公元 1000年左右，北欧的本笃会修道士发明了碾磨谷物的磨坊水车。这是第一个真正的自动化装置，30 年后传遍欧洲。西方学习中国印刷术随后 30 年，古登堡发明的活字印刷和木刻印版也开始出现。

从知识到基于知识的创新所需的时间，似乎根植于知识本质。我们不知道原因何在。但是，如果同样的前导时间也适用于新的科学理论，这就不是纯粹的巧合了。托马斯·库恩（Thomas Kuhn）在他的开创性著作《科学革命的结构》（1962 年）中指出，新的科学理论成为新的范式（科学家们注意并将其应用到工作中的一种陈述）大约需要 30 年。

融合

基于知识的创新的第二个特点也是它独一无二的特点，是它们很少只基于一种知识，而是基于几种不同知识的融合，而且这些知识不全是科学知识或技术知识。

在 20 世纪基于知识的创新中，几乎没有其他创新能够比种子培育和牲畜育种更能造福人类了。它使土地养育比 50 年前人们可以想象的多得多的人口。第一个成功培育的新种子是杂交玉米。它是亨利·华莱士（Henry C. Wallace）历经 20 年的努力培育而成的。华莱士曾是艾奥瓦州一家农场报纸出版商，后来是哈定政府和柯立芝政府时期的农业部长（可能是唯一值得铭记的农业部长）。杂交玉米主要以两种知识为基础。一种是杂交优势，它是密歇根植物育种家威廉·毕尔（William J. Beal）于 1880 年左右发现的。另一种是遗传学，它指荷兰生物学家雨果·德弗里斯（Hugo de Vries）对孟德尔遗传学的重新发现。这两个人彼此并不认识，他们的工作目的和工作内容也截然不同。但只有将这两种知识融合起来，才能培育出杂交玉米。

莱特兄弟发明的飞机同样以两种知识为基础。一种是汽油发动机，它设计于 19 世纪 80 年代中期，主要用于卡尔·本茨（Karl Benz）和戈特弗里德·戴姆勒（Gottfried Daimler）生产的汽车。另一种是与数学相关的空气动力学，它是从滑翔机的试验中发展而来的。每种知识都是独立发展而来的，但只有两者的融合，才使飞机成为可能。

前面提到的计算机，至少需要五种不同知识的融合。一项科学发明：三极管；一项重大的数学发现：二进制；一种新的逻辑：穿孔卡的设计概念；还有程序和反馈的概念。要设计计算机，这些条件缺一不可。人们认为有"计算机之父"之称的英国数学家查尔斯·巴贝奇之所以没有制造出计算机，是因为他所在的年代没有合适的金属和电功率。其实这是一个误解。即便巴贝奇当时拥有合适的金属，他至多只能设计出我们现在称为收银机的机械计算器。没有逻辑、穿孔卡设计、程序和反馈的概念，巴贝奇只能想想而已。

1852年，皮埃尔兄弟创办了第一家创业型银行。因为他们只有创业型银行所需的两种知识之一，这家银行很快就失败了。创造性金融理论使他们成为出色的风险投资家，但他们缺乏系统的银行业知识。这种知识当时正在英吉利海峡对岸的英国发展，并被编写在白芝浩（Walter Bagehot）的经典著作《伦巴第街》（*Lombard Street*）中。

在皮埃尔兄弟19世纪60年代初失败之后，有三位年轻人分别从皮埃尔兄弟的失败中吸取教训，在风险投资概念中融入银行业知识并都取得了成功。第一位是 J. P. 摩根，他在伦敦接受培训，同时认真研究了皮埃尔兄弟的工业信贷银行。1865年，摩根在纽约创办了19世纪最为成功的创业型银行。第二位是年轻的德国人西门子，他在莱茵河彼岸创办了他所称的"综合银行"。"综合银行"的意思是指，它既是英国模式的存款银行，也是皮埃尔兄弟模式的创业型银行。另一位年轻人是远在东京的涩泽荣一，他是第一批赴欧学习银行业第一手知识的日本人，在巴黎和伦敦伦巴第街曾度过一段时光。后来，涩泽荣一创办了日本版的"综合银行"，并成为现代日本经济的奠基人之一。目前，西门子的德意志银行和涩泽荣一的第一国立银行仍然分别是德国和日本最大的银行。

美国人詹姆斯·戈登·本尼特（James Gordon Bennett）第一个设想出现代报纸并创办了《纽约先驱报》（*New York Herald*）。本尼特深知报界存在的问题：报纸必须要有足够的收入，才能保证编辑独立性；但发行价要足够低，才能保证发行量。早期的报纸有的为了获得收入而牺牲自己的独立性，充当一些政治派别的代言人。当时大部分美国报纸和几乎所有的欧洲报纸，都处于这种境地。比如当时的贵族报纸《泰晤士报》是为绅士而写的，这种报纸价格昂贵，只有小部分精英人士能够负担得起。

本尼特极其明智地利用了现代报纸的两种基础技术知识，电报和高速印刷。这使他只需用传统成本的一小部分就能生产报纸。他知道他需要高速排版，但直到他去世后高速排版才出现。他也看到两个非科技基础之一，大众教育，这使便宜报纸的大量流通成为可能。但他没有抓住第五个基础：保持编辑独立性的收入来源，大众广告。本尼特取得了辉煌的成功，成为第一位新闻界巨头。但他的报纸既没有获得领导地位，也没有获取经济效益。20年后，大概在 1890 年，三位了解并利用广告的人实现了这一目标。第一位是约瑟夫·普利策（Joseph Pulitzer），他起初在圣路易斯后来去了纽约；第二位是阿道夫·奥克斯（Adolph Ochs），他接管了即将破产的《纽约时报》并将它发展成为美国的主要报纸；第三位是威廉·伦道夫·赫斯特（William Randolph Hearst），他发明了现代报纸连锁业。

以尼龙为起点的塑料也是由 1910 年左右出现的几种新知识（以及因素）融合而成。其一是有机化学，起初是德国人开始研究，后来是在纽约工作的比利时人贝克兰做了改进；其二是 X 光衍射以及依赖此技术对晶体结构的理解；其三是高真空技术；最后是第一次世界大战导致的物资短缺压力。这使德国政府大力投资聚合物的研究以得到橡胶的替代物。但直到足足 20 年后，尼龙才走向市场。

如果某项必需知识没有准备就绪，那么基于知识的创新就还不成熟并且会失败。大多数情况下，只有当所需要的要素已经为人所知并且能够获得，甚至在某些地方已经被使用，创新才可能发生。1865—1875 年的综合银行就是一个很好的案例。第二次世界大战后，电脑的出现同样如此。有时候，创新者会发现缺失部分并去创造它。约瑟夫·普利策、阿道夫·奥克斯和威廉·伦道夫·赫斯特在很大程度上开创了现代广告业，进而催生了我们现在所称的媒体，也就是信息和广告在"大众传播"中的结合。莱特兄弟确定了飞机制造的缺失知识（主要是数学知识）。于是他们通过制造风洞和实际测试来发展这些知识。直到基于知识的创新所需的知识都准备就绪，创新才会发生。否则，它必然夭折。

举个例子，与塞缪尔·兰利（Samuel Langley）同时代的人都认为兰利将会是飞机的发明者。相比于莱特兄弟，兰利更能称得上是训练有素的科学家。作为美国当时重要的科技机构华盛顿史密森研究院的主席，兰利能够调配国家所有科技资源。但是即便他所在的时期已经发明出了汽油发动机，他也会对此置之不理。他更相信蒸汽发动机。结果他设计出的飞机虽然能够飞行，但由于蒸汽发动机的重量，这架飞机不能承载任何重量，更不必说带一个飞行员了。只有将数学知识和发动机知识相融合，才能设计出飞机。

事实上，直到所需知识都融合起来，基于知识的创新的前导时间才算开始。

II

基于知识的创新的要求

基于知识的创新的特点也赋予了它独特的要求。这些要求不同于其他类型创新的要求。

1. 首先，基于知识的创新要对所有必需要素加以分析，无论是知识本身，还是社会、经济或认知要素。该项分析必须能够辨别出缺失的要素，这样企业家可以决定是想办法制造这些缺失的要素（如莱特兄弟在数学知识缺失时的决定）还是由于条件尚不具备而推迟创新。

莱特兄弟的例子很好地诠释了这一要求。他们对制造发动机驱动的载人飞机所需的知识进行全面的深入分析。利用可用的信息，他们开始研究缺失的知识。首先进行理论上的检验，随后进行风洞测试以及实际飞行试验，直到最后获得设计制造副翼和机翼所需要的数学知识。

基于非技术知识的创新需要同样的分析。摩根和西门子都没有发表过论文，但日本的涩泽荣一发表过论文。我们因此得知，涩泽荣一在仔细分析已有知识以及所需的知识后，决定放弃辉煌的政治生涯并开始创办银行。同样地，普利策在创办第一份现代报纸时仔细分析了所需的知识，决定开辟广告业务并相信能够成功。

如果可以讲个人的例子，我作为管理领域的创新者之所以能够成功，也是建立在 20 世纪 40 年代初类似的分析之上。许多必需的知识已经存在，如组织理论，而且还有很多管理员工和工作的知识。但是，我的分析表明这些知识零散于不同学科之中。经过分析我还发现了缺失的关键知识：企业的目的、我们现在所称的企业策略和战略、目标，等等。我认为这些缺失的知识都可以创造。如果没有这些分析，我永远无法弄清楚必需的知识是哪些、缺失的知识是哪些。

如果不进行这种分析，失败是不可避免的。结果可能是基于知识的创新无法实现，就像兰利身上出现的情况一样；也可能是创新者丢失创新的成果或仅仅为他人作嫁衣。

英国人能够基于知识进行创新却不能收获创新成果，这尤其具有启示意义。

英国人首先发现并培育出青霉素，后来这项成果却被美国人接管了。英国科学家做了出色的技术工作，他们研发出青霉素，明确其用途。但他们并没有把生产青霉素的能力视为一种关键知识要素。他们原本可以研究出发酵技术这一必需知识，但是从未去尝试。结果，美国一家小公司辉瑞公司（Pfizer）开始研究发酵技术，并成为世界上主要的青霉素制造商。

同样地，英国人构思、设计并制造了第一架喷气式客机。英国的德哈维兰公司（de Havilland）并没有对需求进行分析，因此也没有发现两个关键要素。一个要素是配置，在为航空公司创造最大利润的前提下，如何根据不同路线安排合适大小的客机和合适的载客量。另一个要素看似同样平凡，如何解决航空公司购买飞机的融资问题。由于德哈维兰公司未曾进行分析，导致喷气式飞机制造被美国的波音公司和道格拉斯公司接手。而德哈维兰公司早已经消失。

这种分析看似显而易见，但是科学或技术创新者却很少进行分析。科学家和技术专家认为自己早已了然于胸，因此不愿意进行精确的分析。这就解释了为什么基于知识的伟大创新通常是由门外汉而非科学家或技术专家创造出来的。美国通用电气公司很大程度上是一个财务人员构想出来的。他的战略使通用成为世界上供应大型蒸汽涡轮的重要企业，并因此成为世界上电力公司的重要供应商（详见第 19 章）。同样地，老托马斯·沃森与其子小托马斯·沃森这两个门外汉使 IBM 成为计算机行业的领导者。杜邦公司为了让尼龙这一基于知识的创新有效并获得成功需要进行的分析，是由执行委员会的商业人士而非技术开发的化学家做的。波音公司之所以成为世界上喷气式飞机的主要制造商，是因为它由对航空公司和大众需求有深入了解的营销人员所领导。

这并非自然法则，它更多是关乎意愿和自律的问题。也有很多科学家和技术专家会强迫自己去思考基于知识的创新的要求，爱迪生就是一个例子。

2. 其次，基于知识的创新要有清晰的战略定位，它不能是试探性的。创新活动令人振奋并广受关注，这意味着创新者必须一举成功，因为他（们）很难有第二次机会。在目前提到的其他几种创新中，创新者一旦成功就能在相当长时间里独享成功，但这一点并不适用于基于知识的创新。他们的竞争者数量很快会超乎想象。稍有差错，他们就会被竞争者超越。

大体上，基于知识的创新只有三个重点。第一，一个完整的系统。这是埃德温·兰德（Edwin Land）在宝丽来公司提出的，开发一个完整的系统然后占领这个领域。这也正是 IBM 早期的做法，向客户出租计算机但不出售计算机。IBM 向客户提供软件和程序，指导程序员学习计算机语言，指导客户管理人员操作计算机，并为客户提供其他服务。20 世纪初，通用电气公司在建立基于知识的大型蒸汽涡轮创新的领导地位时，采取了同样的做法。

第二，市场焦点。基于知识的创新可以旨在为自家产品开拓市场。这正是杜邦公司对尼龙的做法。杜邦公司并不仅仅销售尼龙，而且还同时创造尼龙的需求市场，如尼龙质的女性袜子和内衣的市场、尼龙质的轮胎的市场，等等。然后它将尼龙运送到制造厂，并让这些工厂生产杜邦公司已经创造出需求且实际上已经在销售的产品。同样地，1888 年查尔斯·M. 霍尔（Charles M. Hall）发明铝电解工艺之后，铝业公司就开始创造锅碗瓢盆、铝杆等铝制产品的市场。这些铝业公司直接进行终端产品的生产和销售。它们创造了一个即便没有完全但也有效阻止潜在竞争者进入的市场。

第三，占领战略位置。这是指集中于某项重要职能来占据一个战略位置（详见第 18 章）。在知识密集型行业中，什么样的位置能够使知识创新者最大限度地免受早期震荡的影响呢？美国辉瑞公司对此进行了深入的思考，并决定专注于发酵工艺，最终成为青霉素的早期领导者并一直处于领先地位。波音公司专注于市场营销，即掌握航空公司和大众对飞机结构和资金方面的需求，最终成为客机制造行业的领导者并保持至今。尽管如今计算机制造行业处于动荡时代，一些计算机制造商陷入困境，但半导体等计算机关键部件的主要制造商依旧维持其领导地位。英特尔公司就是一个例子。

同一行业内，基于知识的创新者有时可以进行不同的选择。比如，杜邦公司选择了创造市场需求，而它在美国的最大竞争者陶氏化学公司（Dow Chemical）则试图在每个市场都占有一席之地。100 多年前，摩根选择关键职能法，他将银行定位为欧洲资本流向美国产业，进而流向其他资本短缺国家的通道。而同时期德国的西门子和日本的涩泽荣一都选择了系统法。

爱迪生的成功诠释了明确定位的效力。并非只有爱迪生发明了电灯泡，同时期的英国物理学家约瑟夫·斯旺（Joseph Swan）也发明了电灯泡。就技术而言，斯旺的灯泡更好，以至于爱迪生购买了斯旺的专利并用于电灯泡生产。不过爱迪生不仅仅思考技术需求，还同时考虑自己的定位。在开始玻璃罩、真空管、闭合开关以及发光纤维等技术工作之前，爱迪生就做了系统的决策。他的灯泡是针对电力公司而设计的，为此，他确定好融资，获得灯泡用户用电的接线权并布局好电力分配系统。斯旺作为一个科学家发明了一个产品，而爱迪生却塑造了一个行业。因此爱迪生可以进行电力设备的销售和安装，而斯旺只能寻找对他的科技成果感兴趣的人。

基于知识的创新者必须要有一个清晰的定位，诚然这三个重点处处布满风险。但如果创新者不能确定一个清晰的定位（更不必说尝试两个或更多选择，风险将会更大），最终注定失败。

3. 最后，基于知识的创新者，尤其是基于科学知识或技术知识的创新者，需要学习创业管理并付诸实践（详见第 15 章）。 事实上，相比于其他类型的创新，创业管理对基于知识的创新尤为重要。基于知识的创新具有更高的风险，因此需要更加重视财务和管理上的远见以及市场主导与市场驱动战略。但基于知识的创新，尤其是高技术创新往往缺乏创业管理。在很大程度上，知识密集型行业高失败率的根源在于知识型尤其是高技术型创业者本身的错误行为。他们往往对非"先进知识"的人或物（尤其是他们所在领域的外行）不屑一顾。他们迷恋自己的技术，认为质量就是技术的精密性而非为客户创造的价值。就这一点而言，总的来说，他们依旧是 19 世纪的发明家而非 20 世纪的企业家。

事实上，许多公司的经验表明，只要认真加强创业管理，基于知识的创新（包括高技术创新）的风险就可以大大降低。瑞士药品制造商霍夫曼罗氏是一个例子；惠普公司和英特尔公司也是一个很好的例子。准确地说，基于知识的创新本身具有极高的风险，创业管理因此变得尤为必要和有效。

Ⅲ

独特的风险

即使对基于知识的创新进行严密分析、明确定位并认真加以管理，它仍然具有独特的风险和固有的不确定性。

首先，就其本质而言，它是动荡不安的。

基于知识的创新的两个特点，即较长的前导时间和知识融合，使它具有独特的节奏。很长时间来，人们认为将会有创新发生，但其实并未发生。然后突然之间，进入爆发期，随后是极度令人兴奋的几年，出现大量创业活动和媒体报道。五年后，市场重新洗牌，只有少数企业存活下来。

1856 年，德国的维尔纳·西门子应用迈克尔·法拉第（Michael Faraday）于 1830 年（1856 年往前 25～26 年）提出的电学原理，首次设计出电动马达和发电机。这在世界上引起了极大轰动。从那时起，人们就确信会出现一个电气行业并成为主要行业。但 22 年来，许多科学家和发明者为之付出努力却毫无收获。究其根源在于缺失一种知识，也就是后来英国物理学家麦克斯韦对法拉第原理的发展。

这种知识出现之后，爱迪生于 1878 年发明了电灯泡，这场电气竞赛开始了。接下来的 5 年，欧洲和美国的主要电气设备公司相继成立。德国西门子公司收购了小型电气设备制造商舒克特（Schuckert）。基于爱迪生的研究成果，德国通用电气公司（AEG）成立了。在美国，现在的通用电气公司和西屋公司（Westinghouse）都是那时成立的。在瑞士，有布朗勃法瑞公司（Brown Boveri）。瑞典的阿西亚公司（ASEA）成立于 1884 年。当时美国、英国、法国、德国、意大利、西班牙、荷兰、比利时、瑞士、奥地利、捷克、匈牙利等国家有上百家这样的公司。这上百家公司备受投资者青睐，都有望成为资产 10 亿美元级别的公司。电气设备行业的兴起催生了第一波科幻小说的热潮，使儒勒·凡尔纳（Jules Verne）和赫伯特·乔治·威尔斯（H. G. Wells）成为享誉世界的畅销作家。但到了 1895—1900 年，大多数公司都消失了，或者停业，或者破产，或者被收购。

1910 年左右，仅仅美国就有多达 200 家汽车公司；到 20 世纪 30 年代初，只剩下 20 家；到 1960 年，就只剩下 4 家了。

20 世纪 20 年代，在美国有数百家公司生产收音机，还有数以百计的广播电台。到 1935 年，美国广播业形成只有三大网鼎立的局面，且收音机制造商也只有几家得以幸存。1880—1900 年，报社如雨后春笋般涌现。当时报业是重要的朝阳行业。但第一次世界大战之后，主要国家的报社数量急剧下降。银行业的处境同样如此。在银行业的开拓者摩根、西门子和涩泽荣一之后，美国和欧洲的银行业几乎进入爆发性增长阶段。但 1890 年左右，也就是仅仅 20 年之后，银行业掀起了兼并浪潮。银行要么停止营业，要么进行合并。第二次世界大战后，每个国家都只剩下几家在全国具有影响力的银行，要么是商业银行，要么是私人银行。

无一例外，每个行业中的幸存者往往都是行业爆发早期创建的。过了这个阶段就很难再进入这个行业了。在任何新的知识密集型行业中，都存在一个为期几年的窗口期。新创企业必须在窗口期内进入该行业。

人们普遍认为，这个窗口期现在变短了。正如人们错误地认为从新知识出现到转化为技术、产品和工艺所需的前导时间变短一样，这个认知也是错误的。

1830 年，乔治·史蒂芬逊（George Stephenson）的"火箭号"在商业铁路上首次成功牵引火车。随后短短几年内，英国成立了 100 多家铁路公司。铁路在 10 年内成为高技术产业，铁路企业家成为媒体关注的焦点。在 1855—1857 年出版的小说《小杜丽》（*Little Dorrit*）中，狄更斯对这种投机活动进行了犀利的讽刺。这种现象与当今硅谷的投机热没有什么差异。1845 年左右，这个窗口突然关闭了。从那时起，英国再也没人去投资建设新的铁路。1845 年还是 100 家左右的公司 50 年后只剩下了五六家。同样地，电气设备业、电话业、汽车业、化工业、家电业及电子消费业的情况也是如此。这种窗口持续时间不会很长。无可否认，如今窗口变得愈加拥挤。19 世纪 30 年代发生的铁路热潮仅仅限于英国；后来，每个国家都经历了完全独立于邻国先前发生的铁路热潮。之后，电气设备的热潮超越国界，25 年后的汽车热潮同样也超越国界。这两个热潮都只限于当时的工业发达地区。如今，工业发达地区的范围更加广泛，包括日本、巴西，而且很快将包括中国香港、中国台湾和新加坡。目前，通信几乎是即时的，交通也很便捷。许多国家或地区都有大批接受过良好训练的人，这些人可以立即参与到基于知识的创新中，尤其是基于科技的创新和基于技术的创新，而 100 多年前，只有极少数国家或地区才拥有这种优势。

这些事实具有两个重要意义。

1. **基于科学或技术的创新者会发现时间与他们作对。** 在其他创新机会源中，包括意外事件、不协调事件、流程需求、产业结构变化、人口统计特征、认知的变化，时间是支持创新者的。在这些创新中，创新者有相当长的时间进行创新而不会被其他人占领先机。即便他们存在失误，也有时间来改正。此外，他们具有多次创业的机会。但在基于知识的创新中，特别是基于科学知识或技术知识的创新，情况就并非如此了。在这类创新中，窗口时间极为有限。创新者必须一举成功，没有再次尝试的机会。外界环境严峻，窗口一旦关闭，机会便随之消逝。

但在某些知识密集型行业中，在第一个窗口关闭之后的二三十年内，可能会出现第二个窗口。计算机行业就是如此。

计算机行业的第一个窗口开始于 1949 年，持续到 1955 年左右。这段时间内，世界上所有的电气设备公司都开展了计算机业务，如美国通用电气公司、西屋公司和美国无线电通信公司（RCA）；英国通用电气公司、普利西半导体公司（Plessey）和费兰蒂技术公司（Ferranti）；德国西门子公司和德国通用电气公司；荷兰飞利浦公司；等等。1970 年，这些大公司又纷纷撤出计算机业。这一领域的占领者是 1948 年尚未成立或者规模很小的公司，包括 IBM 公司、"7 个小矮人"（美国七家小型计算机制造商）；ICL 公司（英国通用电气公司、普利西和费兰蒂公司的计算机事业部剩余部分组成的公司）；法国几家由政府大力扶持的小公司；德国的一家小公司利多富公司

（Nixdorf）；日本几家在政府支持下才得以生存的公司。

随后，在20世纪70年代，微芯片的发明引发了第二个窗口。这催生了文字处理器、小型计算机、个人电脑，并实现了计算机和电话交换机的融合。

但是，在第一回合中失败的公司没有再次参与竞争。第一回合中幸存的公司也没有加入第二回合，或只是不情愿地加入进来。尤尼瓦克公司（Univac）、控制数据公司、霍尼韦尔公司（Honeywell）、宝来公司（Burroughs）、富士通公司和日立公司都没有在小型计算机或个人电脑市场中取得领导地位。IBM公司是唯一的例外，它在第一回合中也是无可争议的冠军。这也是早期以知识为基础的创新模式。

2. 随着窗口更加拥挤，基于知识的创新者存活概率更小。

在窗口打开时，进入者可能会很多。产业结构一旦稳定或者成熟，则至少在一个世纪内都很难变化。当然考虑到技术、资本需求、进入的难易程度、产品是否外销等，不同的产业结构存在很大差异。但在任何一个时间点，任何一个行业都有一个典型结构：在任何给定的市场中有很多公司，包括大、中、小型公司，还有很多专业人员。对于任何一个基于新知识的产业，无论是计算机行业还是现代银行业，都只有一个市场，即世界市场。

当行业进入成熟期或稳定期时，基于知识的创新者的幸存人数并不比传统时期高。随着世界市场和全球通信的出现，窗口期的新进入者会大幅增加。当淘汰期来临时，企业的失败率也会比以往高。淘汰期通常都会出现，不可避免。

淘汰期

窗口一旦关闭，淘汰期随即来临。在窗口期创办的大部分企业，都不能撑过淘汰期。过去的高科技产业如铁路业、电气设备制造业和汽车业的发展，都印证了这一点。在我写本书之时，微处理器、小型计算机和个人电脑公司已经开始经历淘汰期，这距离窗口期的开启也只有五六年。目前仅仅在美国，该产业就有 100 家左右公司。10 年后，也就是 1995 年，无论什么规模或意义，也许只有几家公司才能存活下来。

生存还是毁灭，或是挣扎求生，这是很难预测的。事实上，推测完全没有意义。企业的规模大也许有利于生存，但并不能保证企业在淘汰期依旧成功存活。否则，当今世界上规模最大、最成功的化学公司应该是联合化学公司（Allied Chemical）而不是杜邦公司。当美国化工业窗口于 1920 年开启之际，由于拥有德国化学的专利权（第一次世界大战期间，美国政府没收了这些专利），联合化学公司看似无可匹敌。仅仅七年，淘汰期过后，联合化学公司就变得不堪一击了，再也没能重回往日的巅峰时刻。

1949 年，没人会预想到 IBM 会成为计算机行业的巨头，更不曾想过通用电气或西门子之类经验丰富的行业领袖会一败涂地。1910 年或 1914 年，当汽车股票在纽约证券交易所备受追捧之时，没人会想到通用汽车和福特能够存活并愈加强大，而被寄予厚望的帕卡德（Packard）或哈普（Hupmobile）却消失无踪。19 世纪七八十年代，现代银行业刚刚兴起，也没人料到德意志银行会吞并众多商业银行成为德国的领先银行。

要预测某个行业是否能成为重要行业是很容易的。从历史来看，一个行业如果能进入迅速发展期，也就是我所称的窗口期，就能成为重要行业。问题是：哪些企业能够存活下来并成为行业的领导者？

充斥着狂热投资潮的爆发期之后就是惨烈的淘汰期，这种发展节奏在高科技领域尤其明显。

首先，相比于一般产业，高科技产业备受瞩目，因此吸引更多的新进入者和资金。同样地，它们也承载着更多期望。凭借鞋油生产或手表制造等普通产业变得富有的人远远多于依靠高科技产业致富的人。但是，没人会期望一个鞋油生产公司会成就数十亿美元的事业。即便它们只是一家中等规模的普通家族企业，也没人认为这是失败的。相比之下，高科技产业是一个非赢即输的产业，平淡无奇则毫无价值。这使得高科技创新具有内在的高风险性。

其次，高科技产业在相当长时间内都无法盈利。计算机行业开始于1947—1948年，但30多年后，也就是20世纪80年代初期，整个行业才达到收支平衡点。的确，一些公司（实际上都是美国公司）在较早时候就能盈利。计算机行业的领导者IBM，很早就获得了较高利润。但从整个产业来看，少数几家公司的利润被其他公司的巨额亏损大大抵消了。例如，一些大型国际电气公司想成为计算机制造商却一败涂地。

同样的事情也发生在早期的"高科技"热潮中，如19世纪初的铁路热潮，1880—1914年的电气设备和汽车热潮，20世纪20年代的电子仪器和收音机热潮，等等。

这种现象出现的重要原因是，只有在研究、技术开发和技术服务上投入越来越多的资金，企业才能继续参与比赛。为了维持地位，高科技产业必须奔跑得越来越快。

当然，这也是迷人之处。但这也意味着，当淘汰期到来，哪怕只是一阵短暂的风暴，极少数几家资金雄厚的企业才能存活下来。这不仅仅是为什么高科技新创企业往往需要比其他新创企业在财务上更有远见，也是为什么相比于一般新创企业，有财务远见的高科技新创企业更稀少的原因。

在淘汰期，唯一的生存之道是创业管理（详见第12～15章）。德意志银行当时之所以能在众多金融机构中脱颖而出，全在于乔治·西门子深思熟虑之后成立的世界一流高层管理团队。不同于联合化学公司，杜邦公司在20世纪初成立了世界上第一个系统的组织结构，制定了世界上第一个长期规划，并开发了世界上第一个管理信息和控制系统。联合化学公司则由一个"毫无头脑的极端自大狂"经营。但是，这并非故事的全部。在最近计算机淘汰期失利的许多大公司，如通用电气公司和西门子公司，往往被认为具有一流的管理。虽然在淘汰期福特被诟病管理不善，险些被淘汰，但它还是存活下来了。

因此，创业管理可能是幸存的一个必要条件，并非充分条件。在淘汰期，只有内部人员（也许就算他们也不）能真正了解，在繁荣期迅速成长的基于知识的创新企业是否像杜邦公司一样开展有效管理，或者像联合化学公司一样基本无管理。但等我们搞清楚情况时，大多为时已晚。

接受度赌博

要想获得成功，基于知识的创新必须是成熟的、可接受的。这是基于知识的创新固有的风险，也是它的独特力量。其他类型的创新都是利用已经发生的变化，去满足已经存在的需求。而基于知识的创新则带来变化，创造需求。没人能预知，用户对这种创新是接受、置之不理还是极力排斥。

的确，例外是存在的。发明抗癌药物的人根本不用担心接受度的问题，但这种例子极为罕见。对于大多数基于知识的创新，获得接受度是个赌博。成功的概率是未知的，其实可以说是充满神秘感的。也许本来会有很高的接受度，但没人意识到；也许人们都坚定地认为社会真的迫切需要一种创新，但创新来临时无人接受，甚至还有人抵触。

在基于知识的创新中，这种惰性反应随处可见。一个典型的例子是，普鲁士国王认为："当人们在一天内可以从柏林骑马到波茨坦（不用花钱）时，即便火车只需要一个小时，他们也不会付钱去乘坐火车。"因此断言铁路这一新设施肯定会失败。当时，并非只有普鲁士国王如此判断，同时代的许多专家和他的观点一致。同样地，当计算机出现时，也没有一个专家料想到它在商业界会如此受欢迎。

截然相反的错误反应，同样也很常见。"人人都知道"存在某种真正的需求，但在现实中却对它无动于衷或者大力反对。曾有一个在 1948 年根本无法预想到企业会需要计算机的权威专家，到 1955 年左右，预测计算机将在 10 年之内"使学校发生革命性变化"。

德国人认为"电话之父"是菲利普·赖斯（Philip Reis）而非贝尔。赖斯于 1861 年研制出能够传输音乐的仪器，这很接近语音传输。但后来由于过度沮丧，他放弃了。当时人们普遍认为："电报已经足够满足通信需求了。"赖斯认为没有人会接受电话，对它感兴趣，或者渴望拥有它。但 15 年后，当贝尔申请电话专利时，人们为之振奋。德国人的反应最为热烈。

这 15 年内接受度的改变并不难解释。美国南北战争和普法战争这两大战役暴露了电报的不足。但是，这并非接受度变化的根本原因。1861 年，当赖斯在一个科学会议上展示他的仪器时，与会专家都预测这一发明将备受欢迎。结果，每个权威专家都预测错了。

当然，专家也可能是正确的，而且常常如此。例如，1876—1877 年间，专家们认为灯泡和电话会有很高的接受度。事实证明，他们是正确的。同样地，19 世纪 80 年代，爱迪生发明留声机时也得到了专家的支持。这再次证明专家对新设备的高接受度的预测是正确的。

但是，专家是否能正确判断以知识为基础的创新的可接受度，只能事后评判。

即便在事后，我们也不一定能理解，某个基于知识的创新为什么会受到欢迎或遭到抵制。例如，没人能够解释语音拼写法为何受到极力抵制。人人都认同非语音拼写法是阅读和写作的主要障碍。它使学校不得不在学生阅读技巧上投入过多的时间，还导致很多儿童的阅读能力不足并引发他们的逆反情绪。语音知识至少已经出现一个世纪了。在问题最为严重的两国语言中，语音拼写法的实现方式已经出现：英语中的音标和更早的日语中的 48 个音节的假名表。对于这些国家，它们邻近的国家都有应用语音拼写法并获得成功的例子。19 世纪中期，德国的文字拼写改革对英国来说是个成功的例子。更早时期，韩国的语音改革对日本来说同样是个成功的例子。但是，这样一种具有迫切需求，已被证明是安全、容易、有效的创新，在这两个国家却不被接受。原因何在？外界对此有各种各样的解释，但没有人知道真正的原因。

在基于知识的创新中，这种风险无法消除，甚至根本无法减少。由于无法对不存在的事物开展市场调查，市场研究也毫无效用。意见分析不仅无效，甚至可能会带来危害。要了解基于知识的创新的接受度，应将实践经验和专家意见相结合。

如果想开展基于知识的创新，必须在其接受度上赌一赌。除此之外，别无选择。

基于新的科技知识的创新，风险最高。时下热门的创新领域，如个人电脑、生物技术，风险尤其高。相比之下，一些不受追捧的领域，由于会有更多的时间，风险会低很多。一些基于非科技知识的创新，如社会创新，风险更低。但是，高风险是基于知识的创新的固有属性，也是其高影响力的必要代价。这种变化不仅仅限于产品和服务，还包括我们看待世界本身、我们在世界中的位置，甚至是看待我们自己的方式。

将新知识与其他创新机会源，如意外事件、不协调事件，尤其是流程需求相结合，高科技创新的风险会大幅下降。其他创新机会源中的接受度，或者已经确定，或者很容易进行可靠的检验。而且在这些领域中，创新所需要的知识通常也可以精确无误地加以界定。这也是"项目研究"备受欢迎的原因。不过项目研究需要有组织、有目的，需要大量的系统工作和自我约束。

可见，基于知识的创新对创新者提出了更高的要求。不同于其他领域的创新者，他们承受的风险也不相同，比如时间会与他们作对。但是，风险越高，潜在回报也越高。其他领域的创新者可能会创造财富，但基于知识的创新同时还可能收获荣誉。

聪明的创意

　　基于聪明创意的创新，可能要多于其他种类创新的总和。比如，10 项专利中，有 7~8 项属于这类创新。在企业家和企业家精神的相关书籍中，大多数新创企业都是基于聪明的创意成立的。拉链、圆珠笔、气雾剂喷雾器、软饮料和啤酒罐的拉环等，都是聪明的创意。许多企业中所谓的研究就是发现和利用聪明的创意，或是燕麦早餐和软饮料的新口味，或是更好更轻便舒服的跑鞋，或是不会烧焦衣服的熨斗。

　　但是，聪明的创意是风险最大、成功概率最小的创新机会源。这类创新的失败率是巨大的。这类创新的专利中，能够赚回研发成本和专利申请费用的不足 1%。除去成本支出，能够赚钱的可能只有 0.2%。

　　没人知道，哪些基于聪明创意的创新能够成功，哪些会失败。例如，为什么喷雾器会成功，而其他许多类似的创新却惨败？为什么有的万能扳手销量很好，而其他同类产品却消失了？尽管拉链很容易卡住，礼服、夹克或裤子的拉链如果卡住了，令人十分尴尬，但为什么拉链会被人们接受，甚至取代纽扣呢？

人们曾经试图提高基于聪明创意的创新的可预测性，但并未有所进展。

人们也曾试图找出成功创新者的特质、行为或习惯，同样没有成功。正如一则古老的格言所言："成功的发明家不断地发明，他们只是碰运气而已。如果进行足够多的尝试，他们将会成功。"

"只要你不断去尝试聪明的创意就会成功"这一信念，并不比一个普遍的谬见"只要你持续投钱就能在拉斯维加斯的老虎机里赚大钱"更为合理。老虎机设定的规则是赌场主有 70% 的概率会赢，你投得越多，输得越惨。

根本没有证据表明，持续追求聪明的创意，肯定会有所收获。正如，没有证据表明什么能够击败老虎机一样。一些成功的发明者只有一个聪明的创意，随后就不再寻求新的创意。拉链、圆珠笔的发明者就是如此。也有数以百计的发明者拥有 40 项专利，却无一成功。当然，创新者可以通过实践来改善，但关键前提是正确地实践，即在对创新机会源进行系统分析的基础上开展工作。

基于聪明创意的创新的不可预测性和高失败率的原因，是显而易见的。聪明的创意往往是模糊且难以琢磨的。除了拉链的发明者，恐怕没人会想到纽扣或者挂钩不足以扣紧衣服；除了圆珠笔的发明者，没人会对 19 世纪发明的钢笔不甚满意。20 世纪 60 年代成功进入市场的电动牙刷，如何满足人们的需求呢？毕竟，还是需要用手拿着。

即便能够界定需求，解决方案也难以确定。不难推测，人们在遇到交通堵塞时会想要一些消遣。为满足这种需求，索尼公司于 1965 年推出的小型电视机在市场中惨遭失败，可是更加昂贵的汽车音响却大获成功，这是为什么呢？现在回想起来，这个问题很容易回答。但是，我们是否可以提前预知这个问题的答案呢？

不管成功的故事如何诱人，企业家最好还是放弃基于聪明创意的创新。毕竟，每周总有人能够在拉斯维加斯的老虎机前赢得头奖，但是其他玩家做到最好也就只是没有输到无法承受。系统的、有目的的企业家会分析系统的领域，也就是前面第3~9章提到的7个创新机会源。

这些领域足以使任何一个创业者、创业型的企业或公共服务机构保持忙碌。事实上，机会远远比人们能利用的要多。在这些领域中，我们知道如何观察、观察什么以及应该做什么。

对于追求聪明创意的创新者，我们所能做的就是告诉他们如果成功了，该做些什么。这时，创业型企业的规则就开始有所作用了（详见第15章）。这也是创业文献大都研究如何创办和经营新创企业而非创新本身的根源所在。

但是，创业型经济决不能随意地忽视基于聪明创意的创新。这类创新无法加以预测，不能组织也不能系统化，而且绝大多数会失败。这类创新中很多创新起初微不足道。新的开罐器、假发套和皮带扣的专利总是多于其他事物。在任何新专利的列表中，总会出现一两种对常见物品的创新创意。基于聪明创意的创新是如此之多，极小部分的成功也能为经济带来新的业务、新的工作机会和新的生产力。

在创新与企业家精神的理论和实践中，基于聪明创意的创新是一种附带品。但是它应该得到认可和回报。它代表社会需要的品质：进取心、有志向和独创性。也许，社会很难去做些什么以推动这种创新，毕竟无法去鼓励不了解的事物。但至少，社会不能对这种创新进行打压、惩罚，或者阻碍。发达国家尤其是美国，近期（1984年）以提高专利申请费用等方式阻止基于聪明创意的创新，并将专利视为"反竞争"行为。从这个视角看来，这种做法很短视并且有害。

创新的原则

I

任何一位具有丰富经验的医生都遇到过"奇迹痊愈"的病例。身患绝症的病人突然之间康复了。这种现象有时是自发产生的，有时是求助于信仰，或者通过荒谬的饮食疗法，或者通过黑白颠倒的作息方式。只有偏执的人才会质疑这种痊愈的发生，并批判它是不科学的。这些现象确实存在。但是，没有医生会将这种奇迹痊愈的案例收录在书本里，或在课堂中给医学生讲授。这些案例无法重现，无法传授或学习，这种现象也极为罕见。毕竟，绝大多数绝症患者最终死去。

同样地，一些创新也不是基于前面章节中提到的来源产生的。这些创新并不是按照有组织、有目的、有系统的方式发展的。带来这些创新的创新者得到了"缪斯之吻"，他们的创新是灵光乍现的结果而非来源于有组织、有目标的辛苦工作。这类创新无法重现，不能传授和学习。目前还没有教人成为天才的方法。不同于人们的认知，发明和创新并非都是传奇，灵光乍现的机会很难出现。更糟糕的是，据我所知目前还没有一个"灵光乍现"转变为创新，它们一直都只是聪明的创意而已。

有史以来，最伟大的发明天才非莱奥纳尔多·达·芬奇（Leonardo da Vinci）莫属。他笔记本的每一页都有一个惊人的想法，包括潜水艇、直升机、自动炼钢炉。考虑到1500年的技术水平和材料的限制，这些想法没有一个转化为创新。事实上，在当时的社会经济发展水平下，这些想法也不会被人们接受。

每个学生都知道蒸汽机的发明者是詹姆斯·瓦特（James Watt）。事实并非如此。科技史学家都知道1712年托马斯·纽可曼（Thomas Newcomen）建造了第一台蒸汽机。这台蒸汽机能够做很多有用的工作，如英国一个煤矿用它来抽水。瓦特和纽可曼都是有组织、有系统、有目的的创新者。瓦特的蒸汽机将如何设计平滑的汽缸这一最新知识同压缩机这一"缺失环节"的设计相结合，发展成为一种基于流程需求的创新，更加符合创新的模式。当时已经有几千台纽可曼蒸汽机投入使用，这为瓦特蒸汽机的接受度奠定了基础。但是，具有我们所说的现代技术的内燃机的真正发明者既不是纽可曼，也不是瓦特，而是英裔爱尔兰化学家罗伯特·玻意耳（Robert Boyle）。玻意耳的发明纯粹是"灵光乍现"，但他的发明无法运行，也不可能运行。因为玻意耳通过火力爆破来推动活塞，这会弄脏汽缸。每个冲程之后，都要将汽缸取下来进行清洗。玻意耳的创意起初启发了他制造火力引擎的助手丹尼斯·巴本，随后是纽可曼和瓦特，使他们研发出可以运行的内燃机。玻意耳这个天才仅仅拥有一个聪明的创意。它属于创意史，而非科技史或创新史。

有目的的创新是创新实践的全部，它来源于分析、系统和辛苦的工作。之所以对它进行说明，是因为它至少包含90%的有效创新。与其他领域一样，创新中的卓越表现者必须学习并掌握创新这一学科。

那么，代表创新学科核心的创新原则是什么？有一些必须要做的事情，也有一些最好不要做的事情，另外就是一些条件要素。

II

要做的事情

1. 有目的、有系统的创新起始于对机会的分析。它以对创新机会源的全面思考为起点。不同领域中，不同创新机会源在不同时间的重要性不同。在基础工业工艺中，创新者在寻找生产流程（例如造纸流程）中的缺失环节时，很少会去关注人口统计特征。这种流程中，经济现状之间存在很清晰的不协调情况。同样地，创新者通过创造新的社会工具来满足人口统计特征变化引起的需求时，与新知识的关系也不大。但是，所有创新机会源都应该系统地加以分析和研究。仅仅注意到这些机会源是远远不够的，必须系统地、有规律地来组织研究。

2. 创新同时是概念性和知觉性的。创新的第二件必要的事情是走出去察看、询问、倾听。这种做法无论怎么强调也不为过。成功的创新者同时使用左脑和右脑。他们同时观察数字和人。他们分析满足某个机会所需要的创新。随后，他们走出去观察客户并了解他们的期望、价值观和需求。

这样创新者可以感知创新的接受度和价值，也可以感知这个或那个方案是否符合客户的期望或习惯。然后思考："这项创新需要展现出什么，才能使客户需要用它、愿意用它，并从中看到自己的机会呢？"否则，正确的创新可能会以错误的形式展现。一家为美国学校提供电脑程序的大型制造商就遇到过这种情况。对电脑心生恐惧的老师认为电脑毫无用途甚至是一种威胁，他们并不使用这些优秀高效的程序。

3. 创新必须简单聚焦，才能行之有效。创新应该专注于一件事情，否则容易引起混乱。如果它不够简单，则将很难运作。任何新生事物都会遇到麻烦，如果创新过于复杂，则难以解决。有效的创新往往极其简单。实际上，对创新的最高评价是人们说："这太明显了，为什么我就没想到呢？"

即便是创造新用途和新市场的创新，也要有一个具体清晰、有所设计的应用。它应该专注于所能满足的具体需求和所能产生的具体的终端结果。

4. **有效的创新从小处开始**。它们只是尝试去做一件并非宏大的具体事情。它可能是借助电力使车辆在铁轨上运行，这创造了有轨电车。它也可能是在火柴盒里放置同样数目的火柴（比如过去是 50 根），这催生了全自动火柴生产机，其瑞典发明者几乎长达半世纪垄断了世界火柴市场。那些旨在使产业发生革命性变化的创意或计划，往往最后遭遇失败。

创新最好能从小处开始，只需将少量人员和资金投入一个小而有限的市场。否则，创新者很难有足够的时间来进行调整和改变，而这是成功创新的必要条件。早期的创新很少是完全正确的。只有当规模较小，对人员和资金的需求不高时，才能做出必要的改变。

5. **最后，成功的创新旨在获得领导地位**。这并非指最终要成为一家大型企业。没人能够预言一项特定的创新最终是成就一家大企业还是只不过表现平平。但如果一项创新在初始阶段就不曾想过获得领导地位，它很难会有足够的创新性，也很难会有所成就。旨在获取某个产业或市场中的主导地位，和旨在找到并占领某个流程或市场中的生态利基，不同的战略有很大的区别（详见第 16～19 章）。但是所有创业战略（即旨在利用创新的战略），必须在给定的情境中取得领导地位。否则，就只是为竞争者创造机会罢了。

III

不能做的事情

下面是几项重要的不能做的事情。

1. **首先，不要过于聪明。创新必须能由普通人来运作。**如果想要具有一定规模和重要作用，笨人也要能够操作。毕竟，能力一般的人是充足的，永远能找得到的。而过于聪明的创新，无论是设计上还是操作上的创新，都几乎注定要失败。

2. **其次，不要过于多元化，不要分化，不要试图一次做很多事情。**这是要做的事情（保持专注）的一个推论。偏离核心的创新容易变得混乱，它们只会停留在创意阶段而不能转化为创新。这个核心并非一定是技术或知识。不论是在商业机构还是公共服务机构中，相比于知识和技术，市场知识实际上是企业更好的核心。创新努力必须有一个核心，否则将会四处分散。一项创新需要将各方努力汇聚起来，还需要参与人员互相理解，这些都要求一致的核心。多元化和分化将会破坏这种统一的核心。

3. **最后，不要尝试为未来创新。**要为当下创新！一项创新可能会有深远的影响。它可能需要 20 年才能完全成熟。正如我们所见，第一台计算机引入之后 25 年，也就是 20 世纪 70 年代初，计算机才对企业的运作模式产生重大的影响。但电脑出现之际就具备了现在的具体应用，如科学计算、薪酬支付和模拟训练飞行员等。"25 年后很多人将会需要电脑"这是远远不够的。我们应当说："现在很多人通过电脑改变了生活。随着时光流逝，25 年之后，将会有更多的人需要它。"除非能够即时应用，否则创新就仅仅是莱奥纳尔多·达·芬奇的笔记本中的"聪明创意"而已。现实中很少有人能像达·芬奇那样天赋异禀，仅仅凭借笔记本是很难像他那样万古流芳的。

爱迪生可能是第一个充分理解这一忠告的创新者。1860 年或 1865 年左右，同时代的其他电气发明家都在为电灯泡而努力。但直到十年后各项知识具备之时，爱迪生才着手研制电灯泡。在知识欠缺之时，研制电灯泡是"为未来创新"。在知识具备之后，电灯泡成为当下的产品。爱迪生集聚巨大的力量，组织卓越的人才，几年内都全神贯注于这一机会。

创新机会有时会有很长的前导时间。在药学研究中，10 年的研发工作往往是常态，算不上漫长。没有一家制药公司会研究不能满足现有医疗需求的并可以立即得到应用的药物。

三个条件

最后，还有三个条件。这三个条件明显可见，但往往被忽视。

1. **创新是工作**。创新需要知识，也需要巨大的创造力。显而易见，创新者比普通人更具有聪明才智。创新者很少会在两个或两个以上的领域中工作。尽管爱迪生具有卓越的创新能力，他也只专注于电气领域。金融领域的创新者，如纽约花旗银行，在零售业和医疗保健领域也许就难以创新。正如其他工作，创新也需要才干、独创性和资质。一切准备就绪之后，创新就成了艰苦、专注和有目标的工作，需要极度的勤奋、毅力和投入。如果缺乏这些，才干、独创性和资质将变得毫无效用。

2. **要想成功，创新者必须立足于自身优势**。成功的创新者会多方寻求机会，然后自问："这些机会中，哪项更适合我，并能发挥自身特长？"在这方面，创新与其他工作毫无差异。考虑到创新的固有风险以及知识和工作能力的特有优势，基于自身优势的创新就显得尤为重要了。与其他冒险活动一样，创新也需要"性情相投"。若非真正热爱，企业很难有优异的表现。例如，由具有科学头脑且自认为"严肃"的人所经营的制药公司，不会在口红或香水之类的"轻浮"行业有所成就。同样地，创新者与创新机会也要契合。对创新者而言，这个创新机会必须是重要的、有意义的。否则，他们很难持续投入到成功创新所必需的艰苦且困难重重的工作中。

3. **最后，创新是经济与社会的共同作用**。它是普通人如客户、教师、农民或眼科医生的行为的变化；或者是流程的变化，也就是人们工作和生产方式的变化。因此，创新应该紧密结合市场并专注于市场，事实上创新是市场驱动的。

保守的创新者

一两年前，我参加了一所大学主办的创业研讨会。许多心理学家在会上做了报告。虽然他们的观点各不相同，但他们都认为企业家特质是冒险精神。

随后，一位著名的成功创新创业者受邀进行评论。在过去的 25 年里，他将一项基于流程的创新发展成为一家太空领域的全球性企业。他说："你们的报告令我困惑。我觉得我在认识的很多创新创业者包括我自己身上，从未发现过企业家特质。但是，我所知道的成功者都有且只有一个共同点，那就是他们都不是冒险家。他们尽力界定自己所能承受的最大风险并尽可能降低风险。否则，我们都不会获得成功。至于我自己，如果我曾想过成为冒险家，我会进入房地产或商品贸易业，或者按照母亲的意愿成为一名职业画家。"

这番话和我的体验完全一致。我也认识很多成功的创新创业者，他们之中没有一个人喜欢冒险。

创新者的普遍形象是人们以流行心理学和好莱坞模式为基础勾勒而来。这使得创新者好似超人和圆桌骑士的化身。在真实生活中，大多数创新者并非浪漫人物，他们会花费更多时间预测现金流而不是去寻找冒险机会。当然，创新本身充满风险。开车去超市买面包，同样具有风险。按照定义，所有经济活动都是高风险的。其实"捍卫昨天"（也就是不创新），比"创造明天"更有风险。我所知道的创新者都能成功地界定风险并加以控制。他们成功地对创新机会源进行系统分析，随后找到机会并加以利用。无论是风险较小且能清晰界定的机会，如利用意外事件或流程需求，还是风险较大但能清晰界定的机会，如基于知识创新，同样如此。

成功的创新者是保守的，他们不得不如此。他们并非风险导向的，而是机会导向的。

2

第二部分

企业家精神实践

INNOVATION AND ENTREPRENEURSHIP
PRACTICE AND PRINCIPLES

虽然创业型组织与现有组织所需的管理方式不同，但与现有组织类似，它也需要进行系统的、有组织的和有目的的管理。对创业型组织而言，它们具有相同的基本规则。但是，现有企业、公共服务机构和新创企业面临着不同的挑战和问题，而且必须警惕不同的衰退趋势。此外，个体创业者也需要对其角色和承诺是什么做出决策。

创业管理

　　无论是现有的大型机构还是白手起家的个体创业者，是商业企业还是非商业性公共服务机构，是政府机构还是非政府机构，企业家精神所遵循的原则是一样的，其影响因素也大体相同。此外，创新种类和创新来源也大同小异。上述情形中存在着共通规律，我们称之为"创业管理"。

　　但是，现有企业和个体创业者面临的问题、局限和约束不同，需要学习的东西也不同。比如，现有企业已经知道如何进行管理，需要学习的是如何成为一个创业者和创新者。非商业性公共服务机构也面临着不同的问题，具有不同的学习需求，并容易犯不同的错误。而新创企业首先需要学习如何进行管理，然后再学习如何成为一个创业者和创新者。

　　对于以下三种组织：

- 现有企业
- 公共服务机构
- 新创企业

必须制定具体的企业家精神实践指南，说明不同组织各自需要做什么，注意些什么，以及最好不要做什么。

从时间逻辑上讲，正如医学研究一般从认识胚胎和新生婴儿开始，我们的讨论也应该从新创企业开始。但事实上，医学生首先了解的是成年人的解剖结构和病理学。所以，我们在研究企业家精神的实践时，也应从"成年人"（即现有企业）开始，关注那些促进企业家精神发展管理的策略、实践与问题。

在当前这个快速变化和追求创新的时代，企业（尤其是大型企业）如果没有创业能力将无法生存。从这个观点来看，当今这个时代与经济史上最后一个伟大的创业时期截然不同。那个创业时期持续了五六十年，随着第一次世界大战的爆发而结束。在那个时期，中型企业都不多见，更不用说大型企业了。但在当今这个时代，许多大企业都要学习企业家精神，因为这不仅契合企业自身利益，还是它们应该承担的社会责任。与100年前形成鲜明对比的是，创新会使现有企业（尤其是大型企业）迅速被破坏。引用熊彼特的一句名言："创新者带来了'创造性破坏'。"这种"创造性破坏"对当今的就业、金融稳定、社会秩序和政府责任都构成了真正的社会威胁。

现有企业必须改变，而且必须在各个方面进行彻底的改变。在未来25年里（详见第7章），每个工业发达国家都会意识到，从事制造业的蓝领劳动力总数将减少到现在的1/3，但制造业产值却将增长三四倍。这一发展，好比工业化国家在第二次世界大战后的25年中在农业方面的发展。要想在这样一个巨变时代中稳定发展并保持领先地位，现有企业必须学会生存，以及更重要的是，学会如何繁荣发展。要实现这一目标，它们必须要学习如何成为一个成功的创业者。

在许多情况下，现有企业是企业家精神的唯一来源。今天的一些行业巨头，在未来的25年里可能无法存活下来。但是，一些中型企业却可能通过创业管理成为成功的创业者和创新者。中等规模的现有企业（而不是小企业）

最有能力成为创业界的领导者。因为它们拥有必要的资源（尤其是人力资源），具备管理优势，并已建立管理团队。因此，它们既有机会，也有责任进行有效的创业管理。

这一结论同样适用于公共服务机构，尤其是提供非政治功能的机构（无论该机构是否归政府所有，或是否由税收提供财政资助）。此外，这一结论还适用于医院、各级学校；地方政府的公共服务机构；社区机构和志愿者组织（如红十字会和女童子军）；教堂及其相关组织；以及专业协会和行业协会等。在快速变化的时代，老机构往往会变得陈旧落伍，至少其经营方式变得不合时宜。但也涌现出了很多机会，帮助机构完成新任务、开展新事物以及从事社会创新。

最重要的是，公众的认知和心态发生了重大变化（详见第 8 章）。1776年，亚当·斯密出版了《国富论》，由此开启自由放任主义（Laissez-Faire）的时代。直到 1873 年的大恐慌，这一时代才得以终结。自 1873 年之后的100 年里，"现代化""进步"或"前瞻性"意味着将政府作为社会变革和社会进步的推动者。无论这一观点是好是坏，在所有发达国家中，这一时代已经终结。虽然无法预知下一股"进步主义"浪潮，但我们可以确定，任何仍在鼓吹 20 世纪 30 年代（甚至是 60 年代肯尼迪和约翰逊执政时期）的"自由"或"进步"思想的人，肯定不是"进步分子"，而是"保守分子"。我们不知道私有化[⊖]（由国营转化为非国营，而不是像大多数人认为的那样由私人企业来经营）是否会奏效，但我们知道，任何一个西方发达国家都不会因为对传统承诺的希望、期盼和信念，而走向国有化和政府管制。除非它们在私有化过程中遭受了挫折和失败。如果遇到这种情况，公共服务机构不仅有机会，而且也有责任进行创新、发挥企业家精神。

但正因为它们是公共服务机构，它们会遭遇不同于其他机构的障碍和挑

⊖ 1969 年，我在《不连续的时代》中提出这个词（New York: Harper & Row; London: William Heinemann）。

战，并会犯不同的错误。因此，我们需要单独讨论公共服务机构的企业家精神。

　　最后讨论新创企业的企业家精神。正如在过去所有重要创业时期发挥的作用一样，作为创新的重要载体，新创企业将继续在美国创业型经济中发挥重要作用。美国不乏未来的创业者，也不缺新创企业，但是大部分企业，特别是高科技企业，需要学习创业管理，这是必需的。否则，它们将无法生存。

　　在这三种企业中，普通企业领导者与具有创新和企业家精神的领导者之间的差距巨大。幸运的是，有很多企业成功实践了企业家精神，为我们系统地介绍创业管理的实践和理论、说明和方案提供了充足的例子。

创业型企业

I

　　传统上，人们认为"大企业不创新"，这听起来很有道理。20 世纪的重大创新都不是来自当时的大企业。举例来说，小汽车和卡车都不是由铁路公司发明的，铁路公司甚至都没有尝试过汽车相关的研发。虽然汽车公司曾经尝试过飞行器研发，比如福特和通用汽车公司都是航空领域和航天领域的先驱。但事实上，今天所有的大型飞机公司和航空公司都是由新创企业发展而来的。类似地，当首批现代药物在 50 年前问世时，当今的制药巨头要么尚未成立，要么只是家小公司。计算机行业也大同小异。20 世纪 50 年代，电气工业的巨头们纷纷进入计算机领域，比如美国的通用电气、西屋公司和美国无线电通信公司，欧洲大陆的西门子和飞利浦，日本的东芝，但无一成功。而现今该领域的主导者 IBM 公司，在 40 年前只不过是个中等规模的企业，也算不上是高科技企业。

但是，大企业不创新或不能创新这个普遍的观念，都谈不上是把真假混为一谈，甚至，它完全是一个误解。

首先，很多例子可以说明，大企业是优秀的创业者和创新者。在美国，强生公司在卫生保健领域成绩卓著；3M 公司为工业和消费市场生产高精工艺产品；有 100 多年历史的花旗银行，是美国乃至全球最大的非政府金融机构，同时也是银行业和金融业的重要创新者。在德国，有 125 年历史的赫斯特公司，是全球最大的化工公司之一，同时也是医药领域的创新典范。在瑞典，成立于 1884 年的 ASEA 在过去的六七十年里，不仅规模庞大，还是远程电力传输和工厂自动化机器人领域的真正创新者。

令人困惑的是，众多历史悠久的大企业在一些领域是成功的创业者和创新者，但在其他领域却一败涂地。比如，美国通用电气公司虽然在计算机领域失败了，但在另外三个领域（飞机发动机、工程无机塑料和医疗电子设备）却是成功的创新者。又如，美国无线电通信公司在计算机领域同样惨遭失败，却在彩色电视机领域表现出色。因此，事情并不像传统普遍观念那么简单。

其次，"规模大"是企业家精神和创新的阻碍，这一观点并不正确。当人们在谈论企业家精神时，经常会提到大型组织的"官僚主义"和"保守主义"。的确，这两种现象不仅存在，还严重阻碍了创新与企业家精神，甚至会阻碍企业取得其他成就。但是，历史表明，现有企业中，无论是营利企业还是公共服务机构，小型企业才最缺乏企业家精神和创新意识。而实际上在创业型企业中，有许多都是大型企业和大型公共服务机构。如果要举例的话，我可以轻松地举出世界上 100 个这样的企业。

最具企业家精神的企业可能是中等规模的大企业，比如 20 世纪 80 年代中期，年销售额达 5 亿美元的美国公司[⊖]。而小型企业，却无一出现在创业型企业的名单中。

⊖ 这点长期备受质疑。但是，理查德·卡夫诺和小唐纳德·克利福德于 1983 年秋在《麦肯锡季刊》发表了一篇题为《美国中等规模成长型企业给我们的启示》的研究，为此提供了确凿证据。

创新和企业家精神的真正阻碍不是企业规模，而是企业本身的运作方式，尤其是成功的现有运作方式。对大中型企业而言，它们比小企业更容易克服这一阻碍。任何事物（比如制造工厂、技术、生产线、分销体系）的运作，都需要不懈的努力和关注。而且，每一种运作方式都会经历"日常危机"。危机一经发现，需立即处理，不能拖延。因此，现有的运作方式需要并值得受到优先考虑。

和规模庞大、绩效良好的企业相比，新创企业如此渺小、微不足道以至于前途未卜。事实也的确如此。那些自诩伟大的新生事物，反而不可信。小企业的成功概率很低。但正如前文所述，成功的创新者也都是从小的创新开始的，最重要的是，是从简单的创新开始的。

许多企业声称："10 年后，我们 90% 的收入将来自目前尚未存在的产品。"在很大程度上，这纯属自吹自擂。诚然，在这 10 年里，企业可以对现有产品进行改进或调整，甚至可以开拓现有产品的新市场，以及改变现有产品的最终用途。但是，真正的新创企业或项目需要更长的前导时间，才能推出新产品。目前在正确的市场提供正确的产品和服务的成功企业，10 年后，其 3/4 的收入仍然可能来自现有产品或服务，或者其衍生产品。事实上，如果现有产品或服务无法持续产生大量的现金流，那么这家企业将无力承担创新活动所需的大量投资。

因此，现有企业要想践行创新与企业家精神，确实需要花一番工夫。但是，企业通常将生产资源用以发展现有业务，应付日常危机，提高现有业务的收益。这种诱惑使现有企业总是为满足过去而提供资源，进而舍弃未来。

对企业来说，这的确是一种"致命诱惑"。不创新，就等死。当今时代巨变，创业型经济繁荣发展，企业灭亡速度加快。一旦企业或产业沉迷于过去的成功，就很难向前发展（如果能向前发展的话）。但是，企业现有的成功，确实是其践行创新与企业家精神的阻碍。原因在于，现有企业的成功使其看似如此"健康"，以致人们完全忽略了由官僚主义、繁文缛节或骄傲自满所导致的衰退现象。

这就是为什么列举现有企业成功进行创新的例子是重要的，尤其是那些现有的大型企业和具有相当规模的企业也能成为成功创业者和创新者的例子。这些例子表明，企业的成功所带来的阻碍是能被克服的。我们可以找到一种途径克服这些阻碍，使现有企业和新创企业、成熟企业和初期企业共同获利与共同发展。强生、赫斯特、ASEA、3M 和那 100 家中等规模的"成长型"企业，都是成功的创业者和创新者，都知道如何克服上述阻碍。

传统观念的错误在于，它认为创新与企业家精神是天生的、创造性的或自发的。它认为如果一个组织不创新或缺乏企业家精神，那必定是受到组织内部某些因素的制约。的确，只有少数现有企业能创新或具有企业家精神。因此他们得出以下的结论：现有企业抑制了企业家精神。

但是，企业家精神并不是"天生的"，也不是"创造性的"，而是努力的结果。因此，和一般的看法相反，从上述实例中得出的正确结论是：大量现有企业，包括相当数量的中型、大型和超大型企业，都能成为成功的创业者和创新者。这表明，任何企业都能创新与具备企业家精神。企业必须要有意识地为之奋斗。创新与企业家精神是可以习得的，但需要努力。创业型企业将企业家精神视为一项义务。它们为之训练，对其加以研究，并付诸实践。

具体而言，要进行创业管理，企业需要针对下面四个主要领域制定策略，并付诸实践。

第一，组织必须乐于接受创新，将变化视为机会而非威胁。它们必须付出创业者所应承担的艰辛。它们还应制定策略并付诸实践，以营造创业氛围。

第二，必须对企业作为创业者和创新者的绩效进行系统的衡量和评估，同时建立内部学习机制以提高绩效。

第三，进行创业管理，需要对组织结构、人员任用和管理、薪酬、激励和奖赏制定具体措施。

第四，创业管理存在几点禁忌，即不该做的事情。

Ⅱ

创业策略

一位拉丁诗人认为人类"渴望新事物"。创业管理必须使现有企业的管理者"渴望新事物"。

高层管理者经常问道："如何才能克服现有组织中抵制创新的现象？"即便我们知道答案，这问题依然问错了。正确的问法应该是："如何才能使组织接受创新、渴望创新，并为之努力呢？"如果组织认为创新违反自然规律，犹如逆水行舟，那么除非将创新视为一项"英雄成就"，否则它们绝不会创新。即便创新不是"惯例"，也应该是日常生活中的一部分。

要做到这一点，需要特定的策略。首先，创新，而不是坚持已有的事物，必须能够吸引管理者，让其感到有所收获。组织上下必须清楚地认识到，创新是组织实现长期发展的最佳途径，也是管理者获取稳定的和成功的事业的基础。

其次，必须界定和阐明创新的重要性及其时间期限。

最后，必须制定目标明确的创新计划。

1. **使管理者对创新保持兴趣的唯一方法是：制定系统的策略，摒弃一切陈旧的、过时的、缺乏生产力的事物，以及那些错误的、失败的以及具有误导性的努力。**大约每隔 3 年，企业要对每个产品、流程、技术、市场、分销渠道，甚至每个员工的工作，进行一次全面审查。企业必须扪心自问："现在，我们是否要生产这种产品，进入这个市场，采用这个分销渠道，利用这种技术？"如果答案是"不"，不能就此回应"再研究一下"，而应追问：

"采取何种行动，才能终止在这个产品、市场、分销渠道和员工活动上浪费资源？"

有时候，放弃并非解决之道，甚至放弃是不可能的。但是，企业至少可以限制投入，确保不再将人力、资金等生产资源消耗在"昨日之事"中。这是组织保持健康的正确方式：任何有机体都应清除废弃物，否则将危害自身。如果一个企业有能力、有意愿进行创新，那么放弃过去更是必需的。英国文学家约翰逊常说："如果一个人知道第二天一早自己要被绞死，那没有什么能比这更令他集中注意力了。"类似地，如果管理者知道在可预见的未来，现有产品或服务将被淘汰，那没有什么能比创新更能令他全心投入的了。

创新需要大量的努力，需要有能力的人（这是组织最稀缺的资源）的艰苦工作。正如一句古老的医学谚语所说："没有比保持尸体经久不烂更花费精力的事情了，但也没有比这更徒劳无功的了。"在我所接触的大部分企业中，最优秀的人通常都在做这样的徒劳之事。然而，他们只是在推迟一些必然发生之事的出现，为此却付出了巨大的代价。

不过，如果整个组织都知道不创新就会死亡，那么现在的"生者"才会愿意甚至渴望创新。

若想进行创新，企业必须将高绩效者从无效的工作中解脱出来，以迎接创新的挑战。同样，它还必须为创新投入充足的资金。要做到这两点，企业必须抛却过去的成功与失败，尤其是那些"几近成功"和"本应成功"但并未成功的事情。如果高管知道放弃是公司的策略，他们就会积极寻求新事物，鼓励企业家精神，并促使自己成为企业家。这是第一步，即**塑造健康组织**。

2. 为使现有企业"渴望新事物"，第二个策略是让企业直面现实。现有产品、服务、市场、分销渠道、流程、技术的发展都只有非常有限的健康和生命预期，通常都很短暂。

自 20 世纪 70 年代开始，对现有产品、服务等的生命周期进行分析成为流行。例如，波士顿咨询公司提出的战略概念、哈佛商学院的迈克尔·波特教授出版的战略相关的书籍，以及所谓的投资组合管理。[⊖]

过去的 10 年中，这些战略，尤其是投资组合管理，受到广泛宣传。企业的战略分析结果构成其行动方案。这其实是一种误解，其结果必然令人失望。20 世纪 70 年代末 80 年代初，许多公司纷纷采用这些战略，并发现了这一误解。分析之后应该是"诊断"，随后是判断。要做出正确的判断，必须对企业及其产品、市场、客户和技术进行深入了解。除此之外，还需要具备丰富的经验，而非仅仅进行分析。有人认为，刚从商学院毕业的聪明年轻人，凭借高级分析工具，简单地敲打键盘就能制定关于企业、产品、市场等的生死攸关的决定。这实属无稽之谈。

我将《为成果而管理》一书中所使用的分析方法称作"企业 X 光透视法"。这种分析方法主要用于发现正确的问题，而非给出正确的答案。对具备丰富知识和经验的企业来说，它是一种挑战，并将会（也应该会）引发异议。将某个产品列为"今日赚钱的产品"后所采取的行动，往往有风险。同样，对即将成为"昨日赚钱的产品""不当的特色产品"或"自我投资的产品"所采取的措施，也是有风险的。[⊖]

3. 企业 X 光透视法能够帮助企业明确创新程度、创新领域和创新期限。为此，迈克尔·卡米（Michael J. Kami）提出了最佳也是最简单的方法。卡米是 20 世纪 50 年代纽约大学研究生商学院的"企业家精神研讨会"的成员之一。作为 IBM 企业发展规划部的主管，他将该方案首先应用于 IBM。

⊖ 这些方法源于我在 20 年前出版的一本书《为成果而管理》（New York: Harper & Row, 1964）。据我所知，这是第一本系统阐述企业战略的著作。该书灵感来源是 20 世纪 50 年代末我在纽约大学举办的企业家精神研讨会。该书第 1～5 章的内容是，根据产品和服务的绩效、特点、寿命，将产品和服务归为几个类别，目前仍然是分析产品寿命和产品繁荣的有用工具。

⊖ 这些术语的定义，详见《为成果而管理》第 4 章"我们怎么做"。

60 年代初，他在施乐公司的几年中，继续从事类似的工作，并将其应用于施乐公司。

按照卡米的方法，企业需要列出每项产品或服务，以及它们的目标市场和分销渠道，以估算它们在产品生命周期中所处的位置。企业应该思考："这种产品还能发展多久？在市场中存活多久？何时会老化和衰退，速度如何？何时会被淘汰？"这能使企业知道，如果最大限度地利用现有资源，企业将走向何处。此外，它还能显示企业预期目标与现实状况之间的差距，无论是在销售额、市场地位，还是在盈利能力方面。

如果企业不想走下坡路，必须要填补这一差距。如果不填补差距，企业将走向灭亡。在老产品遭到淘汰之前，企业必须在创业方面取得足够的成就以及时填补这一差距。

但是，创新具有高不确定性、高失败率和更高的延迟率。因此，企业投入的创新努力至少为成功填补差距所需的三倍。

大多数高层管理者认为这一投入过高。然而，经验表明，如果存在失误，那是因为这一投入偏低。当然，有些创新努力的表现高于预期，但其他的则低于预期。此外，每件事情所需的时间和投入，都比我们所估计的要多。最后，任何重大创新都会遇到最后一刻的"故障"和"延误"。如果一切按照计划进行，要求公司投入三倍的努力进行创新，只是基本的预防措施而已。

4. 系统地放弃（过时的产品和服务）。用企业 X 光透视法来分析现有企业及其产品、服务、市场和技术，并确定创新差距和创新需求。基于此，企业能够制定出有创新目标和期限的创业计划。

这一计划可以确保有充足的预算用于创新。此外，它还能确定所需人数，以及这些人所需具备的能力。只有将能力得到验证的人员配备到项目中，向他们提供所需的工具、资金和信息，并明确期限，计划才算真正开始。众所周知，至此，我们才有了"诚意"，并怀揣这种"诚意"要去做一些事情。

这些基本策略可以促使企业进行创业管理，使企业及其管理层渴望新事物，并将创新视为健康、正常且必要的活动。这种方法主要基于"企业 X 光透视法"，即对当前企业及其产品、服务和市场的分析和诊断。因此，该方法确保企业在寻找新事物时，不会忽略现有业务；也不会因为追求新颖性而牺牲现有产品、服务和市场中的机会。

"企业 X 光透视法"是制定决策的工具。它促使我们，事实上是迫使我们，将资源配置到现有企业的有效领域。它还有助于我们确定创建"未来企业"及其新产品、新服务和新市场所需的努力。它使我们将创新诚意转化为创新绩效。

为使现有企业具有企业家精神，管理者必须率先淘汰过时的产品和服务，而不是让竞争对手捷足先登。企业必须把新事物视为机会，而非威胁。只有在当下努力提升产品、服务、流程和技术，企业才能在未来有所不同。

III

创业实践

要培养现有企业的企业家精神，需要以下几种管理实践：

1. **首先，也是最为简单的是，管理层应专注于寻找机会。** 人们往往只看到事物的表面，而忽视未曾显露的部分。比如，大多数管理者只看到"问题"，尤其在未达到预期绩效的领域中，这意味着管理者往往没有注意到机会。机会通常不会展现在人们面前。

管理层，甚至是小企业的管理层，每月都会收到一份经营报告。报告首页通常是绩效低于开支、不达标或者有问题的项目。在月度例会中，每个人都着眼于所谓的问题。直到午餐休会时，整个上午都在讨论这些问题。

　　当然，企业必须要关注这些问题，并严肃对待。但是，如果企业仅仅关注问题，将会失去机会。如果想要拥抱企业家精神，企业必须要特别关注各种机会（详见第 3 章）。

　　这些企业的经营报告通常有两个"首页"：一个是传统的首页，用于罗列问题；另一个则列出绩效高于预期、预算和计划的领域。正如前文所强调的，企业的意外成功是创新机会的一个重要表征。如果对此视而不见，该企业就不可能是创业型企业。事实上，如果企业及其管理者只关注问题，很可能将意外成功视为耗费时间和精力的"不速之客"而置之不理。他们会说："为什么要关注它呢？没有我们的干预，它照样运转良好。"但是，这就使更为敏锐、更加谦虚的竞争对手有了可乘之机。

　　针对经营结果，重视企业家精神的企业通常会举行两次会议：一次专注于问题的解决，另一次聚焦于新机会的探索。

　　一家为医生和医院提供保健品的供应商，在许多新兴的、前景良好的领域中都获得领先地位。每月的第 2 个和最后 1 个周一，该公司都会举行"经营会议"。第一次会议主要讨论问题，即上个月没有达到预期，6 个月后依旧没有达到预期的项目。这个会议与其他运营会议毫无差别。第二次会议，也就是最后 1 周的周一会议，主要讨论表现超出预期的领域：产品销售速度超出预测，或者来自意料之外的市场出现新产品订单。在过去的 20 年里，该公司的规模扩大了 10 倍。企业高层管理者认为这一成功，主要是因为月度会议中对机会的重视。该企业的首席执行官曾多次说："会议中发现机会的确很重要，但更重要的是整个管理层形成的创业氛围和积极寻求机会的习惯。"

　　2. 其次，为培养管理层的企业家精神，公司还开展了以下活动。每隔 6个月，公司举办一次为期两天的管理会议。与会人员是公司各事业部、市场和主要产品线的高层管理者，约四五十人。会议第一天上午，由三四位高管汇报，在过去一年里，作为创业者和创新者，其所在的部门的杰出表现。他们还要汇报何以成功："我们做了哪些努力，事后证明是成功的？""我们如何发现机会？""我们学到了什么？我们现在有哪些关于创新与企业家精神的计划？"

同样，这些会议所传递的态度和价值观，远比汇报内容重要。但是，公司的运营经理仍强调，他们从会议中学到了很多，备受启发，满怀想法且渴望去尝试。

创业型企业总是在寻找表现更好且与众不同的人和部门。它们对此分析，并不断询问："你们做了哪些事情才得以成功？""哪些是其他人没有做的？其他人所做的事情中，哪些是你们不会做的？"

3. 最后，对于大企业极其重要的是，指派一名高层管理者参加研发、工程、生产、营销和会计等部门的基层人员座谈会。这种会议虽不正式，但也需要提前计划，并做好充分准备。高管的开场白应该是："我来这里不是要做报告或告诉你们什么事情，而是想听听你们的想法。我想了解你们渴望什么，最重要的是，你们觉得公司存在什么样的机会和威胁。对尝试新事物、开发新产品、策划市场推广方案，你们有什么想法呢？对公司策略、发展方向，以及在行业、技术和市场中的位置，又有什么看法呢？"

这种座谈会不宜过于频繁。对高层管理者来说，这种会议耗时太长。每次座谈会，高层管理者要与25～30个基层人员交流，要花费一下午或者一晚上的时间。因此，这种会议一年最好不要超过3次。但是，应该系统地坚持召开这种会议。这是向上沟通的重要通道，可以使基层人员（尤其是专业人员）跳出专业局限，从企业层面考虑问题。它还可以使基层人员了解高层管理者真正关切的事情，以及原因何在。反过来，座谈会可以使高层管理者深入了解基层人员的价值观、愿景，还有他们所关心之事。最重要的是这种会议可以促使企业上下共同构建"创业愿景"。

这项实践有一个内在要求。无论该建议是关于全新事物还是改进现有方式，是关于产品或流程，还是市场或服务，建议的提出者都应亲自"去实施"。他们应该在合理的时间内，向主持该会议的高管还有同事提交可行性报告。报告应包括以下内容：如果该建议成为现实，将会如何？为使这个想法有意义，现实应是怎样？对顾客和市场等的假定，又是如何？需要做哪些工作？需要多少资金、人力和时间？预期结果如何？

此外，尽管很多组织都能提出很多具有企业家精神的建议，但这并非会议最重要的结果。最重要的成就则是，整个组织建立了"创业愿景"，乐于接受创新，并"渴望新事物"。

IV

衡量创新绩效

一家重视企业家精神的企业，必须将创新绩效作为自我控制的一个依据。只有对企业的创业绩效进行评价，企业家精神才能转化为行动。人们总是按照期望行事的。

一般的企业评估中，显然没有创新绩效这一项。但是，将创新与企业家精神的绩效纳入企业的控制体系，或至少是定性地评判，并非特别困难。

1. 首先，针对每个创新项目，建立反馈系统，以对比结果和目标之间的差距。这可以体现创新计划和创新努力的质量和可靠性。

很早以前，研发经理就知道在研究项目的启动阶段，要问："我们能从这个项目中获得什么？预计何时能够实现？若要控制项目，何时进行阶段性评估？"他们还知道，要确认实际进程是否与预期相符。这样可以表明他们是否过于乐观或过于悲观，是否过于急于求成或会等待太久，以及是否高估或低估了研究计划的影响力。基于此，他们能够及时纠偏，找出优势领域和薄弱领域。当然，这种反馈系统并非仅仅适用于技术研究和开发项目，它适用于所有的创新努力。

反馈系统的第一个目的是，找出我们的优势领域。人们通常在某一领域表现出色却不知原因何在，但表现依旧突出。第二个目的是，找出限制性因素。例如，高估或低估项目所需的时间；高估某个领域所需的研究工作，却低估研究转化为产品或工艺的过程中所需的资源。还有一种较为常见的倾向，破坏性很大，即在新创企业将要腾飞之际，降低营销和推广力度。

世界上最成功的一家银行，将其成功归因于为创新工作所建立的反馈系统。在该银行进军韩国等新市场，以及提供设备租赁服务或发行信用卡的过程中，反馈系统发挥了重要作用。通过反馈系统，银行及其高层管理者可以对新事业做出预测：投入后何时能产生效果？何时应投入更多努力和资源？

所有的创新工作，如制定或引进新的安全方案或新的薪酬计划，都需要这样的反馈系统。这样我们可以得知，哪些征兆表明创新工作陷入困境，需要重新考虑；哪些征兆表明，虽然暂时遭遇挫折，但创新工作的方向正确，只是需要更多的时间。

2. 其次，对所有的创新工作，进行系统的评估。 每隔几年，企业管理者要对企业的创新工作进行评估，从而确定：现阶段，需要对哪些创新工作提供更多支持，并加以推进？哪些创新工作打开了新的"机会之门"？哪些创新工作与我们的预期不符，应该采取何种举措？是放弃，还是加倍努力呢？如果加倍努力，预期成效以及截至期限又该如何确定呢？

世界上最大且最成功的医药公司之一，其高层管理者每年都会召开专门会议以评估企业的创新工作。首先，他们对每个新药开发项目进行审视，并问："这项药品研发的方向是否正确，速度是否正常？它的产品是否适合现有的产品线，还是转让给其他制药商更好，或者直接放弃？"随后，他们对其他创新工作（尤其是与营销相关的创新工作）进行审视，并询问同样的问题。最后，他们同样仔细地评估主要竞争者的创新绩效。就研究预算和创新支出而言，该企业处于中等水平。但是，作为创业者和创新者，它的表现卓越。

3.最后，创业管理要求，根据企业的创新目标、创新绩效、市场地位和企业的全面绩效，对其综合创新绩效进行评判。

也许每隔5年，高层管理者要与重要领域的相关人员进行座谈："过去5年里，你为公司做出的突出贡献是什么？未来的5年里，你打算做出什么贡献？"

从本质上讲，创新工作是无形的，那该如何评价呢？

的确，我们无法或者没有必要确定某些领域的相对重要性。例如，一项基础研究的突破性成果，多年之后也许能够治愈某种癌症；或者一种全新配方能使病人在家进行古老但有效的药物治疗，而无须每周3次前往医院。孰重孰轻，难以判断。同样，为顾客提供"新的服务方式"，还是"新产品"，企业也难以取舍。前者能为企业留住重要客户，否则将失去客户；后者则能帮助企业成为市场领导者，尽管新市场目前很小，但几年之后可能发展成为规模庞大的重要市场。这些是对创新绩效的判断，而非评价。但是，这些判断并非随意，更非主观臆断。即便无法量化，判断过程也是相当严谨的。最重要的是，做出"评判"意味着促使我们基于知识而非意见和猜测做出有目的的行动。

企业在进行评估时，所面临的最重要问题可能是：我们是否获得了创新领导地位，或至少保持了原有地位？领导地位并非等同于规模，它是指企业作为领导者受到认可，能够制定标准；更重要的是，企业能够主动引领变革，而非仅仅被动跟随。这是对现有企业是否具有成功的企业家精神的决定性考验。

V

结构

策略、实践以及对创新绩效的衡量，使得创新与企业家精神成为可能。它们能够移除或减少可能存在的阻碍。此外，它们还能培养正确的态度，并提供合适的工具。但是，创新要靠人来实现，而人是组织结构的一分子。

为使现有企业具有创新能力，企业必须设计一种组织结构，来培养员工的企业家精神。这种结构应以企业家精神为中心，来设计各种关系，它必须确保所有的奖励和激励措施、薪资待遇、人事决策和策略，都应鼓励而非惩罚创业行为。

1. 这首先表明我们应当将具有企业家精神的项目与现有项目区分开来，采取不同的组织方式。 如果用现有的结构来执行创业项目，注定会失败。当然，对大企业来说，尤为如此。而中等规模的企业同样适用，甚至小企业，也是如此。

其中一个原因是（前文已有相关讨论），现有业务的负责人往往将现有业务视为优先事项，并为此投入大量的时间和精力。相比于规模庞大、正在运营的项目，新项目看起来微不足道、前途渺茫。企业要依靠现有业务支持尚在苦苦挣扎的创新项目，还要时刻关注现有业务的"危机"。因此，现有业务的负责人总是推迟新生事物和具有创新与企业家精神的项目，以致错失良机。过去三四十年来，人们尝试了每一种可能的机制后发现：现有业务只能扩展、改进和适应现有事物。新事物并不能照这样做。

2. 这还表明，组织对新项目要给予特别关注，必须要由高层管理者负责。 就现有规模、收益和市场份额而言，新项目都不及现有项目。但是，作为创业者和创新者，高层管理者必须为新项目的未来而努力。

这并不一定是全职工作。在较小的企业中，它更不可能是全职工作。但是必须清楚地对这项工作加以界定，并指派权威人士全权负责。通常来说，这些负责人还要制定策略以使现有业务具有企业家精神；对要放弃的业务进行分析；对企业执行 X 光透视法；设立创新目标，以填补现有产品和服务的发展水平与企业生存和发展需求之间的缺口。此外，他们还要对创新机会进行系统分析（详见本书第一部分"创新实践"）。最后，他们还要分析企业内部与创新与企业家精神相关的想法，比如前面提到的高层管理者与基层员工之间非正式座谈所产生的想法。

在汇报创新工作，尤其是旨在开发新业务、新产品或新服务的创新工作时，应该直接向"负责该项创新的主管"汇报，而非原有组织中的直属领导汇报，并且决不能向负责企业日常运作的管理者汇报。

这种观点有悖于大多数企业的想法，尤其是"管理完善"的企业。但是，新项目犹如"婴儿"，并且在可预见的未来里，依旧是"婴儿"，需要多加呵护。而负责"成年人"（即现有业务或产品）的管理者，对新项目并不了解，也没有时间去关注它。此外，他们也无法为其解烦忧。

由于无视这一原则，一家大型机床制造商失去了其在机器人领域的领导地位。

这家公司拥有大规模自动化机床生产的基础专利，还拥有出色的工程技术、极高的声誉以及一流的制造工艺。1975 年左右，即工厂自动化初期，人们认为它将成为该领域未来的领导者。然而，10 年后，它却彻底地退出了竞争。究其原因，是因为该公司将自动化机床的发展任务派发给组织的三四级管理部门，并让它们向设计、生产和销售传统机床的负责人汇报。这些人是支持自动化机床的，事实上，机器人就是他们提出的。但是，为了应对新的竞争者（如日本的公司），他们整日忙于重新设计传统生产线，以适应新规格，随后为其做演示、市场推广、融资并提供技术服务。无论何时，当新产品的负责人来征求意见时，他们总回复道："我现在没有时间，下周吧。"毕竟，机器人开发只是公司的一个发展方向，而现有的机床生产线每年创收数百万美元。

不幸的是，这是一个比较常见的错误。

企业若要避免忽视新生事物而使其被扼杀的最佳的，可能也是唯一的办法是，从一开始就将创新项目视为独立业务。

宝洁公司、强生公司以及 3M 公司，这三家美国公司是这一办法的最佳实践者。宝洁公司主要生产肥皂、清洁剂、食用油和食品，是一家富有企业家精神的大型企业；强生公司是卫生和医疗保健品的供应商；3M 公司是工业用品和消费用品的大型制造商。这三家公司的具体实践各不相同，但其策略在本质上是一致的。它们从一开始就将新项目作为独立业务，并由专门的项目经理负责。项目经理要负责到底，直到该项目彻底失败或者获得成功、转变为成熟业务。在整个项目过程中，项目经理人有权调配所需的诸如研究、生产、资金和市场方面的资源，并将其投入到新项目中。

有的企业（尤其是大型企业）会同时开展多项创新工作，并将所有新项目汇报给同一个高层管理者。尽管这些新项目拥有不同的技术、市场和产品，但这无关紧要。它们都是新的小型创业项目，遭受同样的"儿科疾病"之苦。尽管它们的技术、市场和产品不同，但创业项目所面临的问题及其解决方案都是一样的。所以，必须有人为其花费时间，给予它们所需的关注，不辞辛苦地去了解存在的问题、所需的重要决策以及能够起作用的因素。这些人在企业中必须具有足够高的地位，能够代表这个新项目。此外，在新项目毫无希望时，他也有权终止该项目。

3. 之所以要对创新项目单独管理，还有一个原因：使它避开不能承受之重。比如，除非产品面市多年，否则对新产品进行传统的投资收益分析是不合适的。发展中的新业务承担现有业务的全部重担，犹如 6 岁的孩童背负近 30 千克的包裹，难以走远。不过，现有业务在财务、人事、各种汇报上的要求，不可轻易动摇。

不同领域中，创新工作以及其执行部门所需的策略、规则和评价也不相同。例如，如何制定企业的养老金计划？一个合理的解决办法是，让创新部门的人参与未来的利润分红，而非在项目尚未创收、不能提供养老金时，就把他们列入养老金计划。

在关键人员的薪资待遇方面，将创新业务与现有业务区分开来，尤为重要。现有业务的薪酬方案可能会使创新业务夭折，并不适用于创新业务中的关键人员。的确，大企业的薪酬方案主要是基于资产或投资的回报而制定的。这对创新项目来说，几乎是一大阻碍。

多年前，我在一家大型化学公司中学到了这些。众所周知，为了维持公司生存，公司的一个核心部门必须要生产新材料。新材料的生产计划已经制订好，科学研究也准备就绪……，但是毫无产出。年复一年，这个部门总是以各种理由推脱。终于，在一次审查会议中，部门负责人道出实情："我们管理团队的薪酬，主要按照投资回报率计算的。开发新材料需要大量的投入，投资回报率将会降低一半，这种情况至少要持续4年。即便4年后，这些投资产生回报时，我依然在公司里（如果利润一直这么低，公司可能也不会容忍我那么久），但在这之前，全体同事都要节衣缩食。如此一来，我们有何理由去做这件事呢？"后来，公司改变了薪酬核算方式，在计算投资回报率时，不考虑新项目的开发费用。18个月内，新材料就面市了。两年后，该部门取得所在领域的领导地位，并维持至今。4年后，该部门的利润翻倍。

就创新工作的薪酬和奖励而言，与确定需要做的事情相比，确定不该做的事情要容易得多。二者的要求相互冲突：新项目难以承受薪酬负担。但是，公司又必须给予创新人员与其努力相匹配的奖励，以激励他们继续努力。

具体来说，新项目的负责人必须获得适度的报酬。如果他们的待遇低于先前工作的待遇，这是不现实的。他们在现有业务中往往享有优厚的报酬。对他们来说，无论是在企业内部或是外部，重新找一份高薪工作很容易。因此，他们的报酬不应低于他们现有的薪酬和福利。

3M公司和强生公司所采用的方案，极其有效。这个方案是：如果有人成功开发了新产品、新市场或者新服务，并将其发展为新业务，公司将聘用他为该项业务的总经理、副总经理或部门经理，并享受与该职位相匹配的薪酬、红利和优先股。这种报酬相当可观。如果没有成功，公司则不需要任何投入。

另一个方案是，使新项目负责人享有该项目的未来利润。这两种方法如何选择，在很大程度上取决于当时的税法。例如，把新项目当作独立的公司，其创业经理享有一定的股权，比如 25%。当这个项目发展成熟后，公司按照预先的约定，基于销售收入和利润来回购股权。

此外，还需要建立一个风险承担机制。在现有企业中，承担创新项目也是一种"冒险"。为公平起见，雇主也应该承担一定的风险。如果创新失败，创新项目的负责人有权回到原来的工作岗位，并享有原来的报酬。的确，他们不应因失败而获得奖励，但也不能因尝试而遭受惩罚。

4. 正如在讨论个人薪酬时提到的，创新业务的收益不同于现有业务，需要用不同的方式加以衡量。 "希望我们业务的年税前回报率不低于 15%、年增长率不低于 10%"，这句话对现有业务或现有产品，可能是有意义的，但是，对新项目而言，这个要求可能过高，也可能过低，毫无意义。

在很长时间内（很多情况下），新项目可能既没有利润，也没有进展。但是，在随后相当长的时间内，它将快速增长，获得不少于投资 50 倍的收益（否则这个创新就是失败的）。虽然创新起初很渺小，但一旦成功，影响巨大。最终，创新应该开拓新业务，而非仅仅是产品线上的又一个"特色产品"或"优质产品"。

只有对创新经历及创新绩效加以分析，公司才能合理地预测其在产业和市场中的创新表现。多长的时间跨度较为合适？如何才能实现资源最优配置？初始阶段，是否要投资大量的人力和财力，还是只交由一两个人负责？何时应该加大投入？何时发展成为"业务"，来产生丰厚回报？

这些问题都很关键，在书本里也找不到答案。但是，我们不能随意地回答它们，不能凭借直觉判断，也不能刨根问底。创业型企业清楚地知道，在特定行业、技术和市场中，什么是合适的创新模式、节奏和时间跨度。

例如，前面提及的创新的大银行知道，要在一个新的国家建立分行，至少需要 3 年的投资；到第 4 年，达到盈亏平衡；到第 6 年中期，收回所有的投资。如果到第 6 年年底，该分行仍然需要进行投资，那这个项目就很令人失望，放弃可能是最好的选择。

一种重要的新型服务类项目，如租赁，有着类似的周期，也可能更短。在外界看来，宝洁公司知道，新产品需要经过两三年时间才能面市。再过18个月，这些产品将成为市场中的明星产品。IBM向市场推出新产品，可能需要5年的时间。新产品进入市场之后，第1年，开始快速增长；第2年年初，获得市场领导地位；第3年的前几个月，收回全部投资；第5年，到达顶峰并趋于平稳。到那时，新一代产品出现，取而代之。

要了解上述情况，唯一的方法是，对公司及其竞争对手的绩效进行系统分析。也就是说，建立反馈系统，分析创新绩效与创新预期之间的差距，并对企业作为创业者的表现进行定期评估。

只有了解创新工作能产生什么样的绩效，企业才能制定措施加以控制。这些措施可以评估部门和部门经理在创新中的表现，并决定哪些创新工作需要推进，哪些需要重新考虑，哪些需要放弃。

5. 在现有企业中培育企业家精神的最后一个结构性要求是，明确个人或小组的责任。

在前面提到的"中等规模的成长型企业"中，通常由首席执行官（CEO）承担主要责任；在大型企业中，通常指派一位资深高层管理者负责；在小型企业中，负责创新与企业家精神的管理者，可能也同时承担其他任务。

对企业家精神而言，最清晰的组织结构可能是，将创新部门或创新发展部门分离出来。但是，这只适用于大型企业。

这方面的例子最早可以追溯到100多年前。1872年，德国西门子公司聘用的第一位拥有大学学历的工程师赫夫纳·阿尔登涅克（Hefner Alteneck），成立了业界第一个"研究实验室"。该实验室的成员主要负责发明新产品和新工艺。此外，他们还负责发现新用途和新市场。他们不仅从事技术性工作，还负责发展制造工艺，推出新产品并从中获利。

50年后，即20世纪20年代，美国杜邦公司设立类似的独立部门，并称之为"开发部"。该部门负责从公司各处收集创新点子，对其进行研究、思考和分析。然后，向高层管理者提议，应将哪些点子发展成为创新项目。从一开始，该部门就要考虑所需的创新资源，如研究、开发、制造、营销、金融，等等。自始至终，该部门都要负责创新项目，直至新产品或新服务面市多年。

无论创新项目是由首席执行官还是高管团队的其他成员，或某一独立部门负责，无论它是管理者的全部任务还是一部分任务，我们都应将创新项目视为高层管理者的职责，也是一项单独的职责。这项职责包括要系统地、有目的地寻找创新机会。

有人可能会问，这些策略和实践都是必需的吗？难道它们不会阻碍企业家精神和扼杀创造力吗？如果没有这些策略和实践，企业就不具有企业家精神吗？答案是"可能有"，但是企业不会获得巨大成功，也不会长久发展。

当我们谈论企业家精神时，我们主要关注高层管理者的性格和态度，尤其是首席执行官的。⊖诚然，高层管理者可以破坏或扼杀企业家精神，这很容易。只需对每个想法说"不"并持续多年，然后确保新想法的提出者没有奖励和晋升的机会，并很快被辞退。但是，我们很难肯定地说，如果没有合适的策略和实践，仅仅凭借高层管理者的性格和态度，就能够成立创业型企业。而这是大多数关于企业家精神的图书所认同的，至少是如此暗示的。我所知道的一些寿命短暂的企业，都是由创始人经营的。即便企业在获得成功之时，如果不采取创业管理的相关策略和实践，它也会很快失去企业家精神。高层管理者的性格和态度，只能影响比较小的企业或者比较新的企业。究其原因，即便一个中等规模的企业，也是一个相当大的组织。这些公司需要很多知道自己应该做什么并愿意去做的人。企业应该鼓励他们去努力，为之配备所需的工具并给予肯定。否则，光说不做，企业家精神只是首席执行

⊖ 罗莎贝斯·莫斯·坎特的著作《变革大师》（New York: Simon & Schuster, 1983）对这点做了很好的描述。

官的口号而已。

据我所知，除非创始人将创业管理的策略和实践融入组织，否则一旦创始人离开，企业家精神会随之而去。如果缺乏这些策略和实践，几年之内，企业就会变得谨小慎微并停滞不前。这些企业甚至察觉不到其重要特质已经失去，而正是这些特质曾使它们脱颖而出的。等它们意识到时，一切为时已晚。为了及时认识不足，企业应该对创业绩效加以衡量。

有两家创业型企业，在创始人管理时期表现卓越：迪士尼公司和麦当劳。它们的创始人分别是沃尔特·迪斯尼和雷·克罗克。这两人都具有丰富的想象力和充沛的精力，富有创造力，并具有企业家精神和创新思维。他们的公司具有良好的日常运营管理能力。但是，他们自己承担企业的创业责任，依赖于本身的"创业特质"，而非将企业家精神融入具体的策略和实践。他们去世之后的几年内，他们的公司变得古板、保守、谨小慎微。

一些企业将创业管理融入了组织结构，如宝洁、强生、玛莎百货等。无论首席执行官和经济状况如何改变，这些企业数十年如一日，一直是创新者和创业领袖。

VI

人事

为培育创新与企业家精神，现有企业该如何进行人员配置呢？是否有人本身就是"企业家"呢？他们生来如此吗？

文学作品对此进行了广泛的讨论，讲述了"创业型人格"，以及除了创新别无所求的人。根据我们丰富的经验，这些讨论毫无意义。总的来说，那些不愿成为创新者或企业家的人，不会主动从事这样的工作。所以，可将这些人排除在外。我们的经验表明，在其他任务中表现良好的管理者，也是一名合格的企业家。在成功的创业型企业中，没有人会担心某人是否能做好开发工作。显然，无论性情和背景如何，都能表现出色。比如，3M 公司中的任何一个年轻工程师，如果向高层管理者汇报一个有意义的想法，就可能会负责该项开发工作。

同样，没有理由去担心成功的企业家将走向何方。当然，有些人只想从事新项目，而不愿做其他事情。打个比方，大多数英国家庭雇用保姆来照顾婴儿。等孩子会走路和说话时，也就是不再是婴儿时，一些保姆就不愿再继续留下。但是，也有许多保姆非常乐意留下来，而且并不觉得照顾年龄稍大的孩子更为困难。那些只想成为企业家的人，不可能刚进入现有企业就能如愿从事创新项目，即便可以，成功的概率也很小。通常情况下，现有企业中成功的企业家，早已是企业的优秀管理者了。因此，我们可以合理地推测，他们敢于创新，也善于管理。在宝洁公司和 3M 公司内，一些人以"项目经理"为职业，他们成功完成一个项目后，会立即投入到下一个新项目中。但是更高层次的管理者的职业生涯，则是从"项目管理"开始，随后是"产品管理""市场管理"，最后进入公司高层。强生和花旗银行，也是如此。

企业家精神是行为、策略和实践的综合反映，而非性格使然。在美国的大公司里，越来越多的资深人士将创业作为他们的第二职业，为此提供了最好的证明。那些在大公司（通常在同一个公司）度过整个职业生涯的中高层管理者和高级专业人才，在工作 25 或 30 年之后，当意识到自己走到职业生涯的终点时，越来越多的人选择提前退休。在 50 岁或 50 多岁时，这些中年人成了企业家。一些人自主创业；一些人，尤其是技术专家，为新创企业提供咨询服务；一些人在新型小企业中，担任高级职位。他们中的绝大多数人在新事业中获得成功，并感到快乐。

美国退休人员协会的会刊《摩登老人》（*Modern Maturity*）中有很多这类人的故事，也有很多新型小企业招聘这类人的广告。1983 年，我召开的首席执行官的研讨会中，有 48 人参加，其中有 15 位参与者（14 位男性和 1

位女性）将创业作为其第二事业。在针对这些人的特别会议上，我问他们，在大公司工作的这些年里，是否曾因"创业型人格"感到沮丧或压抑。他们认为这个问题十分荒谬。我接着问，他们在转换角色的过程中，是否遇到很多困难。他们认为这一问题同样荒谬。其中一个人说道："好的管理就是好的管理，无论你管理的是通用电气公司中销售额高达 1.8 亿美元的部门（就比如我过去的工作），还是管理一家销售额仅为 600 万美元诊断仪器领域的创新公司（就比如我现在的工作）。当然，我处理的事情不同，处理事情的方式也不同。但是我用的是在通用电气公司学到的理念，所做的分析也完全相同。事实上，相比于 10 年前我从工程师转变为管理者，这种转变更为容易。"其他人对此也深表赞同。

公共服务机构的情况，同样如此。美国近代史上最成功的两位创新者，是高等教育领域的亚历山大·舒尔（Alexander Schure）和欧内斯特·波耶尔（Ernest Boyer）。舒尔起初是电子领域的成功发明家，拥有很多专利。1955年，当他 30 出头时，在没有政府、基金会和大企业的支持下，他创办了一所名为纽约理工学院的私立大学。这所学校在招生对象、教学内容和教学方式方面，都提出了有创见的想法。30 年后，这所学校成为一所领先的技术大学，拥有 4 个校区和 12 000 名学生，其中一个校区是医学院。至今，舒尔仍然是一名极为成功的电子发明家。但是，30 年来，他一直在该校担任全职校长，而且据说建立了一支高效的专业管理团队。

与舒尔相比，波耶尔起初是管理者。他先在加利福尼亚大学任职，后来去了纽约州立大学。纽约州立大学是美国最大、官僚主义最严重的学校，拥有 350 000 名学生和 64 个校区。1970 年，波耶尔在 42 岁时到达事业的顶峰，受命为校长。他很快创办了帝国州立学院（Empire State College）。它甚至还称不上是学院，只是用于解决美国高等教育中由来已久、令人沮丧的问题，即为没有文凭的成人开办能够获得学位的课程项目。

尽管美国曾多次尝试解决这个问题，但一直没有成效。如果这些成人可以与较年轻的"正规"学生一同学习，他们的目标、需求以及经历将不会受到关注。他们会被视为 18 岁的普通学生，因而会感到沮丧，并很快退学。但是，如果像先前多次尝试的那样，让他们参加"继续教育课程"的学习，他们很可能会受到老师轻视。这些课程的老师，都是从大学中随意调配的。而在波耶尔的帝国州立学院中，成年人到纽约州立大学下属的任一学院或大学来学习正规的大学课程。最起初，学校为每个成年学生安排一位"导师"，通常是附近州立大学的老师。这些老师会帮助他们制定计划并确认他们是否需要特别指导，并且还帮助确认他们的哪些经历会使他们获得晋升和进阶工作。随后，作为代理人，导师们帮助每位学生办理入学、选择年级和课程等事宜。

这些听起来像是常识，确实也是如此。但是，它打破了美国学术界的传统，并遭到州立大学的强烈反对。波耶尔依旧坚持自己的做法。他的帝国州立学院拥有 6000 多名学生，退学率很低，设有硕士项目，是美国同类高等教育项目中最早取得成功的。波耶尔这名伟大的创新者并没有止步于做一个"管理者"。在担任纽约州立大学校长之后，他又出任卡特总统时的教育部长，后来成为卡内基教学促进基金会会长，它们分别是美国学术界最"官僚化"、最"传统"的职位。

这些例子并不能说明任何人都能既是官僚，又能成为创新者。舒尔和波耶尔是例外。但他们的经历的确表明，完成特定的任务对"性格"并无要求。而它所需要的是乐于学习、持续的努力工作、自我约束以及采纳和应用正确的策略和实践。这正是企业进行创业管理时，针对人员和人员配置的具体要求。

作为一种新事物，创业项目若想成功，结构和组织必须合适，人际关系处理得当，薪酬和奖励机制合理。当这些准备就绪之后，就要考虑应该由谁来负责这个创业项目，项目完成之后应该如何安置他们的问题。必须基于个人情况而非某种心理理论来考虑，目前尚未有什么被证实有效的心理理论。

创业型企业中的人员决策与其他机构中的决策方式并无差别。当然，这些决策具有风险性，与人有关的决策往往如此。因此，在制定决策时，必须仔细认真并采用正确的方式。首先，必须仔细考虑要做的工作；其次，确定候选人并分析其绩效记录；最后，通过候选人的同事，对其进行核查。这个方式适用于所有的用人决策。在创业型企业中，无论是选择创业者，还是管理者或专业人员，用人决策的成功率是一样的。

Ⅶ

禁忌

下面是现有企业进行创业管理时，不能做的事情。

1. 最重要的警告是，不要将经营部门和创业部门混淆。 不要让现有管理部门负责创业项目，也不要让负责现有业务运营、开发和优化的人员来创新。

如果一个企业不改变它的基本策略和实践就试图成为创业型企业，这一做法是不明智的，事实上，注定会失败。附带做一个创业型企业很难成功。

在过去10~15年中，许多美国大企业试图与创业型企业建立合资企业，但无一成功。创业型企业发现自己受制于策略、基本规则以及古板且保守的官僚风气，而且同时，他们的合作者，即大企业的人员，还无法理解创业型企业的人的行为，认为他们毫无纪律、过于狂妄且不切实际。

总的来说，只有内部人员开展创新项目，大企业才能成为成功的创业型企业。大企业与创新项目负责人互相了解，企业信任负责人，负责人清楚如何在现有企业中进行创新。换言之，就是选择能如合作伙伴般工作的人。但前提是，整个企业都具有企业家精神，即想要创新并为之努力，将创新视为必需品和机会。也就是说，整个组织都"渴望新事物"。

2. **超出现有业务领域的创新工作，很难成功**。创新最好不要"多元化"。无论多元化会带来多少好处，都不能将其和创新与企业家精神相混淆。新事物的发展总是充斥着艰难，在不熟悉的领域中尝试新事物更为困难。现有企业必须在其专业领域内创新，不论是市场领域还是技术领域。任何新事物的发展都会遇到困难，因此企业必须了解其创新业务。除非与现有业务存在共性，无论是市场层面还是技术层面，多元化才可能成功。即便如此，正如我在其他著作中所讨论的⊖，"多元化"仍然存在问题。当多元化存在的困难和要求与实践企业家精神时所面临的困难和要求叠加时，后果将不堪设想。

3. **最后，通过"购买"，也就是收购小型创业型企业，以使企业具有企业家精神，通常毫无效用**。除非收购方愿意并且能够在相当短的时间内管理被收购方，否则收购很难起作用。被收购方的原有管理者很少会长时间停留。如果他们是所有者，他们现在会很富有；如果他们是职业经理人，除非在新的收购方有更多的机会，他们才会继续留任。因此，在一两年内，收购方必须管理其收购的企业。当非创业型企业收购创业型企业时，这一点尤为重要。很快，被收购方的管理者会发现他们难以与母公司员工共同工作，对方也同样如此。据我所知，很少有企业通过"购买"成为创业型企业。

在快速变化的时代里，企业如果想要创新，想要获得成功并繁荣发展，必须将创业管理纳入自身体系中。它必须运用好策略，以使整个组织渴望创新，并具有创新思维与企业家精神。要想成为成功的创业者/创业型企业，现有企业，无论大小，都应将其视为创业型企业进行管理。

⊖ 详见《管理：使命、责任、实践》，尤其是第 56～57 章。

服务机构的企业家精神

I

正如企业一样，公共服务机构，如政府机构、工会、教堂、各级学校、医院、社区和慈善组织、专业学会和行业协会等，也要有创新与企业家精神。事实上，它们对创新与企业家精神的需求更加迫切。对公共服务机构而言，当今社会、技术和经济的快速变化是更大的威胁，同时也是更大的机会。

但是，即便与"官僚化"最为严重的企业相比，公共服务机构创新也更困难。那些"业已存在"的公共服务机构所遇到的创新阻碍，甚至更大。的确，每个服务机构都希望其规模越来越大。服务机构并不以利润为中心，因此规模就成为服务机构成功与否的唯一标准，也是其发展目标。于是，它们就会有很多事情要做。但是，停止做"一直在做的事情"并转向新事物，是服务机构非常厌恶的事情，至少会令它们感到痛苦。

公共服务机构中的创新大都是由局外人或灾难引起的。例如，现代大学是由普鲁士外交官威廉·冯·洪堡创办的。他在教育方面，是个彻底的局外人。1809 年，洪堡创办了柏林大学，当时法国大革命和拿破仑战争几乎完全摧毁了十七八世纪的传统大学。60 年后，美国传统大学无法再吸引学生而日渐消亡，现代大学应运而生。

同样，20 世纪军队的基础创新，无论是结构创新还是战略创新，都源于可耻的错误或惨痛的失败。例如，美国在美西战争惨败后，泰迪·罗斯福（Teddy Roosevelt）任命纽约律师伊莱休·鲁特（Elihu Root）为陆军部长，然后鲁特重新组织了部队，并重新制定作战战略；几年后，英军在布尔战争中同样遭遇惨败，平民出身的战争部长霍尔丹勋爵（Lord Haldane）对军队进行改组并改变了战略；第一次世界大战失败后，德国对其军队也进行了重组，并制定了新的战略。

政府机构的创新，同样如此。近代政治史中最伟大的创新，即 1933～1936 年的罗斯福新政，是由大萧条引起的。这场大萧条如此严重，以至于几乎要瓦解美国的社会结构。

官僚主义的批判者将公共服务机构对创新与企业家精神的抵制归咎到"怯懦的官僚""趋炎附势者"或"热衷权力的政客"身上。这个说法由来已久。事实上，大约 500 年前，马基雅维利倡导这一说法之时，它已经存在很久了。唯一改变的是这一说法的倡导者。20 世纪初，它是所谓的"自由主义者"的口号；现在，它成了所谓的"新保守主义者"的口号。可惜事情并非如此简单。改革派一直将"杰出人士"视为灵丹妙药，其实不过是海市蜃楼罢了。即便是最富有创新与企业家精神的"杰出人士"接管公共服务机构，6 个月后，他也会成为官僚主义者和热衷权力的政客。对于政府机构，更是如此。

阻碍公共服务机构的创新与企业家精神的力量在于机构内部，是机构的一部分，不可分割。[⊖]最有力的证据是企业内部的员工服务部门，也就是企业

⊖　关于公共服务机构及其特征，详见《管理：使命、责任、实践》中第 11～14 章关于服务机构绩效的内容。

内部的"公共服务机构"。该部门的负责人通常来自运营部门，其能力在激烈的市场竞争中已经得到证实。但是，员工服务部门的名气并不如创新部门。他们善于建立自己的帝国，总是想要做同样的事情。此外，他们不愿放弃任何正在做的事情。因此，一旦成立，他们很少再进行创新。

相比于一般的企业，现有公共服务机构进行创新时面临更多阻碍。究其原因，主要有三点。

1.首先，公共服务机构基于"预算"而非"成果"来获得报酬。它的收入取决于自身努力以及从外界获取的资金。无论该资金来自纳税人、慈善组织的捐赠者，还是来自企业人事部门或市场服务部门。公共服务机构越努力，获得的预算就越多。公共服务机构的"成功"在于获得更高的预算，而非产出。如果公共服务机构取消活动或减少努力，自身地位和声望就会受到削弱。另外，公共服务机构还不能承认失败。更糟糕的是，它们不能承认已经达成目标的事实。

2.其次，公共服务机构受众多因素的影响。企业在市场中销售产品，消费者是最重要的因素，其重要性远超过其他因素。企业要想获得成功，只需在市场中占有很小的份额即可，它就可以满足其他利益相关者的需求，如股东、工人、社区，等等。但是，公共服务机构（包括企业内部的员工服务部门）并非基于"成果"获得报酬。任何一个利益相关者，无论多么微不足道，都具有否决权。因此，公共服务机构必须满足每个人的需求。毫无疑问，疏远任何利益相关者所造成的损失，它们都无法承担。

服务机构一旦开启一项活动，就会获得一批"支持者"。随后，这些支持者不愿废除这个项目，甚至不愿对其进行大的改动。但是，任何新事物出现时，总是备受争议。这就意味着，新事物出现时，会遭到现有支持者的反对，而新的支持者尚未形成。

3.最后，最重要的原因是，公共服务机构存在的目的是"做好事"。这意味着，公共服务机构将其使命视为绝对道德行为，而非以成本／收益来分析的经济行为。经济学总是在寻求不同的配置方式，以用同样的资源获取更高的收益。一切经济性行为都是相对的。而在公共服务机构中，根本不存在所谓的更高收益。如果公共服务机构在"做好事"，就不存在"更好的事"。的确，如果没有实现"做好事"的目标，这仅仅意味公共服务机构需要加倍努力。邪恶势力远比预想的更加强大，需要更加努力与之对抗。

几千年来，各种宗教的传教士一直在反对"肉体的罪恶"。至少可以说，他们取得的成效很小。但对传教士而言，这没什么可争论的。这并不能说服他们运用聪明才智去实现更易达到的目标。相反，这只能说明他们需要加倍努力。避免"肉体的罪恶"显然是"德行"，因此是绝对道德行为，不允许进行成本／收益分析。

很少有公共服务机构以如此绝对的方式定义自己的使命。但是，即便是企业的人事服务部门或制造业服务人员，也往往将其使命视为"做好事"，因此是道德的、绝对的行为，而不是经济的、相对的行为。

这意味着公共服务机构力图最大化而非最优化。反饥饿运动的领导人断言："只要地球上有一个孩子挨饿，我们的使命就尚未完成。"如果他说，"如果通过现有分销渠道，绝大多数孩子都有足够的事物，不再发育迟缓，那么我们就完成了使命"，他就会被赶出办公室。但如果目标是最大化，机构将永远无法实现。事实上，越接近目标，机构要付出的努力也越多。一旦机构实现最优化（实现最优化所需的努力是实现理论上的最大化所需努力的75%～80%），边际成本将呈指数上升，边际收益则呈指数下降。因此，公共服务机构遇到的挫折也会更多，继而更加努力去做正在做的事情。

无论公共服务机构取得的成就是大是小，它们的行事方式完全一样。无论成功与否，它们都会将创新或尝试新事物视为对其基本承诺、存在的理由、信念和价值观的攻击，因而加以抵制。

这些都是严重阻碍创新的因素。从大体上来说，它们解释了为何公共服务机构中的创新往往源于新成立的机构，而不是现有机构。

这方面最极端的例子，莫过于工会了。在 20 世纪的发达国家中，工会可能是最成功的机构。显然，它已经实现了最初的目标。西方发达国家中，劳动报酬在国民收入中占比达到 90% 时（在某些国家，如荷兰，该比例已接近 100%），这一目标没有更多增长空间了。但是，工会甚至不去考虑新的挑战、新的目标或新的贡献。它所能做的，只是喊旧口号，打旧仗。因为"劳工问题"是绝对的好事。这不容置疑，也不能重新定义。

大学的情况与工会并无太大差异，造成这一状况的原因也有类似之处，即 20 世纪大学的发展和取得的成功仅次于工会。

但是，公共服务机构中也有很多例外（必须承认的是，政府机构中的例外不多），即便它们历史悠久、规模庞大，也具有创新能力。

例如，美国罗马天主教大主教区是由世俗人民来管理的，并由一名已婚女信徒担任总经理。这位女信徒曾在某百货连锁店担任人事副总裁。除了分发圣餐和主持教会，其他工作都是由世俗专业人员和管理人员负责。尽管美国天主教神职人员短缺，但这个大主教区却有多余的神职人员，能够积极推进教会，拓展宗教方面的服务活动。

美国科学促进会是历史最悠久的科学团体之一。1960—1980 年，它将自己重新定位为"大众组织"，又不失其领袖风范。它把其周刊《科学》彻底改版，使之面向大众和政府的科学发言人，也是科学策略的权威报道。它为外行读者提供了一本富有科学性且备受欢迎的大众读物。

早在 1965 年左右，美国西海岸的一家大型医院认识到，医疗保健因其成功正在发生变化。当其他大城市的医院还在试图抵制这种趋势（如建立连锁医院或独立救护中心），这家医院成了这些领域的创新者和领导者。的确，它最先建立了独立式产科中心。只需以较低的成本，准妈妈就可以待在汽车旅馆式房间，并获得所需的医疗服务。它还首次建立了独立式门诊外科中心。它还开始成立自己的慈善性连锁医院，并与区域内的小医院签订管理合同。

美国女童子军创立于 20 世纪初，是一个拥有数百万名成员的大型组织。

自 1975 年左右，美国女童子军引进创新理念，影响了其会员、项目和志愿者这三个基本要素。它开始积极招募新兴城市中产阶级女性，即非裔、亚裔、拉丁裔。现在，这些人在总人数中占比为 1/5。它意识到，随着女性步入职场、走向管理岗位，女孩需要一些新项目和新榜样，即强调专业性和职业性的工作生涯而非家庭主妇、护士等传统定位。女童子军的管理者认识到，负责当地活动的志愿者越来越少，因为年轻妈妈不再待在家中。但他们也认识到，新的职业女性、新的职业母亲预示着新的机会，女童子军可以为她们提供新的服务。对任何社区来说，志愿者是主要限制因素。因此，她们开始设计一些义务工作，以吸引职业母亲。这些工作可以使她们与孩子一起玩耍，也有利于孩子成长。最后，女童子军还意识到，职业女性没有足够的时间陪伴孩子，也是一个机会。于是，它们开始招收学龄前儿童。由此，女童子军扭转了孩子和志愿者减少的趋势，而男童子军这个规模更大、成立更早、资金更充沛的组织依然飘摇不定。

II

创业策略

上述例子都是我所知道的发生在美国的例子。毫无疑问，在欧洲和日本也有类似的例子。虽然这些例子都存在局限性，但它们足以说明公共服务机构需要创业策略来推动创新。

1. 公共服务机构要明确使命。它想要做什么？为何存在？它应该关注目标，而非计划和项目。计划和项目只是实现目标的手段，因此是临时性的、短暂性的。

2. 公共服务机构要制定合乎现实的目标。它应该说，"我们的工作是缓解饥荒，"而不是"我们的工作是消灭饥饿"。它的目标应该切实可行，能够为之承诺。这样，最后它可以说："我们的任务完成了。"

当然，有些目标永远无法实现。比如，实现和维护社会的公平正义，就是一个无休止的任务。即便以宽松的标准衡量，这一目标也无法实现。但是，对大多数目标来说，我们可以也能够用最优化而非最大化的术语来表述，这样才可能会说："我们已经实现目标了。"

的确，应该满怀崇敬地提到一个学校的校长的传统目标：让每个人都能在学校接受多年教育。在发达国家中，这一目标早已实现。现在需要问的问题是：教育需要做什么？也就是说，与纯粹的"上学"相比，"教育"究竟意味着什么？

3. 如果目标无法实现，表明目标是错误的，至少其定义是错误的。公共服务机构必须假定其目标更具经济意义而非道德意义。如果经过多次尝试仍未达到目标，那说明这个目标是错误的。不能将失败视为反复尝试的充分理由。300多年前，数学家已经发现，随着尝试次数增加，成功的可能性降低。事实上，每次尝试的成功率，不会超过前一次的一半。因此，如果目标无法实现，就要质疑目标的有效性，而大多数公共服务机构的认知恰恰与之相反。

4. 公共服务机构要将持续寻求创新机会纳入其策略和实践。它们应该将变化视为机会，而非威胁。

前面提到的创新型公共服务机构之所以如此成功，就是因为它们采用了这些基本原则。

第二次世界大战后，美国天主教涌现出很多受过良好教育的教徒，这是前所未有的。大多数天主教教区，以及罗马天主教会的大多数机构，都将其视为威胁，至少视其为问题。随着受过良好教育的天主教徒增多，对主教和神职人员的完全认可不再被视为理所当然。然而，在天主教会的结构和管理体系中，却没有这些平民信徒的一席之地。自1965年或1970年以来，美国罗马天主教教区的年轻神职人员急剧减少，这被视为一个重大威胁。只有一个天主教教区将这两种情况视为机会。（结果，出现了不同的境况。美国的年轻神职人员都想进入这个教区。这些神职人员在此可以发挥自身才能,这也是他们成为神职人员的原因。)

从 1970 年或 1975 年开始,美国医院都察觉到医疗保健领域的变化。大多数医院都抵抗这种变化,并告诉人们"这种变化是灾难性的"。只有一家医院将变化视为机会。

美国科学促进会认为,具有科学背景和从事科学工作的人数不断增长,这为其在科学界及其他领域树立领导地位提供了巨大机会。

美国女童子军看到人口统计数据,便自问:"我们如何才能把人口变化趋势转化为新机会?"

只要遵循这些基本原则,甚至连政府机构也能创新。下面举个例子。

120 年前,美国内布拉斯加州的林肯市将公共交通、电力、天然气、水等公共服务纳为市政所有,这在西方世界是首次尝试。过去 10 年里,在女市长海伦·布萨里斯的领导下,政府开始将垃圾收集、学校交通等服务进行私有化改造。市政府提供资金,由私营企业进行竞标。这种做法大大降低了成本,并提高了服务质量。

海伦在林肯市看到的机会,就是将公共服务的"提供者"(即政府)和"供应商"分开。通过引入竞争机制,这使得以低成本获得高标准、高效率、高可靠性的服务成为可能。

如果公共服务机构想要能够创新与具有企业家精神,上述 4 条原则构成其所需的具体策略和实践。此外,公共服务机构也可以借鉴现有组织成为创业型企业所采用的策略和实践(详见上一章"创业型企业")。

Ⅲ

创新的必要性

为何公共服务机构的创新如此重要?为何我们不能像从前一样,保持现有的公共服务机构不变，成立新机构来进行我们所需的创新呢？

这是因为在发达国家中，公共服务机构愈加重要，其规模也愈加庞大。公共服务部门（政府部门和民间非营利部门）在 20 世纪快速增长，其增长速度大概是私营部门的 3～5 倍。第二次世界大战后，公共服务机构的发展更为迅速。

从某种程度上讲，这种发展过快。只要公共服务机构可以转化为营利性企业，就应如此转变。这种转变不仅仅适用于将内布拉斯加州林肯市的市政服务进行"私有化"。美国医院在非营利组织向营利组织转变的过程中，已经走得很远。我认为，这种转变将在职业教育和研究生教育中掀起热潮。在发达国家中，对高收入人群，也就是拥有高学历的人，进行补助，是不合理的。

在未来的二三十年中，发达国家的主要经济问题必定是资本形成的问题。现在只有日本，资本能够满足其经济发展需要。因此，只有非营利组织转变其活动方式，使其能够形成资本、获得利润，否则，我们无力承担这些非营利活动。因为这些活动只是吞噬资本，而不能形成资本。

但是，公共服务机构负责的很多活动，将仍是公共服务活动。这些活动既不会消失，也不会转变。因此，公共服务机构必须具有生产力，并取得生产效益。它们必须成为创新者，并用企业家精神进行自我管理。要实现这些目标，在社会、技术、经济和人口等快速变化的时代里，公共服务机构应将这些领域的转变视为机会。否则，它们将成为阻碍。如果公共服务机构固守于快速变化的环境中无法运行的项目和计划，它们将不能实现其使命。可是，它们又不能也不愿放弃这些使命。渐渐地，它们就像 14 世纪丧失社会功能的封建贵族一样：如寄生虫般毫无能力，只会妨碍和剥削他人。它们将变得自以为是，渐渐失去合法性。显然，公共服务机构中最强大的工会，已经出现这样的情况。但是，在快速变化的社会中，充满了新挑战、新需求和新机会，公共服务机构仍是必需的。

美国公立学校同样面临着机会与风险并存的局面。除非它能够引领创新，否则将很难在 20 世纪生存下去（不包括面向贫民窟里少数人的学校）。在美国教育史中，学校首次面临阶层结构的威胁。原有的教育制度规定：除了极其贫困的学生外，其余学生都要在公立学校上学。至少在拥有多数人口的城市和郊区，情况如此。这种情况正是公立学校自身的错误造成的，这也是众所周知公立学校需要改革的地方（详见第 9 章）。

许多其他公共服务机构也面临着类似的情况。创新所需的知识已经存在，它们的创新需求也很清晰。现在它们需要做的就是，将创新与企业家精神融入自身体系中。否则，外来者将会创办具有企业家精神的竞争性公共服务机构，现有的公共服务机构将被取代。

在 19 世纪末和 20 世纪初这段时期，公共服务领域创造力强大，创新活跃。在这 75 年里（直到 20 世纪 30 年代），相比于技术创新，社会创新即便不是更为突出，也同样活跃、高效、发展迅速。但在这段时期里，创新表现为新型公共服务机构的创立。目前的公共服务机构，大都是六七十年前创立的，只是形式和使命有所转变。在接下来的二三十年里，情况将会大不相同。社会创新的需求将更为强烈，但主要是现有公共服务机构中的社会创新。因此，这代人的首要政治任务就是，将创业管理纳入现有公共服务机构体系。

新创企业

对现有企业来说，无论是商业企业还是公共服务机构，"创业管理"一词的核心是"创业"；而对新创企业来说，"创业管理"的核心则是"管理"。在现有企业中，"有"是企业家精神的主要阻碍；而在新创企业中，主要阻碍则是"没有"。

新创企业具有创意，也可能有产品或服务，甚至可能有销售额，有时销售额很大。当然，它有成本费用，有收入，甚至也有利润。它"没有"的是一种可实现的、可经营的"业务"，是一个完善的"现有"组织架构，让人们明确组织的前进方向、应做之事以及预期结果。除非新创企业发展成为真正的企业，并确保可加以管理，否则无论它的创意多么出色，吸引多少投资，产品多么优质，甚至无论市场需求多么大，它都无法生存。

由于拒绝接受这些事实，19 世纪最伟大的发明家托马斯·爱迪生所创办的企业都惨遭失败。爱迪生立志成为成功的商人和大企业的负责人。考虑到他是一名出色的商务策划师，这一目标本可以实现。他清楚地知道，如何利用自己发明的电灯泡成立一家电力公司。他也清楚地知道，如何获取新创企业需要的资金。他的产品一经面市，就大获成功，并且拥有巨大的市场需求。但是，爱迪生仍然只是创业者。更确切地说，他认为"管理"就是当老板，他不愿成立管理团队。因此，他的四五个企业在发展到中等规模时，都毫无例外地失败了。只有当专业管理者取代爱迪生时，企业才得以存活。

新创企业的创业管理有以下四点需求：

第一，要关注市场。

第二，要有财务远见，特别要提前规划现金流和资金需求。

第三，尽早组建高层管理团队，要在新创企业真正需要并能够承担一支高层管理团队之前，就建立起来。

第四，新创企业的创始人要明确自身角色、工作范围以及与他人的关系。

Ⅰ

市场焦点的必要性

新创企业在没有实现预期目标，甚至难以生存时，往往会解释道："我们起初做得很好，后来其他新进入者却占领了市场。我们百思不得其解，它们的产品与我们的并无太大差异。"或者解释说："我们本来做得很好，但其他企业却向我们未曾听说过的客户销售产品。突然之间，它们就占领了市场。"

当新创企业获得成功时，通常情况下，它的市场与预期市场有很大不同；产品和服务也与最初的设想不同；客户群体也在预料之外；产品的最终用途比起初的设计要多。如果新创企业没有预见到这些差异，不能利用这些未曾预料到和未曾留意的市场并加以组织，如果它并非完全以市场为中心，并非以市场为导向，那么它只不过是为竞争对手创造机会罢了。

当然，例外总会存在。为某种特定用途而设计的产品，尤其是科技产品，其市场和最终用途通常符合预期，但并非总是如此。针对特定疾病设计并测试的处方药，也会用于治疗完全不同的疾病。用于治疗胃溃疡的一种药物，就是一个例子。另一个例子是，一种起初用于治疗人类疾病的药物，最终却主要进入了兽医药品市场。

任何真正的新生事物，都能创造出预期之外的市场。在1960年第一台施乐复印机问世之前，没人想到办公室复印机会有市场；5年后，企业无法想象，如果没有复印机，将会如何。当第一架喷气式飞机试飞时，最权威的市场研究指出，就现有的以及正在建造的横跨大西洋的航班飞机而言，根本不会有足够多的乘客；5年后，跨大西洋航班的每年载客量，是以往横跨大西洋总人数的50～100倍。

创新者的视野有一定的局限性。事实上，创新者视野狭隘，他们往往只关注熟悉的领域，而忽视其他领域。

DDT就是一个例子。第二次世界大战期间，人们发明了DDT以使美军避免遭受热带昆虫和寄生虫的侵扰，最终却被广泛应用于农业中保护牲畜和农作物。后来由于过于有效，而遭到禁用。然而，那些发明DDT的杰出发明家，无一设想过DDT的这些用途。当然，他们知道许多婴儿死于苍蝇引起的"夏季"腹泻，也知道牲畜和农作物被昆虫和寄生虫侵害。但是，对于这些事情，他们只是"门外汉"。作为专家，他们只关注人类的热带疾病。一个普通的美国士兵，将DDT用于他家的牛群和棉花田里，他才是这些领域的"专家"。

同样，3M公司未曾想到，起初为工业界开发的胶带最终却广泛用于家庭和办公室（后来，这种胶带发展成为透明胶带）。多年来，3M公司一直为工业界提供研磨剂和黏合剂，并取得了一定的成功。不过它甚至从未想过进入消费市场。一位工程师研制出工业胶带却没有工业用户，不过他意识到这种产品可能在消费市场大卖。据说，当时公司已经放弃这种产品，这名工程师将一些样品带回了家。令他吃惊的是，他的十几岁的女儿整夜用它固定卷发。这件不寻常之事，使他和他老板发现了一个新市场。

1905 年，一名德国化学家首次研发出局部麻醉剂，即奴佛卡因（Novocain，也称为普鲁卡因）。但是，他无法说服医生使用这种麻醉剂，医生更愿意使用全身麻醉剂（第一次世界大战期间，他们才接受奴佛卡因）。但是，牙医竟然开始使用这种局部麻醉剂，这完全出人意料。于是，这位化学家在德国四处奔走，发表演讲，反对将奴佛卡因用于牙科。毕竟，他研发奴佛卡因的初衷，并不是用于牙科领域。

我承认，这种反应未免过于极端。但是，创新者清楚地知道，他们的创新意欲何为。如果用于其他用途，他们往往会抵触反抗。虽然不会拒绝意料之外的顾客，但他们会明确表示，不欢迎这些顾客。

计算机领域就发生过这种情况。尤尼瓦克公司曾推出世界上第一台计算机，也清楚地知道这种伟大的机器是为科学工作而设计的。因此，当企业对此表现出兴趣时，它甚至没有派销售人员去提供服务。它认为，企业根本不知道计算机到底为何物。同样，IBM 公司也深信，计算机是科学工作的工具，它的计算机就是专为天文计算而设计的。但是，IBM 愿意接受企业的订单，并为它们提供服务。10 年后，即 1960 年左右，尤尼瓦克仍然拥有当时最先进也是最好的计算机，而 IBM 则占有整个计算机市场。

教科书认为上述问题的解决方案是开展"市场调查"。但这个方案并不合理。

人们不能对真正的新生事物开展市场调查，也不能对尚未上市的事物进行市场调查。1950 年左右，尤尼瓦克的市场调查显示，到 2000 年，计算机的销量将为 1 000 台。事实上，1984 年，计算机的销量已经达到 100 万台。然而，它做的那次市场调查是有史以来最科学、最认真、最严谨的市场调查了。唯一的错误是，它假定计算机只能用于先进的科学工作（这也是当时人们的共识）。这样一来，销量的确有限。类似地，数家企业在进行全面的市场调查后，发现印刷厂不需要复印机，于是拒绝了施乐公司的专利。但是，没人想到，企业、学校和一些个人需要复印机。

因此，新创企业在创立之初就要假定，它的产品或服务能在预料之外的市场中找到客户，会对应不同于预期的用途，也会有一些意料之外的顾客前来购买，有些顾客甚至是新创企业从未听说过的。

如果新创企业在创立之初并没有聚焦于市场，那就可能是在为竞争对手创造市场。几年后，竞争对手将会占领"我们的市场"；或者开始"向我们未曾听说过的顾客推销"，突然就占领了市场。

事实上，要使新创企业聚焦于市场，并非特别困难。但是，它所需具备的条件却与典型企业家的意愿背道而驰。首先，它要求新创企业系统地找出意料之外的成功和失败（详见第3章）。企业家不应把意外事件视为"例外"而不予理会。他们应该走出去，仔细观察，并将意外事件视为独特的机会。

第二次世界大战后不久，印度一家小型工程公司获得了一种欧洲设计的、配有轻型发动机的自行车生产许可证。这种自行车看似很适合印度市场，却表现不佳。这家小公司的老板注意到，轻型发动机收到了大量订单。起初，他并不愿意接受这些订单，并寻思这些发动机能有什么用途呢？好奇心驱使他亲自到订单来源地察看。他发现，农民拆卸下自行车上的发动机，用它为灌溉水泵提供动力。在此之前，灌溉水泵依靠人工提供动力。现在，这家制造商成了全球最大的小型灌溉水泵制造商，销量达到数百万台。由于它的水泵，东南亚的农作方式出现革命性变化。

要以市场为导向，新创企业也要乐于尝试。如果有意料之外的顾客或市场对产品或服务感兴趣，新创企业可以在新市场中寻找志愿者来测试产品或服务，以发现新的用途。新创企业也可以向"不可能"市场的人发放样品，观察新产品是否能为其所用，用于何处，如何改造，才能吸引顾客。此外，新创企业可以在业界的商业报纸上宣传，了解顾客的兴趣从何而来。

杜邦公司在开发新型尼龙纤维时，从未想过它将主要用于汽车轮胎中。

但是，当阿克伦（Akron）一家轮胎制造商对尼龙表现出兴趣时，杜邦公司为此建立了一家工厂。几年后，轮胎成为尼龙最大的且利润最高的市场。

不需要大量资金，新创企业就能发现，意外市场的出现是纯属偶然，还是由于产品的潜力。这就需要新创企业具有敏锐的市场洞察力，并开展一些系统性工作。

最重要的是，新创企业的经营者要走出企业，走进市场，与顾客和销售人员交流，聆听外界的声音。新创企业还要建立一套系统的实践方式，使其认识到产品或服务是由客户定义的，而非由生产者。最后，新创企业还需要不断地改善产品或服务，为顾客带来更大的效用和价值。

对新创企业而言，最大的危险是自认为比客户"更了解"产品或服务是什么或应该是什么，应该如何购买以及如何应用。最重要的是，新创企业应将意外的成功视为机会，而非对其专业知识的侵犯。最后，它还需要铭记一句营销格言：企业不是要改变客户，而是要满足客户。

II

财务远见

对市场缺乏关注是"新生儿"（即新创企业）的通病。这也是新创企业早期面临的最严重的问题。即便新创企业得以生存，这也可能阻碍它的长期发展。

相比之下，对财务缺乏关注和财务策略缺失是新创企业在成长的第二阶段的最大威胁。对快速发展的新创企业而言，它更是个威胁。新创企业越成功，财务远见的缺失更为危险。

设想一家新创企业成功地推出了产品或服务，并处于快速发展阶段。企业报告道"利润快速增长"，对未来持乐观态度。随后，股票市场将会"发现"这家新创企业。当新创企业属于高科技领域或当下热门领域时，它会更受关注。各种预测比比皆是，都声称未来 5 年内，新创企业的销售额将达到 10 亿美元。18 个月后，该新创企业垮台了。它可能并非倒闭或者破产了，但突然陷入赤字困境，从 275 名员工中裁掉 180 名，解雇了总裁，或者被大企业低价收购。出现这种情况的原因，总是大同小异：资金不足；无法筹集扩张所需的资金；费用、存货和应收账款一片混乱，失去控制。这三种财务困境往往同时出现。但是，任何财务困境都会危及新创企业的健康发展，甚至会危及其生存。

一旦出现财务危机，新创企业必须历经重重磨难，经受巨大痛苦，才能渡过危机。但是，财务危机是可以有效预防的。

新创企业的企业家很少会忽视金钱。他们往往很贪婪，比较重视利润。但对新创企业而言，利润不应是关注点。更确切地说，新创企业应把利润放在末位，而非首位。他们应该重点关注现金流、资本以及资金管理。如果没有它们，利润纯属虚幻，可能在 12 个月或 18 个月后，就消失无踪了。

成长需要滋养。从财务角度来看，这意味着新创企业若要成长，需要增加财务资源，而非减少供给。成长需要更多的现金和资本。成长中的新创企业所谓的"盈利"，只是假象而已，只是用于平衡账目的记账方式。大多数国家中，企业根据利润来缴纳税费。因此，利润反而造成企业的负债和资金外流，而非"盈余"。新创企业愈是健康，发展越快，所需的资金也越多。那些报纸和股市所称的"宠儿"，那些利润快速增长、获得"破纪录利润"的新创企业，在几年后，反而更容易陷入绝境。

新创企业需要进行现金流分析、现金流预测和现金管理。相比于先前的新创企业，最近几年的美国新创企业在这方面的表现更好（不包括高科技企业）。这主要是因为，新的一批企业家意识到，企业家精神需要财务管理。

如果现金流预测比较可靠，那么现金管理便相当容易。这里的"可靠"是指立足于"最坏情况"，而非"希望"。银行界有一个古老的经验法则：在进行现金收入和支出预测时，对应付账款按提前 60 天支付计算，而应收账款按延后 60 天入账计算。如果这种预测过于保守，那最坏的情况只是出现短暂的现金盈余。而这在正成长的新创企业中，实属少见。

对成长中的新创企业来说，它们应该提前 12 个月明确现金需求量、何时需要、所为何用？由于有 1 年的时间，它们往往能够满足现金需求。但是，即便新创企业经营良好，仓促筹集资金或在"危机"时筹集资金也并非易事，而且往往代价巨大。最重要的是，这会使企业的重要人员在关键时刻偏离正确路线。几个月来，他们花费大量时间和精力奔走于各金融机构中，制定一系列可能存在问题的财务预测。最后，他们通常拿企业的未来做抵押，以度过 90 天的资金周转困难期。等到他们能够再次将时间和精力投入到企业时，早已错失良机。几乎可以断定，新创企业在面临资金危机的时候，往往也是机会最大的时候。

成功的新创企业的发展，也会使现有的资本结构不合时宜。经验法则表明，新创企业的销售额（或订单额）每增长 40%～50%，其资本基础就不再适用。一般来说，这种增长之后，新创企业要有一个全新的、不同的资本结构。随着新创企业的发展，私有资本（无论是个人资金，还是家人或外界的资金）将不再充足。它必须拓展更多资金来源，如公开"上市"，在现有企业中寻找合作伙伴，或向保险公司和养老基金筹集资金。如果新创企业原先是以股权融资方式获得资金，则需要转为长期负债，反之亦然。随着新创企业的成长，现有的资本结构往往变得不合时宜，成为企业发展的障碍。

对某些新创企业而言，资本规划相对容易些。有些企业是由不同地区的分部按照同一标准组成的，这样每个分部可以作为分公司来融资，如连锁餐厅、不同城市的独立外科中心或独立医院、各个城市独立的房屋建筑商、专卖店，等等。一种解决方案是，特许经营（本质上是一种为快速扩张而融资的方式）。另一种解决方案是，将分部转为独立的分公司，并由当地投资者担任有限合伙人。因此，企业可以逐步地筹集资金以获得成长和扩张。此外，前一分部的成功，会为后续分部的投资者带来信心。这种融资方式起作用的前提是：①每个分部要能够尽快达到收支平衡，至多两三年内；②当分部步入正轨后，那些管理能力有限的人，如特许经营者或独立外科中心的业务经理，要能够独立地完成工作；③分部要能够自主地发展到一定规模，不再需要更多资金投入，而是产生现金盈余用以建立新分部。

对于不能以独立分部进行融资的新创企业，资本规划是其赖以生存的必要条件。如果成长中的新创企业为未来 3 年的资本需求和资本结构做好规划，那它对资金获取、获取时间以及获取方式就不会有困难了。当然，这意味着，要按资金的最大需求而非最小需求来进行资本规划。如果资本基础和资本结构无法满足企业发展需求时，那新创企业无疑是拿自己的生存（至少是独立性）开玩笑。最终新创企业的创始人所承担的创业风险、艰苦的工作，只是为他人作嫁衣裳。他们从所有者变为雇员，新的投资者却控制一切。

最后，新创企业需要建立一个完整的财务系统，以适应企业的增长。这种现象一再地发生：成长中的新创企业在成立之初，拥有出色的产品、卓越的市场地位和良好的发展前景。突然之间，一切都失去控制了，包括应收账款、库存、制造成本、管理成本、服务、分销，等等。只要其中一项失去控制，其他各项也会随之失控。这是因为，新创企业的发展超出其可控范围。等它重新控制局面时，市场已不在了，客户即便没有敌意也会有所不满，分销商也对企业丧失信心。最糟糕的是，员工不再信任企业管理层，当然这情有可原。这样的例子比比皆是。

企业如果过快增长，会导致现有的控制结构不合时宜。当销售额增长40%～50% 时，这种现象就会发生。

企业一旦失控，就难以回归常态。不过，失控可以很容易地避免。首先要考虑的是，特定企业的关键领域是什么，可能包括：第一是产品质量，第二是服务，第三是应收账款和存货，第四是制造成本。对任何企业而言，关键领域很可能不会超过四五个。但是，企业要关注管理费用和行政费用。如果这两项费用占总收入的比例过高，意味着管理人员和行政人员的雇用人数超过企业的增速。这往往是企业失控的第一征兆，表明企业的管理结构和实践与任务不匹配。

要达到增长预期，新创企业必须提前 3 年为这些关键领域建立控制系统。精细的控制系统并不是必要的，事实上也无关紧要，只是大概数字而已。真正重要的是，新创企业的管理者对关键领域要加以关注，时刻想到它们。这样，如果需要，企业能够及时响应。如果新创企业足够重视关键领域，往往就不会出现混乱。因为只要有需求，它们就会对其加以控制。

进行财务预测，并不需要花费很多时间。但是，它需要企业进行深入思考。这项工作的技术工具很容易获得，许多管理会计教科书里都有阐述。不过，这项工作必须要由企业来完成。

Ⅲ

建立高层管理团队

一家新创企业，找到合适的市场并成功地获得了一席之地，随后成功地建立了所需的财务结构和财务系统。但是，几年后，它仍然可能陷到严重的危机之中。在它即将"成人"（即成为一家成功的且能持续发展的现有企业）之际，它会陷入难以理解的困境。企业拥有一流的产品和良好的前景，但却无法发展。无论是盈利能力、质量，还是其他方面，都表现欠佳。

究其原因，这些企业都缺乏一个高层管理团队。企业已经发展到一定阶段，非一两个人所能管理。现在，它需要一个高层管理团队。如果尚未有一个高层管理团队，那为时已晚，事实上是很晚了。到那时，企业能够存活下来，就是最大的奢求。企业可能因此遭受重创，这重创或如同难以愈合的伤疤，会影响企业发展。士气一落千丈，员工大失所望并变得愤世嫉俗。企业的创始人可能就此离去，满怀怨恨，心灰意冷。

补救的方法很简单：在新创企业需要高层管理团队之前，就将其建立。团队并非一夜建成的。要想让它真正发挥作用，需要很长一段时间。实际上它需要很长一段时间，才能够真正发挥作用。团队赖以成立的基础是相互信任和相互理解，这需要一定的时间来培养。以我的经验，3年为最低年限。

但是，对发展中的小型新创企业来说，高层管理团队是难以承受的负担。它无力承担6个高管的薪资。事实上，小型新创企业在成长阶段，一般都是由少数几个人包办一切事务。那么，如何才能打破这个怪圈呢？

同样，办法也很简单。但是，它要求创始人愿意组建团队，而不是凡事亲力亲为。如果高层管理者中有一两个人认为，他们必须独自实现一切。那么，几个月后，或者至多几年后，管理危机将不可避免。

无论何时，当客观经济指标（如市场调查或人口统计分析）显示，新创企业的业务将在三五年内翻番时，创始人就应该建立高层管理团队。很快，它将需要这一团队。这就是所谓的"防患于未然"。

首先，创始人和企业的其他关键人物，要共同考虑企业的关键活动：企业赖以生存和成功的具体领域是什么？每个人都会列出大多数关键领域。如果存在分歧和异议，他们要严肃对待，因为这是一个重要问题。最后，小组成员考虑到的关键领域，都应包含在最终清单中。

关键活动并非来自书本，而是源于对特定企业的分析。对局外人来说，同一行业中的两个企业对关键活动的界定，可能完全不同。比如，一个企业可能以生产为中心，另一个则以客户服务为中心。只有两项关键活动是所有组织共有的，即人员管理和资金管理。其他活动则由企业内部人员根据企业、自身工作、价值观和目标而定。

下一步是，团队中的每个成员，从创始人开始，要自问："我所擅长的活动是什么？我的同事所擅长的活动是什么？"再次强调，要对大部分成员及其优势达成共识。同样，任何分歧，都要严肃认真对待。

接下来，继续问："根据自身优势，每个人应承担哪项关键活动，并作为其首要责任呢？某个关键活动，应该由谁负责呢？"

随后就可以开始组建团队了。创始人要自我约束，如果自己并非最佳人选，就不要对人事管理和相关问题加以干预。也许他的核心优势是新产品和新技术；也许他的关键活动是运营、制造、物流和服务；也许他擅长资金和财务，而其他人更擅长人事管理。但是，所有关键活动应与负责人的关键能力匹配。

从来没有规定要求"首席执行官必须负责某件事"。当然，首席执行官是最终决策者，负有最终责任。此外，首席执行官要确保可以获得必要的信息，以履行这一最终责任。首席执行官的工作取决于企业的需求以及自身条件。只要首席执行官的工作内容包含了关键活动，他就履行了首席执行官的责任。首席执行官要确保所有关键活动都由合适的人负责。

最后，企业要对每个关键领域设定目标。关键活动的主要负责人，无论是产品开发、人事，还是财务管理，都要思考："你能为企业做什么？你应该负责什么？你能完成什么事情，何时完成？"当然，这是管理的基本问题。

在一开始，建立一个非正式的高层管理团队是十分明智的。对发展中的新创企业来说，无须给予员工头衔，也不必公开宣布，甚至不需要支付额外薪酬。大约 1 年后，等新的团队确实发挥作用之时，再实施这些举措。在此期间，团队所有的成员可以学到很多：他们如何工作，如何协同工作，如何协助首席执行官和同事工作。两三年后，当企业发展到需要高层管理团队时，高层管理团队就在那里。

但是，如果企业需要高层管理团队时却无法具备这样一个高层管理团队的话，那事实上，早在这个需求产生之前，企业已丧失了自我管理能力。创始人肩上的担子过重，以致他无法完成重要的工作。此时，企业可能出现两种情况。第一种可能性是，创始人基于自身能力和兴趣，专注于一两个领域。这些领域的确关键，但并非所有的关键领域，其他关键领域将无人顾及。两年后，由于重要领域遭到忽视，企业再次陷入困境。另一种可能性是，创始人富有责任心，这更为糟糕。创始人清楚地知道人员和资金是关键要素，需要多加关注。他的能力和兴趣在于新产品的设计和开发，事实上也是该企业赖以成立的基础。但是，出于强烈的责任心，创始人强迫自己管理人员和资金。由于缺乏相应的能力，他在这两个领域都表现不佳。此外，针对这些领域，他要花费时间制定决策并开展工作。这样，他就忽视了自己真正擅长且企业也依赖于他的领域，即开发新技术和新产品。三年后，这家企业成为一个空壳，没有产品，没有人事管理，也没有资金管理。

在第一种情况下，企业也许能得以挽救。毕竟，它还有产品。但是，无论谁来拯救企业，创始人终将被其取代。在第二种情况下，企业已无重生机会，只能被迫出售或清算。

新创企业在需要之前，就应该着手建立高层管理团队。在个人管理无法奏效，出现管理混乱之前，创始人就应该学习与同事协作、信任他人、让他人承担责任。创始人必须学习成为团队的领导者，而非有很多"帮手"的"明星"。

VI

"我将在哪里贡献自己的才智"

建立高层管理团队可能是新创企业进行创业管理最重要的一步。但是，对创始人来说，这只是第一步，他们还要考虑自己的未来。

随着新创企业的发展，创业者的角色和关系出现无法阻挡的变化。如果创始人不愿接受这一事实，他们可能会阻碍企业的发展，甚至使其走向灭亡。

每个企业创始人都认同这一观点。每个人都曾听说，有的创始人由于没有根据企业的变化而加以改变，致使企业和自身毁灭的可怕故事。但是，有些创始人即便知道要有所行动，却很少知道如何应对自身角色和关系的变化。一开始，他们往往会自问："我喜欢做什么？"最好的情况下，他们可能会问："我适合做什么？"而正确的问题应该是："客观来看，企业的未来发展需要何种管理方式？"对于成长中的新创企业，无论何时，当企业（或公共服务机构）显著发展时，或者改变方向和特征（即改变产品、服务、市场或人才）时，创始人必须自问这个问题。

接下来，创始人还必须自问："我擅长什么？在企业的所有需求中，我能有什么独特的贡献呢？"只有对这两个问题仔细思考之后，创始人才应该问："我真正想做什么？我的信念是什么？如果不是讲余生所有时间，那未来几年我最想做什么？这是企业真正的需求吗？这是重要的、必要的、不可或缺的贡献吗？"

第二次世界大战后，美国纽约的佩斯大学，就是一个成功的例子。1947年，爱德华·莫托拉（Edward Mortola）博士白手起家创办了这所学校。这所学校发展很快，已经成为纽约第三大的学校，拥有 25 000 名学生和几个著名的研究生院。在大学创立初期，莫托拉是一个激进的创新者。但是，大约在 1950 年，佩斯大学的规模尚小，他就开始建立强大的高层管理团队。团队成员都有明确的职责分工，对此承担全部责任并发挥领导作用。几年后，莫托拉明确自身角色，即成为一名传统的大学校长。与此同时，他成立一个强大的理事会，以获取建议和支持。

但是，企业需要什么，企业创始人的优势是什么，创始人想做什么，这些问题的答案可能截然不同。

例如，埃德温·兰德，即宝丽来镜片和宝丽来相机的发明者，从企业创立开始，到 20 世纪 50 年代初，这 12～15 年间一直负责企业的经营。随后，企业开始快速成长。兰德着手组建了一个高层管理团队，并付诸实践。至于他自己，他认为自己并非高层管理者的最佳人选。他所能做的就是科技创新，而且只有他能胜任。因此，兰德创建了一个实验室，并担任企业基础研究的咨询总监。企业的日常运营，则由其他人负责。

麦当劳的创始人雷·克罗克，也做出过类似的结论。克罗克在去世之前，即 80 多岁时，一直担任企业的董事长。但是，他组建了高层管理团队来管理企业，并自我任命为企业的"营销良心"。在他去世前不久，他每周都会光顾两三家麦当劳餐厅，审查它们的质量、卫生状况和服务态度。最重要的是，他会去了解顾客，与他们交流，倾听他们的声音。这使得企业做出必要的改变，以维持其在快餐界的领导地位。

美国太平洋西北地区的一个建筑供应商，是一家规模较小的新创企业，也是类似的例子。年轻的创始人认为他的职责不是经营企业，而是发展企业的关键资源，即支持位于小城镇和郊区的 200 个分公司的经理。事实上，这些经理都在经营本地业务。他们得到了总部的大力支持：统一采购、质量控制、信贷控制和应收账款控制，等等。不过，分公司经理负责销售工作，得到的帮助也有限，可能只有一个销售人员和两三个卡车司机。

企业的发展取决于这些独立的、经验不足的分公司经理的动机、内驱力、工作能力和工作热情。他们都没有大学文凭，有些甚至连高中都没毕业。因此，该企业的创始人每月都会花 12～15 天去分公司实地察看，花上半天时间与分公司经理讨论他们的业务、计划和志向。这可能是该企业区别于其他建筑商的唯一之处。除此之外，所有的建筑商都是一样的。但是，首席执行官的这一关键举措，使得企业的增长速度是竞争者的三四倍。即便在经济衰退时期，也是如此。

然而，对于同样的问题，有三位科学家的回答完全不同。他们合伙创办了一家企业，现在是业内最大、最成功的半导体企业之一。他们自问"企业的需求是什么"，有三个答案："一个是基本业务战略，一个是科学研究和开发，还有一个是人才培养，尤其是科技人才。"随后，根据个人专长，他们分配最适合每个人的任务。负责人际关系和员工发展的是一位出色的科技创新者，并在科技界享有盛名。而他和同伴都认为，他适合管理工作，尤其是人事管理。于是，他接受了这项工作。在一次演讲中，他曾说："这并非我真正想做的事，却是我能做出最大贡献的地方。"

这些事情的结局并非总是皆大欢喜，有时它们甚至会导致创业者出走。

美国一家成功的新型金融服务企业的创始人，就遇到了这种情况。他确实创建了高层管理团队，并探讨了企业的需求。在自我审视之后，他发现自身能力与企业需求不符，更不必说自己真正想做的事情与企业需求的相关性了。他说："我用 18 个月培养了一个接班人，将企业交接给他，然后离职。"随后，他又创办了三家企业，无一属于金融领域。等企业发展到中等规模时，他再次离职。他想要创办新企业，但不愿经营它们。他早已接受这一事实：到某个阶段，他必须离开企业。

同样的情况下，其他创业者可能会有不同的结果。一家知名医疗诊所的创始人，也是某个领域的领军人物，面临着类似的困境。该诊所需要的是管理者和筹资人。但是，创始人却想要成为研究员和临床医生。他认识到，自己擅长于筹集资金，也能学会担任大规模医疗机构的首席执行官。他说："我应该承担起对诊所和同事的责任。因此，我克制自己的欲望，成为管理者和筹资人。但是，如果不是我认为自己具备相应的能力，并且我的顾问和董事会也让我深信于此，我可能永远不会担任如此重任。"

一旦新创企业有成功的征兆，企业创始人就要思考："我到底属于哪个领域？"当然，创始人也可以提前思考这一问题。事实上，早在新创企业创立之前，就可以对其加以思考。

日本本田汽车公司的创始人本田宗一郎，就是这样做的。第二次世界大战惨败后，日本陷入黑暗时代时，本田宗一郎打算创办一家小企业。直到找到合适的合伙人来负责行政、财务、分销、营销、销售和人事之后，他才开始创办企业。因为本田宗一郎从一开始就清楚地知道，他属于工程和生产领域，不会处理其他业务。正是这一决策，成就了本田汽车公司。

亨利·福特的事例更早，也更有启示意义。1903 年，亨利·福特决定从商，他的做法与 40 多年后的本田如出一辙：在创办企业之前，找到最佳合伙人来负责他不擅长的领域，如行政、财务、分销、营销、销售和人事。和本田一样，亨利·福特也知道自己属于工程和制造领域，而且只负责这两个领域。他的合伙人是詹姆斯·卡曾斯（James Couzens）⊖，他为企业做出的贡献堪比亨利·福特。福特汽车公司有许多著名的策略和做法，例如，1913 年著名的 5 美元日薪制、开拓性的分销和服务策略。这些成就曾被归功于亨利·福特，但其实是卡曾斯的想法，甚至起初还遭到亨利的反对。卡曾斯的成就如此之高，使得亨利·福特越来越嫉妒他，最终于 1917 年卡曾斯不得已退出福特公司。导致其退出的最后一根稻草是，卡曾斯坚持认为 T 型车已经过时，并建议将巨额利润的一部分用于研制后继车型。

就在卡曾斯退出之日，福特汽车公司的发展和繁荣随之结束。短短几个月内，福特掌握了高层管理者的所有职权，将先前的自我认知完全抛到脑后。很快，福特汽车公司江河日下。在长达 10 年内，亨利·福特依然固守 T 型车，一直到它无人问津。在卡曾斯被解雇后的 30 年里，福特公司一直在走下坡路，无法扭转。等亨利·福特去世，他的孙子亨利·福特二世接管公司时，福特公司已濒临破产。

局外人建议的必要性

上述例子表明，在新创企业处于发展阶段时，企业家需要局外人的独

⊖ 卡曾斯后来当选底特律市长和密歇根州参议员。如果不是出生在加拿大，他甚至可能会当选美国总统。

立、客观的建议。

发展中的新创企业也许并不需要正式的董事会。通常情况下，董事会也不能为创始人提供所需的建议和忠告。但是，创始人确实需要与他人讨论基本决策，并获取建议。企业内部却很少有这样的人。对创始人、对企业需求和个人能力的评估，他们要客观地评判。作为企业发展的旁观者，他们要提出问题和审视决策，最重要的是，他们要持续推动企业，使其以市场为中心，具有财务远见，并拥有高效的高层管理团队，最终实现新创企业的长期生存。这是新创企业进行创业管理的最终要求。

如果新创企业能将创业管理融入自身策略和实践，那它一定能成为一个蓬勃向上的大企业。[⊖]

许多新创企业，尤其是高科技企业，对本章讨论的方法不屑一顾。他们认为：这些只构成"管理"，但"我们是企业家"。这并不是随意说说，而是不负责任的说法。这是对行为和实质的一种混淆。有一句古话是这样说的：自由是法律之内的自由。没有法律的自由只是特许，很快就会成为无政府状态，不久之后沦为暴政。正因为新创企业必须保持和加强企业家精神，它必须要有远见和规则。新创企业要想成功，就要达到成功所需的条件。最重要的是，它需要人们有责任感，这就是创业管理赋予新创企业的。

关于新创企业的管理、融资、人事、营销等，还有很多可以讨论，但这些问题在许多出版物中已经详细阐述。[⊜]本章主要是找出并讨论，对新创企业的生存和成功都至关重要的一些简单策略。此处新创企业可以是商业机构或公共服务机构，是"高科技企业""低科技企业"或"非科技企业"，是由个人经营的企业或团体创立的企业，也可以是愿意保持小规模的企业或要成为"另一个 IBM"的企业。

⊖　关于此过程的阐述，详见《高产出管理》（New York: Random House，1983），作者是英特尔公司总裁安迪·格鲁夫，也是英特尔的创始人之一。英特尔公司是世界上最大的半导体制造商之一。

⊜　请参考本书结尾的推荐书目。

3

创业战略

INNOVATION AND ENTREPRENEURSHIP
PRACTICE AND PRINCIPLES

正如企业家精神需要创业管理（即企业内部的实践和策略），同样地，企业家精神也需要企业外部的实践和策略，即在市场中开展创业战略。

"孤注一掷"

近年来，"企业战略"⊖已成为一个时髦词汇。市面上关于企业战略的书籍有很多⊜。但是，我至今尚未看到任何专注于创业战略的讨论。尽管如此，创业战略依然十分重要和与众不同。

具体来说，主要有以下四种创业战略：

- 孤注一掷。

- 攻其软肋。

- 寻找并占据一个"生态利基"。

⊖ 根据《简明牛津词典》1952 年版，战略一词仍被定义为："将才；战争的艺术；对军队或对竞选团体的管理。" 1962 年，钱德勒（Alfred D. Chandler, Jr.）在其开创性著作《战略与结构》中，首次将"战略"一词引入商业领域。该书阐述大公司中管理的演变。但此后不久，当我于 1963 年首次撰写关于企业战略的著作时，我和出版商都发现，用"战略"作为书名会引起严重的误解。书商、杂志编辑及资深企业管理者都一致认为，对他们来说，"战略"意味着军事或选举活动。因此，尽管我在书中使用了"战略"一词，但书名是《为成果而管理》。事实上，我的那本书所讨论的大部分内容，就是今天人们所说的"战略"。

⊜ 在这其中，我认为迈克尔·波特（Michael Porter）的《竞争战略》（New York: Free Press, 1980）最为有用。

• 改变产品、市场或一个产业的经济特征。

这四种战略并非相互排斥。企业家通常会把两个，有时甚至是三个战略的要素整合到一个战略中。而且，这四个战略并非总是界线分明的。例如，相同的战略行为既可以归入"攻其软肋"，又能归入"寻找并占据一个'生态利基'"。不过，这四个战略都有其先决条件。每个战略通常只适用于某些特定类型的创新，需要企业家执行特定的行为，最后，每个战略都具有独特的局限性和风险。

I

孤注一掷

美国南北战时期，南部联邦骑兵部队的一位将军凭借"孤注一掷"（Fastest with the Mostest）连连取胜。采用这种战略的企业家的目标是：即便不在新市场或新产业中占据主导地位（统治），也要取得领导地位（领先）。尽管"孤注一掷"并非要立刻成立一家大企业，但这通常是它的终极目标。该战略从一开始就旨在获取永久性的领导地位。

许多人都将"孤注一掷"视为一项杰出的创业战略。如果按照现在畅销的创业书籍所传达的观点[⊖]，人们确实会认为"孤注一掷"是唯一的创业战略。许多企业家，特别是高科技企业家，似乎也持有相同的观点。

然而，他们都错了。不可否认，有很多企业家选择了这一战略。然而，"孤注一掷"甚至称不上是主要的创业战略，更谈不上是创业战略中风险最低或成功率最高的那一个。恰恰相反，在所有的创业战略中，这个战略的风险最大，犹如一场赌博。因为它不允许出现任何失误，也没有重来的机会。

⊖ 乔治·吉尔德（George Gilder）的 *The Spirit of Enterprise* （New York: Simon & Schuster, 1984），也许是这一流派值得阅读的一书。

但实施该战略一旦成功，"孤注一掷"就会为企业带来十分可观的回报。

下面几个例子说明了"孤注一掷"的战略内容和战略要求。

多年来，瑞士的霍夫曼罗氏公司一直是全球最大、也可能最赚钱的制药公司。但在成立之初，它极不显眼。20世纪20年代中期之前，霍夫曼罗氏公司只生产几种纺织染料，为了生存而苦苦挣扎，它被德国的大型印染制造商和两三家国内比它规模大得多的化学公司压得喘不过气。当时，研究者新发现的维生素尚未得到科学界的普遍认可。但是，霍夫曼罗氏公司仍决定将赌注押到这些新物质上。它先是买下这些无人问津的维生素专利，并用高于大学教授几倍的薪资待遇，从苏黎世大学聘请了维生素的那些发现者，这种待遇在业界闻所未闻。随后，霍夫曼罗氏公司又将全部资金和贷款用于生产和销售维生素。

60年后，即便维生素的专利早已过了有效期，霍夫曼罗氏公司也已经占据了世界维生素市场近一半的份额。如今，它已经成长为年收入高达几十亿美元的制药巨头。后来，这家公司又两度使用了该战略：一次是在20世纪30年代，当时，大多数科学家都认为磺胺类药品不能有效抗感染，霍夫曼罗氏公司却毅然进军磺胺类药品市场；另一次是在20年后，即20世纪50年代中期，当时几乎所有科学家都对镇静剂持怀疑态度，认为这些东西是"异类"，霍夫曼罗氏公司仍全力投产了利眠宁（也称为氯氮卓）和安定两种镇静剂药物。

杜邦公司也采用过同样的战略来获取成功。经过了15年的艰苦探索和无数次失败的洗礼，杜邦公司成功发明了尼龙，这是第一种真正意义上的合成纤维。随即，杜邦公司付出了巨大努力，建立大型工厂、投放大量的广告（它先前从未对消费品做过广告），最终，它开创了我们现在所称的塑胶行业。

也许有人会说，这些都是"大公司"的故事，但事实上，霍夫曼罗氏公司在创立之初只是一家默默无闻的小公司。下面是近年来的一些企业的事例。这些企业起初一无所有，凭借实施"孤注一掷"战略取得成功。

文字处理器并不能称得上是"科学"发明。它只是将打字机、显示器和比较基础的计算机，这三种现有仪器整合在一起。但是，这些现有仪器的组合却带来了真正的创新，并从根本上改变了办公室内的工作方式。20世纪50年代中期，当王安博士（Dr. An Wang）构思这种组合时，他只是一个没有任何创业经验和财务支持的个体创业者。但显然，他从一开始就决心要改变传统办公室的工作模式，创立一个全新产业。如今，王安实验室确实成了一家规模庞大的公司。

苹果公司在成立之初的境况，同样如此。两名年轻的工程师在车库里白手起家，没有财务支持，也没有商业经验。但是从一开始，他们就立志创立一个产业，并成为这个产业的主导者。

尽管"孤注一掷"旨在创办能够主导市场的企业，但并非所有采用这一战略的企业都想成为大企业。明尼苏达州圣保罗市的3M公司，从未尝试通过创新（这似乎是经过深思熟虑的商业策略）成为大企业。强生公司，作为一个卫生保健用品制造商，也采取了同样的策略。这两家企业都是成功的创新者，利润也很高。它们开展创新并非为了成为巨头企业，而是成为中等规模的企业。然而，正是这使它们成了市场主导者。

"孤注一掷"并非仅限于商业企业，也适用于公共服务机构。正如前文提到的，1809年，当洪堡创办柏林大学时，他显然也运用了"孤注一掷"战略。当时，普鲁士被拿破仑打得一败涂地，差点惨遭解体。无论从政治、军事，还是财务来看，普鲁士都已陷入破产困境。这种境况与1945年希特勒战败后的德国非常相似。但是，洪堡却创办了西方世界有史以来规模最大的大学，其规模是当时已有的单所大学的三四倍。随后，他开始聘请各个学科的顶尖学者，受聘的第一位学者是当时的哲学泰斗黑格尔（Georg W. F. Hegel）。拿破仑战争后，很多历史悠久的知名大学被迫解体，许多一流学者即将沦为乞丐。然而，洪堡支付给教授们的薪资，是他们先前薪资的10倍。

100 年后，也就是 20 世纪初，罗彻斯特（Rochester）小镇的两名外科医生梅奥兄弟决定建立一个医疗中心。罗彻斯特是明尼苏达州的一个偏远小镇，远离人口中心和医学院。这个医疗中心应用了全新的医疗理念（在当时被视为"异端"），并拥有一支由杰出专家和一名负责协调的领导组成的医疗团队。被誉为"科学管理之父"的弗雷德里克·泰勒（Frederick William Taylor）从未见过梅奥兄弟，但在 1911 年著名的国会听证会上，他宣称梅奥诊所是他所知的"唯一彻底地实践科学管理，并大获成功的机构"。从一开始，这两个不知名的地方医生就旨在获得该领域的主导地位，力求吸引医学各分支领域内杰出的临床医生和最有天赋的年轻人，并吸引那些有能力也愿意支付高昂医疗费用的病人。

25 年后，美国出生缺陷基金会（March of Dimes）在研究小儿麻痹症时，也采用了"孤注一掷"战略。早期的医疗研究机构都是一步一步地收集新知识。而美国出生缺陷基金会从一开始就决心攻克这种神秘疾病。在此之前，从未有人组织过"无界研究实验室"（research lab without walls），即针对事先拟定的研究项目，委派许多研究机构的大批科学家，负责特定阶段的工作。美国出生缺陷基金会建立了这种模式。后来，美国将其用于组织第二次世界大战中的第一批伟大的研究项目：原子弹、雷达实验室、低空爆炸引信，还有 15 年后的登月计划。这些创新工作都采用了"孤注一掷"战略。

这些例子表明，"孤注一掷"首先要有一个雄心勃勃的目标，否则它必将失败。它通常旨在建立一个新产业或开拓一个新市场。至少，如同梅奥诊所或美国出生缺陷基金会一样，创建一个非同寻常的流程。20 世纪 20 年代中期，当杜邦公司邀请卡罗瑟斯时，企业人员肯定没有宣称"我们要建立塑胶产业"（事实上，塑胶这个术语直到 20 世纪 50 年代才被使用），但是，当时大量的内部出版物显示，杜邦的高层管理者确实打算创建一个新产业。他们无法确定卡罗瑟斯以及他的研究是否会成功。但是，他们知道，一旦成功，他们将会获得一项全新的发现，这项新发现远远超过了一种产品或一条重要的产品线。据我所知，王安博士并没有创造"未来办公室"一词。但是，在他的第一支广告中，他描绘了一个全新的办公环境，并提出了办公室工作的新理念。从一开始，杜邦公司和王安实验室就旨在创办一个新产业，并成为该产业的主导者。

要说最能体现"孤注一掷"的例子并非企业，而是洪堡创办的柏林大学。事实上，洪堡对大学毫无兴趣。对他来说，大学只是用来建立新政治秩序的手段而已。这种新秩序不同于18世纪的君主专制，也不同于资产阶级主导的法国大革命所倡导的民主制。确切地说，它是一种均衡制度。在这种制度下，公务员与军官的选拔和晋升，都严格按照功绩遴选，与政治无关。他们在自己的工作领域内，享有充分的自主权。这些人，即我们现在所说的技术专家，只承担有限的任务，并受独立的专职司法机构的严格监管。但是，在自己从事的领域内，他们就是主人。而资产阶级在两个领域内仍享有个人自由的权利，一个是道德和文化自由，另一个是经济自由。

洪堡还著书立说，阐述这些思想。[○]1806年，拿破仑彻底摧毁了普鲁士的君主专制制度。国王、贵族、军队等（这些可能会阻碍洪堡的新思想）随之瓦解。洪堡抓住机会，创办柏林大学，并将其视为传播政治思想的主要载体，大获成功。的确，柏林大学建立了独特的政治结构，也就是19世纪的德国人所称的"法治国家"。在这个政治结构中，公务员和参谋员等自主自治的精英，控制了政治和军事领域；知识分子中的自主自治的精英与自治的大学，共同营造了"自由的"文化氛围；还创造了一种自主的、不受限制的经济社会。这种政治结构首先赋予了普鲁士道德和文化上的优越感，随后又使德国获得了政治和经济上的优势。很快，德国在欧洲取得领导地位，受到外界的推崇，特别是英国和德国。直到1890年左右，它们依旧将德国视为文化和知识领域的标杆。这一切都是洪堡在普鲁士惨败后陷入绝望时所设想

○ 书名为 *The Limits on the Effectiveness of Government*，这是少数几本由德国人撰写的关于政治哲学方面的早期著作之一。

出来的。事实上，在柏林大学的计划书和章程中，他已明确这一目标。

也许因为"孤注一掷"必须要建立前所未有的新事物，因此非专业人士和局外人的表现与专家似乎一样好。事实上，相比专家，他们的表现更为出色。比如，霍夫曼罗氏公司战略的制定者不是化学家，而是音乐家。这位音乐家是创始人的孙女婿。他之所以如此，是因为公司的微薄红利不足以支持他的管弦乐队。直至今日，霍夫曼罗氏公司也从未交由化学家管理，通常由曾在瑞士大型银行任职的金融人士管理。洪堡则是一名外交官，之前与学术界从未有过交集。杜邦公司的高层管理者都是商人，而非化学家或研究人员。虽然梅奥兄弟是受过良好训练的外科医生，但他们与医疗中心并无接触。

当然，也有真正的"业内人士"，如王安博士、3M 公司的人员、设计苹果电脑的年轻计算机工程师。但是，就"孤注一掷"来说，局外人可能具有独特优势。局外人不知道业内众所周知的知识，因此也不知道其中的禁忌。

II

"孤注一掷"战略必须一举击中，否则就会失去一切。打个比方，"孤注一掷"犹如登月发射：角度稍有 1 度偏差，火箭就会消失在外太空中。"孤注一掷"战略一旦实施，就很难加以调整或修正。

也就是说，要采用这种战略，需要仔细思考和审慎分析。大众文学或好莱坞电影中所描述的创业者，突然灵光乍现，并迅速付诸实践，这并不会取得成功。事实上，要使这个战略成功，创新必须是在深思熟虑的基础上，充分挖掘一个重要的创新机会（第 3～9 章提到的）。

例如，洪堡的柏林大学就是利用"认知变化"的最佳案例。在法国大革命和拿破仑战争后，资产阶级知识分子对政治失去了幻想。他们不愿重回18 世纪的君主专制时代，更不用说封建时代了。他们需要一种毫无政治色彩的"自由的"氛围，也需要一个不带政治色彩的政府，即一个基于他们所信奉的法律和教育原则而建立的政府。这些资产阶级知识分子都是亚当·斯密的追随者。在那个时代，斯密的《国富论》可能是读者最多和最受推崇的政治书籍。洪堡的政治结构正是利用这一机会，使得他的柏林大学从计划变为现实。

王安的文字处理器则是巧妙地利用了流程需求。20世纪70年代，办公人员对计算机的恐惧刚刚消除，转而好奇道："计算机能为我做什么？"那时，他们逐渐熟悉利用计算机来工作，如编制工资单或控制库存，而且他们也有了复印机，办公室用纸量随之快速上升。就在这时，王安的文字处理器出现了。它主要针对那些不能自动化处理，同时也是办公人员所痛恨的琐事：誊写信函、发言稿、报告、手稿。这些文件往往需要小的改动，而不得不一遍又一遍地重做。

20世纪20年代初，霍夫曼罗氏公司利用新知识，将维生素作为发展方向。众所周知，哲学家托马斯·库恩写了著名的《科学革命的结构》一书。而早在30年前，那个音乐家，也就是霍夫曼罗氏公司的战略制定者，就深知"科学革命的结构"的内涵。他知道一项基本科学原理即便已经有大量证据支持，如果它与科学家所信奉的基本原理相违背，那么也不会被科学家认可。直到旧"范式"和旧理论不再适用，他们才会关注这个新原理，否则很长一段时间内，他们都会置之不理。在此期间，那些接受新原理并付诸实践的人，就拥有了新领域。

只有审慎地分析，"孤注一掷"才可能取得成功。

即便如此，它还需要极度专注。创新者必须要有明确的目标，并为之倾注一切努力。当努力有所成效时，他要做好大规模资源调配的准备。杜邦公司刚刚研制出可用的合成纤维时，就立刻着手建立大型工厂，向纺织制造商和普通公众投放广告，进行产品试验演示，发放样品。而这一切，都早在市场有所回应之前。

然后，当创新成功之时，才是工作的真正开始。"孤注一掷"要求创新者投入持续的努力，才能保持领导地位。否则，它所做的一切只是为竞争者创造市场而已。居于主导地位的创新者要比之前更加努力，持续大规模地推进创新工作。相比之前，创新成功之后的研究预算也要更多。此外，还要探索新用途，开拓新客户并说服他们尝试新产品。最重要的是，成功实施"孤注一掷"的企业家必须赶在竞争者之前，淘汰自己的产品或工艺。对于成功的产品或工艺，要立即研发其后继产品，与先前一样专注，投入同样的资源。

最后，通过"孤注一掷"取得领导地位的企业家，必须系统地降低其产品和工艺的价格。维持高价只是为潜在的竞争者撑起"保护伞"而已，并给予他们激励（详见下一章"攻其软肋"）。

这是由经济史中最长久的私人垄断组织（即炸药卡特尔）所提出的。阿尔弗雷德·诺贝尔（Alfred Nobel）发明炸药后，建立了这个组织。直到第一次世界大战，甚至之后，炸药卡特尔一直占据全球垄断地位。当时，诺贝尔的专利早已失效。它之所以能够维持地位，是因为采取了降价策略：每当需求增加 10%～20%，它就会降价。当时，卡特尔组织内的企业已经收回全部投资，可以用这种方式来消化剩余产能。这样，潜在竞争者就不愿建立新的炸药厂，而卡特尔依然盈利。毫不意外，杜邦公司在美国也始终遵循这一策略，因为它也是炸药卡特尔的美国成员。王安的文字处理器、苹果的计算机、3M 的所有产品，也都贯彻这个策略。

III

这些都是成功的案例。它们并没有表明"孤注一掷"的风险究竟有多大。因为这些例子没有提到任何失败。我们知道，尽管很多人凭借这个战略而成功，但更多人以失败告终。在运用"孤注一掷"战略时，只有一次机会。

如果没有即刻奏效，它就会一败涂地。

瑞士神箭手威廉·泰尔（Wilhelm Tell）的故事家喻户晓。只有他第一箭能够射中儿子头上的苹果，暴君才会赦免他；否则，要么儿子中箭身亡，要么他被杀死。这正是企业家实施"孤注一掷"时的处境。"孤注一掷"，没有"几乎成功"或"差点失败"，只有成功或失败。

成功往往在事后才为人所知。但至少，我们从以下例子得知，它们离失败只有一步之遥，因为运气和机会才幸免于难。

尼龙算是侥幸的成功。在 20 世纪 30 年代中期，合成纤维根本没有市场。相比于棉纱和人造纤维（也就是当时比较便宜的纤维），尼龙价格过高而没有竞争力。事实上，它甚至比丝绸还要昂贵。丝绸是一种奢侈纤维，30 年代末期，日本陷入经济大萧条，被迫抛售丝绸。第二次世界大战爆发后，日本停止出口丝绸，这使尼龙得以生存。等到 1950 年左右，日本重振丝绸产业时，尼龙已经稳占市场，其成本和价格只是 30 年代末期的一小部分。3M公司的著名产品，即透明胶带，同样如此。若非意外事件，它也难逃失败。

"孤注一掷"的风险如此之高，另一个重要战略就是基于"孤注一掷"的失败的可能性远高于成功的可能性这一假定提出的（该重要战略是"创造性模仿"，我们将在下一章讨论）。"孤注一掷"战略之所以失败，可能是因为意志力不足，也可能是因为努力不够。尽管创新取得成功，但是由于资源不足，资源不能充分发挥效用等，该战略仍会失败。虽然"孤注一掷"的成功会带来巨额回报，但由于风险和难度较高，它只适用于重大创新。例如，洪堡成功地创建一个新政治秩序；霍夫曼罗氏公司利用维生素开拓一个新的医药领域；梅奥兄弟开创医疗诊断和实践的新方式。事实上，它只适用于极少部分创新。它要求对创新的来源及动态进行深入分析，并做到真正了解。它需要极度专注，以及大量资源投入。在大多数情况下，其他可用的战略更为合适。这并非因为其他战略风险较低，而是因为大多数创新所带来的机会不足以弥补"孤注一掷"战略所需的成本、努力和资源。

第 17 章 │ CHAPTER 17

"攻其软肋"

美国南北战争时期，一位南方常胜将军说道："攻击敌人脆弱的地方。"这句话提出两种不同的创业战略："创造性模仿"和"创业柔道"。

I

创造性模仿

从字面上看，"创造性模仿"[⊖]显然自相矛盾。"创造性"必然是"原创"，而"原创"意味着不是模仿。但是，这个词很贴切。它描述了一种本质上是"模仿"的战略。企业家所做的事情，是他人已经做过的。之所以称它是"创造性"，是因为相比于最初的创新者，运用"创造性模仿"的企业家更加深

⊖ 这个词由哈佛商学院的西奥多·莱维特（Theodore Levitt）提出。

知该项创新的意义。

IBM 最早采用了这一战略，并取得了极大的成功。为获得并保持在肥皂、清洁剂和化妆品市场的领导地位，宝洁公司也广泛地采用这一战略。另外，日本服部精工株式会社也将其市场主导地位归功于创造性模仿，其精工手表已成为世界领导者。

20 世纪 30 年代初期，为了纽约哥伦比亚大学的天文学家的计算工作，IBM 制造了一台高速计算器。几年后，为了哈佛大学的天文计算，它又研制了一台类似于计算机的机器。第二次世界大战末期，IBM 制造出第一台真正意义上的计算机，具备真正计算机的特征："内存"和"编程能力"。但是，很少有历史书将 IBM 视为计算机的发明者，这一点很好解释。IBM 在 1945 年刚研制出高级计算机（这是在纽约市中心展示厅的第一台计算机，吸引大批观众观看）后不久，就放弃了自己的设计，转而采用了竞争对手的设计，即宾夕法尼亚大学研发的 ENIAC。ENIAC 更适用于商业用途，如薪酬发放，但其设计者并未发现这一点。IBM 对 ENIAC 进行重新设计，使它能够大批量生产和维修，并进行普通的"数据处理"。当 IBM 生产的 ENIAC 于 1953 年推出时，立刻成为多功能大型商用计算机的标准。

这就是"创造性模仿"。当其他企业创造出新事物，有待改进之时，它才开始采取行动。很快，它就知道如何满足客户需求，为客户想要并愿意为之买单的产品而工作。随后，"创造性模仿"制定标准，占领市场。

在个人电脑方面，IBM 再次采用了创造性模仿战略。个人电脑的构想源于苹果公司。如前所述（详见第 3 章），IBM 的人都"知道"，这种独立式小型电脑是个错误。它既不经济，也远非完善，而且很昂贵。然而，它却大获成功。随后，IBM 立即着手设计一种机器，以使其成为个人电脑领域的标准，主导该领域，至少成为该领域的领先者。结果，PC 机出现了。两年之内，它就取代苹果公司成为个人电脑领域的领导者，并成为最畅销的品牌和行业标准。

宝洁公司在清洁用品、肥皂、化妆品及加工食品领域，也采用了同样的做法。

半导体问世后，钟表行业的业内人士都清楚，相比于传统手表，用半导体做动力的手表走得更精确、更可靠，而且也更便宜。瑞士钟表公司很快拿出了石英电子表方案。但是，由于之前在传统手表中的大量投入，它们决定逐步推出石英电子表。在这段漫长的时间里，这些新手表依然是昂贵的奢侈品。

与此同时，日本服部精工株式会社（原本是日本市场中的传统手表制造商），看到了这个机会。随后，它立即采取了创造性模仿战略，将石英电子表发展成为业界标准。等到瑞士钟表公司觉醒时，一切为时已晚。精工手表已成为世界上的畅销手表，而瑞士钟表公司几乎被挤出市场。

正如"孤注一掷"，创造性模仿战略也旨在成为市场或产业中的主导者，至少是市场或行业中的领导者。但是，相比之下，创造性模仿战略的风险要小得多。当创造性模仿者开始行动时，市场已形成，新生事物也已得到认可。事实上，市场需求已超过原始创新者的供应能力。市场细分已经形成，或正在形成。到这个时候，通过市场研究，可以了解客户购买什么、如何购买，以及什么对他们才是有价值的，等等。原始创新者所面临的不确定性大多已消除，至少可以加以分析和研究。企业无须费心解释，个人电脑或电子手表是什么，以及功能如何。

当然，原始创新者也可能一击即中，这样创造性模仿的机会之门就关闭了。从瑞士霍夫曼罗氏公司的维生素、杜邦公司的尼龙或王安实验室的文字处理器来看，创新虽然能成功，但仍存在风险。不过，从采取创造性模仿战略的企业家，以及他们所取得的巨大成功来看，他们通过一击即中抢占市场先机所抢占的优势也并非很大。

另外一个关于创造性模仿的例子是泰诺，它是"非阿司匹林的阿司匹林"。据我所知，这个例子最能说明创造性模仿战略的内容、要求以及如何运用。

对乙酰氨基酚（美国市场的"泰诺"的主要成分）多年来一直被用作止痛药，直到最近，美国才将它列为处方药。在这之前，作为传统的止痛药，阿司匹林一直被认为是绝对安全的，占据止痛药市场。相比之下，对乙酰氨基酚的药性较弱。它能够有效止痛，但没有抗炎作用，对凝血机制也没有影响。因此，对乙酰氨基酚没有副作用。而为治疗关节炎之类的疾病长期大量服用阿司匹林，则会引起副作用，尤其是胃部不适或胃出血。

当乙酰氨基酚还是非处方药时，以其为成分的第一个药剂品牌将目标人群定为那些饱受阿司匹林副作用之苦的患者。它大获成功，事实上，远远超出制造商的预期。正是这项成功，提供了创造性模仿的机会。强生公司意识到抗炎和凝血的问题，阿司匹林的市场有限。取代阿司匹林的止痛药，将会有广阔的市场。从一开始，泰诺就被定位为安全的、适用范围广泛的止痛药。结果，只用了一两年时间，它就占领了市场。

这些例子表明，不同于人们的普遍理解，创造性模仿战略并非利用先行者的失败。相反，先行者必须是成功的。苹果计算机大获成功。在泰诺之前，最早推出对乙酰氨基酚的先行者也曾是市场领导者。但是，当时这些原始创新者并没有理解成功的真正含义。苹果公司以产品为中心，而非客户。在客户需要程序和软件时，它却推出更多的硬件。泰诺的例子也说明了，其原始创新者并未领会他们自己的成功的意义。

创造性模仿者利用了他人的成功。创造性模仿并非通常意义上的"创新"，他们并非发明产品或服务，而是将其完善并重新定位。新事物首次出现时，或多或少会少点什么。可能是产品的额外功能；可能是产品或服务需要进行细分，以满足不同市场的需求；也可能是更合适的市场定位；等等。而创造性模仿则能弥补现有不足。

创造性模仿者从客户的角度来审视产品或服务。从技术层面看，IBM 的个人电脑和苹果并无实质性差异，但 IBM 从一开始将程序和软件提供给客户。苹果利用传统的销售渠道，即专卖店，来进行销售；IBM 则打破自己多年的传统，开拓各种销售渠道，如专卖店、西尔斯之类的主要零售商，自家的零售店，等等。这使客户更容易购买并使用它的产品。恰好这些非硬件，是使得 IBM 占领个人电脑市场的"创新"。

总的来说，"创造性模仿"始于市场而非产品，始于客户而非制造商。它既以市场为中心，又是由市场驱动的。

这些例子表明了创造性模仿战略的要求：

它需要一个快速增长的市场。创造性模仿者获得成功，并不是要从引进新产品或服务的先行者手中抢走客户，而是要为先行者开拓的但并未满足其需求的市场提供服务。创造性模仿战略是要满足现有的需求，而非创造新的需求。

这一战略存在固有的风险，而且风险很大。创造性模仿者往往会分散力量，以规避风险。另外，创造性模仿者可能会误判市场趋势，对那些不能赢得未来市场的创新进行模仿。

作为世界上最杰出的创造性模仿者，IBM 的发展很好地诠释了这些风险。IBM 对办公自动化领域的重要发明都成功地进行了模仿。结果，在每个领域，它都拥有主导产品。但是，由于这些产品都是模仿而来的，种类繁多，彼此之间很难兼容，致使人们无法利用 IBM 的产品建立一个完整的自动化办公系统。IBM 能否保持办公自动化领域的领导地位，并提供一套办公集成系统，实在令人怀疑。而集成系统正是电脑市场的未来发展趋势。由此说明，"过于聪明"是创造性模仿战略的固有风险。

创造性模仿战略在高科技领域可能更为有效，原因很简单：高科技创新者更倾向于以技术或产品为中心，最不可能以市场为中心。因此，他们往往会误解自身的成功，而无法利用并满足他们所创造的需求。正如对乙酰氨基酚和精工表的例子中讲到的一样，它们绝非个例。

由于创造性模仿战略旨在主导市场，它最适用于主流产品、流程或服

务：个人电脑市场、全球手表市场，或者像止痛药这样的巨大市场。相比于
"孤注一掷"，该战略对市场的要求较少，风险也较小。在创造性模仿者开始
行动时，市场已经形成，需求也已经产生。为了弥补风险，在实施创造性模
仿战略时，要高度警惕和灵活，要乐于接受市场的反馈。最重要的是，必须
要努力工作，并投入巨大的努力。

II

创业柔道

1947 年，贝尔实验室发明了晶体管。他们立即意识到，晶体管将取代
真空管，尤其是用于收音机和电视机等消费电子品。每个人都知道这一点，
但是，没有人对此采取行动。当时的领先制造商（都是美国公司）开始研究
晶体管，并计划到"1970 年左右的某个时候"将其转化为真正的产品。他
们宣称，晶体管"尚未准备就绪"。当时的索尼公司（除了在日本，几乎没
人知道）甚至从未涉足消费电子领域。但是，索尼总裁盛田昭夫从报纸上了
解到晶体管后，立即前往美国，并以 2.5 万美元的荒谬价格从贝尔实验室获
得晶体管的许可权。两年后，索尼推出了第一台便携式晶体管收音机，重量
不足市场中真空管收音机的 1/5，成本还不到它的 1/3。三年后，索尼占领了
美国低端收音机市场；五年后，日本占领了全球收音机市场。

当然，这也是一个拒绝意外成功的经典案例。美国人之所以拒绝晶体
管，是因为它是"非我发明"，即并非由电气和电子行业领导者美国无线电
通信公司和通用电气公司所发明的。另外，这个案例也是一个因自大而自
食恶果的典型案例。当时美国人以优质收音机为傲，认为超外差式收音机
（Super Heterodyne sets）彰显其精湛工艺。对比之下，他们对硅片嗤之以鼻，
甚至认为它们有损尊严。

然而，索尼的成功并非个例。日本人一再应用这一战略，一再获得成功，并令美国人惊讶，这该如何解释呢？他们在电视机、电子表和掌上计算器领域，重复采用该战略。他们在进军复印机市场时，也采用这一战略，从原始创新者施乐公司手中夺走大部分市场份额。换句话说，日本人一再地使用"创业柔道"来战胜美国人。

MCI 公司和斯普林特公司也采用了这一战略。它们利用贝尔电话系统的定价体系，拿走了贝尔电话系统的大部分长途电话业务（详见第 6 章）。罗尔姆公司在利用贝尔系统的策略，夺取大部分用户交换机市场时，采用了同样的战略。花旗银行同样如此，它在德国创办了消费者银行，即"家庭银行"。短短几年内，花旗银行就占领了德国的消费金融市场。

德国银行意识到，普通消费者已经拥有购买力，并已是理想的客户。它们走走过场为消费者提供银行服务。但是，事实上，它们并不想要这些客户。它们认为，相比于商业客户和富有的投资者来说，这些散户有损银行的尊严。如果一个消费者确实想要开户，应该去邮政储蓄银行。无论它们的广告如何宣传，当消费者走进当地银行的办事处时，从银行的行为中可以清楚地感知到这些银行对自己没有什么用处。

花旗银行正是利用了这一机遇，在德国创办了家庭银行。它专注于个人消费者，为消费者设计所需的业务，使消费者更易于与银行进行业务往来。尽管德国银行实力雄厚，覆盖面极广，几乎在每个市中心的街道上都有分支机构，但是，仅仅 5 年左右，花旗银行旗下的家庭银行就成了消费者银行业务的主导者。

日本人、MCI 公司、罗尔姆公司以及花旗银行等新进入者，都采用了"创业柔道"。在所有创业战略中，尤其是那些旨在领导或主导某个产业或市场的战略中，"创业柔道"可能是风险最低、成功率最高的战略。

每个警察都知道，惯犯总是以同样的手法作案，无论是撬保险箱还是进大厦抢劫。他都会留下"签名"，如同指纹一般，独一无二。即便这个"签名"会导致他多次被捕，他也不会有所改变。

并非只有罪犯才有这种习惯。人都是如此，企业和产业也是如此。即便某种习惯致使企业一再失去领导地位、失去市场份额，企业依旧会坚守这一习惯。正是由于美国制造商所固守的习惯，日本人才"一而再，再而三"地夺走它们的市场。

如果罪犯被抓，他很少会认为是习惯出卖了他。相反，他会找出各种理由来解释，并坚持使其被捕的习惯。同样，企业也很少会将失败归咎于习惯，反而会找出各种理由来解释。比如，美国电子产品制造商就将日本人的成功归因于日本的廉价劳动力。不过，少数几家美国制造商能够直面现实。例如，电视机制造商美国无线电公司和美国米罗华公司（Magnavox），尽管支付了较高的薪水和福利，但它们的产品在价格和质量上都可以与日本的产品相抗衡。德国银行一致将花旗银行旗下的家庭银行的成功归功于冒险精神，而它们自己不愿冒这种风险。然而，家庭银行在消费贷款方面的信贷损失率低于德国银行，而且其贷款条件同德国银行一样严格。当然，德国银行知道这些情况。不过，它们始终不愿直面自己的失败和家庭银行的成功。这种情况十分典型。这也解释了同一战略，即创业柔道战略，为何可以经久不衰。

在下面五种常见的坏习惯中，新进入者可以采用创业柔道战略，与偏执的现有企业相抗衡，并夺取业界领导地位。

1. 第一个坏习惯是美国俚语所称的"非我发明"（Not Invented Here）。 这种傲慢会使企业或者产业认为，如果一个新事物不是自己发明的，就没有价值。这样，新发明就会遭到轻视。美国电子制造商就是如此对待晶体管的。

2. 第二个坏习惯是从市场撇脂，即只关注高利润领域。

正是由于施乐公司采取了这种做法，复印机才成为日本模仿者的目标。施乐公司把目标瞄准大客户，批量设备或者昂贵的高性能设备的购买者。它并没有拒绝其他客户，但不会主动寻找他们，也没有向他们提供优质的服务。最后，小客户对施乐公司的服务（或者是根本没有服务）不甚满意，进而转向竞争对手。

"撇脂"的做法违背了管理和经济的基本原则，最终受到失去市场的惩罚。

施乐公司取得成功后，便不思进取。的确，它获利颇丰，但企业不能过分地依赖曾经的辉煌。"撇脂"就是试图从过去的成就中获利。这个习惯一旦形成，企业这样持续下去，将很容易遭受创业柔道战略的攻击。

3. 第三个坏习惯更为糟糕，就是迷信"品质"。 产品或服务的"品质"，并非取决于供应商的投入，而是取决于客户所能利用并为之买单的东西。制造商的普遍看法是，产品之所以具有"品质"，是因为它难以生产和成本很高。这纯属谬误。客户只会为那些能够为他们所用并带来价值的东西买单。对"品质"来说，除此之外，别无其他。

20 世纪 50 年代，美国电子制造商深信，具有很棒的真空管的收音机才是有"品质"的产品。这是因为，经过 30 年的努力，它们才制造出更复杂、更庞大、更昂贵的收音机。整个过程需要大量的技术，赋予了真空管收音机更高的"品质"。相比之下，晶体管收音机如此简单，仅仅靠不熟练的流水线工人就能生产出来。但是，从消费者的角度来看，晶体管收音机的"品质"更高。它足够轻便，可以随身携带去海滩或野餐。它也很少出故障，不需要更换晶体管。它价格更低。从接收范围和接收效果来看，与拥有 16 根真空管的超豪华外差式收音机相比，晶体管收音机更为出色。除此之外，真空管容易烧坏，令人困扰。

4. 第四个坏习惯与"撇脂"和"品质"紧密联系，就是对"高价"的错觉。 "高价"容易创造竞争对手。

自法国萨伊和英国大卫·李嘉图（David Ricardo）所处的 19 世纪初期开始，200 多年来，经济学家普遍认为，获取高额利润的唯一方式，除了垄断，就是降低成本。通过抬高价格来获取高额利润，往往会弄巧成拙。这为竞争者撑起"保护伞"。在位的领先企业看似获得高额利润，实际上在补贴新进入者。几年后，这些新进入者会攻击现有企业，取代其领导地位。"高价"并不是享受胜利，也不是提高股价或市盈率的方式，它会引致攻击行为，遭受威胁。

尽管"高价"会为竞争对手采取"创业柔道"提供可乘之机，但为获取高额利润而迷恋"高价"依然是普遍行为。

5. 最后一个坏习惯是力求最大化而非最优化。这个坏习惯常见于现有企业，它会导致企业失败，施乐公司就是一个很好的例子。随着市场的发展，它们试图用同样的产品或服务来满足每个客户的需求。

举个例子来说，用于测试化学反应的新型分析仪器，起初，这个产品的市场有限，假定为产业实验室。随后，大学实验室、研究机构和医院都开始采购这种仪器，但它们的需求有些许不同。于是，为满足不同客户的需求，制造商数次增加产品的功能，直到原本简单的仪器变得异常复杂。制造商将仪器的功能最大化，最后却无法满足任何人的需求。为了尽力满足每个人的需求，结果却适得其反。这种仪器变得非常昂贵，而且难以操作和维护。制造商却以此为傲，用整页的广告列出该仪器的 64 种功能。

毫无疑问，这家制造商将成为创业柔道战略的牺牲品。它自认为的优势，将会阻碍其发展。新进入者将推出满足特定市场（如医院）的仪器。它并不包含医院所不需要的功能，但具备医院所需的全部功能。而且，相比于多功能仪器，它的性能更为完善。随后，这个制造商将陆续推出针对研究实验室、政府实验室、产业实验室的专用仪器。很快，依靠这些为客户量身定制的仪器，新进入者就会占领市场。它所采用的理念是最优化，而非最大化。

同样，当日本人进军复印机市场与施乐公司竞争时，他们也是针对特定客户群体设计机器，如办公室复印机特别适用于牙医、医生和校长的办公室。他们并不推崇产品要具备施乐公司引以为傲的功能（如复印速度、高清晰度等）。他们为小型办公室提供它们迫切需要的产品，即低价的简单复印机。一旦他们在这个市场站稳脚跟，接着就进入其他市场，即针对每个特定细分市场专门设计产品。

索尼公司也采取了同样的策略，首先进军低端收音机市场，即价格低廉、接收范围有限的便携式收音机。一旦在这个市场站稳脚跟，它就开始转向其他细分市场。

"创业柔道"旨在先攻占一个"滩头堡"，也就是领先企业忽略或轻视的环节。比如，花旗银行建立家庭银行时，德国银行置之不理。一旦占领"滩头堡"，也就是说，一旦新进入者赢得足够的市场并获得可观的收益，它们将会拓展到其他"沙滩"，最终占领整个"岛屿"。上述每一个案例中，新进入者采用了同样的战略。它们针对特定的细分市场设计产品或服务，使之最优化。在这场竞争中，领先企业很难战胜它们。在新进入者取得领导地位并主导市场之前，领先企业甚至没有改变自己的行为。

对于下面三种情况，采用"创业柔道"，尤为成功。

第一种情况比较常见，领先企业对意外事件置之不理，无论是意外成功，还是意外失败（要么忽视它，要么拒之门外）。索尼公司就是在这种情况下，抓住了机会。

第二种情况就是施乐公司的那种情况。一项新技术出现，并迅速发展。但是，新技术（或新服务）的创新者，犹如传统的"垄断者"：利用自身的领导地位从市场"撇脂"，制定"高价"。它们或许是不知道，或许是拒绝接受这一既定事实：只有"仁慈的垄断者"（熊彼特提出的名词）才能保持领导地位，更不必说是垄断地位了。

在竞争者降低价格之前，"仁慈的垄断者"会主动降价。在竞争对手推出新产品之前，它就会主动淘汰自己的产品，并推出新产品。有很多例子可以证明这一论点的有效性。多年以来，杜邦公司一直如此行事。贝尔电话公司在 20 世纪 70 年代由于通胀而衰败之前，也是采取这种策略。如果领导者利用领导地位而非低成本，来提高价格获取利润，那么任何创业柔道战略实施者都能将其击败。

同样，快速发展的新市场或新技术的领导者，如果力求最大化而非最优化，也会受到创业柔道战略实施者的攻击。

最后一种情况，当市场或产业结构快速变化时，"创业柔道"尤其有效，这就是家庭银行抓住的那种情况。20 世纪五六十年代，德国日渐繁荣，除了传统储蓄或抵押贷款之外，普通群众对其他金融业务也有需求。但是，德国银行却固守于先前的市场。

"创业柔道"通常以市场为中心，以市场为导向。它可能以技术为起点，如盛田昭夫从二战后刚刚复苏的日本前往美国，以获取晶体管的许可权。他发现，由于真空管笨重且脆弱，当时的技术无法满足便捷式收音机市场的需求。这个市场的客户群体主要是年轻人，他们收入较低，对收音机的接收范围和音质要求不高。因此，针对这一细分市场，索尼公司设计了新型收音机。

同样，美国的长途电话业务折扣公司发现一个机会，从贝尔电话公司批量购买长途电话业务，然后以零售价转卖给客户。它们首次为那些拥有一定的长途电话业务需求的企业提供服务，这些业务不足以建立自己的长途电话系统，但花费很大。等获得足够的市场份额后，它们开始转向很大的客户或者小客户。

要采用"创业柔道"，首先要对所在产业进行分析，对生产商和供应商的习惯，尤其是坏习惯，以及它们的策略进行分析。然后，再关注整个市场，设法找到一个突破口，使替代战略能取得最大成功，使遭遇的阻力最小。

"创业柔道"需要一定程度上的真正创新。一般来说，仅仅以较低价格提供同样的产品或服务，是远远不够的。它们必须要与现有事物有所区别。为了与贝尔电话公司竞争，罗尔姆公司推出专用小交换机（用于企业和办公室的电话总机）并为小型计算机增添了其他附加功能。这些创新并非高科技，更不必说是新发明了。事实上，贝尔系统也设计了类似的功能，只是没有将其推向市场。同样，当花旗银行在德国创建家庭银行时，提供了一些创新服务，如旅行支票或税务咨询，而德国银行通常不会为小储户提供这些服务。

换言之，对新进入者而言，仅仅以较低的价格或更好的服务提供与现有企业同样产品或服务，是远远不够的。它们必须具有独特之处。

与"孤注一掷"和"创造性模仿"一样，新创企业实施"创业柔道"旨在获取领导地位，最终主导市场。但是，它并不与领先企业展开竞争，至少不会进军使领先企业感到竞争威胁的领域。创业柔道就是"攻其软肋"。

生态利基

到目前为止，我们讨论了"孤注一掷""创造性模仿"和"创业柔道"这三种创业战略。它们都旨在获取领导地位，甚至主导市场，而本章所讨论的"生态利基"则旨在取得控制权。前面讨论的三种战略是使企业在一个巨大市场或重要行业中占据一席之地，而"生态利基"则旨在小领域内取得垄断地位。前三个战略都是竞争性战略，而"生态利基"则力求使企业免遭竞争和挑战。成功实施前三个战略的企业，会成为大企业，享有高知名度，甚至家喻户晓，而成功实施"生态利基"的企业则享有实利，不慕虚名。它们默默无闻，却怡然自得。事实上，最成功的"生态利基"战略的重点是，尽管一个产品在某个流程中必不可少，它依旧看似不起眼，以至无人想要与之竞争。

我们将讨论以下三种不同的利基战略，以及它们的独特要求、局限性和风险。

- 收费站战略。

- 专门技术战略。

- 专门市场战略。

I

收费站战略

在本书的第 4 章，我讨论了爱尔康公司所采取的战略。该公司研制出一种酶，使眼科医生在进行老年白内障外科手术时，减少一个步骤，而这个步骤会使整个手术流程不协调。一旦研制出这种酶，并获得专利，爱尔康公司就占据了"收费站"位置。所有眼科医生都需要这种酶。不管爱尔康公司对这种酶如何要价，与整个白内障手术的成本相比，这点花费微不足道。我估计眼科医生或医院甚至都不会去询问酶的价格。这种酶的市场如此之小，一年的销售总额只有 5000 万美元，以至于没有人会想要研发新的竞品。即便这种酶的价格降低，世界上的白内障手术也不会多出一例。因此，潜在竞争者若想进入，所做的只可能是降低酶的价格，而这样做自己却无利可得。

同样，五六十年前，一家中等规模的企业因研制出一种防井喷装置，多年来一直占据"收费站"位置。钻一口油井的成本高达数百万美元，但一次井喷就会破坏整个油井，让所有努力毁于一旦。在钻井的时候，这种防井喷装置能够保护油井。无论价格如何，它都是一部廉价的保护装置。与前一个案例相似，防井喷装置的市场如此狭小，以至无法吸引任何潜在竞争者。这种装置的价格只是钻油井成本的 1%，即便价格降低，人们也不会去打更多油井。竞争只会降低价格，但无法刺激需求。

另一个采用收费站战略的例子是杜威－阿尔米公司（Dewey & Almy），如今它是美国格雷斯公司（W. R. Grace）的一个分支机构。20 世纪 30 年代，这家公司研制了一种能密封锡罐的化合物。密封流程是罐头工艺流程中必不可少的环节：如果一个罐头食品变质，后果将不堪设想。任何一个因罐头变质而发生中毒的事故，都可以轻易毁掉一家罐头食品厂。因此，能够防止食物变质的密封化合物，无论价格多高，都不算贵。相较于整个罐头的成本以及食物变质引致的风险，密封成本实在微不足道（最高不到 1 美分），以至于没人会关心它的价格。人们更关心的是它的密封性能，而非价格。与白内障手术中的酶或防井喷装置相比，这种化合物的市场要大一些，但仍然有限。即便密封罐头的化合物的价格降低，罐头的需求量也很难增加。

从很多方面来看，收费站位置是企业最渴望占据的位置，但是它要求严苛。首先，该产品必须是某个流程的必要环节。如果不使用这项产品，所带来的风险将远远高于产品的成本。在上述例子中，不使用这些产品，可能会导致失明、失去一口油井，或罐头变质。其次，该产品的市场规模有限，先占领者可以独占。最后，它必须是真正的"生态利基"，一种产品就足够满足需求，同时，这个市场要足够小且低调，不足以吸引竞争对手。

这种收费站位置很难被发现。通常情况下，它们只出现在不协调的情况下（详见第 4 章）。在爱尔康公司酶的例子中，这种不协调是流程的节奏或逻辑的不协调，而在油井防喷装置或密封罐头的化合物的例子中，是经济现实中的不协调，即故障引致的成本与保护措施的花费之间的不协调。

收费站位置也存在严重的局限性和风险。从基本上讲，这个位置是静止不变的。生态利基一旦被占据，就很难会发展。处于收费站位置的企业，很难增加或控制其业务。"收费站"产品属于产品或流程的一部分，无论其质量多好，价格多低，它的需求都取决于产品或流程的需求。

对于爱尔康公司，这点可能并不重要。无论经济繁荣或萧条，白内障手术的数量都不会受经济波动的影响。但是，生产防井喷装置的企业对经济波动深有感触。1973 年的石油危机和 1979 年的石油恐慌，导致石油钻井数量攀升，该企业不得不大量增资建厂。即便它意识到，繁荣不会永久，投资可能难以收回，但它依旧要加大投资。如果不这样做，企业会永久失去市场。几年后，石油繁荣的局面彻底崩溃，石油钻井数量在 12 个月内骤降了 80%，钻井设备需求随之下降。面对这种情况，企业完全无能为力。

采用收费站战略的企业一旦实现目标，企业就"成熟"了。它的发展速度只能与最终用户保持一致。但是，它也可能迅速衰败。如果某种方式同样满足最终需求，它可能一夜之间就惨遭淘汰。比如，杜威－阿米尔公司对锡罐的替代品（如玻璃、纸张或塑料）以及食物的其他保存方法（如冷冻或放射线处理）都毫无防备。

此外，采用收费站战略的企业决不能利用自己的垄断地位成为德国人所称的强盗贵族（德语为 Raubritter，与英语"robber baron"意思并不完全相同）。强盗贵族的城堡占据附近的重要山口、河谷，他们借此来敲诈旅客。如果企业像他们一样行事，客户将会引入其他供应商，或者转向虽然不太有效但能够加以控制的替代品。

40 多年来，杜威－阿米尔公司都成功地执行正确的战略。它为客户，尤其是第三世界的客户，提供广泛的技术服务和员工培训，还为它们设计更新、更好的装罐机和封罐机，来与罐头密封化合物共同供客户使用。它还不断对这个化合物进行升级换代。

收费站位置可能坚不可摧，或几乎不可摧。但是，它只能控制一个狭窄的领域。为了克服这种局限性，爱尔康公司实施多元化战略，进军与眼睛相关的消费品市场，如人工泪液、隐形眼镜清洗液、抗过敏眼药水，等等。从某种程度上讲，这项举措非常成功。它引起瑞士雀巢公司（一家全球领先的消费品跨国公司）的注意，并被其以一个优厚的价格收购。据我所知，在占据收费站位置的公司中，爱尔康公司是唯一一家在其原有位置之外拥有一席之地并获得成功的公司。此外，它的新产品的经济特征与原有的产品并不相同。但是，一家企业以多元化方式进入自己不甚了解的高度竞争的消费品市场，是否能够获利，我们就不得而知了。

Ⅱ

专门技术战略

大型汽车品牌，众人皆知。但是，为这些汽车提供电力和照明系统的企业，却少有人知。而且，这些企业的数量远远少于汽车品牌。在美国，有通用汽车公司的德科集团（Delco）；在德国，有博世公司（Robert Bosch）；在英国，有卢卡斯公司（Lucas）；等等。几十年来，美国客车的车架都是由密尔沃基市的 A.O. 史密斯公司（A. O. Smith）生产的；美国汽车业的刹车装置都是由本迪克斯公司（Bendix）制造的。然而在汽车行业之外，很少有人知道这些。

这些企业如今都是历史悠久的企业了，但这只是因为汽车行业具有悠久的历史。早在第一次世界大战之前，汽车业尚处于萌芽期，这些企业就在市场中取得了控制地位。例如，罗伯特·博世（Robert Bosch）在 19 世纪 80 年代就创办了自己的公司。他与同时期的卡尔·奔驰（Carl Benz）和戈特弗里德·戴姆勒（Gottfried Daimler）这两位德国汽车业先驱是好友。

一旦这些企业在专门技术领域取得控制地位，就会保持这一地位。不同于占据收费站位置的企业（它们的利基更大），但依然独特。这种利基的取得，是因为它们在较早期就开始发展高水平技术。第一次世界大战期间及之后不久，A.O. 史密斯公司就发展出了我们如今所称的汽车车架的"自动化"制造技术。早在 1911 年左右，德国博世公司就为奔驰的指挥车设计了先进的电力系统，直到第二次世界大战结束后，这种系统也只用于豪华汽车中。俄亥俄州代顿市的德科集团在 1914 年加入通用汽车公司之前，就研发出了汽车自动启动器。这些专门技术使它们在各自的领域内遥遥领先，其他人很少会去挑战。它们就是业界"标准"。

专门技术战略并非局限于制造业。过去 10 年来，一些私营贸易公司（大部分位于奥地利维也纳）也建立了相似的利基市场。这种市场，人们过去称之为"易货贸易"（barter），如今称之为"对等贸易"（counter-trade），即用发达国家的商品（如火车头、机械设备或医药）来交换发展中国家的商品（如保加利亚的烟草、巴西制造的灌溉水泵）。更早之前，一位富有开拓精神的德国人掌握了一个专门技术利基。如今，很多旅行指南还以他的名字，即"贝德克尔"（Baedeker）命名。

这些例子表明，要想建立一个专门技术利基，时机至关重要。在新产业、新习惯、新市场、新趋势形成之初，就要有所行动。当莱茵河上的蒸汽轮船首次向中产阶级提供旅行服务时，卡尔·贝德克尔（Karl Baedeker）就于 1828 年出版了他的第一本旅游指南。直到第一次世界大战爆发，西方国家抵制德国书籍之前，贝德克尔一直占据着这一市场。维也纳的对等贸易开始于 1960 年左右，当时这种贸易实属罕见，大都局限于当时同为苏联成员的小国家中（这也说明了为什么对等贸易集中在奥地利）。10 年后，当第三世界国家的耐用消费品短缺时，它们已能熟练地开展对等贸易，并成为该领域的"专家"。

要占据专门技术利基市场，往往需要一些新的东西、额外的东西或某种真正创新的东西。早在贝德克尔之前，就有旅游指南了。但是，这些旅游指南只介绍文化方面的知识，如教会、景点等，而对旅行中的具体问题，如旅馆、马车租金、路程以及小费标准，却不曾涉及。因此，当时英国绅士旅行时，会携带专门的仆从负责这些事务。然而，中产阶级却无力雇用专门的旅行仆从，这正是机会所在。当弄清楚了旅客所需信息，如何获取这些信息并以何种方式呈现（目前许多旅游指南依然遵循这一呈现方式），贝德克尔就出版了更为全面的旅游指南。其他人如果重复同样的工作，创办与之竞争的产品，将一无所获。

在重大创新的初始阶段，专门技术战略有助于赢得重要机会。这种例子比比皆是。比如，多年来，美国只有两家企业生产飞机螺旋桨，而它们早在第一次世界大战之前就已创立。

专门技术利基市场，很少出于偶然。上述例子中，专门技术利基都源于对创新机会的系统分析；企业家都在寻找专门技术可以发展的领域，以使新创企业取得控制地位。罗伯特·博世在新兴汽车产业上花费多年时间，来找到自己的新创企业的定位，使其迅速成为业界领导者。多年来，汉密尔顿公司一直是美国领先的飞机螺旋桨制造商，这主要得益于其创始人早期在动力飞行领域所进行的系统研究。在决定出版旅游指南之前，贝德克尔也多次尝试为游客提供服务。这本旅游指南以他的名字命名，使他声名远扬。

由此看来，专门技术战略有三个要点。第一个要点是，在新产业、新市场或新趋势形成初期，通过系统地研究，找到发展专门技术的机会，这样就有足够的时间发展这一独特技术。

第二个要点是，专门技术战略要求技术必须是独特且不同的。毫无例外，早期的汽车先驱都是机械师。他们熟知机械、金属和发动机的相关知识，但对电学一窍不通。他们既没有电学的理论知识，也不知如何获取这些知识。这就为汽车电气设备制造商创造了机会。在贝德克尔所处的时代，也有很多其他的出版商。但是，旅游指南需要实地搜集大量信息、持续考察、聘请旅游顾问，这些并不在出版商关注的范围内。"对等贸易"既不是贸易业务，也不是银行业务。

因此，如果一个企业拥有专门技术利基市场，它将不易遭受客户或供应商的威胁。无论客户或供应商，都不会盲目涉足自己不熟悉的领域。

第三个要点是，拥有专门技术利基市场的企业，必须不断提升自身能力。它必须要保持技术上的领先地位，要不断自我超越。早期的汽车制造商经常抱怨道，德科公司和博世公司给它们施加了很大的压力。这两家企业的照明系统非常先进，远远超出普通汽车的需求，也超出当时的它们对客户需求以及支付能力的预期，还超出它们的装配能力。

虽然专门技术战略具有独特的优势，但也有严重的局限性。首先，它会使企业陷入"视野狭隘"的状态。为了保持控制地位，企业不能左顾右盼，只能专注于狭窄的专业领域内。在早期，飞机电子系统与汽车电子系统并无显著差异。但是，德科、博世和莱卡斯等汽车电气设备制造商并没有成为飞机电子系统领域的领先者。它们甚至未曾发现这一领域，也从未尝试进军该领域。

其次，拥有专门技术利基市场的企业，需要依赖他人才能将产品或服务推向市场。它的产品或服务只是一个组件而已。汽车电气设备公司的一个优势是，客户根本不知道它们的存在。但是，这也是它们的劣势。如果英国汽车工业衰落了，卢卡斯工业公司也将走向衰落。能源危机爆发后，A.O. 史密斯公司的汽车车架业务也不再繁荣。美国汽车制造商开始转向无车架式汽车。相比于有车架汽车，这种汽车更为昂贵，但更为轻便、油耗更低。面对这种局面，A.O. 史密斯公司完全束手无策。

最后，拥有专门技术利基市场的企业所面临的最大危险是，专门技术不再独特，成为通用技术。

20 世纪二三十年代，外汇交易商（大都是瑞士人）就开展了维也纳商人现在所从事的对等交易。当时的银行家（他们深信，货币会保持稳定）发迹于第一次世界大战之前。当货币不再稳定，冻结货币随处可见。货币由于交易目的不同，汇率也不同。此外，还有一些畸形的"交易"。在这种情况下，银行家甚至不愿处理交易业务。他们只希望瑞士的外汇交易商能接手这些不堪的交易。因此，小部分外汇交易商占据了这个获利颇丰的专门技术利基市场。第二次世界大战后，世界贸易迅速发展，外汇交易成为常态。如今，每家银行在重要的金融中心都有外汇交易商。

与其他生态利基一样，专门技术利基在范围和时间上都有所局限。生物学告诉我们，对占据某一利基的物种来说，外界环境稍有变化，它们就难以适应。专门技术战略亦是如此。尽管存在这些局限性，专门技术利基仍然是有利位置。在快速扩张的新技术领域、新产业或新市场中，专门技术战略或许是最优战略。1920 年的汽车制造商已所剩无几，但电气和照明系统的制造商却存活至今。企业一旦占据专门技术利基，并维持这个地位，就可以避免竞争。汽车买家不知道也不会关心汽车的前灯或刹车出自谁手，也不会为此货比三家。一旦"贝德克尔"成为旅游指南的代名词，只要市场不出现急剧变化，就不需要担心竞争对手的攻击。在新技术领域、新产业或新市场中，专门技术战略的成功率最高，风险最低。

III

专门市场战略

专门技术战略与专门市场战略非常相似，二者的主要区别在于，前者以产品或服务为基础，后者则以市场的专门知识为基础。

有两家中等规模的企业，一家在北英格兰，另一家在丹麦。它们生产的用来烘制西点的自动烤箱，在西方国家占据大部分市场份额。几十年来，两家最早的旅行社，欧洲的托马斯·库克公司（Thomas Cook）和美国运通公司（American Express），一直垄断旅行支票业务。

据我所闻，制造烤箱并不需要什么深奥或独特的技术。许多企业都能生产出这种产品，而且同英国和丹麦的这两家企业的产品一样好。不过这两家企业熟知市场：它们了解每个知名面包师，这些面包师也了解它们。只要这两家企业表现尚可，这个不大的市场也就不足以吸引他人参与竞争。同样的，在第二次世界大战战后时期的旅游热潮之前，旅行支票领域犹如一潭死水。事实上，这项业务获利颇丰。在旅行支票被兑现之前（有的支票售出之后，数月才被兑现），其发行商，无论是库克公司还是美国运通公司，都可以使用这笔资金，获取利息。但是，这一市场规模并不大，不足以吸引他人进入。此外，旅行支票发行商要成为全球性组织，才能更好地服务旅客。除了这两家企业外，尚无企业愿意涉足这一领域。

要发现一个专门市场，要带着以下问题来审视一项新进展：这项新进展存在哪些机会来提供一个独特的利基市场？为占据这个利基市场，我们需要做什么？旅行支票不是伟大的"发明"，它与已经存在几百年的信用证并无二致。它的创新之处在于，旅行支票的面额是标准化的。库克公司和美国通运公司先向自己的客户发售，随后向普通大众公开发售。购买者可以在库克公司或美国运通公司的全球范围内的任意一个分支机构或代理处兑换。对那些不愿携带大量现金，又没有资格从银行获取信用证的旅客来说，这具有独特的吸引力。

早期的烤箱也没什么特别之处，就算是今天的烤箱，也没什么高科技含量。这两家企业之所以领先，是因为它们意识到西点烘焙正在从家庭转向工厂。于是，它们开始研究职业面包师的需求，以制造出在杂货店和超市里受欢迎的产品，进而吸引家庭主妇购买。烤箱的成功并不在于工艺，而在于市场调研。实际上，任何人都可以采用这种工艺。

同专门技术战略一样，专门市场战略具有同样的要求：对新趋势、新产业、新市场进行系统分析；具体的创新或许只是一个"转变"，如将传统的信用证转变为现代的旅行支票；持续改进产品，尤其是服务，这样才能保持所获得的领导地位。

专门市场战略也具有与专门技术战略同样的局限性。对占据专门市场位置的企业而言，最大的威胁是市场的成功，也就是专门市场发展成为大众市场。

如今，旅行支票已成为大众商品，竞争激烈。这主要是因为旅游市场成了大众市场。

香水产业同样如此。法国科蒂集团（Coty）开创了现代香水业。它意识到，第一次世界大战改变了人们对化妆品的态度。在此之前，只有"开放型女性"才使用化妆品,或者敢于承认自己使用了化妆品。第一次世界大战后,化妆品开始为人接受,并受到尊重。到 20 世纪 20 年代中期,科蒂集团在大西洋两岸几乎都建立了自己的垄断地位。1929 年之前,化妆品市场是"专门市场",只针对中上流人士。在经济大萧条时期,它发展成为一个真正的大众市场。这时,出现了两个细分市场:一个以昂贵的价格、专门的分销渠道和包装为特色的高端市场;另一个是以亲民的价格在一般销售点(包括超市、杂货店和药店)出售的大众市场。短短几年,由科蒂集团主导的专门市场就消失无踪了。它试图停留在那个不复存在的市场之中,在化妆品大众市场营销商和奢侈品制造商之间摇摆,结果一直处于飘摇不定的状态。

改变价值和特征

到目前为止，本书所讨论的创业战略都旨在推出创新。本章所讨论的创业战略，其本身就是创新。本章所提到的产品或服务，可能存在已久（本章第一个例子中的邮政服务，大约有 2000 年之久）。但是，战略将这种已存在的产品或服务转换成新事物。它改变了产品或服务的效用、价值和经济特征。从物质意义上看，这些产品或服务并无变化，但从经济意义上看，它们有所改变。

本章讨论的战略具有一个共同点，即创造客户。这是企业的终极目的，事实上，也是经济活动的终极目的。[⊖]不过，它们以如下四种不同的方式来实现这一目的。

- 创造效用。
- 定价。

⊖ 正如 30 多年前，我在《管理的实践》(New York: Harper & Row, 1954) 提到的。

- 适应客户的社会和经济现实。
- 向客户提供所需的价值。

I

创造客户所需的效用

英国学生曾被教导，罗兰·希尔（Rowland Hill）于1836年"发明"了邮政服务。这纯属谬论。早在恺撒大帝执政时期，罗马的邮政服务就已相当完善，信使定期将邮件投递到罗马帝国的每个角落。1 000年后，即1952年，德国国王查理五世重现文艺复兴时期的风格，效仿古罗马，将邮件服务全权交由王室成员特恩（Thurn）和塔克西斯（Taxis）家族负责（这两个家族为查理五世竞选慷慨捐赠，使他获得足够多选民的支持，最终赢得王位）。集邮爱好者知道，直至1866年，特恩和塔克西斯的后代依然为德国境内很多地方提供邮政服务。到17世纪中期，欧洲国家都纷纷效仿德国，开创自己的邮政服务。100年以后，美国殖民地也是如此。事实上，早在希尔"发明"邮政服务之前，所有西方传统的伟大作家（书信作家），从西塞罗（Cicero）到塞维尼夫人（Madame de Sévigné），从查斯特菲尔德勋爵（Lord Chesterfield）到伏尔泰（Voltaire），就已开始写信寄信了。

然而，希尔的确创造了我们今天所称的"邮件"。他既没有发明新技术或新"事物"，也没有什么成果能够申请专利。过去邮资通常按照距离和重量计算，由收件人支付。每封信件都要送到邮局，这使邮件服务既昂贵又耗时。希尔提议，只要在英国境内，无论距离，邮资要统一；邮资由寄件人预付；邮资通过贴邮票的方式支付，这种方式一直被用于支付各种费用和税费。一夜之间，邮政服务变得简单便捷，寄件人只需直接将邮件投递到邮箱。同时，邮资也变得极其便宜。以往至少要花费1先令的邮件（1先令当时相当于一个手艺人一天的收入），现在只需 1 便士。人们的寄件量多了起来。简言之，"邮件"诞生了。

希尔创造了效用。他也许曾问道：邮政服务到底能为客户提供什么服务？在改变效用、价值和经济特征的创业战略中，这往往是首要问题。事实上，尽管邮资至少降低了 80%，但这只是次要的。更重要的是，邮件服务变得更为便利，人人可用。邮件不再仅仅限于"书信"，比如裁缝也可以用它来寄送账单。邮件数量大增，在邮件改革的最初 4 年，翻了一番；10 年后，又翻了两番。邮资随之下降，在很长一段时间里，邮资根本微不足道。

在创造效用战略中，价格几乎无关紧要。这个战略的作用在于，满足客户需求，并回答"对客户而言，何为真正的'服务'，何为真正的'效用'"的问题。美国新娘都想入手一套"优质瓷器"。然而，作为结婚礼物，整套瓷器过于昂贵，送礼人也不知道新娘的喜好以及她已有哪些瓷器。后来，他们都改送了其他礼物。换句话说，客户需求已经存在，但效用不能使其满足。一个生产餐具的中型企业，雷诺克斯瓷器公司（Lenox China Company），从中发现了创新机会。它采用了"结婚登记簿"这一老方法。这种簿子只能登记雷诺克斯的瓷器。准新娘选择一家瓷器零售商，告诉它自己心仪的雷诺克斯的瓷器，然后递交一份可能的送礼人名单。这个零售商会逐个询问送礼人："你的预算大概是多少？"然后解释道："这可以买两只带茶托的咖啡杯。"或者回答："她已经有咖啡杯了，现在需要一个甜点盘。"最后的结果皆大欢喜，新娘、送礼人和雷诺克斯公司都心满意足。

同样，这个例子也与高科技、专利无关，仅仅是关注了客户需求。虽然"结婚登记簿"这一方式相当简单，或许正因如此，雷诺克斯公司成为备受欢迎的"优质瓷器"制造商，也是发展最为迅速的美国中型制造企业之一。

创造效用战略，是指人们以自己的方式满足自身需求。如果裁缝花 3 个小时将信件交给邮递员，随后收信人还要支付一大笔邮费（甚至与账单金额一样），那么他就不会以邮寄方式将账单交由顾客。希尔并没有为邮政服务增添什么新服务。邮局营业员并未改变，邮车和邮递员也没有变化。但是，希尔提出的邮政服务的确是一种完全不同的"服务"。这种邮政服务具有独特的功能。

II

定价

多年来，世界上最熟悉的美国人面孔，非金·吉列（King Gillette）莫属。他的头像印制在吉列剃须刀的包装上，这种刀片销往世界各地。每天早晨，世界上数百万男士都使用吉列刀片。

安全剃须刀并非吉列发明的。19 世纪末，许多安全剃须刀已经获得了专利。直到 1860 年或 1870 年以前，只有贵族、一些专业人士和商人等少数男士会注意面部修饰，也只有他们才请得起理发师。突然之间，商人、店主、职员等大多数男士，都想让自己看起来"体面"。人们很少会使用剃刀，或者对这种危险工具感到不舒适，但是光顾理发店又过于昂贵，而且也很耗时。许多人发明了"自助式"安全剃刀，却都没有销路。究其原因，当时日薪 1 美元算是很高的工资了，去一趟理发店的花费是 10 美分，而最便宜的剃须刀也需要 5 美元。

吉列的安全剃刀并非最优，它生产成本更高。但是，吉列"卖"的并非剃刀。吉列剃刀的零售价为 55 美分，批发价为 20 美分，不超过生产成本的 1/5。但是，这种剃刀只能用吉列刀片。吉列刀片的生产成本不到 1 美分，售价为 5 美分。由于每片刀片可以用六七次，一次刮脸的花费不到 1 美分，不到去一趟理发店花费的 1/10。

吉列根据客户购买的服务，即修面，而非产品本身来定价。如果花 5 美元购买竞争对手的安全剃刀，然后再花 1 美分或 2 美分购买竞争对手的刀片，这样比购买吉列的产品更为划算。吉列的客户清楚地知道这点，其实客户比广告商或拉尔夫·纳德尔（Ralph Nader）所预想的更为明智。但是，在他们看来，吉列的定价很合理。他们购买的是修面服务，而非一件"物品"。而且，相比于危险的折叠式剃刀，吉列的产品（剃刀和刀片）给他们带来更为愉悦的体验，而且花费远比附近的理发店要低。

为何复印机的专利权会落到纽约罗彻斯特一家不知名的小企业（后来称为哈罗伊德公司（Haloid））手中，而不是大型印刷制造商手中？一个原因是，大型印刷制造商并未看到复印机的销路。经计算，它们认为一台复印机的售价至少为 4000 美元。在复写纸如此廉价的情况下，没人会愿意为一台复印机支付这一高价。此外，要花费 4000 美元购买机器，必须要向董事会申请资金拨付，并附上投资收益分析报告。从这两点看，为秘书购买这样的"玩意儿"，实属不可思议。哈罗伊德公司，也就是现在的施乐公司，做了大量技术性工作来设计复印机。但是，它的主要贡献在于定价。它销售的并非机器，而是复印件。一份复印件只需 5～10 美分，无须申请资金拨付。这属于"小额备用金"，秘书可以自主决定，无须上报。施乐公司将复印机定价为"每张复印件 5 美分"，是一项真正的创新。

大多数供应商，包括公共服务机构，从未想过将定价视为一项战略。但是，定价使客户愿意为其所需（如修面、复印件）买单，而不是供应商的产品。当然，客户最终支付的金额是一样的。但是，支付方式根据客户需求和实际情况来确定。价格代表的应是客户的"价值"，而不是供应商的"成本"。

Ⅲ

客户的实际情况

美国通用电气公司之所以能在大型汽轮机领域取得领先地位，是因为早在第一次世界大战之前，它就考虑到了客户的实际情况。不同于活塞蒸汽机，汽轮机结构复杂，其设计需要高水平的工程技术，建造和安装也需要一定的技能。单个电力公司根本无法做到这一点。也许每隔 5 年或 10 年，当建立新的发电站时，它才会购买一台汽轮机。由于汽轮机对技术要求比较高，制造商必须要有一个咨询机构，以向客户提供技术服务。

但是，通用电气公司很快发现，电力公司根本不会为咨询服务买单。根据美国法律，这项开支需经国家公用事业委员会批准。委员会认为，电力公司能够自行解决这个问题。通用电气公司也发现，它不能将咨询服务的费用追加到汽轮机的价格中，因为国家公用事业委员会不会批准这项提议。由于汽轮机的寿命很长，需要经常更换叶片（也许每隔 5～7 年），而这些叶片必须出自该汽轮机的原始制造商。于是，通用电气公司成立了世界上第一家工程咨询服务机构（为谨慎起见，通用电气公司称之为"设备销售部"而非"咨询工程部"），为电力公司免费提供咨询服务。相比于竞争对手，通用电气的汽轮机不再昂贵。但是，它将咨询费用和一大笔利润加到更换叶片的价格中。10 年内，其他汽轮机制造商业纷纷采用了这一价格体系。彼时，通用电气公司已取得世界领导地位。

早在 19 世纪 40 年代，就存在基于客户的实际情况进行类似产品或流程的设计，由此催生了分期付款。当时，许多美国人发明了收割机，赛勒斯·麦考密克就是其中之一。但是，他却发现，这种收割机根本没有销量，其他发明者也遇到同样的难题。虽然农民对收割机的需求显而易见，他们却无力购买。众所周知，购买这一机器，只需两三季度就可回本。但是，没有银行愿意借钱给美国农民来购买机器。麦考密克提出了分期付款方式，在接下来的 3 年内，农民可以将收入的一部分用于偿付机器款项。如此一来，农民就有能力而且的确购买了收割机。

事实上，制造商常提到的"非理性客户"（经济学家、心理学家、伦理学家也是如此称呼）根本不存在。正如古话所说："只有懒惰的制造商。"我们应该假定客户是理性的，但客户的实际情况与制造商的实际情况往往相去甚远。比如，公用事业委员会制定的规章制度看似毫无意义，主观武断。但是，这是受其管辖的电力公司所面临的实际情况。19 世纪 40 年代，美国农民的信用风险可能低于银行家的预期。但是，那个时期的美国银行家并不愿意借钱给农民来购买机器。因此，客户的实际情况这一创新战略包含一个观念：实际情况与产品并非毫无关联，对客户而言，二者紧密相关。客户购买的产品必须符合其实际情况，否则这种产品毫无用处可言。

Ⅳ

向客户提供所需的价值

最后一个创新战略是向客户提供所需的"价值"，而不是制造商所生产的"产品"。实际上，这只是将"接受客户的实际情况，并将其视为产品或客户所购买的东西的一部分"这一战略，向前推进一步。

美国中西部有一家中型企业，为大型推土机和牵引机（如承包商修建公路所用的推土机和拉铲挖土机；清理露天矿覆盖物的重型设备；煤矿运煤的重型矿车；等等）提供专用润滑油。这家企业的竞争对手是大型石油公司，这些石油公司拥有众多润滑油专家。但是，它并不以销售润滑油而是以"保障"服务来提升竞争力。对工程承包商而言，真正的"价值"不是润滑油，而是设备的正常运转。重型设备由于无法正常运转在 1 小时内造成的损失，远远高于承包商全年在润滑油上的花费。一般的工程项目中，如果承包商未能如期完工，将受到严重惩罚。只有争分夺秒，最大可能缩短工期，承包商才能中标。这个润滑油制造商采取的做法是：首先，向承包商提供机器维护的需求分析。然后，制定维护方案以及相应的年度维护费用，并向它们保证，重型设备因润滑问题停止运转的时间，在一年之内不会超过特定时长。毋庸置疑，这个维护方案只针对该润滑油制造商的客户。但是，承包商购买的并非润滑油，而是机器正常运转的保障。对他们来说，这种保障尤为重要。

最后一个例子，可以被称为"从产品到系统"，是关于美国密歇根齐兰的赫曼米勒家具公司（Herman Miller）的。这家公司最初因设计和生产现代家具（埃姆斯椅）而著称。当其他制造商开始跟风效仿时，它却转向了生产和销售整体办公室和医院工作台，都大获成功。最后，当"未来办公室"开始流行时，赫曼米勒公司成立了设备管理机构。这个机构并不出售家具或设备，而是向企业提供办公室设计咨询，即如何以最低成本获得最佳工作流程，提高生产率和员工士气。赫曼米勒公司所做的是，为客户定义"价值"。它告诉客户："你也许是为家具买单，但实际上购买的是工作、士气、生产率。因此，这些才是你应该花钱的地方。"

这些例子看似明显，似乎只要稍加思考就能想出类似的战略。系统经济学之父大卫·李嘉图曾说过："利润并非源于与众不同的聪明，而是源于与众不同的愚蠢。"上述战略之所以成功，不是因为他们很聪明，而是因为大多数产品或服务的供应商（企业和公共服务机构）未曾思考。正是因为如此"显而易见"，这些战略才得以成功。那么，为什么采用这些战略的人如此之少呢？上述例子表明，任何人只要问"客户真正想买什么"，就会赢得比赛。由于没有其他参赛者，这甚至不能称为比赛。到底原因何在？

其中一个因素是经济学家以及他们所称的"价值"。经济学书籍都指出，客户购买的不是"产品"，而是产品所带来的价值。随后，这些经济学书籍立即摒弃一切，只考虑产品的"价格"。"价格"的定义是，客户为获得产品或服务的所有权需要支付的金额。至于产品对客户的价值，却不再提及。遗憾的是，产品或服务的供应商往往会遵循经济学家的思路。

"产品 A 的成本是 X 美元"，这句话是有道理的。"我们应将产品定价为 Y 美元，这样可以抵消生产成本和资本成本，获得足额利润"，这句话也是有道理的。但是，"……因此，客户若购买产品 A，就必须支付 Y 美元"，这一结论就毫无道理可言。正确的结论应该是："对我们来说，客户为每件产品支付的金额必须是 Y 美元。但是，客户如何支付取决于什么对他更重要，产品能为他带来什么，什么符合他的实际情况，以及他所认为的'价值'。"

价格不是"定价"，也不是"价值"。正是由于洞悉这一点，吉列得以在长达 40 年的时间里垄断修面市场；小小的哈洛德公司在 10 年内成为价值数十亿美元的施乐公司；通用电气公司在汽轮机市场占据领导地位。这三家公司都获得了超高利润，而且理所应当。它们提高了客户满意度，为客户提供所需，换句话说，它们让客户觉得物有所值。

多数读者可能会断言："这只不过是基本的营销理论罢了。"的确如此，这只是基本的营销理论，主要从客户的效用、客户购买的东西、客户的实际情况以及客户所需的价值着手分析。但是，为何对营销理论历经 40 年的宣传、教育、传授之后，依然只有少数企业愿意采用这些理论呢？对此，我无法解释。到目前为止，事实依旧如此。任何企业如果将营销理论视为战略基础，可能会在几乎没有风险的情况下，以最快的速度取得产业或市场的领导地位。

正如有目的的创新和创业管理，创业战略也同样重要。这三者共同构成了创新与企业家精神。

创业战略为数不多，且清晰易懂。但是，与有目的的创新和创业管理相比，创业战略的具体实施要困难得多。我们知道从哪里找到创新机会，以及如何对它们加以分析。我们知道，要使现有企业或公共服务机构具有企业家精神，何为正确的策略和实践，何为错误的策略和实践；对于小企业，同样如此。但是，为特定创新选择创业战略，风险很大。一些创业战略更适用于某种情况，如我所称的"创业柔道"，就比较适合行业领先者多年持续骄傲自大的情形。我们还可以描述某个创业战略的典型优势和不足。

更重要的是，我们知道，越是从用户出发（考虑用户的效用、价值和实际情况），创业战略越容易成功。所谓的创新，就是市场或社会的变化。它为用户创造收益，为社会创造财富，还会创造更高的价值和满足感。创新的检验标准永远是：为用户带来什么。因此，企业家精神必须以市场为中心，以市场为导向。

即便如此，创业战略依旧属于创业决策范畴，具有风险性。它绝非赌博，也不是精准的科学。确切地说，它是一种判断。

创业型社会

I

"每代人都需要新的革命",这是托马斯·杰斐逊(Thomas Jefferson)在漫长生命终结之时的感悟。与他同时代的德国伟大诗人歌德(Goethe),虽然是保守主义者,在暮年时期也道出同样的心声:

> 理性成为胡言
> 恩惠成为苦难

杰斐逊和歌德都表达了他们那一代人对启蒙运动和法国大革命的遗产不抱任何希望。也许,150年后,他们对今日的遗产,即"福利国家"这一伟大承诺,也会感到不满。福利国家始于德意志帝国,初衷是为贫民和残疾人谋取福利,如今却成为"公民权利",并逐渐成为财富创造者的重担。正如产品、流程和服务终将不合时宜，制度、系统和策略也会变得陈旧迂腐。无论预期目标实现与否，它们终将退出历史舞台。它们的机制或许依旧发挥作用，但是起初设计它们的前提已不再成立。例如，过去 100 年来，发达国家在制定医疗保健计划和退休计划时，都基于人口统计学的假设。随后，理性成为胡言，恩惠成为苦难。

自杰斐逊时期开始，我们就认识到"革命"并非一剂良药。人们对革命无法进行预测，也不能加以指导或控制。革命来的权力甚至会沦落到错误的人手中。更糟糕的是，结果可能与最初的承诺完全相反。1826 年，杰斐逊逝世后不久，素有"政府和政治的伟大解读者"之称的亚历克西·德·托克维尔（Alexis de Tocqueville）就指出，革命并不能摧毁旧政权，反而会强化它。托克维尔证明，相比于之前，大革命后的法国被枷锁束缚得更紧；整个国家由一个不受控制且无法控制的官僚机构所掌控，政治、知识、艺术和经济活动都集中在巴黎。而俄国革命的主要影响是，产生了新型的农奴制度，无所不能的秘密警察，以及僵化、腐败、令人窒息的官僚主义。这与沙皇政权如出一辙，那俄国的自由主义者和革命者究竟推翻了什么？

我们现在知道，"革命"是一种错觉，是 19 世纪普遍存在的错觉。如今，它可能是最令人难以置信的神话。我们现在知道，"革命"不是一项成就，也不是新的曙光。它是陈旧腐朽、思想和制度的破产或自我更新失败的产物。

我们也知道，理论、价值以及人类思想和技术的产物都会老化、僵化，变得不合时宜，最后成为"苦难"。

无论是社会还是经济，是公共服务机构还是企业，都需要创新与企业家精神。这是因为：首先，创新与企业家精神并非对现有事物"连根拔除"，而是"循序渐进"地推出一个新产品，随后制定一项新策略，进而改善公共服务。其次，它们并不是事先计划好的，而是专注于机会和需求。最后，它们是试探性的。如果不能实现预期，它们就会消失。换句话说，它们是务实的而非武断的，是谦虚的而非浮夸的。创新与企业家精神可以使社会、经济、产业、公共服务或企业保持灵活性，并自我更新。无须通过流血、内战、集中营和经济危机的方式，创新与企业家精神就可以在有目的、有方向、可控的情况下，实现杰斐逊希望通过革命达到的目标。

我们需要的是一个创业型社会。在创业型社会中，创新与企业家精神实属常态，是稳定的、持续的活动。正如管理已成为当今机构的特殊器官、当代社会的整合器官一样，创新与企业家精神也要成为组织、经济和社会的重要生命活动。

这就要求，所有机构的高层管理者要将创新与企业家精神视为正常的、持续的日常活动，他们自身工作和组织工作中的实践。本书的目的，就是为完成这项任务提供所需的概念和工具。

II

无效的策略

在讨论创业型社会所需的公共策略和政府举措时，首先要明确哪些是无效的策略，尤其是在无效策略颇为盛行的当今时代。

人们通常所理解的"规划"与创业型社会和经济格格不入。的确，创新要有目的性，企业家精神要能加以管理。但是几乎可以肯定，创新应该是分散式的、自主的、具体的，是一种微观经济活动。创新最好始于小规模事物，试探性地、灵活地加以实施。总体来说，只有接近现实事件，才能发掘创新机会。它们并非出现在规划者必须处理的大量事物中。反之，偏差之中（如意外事件中，不协调事件中，"杯子是半满的"与"杯子是半空的"这两种不同的认知中，以及流程的薄弱环节中）孕育创新机会。当这种偏差具有"统计上的显著性"，并为规划者所知时，为时已晚。创新机会并不会随"暴风雨"降临，而是如微风般悄然而至。

如今，人们普遍认为国家靠自身的力量能够产生"高科技企业家精神"。在欧洲国家，这种观点尤为盛行。法国、德国，甚至英国在制定国策时，都以此为前提。这只是假象而已。事实上，提倡高科技的策略和高科技本身，甚至无法推动高科技的发展，反而会导致对企业家精神的敌视（法国、德国，甚至英国就遭遇过如此状况）。其最终结果是，又一次代价昂贵的失败，或是重蹈协和式超音速飞机的覆辙——赢得一丝"荣耀"，却收获巨额赤字；既没有创造就业岗位，也没有实现技术领先。

高科技只是创新与企业家精神的一部分，当然，它的确是本书的重要前提之一。实际上绝大多数创新源于其他领域。推行高科技策略也会遭遇政治阻碍，可能会被一道命令即刻废止。从创造就业岗位来说，高科技是未来就业岗位的创造者，而非当下。正如我们最初看到的（详见引言部分），1970—1985年期间，美国"高科技"产业所创造的五六百个就业岗位，还不足以弥补"烟囱工业"所失去的就业岗位。同期，美国经济的其他新增就业岗位（共3500万个）都是由新创企业创造的，这些新创企业都不是"高科技"企业，而是"中科技""低科技"，甚至"零科技"企业。由于就业人员不断增加，欧洲国家面临的就业压力也随之增加。如果创新与企业家精神的重心是高科技，政府将会牺牲当今其他产业的需求（支持深陷困境的巨头），而高科技的未来却扑朔迷离。这正是法国所面临的问题。1984年，法国共产党退出了密特朗总统的内阁，而密特朗本人所领导的社会党左翼分子对高科技策略也愈加感到不满和不安。

最重要的是，如果只在"高科技"中强调企业家精神，而不将其纳入广泛的创业型经济（包括"零科技""低科技"和"中科技"），犹如无本之木。在这种情况下，高科技人员甚至都不愿任职于高风险的新兴高科技企业，反而偏向"安全的"大型企业或政府机构。当然，高科技企业也需要许多非高科技人员，如会计、销售人员、管理者。在一个只有"耀眼的高科技企业"

才重视创新与企业家精神的经济中，高科技人员会追求在"安全的"大型机构中获得就业机会并实现职业发展。这是因为，他们在社会和经济上的相关人（也就是，同学、父母和老师）都是如此劝导的。结果，分销商不愿销售新创企业的产品，投资者也不愿给予资金支持。

但是，其他创新型企业也需要向高科技企业提供所需的资本。就基于知识的创新来说，尤其是高科技创新，其投资和收益的间隔时间最长。直到20世纪70年代末，在30年的亏损后，世界计算机行业才实现盈亏平衡。当然，IBM很早就实现盈利了。20世纪60年代末期，有"7个小矮人"之称的美国小型计算机制造商也逐渐开始盈利。但是，这些利润远远不足以抵消其他计算机制造商的巨额亏损，尤其是那些历史悠久的大型企业（如美国通用电气公司、西屋电器、国际电报电话公司和美国无线电通信公司；英国通用电气公司、普利西半导体公司和费兰蒂技术公司；法国汤姆森休斯敦公司；德国西门子公司和德国通用电气公司；荷兰飞利浦公司；等等）在计算机领域的溃败。如今，历史在重演，微型计算机和个人电脑也面临着同样状况：多年以后，该产业才能在全球范围内盈利。生物技术行业，也是如此。100年前，19世纪80年代的电气设备行业，还有1900或1910年的汽车工业也历经同样的发展模式。

在高科技企业的漫长孕育期中，非高科技企业必须创造足够的利润，才能弥补高科技企业的亏损，并为它们提供所需的资本。

当然，法国推动高科技的举措是正确的。当今时代，一个国家的经济和政治力量取决于高科技地位，无论是信息技术、生物学，还是自动化。的确，法国具有科技实力。但是，如果一个国家不发展创业型经济，其高科技领域也将很难具有创新与企业家精神（我认为是不可能的）。高科技的确属于前沿领域，然而刀若不存，何来刀刃？高科技产业根本不能独立存在，犹如健康大脑不能脱离身体而存在。经济中必须充满创新者和创业者，具备创业理念和创业价值观，能够获取风险资本，并保持创业活力。

Ⅲ

社会创新的需要

在创业型社会中，两个领域需要开展社会创新。

1. 第一，制定策略来安置剩余劳动力。 剩余劳动力的数量并不大。"烟囱工业"中的蓝领工人集中在少数几个地方，比如，3/4 的汽车工人集中在 20 个县。他们备受瞩目，具有高度组织性。更重要的是，他们没有能力安置自己，也不知如何改行或更换工作。他们的教育水平低，也没有良好的技术和社交能力。更糟糕的是，他们大都缺乏自信。终其一生，他们从未有自主求职经历。当他们准备进入就业市场时，在汽车厂工作的亲戚就会将它们引荐给主管，或者教区牧师将其介绍给在工厂工作的教区居民。英国"烟囱工业"的工人（如威尔士的煤矿工人），德国鲁尔、法国洛林或比利时博里纳日的蓝领工人，大都如此。20 世纪初，发达国家的教育和知识水平都大幅提升，然而这些工人并未因此受益。就能力、经验、技能和受教育水平来看，他们与 1900 年的非熟练工人并无差异。不同之处在于，他们的工资和政治权力大幅提升。如果把工资和福利加总，他们是工业社会中收入最高的群体。无论作为个体或群体而言，他们都不具备自我帮助能力，但却有足够的权利去反对、否决和干涉。如果社会不能妥善安置他们，只提供一份低收入工作，他们将成为一股纯粹的消极力量。

如果是创业型经济，这个问题即可迎刃而解。因为创业型经济中的新创企业能够创造新的就业岗位，正如过去 10 年来美国所发生的情况（这也解释了，为何美国"烟囱工业"中的大规模失业，至今尚未引发政治危机，甚至没有引发大规模的贸易保护主义者的抗议）。即便创业型经济能够创造新的就业岗位，也需要对"烟囱工业"的剩余劳动力有组织地加以培训和安置，他们自己力所不及。否则，"烟囱工业"的剩余劳动力将会愈加抵制新事物，甚至包括那些拯救他们的举措。"迷你钢铁厂"能够为过剩的钢铁工人提供就业机会。自动化汽车公司是汽车工人的最佳去处。但是，在"迷你钢铁厂"和自动化汽车公司中，在岗职工知道自己的工作也不是固定的，他们之间竞争激烈。除非"烟囱工业"的剩余劳动力能够利用创新机会，否则他们会感到无力、恐惧、受困于社会，进而抵制创新；英国（或美国邮政机构）就出现了这种状况。历史上有妥善安置剩余劳动力的成功案例。1906 年日俄战争后，日本陷入经济大萧条，三井财阀就安置了不少剩余劳动力。类似地，第二次世界大战后，瑞典经过深思熟虑制定一项策略，使得自己从一个拥有大量贫民和林业工人的国家转变为一个高度工业化和高度繁荣的国家。正如前面所提到的，剩余劳动力的数量并非特别大，尤其是 1/3 的 55 岁以上的人群可以提前退休，1/3 的 30 岁以下的人群可以自我安排。剩余的 1/3 人群，规模虽小但是核心力量，必须制定一套策略来培训和安置这些"烟囱工业"工人。

2. 第二，有组织、有系统地放弃不合时宜的社会策略和公共服务机构，这项社会创新史无前例，更为激进，也更为困难。在上一个伟大创业时代中，这根本就不是个问题。100 年前，类似的策略和机构少之又少。如今，它们过于多余。我们现在也清楚，很少有策略或机构能够永存，连能发挥短期效应的也寥寥无几。

过去 20 年来，人们的世界观和认知出现了一个根本性变化，也是真正具有里程碑意义的转变。人们认识到政府策略和机构是人为的，而非神赐的。因此，可以确定的是，这些策略和机构很快会变得不合时宜。但是，政治活动以一个古老的假设为基础，即政府的所作所为都根植于人类社会的本质，因此是"永恒"的。结果，迄今尚未出现一种政治机制，能够摒弃陈旧的、过时的、不再有效的政府机构和策略。

或者更确切地说，现有的政府机构和策略，还未真正发挥效用。最近，美国出台了一系列"日落条款"（sunset laws）。该条款规定，在一定的时间内，如果政府机构或公共法律没有进行重新修订，将自动失效。但是，这些条款并未发挥作用。一部分原因是，缺乏一个客观标准来评判机构和法律何时无效；还有一部分原因是，至今没有一个有组织的废除流程；但最主要的原因可能是，还没有找到一个替代方案，能够实现这些无效的法律和机构的最初目标。制定一套原则和流程，以使"日落条款"有效实施并颇具意义，是亟待解决的重要社会创新。我们的社会已准备就绪，迎接这一重要的社会创新。

IV

新任务

上面提到的两项社会策略，只是举例而已。更深层次的需求是，对策略、态度，尤其是优先事项的重新定位。无论是机构还是个人，我们都应倡导他们要灵活应变、持续学习，将变化视为常态和机会。

税收政策是一个重要领域。它深刻地影响着人们的行为，也是社会价值观和优先事项的表征。在发达国家，税制将对"摆脱昨天"的行为处以严罚。比如，美国税务人员将出售或清算业务或产品线的所得计为收入。实际上，这些收入当然应该视为资本回收额。但是，在现行税制下，企业要为这笔钱缴纳企业所得税。如果企业将这笔钱分发给股东，股东就要缴纳个人所得税。税制将这笔钱视为普通的"分红"，也就是"利润"分配。结果，企业宁愿苦苦挣扎、持续投资，也不愿放弃陈旧、过时、低效的事物。更糟糕的是，它们派遣能力最突出的人去"捍卫"陈旧事物，这是对人才这种稀有宝贵资源最严重的错误配置。企业应该将这些资源用于创造明天（如果企业还有明天的话）。当企业最终清算或出售陈旧、过时、低效的业务或产品线时，它不会把收益分发给股东。因此，股东也无法将它们投资到市场中，不能用于投资创新创业机会。相反，企业会保留这些资金，并投资于其他陈旧、传统、衰落的业务或产品，也就是说，将资金用于难以从资本市场募资的业务和活动。结果，这又一次导致稀缺资源的错误配置。

创业型社会所需的税制，要鼓励资本从旧事物转向新事物，而非阻止甚至惩罚这种行为。

我们还要利用税制来缓解成长中的新创企业最紧迫的财务问题，即资金短缺。一个方法可能是，接受经济现实：对于新创企业，尤其是成长中的新创企业，在最初的五六年中，"利润"只不过是账面上的数字游戏而已。在这段时期，企业所需的经营成本总是大于昨日的运营盈余（即本期收入与上期支出的差额）。这实际上意味着，成长中的新创企业要将所有的运营盈余用以维持生存；特别是当企业快速发展时，企业需要投入更多资金，远远高于它的"当期盈余"（即账面"利润"）。因此，在最初的几年中，成长中的新创企业（无论是独立企业，还是现有企业的一个分支机构）都应免缴税费。这与我们不能指望一个快速成长的小孩创造"盈余"来支持一个成人，是同样的道理。此外，税收是生产者支持其他人（即非生产者）的一种方式。待到新创企业发展壮大时再收税，它们肯定可以缴纳更多税费。

如果政府认为这种做法过于激进，至少应该对新创企业初始阶段的税费予以缓征。在新创企业面临严重的资金压力时，新创企业可以保留收益。而且，政府不能对此加以惩罚或征收利息。总而言之，创业型社会和经济需要一套鼓励资本形成的税收策略。

在资本形成方面，日本有一个秘诀，那就是官方鼓励"逃税"（tax evasion）。从法律上讲，日本成年人可以拥有一个中等规模的储蓄账户，这个账户的利息不需要缴税。但实际上，在日本，这类账户的数量是其人口（包括小孩和未成年人）的5倍之多。当然，报纸和政客经常抨击这个"丑闻"。日本对此持谨慎态度，并未采取任何措施来"根除弊端"。结果，日本的资本形成率居世界首位。这也许是摆脱现代社会困境的一种迂回战术。这种困境就是一种冲突：一方面对高水平资本形成率的强烈需求，另一方面又将利息和红利视为"非劳动所得"和"资本主义作风"，并加以谴责（甚至认为是罪恶的和不道德的）。但一个国家如果要在创业时代保持竞争力，就要效仿日本的策略，以半官方形式鼓励资本形成。

与激发企业家精神（至少不加以惩罚）的税收和政策同样重要的是，保护新创企业免受政府规制、限制条件、报告和文书工作的妨碍。我个人的建议是（尽管我认为它不会被接受），新创企业（无论是独立企业还是现有企业的分支机构）因政府规制、报告和文书工作所产生的费用，如果超过总收入的一定比例（如 5%），可以向政府申请补贴。这对公共服务领域中的新创企业尤其有益，如独立的外科诊所。在发达国家，公共服务机构深受政府繁文缛节的困扰，处理的政府琐事比自身业务还要多。就公共服务机构的财力和人力来讲，它们甚至无力承受这些重担。

在发达国家，政府机构所引致的无形成本持续增加，这已成为一种隐伏的恶疾。如果将我的提议拟定为政策，它将是治疗这种疾病的良方，也可能是唯一药方。政府琐事耗费大量资金，甚至会耗费优质人才大量时间和精力。这是"看不见的成本"，它并不体现在政府预算上，而是隐含在医生的账目中，这些医生的护士要花费一半的工作时间来填写政府表格和报告；也隐含在大学的预算中，大学里有 16 名高级管理者专门负责满足政府命令和法规要求；也隐含在小企业的损益表中，一个有 275 名员工的企业，19 名员工专门处理与政府相关的税务工作，包括从员工薪水中扣除税费和社会保障金，收集供应商和客户的税号，并报告给政府（或像欧洲一样征收增值税）。这些无形的政府相关费用，不能产生任何效益。例如，难道有人会相信，无论是精神上还是物质上，税务会计师能为国家财富、生产力和社会福利做出贡献？但是，发达国家政府却将越来越多的最稀缺资源，即有能力、勤奋且训练有素的人们，安排到无效的工作中。

要想控制政府无形成本这个"肿瘤"，也许只是奢望而已，更不用说将它彻底治愈。但是，我们至少可以保护新的创业型企业免受其害。

对于新的政府策略或措施，我们应该问以下问题：它是否能提升社会创新能力？它是否能推进社会和经济灵活性？或者，它是否阻碍或惩罚创新与企业家精神？当然，对社会创新能力的推动作用，不能也不应是决定性因素，更不用说是唯一标准。但是，在制定某项新策略或新措施之前，应将它们的影响考虑在内。然而当下，也许除了日本，没有一个国家或策略制定者做到了这一点。

V

创业型社会中的个人

在创业型社会中，个人面临着巨大的挑战：需要不断学习、再学习。他们应该将这个挑战视为机会，并加以利用。

在传统社会中，人们认为或者曾经认为，学习随着青春期的结束而终止，最迟也会终止于成年之际。一个人 21 岁时没有学到的知识，永不会再学到；一个人 21 岁时已经习得的知识，将保持不变、受用余生。传统学徒制、传统工艺、传统职业，以及传统教育制度和学校都以此为前提。直到现在，工艺、职业、教育制度和学校大体也都以此为前提。但例外总会存在。一些群体在不断学习，再学习，比如，伟大的艺术家和学者、禅僧、神秘主义者和耶稣会士。这些特例如此之少，以致往往被忽略。

但是，在创业型社会中，这些"例外"成为典范。在创业型社会中，正确的假设是：即便已经是成年人了，也要持续学习（类似的学习，也许不止一次）。5～10 年后，个人在 21 岁时所学到的知识就会过时，因此要不断习得新知识、新技能以替换或更新以前所学的知识。

这意味着，每个人都需要不断学习再学习，为自身发展和职业发展负责。他们不再认为，孩提时代和青少年时代所学的知识是未来发展的"基础"。这些知识应是"发射台"、未来的起点，而非依赖或休息之地。他们也不再认为，"进入某个职业领域"，随后按照预先确定的、规划清晰的、充满光明的"职业路径"，进而到达既定目的地。这就是美国军队所称的"进阶之路"（progressing in grade）。自此以后，每个人在其职业生涯中，都要寻找、决定并发展多个"职业"。

一个人受教育程度越高，所从事的职业越具有企业家精神，在学习中遇到的挑战也越大。木匠可能认为，他们在学徒工和熟练工时期所获得的技能，40年后依旧有用。但医生、工程师、冶金学家、化学家、会计师、律师、教师和管理者最好能意识到，他们15年后需要掌握和应用的技能、知识和工具与今日完全不同。事实上，他们最好假定，他们15年后将做不同的事情，具有不同的目标，在多数情况下，甚至从事不同的职业。因此，他们必须不断学习和再学习，并自我指导。传统、惯例和"公司策略"将成为个人进步的阻碍，而非帮助。

这也意味着，创业型社会对现有教育和学习的习惯和假设是一个挑战。全球当代教育体制起源于17世纪的欧洲，在此基础上进行优化拓展。但是，学校和大学的基本架构可以追溯到300多年前。现在各级学校都需要采用全新的（甚至是激进的）思维方式和教学方法。学龄前儿童使用计算机只是一时的狂热。但是，现在的孩子在4岁就开始接触电视，与50年前的同龄儿童相比，他们对教育的期望、要求及回应截然不同。又比如，将要奔赴职场的年轻人，也就是当今4/5的大学生，都需要接受"博雅教育"（liberal education）。这显然不是17世纪英语国家的"liberal education"课程（或者德国的"Aligemeine Bildung"课程）的19世纪新版本。如果不正视这一变化，我们将丧失"博雅教育"的真正内涵，将沦落为纯粹的职业化、专业化教育。这会危及社区教育的基础，最终危及社区本身。教育者必须接受这一事实，即教育不仅仅限于年轻人。最大的挑战（也是最大的机会）是学校也要是受过高等教育的成人继续学习的场所。

迄今为止，尚未有一套教育理论体系，可以指导我们完成这些任务。也没有人能比得上捷克 17 世纪的教育学伟大改革者科梅纽斯（Johann Comenius）和普遍的耶稣会的教士（他们为现在所称的"现代"学校和"现代"大学的发展，做出了巨大贡献）。但至少在美国，教育实践的发展远远超过教育理论的发展。在我看来，过去 20 年来，最积极和振奋人心的教育成就是，针对需要学习和再学习的成人，尤其是受过高等教育的专业人士，美国教育所做出的努力。这也是美国不设"教育部"以后，一个令人愉悦的意外收获。虽然没有"总体规划"，也没有"教育理念"，甚至没有教育机构的大力支持，但为受过良好教育并取得一定成就的成人提供的继续教育和培训项目，成为美国过去 20 年来真正的"增长型产业"。

创业型社会的出现可能是历史上的一个重要转折点。

1776 年，亚当·斯密出版了《国富论》，自由放任主义随之出现。1873年，席卷全球的经济恐慌终结了自由放任主义，现代福利国家取而代之。众所周知，100 年后，现代福利国家也将走到终点。尽管遭遇人口老龄化和出生率下降的冲击，现代福利国家不会马上结束。但是，只有当创业型经济大幅提高生产力时，现代福利国家才能维持下去。我们甚至仍可以多多少少对福利体系"添砖加瓦"，如建点新的房屋或搞点新的福利。但即便最偏执的自由主义者也意识到，如今福利国家时代已经一去不返。

福利国家时代之后，会是创业型社会吗？

推荐书目

关于企业家精神的书籍大都描述奇闻逸事和街头趣闻。这类书中，最好的当属乔治·吉尔德（George Gilder）的 *The Spirit of Enterprise*（New York: Simon & Schuster, 1984）。这本书介绍了几个企业家的奋斗故事，但并没有过多讨论我们从中能学到什么。另外，本书仅仅限于新创企业，并未涉及现有企业和公共服务机构的企业家精神。但是，吉尔德至少没有将企业家精神错误地等同于高科技。

对企业家和想要了解企业家精神的人来说，华盛顿大学西雅图分校的卡尔·H.维斯珀（Karl H. Vesper）更有帮助，尤其是他的 *New Venture Strategy*（Englewood Cliffs, N.J.: Prentice-Hall, 1980）和年度出版物 *Frontiers of Entrepreneurship Research*（Babson Park, Mass.: Babson College）。维斯珀的研究也仅限于新创企业，尤其是小企业。虽然存在一定的局限性，但他的研究成果充满了真知灼见。

约瑟夫·R.曼库索（Joseph R. Mancuso）在纽约创办并主导的创业管理中心（83 Spring Street, New York, N.Y. 10012）以及其举世闻名的著作 *How to Start, Finance and Manage Your Own Small Business*（Englewood Cliffs, N.J.: Prentice-HaIl, 1978）都只专注于小企业。

　　有两本书籍探讨了现有企业，尤其是大型企业中的创业管理。这两本书有很大不同，但互为补充。一本是安德鲁·S.格罗夫（Andrew S. Grove）的著作《高产出管理》（*High-Output Management*，New York: Random House, 1983）。格罗夫现在是英特尔公司的总裁，也是公司创始人之一。书中探讨了快速发展中的大企业要保持企业家精神，所需的策略和实践。另一本是耶鲁大学组织心理学家罗莎贝斯·莫斯·坎特（Rosabeth M. Kanter）的著作《变革大师》（*The Change Master*，New York: Simon & Schuster, 1983），书中探讨创业型企业领导者的态度和行为。到目前为止，对现有企业中企业家精神的最具洞察力的讨论，当属麦肯锡咨询公司的两位成员，理查德·卡夫诺（Richard E. Cavenaugh）和小唐纳德·克利福德（Donald K. Clifford, Jr.）的文章。这篇文章发表在1983年秋的《麦肯锡季刊》，题为《美国中等规模成长型企业给我们的启示》（"*Lessons from America's Mid-Sized Growth Companies*"）。这两个人还将他们的文章和研究成果聚集成书，将于1985年或1986年出版。

　　在战略类书籍中，最好的当属迈克尔·波特（Michael Porter）的《竞争战略》（*Competitive Strategies*，New York: Free Press, 1980）。

　　在我早期的著作中，《为成果而管理》（New York: Harper & Row, 1964），尤其是第1～5章，以及《管理：使命、责任、实践》（New York: Harper & Row, 1973）中的第11～14章（服务机构）、第53～61章（战略和结构），也对企业家精神和创业管理进行了探讨。

This book presents innovation and entrepreneurship as a practice and a discipline. It does not talk of the psychology and the character traits of entrepreneurs; it talks of their actions and behavior. It uses cases, but primarily to exemplify a point, a rule, or a warning, rather than as success stories. The work thus differs, in both intention and execution, from many of the books and articles on innovation and entrepreneurship that are being published today. It shares with them the belief in the importance of innovation and entrepreneurship. Indeed, it considers the emergence of a truly entrepreneurial economy in the United States during the last ten to fifteen years the most significant and hopeful event to have occurred in recent economic and social history. But whereas much of today's discussion treats entrepreneurship as something slightly mysterious, whether gift, talent, inspiration, or "flash of genius," this book represents innovation and entrepreneurship as purposeful tasks that can be organized—are in need of being organized—and as systematic work. It treats innovation and entrepreneurship, in fact, as part of the executive's job.

This is a practical book, but it is not a "how-to" book. Instead, it deals with the what, when, and why; with such tangibles as policies and decisions; opportunities and risks; structures and strategies; staffing, compensation, and rewards.

Innovation and entrepreneurship are discussed under three main headings: The Practice of Innovation; The Practice of Entrepreneurship; and Entrepreneurial Strategies. Each of these is an "aspect" of innovation and entrepreneurship rather than a stage.

Part I on the Practice of Innovation presents innovation alike as purposeful and as a discipline. It shows first where and how the entrepreneur searches for innovative opportunities. It then discusses the Do's and Dont's of developing an innovative idea into a viable business or service.

Part II, The Practice of Entrepreneurship, focuses on the institution that is the carrier of innovation, It deals with entrepreneurial management in three areas: the existing business; the public-service institution; and the new venture. What are the policies and practices that enable an institution, whether business or public-service, to be a successful entrepreneur? How does one organize and staff for entrepreneurship? What are the obstacles, the impediments, the traps, the common mistakes? The section concludes with a discussion of individual entrepreneurs, their roles and their decisions.

Finally, Part III, Entrepreneurial Strategies, talks of bringing an innovation successfully to market. The test of an innovation, after all, lies not its novelty, its scientific content, or its cleverness. It lies in its success in the marketplace.

These three parts are flanked by an Introduction that relates innovation and entrepreneurship to the economy, and by a Conclusion that relates them to society.

Entrepreneurship is neither a science nor an art. It is a practice.It has a knowledge base, of course, which this book attempts to present in organized fashion. But as in all practices, medicine, for instance, or engineering, knowledge in entrepreneurship is a means to an end.Indeed, what constitutes knowledge in a practice is largely defined by the ends, that is, by the practice. Hence a book like this should be backed by long years of practice.

My work on innovation and entrepreneurship began thirty years ago, in the mid-fifties. For two years, then, a small group met under my leadership at the Graduate Business School of New York University every week for a long evening's seminar on Innovation and Entrepreneurship. The group included people who were just launching their own new ventures, most of them successfully. It included mid-career executives from a wide variety of established, mostly large organizations: two big hospitals; IBM and General Electric; one or two major banks; a brokerage house; magazine and book publishers; pharmaceuticals; a worldwide charitable organization; the Catholic Archdiocese of New York and the Presbyterian Church; and so on.

The concepts and ideas developed in this seminar were tested by its members week by week during those two years in their own work and their own institutions. Since then they have been tested, validated, refined, and revised in more than twenty years of my own consulting work. Again, a wide variety of institutions has been involved. Some were businesses, including high-tech ones such as pharmaceuticals and computer companies; "no-tech" ones such as casualty insurance companies;

"world-class" banks, both American and European; one-man startup ventures; regional wholesalers of building products; and Japanese multinationals. But a host of "nonbusinesses" also were included:several major labor unions; major community organizations such as the Girl Scouts of the U.S.A. or C.A.R.E., the international relief and development cooperative; quite a few hospitals; universities and research labs; and religious organizations from a diversity of denominations.

Because this book distills years of observation, study, and practice, I was able to use actual "mini-cases," examples and illustrations both of the right and the wrong policies and practices. Wherever the name of an institution is mentioned in the text, it has either never been a client of mine (e.g., IBM) and the story is in the public domain, or the institution itself has disclosed the story. Otherwise organizations with whom I have worked remain anonymous, as has been my practice in all my management books. But the cases themselves report actual events and deal with actual enterprises.

Only in the last few years have writers on management begun to pay much attention to innovation and entrepreneurship. I have been discussing aspects of both in all my management books for decades. Yet this is the first work that attempts to present the subject in its entirety and in systematic form. This is surely a first book on a major topic rather than the last word—but I do hope it will be accepted as a seminal work.

Claremont, California
Christmas 1984

The Entrepreneurial Economy

I

Since the mid-seventies, such slogans as "the no-growth economy;" the "deindustrialization of America," and a long-term "Kondratieff stagnation of the economy" have become popular and are invoked as if axioms. Yet the facts and figures belie every one of these slogans. What is happening in the United States is something quite different: a profound shift from a "managerial" to an "entrepreneurial" economy.

In the two decades 1965 to 1985, the number of Americans over sixteen (thereby counted as being in the work force under the conventions of American statistics) grew by two-fifths, from 129 to 180 million.But the number of Americans in paid jobs grew in the same period by one-half, from 71 to 106 million. The labor force growth was fastest in the second decade of that period, the decade from 1974 to 1984, when total jobs in the American economy grew by a full 24 million.

In no other peacetime period has the United States created as many new jobs, whether measured in percentages or in absolute numbers. And yet the ten years that began with the "oil shock" in the late fall of 1973 were years of extreme turbulence, of "energy crises," of the near-collapse of the "smokestack" industries, and of two sizable recessions.

The American development is unique. Nothing like it has happened yet in any other country. Western Europe during the period 1970 to 1984 actually *lost* jobs, 3 to 4 million of them. In 1970, western Europe still had 20 million more jobs than the United States; in 1984, it had almost 10 million less. Even Japan did far less well in job creation than the United States. During the twelve years from 1970 through 1982, jobs in Japan grew by a mere 10 percent, that is, at less than half the U.S. rate.

But America's performance in creating jobs during the seventies and early eighties also ran counter to what every expert had predicted twenty-five years ago. Then most labor force analysts expected the economy, even at its most rapid growth, to be unable to provide jobs for all the boys of the "baby boom" who were going to reach working age in the seventies and early eighties—the first large cohorts of "baby boom" babies having been born in 1949 and 1950. Actually, the American economy had to absorb twice that number. For—something nobody even dreamed of in 1970—married women began to rush into the labor force in the mid-seventies. The result is that today, in the mid-eighties, every other married woman with young children holds a paid job, whereas only one out of every five did so in 1970. And the American economy found jobs for these, too, in many cases far better jobs than women had ever held before.

And yet "everyone knows" that the seventies and early eighties were periods of "no growth," of stagnation and decline, of a "deindustrializing America," because everyone still focuses on what were the growth areas in the twenty-five years after World War II, the years that came to an end around 1970.

In those earlier years, America's economic dynamics centered in institutions that were already big and were getting bigger: the Fortune 500, that is, the country's largest businesses; governments, whether federal, state, or local; the large and super-large universities; the large consolidated high school with its six thousand or more students; and the large and growing hospital. These institutions created practically all the new jobs provided in the American economy in the quarter century after World War II. And in every recession during this period, job loss and unemployment occurred predominantly in small institutions and, of course, mainly in small businesses.

But since the late 1960s, job creation and job growth in the United States have shifted to a new sector. The old job creators have actually *lost* jobs in these last twenty years. Permanent jobs (not counting recession unemployment) in the Fortune 500 have been shrinking steadily year by year since around 1970, at first slowly, but since 1977 or 1978 at a pretty fast clip. By 1984, the Fortune 500 had lost permanently at least 4 to 6 million jobs. And governments in America, too, now employ fewer people than they did ten or fifteen years ago, if only because the number of schoolteachers has been falling as school enrollment dropped in the wake of the "baby bust" of the early sixties. Universities grew until 1980; since then, employment there has been declining. And in the early eighties, even hospital employment stopped increasing. In other words, we have not in fact created 35 million new jobs; we have created 40 million or more, since we had to offset a permanent job shrinkage of at least 5 million jobs in the traditional employing institutions. And all these new jobs must have been created by small and medium-sized institutions, most of them small and medium-sized businesses, and a great many of them, if not the majority, *new* businesses that did not even exist twenty years ago. According to *The Economist*, 600,000 new businesses are being started in the United States every year now—about seven times as many as were started in each of the boom years of the fifties and sixties.

II

"Ah," everybody will say immediately, "high tech." But things are not quite that simple. Of the 40 million-plus jobs created since 1965 in the economy, high technology did not contribute more than 5 or 6 million. High tech thus contributed no more than "smokestack" lost. All the additional jobs in the economy were generated elsewhere. And only one or two out of every hundred new businesses— a total of ten thousand a year—are remotely "high-tech," even in the loosest sense of the term.

We are indeed in the early stages of a major technological transformation, one that is far more sweeping than the most ecstatic of the "futurologists" yet realize, greater even than *Megatrends* or *Future Shock*. Three hundred years of technology came to an end after World War II. During those three centuries the model for technology was a mechanical one: the events that go on inside a star such as the sun. This period began when an otherwise almost unknown French physicist, Denis Papin, [⊖]envisaged the steam engine around 1680. They ended when we replicated in the nuclear explosion the events inside a star. For these three centuries advance in technology meant—as it does in mechanical processes—more speed, higher temperatures, higher pressures. Since the end of World War II, however, the model of technology has become the biological process, the events inside an organism. And in an organism, processes are not organized around energy in the physicist's meaning of the term. They are organized around information.

There is no doubt that high tech, whether in the form of computers or telecommunication, robots on the factory floor or office automation, biogenetics

---

⊖ The dates of all persons mentioned in the text will be found in the Index.

or bioengineering, is of immeasurable qualitative importance. High tech provides the excitement and the headlines. It creates the vision for entrepreneurship and innovation in the community, and the receptivity for them. The willingness of young, highly trained people to go to work for small and unknown employers rather than for the giant bank or the worldwide electrical equipment maker is surely rooted in the mystique of "high tech"—even though the overwhelming majority of these young people work for employers whose technology is prosaic and mundane. High tech also probably stimulated the astonishing transformation of the American capital market from near-absence of venture capital as recently as the mid-sixties to near-surplus in the mid-eighties. High tech is thus what the logicians used to call the *ratio cognoscendi*, the reason why we perceive and understand a phenomenon rather than the explanation of its emergence and the cause of its existence.

Quantitatively, as has already been said, high tech is quite small still, accounting for not much more than one-eighth of the new jobs. Nor will it become much more important in terms of new jobs within the near future. Between now and the year 2000, no more than one-sixth of the jobs we can expect to create in the American economy will be high-tech jobs in all likelihood. In fact, if high tech were, as most people think, the entrepreneurial sector of the U.S. economy, then we would indeed face a "no-growth" period and a period of long-term stagnation in the trough of a "Kondratieff wave."

The Russian economist Nikolai Kondratieff in the mid-1930s, using his econometric model, predicted, accurately as it turned out, that collectivization of Russian agriculture would lead to a sharp decline in farm production. The "fifty-year Kondratieff cycle" was based on the inherent dynamics of technology. Every fifty years, so Kondratieff asserted, a long technological wave crests. For the last twenty years of this cycle, the growth industries of the last technological advance seem to be doing exceptionally well. But what look like record profits are actually repayments of capital which is no longer needed in industries that have ceased to grow. This situation never lasts longer than twenty years, then there is a sudden crisis, usually signaled by some sort of panic. There follow twenty years of stagnation, during which the new, emerging technologies cannot generate enough jobs to make the economy itself grow again—and no one, least of all government, can do much about this.[⊖]

The industries that fueled the long economic expansion after World War II—

[⊖] Kondratieff's long-wave cycle was popularized in the West by the Austro-Americaneconomist Joseph Schumpeter, in his monumental book *Business Cycles* (1939). Kondratieff's best known, most serious, and most important disciple today—and also the most serious and most knowledgeable of the prophets of "long-term stagnation" —is the MIT scientist Jay Forrester.

automobiles, steel, rubber, electrical apparatus, consumer electronics, telephone, but also petroleum⊖—perfectly fit the Kondratieff cycle. Technologically, all of them go back to the fourth quarter of the nineteenth century or, at the very latest, to before World War I. In none of them has there been a significant breakthrough since the 1920s, whether in technology or in business concepts. When the economic growth began after World War II, they were all thoroughly mature industries. They could expand and create jobs with relatively little new capital investment, which explains why they could pay skyrocketing wages and workers' benefits and simultaneously show record profits. Yet, as Kondratieff had predicted, these signs of robust health were as deceptive as the flush on a consumptive's cheek. The industries were corroding from within. They did not become stagnant or decline slowly. Rather, they collapsed as soon as the "oil shocks" of 1973 and 1979 dealt them the first blows. Within a few years they went from record profits to near-bankruptcy. As soon became abundantly clear, they will not be able to return to their earlier employment levels for a long time, if ever.

The high-tech industries, too, fit Kondratieff's theory. As Kondratieff had predicted, they have so far not been able to generate more jobs than the old industries have been losing. All projections indicate that they will not do much more for long years to come, at least for the rest of the century. Despite the explosive growth of computers, for instance, data processing and information handling in all their phases (design and engineering of both hardware and software, production, sales and service) are not expected to add as many jobs to the American economy in the late 1980s and early 1990s as the steel and automotive industries are almost certain to lose.

But the Kondratieff theory fails totally to account for the 40 million jobs which the American economy actually did create. Western Europe, to be sure, has so far been following the Kondratieff script. But not the United States, and perhaps not Japan either. Something in the United States offsets the Kondratieff "long wave of technology." Something has already happened that is incompatible with the theory of long-term stagnation.

Nor does it appear at all likely that we have simply postponed the Kondratieff cycle. For in the next twenty years the need to create new jobs in the U.S. economy will be a great deal lower than it has been in the last twenty years, so that economic growth will depend far less on job creation. The number of new entrants into the

---

⊖ Which, contrary to common belief, was the first one to start declining. In fact, petroleum ceased to be a growth industry around 1950. Since then the incremental unit of petroleum needed for an additional unit of output, whether in manufacturing, in transportation, or in heating and air conditioning, has been falling—slowly at first but rapidly since 1973.

American work force will be up to one-third smaller for the rest of the century—and indeed through the year 2010—than it was in the years when the children of the "baby boom" reached adulthood, that is, 1965 until 1980 or so. Since the "baby bust" of 1960-61, the birth cohorts have been 30 percent lower than they were during the "baby boom" years. And with the labor force participation of women under fifty already equal to that of men, additions to the number of women available for paid jobs will from now on be limited to natural growth, which means that they will also be down by about 30 percent.

For the future of the traditional "smokestack" industries, the Kondratieff theory must be accepted as a serious hypothesis, if not indeed as the most plausible of the available explanations. And as far as the inability of new high-tech industries to offset the stagnation of yesterday's growth industries is concerned, Kondratieff again deserves to be taken seriously. For all their tremendous qualitative importance as vision makers and pacesetters, quantitatively the high-tech industries represent tomorrow rather than today, especially as creators of jobs. They are the makers of the future rather than the makers of the present.

But as a theory of the American economy that can explain its behavior and predict its direction, Kondratieff can be considered disproven and discredited. The 40 million new jobs created in the U.S. economy during a "Kondratieff long-term stagnation" cannot be explained in Kondratieff's terms.

I do not mean to imply that there are no economic problems or dangers. Quite the contrary. A major shift in the technological foundations of the economy such as we are experiencing in the closing quarter of the twentieth century surely presents tremendous problems, economic, social, and political. We are also in the throes of a major political crisis, the crisis of that great twentieth-century success the Welfare State, with the attendant danger of an uncontrolled and seemingly uncontrollable but highly inflationary deficit. There is surely sufficient danger in the international economy, with the world's rapidly industrializing nations, such as Brazil or Mexico, suspended between rapid economic takeoff and disastrous crash, to make possible a prolonged global depression of 1930 proportions. And then there is the frightening specter of the runaway armaments race. But at least one of the fears abroad these days, that of a Kondratieff stagnation, can be considered more a figment of the imagination than reality for the United States. There we have a new, an entrepreneurial economy.

It is still too early to say whether the entrepreneurial economy will remain primarily an American phenomenon or whether it will emerge in other industrially developed countries. In Japan, there is good reason to believe that it is emerging, albeit in its own, Japanese form. But whether the same shift to an entrepreneurial economy will occur in western Europe, no one can yet say. Demographically, western Europe lags some ten to fifteen years behind America: both the "baby boom" and the "baby bust" came later in Europe than in the United States. Equally, the shift to much longer years of schooling started in western Europe some ten years later than in the United States or in Japan; and in Great Britain it has barely started yet. If, as is quite likely, demographics has been a factor in the emergence of the entrepreneurial economy in the United States, we could well see a similar development in Europe by 1990 or 1995. But this is speculation. So far, the entrepreneurial economy is purely an American phenomenon.

III

Where did all the new jobs come from? The answer is from anywhere and nowhere; in other words, from no one single source.

The magazine *Inc.*, published in Boston, has printed each year since 1982 a list of the one hundred fastest-growing, publicly owned American companies more than five years and less than fifteen years old. Being confined to publicly owned companies, the list is heavily biased toward high tech, which has easy access to underwriters, to stock market money, and to being traded on one of the stock exchanges or over the counter. High tech is fashionable. Other new ventures, as a rule, can go public only after long years of seasoning, and of showing profits for a good deal more than five years. Yet only one-quarter of the "*Inc.* 100" are high-tech; three-quarters remain most decidedly "low-tech," year after year.

In 1982, for instance, there were five restaurant chains, two women's wear manufacturers, and twenty health-care providers on the list, but only twenty to thirty high-tech companies. And whilst America's newspapers in 1982 ran one article after the other bemoaning the "deindustrialization of America," a full half of the *Inc.* firms were manufacturing companies; only one-third were in services. Although word had it in 1982 that the Frost Belt was dying, with the Sun Belt the only possible growth area, only one-third of the "*Inc.* 100" that year were in the Sun Belt. New York had as many of these fast-growing, young, publicly owned companies as California or Texas. And Pennsylvania, New Jersey, and Massachusetts—while supposedly dying, if not already dead—also had as many as California or Texas, and as many as New York. Snowy, Minnesota, had seven. The *Inc.* lists for 1983 and 1984 showed a very similar distribution, in respect both to industry and to geography.

In 1983, the first and second companies on another *Inc.* list—the "*Inc.* 500" list of fast-growing, young, privately held companies—were, respectively, a building contractor in the Pacific Northwest (in a year in which construction was supposedly at an all-time low) and a California manufacturer of physical exercise equipment for the home.

Any inquiry among venture capitalists yields the same pattern. Indeed, in their portfolios, high tech is usually even less prominent. The portfolio of one of the most successful venture capital investors does include several high-tech companies: a new computer software producer, a new venture in medical technology, and so on. But the most profitable investment in this portfolio, the new company that has been growing the fastest in both revenues and profitability during the three years 1981- 83, is that most mundane and least high-tech of businesses, a chain of barbershops. And next to it, both in sales growth and profitability, comes a chain of dentistry offices, followed by a manufacturer of handtools and by a finance company that leases machinery to small businesses.

Among the businesses I know personally, the one that has created the most jobs during the five years 1979-84, and has also grown the fastest in revenues and profits, is a financial services firm. Within five years this firm alone has created two thousand new jobs, most of them exceedingly well paid. Though a member of the New York Stock Exchange, only about one-eighth of its business is in stocks. The rest is in annuities, tax-exempt bonds, money-market funds and mutual funds, mortgage-trust certificates, tax-shelter partnerships, and a host of similar investments for what the firm calls "the intelligent investor." Such investors are defined as the well-to-do but not rich professional, small businessman, or farmer, in small towns or in the suburbs, who makes more money than he spends and thus looks for places to put his savings, but who is also realistic enough not to expect to become rich through investment.

The most revealing source of information about the growth sectors of the U.S. economy I have been able to find is a study of the one hundred fastest-growing "mid-size" companies, that is, companies with revenues of between $25 million and $1 billion. This study was conducted during 1981-83 for the American Business Conference by two senior partners of McKinsey & Company, the consulting firm.[⊖]

These mid-sized growth companies grew at three times the rate of the Fortune 500 in sales and in profits. The Fortune 500 have been losing jobs steadily since 1970. But these mid-sized growth companies added jobs between 1970 and 1983 at three times the rate of job growth in the entire U.S. economy. Even in the depression years 1981-82 when jobs in U.S. industry declined by almost 2 percent, the hundred mid-sized growth companies increased their employment by one full percentage

---

⊖ It was published under the title "Lessons from America's Mid-sized Growth Companies," by Richard E. Cavenaugh and Donald K. Clifford, Jr., in the Autumn 1983 issue of the *McKinsey Quarterly*.

point. The companies span the economic spectrum. There are high-tech ones among them, to be sure. But there are also financial services companies—the New York investment and brokerage firm of Donaldson, Lufkin & Jenrette, for instance. One of the best performers in the group is a company making and selling living-room furniture; another one is making and marketing doughnuts; a third, high-quality chinaware; a fourth, writing instruments; a fifth, household paints; a sixth has expanded from printing and publishing local newspapers into consumer marketing services; a seventh produces yarns for the textile industry; and so forth. And where "everybody knows" that growth in the American economy is exclusively in services, more than half of these "mid-sized growth" companies are in manufacturing.

To make things more confusing still, the growth sector of the U.S. economy during the last ten to fifteen years, while entirely nongovernmental, includes a fairly large and growing number of enterprises that are not normally considered businesses, though quite a few are now being organized as profit-making companies. The most visible of these are, of course, in the health-care field. The traditional American community hospital is in deep trouble these days. But there are fast-growing and flourishing hospital chains, both "profit" and (increasingly) "not-for-profit" ones. Even faster growing are the "freestanding" health facilities, such as hospices for the terminally ill, medical and diagnostic laboratories, freestanding surgery centers, freestanding maternity homes, psychiatric "walk-in" clinics, or centers for geriatric diagnosis and treatment.

The public schools are shrinking in almost every American community. But despite the decline in the total number of children of school age as a result of the "baby bust" of the 1960s, a whole new species of non-profit but private schools is flourishing. In the small California city in which I live, a neighborhood babysitting cooperative, founded around 1980 by a few mothers for their own children, had by 1984 grown into a school with two hundred students going on into the fourth grade. And a "Christian" school founded a few years ago by the local Baptists is taking over from the city of Claremont a junior high school built fifteen years ago and left standing vacant for lack of pupils for the last five years. Continuing education of all kinds, whether in the form of executive management programs for mid-career managers or refresher courses for doctors, engineers, lawyers, and physical therapists, is booming; even during the severe 1982-83 recession, such programs suffered only a short setback.

One additional area of entrepreneurship, and a very important one, is the emerging "Fourth Sector" of public-private partnerships in which government units, either states or municipalities, determine performance standards and provide the money. But then they contract out a service—fire protection, garbage collection, or bus transportation—to a private business on the basis of competitive bids, thus ensuring both better service and substantially lower costs. The city of Lincoln, Nebraska, has been a pioneer in this area since Helen Boosalis was first elected mayor in 1975—the same Lincoln, Nebraska, where a hundred years ago the Populists and William Jennings Bryan first started us on the road to municipal ownership of public services. Pioneering work in this area is also being done in Texas—in San Antonio and in Houston, for instance—and especially in Minneapolis at the Hubert Humphrey Institute of the University of Minnesota. Control Data Corporation, a leading computer manufacturer also in Minneapolis, is building public-private partnerships in education and even in the management and rehabilitation of prisoners. And if there is one action that can save the postal service in the long run—for surely there is a limit to the public's willingness to pay ever larger subsidies and ever higher rates for ever-shrinking service—it may be the contracting out of first-class service (or what's still left of it ten years hence) to the "Fourth Sector," through competitive bids.

IV

Is there anything at all that these growth enterprises have in common other than growth and defiance of the Kondratieff stagnation? Actually, they are all examples of "new technology," all new applications of knowledge to human work, which is, after all, the definition of technology. Only the "technology" is not electronics or genetics or new materials. The "new technology" is entrepreneurial management.

Once this is seen, then the astonishing job growth of the American economy during the last twenty, and especially the last ten years can be explained. It can even be reconciled with the Kondratieff theory. The United States—and to some extent also Japan—is experiencing what might be called an "atypical Kondratieff cycle."

Since Joseph Schumpeter first pointed it out in 1939, we have known that what actually happened in the United States and in Germany in the fifty years between 1873 and World War I does not fit the Kondratieff cycle. The first Kondratieff cycle, based on the railway boom, came to an end with the crash of the Vienna Stock Exchange in 1873, a crash that brought down stock exchanges worldwide and ushered in a severe depression. Great Britain and France did then enter a long period of industrial stagnation during which the new emerging technologies—steel, chemicals, electrical apparatus, telephone, and finally, automobiles—could not create enough jobs to offset the stagnation in the old industries, such as railway construction, coal mining, or textiles.

But this did not happen in the United States or in Germany, nor indeed in

Austria, despite the traumatic impact of the Viennese stock market crash from which Austrian politics never quite recovered.These countries were severely jolted at first. Five years later they had pulled out of the slump and were growing again, fast. In terms of "technology," these countries were no different from stagnating Britain or France. What explains their different economic behavior was one factor, and one factor only: the entrepreneur. In Germany, for instance, the single most important economic event in the years between 1870 and 1914 was surely the creation of the Universal Bank. The first of these, the Deutsche Bank, was founded by Georg Siemens in 1870$^\ominus$ with the specific mission of finding entrepreneurs, financing entrepreneurs, and forcing upon them organized, disciplined management. In the economic history of the United States the entrepreneurial bankers such as J. P. Morgan in New York played a similar role.

Today, something very similar seems to be happening in the United States and perhaps also to some extent in Japan.

Indeed, high tech is the one sector that is not part of this new "technology, " this "entrepreneurial management. " The Silicon Valley high-tech entrepreneurs still operate mainly in the nineteenth-century mold. They still believe in Benjamin Franklin's dictum: "If you invent a better mousetrap the world will beat a path to your door." It does not yet occur to them to ask what makes a mousetrap "better" or for whom?

There are, of course, plenty of exceptions, high-tech companies that know well how to manage entrepreneurship and innovation. But then there were exceptions during the nineteenth century, too. There was the German, Werner Siemens, who founded and built the company that still bears his name. There was George Westinghouse, the American, a great inventor but also a great business builder, who left behind two companies that still bear his name, one a leader in the field of transportation, the other a major force in the electrical apparatus industry.

But for the "high-tech" entrepreneur, the archetype still seems to be Thomas Edison. Edison, the nineteenth century's most successful inventor, converted invention into the discipline we now call research. His real ambition, however, was to be a business builder and to become a tycoon. Yet he so totally mismanaged the businesses he started that he had to be removed from every one of them to save it. Much, if not most high tech is still being managed, or more accurately mismanaged, Edison's way.

This explains, first, why the high-tech industries follow the traditional pattern of great excitement, rapid expansion, and then sudden shakeout and collapse, the pattern of "from rags to riches and back to rags again" in five years. Most of

---

$\ominus$ On Georg Siemens and the Universal Bank, see Chapter 9.

Silicon Valley—but most of the new biological high-tech companies as well—are still inventors rather than innovators, still speculators rather than entrepreneurs. And this, too, perhaps explains why high tech so far conforms to the Kondratieff prediction and does not generate enough jobs to make the whole economy grow again.

But the "low tech" of systematic, purposeful, managed entrepreneurship does.

V

Of all the major modern economists only Joseph Schumpeter concerned himself with the entrepreneur and his impact on the economy. Every economist knows that the entrepreneur is important and has impact. But, for economists, entrepreneurship is a "meta-economic" event, something that profoundly influences and indeed shapes the economy without itself being part of it. And so too, for economists, is technology. Economists do not, in other words, have any explanation as to why entrepreneurship emerged as it did in the late nineteenth century and as it seems to be doing again today, nor why it is limited to one country or to one culture. Indeed, the events that explain why entrepreneurship becomes effective are probably not in themselves economic events. The causes are likely to lie in changes in values, perception, and attitude, changes perhaps in demographics, in institutions (such as the creation of entrepreneurial banks in Germany and the United States around 1870), perhaps changes in education as well.

Something, surely, has happened to young Americans—and to fairly large numbers of them—to their attitudes, their values, their ambitions, in the last twenty to twenty-five years. Only it is clearly not what anyone looking at the young Americans of the late 1960s could possibly have predicted. How do we explain, for instance, that all of a sudden there are such large numbers of people willing both to work like demons for long years and to choose grave risks rather than big organization security? Where are the hedonists, the status seekers, the "me-too-ers," the conformists? Conversely, where are all the young people who, we were told fifteen years ago, were turning their backs on material values, on money, goods, and worldly success, and were going to restore to America a "laid-back," if not a pastoral "greenness"? Whatever the explanation; it does not fit in with what all the soothsayers of the last thirty years—David Riesman in *The Lonely Crowd*, William H. Whyte in *The Organization Man*, Charles Reich in *The Greening of America*, or Herbert Marcuse—predicted about the younger generation. Surely the emergence of the entrepreneurial economy is as much a cultural and psychological as it is an economic or technological event. Yet whatever the causes, the effects are above all economic ones.

And the vehicle of this profound change in attitudes, values, and above all in behavior is a "technology." It is called management. What has made possible the emergence of the entrepreneurial economy in America is new applications of management:

- to new enterprises, whether businesses or not, whereas most people until now have considered management applicable to existing enterprises only;
- to small enterprises, whereas most people were absolutely sure only a few years ago that management was for the "big boys" only;
- to nonbusinesses (health care, education, and so on), whereas most people still hear "business" when they encounter the word "management";
- to activities that were simply not considered to be "enterprises" at all, such as local restaurants;
- and above all, to systematic innovation: to the search for and the exploitation of new opportunities for satisfying human wants and human needs.

As a "useful knowledge," a *techné*, management is the same age as the other major areas of knowledge that underlie today's high-tech industries, whether electronics, solid-state physics, genetics, or immunology. Management's roots lie in the time around World War I. Its early shoots came up in the mid-1920s. But management is a "useful knowledge" like engineering or medicine, and as such it first had to develop as a practice before it could become a discipline. By the late 1930s, there were a few major enterprises around—at that time mostly businesses—that practiced "management" in the United States: the DuPont Company and its half brother, General Motors, but also a large retailer, Sears, Roebuck. On the other side of the Atlantic there was Siemens in Germany, or the department store chain of Marks and Spencer in Great Britain. But management as a discipline originated during and right after World War II.[⊖]

Beginning around 1955, the entire developed world experienced a "management boom." [⊖] The social technology we call management was first presented to the general public, including managers themselves, some forty years ago. It then rapidly became a discipline rather than the hit-or-miss practice of a few isolated

---

⊖ My first two management books, *Concept of the Corporation* (1946; a study of General Motors), and *The Practice of Management* (1954) were indeed the original attempts to organize and present management as a systematic body of knowledge, that is, as a discipline.

⊖ This by now has even reached Communist China. One of the first actions of the Chinese government after the fall of the "Gang of Four" was to establish an Enterprise Management Agency directly responsible to the prime minister, and to import a Graduate Business School from the United States.

true believers. And in these forty years management has had as much impact as any of the "scientific breakthroughs" of the period—perhaps a good deal more. It may not be solely or even primarily responsible for the fact that society in every single developed country has become since World War II a society of organizations. It may not be solely or even primarily responsible for the fact that in every developed society today the great majority of people—and the overwhelming majority of educated people—work as employees in organizations, including of course the bosses themselves, who increasingly tend to be "professional managers," that is, hired hands, rather than owners. But surely if management had not emerged as a systematic discipline, we could not have organized what is now a social reality in every developed country: the society of organizations and the "employee society."

We still have quite a bit to learn about management, admittedly, and above all about the management of the knowledge worker. But the fundamentals are reasonably well known by now. Indeed, what was an esoteric cult only forty years ago, when most executives even in large companies did not in fact realize that they practiced management, now has become commonplace.

But by and large management until recently was seen as being confined to business, and within business, to "big business." In the early seventies, when the American Management Association invited the heads of small business to its "Presidents' Course" in Management, it was told again and again: "Management? That's not for me—that's only for big companies." Up to 1970 or 1975, American hospital administrators still rejected anything that was labeled "management." "We're hospital people, not business people," they said. (In the universities the faculties are still saying the same thing even though they will simultaneously complain how "badly managed" their institution is.) And indeed for a long time, from the end of World War II until 1970, "progress" meant building bigger institutions.

This twenty-five-year trend toward building bigger organizations in every social sphere—business, labor union, hospital, school, university, and so on— had many causes. But the belief that we knew how to manage bigness and did not really know how to manage small enterprises was surely a major factor. It had, for instance, a great deal to do with the rush toward the very large consolidated American high school. "Education," it was argued, "requires professional administration, and this in turn works only in large rather than small enterprises."

During the last ten or fifteen years we have reversed this trend. In fact, we might now have a trend toward "deinstitutionalizing" America rather than one toward "deindustrializing" it. For almost fifty years, ever since the 1930s, it was widely believed in the United States and in western Europe too that the hospital was the best place for anyone not quite well, let alone for anyone seriously sick. "The sooner the patient gets to the hospital, the better care we can take of him," was the prevailing belief, shared by doctors and patients alike. In the last few years, we have been reversing this trend. We now increasingly believe that the longer we can keep patients away from the hospital and the sooner we can get them out, the better. Surely this reversal has little to do with either health care or with management. It is a reaction—whether permanent or short-lived—against the worship of centralization, of "planning," of government which began in the 1920s and 1930s, and which in the United States reached its peak in the Kennedy and Johnson administrations of the 1960s. However, we could not indulge in this "deinstitutionalization" in the health-care field if we had not acquired the competence and the confidence to manage small institutions and "non-businesses," that is, health-care institutions.

All told we are learning that management may well both be more needed and have greater impact on the small entrepreneurial organization than it has in the big "managed" one. Above all, management, we are learning now, has as much to contribute to the new, the entrepreneurial enterprise, as to the existing, ongoing "managerial" one.

To take a specific example, hamburger stands have been around in the United States since the nineteenth century; after World War II they sprang up on big-city street corners. But in the McDonald's hamburger chain—one of the success stories of the last twenty-five years—management was being applied to what had always been a hit-and-miss, mom-and-pop operation. McDonald's first designed the end product; then it redesigned the entire process of making it; then it redesigned or in many cases invented the tools so that every piece of meat, every slice of onion, every bun, every piece of fried potato would be identical, turned out in a precisely timed and fully automated process. Finally, McDonald's studied what "value" meant to the customer, defined it as quality and predictability of product, speed of service, absolute cleanliness, and friendliness, then set standards for all of these, trained for them, and geared compensation to them.

All of which is management, and fairly advanced management at that.

Management is the new technology (rather than any specific new science or invention) that is making the American economy into an entrepreneurial economy. It is also about to make America into an entrepreneurial *society*. Indeed, there may be greater scope in the United States—and in developed societies generally—for social innovation in education, health care, government, and politics than there is in business and the economy. And again, entrepreneurship in society—and it is badly needed—requires above all application of the basic concepts, the basic *techné*, of management to new problems and new opportunities.

This means that the time has now come to do for entrepreneurship and innovation what we first did for management in general some thirty years ago: to develop the principles, the practice, and the discipline.

1

THE PRACTICE OF INNOVATION

INNOVATION AND ENTREPRENEURSHIP
PRACTICE AND PRINCIPLES

Innovation is the specific tool of entrepreneurs, the means by which they exploit change as an opportunity for a different business or a different service. It is capable of being presented as a discipline, capable of being learned, capable of being practiced. Entrepreneurs need to search purposefully for the sources of innovation, the changes and their symptoms that indicate opportunities for successful innovation. And they need to know and to apply the principles of successful innovation.

CHAPTER 1

Systematic Entrepreneurship

I

"The entrepreneur," said the French economist J. B. Say around 1800,"shifts economic resources out of an area of lower and into an area of higher productivity and greater yield." But Say's definition does not tell us who this "entrepreneur" is. And since Say coined the term almost two hundred years ago, there has been total confusion over the definitions of "entrepreneur" and "entrepreneurship."

In the United States, for instance, the entrepreneur is often defined as one who starts *his own, new* and *small business*. Indeed, the courses in "Entrepreneurship" that have become popular of late in American business schools are the linear descendants of the course in starting one's own small business that was offered thirty years ago, and in many cases, not very different.

But not every new small business is entrepreneurial or represents entrepreneurship.

The husband and wife who open another delicatessen store or another Mexican restaurant in the American suburb surely take a risk. But are they entrepreneurs? All they do is what has been done many times before. They gamble on the increasing popularity of eating out in their area, but create neither a new satisfaction nor new consumer demand.Seen under this perspective they are surely not entrepreneurs even though theirs is a new venture.

McDonald's, however, was entrepreneurship. It did not invent anything, to be sure. Its final product was what any decent American restaurant had produced years ago. But by applying management concepts and management techniques (asking, What is "value" to the customer?), standardizing the "product," designing process and tools, and by basing training on the analysis of the work to be done and then setting the standards it required, McDonald's both drastically upgraded the yield from resources, and created a new market and a new customer. This is entrepreneurship.

Equally entrepreneurial is the growing foundry started by a husband and wife team a few years ago in America's Midwest, to heat-treat ferrous castings to high-performance specifications—for example, the axles for the huge bulldozers used to clear the land and dig the ditches for a natural gas pipeline across Alaska. The science needed is well known; indeed, the company does little that has not been done before. But in the first place the founders systematized the technical information: they can now punch the performance specifications into their computer and get an immediate printout of the treatment required. Secondly, the founders systematized the process. Few orders run to more than half a dozen pieces of the same dimension, the same metallic composition, the same weight, and the same performance specifications. Yet the castings are being produced in what is, in effect, a flow process rather than in batches, with computer-controlled machines and ovens adjusting themselves.

Precision castings of this kind used to have a rejection rate of 30 to 40 percent; in this new foundry, 90 percent or more are flawless when they come off the line. And the costs are less than two-thirds of those of the cheapest competitor (a Korean shipyard), even though the Midwestern foundry pays full American union wages and benefits. What is "entrepreneurial" in this business is not that it is new and still small (though growing rapidly). It is the realization that castings of this kind are distinct and separate; that demand for them has grown so big as to create a "market niche"; and that technology, especially computer technology, now makes possible the conversion of an art into a scientific process.

Admittedly, all new small businesses have many factors in common. But to be entrepreneurial, an enterprise has to have special characteristics over and above being new and small. Indeed, entrepreneurs are a minority among new businesses. They create something new, something different; they change or transmute values.

An enterprise also does not need to be small and new to be an entrepreneur. Indeed, entrepreneurship is being practiced by large and often old enterprises. The General Electric Company (G.E.), one of the world's biggest businesses and more than a hundred years old, has a long history of starting new entrepreneurial businesses from scratch and raising them into sizable industries. And G.E. has not confined itself to entrepreneurship in manufacturing. Its financing arm, G.E.

Credit Corporation, in large measure triggered the upheaval that is transforming the American financial system and is now spreading rapidly to Great Britain and western Europe as well. G.E. Credit in the sixties ran around the Maginot Line of the financial world when it discovered that commercial paper could be used to finance industry. This broke the banks' traditional monopoly on commercial loans.

Marks and Spencer, the very large British retailer, has probably been more entrepreneurial and innovative than any other company in western Europe these last fifty years, and may have had greater impact on the British economy and even on British society, than any other change agent in Britain, and arguably more than government or laws.

Again, G.E. and Marks and Spencer have many things in common with large and established businesses that are totally unentrepreneurial. What makes them "entrepreneurial" are specific characteristics other than size or growth.

Finally, entrepreneurship is by no means confined solely to economic institutions.

No better text for a *History of Entrepreneurship* could be found than the creation and development of the modern university, and especially the modern American university. The modern university as we know it started out as the invention of a German diplomat and civil servant, Wilhelm von Humboldt, who in 1809 conceived and founded the University of Berlin with two clear objectives: to take intellectual and scientific leadership away from the French and give it to the Germans; and to capture the energies released by the French Revolution and turn them against the French themselves, especially Napoleon. Sixty years later, around 1870, when the German university itself had peaked, Humboldt's idea of the university as a change agent was picked up across the Atlantic, in the United States. There, by the end of the Civil War, the old "colleges" of the colonial period were dying of senility. In 1870, the United States had no more than half the college students it had had in 1830, even though the population had nearly tripled. But in the next thirty years a galaxy of American university presidents$^{\ominus}$ created and built a new "American university"—both distinctly new and distinctly American—which then, after World War I, soon gained for the United States worldwide leadership in scholarship and research, just as Humboldt's university had gained worldwide leadership in scholarship and research for Germany a century earlier.

After World War II a new generation of American academic entrepreneurs innovated once again, building new "private" and "metropolitan" universities: Pace University, Fairleigh-Dickinson, and the New York Institute of Technology in

---

$\ominus$ See the section on The American University in my book *Management : Tasks, Responsibilities, Practices* (New York: Harper & Row, 1973), pages 150-152.

the New York area; Northeastern in Boston; Santa Clara and Golden Gate on the West Coast; and so on. They have constituted a major growth sector in American higher education in the last thirty years. Most of these new schools seem to differ little from the older institutions in their curriculum. But they were deliberately designed for a new and different "market"—for people in mid-career rather than for youngsters fresh out of high school; for big-city students commuting to the university at all hours of the day and night rather than for students living on campus and going to school full time, five days a week from nine to five; and for students of widely diversified, indeed, heterogenous backgrounds rather than for the "college kid" of the American tradition. They were a response to a major shift in the market, a shift in the status of the college degree from "upper-class" to "middle-class," and to a major shift in what "going to college" means. They represent entrepreneurship.

One could equally write a casebook on entrepreneurship based on the history of the hospital, from the first appearance of the modern hospital in the late eighteenth century in Edinburgh and Vienna, to the creation of the various forms of the "community hospital" in nine-teenth-century America, to the great specialized centers of the early twentieth century, the Mayo Clinic or the Menninger Foundation, to the emergence of the hospital as health-care center in the post-World War II period. And now new entrepreneurs are busily changing the hospital again into specialized "treatment centers": ambulatory surgical clinics, freestanding maternity centers or psychiatric centers where the emphasis is not, as in the traditional hospital, on caring for the patient but on specialized "needs."

Again, not every nonbusiness service institution is entrepreneurial; far from it. And the minority that is still has all the characteristics, all the problems, all the identifying marks of the service institution.$^{\ominus}$ What makes these service institutions entrepreneurial is something different, something specific.

Whereas English speakers identify entrepreneurship with the new, small business, the Germans identify it with power and property, which is even more misleading. The *Unternehmer*—the literal translation into German of Say's *entrepreneur*—is the person who both owns and runs a business (the English term would be "owner-manager"). And the word is used primarily to distinguish the "boss," who also owns the business, from the "professional manager" and from "hired hands"altogether.

But the first attempts to create systematic entrepreneurship—the entrepreneurial bank founded in France in 1857 by the Brothers Pereire in their Crédit Mobilier, then

---

$\ominus$　On this, see the section Performance in the Service Institution (Chapters 11-14) in *Management: Tasks, Responsibilities, Practices*, but also Chapter 14 of this book, Entre-preneurship in the Service Institution.

perfected in 1870 across the Rhine by Georg Siemens in his Deutsche Bank, and brought across the Atlantic to New York at about the same time by the young J. P. Morgan—did not aim at ownership. The task of the banker as entrepreneur was to mobilize *other people's money* for allocation to areas of higher productivity and greater yield. The earlier bankers, the Rothschilds, for example, became owners. Whenever they built a railroad, they financed it with their own money. The entrepreneurial banker, by contrast, never wanted to be an owner. He made his money by selling to the general public the shares of the enterprises he had financed in their infancy, And he got the money for his ventures by borrowing from the general public.

Nor are entrepreneurs capitalists, although of course they need capital as do all economic (and most noneconomic) activities. They are not investors, either. They take risks, of course, but so does anyone engaged in any kind of economic activity. The essence of economic activity is the commitment of present resources to future expectations, and that means to uncertainty and risk. The entrepreneur is also not an employer, but can be, and often is, an employee—or someone who works alone and entirely by himself or herself.

Entrepreneurship is thus a distinct feature whether of an individual or of an institution. It is not a personality trait; in thirty years I have seen people of the most diverse personalities and temperaments perform well in entrepreneurial challenges. To be sure, people who need certainty are unlikely to make good entrepreneurs. But such people are unlikely to do well in a host of other activities as well—in politics, for instance, or in command positions in a military service, or as the captain of an ocean liner. In all such pursuits decisions have to be made, and the essence of any decision is uncertainty.

But everyone who can face up to decision making can learn to be an entrepreneur and to behave entrepreneurially. Entrepreneurship, then, is behavior rather than personality trait. And its foundation lies in concept and theory rather than in intuition.

II

Every practice rests on theory, even if the practitioners themselves are unaware of it. Entrepreneurship rests on a theory of economy and society. The theory sees change as normal and indeed as healthy. And it sees the major task in society— and especially in the economy—as doing something different rather than doing better what is already being done. This is basically what Say, two hundred years ago, meant when he coined the term *entrepreneur*. It was intended as a manifesto and as a declaration of dissent: the entrepreneur upsets and disorganizes. As Joseph Schumpeter formulated it, his task is "creative destruction."

Say was an admirer of Adam Smith. He translated Smith's *Wealth of Nations* (1776) into French and tirelessly propagated throughout his life Smith's ideas and policies. But his own contribution to economic thought, the concept of the entrepreneur and of entrepreneurship, is independent of classical economics and indeed incompatible with it. Classical economics optimizes what already exists, as does mainstream economic theory to this day, including the Keynesians, the Friedmanites, and the Supply-siders. It focuses on getting the most out of existing resources and aims at establishing equilibrium. It cannot handle the entrepreneur but consigns him to the shadowy realm of "external forces," together with climate and weather, government and politics, pestilence and war, but also technology. The traditional economist, regardless of school or "ism," does not deny, of course, that these external forces exist or that they matter. But they are not part of his world, not accounted for in his model, his equations, or his predictions.

Joseph Schumpeter was the first major economist to go back to Say. In his classic *Die Theorie der Wirtschaftlichen Entwicklung* (*The Theory of Economic Dynamics*), published in 1911, Schumpeter broke with traditional economics—far more radically than John Maynard Keynes was to do twenty years later. He postulated that dynamic disequilibrium brought on by the innovating entrepreneur, rather than equilibrium and optimization, is the "norm" of a healthy economy and the central reality for economic theory and economic practice.

Say was primarily concerned with the economic sphere. But his definition only calls for the resources to be "economic." The purpose to which these resources are dedicated need not be what is traditionally thought of as economic. Education is not normally considered "economic"; and certainly economic criteria are hardly appropriate to determine the "yield" of education (though no one knows what other criteria might pertain). But the resources of education are, of course, economic. They are in fact identical with those used for the most unambiguously economic purpose such as making soap for sale. Indeed, the resources for all *social* activities of human beings are the same and are "economic" resources: capital (that is, the resources withheld from current consumption and allocated instead to future expectations), physical resources, whether land, seed corn, copper, the classroom, or the hospital bed; labor, management, and time. Hence entrepreneurship is by no means limited to the economic sphere although the term originated there. It pertains to all activities of human beings other than those one might term "existential" rather than "social." And we now know that there is little difference between entrepreneurship whatever the sphere. The entrepreneur in education and the entrepreneur in health care—both have been fertile fields—do very much the same things, use very much the same tools, and encounter very much the same problems as the entrepreneur in a business or a labor union.

Entrepreneurs see change as the norm and as healthy. Usually, they do not bring about the change themselves. But—and this defines entrepreneur and entrepreneurship—*the entrepreneur always searches for change, responds to it, and exploits it as an opportunity.*

III

Entrepreneurship, it is commonly believed, is enormously risky. And, indeed, in such highly visible areas of innovation as high tech—microcomputers, for instance, or biogenetics—the casualty rate is high and the chances of success or even of survival seem to be quite low.

But why should this be so? Entrepreneurs, by definition, shift resources from areas of low productivity and yield to areas of higher productivity and yield. Of course, there is a risk they may not succeed. But if they are even moderately successful, the returns should be more than adequate to offset whatever risk there might be. One should thus expect entrepreneurship to be considerably less risky than optimization. Indeed, nothing could be as risky as optimizing resources in areas where the proper and profitable course is innovation, that is, where the opportunities for innovation already exist. Theoretically, entrepreneurship should be the least risky rather than the most risky course.

In fact, there are plenty of entrepreneurial organizations around whose batting average is so high as to give the lie to the all but universal belief in the high risk of entrepreneurship and innovation.

In the United States, for instance, there is Bell Lab, the innovative arm of the Bell Telephone System. For more than seventy years—from the design of the first automatic switchboard around 1911 until the design of the optical fiber cable around 1980, including the invention of transistor and semiconductor, but also basic theoretical and engineering work on the computer—Bell Lab produced one winner after another. The Bell Lab record would indicate that even in the high-tech field, entrepreneurship and innovation can be low-risk.

IBM, in a fast-moving high-tech field, that of the computer, and in competition with the "old pros" in electricity and electronics, has so far not had one major failure. Nor, in a far more prosaic industry, has the most entrepreneurial of the world's major retailers, the British department store chain Marks and Spencer. The world's largest producer of branded and packaged consumer goods, Procter & Gamble, similarly has had a near-perfect record of successful innovations. And a "middle-tech" company, 3M in St. Paul, Minnesota, which has created around one hundred new businesses or new major product lines in the last sixty years, has been successful four out of every five times in its ventures. This is only a small sample of the entrepreneurs who somehow innovate at low risk. Surely there are far too many of them for low-risk entrepreneurship to be a fluke, a special dispensation of the gods, an accident, or mere chance.

There are also enough individual entrepreneurs around whose batting average in starting new ventures is so high as to disprove the popular belief of the high risk of entrepreneurship.

Entrepreneurship is "risky" mainly because so few of the so-called entrepreneurs know what they are doing. They lack the methodology. They violate elementary and well-known rules. This is particularly true of high-tech entrepreneurs. To be sure (as will be discussed in Chapter 9), high-tech entrepreneurship and innovation are intrinsically more difficult and more risky than innovation based on economics and market structure, on demographics, or even on something as seemingly nebulous and intangible as *Weltanschauung* perceptions and moods. But even high-tech entrepreneurship need not be "high-risk," as Bell Lab and IBM prove. It does need, however, to be systematic. It needs to be managed. Above all, it needs to be based on *purposeful innovation*.

CHAPTER 2

Purposeful Innovation and the Seven Sources for Innovative Opportunity

Entrepreneurs innovate. Innovation is the specific instrument of entrepreneurship. It is the act that endows resources with a new capacity to create wealth. Innovation, indeed, creates a resource. There is no such thing as a "resource" until man finds a use for something in nature and thus endows it with economic value. Until then, every plant is a weed and every mineral just another rock. Not much more than a century ago, neither mineral oil seeping out of the ground nor bauxite, the ore of aluminum, were resources. They were nuisances; both render the soil infertile. The penicillin mold was a pest, not a resource. Bacteriologists went to great lengths to protect their bacterial cultures against contamination by it. Then in the 1920s, a London doctor, Alexander Fleming, realized that this "pest" was exactly the bacterial killer bacteriologists had been looking for—and the penicillin mold became a valuable resource.

The same holds just as true in the social and economic spheres. There is no greater resource in an economy than "purchasing power." But purchasing power is the creation of the innovating entrepreneur.

The American farmer had virtually no purchasing power in the early nineteenth century; he therefore could not buy farm machinery. There were dozens of harvesting machines on the market, but however much he might have wanted them, the farmer could not pay for them. Then one of the many harvesting-machine inventors, Cyrus McCormick, invented installment buying. This enabled the farmer to pay for a harvesting machine out of his future earnings rather than out of past savings—and suddenly the farmer had "purchasing power" to buy farm equipment.

Equally, whatever changes the wealth-producing potential of already existing resources constitutes innovation.

There was not much new technology involved in the idea of moving a truck body off its wheels and onto a cargo vessel. This "innovation," the container, did not grow out of technology at all but out of a new perception of the "cargo vessel" as a materials-handling device rather than a "ship," which meant that what really mattered was to make the time in port as short as possible. But this humdrum innovation roughly quadrupled the productivity of the ocean-going freighter and probably saved shipping. Without it, the tremendous expansion of world trade in the last forty years—the fastest growth in any major economic activity ever recorded—could not possibly have taken place.

What really made universal schooling possible more so than the popular commitment to the value of education, the systematic training of teachers in schools of education, or pedagogic theory—was that lowly innovation, the textbook. (The textbook was probably the invention of the great Czech educational reformer Johann Amos Comenius, who designed and used the first Latin primers in the mid-seventeenth century.) Without the textbook, even a very good teacher cannot teach more than one or two children at a time; with it, even a pretty poor teacher can get a little learning into the heads of thirty or thirty-five students.

Innovation, as these examples show, does not have to be technical, does not indeed have to be a "thing" altogether. Few technical innovations can compete in terms of impact with such social innovations as the newspaper or insurance. Installment buying literally transforms economies. Wherever introduced, it changes the economy from supply-driven to demand-driven, regardless almost of the productive level of the economy. The hospital, in its modern form a social innovation of the Enlightenment of the eighteenth century, has had greater impact on health care than many advances in medicine. Management, that is, the "useful knowledge" that enables man for the first time to render productive people of different skills and knowledge working together in an "organization," is an innovation of this century. It has converted modern society into something brand new, something, by the way, for which we have neither political nor social theory: a society of organizations.

Books on economic history mention August Borsig as the first man to build steam locomotives in Germany. But surely far more important was his innovation—against strenuous opposition from craft guilds, teachers, and government bureaucrats—of what to this day is the German system of factory organization and the foundation of Germany's industrial strength. It was Borsig who devised the idea of the *Meister* (Master), the highly skilled and highly respected senior worker who runs the shop with considerable autonomy; and the *Lehrling System* (apprenticeship system), which combines practical training (*Lehre*) on the job with schooling (*Ausbildung*) in the classroom. And the twin inventions of modern government by Machiavelli in *The Prince* (1513) and of the modern national state by his early follower, Jean Bodin, sixty years later, have surely had more lasting impacts than most technologies.

One of the most interesting examples of social innovation and its importance can be seen in modern Japan.

From the time she opened her doors to the modern world in 1867, Japan has been consistently underrated by westerners, despite her successful defeats of China and then Russia in 1894 and 1905, respectively; despite Pearl Harbor; and despite her sudden emergence as an economic superpower and the toughest competitor in the world market of the 1970s and 1980s. A major reason, perhaps the major one, is the prevailing belief that innovation has to do with things and is based on science or technology. And the Japanese, so the common belief has held (in Japan as well as in the West, by the way), are not innovators but imitators. For the Japanese have not, by and large, produced outstanding technical or scientific innovations. Their success is based on social innovation.

When the Japanese, in the Meiji Restoration of 1867, most reluctantly opened their country to the world, it was to avoid the fates of India and nineteenth-century China, both of which were conquered, colonized, and "westernized" by the West. The basic aim, in true Judo fashion, was to use the weapons of the West to hold the West at bay; and to remain Japanese.

This meant that social innovation was far more critical than steam locomotives or the telegraph. And social innovation, in terms of the development of such institutions as schools and universities, a civil service, banks and labor relations, was far more difficult to achieve than building locomotives and telegraphs. A locomotive that will pull a train from London to Liverpool will equally, without adaptation or change, pull a train from Tokyo to Osaka. But the social institutions had to be at once quintessentially "Japanese" and yet "modern." They had to be run by Japanese and yet serve an economy that was "Western" and highly technical. Technology can be imported at low cost and with a minimum of cultural risk. Institutions, by contrast, need cultural roots to grow and to prosper. The Japanese made a deliberate decision a hundred years ago to concentrate their resources on social innovations, and to imitate, import, and adapt technical innovations—with startling success. Indeed, this policy may still be the right one for them. For, as will be discussed in Chapter 17, what is sometimes half-facetiously called creative imitation is a perfectly respectable and often very successful entrepreneurial strategy.

Even if the Japanese now have to move beyond imitating, importing, and adapting other people's technology and learn to undertake genuine technical innovation of their own, it might be prudent not to underrate them. Scientific research is in itself a fairly recent "social innovation." And the Japanese, whenever they have had to do so in the past, have always shown tremendous capacity for such innovation. Above all, they have shown a superior grasp of entrepreneurial strategies.

"Innovation," then, is an economic or social rather than a technical term. It can be defined the way J. B. Say defined entrepreneurship, as changing the yield of resources. Or, as a modern economist would tend to do, it can be defined in demand terms rather than in supply terms, that is, as changing the value and satisfaction obtained from resources by the consumer.

Which of the two is more applicable depends, I would argue, on the specific case rather than on the theoretical model. The shift from the integrated steel mill to the "mini-mill," which starts with steel scrap rather than iron ore and ends with one final product (e.g., beams and rods, rather than raw steel that then has to be fabricated), is best described and analyzed in supply terms. The end product, the end uses, and the customers are the same, though the costs are substantially lower. And the same supply definition probably fits the container. But the audiocassette or the videocassette, though equally "technical," if not more so, are better described or analyzed in terms of consumer values and consumer satisfactions, as are such social innovations as the news magazines developed by Henry Luce of Time-Life-Fortune in the 1920s, or the money-market fund of the late 1970s and early 1980s.

We cannot yet develop a theory of innovation. But we already know enough to say when, where, and how one looks systematically for innovative opportunities, and how one judges the chances for their success or the risks of their failure. We know enough to develop, though still only in outline form, the practice of innovation.

It has become almost a cliché for historians of technology that one of the great achievements of the nineteenth century was the "invention of invention." Before 1880 or so, invention was mysterious; early nine-teenth-century books talk incessantly of the "flash of genius." The inventor himself was a half-romantic, half-ridiculous figure, tinkering away in a lonely garret. By 1914, the time World War I broke out, "invention" had become "research," a systematic, purposeful activity, which is planned and organized with high predictability both of the results aimed at and likely to be achieved.

Something similar now has to be done with respect to innovation. Entrepreneurs will have to learn to *practice systematic innovation*.

Successful entrepreneurs do not wait until "the Muse kisses them" and gives them a "bright idea"; they go to work. Altogether, they do not look for the "biggie," the innovation that will "revolutionize the industry," create a "billion-dollar business," or "make one rich over-night." Those entrepreneurs who start out with the idea that they'll make it big—and in a hurry—can be guaranteed failure. They are almost bound to do the wrong things. An innovation that looks very big may turn out to be nothing but technical virtuosity; and innovations with modest intellectual pretensions, a McDonald's, for instance, may turn into gigantic, highly profitable businesses. The same applies to nonbusiness, public-service innovations.

Successful entrepreneurs, whatever their individual motivation—be it money, power, curiosity, or the desire for fame and recognition—try to create value and to make a contribution. Still, successful entrepreneurs aim high. They are not content simply to improve on what already exists, or to modify it. They try to create new and different values and new and different satisfactions, to convert a "material" into a "resource," or to combine existing resources in a new and more productive configuration.

And it is change that always provides the opportunity for the new and different. *Systematic innovation therefore consists in the purposeful and organized search for changes, and in the systematic analysis of the opportunities such changes might offer for economic or social innovation.*

As a rule, these are changes that have already occurred or are under way. The overwhelming majority of successful innovations *exploit* change. To be sure, there are innovations that in themselves constitute a major change; some of the major technical innovations, such as the Wright Brothers' airplane, are examples. But these are exceptions, and fairly uncommon ones. Most successful innovations are far more prosaic; they exploit change. And thus the discipline of innovation (and it is the knowledge base of entrepreneurship) is a diagnostic discipline: a systematic examination of the areas of change that typically offer entrepreneurial opportunities.

Specifically, systematic innovation means monitoring *seven sources* for innovative opportunity.

The first four sources lie within the enterprise, whether business or public-service institution, or within an industry or service sector. They are therefore visible primarily to people within that industry or service sector. They are basically symptoms. But they are highly reliable indicators of changes that have already happened or can be made to happen with little effort. These four source areas are:

- The *unexpected*—the unexpected success, the unexpected failure, the unexpected outside event;
- *The incongruity*—between reality as it actually is and reality as it is assumed to be or as it "ought to be";

- *Innovation based on process need;*
- *Changes in industry structure or market structure* that catch everyone unawares.
- The second set of sources for innovative opportunity, a set of three, involves changes outside the enterprise or industry:
- *Demographics* (population changes);
- *Changes in perception, mood, and meaning;*
- *New knowledge,* both scientific and nonscientific.

The lines between these seven source areas of innovative opportunities are blurred, and there is considerable overlap between them. They can be likened to seven windows, each on a different side of the same building. Each window shows some features that can also be seen from the window on either side of it. But the view from the center of each is distinct and different.

The seven sources require separate analysis, for each has its own distinct characteristic. No area is, however, inherently more important or more productive than the other. Major innovations are as likely to come out of an analysis of symptoms of change (such as the unexpected success of what was considered an insignificant change in product or pricing) as they are to come out of the massive application of new knowledge resulting from a great scientific breakthrough.

But the order in which these sources will be discussed is not arbitrary. They are listed in descending order of reliability and predictability. For, contrary to almost universal belief, new knowledge—and especially new scientific knowledge—is not the most reliable or most predictable source of successful innovations. For all the visibility, glamour, and importance of science-based innovation, it is actually the least reliable and least predictable one. Conversely, the mundane and unglamorous analysis of such symptoms of underlying changes as the unexpected success or the unexpected failure carry fairly low risk and uncertainty. And the innovations arising therefrom have, typically, the shortest lead time between the start of a venture and its measurable results, whether success or failure.

CHAPTER 3

Source: The Unexpected

I

The Unexpected Success

No other area offers richer opportunities for successful innovation than the unexpected success. In no other area are innovative opportunities less risky and their pursuit less arduous. Yet the unexpected success is almost totally neglected; worse, managements tend actively to reject it.

Here is one example.

More than thirty years ago, I was told by the chairman of New York's largest department store, R. H. Macy, "We don't know how to stop the growth of appliance sales."

"Why do you want to stop them?" I asked, quite mystified. "Are you losing money on them?"

"On the contrary," the chairman said, "profit margins are better than on fashion goods; there are no returns, and practically no pilferage."

"Do the appliance customers keep away the fashion customers?" I asked.

"Oh, no," was the answer. "Where we used to sell appliances primarily to people who came in to buy fashions, we now sell fashions very often to people who come in to buy appliances. But," the chairman continued, "in this kind of store, it is normal and healthy for fashion to produce seventy percent of sales. Appliance sales have grown so fast that they now account for three-fifths. And that's abnormal. We've tried everything we know to make fashion grow to restore the normal ratio, but nothing works. The only thing left now is to push appliance sales down to where they should be."

For almost twenty years after this episode, Macy's New York continued to drift. Any number of explanations were given for Macy's inability to exploit its dominant position in the New York retail market: the decay of the inner city, the poor economics of a store supposedly "too big," and many others. Actually, once a new management came in after 1970, reversed the emphasis, and accepted the contribution of appliances to sales, Macy's—despite inner-city decay, despite its high labor costs, and despite its enormous size—promptly began to prosper again.

At the same time that Macy's rejected the unexpected success, another New York retail store, Bloomingdale's, used the identical unexpected success to propel itself into the number two spot in the New York market. Bloomingdale's, at best a weak number four, had been even more of a fashion store than Macy's. But when appliance sales began to climb in the early 1950s, Bloomingdale's ran with the opportunity. It realized that something unexpected was happening and analyzed it. It then built a new position in the marketplace around its Housewares Department. It also refocused its fashion and apparel sales to reach a new customer: the customer of whose emergence the explosion in appliance sales was only a symptom. Macy's is still number one in New York in volume. But Bloomingdale's has become the "smart New York store." And the stores that were the contenders for this title thirty years ago—the stores that were then strong number twos, the fashion leaders of 1950 such as Best—have disappeared (for additional examples, see Chapter 15).

The Macy's story will be called extreme. But the only uncommon aspect about it is that the chairman was aware of what he was doing. Though not conscious of their folly, far too many managements act the way Macy's did. It is never easy for a management to accept the unexpected success. It takes determination, specific policies, a willingness to look at reality, and the humility to say, "We were wrong!"

One reason why it is difficult for management to accept unexpected success is that all of us tend to believe that anything that has lasted a fair amount of time must be "normal" and go on "forever." Anything that contradicts what we have come to consider a law of nature is then rejected as unsound, unhealthy, and obviously abnormal.

This explains, for instance, why one of the major U.S. steel companies, around 1970, rejected the "mini-mill."⊖ Management knew that its steelworks were

---

⊖   On the "mini-mill," see Chapter 4.

rapidly becoming obsolete and would need billions of dollars of investment to be modernized. It also knew that it could not obtain the necessary sums. A new, smaller "mini-mill" was the solution.

Almost by accident, such a "mini-mill" was acquired. It soon began to grow rapidly and to generate cash and profits. Some of the younger men within the steel company therefore proposed that the available investment funds be used to acquire additional "mini-mills" and to build new ones. Within a few years, the "mini-mills" would then give the steel company several million tons of steel capacity based on modern technology, low labor costs, and pinpointed markets. Top management indignantly vetoed the proposal; indeed, all the men who had been connected with it found themselves "ex-employees" within a few years. "The integrated steelmaking process is the only right one," top management argued. "Everything else is cheating—a fad, unhealthy, and unlikely to endure." Needless to say, ten years later the only parts of the steel industry in America that were still healthy, growing, and reasonably prosperous were "mini-mills."

To a steelmaker who has spent his entire life working to perfect the integrated steelmaking process, who is at home in the big steel mill, and who may himself be the son of a steelworker (as a great many American steel company executives have been), anything but "big steel" is strange and alien, indeed a threat. It takes an effort to perceive in the "enemy" one's own best opportunity.

Top management people in most organizations, whether small or large, public-service institution or business, have typically grown up in one function or one area. To them, this is the area in which they feel comfortable. When I sat down with the chairman of R. H. Macy, for instance, there was only one member of top management, the personnel vice-president, who had not started as a fashion buyer and made his career in the fashion end of the business. Appliances, to these men, were something that other people dealt with.

The unexpected success can be galling. Consider the company that has worked diligently on modifying and perfecting an old product, a product that has been the "flagship" of the company for years, the product that represents "quality." At the same time, most reluctantly, the company puts through what everyone in the firm knows is a perfectly meaningless modification of an old, obsolete, and "low-quality" product. It is done only because one of the company's leading salesmen lobbied for it, or because a good customer asked for it and could not be turned down. But nobody expects it to sell; in fact, nobody wants it to sell. And then this "dog" runs away with the market and even takes the sales which plans and forecasts had promised for the "prestige," "quality" line. No wonder that everybody is appalled and considers the success a "cuckoo in the nest" (a term I have heard more than once).Everybody is likely to react precisely the way the chairman of R. H. Macy reacted when he saw the unwanted and unloved appliances overtake his beloved fashions, on which he himself had spent his working life and his energy.

The unexpected success is a challenge to management's judgment. "If the mini-mills were an opportunity, we surely would have seen it ourselves," the chairman of the big steel company is quoted as saying when he turned the mini-mill proposal down. Managements are paid for their judgment, but they are not being paid to be infallible. In fact, they are being paid to realize and admit that they have been wrong—especially when their admission opens up an opportunity. But this is by no means common.

A Swiss pharmaceutical company today has world leadership in veterinary medicines, yet it has not itself developed a single veterinary drug. But the companies that developed these medicines refused to serve the veterinary market. The medicines, mostly antibiotics, were of course developed for treating human diseases. When the veterinarians discovered that they were just as effective for animals and began to send in their orders, the original manufacturers were far from pleased. In some cases they refused to supply the veterinarians; in many others, they disliked having to reformulate the drugs for animal use, to repackage them, and so on. The medical director of a leading pharmaceutical company protested around 1953 that to apply a new antibiotic to the treatment of animals was a "misuse of a noble medicine." Consequently, when the Swiss approached this manufacturer and several others, they obtained licenses for veterinary use without any difficulty and at low cost. Some of the manufacturers were only too happy to get rid of the embarrassing success.

Human medications have since come under price pressure and are carefully scrutinized by regulatory authorities. This has made veterinary medications the most profitable segment of the pharmaceutical industry. But the companies that developed the compounds in the first place are not the ones who get these profits.

Far more often, the unexpected success is simply not seen at all. Nobody pays any attention to it. Hence, nobody exploits it, with the inevitable result that the competitor runs with it and reaps the rewards.

A leading hospital supplier introduced a new line of instruments for biological and clinical tests. The new products were doing quite well. Then, suddenly, orders came in from industrial and university laboratories. Nobody was told about them, nobody noticed them; nobody realized that, by pure accident, the company had developed products with more and better customers outside the market for which those products had been developed. No salesman was being sent out to call on these new customers, no service force was being set up. Five or eight years later, another company had taken over these new markets. And because of the volume of business these markets produced, the newcomer could soon invade the hospital market offering lower prices and better services than the original market leader.

One reason for this blindness to the unexpected success is that our existing reporting systems do not as a rule report it, let alone clamor for management's attention.

Practically every company—but every public-service institution as well—has a monthly or quarterly report. The first sheet lists the areas in which performance is below expectations: it lists the problems and the shortfalls. At the monthly meetings of the management group and the board of directors, everybody therefore focuses on the problem areas. No one even looks at the areas where the company has done better than expected. And if the unexpected success is not quantitative but qualitative—as in the case of the hospital instruments mentioned above, which opened up new major markets outside the company's traditional ones—the figures will not even show the unexpected success as a rule.

To exploit the opportunity for innovation offered by unexpected success requires analysis. Unexpected success is a symptom. But a symptom of what? The underlying phenomenon may be nothing more than a limitation on our own vision, knowledge, and understanding. That the pharmaceutical companies, for instance, rejected the unexpected success of their new drugs in the animal market was a symptom of their own failure to know how big—and how important—livestock raising throughout the world is; of their blindness to the sharp increase in demand for animal proteins throughout the world after World War II, and to the tremendous changes in knowledge, sophistication, and management capacity of the world's farmers.

The unexpected success of appliances at R. H. Macy's was a symptom of a fundamental change in the behavior, expectations, and values of substantial numbers of consumers—as the people at Bloomingdale's realized. Up until World War II, department store consumers in the United States bought primarily by socioeconomic status, that is, by income group. After World War II, the market increasingly segmented itself by what we now call "lifestyles." Bloomingdale's was the first of the major department stores, especially on the East Coast, to realize this, to capitalize on it, and to innovate a new retail image.

The unexpected success of laboratory instruments designed for the hospital in industrial and university laboratories was a symptom of the disappearance of distinctions between the various users of scientific instruments, which for almost a century had created sharply different markets, with different end uses, specifications, and expectations. What it symptomized—and the company never realized this—was not just that a product line had uses that were not originally envisaged. It signaled the end of the specific market niche the company had enjoyed in the hospital market. So the company that for thirty or forty years had successfully defined itself as a designer, maker, and marketer of hospital laboratory equipment was forced eventually to redefine itself as a maker of laboratory instruments, and to develop capabilities to design, manufacture, distribute, and service way beyond its original field. By then, however, it had lost a large part of the market for good.

Thus the unexpected success is not just an opportunity for innovation; it demands innovation. It forces us to ask, What basic changes are now appropriate for this organization in the way it defines its business? Its technology? Its markets? If these questions are faced up to, then the unexpected success is likely to open up the most rewarding and least risky of all innovative opportunities.

Two of the world's biggest businesses, DuPont, the world's largest chemical company, and IBM, the giant of the computer industry, owe their preeminence to their willingness to exploit the unexpected success as an innovative opportunity.

DuPont, for 130 years, had confined itself to making munitions and explosives. In the mid-1920s it then organized its first research efforts in other areas, one of them the brand-new field of polymer chemistry, which the Germans had pioneered during World War I. For several years there were no results at all. Then, in 1928, an assistant left a burner on over the weekend. On Monday morning, Wallace H. Carothers, the chemist in charge, found that the stuff in the kettle had congealed into fibers. It took another ten years before DuPont found out how to make Nylon intentionally. The point of the story is, however, that the same accident had occurred several times in the laboratories of the big German chemical companies with the same results, and much earlier. The Germans were, of course, looking for a polymerized fiber—and they could have had it, along with world leadership in the chemical industry, ten years before DuPont had Nylon. But because they had not planned the experiment, they dismissed its results, poured out the accidentally produced fibers, and started all over again.

The history of IBM equally shows what paying attention to the unexpected success can do. For IBM is largely the result of the willingness to exploit the unexpected success not once, but twice. In the early 1930s, IBM almost went under. It had spent its available money on designing the first electro-mechanical bookkeeping machine, meant for banks. But American banks did not buy new equipment in the Depression days of the early thirties. IBM even then had a policy of not laying off people, so it continued to manufacture the machines, which it had to put in storage.

When IBM was at its lowest point—so the story goes—Thomas Watson, Sr., the founder, found himself at a dinner party sitting next to a lady. When she heard his name, she said: "Are you the Mr. Watson of IBM? Why does your sales manager refuse to demonstrate your machine to me?" What a lady would want with an accounting machine Thomas Watson could not possibly figure out, nor did it help him much when she told him she was the director of the New York Public Library; it turned out he had never been in a public library. But next morning, he appeared there as soon as its doors opened.

In those days, libraries had fair amounts of government money. Watson walked out two hours later with enough of an order to cover next month's payroll. And, as he added with a chuckle whenever he told the story, "I invented a new policy on the spot: we get cash in advance before we deliver."

Fifteen years later, IBM had one of the early computers. Like the other early American computers, the IBM computer was designed for scientific purposes only. Indeed, IBM got into computer work largely because of Watson's interest in astronomy. And when first demonstrated in IBM's show window on Madison Avenue, where it drew enormous crowds, IBM's computer was programmed to calculate all past, present, and future phases of the moon.

But then businesses began to buy this "scientific marvel" for the most mundane of purposes, such as payroll. Univac, which had the most advanced computer and the one most suitable for business uses, did not really want to "demean" its scientific miracle by supplying business. But IBM, though equally surprised by the business demand for computers, responded immediately. Indeed, it was willing to sacrifice its own computer design, which was not particularly suitable for accounting, and instead use what its rival and competitor (Univac) had developed. Within four years IBM had attained leadership in the computer market, even though for another decade its own computers were technically inferior to those produced by Univac. IBM was willing to satisfy business and to satisfy it on business' terms—to train programmers for business, for instance.

Similarly, Japan's foremost electronic company, Matsushita (better known by its brand names Panasonic and National), owes its rise to its willingness to run with unexpected success.

Matsushita was a fairly small and undistinguished company in the early 1950s, outranked on every count by such older and deeply entrenched giants as Toshiba or Hitachi. Matsushita "knew," as did every other Japanese manufacturer of the time, that "television would not grow fast in Japan." "Japan is much too poor to afford such a luxury," the chairman of Toshiba had said at a New York meeting around 1954 or 1955. Matsushita, however, was intelligent enough to accept that the Japanese farmers apparently did not know that they were too poor for television. What they knew was that television offered them, for the first time, access to a big world. They could not afford television sets, but they were prepared to buy them anyhow and pay for them. Toshiba and Hitachi made better sets at the time, only they showed them on the Ginza in Tokyo and in the big-city department stores, making it pretty clear that farmers were not particularly welcome in such elegant surroundings. Matsushita went to the farmers and sold its televisions door-to-door, something no one in Japan had ever done before for anything more expensive than cotton pants or aprons.

Of course, it is not enough to depend on accidents, nor to wait for the lady at the dinner table to express unexpected interest in one's apparently failing product. The search has to be organized.

The first thing is to ensure that the unexpected is being seen; indeed, that it clamors for attention. It must be properly featured in the information management obtains and studies. (How to do this is described in some detail in Chapter 13.)

Managements must look at every unexpected success with the questions: (1) What would it mean to us if we exploited it? (2) Where could it lead us? (3) What would we have to do to convert it into an opportunity? And (4) How do we go about it? This means, first, that managements need to set aside specific time in which to discuss unexpected successes; and second, that someone should always be designated to analyze an unexpected success and to think through how it could be exploited.

But management also needs to learn what the unexpected success demands of them. Again, this might best be explained by an example.

A major university on the eastern seaboard of the United States started, in the early 1950s, an evening program of "continuing education" for adults, in which the normal undergraduate curriculum leading to an undergraduate degree was offered to adults with a high school diploma.

Nobody on the faculty really believed in the program. The only reason it was offered at all was that a small number of returning World War II veterans had been forced to go to work before obtaining their undergraduate degrees and were clamoring for an opportunity to get the credits they still lacked. To everybody's surprise, however, the program proved immensely successful, with qualified students applying in large numbers. And the students in the program actually outperformed the regular undergraduates. This, in turn, created a dilemma. To exploit the unexpected success, the university would have had to build a fairly big first-rate faculty. But this would have weakened its main program; at the least, it would have diverted the university from what it saw as its main mission, the training of undergraduates. The alternative was to close down the new program. Either decision would have been a responsible one. Instead, the university decided to staff the program with cheap, temporary faculty, mostly teaching assistants working on their own advanced degrees. As a result, it destroyed the program within a few years; but worse, it also seriously damaged its own reputation.

The unexpected success is an opportunity, but it makes demands. It demands to be taken seriously. It demands to be staffed with the ablest people available, rather than with whoever we can spare. It demands seriousness and support on the part of management equal to the size of the opportunity. And the opportunity is considerable.

II

The Unexpected Failure

Failures, unlike successes, cannot be rejected and rarely go unnoticed. But they are seldom seen as symptoms of opportunity. A good many failures are, of course, nothing but mistakes, the results of greed, stupidity, thoughtless bandwagon-climbing, or incompetence whether in design or execution. Yet if something fails despite being carefully planned, carefully designed, and conscientiously executed, that failure often bespeaks underlying change and, with it, opportunity.

The assumptions on which a product or service, its design or its marketing strategy, were based may no longer fit reality. Perhaps customers have changed their values and perceptions; while they still buy the same "thing," they are actually purchasing a very different "value." Or perhaps what has always been one market or one end use is splitting itself into two or more, each demanding something quite different. Any change like this is an opportunity for innovation.

I had my first experience with an unexpected failure at the very beginning of my working life, almost sixty years ago, just out of high school. My first job was as a trainee in an old export firm, which for more than a century had been selling hardware to British India. Its best seller for years had been a cheap padlock, of which it exported whole shiploads every month. The padlock was flimsy; a pin easily opened the lock. As incomes in India went up during the 1920s, padlock sales, instead of going up, began to decline quite sharply. My employer thereupon did the obvious: he redesigned the padlock to give it a sturdier lock, that is, to make it "better quality." The added cost was minimal and the improvement in quality substantial. But the improved padlock turned out to be unsalable. Four years later, the firm went into liquidation, the decline of its Indian padlock business a major factor in its demise.

A very small competitor of this firm in the Indian export business—no more than a tenth of the size of my employer and until then barely able to survive—realized that this unexpected failure was a symptom of basic change. For the bulk of Indians, the peasants in the villages, the padlock was (and for all I know, still is) a magical symbol; no thief would have dared open a padlock. The key was never used, and usually disappeared. To get a padlock that could not easily be opened without a key—the improved padlock my employer had worked so hard to perfect without additional cost—was thus not a boon but a disaster.

A small but rapidly growing middle-class minority in the cities, however, needed a real lock. That it was not sturdy enough for their needs was the main reason why the old lock had begun to lose sales and market. But for them the redesigned product was still inadequate.

My employer's competitor broke down the padlock into two separate products: one without lock and key, with only a simple trigger release, and selling for one-third less than the old padlock but with twice its profit margin; and the other with a good sturdy lock and three keys, selling at twice the price of the old product and also with a substantially larger profit margin. Both lines immediately began to sell. Within two years, the competitor had become the largest European hardware exporter to India. He maintained this position for ten years, until World War II put an end to European exports to India altogether.

A quaint tale from horse and buggy days, some might say. Surely we have become more sophisticated in this age of computers, of market research, and of business school MBAs.

But here is another case, half a century later and from a very "sophisticated" industry. Yet it teaches exactly the same lesson.

Just at the time when the first cohorts of the "baby boom" were reaching their mid-twenties—that is, the age to form families and to buy their first house—the 1973-74 recession hit. Inflation was becoming rampant, particularly in housing prices, which rose much faster than anything else. At the same time, interest rates on home mortgages were skyrocketing. And so the mass builders in America began to design and offer what they called a "basic house," smaller, simpler, and cheaper than the house that had become standard.

But despite its being such "good value" and well within the means of the first-time homebuyer, the "basic house" was a thumping failure. The builders tried to salvage it by offering low-interest financing and long repayment terms, and by slashing prices. Still, no one bought the "basic house."

Most homebuilders did what businessmen do in an unexpected failure: they blamed that old bogeyman, the "irrational customer." But one builder, still very small, decided to look around. He found that there had been a change in what the young American couple wants in its first house. This no longer represents the family's permanent home as it had done for their grandparents, a house in which the couple expects to live the rest of its life, or at least a long time. In the 1970s, young couples were buying not one, but two separate "values" in purchasing their first home. They bought shelter for a few short years; and they also bought an option to buy—a few years later—their "real" house, a much bigger and more luxurious home, in a better neighborhood, with better schools. To make the down payment on this far more expensive permanent home, they would, however, need the equity they had built up in the first house. The young people knew very well that the "basic house" was not what they and their contemporaries really wanted, even though it was all they could afford. They feared therefore—and perfectly rationally—that they would not be able to resell the "basic house" at a decent price. So the "basic house," instead of being an option to buy the "real house" later on, would become a serious impediment to the fulfillment of their true housing needs and wants.

The young couple of 1950 had still perceived itself as "working-class," by and large. And "working-class" people in the West do not expect their incomes and their standards of living to rise materially once they are out of their apprenticeship and into a full-time job. Seniority, for working-class people (with Japan being the major exception), means greater job security rather than larger incomes. But the "middle class" traditionally can expect a steady increase in its income until the head of the household reaches age forty-five or forty-eight. Between 1950 and 1975, both the reality and the self-image of young American adults—their educations, their expectations, their jobs—had changed from "working-class" to "middle-class." And with this change had come a sharp change in what the young people's first home represented, and what "value" was connected with it.

Once this was understood—and all it took was to listen to prospective homebuyers for a few weekends—successful innovation came about easily. Almost no change was made in the physical plant itself; only the kitchen was redesigned and made somewhat roomier. Otherwise, the building remained the same "basic house." the homebuilders had not been able to sell. But instead of being offered as "your house," it was offered as "your *first* house," and as a "building block toward the house you want." Specifically, this meant that the young couple was shown both the house as it was standing—that is, the "basic house"—and a model of the same house in which future additions such as an extra bathroom, one or two more bedrooms, and a basement "family den" had been built. Indeed, the builder had already obtained the necessary city permits for conversion of the "basic house" to a "permanent home." Furthermore, the builder guaranteed the young couple a fixed resale price for their first house, to be credited against their purchase from his firm of a second, bigger, "permanent" home within five to seven years. "This entailed practically no risk," he explained. "The demographics were such, after all, as to guarantee a steady increase in the demand for 'first houses' until the late 1980s or 1990s, during which time the babies of the 'baby bust' of 1961 will have become twenty-five themselves and will start forming their own families."

Before this homebuilder transformed failure into innovation, he had operated in only one metropolitan area and was a small factor in it. Five years later, the firm was operating in seven metropolitan areas and was either number one or a strong number two in each of them. Even during the building recession of 1981-82— a recession so severe that some of the largest American builders did not sell one single new house during an entire season—this innovative homebuilder continued to grow. "One reason," the firm's founder explained, "was something even I had not seen when I decided to offer first-time homebuyers a repurchase guarantee. It gave us a steady supply of well-built and still fairly new houses that needed only a little fixing up and could then be resold at a very decent profit to the next crop of first-home buyers."

Faced with unexpected failure, executives, especially in large organizations, tend to call for more study and more analysis. But as both the padlock story and the "basic house" story show, this is the wrong response. The unexpected failure demands that you go out, look around, and listen. Failure should always be considered a symptom of an innovative opportunity, and taken seriously as such.

It is equally important to watch out for the unexpected event in a supplier's business, and among the customers. McDonald's, for instance, started because the company's founder, Ray Kroc, paid attention to the unexpected success of one of his customers. At that time Kroc was selling milkshake machines to hamburger joints. He noticed that one of his customers, a small hamburger stand in a remote California town, bought several times the number of milkshake machines its location and size could justify. He investigated and found an old man who had, in effect, reinvented the fast-food business by systematizing it. Kroc bought his outfit and built it into a billion-dollar business based on the original owner's unexpected success.

A competitor's unexpected success or failure is equally important. In either case, one takes the event seriously as a possible symptom of innovative opportunity. One does not just "analyze." One goes out to investigate.

Innovation—and this is a main thesis of this book—is organized, systematic, rational work. But it is perceptual fully as much as conceptual. To be sure, what the innovator sees and learns has to be subjected to rigorous logical analysis. Intuition is not good enough; indeed, it is no good at all if by "intuition" is meant "what I feel." For that usually is another way of saying "What I like it to be" rather than "What I perceive it to be." But the analysis, with all its rigor—its requirements for testing, piloting, and evaluating—has to be based on a perception of change, of opportunity, of the new realities, of the incongruity between what most people still are quite sure is the reality and what has actually become a new reality. This requires the willingness to say: "I don't know enough to analyze, but I shall find out. I'll go out, look around, ask questions, and *listen*. "

It is precisely because the unexpected jolts us out of our preconceived notions, our assumptions, our certainties, that it is such a fertile source of innovation.

It is not in fact even necessary for the entrepreneur to understand why reality has changed. In the two cases above, it was easy to find out what had happened and why. More often, we find out what is happening without much clue as to why. And yet we can still innovate successfully.

Here is one example.

The failure of the Ford Motor Company's Edsel in 1957 has become American folklore. Even people who were not yet born when the Edsel failed have heard about it, at least in the United States. But the general belief that the Edsel was a slapdash gamble is totally mistaken.

Very few products were ever more carefully designed, more carefully introduced, more skillfully marketed. The Edsel was intended to be the final step in the most thoroughly planned strategy in American business history: a ten-year campaign during which the Ford Motor Company converted itself after World War II from near-bankruptcy into an aggressive competitor, a strong number two in the United States, and a few years later, a strong contender for the number one spot in the rapidly growing European market.

By 1957, Ford had already successfully reestablished itself as a strong competitor in three of the four main American automobile markets: the "standard" one with the Ford nameplate; the "lower-middle" one with Mercury; and the "upper" one with the Continental. The Edsel was then designed for the only remaining segment, the upper-middle one, the one for which Ford's big rival, General Motors, produced the Buick and the Oldsmobile. This "upper-middle" segment was, in the period after World War II, the fastest-growing part of the automobile market and yet the one for which the third automobile producer, Chrysler, did not have a strong entry, thereby leaving the door wide open for Ford.

Ford went to extreme lengths to plan and design the Edsel, embodying in its design the best information from market research, the best information about customer preferences in appearance and styling, and the highest standards of quality control.

Yet the Edsel became a total failure right away.

The reaction of the Ford Motor Company was very revealing. Instead of blaming the "irrational consumer," the Ford people decided there was something happening that did not jibe with the assumptions about reality everyone in the automobile industry had been making about consumer behavior—and for so long that they had become unquestioned axioms.

The result of Ford's decision to go out and investigate was the one genuine innovation in the American automobile industry since Alfred P. Sloan, in the 1920s, had defined the socioeconomic segmentation of the American market into "low," "lower-middle," "upper-middle," and "upper" segments, the insight on which he then built the General Motors Company. When the Ford people went out, they discovered that this segmentation was rapidly being replaced—or at least paralleled—by another quite different one, the one we would now call "lifestyle segmentation." The result, within a short period after the Edsel's failure, was the appearance of Ford's Thunderbird, the greatest success of any American car since Henry Ford, Sr., had introduced his Model T in 1908. The Thunderbird established Ford again as a major producer in its own right, rather than as GM's kid brother and a perennial imitator.

And yet to this day we really do not know what caused the change.It occurred well *before* any of the events by which it is usually explained, such as the shift of the center of demographic gravity to the teenagers as a result of the "baby boom," the explosive expansion of higher education, or the change in sexual mores. Nor do we really know what is meant by "lifestyle." All attempts to describe it have been futile so far. All we know is that something happened.

But that is enough to convert the unexpected, whether success or failure, into an opportunity for effective and purposeful innovation.

III

The Unexpected Outside Event

Unexpected successes and unexpected failure have so far been discussed as occurring within a business or an industry. But outside events, that is, events that are not recorded in the information and the figures by which a management steers its institution, are just as important. Indeed, they often are more important.

Here are some examples showing typical unexpected outside events and their exploitation as major opportunities for successful innovation.

One example concerns IBM and the personal computer.

However much executives and engineers at IBM may have disagreed with each other, there apparently was total agreement within the company on one point until well into the seventies: the future belonged to the centralized "main-frame" computer, with an ever larger memory and an ever larger calculating capacity. Everything else, every IBM engineer could prove convincingly, would be far too expensive, far too confusing, and far too limited in its performance capacity. And so IBM concentrated its efforts and resources on maintaining its leadership in the main-frame market.

And then around 1975 or 1976, to everybody's total surprise, ten and eleven-year-old kids began to play computer games. Right away their fathers wanted their own office computer or personal computer, that is, a separate, small, freestanding machine with far less capacity than even the smallest main-frame has. All the dire things the IBM people had predicted actually did happen. The freestanding machines cost many times what a plug-in "terminal" costs, and they have far less capacity; there is such a proliferation of them and their programs, and so few of them are truly compatible with one another, that the whole field has become chaotic, with service and repairs in shambles. But this does not seem to bother the customers. On the contrary, in the U.S. market the personal computers in five short years—from 1979 to 1984—reached the annual sales volume it had taken the "main-frames" thirty years to reach, that is, $15-$16 billion.

IBM could have been expected to dismiss this development. Instead, as early as 1977, when personal computer sales worldwide were still less than $200 million (as against main-frame sales of $7 billion for the same year), IBM set up task forces in competition with one another to develop personal computers for the company. As a result, IBM produced its own personal computer in 1980, just when the market was exploding. Three years later, in 1983, IBM had become the world's leading personal computer producer with nearly as much of a leadership position in the new field as it had in main-frames. Also in 1983 IBM then introduced its own very small "home computer," the "Peanut."

When I discuss all this with the IBM people, I always ask the same question: "What explains that IBM, of all people, saw this change as an opportunity when everybody at IBM was so totally sure that it couldn't happen and made no sense?" And I always get the same answer: "Precisely because we *knew* that this couldn't happen, and that it would make no sense at all, the development came as a profound shock to us. We realized that everything we'd assumed, everything we were so absolutely certain of, was suddenly being thrown into a cocked hat, and that we had to go out and organize ourselves to take advantage of a development we knew couldn't happen, but which then did happen."

The second example is far more mundane. But is it no less instructive despite its lack of glamour.

The United States has never been a book-*buying* country, in part because of the ubiquitous free public library. When TV appeared in the early fifties and more and more Americans began to spend more and more of their time in front of the tube—particularly people in their prime book-reading years, that is, people of high school and college age—"everyone knew" that book sales would drop drastically. Book publishers frantically began to diversify into "high-tech media": educational movies, or computer programs (in most cases, with total lack of success).But instead of collapsing, book sales in the United States have soared since TV first came in. They have grown several times as fast as every indicator had predicted, whether family incomes, total population in the "book-reading years," or even people with higher degrees.

No one knows why this happened. Indeed, no one quite knows what really happened. Books are still as rare in the typical American home as before.[⊖] Where, then, do all these books go? That we have no answer to this question does not alter the fact that books are being bought and paid for in increasing numbers.

Both the publishers and the existing bookstores knew, of course, all along that book sales were soaring. Neither, however, did anything about it. The unexpected event was exploited, instead, by a few mass retailers such as department stores in Minneapolis and Los Angeles. None of these people had ever had anything to do with books, but they knew the retail business. They started bookstore chains that are quite different from any earlier bookstore in America. Basically, these are supermarkets. They do not treat books as literature but as "mass merchandise," and they concentrate on the fast-moving items that generate the largest dollar sales per unit of shelf space. They are located in shopping centers with high rents but also with high traffic, whereas everybody in the book business had known all along that a bookstore has to be in a low-rent location, preferably near a university. Traditionally, booksellers were themselves "literary types" and tried to hire people who "love books." The managers of the new bookstores are former cosmetics salespeople. The standing joke among them is that any salesperson who wants to read anything besides the price tag on the book is hopelessly overqualified.

For ten years now, these new bookstore chains have been among the most successful and fastest-growing segments in American retailing and among the fastest-growing new businesses in this country altogether.

Each of these cases represents genuine innovation. But not one of them represents diversification.

IBM stayed in the computer business. And the chain bookstores are run by people who all along have been in retailing, in shopping centers, or managing "boutiques."

It is a condition of success in exploiting the unexpected outside event that it must fit the knowledge and expertise of one's own business. Companies, even large companies, that went into the new book market or into mass merchandising without the retail expertise have uniformly come to grief.

The unexpected outside event may thus be, above all, an opportunity to apply

---

⊖   This is also true of Japan, the country that, *per capita*, buys more books than any other and twice as many as the United States.

already existing expertise to a new application, but to an application that does not change the nature of the "business we are in." It may be extension rather than diversification. Yet as the above examples show, it also demands innovation in product and often in service and distribution channels.

The second point about these cases is that they all are big-company cases. Of course, a good many of the cases in this book, as in any management book, have to be big-company cases. They are the only available ones, as a rule, the only ones that can be found in the published records, the only ones discussed on the business page of newspapers or in magazines. Small-company cases are much harder to come by and often cannot be discussed without violating confidences.

But exploiting the unexpected outside event appears to be something that particularly fits the existing enterprise, and a fairly sizable one at that. I know of few small companies that have successfully exploited the unexpected outside event; nor does any other student of entrepreneurship and innovation whom I could consult. This may be coincidence. But perhaps the existing large enterprise is more likely to see the "big picture."

It is the large retailer in the United States who is used to looking at figures that show where and how consumers spend retail dollars. The large retailer also knows about shopping-center locations and how to get the good ones. And could a small company have done what IBM did and detach four task forces of first-rate designers and engineers to work on new product lines? Smaller high-tech companies in a rapidly growing industry usually do not have enough of such people even for their existing work.

It may well be that the unexpected outside event is the innovative area that offers the large enterprise the greatest opportunity along with the lowest risk. It may be the area that is particularly suited for innovation by the large and established enterprise. It may be the area in which expertise matters the most, and in which the ability to mobilize substantial resources fast makes the greatest difference.

But as these cases also show, being big and established does not guarantee that an enterprise will perceive the unexpected event and successfully organize itself to exploit it. IBM's American competitors are all big businesses with sales in the billions. Not one of them exploited the personal computer—they were all too busy fighting IBM. And not one of the old large bookstore chains in the United States, Brentano's in New York, for instance, exploited the new book market.

The opportunity is there, in other words. It is a major opportunity, occurring frequently. And when it occurs, it holds out great promise, particularly for existing and sizable enterprises. But such opportunities require more than mere luck or intuition. They demand that the enterprise search for innovation, be organized for it, and be managed so as to exploit it.

CHAPTER 4

Source: Incongruities

An incongruity is a discrepancy, a dissonance, between what is and what "ought" to be, or between what is and what everybody assumes it to be. We may not understand the reason for it; indeed, we often cannot figure it out. Still, an incongruity is a symptom of an opportunity to innovate. It bespeaks an underlying "fault," to use the geologist's term. Such a fault is an invitation to innovate. It creates an instability in which quite minor efforts can move large masses and bring about a restructuring of the economic or social configuration. Incongruities do not, however, usually manifest themselves in the figures or reports executives receive and pay attention to. They are qualitative rather than quantitative.

Like the unexpected event, whether success or failure, incongruity is a symptom of change, either change that has already occurred or change that can be made to happen. Like the changes that underlie the unexpected event, the changes that underlie incongruity are changes *within* an industry, a market, a process. The incongruity is thus clearly visible to the people within or close to the industry, market, or process; it is directly in front of their eyes. Yet it is often overlooked by the insiders, who tend to take it for granted—"This is the way it's always been," they say, even though "always" may be a very recent development.

There are several kinds of incongruity:

- An incongruity between the economic realities of an industry (or of a public-service area);

- An incongruity between the reality of an industry (or of a public-service area) and the assumptions about it;
- An incongruity between the efforts of an industry (or a public-service area) and the values and expectations of its customers;
- An internal incongruity within the rhythm or the logic of a process.

I

Incongruous Economic Realities

If the demand for a product or a service is growing steadily, its economic performance should steadily improve, too. It should be easy to be profitable in an industry with steadily rising demand. The tide carries it. A lack of profitability and results in such an industry bespeaks an incongruity between economic realities.

Typically, these incongruities are macro-phenomena, which occur within a whole industry or a whole service sector. The major opportunities for innovation exist, however, normally for the small and highly focused new enterprise, new process, or new service. And usually the innovator who exploits this incongruity can count on being left alone for a long time before the existing businesses or suppliers wake up to the fact that they have new and dangerous competition. For they are so busy trying to bridge the gap between rising demand and lagging results that they barely even notice somebody is doing something different—something that produces results, that exploits the rising demand.

Sometimes we understand what is going on. But sometimes it is impossible to figure out why rising demand does not result in better performance. The innovator, therefore, need not always try to understand why things do not work as they should. He should ask instead: "What would exploit this incongruity? What would convert it into an opportunity? What can be done?" Incongruity between economic realities is a call to action. Sometimes the action to be taken is rather obvious, even though the problem itself is quite obscure. And sometimes we understand the problem thoroughly and yet cannot figure out what to do about it.

The steel "mini-mill" is a good example of an innovation that successfully exploited incongruity.

For more than fifty years, since the end of World War I, the large, integrated steel mill in developed countries did well only in wartime. In times of peace its results were consistently disappointing, even though the demand for steel appeared to be going up steadily, at least until 1973.

The explanation of this incongruity has long been known. The minimum incremental unit needed to satisfy additional demand in an integrated steel mill is a very big investment and adds substantially to capacity. Any expansion to an existing steel mill is thus likely to operate for a good many years at a low utilization rate, until demand—which always goes up in small, incremental steps except in wartime—reaches the new capacity level. But not to expand when demand creeps up means losing market share, and permanently. No company can afford to take that risk. The industry can therefore only be profitable for a few short years: between the time when everybody begins to build new capacity and the time when all this new capacity comes on stream.

Further, the steelmaking process invented in the 1870s is fundamentally uneconomical, as also has been known for many years. It tries to defy the laws of physics—and that means violating the laws of economics. Nothing in physics requires as much work as the creation of temperatures, whether hot or cold, unless it is working against the laws of gravity and of inertia. The integrated steel process creates very high temperatures four times, only to quench them again. And it lifts heavy masses of hot materials and then moves them over considerable distances.

It had been clear for many years that the first innovation in process that would assuage these inherent weaknesses would substantially lower costs. This is exactly what the "mini-mill" does. A mini-mill is not a "small" plant; the minimum economical size produces around $100 million of sales. But that is still about one-sixth to one-tenth the minimum economic size of an integrated steel mill. A mini-mill can thus be built to provide, economically, a fairly small additional increment of steel production for which the market already exists. The mini-mill creates heat only once, and does not quench it, but uses it for the rest of the process. It starts with steel scrap instead of iron ore, and then concentrates on one end product: sheet, for instance, or beams, or rods. And while the integrated steel mill is highly labor-intensive, the mini-mill can be automated. Its costs thus come to less than half those of the traditional steel process.

Governments, labor unions, and the integrated steel companies have been fighting the mini-mill every step of the way. But it is steadily encroaching. By the year 2000, fifty percent or more of the steel used in the United States is likely to come out of mini-mills, while the large, integrated steel mills will be in irreversible decline.

There is a catch, however, and it is an important one. A similar incongruity between the economic reality of demand and the economic reality of the process exists in the paper industry. Only in this case, we do not know how to convert it into innovation and opportunity.

Despite the constant efforts of the governments of all developed and most developing countries to increase the demand for paper—perhaps the only objective on which the governments of all countries agree—the paper industry has not been doing well. Three years of "record profits" are invariably followed by five years of "excess capacity" and losses. Yet we do not, so far, have anything like a "mini-mill" process for paper. For eighty or ninety years, it has been known that wood fiber is a monomer; and it should not be too difficult, one would say, to find a plasticizer that converts it into a polymer. This would convert paper-making from an inherently inefficient and wasteful mechanical process into an inherently efficient chemical process. Indeed, almost a hundred years ago this was achieved as far as making textile fibers out of wood pulp is concerned—in the rayon process, which dates back to the 1880s. But despite millions spent in research, nobody has so far found a technique to produce paper that way.

In an incongruity, as these cases exemplify, the innovative solution has to be clearly definable. It has to be feasible with the existing, known technology, and with easily available resources. It requires hard developmental work, of course. But if a great deal of research and new knowledge is still needed, it is not yet ready for the entrepreneur, not yet "ripe." The innovation that successfully exploits an incongruity between economic realities has to be simple rather than complicated, "obvious" rather than grandiose.

In public-service areas, too, major incongruities between economic realities can be found.

Health care in developed countries offers one example. As recently as 1929, health care represented an insignificant portion of national expenditure in all developed countries, taking up a good deal less than 1 percent of gross national product or of consumer expenditures. Now, half a century later, health care, and especially the hospital, accounts in all developed countries for 7 to 11 percent of a much larger gross national product. Yet economic performance has been going down rather than up. Costs have risen much faster than services—perhaps three or four times as fast. The demand will continue to rise with the steady growth in the number of older people in all developed countries over the next thirty years. And so will the costs, which are closely tied to the age of the population.

We do not understand the phenomenon.⊖ But successful innovations, simple, targeted and focused on specific objectives, have emerged in Great Britain and the United States. These innovations are quite different simply because the two countries have such radically different systems. But each exploits the specific

---

⊖   This is brought out clearly in the best discussion of the health-care problem that has appeared so far, and the only one that looks at health care across national boundaries, in all developed countries. It is given in *The Economist* of April 29, 1984.

vulnerability of its country's system and converts it into an opportunity.

In Britain, the "radical innovation" is private health insurance, which has become the fastest-growing and most popular employee benefit. All it does is to enable policyholders to be seen immediately by a specialist and to jump to the head of the queue and avoid having to wait should they need "elective surgery." [⊖] For the British system has attempted to keep health-care costs down by *"triage"* which, in effect, reserves immediate attention and treatment to routine illnesses on the one hand and to "life-threatening" ailments on the other, but puts everything else, and especially elective surgery, on hold with waiting periods now running into years (e.g., for replacing a hip destroyed by arthritis). Health insurance policyholders, however, are operated on right away.

In contrast to Great Britain, the United States has so far tried to satisfy all demands of health care regardless of cost. As a result, hospital costs in America have exploded. This created a different innovative opportunity: to "unbundle," that is, to move out of the hospital into separate locations a host of services that do not require such high-cost hospital facilities as a body scanner or cobalt X-Ray to treat cancers, the highly instrumented and automated medical laboratory, or physical rehabilitation. Each of these innovative responses is small and specific: a freestanding maternity center, which basically offers motel facilities for mother and new baby; a freestanding "ambulatory" surgical center for surgery that does not require a hospital stay and post-operative care; a psychiatric diagnostic and referral center; geriatric centers of a similar nature; and so on.

These new facilities do not substitute for the hospital. What they do in effect is to push the American hospital toward the same role the British have assigned to their hospitals: as a place for emergencies, for life-threatening diseases, and for intensive and acute sickness care. But these innovations which, as in Britain, are embodied primarily in profit-making "businesses," convert the incongruity between the economic reality of rising health-care demand and the economic reality of falling health-care performance into an opportunity for innovation.

These are "big" examples, taken from major industries and public services. It is this fact, however, that makes them accessible, visible, and understandable. Above all, these examples show why the incongruity between economic realities offers such great innovative opportunities. The people who work within these industries or public services know that there are basic flaws. But they are almost forced to ignore them and to concentrate instead on patching here, improving there,

---

⊖ Surgery for complaints that yield to surgery, will not improve without it, but are not "life-threatening." Examples are cataracts, hip replacements and orthopedic surgery generally, or a prolapsed uterus.

fighting this fire or caulking that crack. They are thus unable to take the innovation seriously, let alone to try to compete with it. They do not, as a rule, even notice it until it has grown so big as to encroach on their industry or service, by which time it has become irreversible. In the meantime, the innovators have the field to themselves.

II

The Incongruity Between Reality and the Assumptions About It

Whenever the people in an industry or a service misconceive reality, whenever they therefore make erroneous assumptions about it, their efforts will be misdirected. They will concentrate on the area where results do not exist. Then there is an incongruity between reality and behavior, an incongruity that once again offers opportunity for successful innovation to whoever can perceive and exploit it.

A simple example is that old workhorse of world trade, the ocean-going general cargo vessel.

Thirty-five years ago, in the early 1950s, the ocean-going freighter was believed to be dying. The general forecast was that it would be replaced by air freight, except for bulk commodities. Costs of ocean freight were rising at a fast clip, and it took longer and longer to get merchandise delivered by freighter as one port after another became badly congested. This, in turn, increased pilferage at the docks as more and more merchandise piled up waiting to be loaded while vessels could not make it to the pier.

The basic reason was that the shipping industry had misdirected its efforts toward nonresults for many years. It had tried to design and build faster ships, and ships that required less fuel and a smaller crew. It concentrated on the economics of the ship while at sea and in transit from one port to another.

But a ship is capital equipment; and for all capital equipment the biggest cost is the cost of not working, during which interest has to be paid while the equipment does not earn. Everybody in the industry knew, of course, that the main expense of a ship is interest on the investment. Yet the industry kept on concentrating its efforts on costs that were already quite low—the costs of the ship while at sea and doing work.

The solution was simple: Uncouple loading from stowing. Do the loading on land, where there is ample space and where it can be performed before the ship is in port, so that all that has to be done is to put on and take off pre-loaded freight.

Concentrate, in other words, on the costs of not working rather than on those of working. The answer was the roll-on, roll-off ship and the container ship.

The results of these simple innovations have been startling. Freighter traffic in the last thirty years has increased up to five-fold. Costs, overall, are down by 60 percent. Port time has been cut by three-quarters in many cases, and with it congestion and pilferage.

Incongruity between perceived reality and actual reality often declares itself. But whenever serious, concentrated efforts do not, make things better but, on the contrary, make things worse—where faster ships only mean more port congestion and longer delivery times—it is highly probable that efforts are being misdirected. In all likelihood, refocusing on where the results are will yield substantial returns easily and fast.

Indeed, the incongruity between perceived and actual reality rarely requires "heroic" innovations. Uncoupling the loading of freight from the stowing thereof required little but adapting to the ocean-going freighter methods which, much earlier, had been developed for trucks and railroads.

The incongruity between perceived and actual reality typically characterizes a whole industry or a whole service area. The solution, however, should again be small and simple, focused and highly specific.

III

The Incongruity Between Perceived and Actual Customer Values and Expectations

In Chapter 3, I mentioned the case of television in Japan as an example of the unexpected success. It is also a good example of the incongruity between actual and perceived customer values and customer expectations. Long before the Japanese industrialist told his American audience that the poor in his country would not buy a TV set because they could not afford it, the poor in the United States and in Europe had already shown that TV satisfies expectations which have little to do with traditional economics. But this highly intelligent Japanese simply could not conceive that for customers—and especially for poor customers—the TV set is not just a "thing." It represents access to a new world; access, perhaps, to a whole new life.

Similarly, Khrushchev could not conceive that the automobile is not a "thing" when he said on his visit to the United States in 1956 that "Russians will never want to own automobiles; cheap taxis make much more sense." Any teenager could have told him that "wheels" are not mere transportation but freedom, mobility, power, romance. And Khrushchev's misperception created one of the wildest entrepreneurial opportunities: the shortage of automobiles in Russia has brought forth the biggest and liveliest black market.

These, it will be said, are again "cosmic" examples, not much use to a businessman or to an executive in a hospital, a university, or a trade association. But they are examples of a common phenomenon. What follows is a different case, in its own way equally "cosmic" but very definitely of operational significance.

One of the fastest-growing American financial institutions for the last several years has been a securities firm located not in New York but in a suburb of a Midwestern city. It now has two thousand branch offices all over the United States. And it owes its success and growth to having exploited an incongruity.

The large financial institutions, the Merrill Lynches and Dean Witters and E. F. Huttons, assume that their customers have the same values they have. To them it is obvious, if not axiomatic, that people invest in order to get rich. This is, after all, what motivates the members of the New York Stock Exchange, and determines what they consider "success." However, this assumption holds true only for a part of the investing public, and surely not even for the majority. They are not "financial people." They know that in order to "get rich" by investing, one has to work full time at managing money and be pretty knowledgeable about it. The local professional men, the local small businessmen, the local substantial farmers, however, have neither such time nor such knowledge; they are much too busy earning their money to have time to manage it.

This is the incongruity which the Midwestern securities firm exploits. Outwardly, it looks just like any other securities firm. It is a member of the New York Stock Exchange. But only a very small portion of its business, around one-eighth, is Stock Exchange business. It stays away from the items the big trading houses on Wall Street push the hardest: options, commodity futures, and so on, appealing instead to what it calls "the intelligent investor." It does not promise— and this is a genuine innovation among American financial service institutions— that its customers will make a fortune. It does not even want customers who trade. It wants customers who earn more money than they spend, which is typical for the successful professional, the substantial farmer, or the small-town businessman, less because their incomes are high than because their spending habits are modest. And then it appeals to their psychological need to protect their money. What this firm sells is a chance to maintain one's savings—through investment in bonds and stocks, to be sure, but also in deferred annuities, tax-sheltered partnerships, real estate trust, and so on. The "product" the firm delivers is a different one and one that no Wall Street house has ever sold before: peace of mind. And this is what really represents "value" for the "intelligent investor."

The big Wall Street houses cannot even imagine that such customers exist since they defy everything the houses believe in and hold true. This successful firm has now been widely publicized. It is on every list of large and growing Stock Exchange firms. Yet the senior people in the big firms have not yet accepted that their competitor exists, let alone that it is successful.

Behind the incongruity between actual and perceived reality, there always lies an element of intellectual arrogance, of intellectual rigor and dogmatism. "It is I, not they, who know what poor people can afford," the Japanese industrialist in effect asserted. This explains why the incongruity is so easily exploited by innovators: they are left alone and undisturbed.

Of all incongruities, that between perceived and actual reality may be the most common. Producers and suppliers almost always misconceive what it is the customer actually buys. They must assume that what represents "value" to the producer and supplier is equally "value" to the customer. To succeed in doing a job, any job, one has to believe in it and take it seriously. People who make cosmetics must believe in them; otherwise, they turn out shoddy products and soon lose their customers. People who run a hospital must believe in health care as an absolute good, or the quality of medical and patient care will deteriorate fast. And yet, no customer ever perceives himself as buying what the producer or supplier delivers. Their expectations and values are always different.

The reaction of the typical producer and supplier is then to complain that customers are "irrational" or "unwilling to pay for quality." Whenever such a complaint is heard, there is reason to assume that the values and expectations the producer or supplier holds to be real are incongruous with the actual values and expectations of customers and clients. Then there is reason to look for an opportunity for innovation that is highly specific, and carries a good chance of success.

IV

Incongruity Within the Rhythm or Logic of a Process

Twenty-five years or so ago, during the late 1950s, a pharmaceutical company salesman decided that he wanted to go into business for himself. He therefore looked for an incongruity within a process in medical practice. He found one almost immediately. One of the most common surgical operations is the operation for senile cataract in the eye. Over the years the procedure had become refined, routinized and instrumented to the point where it was conducted with the rhythm of a perfectly rehearsed dance—and with total control. But there was one point in this operation that was out of character and out of rhythm: at one phase the eye surgeon had to cut a ligament, to tie blood vessels and so risk bleeding, which then endangered the eye. This procedure was done successfully in more than 99 percent of all operations; indeed, it was not very difficult. But it greatly bothered the surgeons. It forced them to change their rhythm and induced anxiety in them. Eye surgeons, no matter how often they had done the operation, dreaded this one, quick procedure.

The pharmaceutical company salesman—his name is William Connor—found out without much research that an enzyme had been isolated in the 1890s which almost instantaneously dissolves this particular ligament. Only nobody then, sixty years earlier, had been able to store this enzyme even under refrigeration for more than a few short hours. Preservation techniques have, however, made quite a bit of progress since 1890. And so Connor, within a few months, was able by trial and error to find a preservative that gives the enzyme substantial shelf life without destroying its potency. Within a few years, every eye surgeon in the world was using Connor's patented compound. Twenty years later he sold his company, Alcon Laboratories, to one of the multinationals for a very large amount.

And another telling example:

O. M. Scott & Co. is the leader among American producers of lawn-care products: grass seed, fertilizer, pesticides, and so on. Though it is now a subsidiary of a large corporation (ITT), it attained leadership while a small independent company in fierce competition with firms many times its size, ranging from Sears, Roebuck to Dow Chemicals. Its products are good but so are those of the competition. Its leadership rests on a simple, mechanical gadget called a Spreader, a small, light-weight wheelbarrow with holes that can be set to allow the proper quantities of Scott's products to pass through in an even flow. Products for the lawn all claim to be "scientific" and are compounded on the basis of extensive tests. All prescribe in meticulous detail how much of the stuff should be applied, given soil conditions and temperatures. All try to convey to the consumer that growing a lawn is "precise," "controlled," if not "scientific." But before the Scott Spreader, no supplier of lawn-care products gave the customer a tool to control the process. And without such a tool, there was an internal incongruity in the logic of the process that upset and frustrated customers.

Does the identification of such internal incongruity within a process rest on "intuition" and on accident? Or can it be organized and systematized?

William Connor is said to have started out by asking surgeons where they felt uncomfortable about their work. O. M. Scott grew from a tiny local seed retailer into a fair-sized national company because it asked dealers and customers what they missed in available products. Then it designed its product line around the Spreader.

The incongruity within a process, its rhythm or its logic, is not a very subtle matter. Users are always aware of it. Every eye surgeon knew about the discomfort he felt when he had to cut eye muscle—and talked about it. Every hardware-store clerk knew about the frustration of his lawn customers—and talked about it. What was lacking, however, was someone willing to listen, somebody who took seriously what everybody proclaims: That the purpose of a product or a service is to satisfy the customer. If this axiom is accepted and acted upon, using incongruity as an opportunity for innovation becomes fairly easy—and highly effective.

There is, however, one serious limitation. The incongruity is usually available only to people within a given industry or service. It is not something that somebody from the outside is likely to spot, to understand, and hence is able to exploit.

CHAPTER 5

Source: Process Need

"Opportunity is the source of innovation" has been the leitmotif of the preceding chapters. But an old proverb says, "Necessity is the mother of invention." This chapter looks at *need* as a source of innovation, and indeed as a major innovative opportunity.

The need we shall discuss as a source of innovative opportunity is a very specific one: I call it "process need." It is not vague or general but quite concrete. Like the unexpected, or the incongruities, it exists within the process of a business, an industry, or a service. Some innovations based on process need exploit incongruities, others demographics. Indeed, process need, unlike the other sources of innovation, does not start out with an event in the environment, whether internal or external. It starts out with the job to be done. It is task-focused rather than situation-focused. It perfects a process that already exists, replaces a link that is weak, redesigns an existing old process around newly available knowledge. Sometimes it makes possible a process by supplying the "missing link."

In innovations that are based on process need, everybody in the organization always knows that the need exists. Yet usually no one does anything about it. However, when the innovation appears, it is immediately accepted as "obvious" and soon becomes "standard."

One example has been mentioned earlier in Chapter 4. It is William Connor's conversion of the enzyme that dissolves a ligament in cataract surgery of the eye from a textbook curiosity into an indispensable product. The process of cataract surgery itself was a very old one. The enzyme to perfect the process had been known for decades. The innovation was the preservative to keep the enzyme fresh under refrigeration. Once that process need had been satisfied, no eye surgeon could possibly imagine doing without Connor's compound.

Very few innovations based on process need are so sharply focused as this one, in which formulating the need right away produced the required solution. But in their essentials, most, if not all, innovations based on process need have the same elements.

Here is another example of a similar process-need innovation.

Ottmar Mergenthaler designed the linotype for typesetting in 1885. During the preceding decades, printed materials of all kinds—magazines, newspapers, books—had all been growing at an exponential rate with the spread of literacy and the development of transportation and communication. All the other elements of the printing process had already changed. There were high-speed printing presses, for instance, and paper was being made on high-speed paper machines. Only typesetting had gone unchanged from the days of Gutenberg four hundred years earlier. It remained slow and expensive manual work, requiring high skill and long years of apprenticeship. Mergenthaler, like Connor, defined what was needed: a keyboard that would make possible the mechanical selection of the right letter from the typefont; a mechanism to assemble the letters and to adjust them in a line; and—the most difficult, by the way—a mechanism to return each letter to its proper receptacle for future use. Each of these required several years of hard work and considerable ingenuity. But none required new knowledge, let alone new science. Mergenthaler's linotype became the "standard" in less than five years, despite vigorous resistance from the old craftsmen-typesetters.

In both these cases—William Connor's enzyme and the linotype machine—the process need was based on an incongruity in the process. Demographics, however, are very often an equally powerful source of process need and an opportunity for process innovation.

In 1909 or thereabouts a statistician at the Bell Telephone System projected two curves fifteen years ahead: the curve for American population growth and the curve for the number of people required as central-station operators to handle the growing volume of telephone calls. These projections showed that every American woman between age seventeen and sixty would have to work as a switchboard operator by the year 1925 or 1930 if the manual system of handling calls were to be continued. Two years later, Bell engineers had designed and put into service the first automatic switchboard.

Similarly, the present rush into robotics is largely the result of a process need caused by demographics. Most of the knowledge has been around for years. But until the consequences of the "baby bust" became apparent to major manufacturers in the industrial countries, especially in Japan and the United States, the need to replace semi-skilled assembly-line labor with machines was not felt. The Japanese are not ahead in robotics because of technical superiority; their designs have mostly come from the United States. But the Japanese had their "baby bust" four or five years earlier than America and almost ten years earlier than West Germany. It took the Japanese just as long as it did the Americans or the Germans—ten years—to realize that they were facing a labor shortage. But these ten years started in Japan a good deal sooner than in the United States, and in West Germany the ten years are still not quite over as these lines are being written.

Mergenthaler's linotype was also in large measure the result of demographic pressures. With the demand for printed materials exploding, the supply of typesetters requiring an apprenticeship of six to eight years was fast becoming inadequate, and wages for typesetters were skyrocketing. As a result, printers became conscious of the "weak link" but also willing to pay good money for a machine that replaced five very expensive craftsmen with one semi-skilled machine operator.

Incongruities and demographics may be the most common causes of a process need. But there is another category, far more difficult and risky yet in many cases of even greater importance: what is now being called program research (as contrasted with the traditional "pure research" of scientists). There is a "weak link" and it is definable, indeed, clearly seen and acutely felt. But to satisfy the process need, considerable *new knowledge* has to be produced.

Very few inventions have succeeded faster than photography. Within twenty years after its invention, it had become popular worldwide. Within twenty years or so, there were great photographers in every country; Mathew Brady's photographs of the American Civil War are still unsurpassed. By 1860, every bride had to have her photograph taken. Photography was the first Western technology to invade Japan, well before the Meiji Restoration and at a time when Japan otherwise was still firmly closed to foreigners and foreign ideas.

Amateur photographers were fully established by 1870. But the available technology made things difficult for them. Photography required heavy and fragile glass plates, which had to be lugged around and treated with extreme care. It required an equally heavy camera, long preparations before a picture could be taken, elaborate settings, and so on. Everybody knew this. Indeed, the photography magazines of the time—and photography magazines were among the first specialty mass magazines—are full of complaints about the extreme difficulty of taking photographs and of suggestions what to do. But the problems could not be solved with the science and technology available in 1870.

By the mid-1880s, however, new knowledge had become available which then enabled George Eastman, the founder of Kodak, to replace the heavy glass plates with a cellulose film weighing practically nothing and impervious even to very rough handling, and to design a light-weight camera around his film. Within ten years, Eastman Kodak had taken world leadership in photography, which it still retains.

"Program research" is often needed to convert a process from potential into reality. Again, the need must be felt, and it must be possible to identify what is needed. Then the new knowledge has to be produced. The prototype innovator for this kind of process-need innovation was Edison (see also Chapter 9). For twenty-odd years, everybody had known that there was going to be an "electric power industry." For the last five or six years of that period, it had become abundantly clear what the "missing link" was: the light bulb. Without it, there could be no electric power industry. Edison defined the new knowledge needed to convert this potential electric power industry into an actual one, went to work, and had a light bulb within two years.

Program research to convert a potential into reality has become the central methodology of the first-rate industrial research laboratory and, of course, of research for defense, for agriculture, for medicine, and for environmental protection.

Program research sounds big. To many people it means "putting a man on the moon" or finding a vaccine against polio. But its most successful applications are in small and clearly defined projects—the smaller and the more sharply focused the better. Indeed, the best example—and perhaps the best single example of successful process need-based innovation—is a very small one, the highway reflector that cut the Japanese automobile accident rate by almost two-thirds.

As late as 1965, Japan had almost no paved roads outside of the big cities. But the country was rapidly shifting to the automobile, so the government frantically paved the roads. Now automobiles could—and did—travel at high speed. But the roads were the same old ones that had been laid down by the oxcarts of the tenth century—barely wide enough for two cars to pass, full of blind corners and hidden entrances, and with junctions every few kilometers at which half a dozen roads meet at every conceivable angle. Accidents began to mount at an alarming rate, especially at night. Press, radio and TV, and the opposition parties in Parliament soon began to clamor for the government to "do something." But, of course, rebuilding the roads was out of the question; it would have taken twenty years anyhow. And a massive publicity campaign to make automobilists "drive carefully" had the result such campaigns generally have, namely, none at all.

A young Japanese, Tamon Iwasa, seized on this crisis as an innovative opportunity. He redesigned the traditional highway reflector so that the little glass beads that serve as its mirrors could be adjusted to reflect the headlights of oncoming cars from any direction onto any direction. The government rushed to install Iwasa reflectors by the hundreds of thousands. And the accident rate plummeted.

To take another example.

World War I had created a public in the United States for national and international news. Everybody was aware of this. Indeed, the newspapers and magazines of those early post-World War I years are full of discussions as to how this need could be satisfied. But the local newspaper could not do the job. Several leading publishers tried, among them *The New York Times*; none of them succeeded. Then Henry Luce identified the process need and defined what was required to satisfy it. It could not be a local publication, it had to be a national one, otherwise, there would be neither enough readers nor enough advertisers. And it could not be a daily—there was not enough news of interest to a large public. The development of the editorial format was then practically dictated by these specifications. When *Time* magazine came out as the first news magazine in the world, it was an immediate success.

These examples, and especially the Iwasa story, show that successful innovations based on process needs require five basic criteria:

- A self-contained process;
- One "weak" or "missing" link;
- A clear definition of the objective;
- That the specifications for the solution can be defined clearly;
- Widespread realization that "there ought to be a better way," that is, high receptivity.

There are, however, some important caveats.

1. The need must be *understood*. It is not enough for it to be "felt." Otherwise one cannot define the specifications for the solution.

We have known, for instance, for several hundred years that mathematics is a problem subject in school. A small minority of students, certainly no more than one-fifth, seem to have no difficulty with mathematics and learn it easily. The rest never really learn it. It is possible, of course, to drill a very much larger percentage to pass mathematics tests. The Japanese do this through heavy emphasis on the subject. But that does not mean that Japanese children learn mathematics. They learn to pass the tests and then immediately forget mathematics. Ten years later, by the time they are in their late twenties, Japanese do just as poorly on mathematics tests as do westerners. In every generation there is a mathematics teacher of genius who somehow can make even the untalented learn, or at least learn a good deal better. But nobody has ever been able, then, to replicate what this one person does. The need is acutely felt, but we do not understand the problem. Is it a lack of native ability? Is it that we are using the wrong methods? Are there psychological and emotional problems? No one knows the answer. And without understanding the problem, we have not been able to find any solution.

2. We may even understand a process and still not have the knowledge to do the job. The preceding chapter told of the clear and understood incongruity in paper making: to find a process that is less wasteful and less uneconomical than the existing one. For a century, able people have worked on the problem. We know exactly what is needed: polymerization of the lignin molecule. It should be easy—we have polymerized many molecules that are similar. But we lack the knowledge to do it, despite a hundred years of assiduous work by well-trained people. One can only say, "Let's try something else."

3. The solution must fit the way people do the work and want to do it. Amateur photographers had no psychological investment in the complicated technology of the early photographic process. All they wanted was to get a decent photograph, as easily as possible. They were receptive, therefore, to a process that took the labor and skill out of taking pictures. Similarly, eye surgeons were interested only in an elegant, logical, bloodless process. An enzyme that gave this to them therefore satisfied their expectations and values.

But here is an example of an innovation based on a clear and substantial process need that apparently does not quite fit, and therefore has not been readily accepted.

For many years the information required by a number of professionals such as lawyers, accountants, engineers, and physicians has grown much faster than the capacity to find it. Professionals have been complaining that they have to spend more and more time hunting for information in the law library, in handbooks and textbooks, in looseleaf services, and so on. One would therefore expect a "databank" to be an immediate success. It gives the professionals immediate information through a computer program and a display terminal: court decisions for the lawyers, tax rulings for the accountants, information on drugs and poisons for the physicians. Yet these services have found it very hard to gather enough subscribers to break even. In some cases, such as Lexis, a service for lawyers, it has taken more than ten years and huge sums of money to get subscribers. The reason is probably that the databanks make it *too* easy. Professionals pride themselves on their "memory," that is, on their ability either to remember the information they need or to know where to find it. "You have to remember the court decisions you need and where to find them," is still the injunction the beginning lawyer gets from the seniors.

So the databank, however helpful in the work and however much time and money it saves, goes against the very values of the professional. "What would you need *me* for if it can be looked up?" an eminent physician once said when asked by one of his patients why he did not use the service that would give him the information to check and confirm his diagnosis, and then decide which alternative method of treatment might be the best in a given case.

Opportunities for innovation based on process need can be found systematically. This is what Edison did for electricity and electronics. This is what Henry Luce did while still an undergraduate at Yale. This is what William Connor did. In fact, the area lends itself to systematic search and analysis.

But once a process need has been found, it has to be tested against the five basic criteria given above. Then, finally, the process need opportunity has to be tested also against the three constraints. Do we understand what is needed? Is the knowledge available or can it be procured within the "state of the art"? And does the solution fit, or does it violate the mores and values of the intended users?

CHAPTER 6

Source: Industry and Market Structures

Industry and market structures sometimes last for many, many years and seem completely stable. The world aluminum industry, for instance, after one century is still led by the Pittsburgh-based Aluminum Company of America which held the original patents, and by its Canadian offspring, Alcan of Montreal. There has only been one major newcomer in the world's cigarette industry since the 1920s, the South African Rembrandt group. And in an entire century only two newcomers have emerged as leading electrical apparatus manufacturers in the world: Philips in Holland and Hitachi in Japan. Similarly no major new retail chain emerged in the United States for forty years, between the early twenties when Sears, Roebuck began to move from mail order into retail stores, and the mid-sixties when an old dime-store chain, Kresge, launched the K-Mart discount stores. Indeed, industry and market structures appear so solid that the people in an industry are likely to consider them foreordained, part of the order of nature, and certain to endure forever.

Actually, market and industry structures are quite brittle. One small scratch and they disintegrate, often fast. When this happens, every member of the industry has to act. To continue to do business as before is almost a guarantee of disaster and might well condemn a company to extinction. At the very least the company will lose its leadership position; and once lost, such leadership is almost never regained. But a change in market or industry structure is also a major opportunity for innovation.

In industry structure, a change requires entrepreneurship from every member of the industry. It requires that each one ask anew: "What is our business?" And each of the members will have to give a different, but above all a new, answer to that question.

I

The Automobile Story

The automobile industry in the early years of this century grew so fast that its markets changed drastically. There were four different responses to this change, all of them successful. The early industry through 1900 had basically been a provider of a luxury product for the very rich. By then, however, it was outgrowing this narrow market with a rate of growth that doubled the industry's sales volume every three years. Yet the existing companies all still concentrated on the "carriage trade."

One response to this was the British company, Rolls-Royce, founded in 1904. The founders realized that automobiles were growing so plentiful as to become "common," and set out to build and sell an automobile which, as an early Rolls-Royce prospectus put it, would have "the cachet of royalty." They deliberately went back to earlier, already obsolete, manufacturing methods in which each car was machined by a skilled mechanic and assembled individually with hand tools. And then they promised that the car would never wear out. They designed it to be driven by a professional chauffeur trained by Rolls-Royce for the job. They restricted sales to customers of whom they approved—preferably titled ones, of course. And to make sure that no "riff-raff" bought their car, they priced the Rolls-Royce as high as a small yacht, at about forty times the annual income of a skilled mechanic or prosperous tradesman.

A few years later in Detroit, the young Henry Ford also saw that the market structure was changing and that automobiles in America were no longer a rich man's toy. His response was to design a car that could be totally mass-produced, largely by semi-skilled labor, and that could be driven by the owner and repaired by him. Contrary to legend, the 1908 Model T was not "cheap": it was priced at a little over what the world's highest-priced skilled mechanic, the American one, earned in a full year. (These days, the cheapest new car on the American market costs about one-tenth of what an unskilled assembly-line worker gets in wages and benefits in a year.) But the Model T cost one-fifth of the cheapest model then on the market and was infinitely easier to drive and to maintain.

Another American, William Crapo Durant, saw the change in market structure as an opportunity to put together a professionally managed large automobile company that would satisfy all segments of what he foresaw would be a huge "universal" market. He founded General Motors in 1905, began to buy existing automobile companies, and integrated them into a large modern business.

A little earlier, in 1899, the young Italian Giovanni Agnelli had seen that the automobile would become a military necessity, especially as a staff car for officers. He founded FIAT in Turin, which within a few years became the leading supplier of staff cars to the Italian, Russian, and Austro-Hungarian armies.

Market structures in the world automobile industry changed once again between 1960 and 1980. For forty years after World War I, the automobile industry had consisted of national suppliers dominating national markets. All one saw on Italy's roads and parking lots were Fiats and a few Alfa Romeos and Lancias; outside of Italy, these makes were fairly rare. In France, there were Renaults, Peugeots, and Citroens; in Germany, Mercedes, Opels, and the German Fords; in the United States, GM cars, Fords, and Chryslers. Then around 1960 the automobile industry all of a sudden became a "global" industry.

Different companies reacted quite differently. The Japanese, who had remained the most insular and had barely exported their cars, decided to become world exporters. Their first attempt at the U.S. market in the late sixties was a fiasco. They regrouped, thought through again what their policy should be, and redefined it as offering an American-type car with American styling, American comfort, and American performance characteristics, but smaller, with better fuel consumption, much more rigorous quality control and, above all, better customer service. And when they got a second chance with the petroleum panic of 1979, they succeeded brilliantly. The Ford Motor Company, too, decided to go "global" through a "European" strategy. Ten years later, in the mid-seventies, Ford had become a strong contender for the number one spot in Europe.

Fiat decided to become a European rather than merely an Italian company, aiming to be a strong number two in every important European country while retaining its primary position in Italy. General Motors at first decided to remain American and to retain its traditional 50 percent share of the American market, but in such a way as to reap something like 70 percent of all profits from automobile sales in North America. And it succeeded. Ten years later, in the mid-seventies, GM shifted gears and decided to contend with Ford and Fiat for leadership in Europe— and again it succeeded. In 1983—84, GM, it would seem, decided finally to become a truly global company and to link up with a number of Japanese; first with two smaller companies, and in the end with Toyota. And Mercedes in West Germany decided on yet another strategy—again a global one—where it limited itself to narrow segments of the world market, to luxury cars, taxicabs, and buses.

All these strategies worked reasonably well. Indeed, it is impossible to say which one worked better than another. But the companies that refused to make hard choices, or refused to admit that anything much was happening, fared badly. If they survive, it is only because their respective governments will not let them go under.

One example is, of course, Chrysler. The people at Chrysler knew what was happening—everybody in the industry did. But they ducked instead of deciding. Chrysler might have chosen an "American" strategy and put all its resources into strengthening its position within the United States, still the world's largest automobile market. Or it might have merged with a strong European firm and aimed at taking third place in the world's most important automobile markets, the United States and Europe. It is known that Mercedes was seriously interested —but Chrysler was not. Instead, Chrysler frittered away its resources on make-believe. It acquired defeated "also-rans" in Europe to make itself look multinational. But this, while giving Chrysler no additional strength, drained its resources and left no money for the investment needed to give Chrysler a chance in the American market. When the day of reckoning came after the petroleum shock of 1979, Chrysler had nothing in Europe and not much more in the United States. Only the U.S. government saved it.

The story is not much different for British Leyland, once Britain's largest automobile company and a strong contender for leadership in Europe; nor for the big French automobile company, Peugeot. Both refused to face up to the fact that a decision was needed. As a result, they rapidly lost both market position and profitability. Today all three—Chrysler, British Leyland, and Peugeot—have become more or less marginal.

But the most interesting and important examples are those of much smaller companies. Every one of the world's automobile manufacturers, large or small, has had to act or face permanent eclipse. However, three small and quite marginal companies saw in this a major opportunity to innovate: Volvo, BMW, and Porsche.

Around 1960, when the automobile industry market suddenly changed, the informed betting was heavily on the disappearance of these three companies during the coming "shakeout." Instead, all three have done well and have created for themselves market niches in which they are the leaders. They have done so through an innovative strategy which, in effect, has reshaped them into different businesses. Volvo in 1965 was small, struggling and barely breaking even. For a few critical years, it did lose large amounts of money. But Volvo went to work reinventing itself, so to speak. It became an aggressive worldwide marketer—especially strong in the United States— of what one might call the "sensible" car; not very luxurious, far from low-priced, not at all fashionable, but sturdy and radiating common sense and "better value." Volvo has marketed itself as the car for professionals who do not need to demonstrate how successful they are through the car they drive, but who value being known for their "good judgment."

BMW, equally marginal in 1960 if not more so, has been equally successful, especially in countries like Italy and France. It has marketed itself as the car for "young comers," for people who want to be taken as young but who already have attained substantial success in their work and profession, people who want to demonstrate that they "know the difference" and are willing to pay for it. BMW is unashamedly a luxury car for the well-to-do, but it appeals to those among the affluent who want to appear "nonestablishment." Whereas Mercedes and Cadillac are the cars for company presidents and for heads of state, BMW is *muy macho*, and bills itself as the "ultimate driving machine."

Finally Porsche (originally a Volkswagen with extra styling) repositioned itself as *the* sports car, the one and only car for those who still do not want transportation but excitement in an automobile.

But those smaller automobile manufacturers who did not innovate and present themselves differently in what is, in effect, a different business—those who continued their established ways—have become casualties. The British MG, for instance, was thirty years ago what Porsche has now become, the sports car *par excellence*. It is almost extinct by now. And where is Citroen? Thirty years ago it was the car that had the solid innovative engineering, the sturdy construction, the middle-class reliability. Citroen would have seemed to be ideally positioned for the market niche Volvo has taken over. But Citroen failed to think through its business and to innovate; as a result, it has neither product nor strategy.

II

The Opportunity

A change in industry structure offers exceptional opportunities, highly visible and quite predictable to outsiders. But the insiders perceive these same changes primarily as threats. The outsiders who innovate can thus become a major factor in an important industry or area quite fast, and at relatively low risk.

Here are some examples.

In the late 1950s three young men met, almost by accident, in New York City. Each of them worked for financial institutions, mostly Wall Street houses. They found themselves in agreement on one point: the securities business—unchanged since the Depression twenty years earlier—was poised for rapid structural change. They decided that this change had to offer opportunities. So they systematically studied the financial industry and the financial markets to find an opportunity for newcomers with limited capital resources and practically no connections. The result was a new firm: Donaldson, Lufkin & Jenrette. Five years after it had been started in 1959, it had become a major force on Wall Street.

What these three young men found was that a whole new group of customers was emerging fast: the pension fund administrators. These new customers did not need anything that was particularly difficult to supply, but they needed something different. And no existing firm had organized itself to give it to them. Donaldson, Lufkin & Jenrette established a brokerage firm to focus on these new customers and to give them the "research" they needed.

About the same time, another young man in the securities business also realized that the industry was in the throes of structural change and that this could offer him an opportunity to build a different securities business of his own. The opportunity he found was "the intelligent investor" mentioned earlier. On this, he then built what is now a big and still fast-growing firm.

During the early or mid-sixties, the structure of American health care began to change very fast. Three young people, the oldest not quite thirty, then working as junior managers in a large Midwestern hospital, decided that this offered them an opportunity to start their own innovative business. They concluded that hospitals would increasingly need expertise in running such housekeeping services as kitchen, laundry, maintenance, and so on. They systematized the work to be done. Then they offered contracts to hospitals under which their new firm would put in its own trained people to run these services, with the fee a portion of the resultant savings. Twenty years later, this company billed almost a billion dollars of services.

The final case is that of the discounters like MCI and Sprint in the American long-distance telephone market. They were total outsiders; Sprint, for instance, was started by a railroad, the Southern Pacific. These outsiders began to look for the chink in Bell System's armor. They found it in the pricing structure of long-distance services. Until World War II, long-distance calls had been a luxury confined to government and large businesses, or to emergencies such as a death in the family. After World War II, they became commonplace. Indeed, they became the growth sector of telecommunications. But under pressure from the regulatory authorities for the various states which control telephone rates, the Bell System continued to price long-distance as a luxury, way above costs, with the profits being used to subsidize local service. To sweeten the pill, however, the Bell System gave substantial discounts to large buyers of long-distance service.

By 1970, revenues from long-distance service had come to equal those from local service and were fast outgrowing them. Still, the original price structure was maintained. And this is what the newcomers exploited. They signed up for volume service at the discount and then retailed it to smaller users, splitting the discount with them. This gave them a substantial profit while also giving their subscribers long-dis-tance service at substantially lower cost. Ten years later, in the early eighties, the long-distance discounters handled a larger volume of calls than the entire Bell System had handled when the discounters first started.

These cases would just be anecdotes except for one fact: each of the innovators concerned *knew* that there was a major innovative opportunity in the industry. Each was reasonably sure that an innovation would succeed, and succeed with minimal risk. How could they be so sure?

III

When Industry Structure Changes

Four near-certain, highly visible indicators of impending change in industry structure can be pinpointed.

1. The most reliable and the most easily spotted of these indicators is rapid growth of an industry. This is, in effect, what each of the above examples (but also the automobile industry examples) have in common. If an industry grows significantly faster than economy or population, it can be predicted with high probability that its structure will change drastically—at the very latest by the time it has doubled in volume. Existing practices are still highly successful, so nobody is inclined to tamper with them. Yet they are becoming obsolete. Neither the people at Citroen nor those at Bell Telephone were willing to accept this, however—which explains why "newcomers," "outsiders," or former "second-raters" could beat them in their own markets.

2. By the time an industry growing rapidly has doubled in volume, the way it perceives and services its market is likely to have become inappropriate. In particular, the ways in which the traditional leaders define and segment the market no longer reflect reality, they reflect history. Yet reports and figures still represent the traditional view of the market. This is the explanation for the success of two such different innovators as Donaldson, Lufkin & Jenrette and the Midwestern "intelligent investor" brokerage house. Each found a segment that the existing financial services institutions had not perceived and therefore did not serve adequately; the pension funds because they were too new, the "intelligent investor"

because he did not fit the Wall Street stereotype.

But the hospital management story is also one of traditional aggregates no longer being adequate after a period of rapid growth. What grew in the years after World War II were the "paramedics," that is, the hospital professions: X-Ray, pathology, the medical lab, therapists of all kinds, and so on. Before World War II these had barely existed. And hospital administration itself became a profession. The traditional "housekeeping" services, which had dominated hospital operations in earlier times, thus steadily became a problem for the administrator, proving increasingly difficult and costly as hospital employees, especially the low-paid ones, began to unionize.

And the case of the book chains reported earlier (in Chapter 3) is also a story of structural change because of rapid growth. What neither the publishers nor the traditional American bookstores realized was that new customers, the "shoppers," were emerging side by side with the old customers, the traditional readers. The traditional bookstore simply did not perceive these new customers and never attempted to serve them.

But there is also the tendency if an industry grows very fast to become complacent and, above all, to try to "skim the cream." This is what the Bell System did with respect to long-distance calls. The sole result is to invite competition (on this see also Chapter 17).

Yet another example is to be found in the American art field. Before World War II, museums were considered "upper-class." After World War II, going to museums became a middle-class habit; in city after city new museums were founded. Before World War II, collecting art was something a few very rich people did. After World War II, collecting all kinds of art became increasingly popular, with thousands of people getting into the act, some of them people of fairly limited means.

One young man working in a museum saw this as an opportunity for innovation. He found it in the most unexpected place—in fact, in a place he had never heard of before, insurance. He established himself as an insurance broker specializing in art and insuring both museums and collectors. Because of his art expertise, the underwriters in the major insurance companies, who had been reluctant to insure art collections, became willing to take the risk, and at premiums up to 70 percent below those charged before. This young man now has a large insurance brokerage firm.

3. Another development that will predictably lead to sudden changes in industry structure is the convergence of technologies that hitherto were seen as distinctly separate.

One example is that of the private branch exchange (PBX), that is, the switchboard for offices and other large telephone users. Basically, all the scientific and technical work on this in the United States has been done by Bell Labs, the research arm of the Bell System. But the main beneficiaries have been a few newcomers such as ROLM Corporation. In the new PBX, two different technologies converge: telephone technology and computer technology. The PBX can be seen as a telecommunications instrument that uses a computer, or as a computer that is being used in telecommunications. Technically, the Bell System would have been perfectly capable of handling this—in fact, it has all along been a computer pioneer. In its view of the market, however, and of the user, Bell System saw the computer as something totally different and far away. While it designed and actually introduced a computer-type PBX, it never pushed it. As a result, a total newcomer has become a major competitor. In fact, ROLM, started by four young engineers, was founded to build a small computer for fighter aircraft, and only stumbled by accident into the telephone business. The Bell System now has not much more than one-third of that market, despite its technical leadership.

4. An industry is ripe for basic structural change if the way in which it does business is changing rapidly.

Thirty years ago, the overwhelming majority of American physicians practiced on their own. By 1980, only 60 percent were doing so. Now, 40 percent (and 75 percent of the younger ones) practice in a group, either in a partnership or as employees of a Health Maintenance Organization or a hospital. A few people who saw what was happening early on, around 1970, realized that it offered an opportunity for innovation. A service company could design the group's office, tell the physicians what equipment they needed, and either manage their group practice for them or train their managers.

Innovations that exploit changes in industry structure are particularly effective if the industry and its markets are dominated by one very large manufacturer or supplier, or by a very few. Even if there is no true monopoly, these large, dominant producers and suppliers, having been successful and unchallenged for many years, tend to be arrogant. At first they dismiss the newcomer as insignificant and, indeed, amateurish. But even when the newcomer takes a larger and larger share of their business, they find it hard to mobilize themselves for counteraction. It took the Bell System almost ten years before it first responded to the long-distance discounters and to the challenge from the PBX manufacturers.

Equally sluggish, however, was the response of the American producers of aspirin when the "non-aspirin aspirins"—Tylenol and Datril —first appeared (on this see also Chapter 17). Again, the innovators diagnosed an opportunity because of an impending change in industry structure, based very largely on rapid growth. There was no reason whatever why the existing aspirin manufacturers, a very small number of very large companies, could not have brought out "non-aspirin aspirin" and sold it effectively. After all, the dangers and limitations of aspirin were no secret; medical literature was full of them. Yet, for the first five or eight years, the newcomers had the market to themselves.

Similarly, the United States Postal Service did not react for many years to innovators who took away larger and larger chunks of the most profitable services. First, United Parcel Service took away ordinary parcel post; then Emery Air Freight and Federal Express took away the even more profitable delivery of urgent or high-value merchandise and letters. What made the Postal Service so vulnerable was its rapid growth. Volume grew so fast that it neglected what seemed to be minor categories, and thus practically delivered an invitation to the innovators.

Again and again when market or industry structure changes, the producers or suppliers who are today's industry leaders will be found neglecting the fastest-growing market segments. They will cling to practices that are rapidly becoming dysfunctional and obsolete. The new growth opportunities rarely fit the way the industry has "always" approached the market, been organized for it, and defines it. The innovator in this area therefore has a good chance of being left alone. For some time, the old businesses or services in the field will still be doing well serving the old market the old way. They are likely to pay little attention to the new challenge, either treating it with condescension or ignoring it altogether.

But there is one important caveat. It is absolutely essential to keep the innovation in this area simple. Complicated innovations do not work. Here is one example, the most intelligent business strategy I know of and one of the most dismal failures.

Volkswagen triggered the change which converted the automobile industry around 1960 into a global market. The Volkswagen Beetle was the first car since the Model T forty years earlier that became a truly international car. It was as ubiquitous in the United States as it was in its native Germany, and as familiar in Tanganyika as it was in the Solomon Islands. And yet Volkswagen missed the opportunity it had created itself—primarily by being *too* clever.

By 1970, ten years after its breakthrough into the world market, the Beetle was becoming obsolete in Europe. In the United States, the Beetle's second-best market, it still sold moderately well. And in Brazil, the Beetle's third-largest market, it apparently still had substantial growth ahead. Obviously, new strategy was called for.

The chief executive officer of Volkswagen proposed switching the German plants entirely to the new model, the successor to the Beetle, which the German plants would also supply to the United States market. But the continuing demand for Beetles in the United States would be satisfied out of Brazil, which would then give Volkswagen do Brasil the needed capacity to enlarge its plants and to maintain for another ten years the Beetle's leadership in the growing Brazilian market. To assure the American customers of the "German quality" that was one of the Beetle's main attractions, the critical parts such as engines and transmissions for all cars sold in North America would, however, still be made in Germany, with the finished car for the North American market then assembled in the United States.

In its way, this was the first genuinely global strategy, with different parts to be made in different countries and assembled in different places according to the needs of different markets. Had it worked, it would have been the right strategy, and a highly innovative one at that. It was killed primarily by the German labor unions. "Assembling Beetles in the United States means exporting German jobs," they said, "and we won't stand for it." But the American dealers were also doubtful about a car that was "made in Brazil," even though the critical parts would still be "made in Germany." And so Volkswagen had to give up its brilliant plan.

The result has been the loss of Volkswagen's second market, the United States. Volkswagen, and not the Japanese, should have had the small car market when small cars became all the rage after the fall of the Shah of Iran triggered the second petroleum panic. Only the Germans had no product. And when, a few years later, Brazil went into a severe economic crisis and automobile sales dropped, Volkswagen do Brasil got into difficulties. There were no export customers for the capacity it had had to build there during the seventies.

The specific reasons why Volkswagen's brilliant strategy failed—to the point where the long-term future of the company may have become problematical—are secondary. The moral of the story is that a "clever" innovative strategy always fails, particularly if it is aimed at exploiting an opportunity created by a change in industry structure. Then only the very simple, specific strategy has a chance of succeeding.

CHAPTER 7

Source: Demographics

The unexpected; incongruities; changes in market and industry structure; and process needs—the sources of innovative opportunity discussed so far in Chapters 3 through 6—manifest themselves within a business, an industry, or a market. They may actually be symptoms of changes outside, in the economy, in society, and in knowledge. But they show up internally.

The remaining sources of innovative opportunity:

- Demographics;
- Changes in perception, meaning, and mood;
- New knowledge

are external. They are changes in the social, philosophical, political, and intellectual environment.

I

Of all external changes, demographics—defined as changes in population, its size, age structure, composition, employment, educational status, and income—are the clearest. They are unambiguous. They have the most predictable consequences.

They also have known and almost certain lead times. Anyone in the American labor force in the year 2000 is alive by now (though not necessarily living in the United States; a good many of America's workers fifteen years hence may now be children in a Mexican *pueblo*, for example). All people reaching retirement age in 2030 in the developed countries are already in the labor force, and in most cases in the occupational group in which they will stay until they retire or die. And the educational attainment of the people now in their early or mid-twenties will largely determine their career paths for another forty years.

Demographics have major impact on what will be bought, by whom, and in what quantities. American teenagers, for instance, buy a good many pairs of cheap shoes a year; they buy for fashion, not durability, and their purses are limited. The same people, ten years later, will buy very few pairs of shoes a year—a sixth as many as they bought when they were seventeen—but they will buy them for comfort and durability first and for fashion second. People in their sixties and seventies in the developed countries—that is, people in their early retirement years — form the prime travel and vacation market. Ten years later the same people are customers for retirement communities, nursing homes, and extended (and expensive) medical care. Two-earner families have more money than they have time, and spend accordingly. People who have acquired extensive schooling in their younger years, especially professional or technical schooling, will, ten to twenty years later, become customers for advanced professional training.

But people with extensive schooling are also available primarily for employment as knowledge workers. Even without competition from low-wage countries with tremendous surpluses of young people trained only for unskilled or semi-skilled manual jobs—the surge of young people in the Third World countries resulting from the drop in infant mortality after 1955—the industrially developed countries of the West and of Japan would have had to automate. Demographics alone, the combined effects of the sharp drop in birth rates and of the "educational explosion"—makes it near-certain that traditional manual blue-collar employment in manufacturing in developed countries, by the year 2010, cannot be more than one-third or less than what it was in 1970. (Though manufacturing production, as a result of automation, may be three to four times what it was then.)

All this is so obvious that no one, one should think, needs to be reminded of the importance of demographics. And indeed businessmen, economists, and politicians have always acknowledged the critical importance of population trends, movements, and dynamics. But they also believed that they did not have to pay attention to demographics in their day-to-day decisions. Population changes—whether in birth rates or mortality rates, in educational attainment, in labor force composition and participation, or in the location and movement of people —were thought to occur so slowly and over such long time spans as to be of little practical concern. Great demographic catastrophes such as the Black Death in Europe in the fourteenth century were admitted to have immediate impacts on society and economy. But otherwise, demographic changes were "secular" changes, of interest to the historian and the statistician rather than to the businessman or the administrator.

This was always a dangerous error. The massive nineteenth-century migration from Europe to the Americas, both North and South, and to Australia and New Zealand, changed the economic and political geography of the world beyond recognition. It created an abundance of entrepreneurial opportunities. It made obsolete the geopolitical concepts on which European politics and military strategies had been based for several centuries. Yet it took place in a mere fifty years, from the mid-1860s to 1914. Whoever disregarded it was likely to be left behind, and fast.

Until 1860, for instance, the House of Rothschild was the world's dominant financial power. The Rothschilds failed, however, to recognize the meaning of the transatlantic migration; only "riff-raff," they thought, would leave Europe. As a result, the Rothschilds ceased to be important around 1870. They had become merely rich individuals. It was J. P. Morgan who took over. His "secret" was to spot the transatlantic migration at its very onset, to understand immediately its significance, and to exploit it as an opportunity by establishing a worldwide bank in New York rather than in Europe, and as the medium for financing the American industries that immigrant labor was making possible. It also took only thirty years, from 1830 to 1860, to transform both western Europe and the eastern United States from rural and farmbased societies into industry-dominated big-city civilizations.

Demographic changes tended to be just as fast, just as abrupt, and to have fully as much impact, in earlier times. The belief that populations changed slowly in times past is pure myth. Or rather, static populations staying in one place for long periods of time have been the exception historically rather than the rule. [⊖]

In the twentieth century it is sheer folly to disregard demographics. The basic assumption for our time must be that populations are inherently unstable and subject to sudden sharp changes—and that they are the first environmental factor that a decision maker, whether businessman or politician, analyzes and thinks through. Few issues in this century, for instance, will be as critical to both domestic and international politics as the aging of the population in the developed countries on the one hand and the tidal wave of young adults in the Third World on the other hand. Whatever the reasons, twentieth-century societies, both developed and developing ones, have become prone to extremely rapid and radical demographic

---

⊖ Here the work of the modern French historians of civilization is definitive.

changes, which occur without advance warning.

The most prominent American population experts called together by Franklin D. Roosevelt predicted unanimously in 1938 that the U.S. population would peak at around 140 million people in 1943 or 1944, and then slowly decline. The American population—with a minimum of immigration—now stands at 240 million. For in 1949, without the slightest advance warning, the United States kicked off a "baby boom" that for twelve years produced unprecedentedly large families, only to turn just as suddenly in 1960 into a "baby bust," producing equally unprecedented small families. The demographers of 1938 were not incompetents or fools; there was just no indication then of a "baby boom."

Twenty years later another American President, John F. Kennedy, called together a group of eminent experts to work out his Latin-American aid and development program, the "Alliance for Progress." Not one of the experts paid attention in 1961 to the precipitous drop in infant mortality which, within another fifteen years, totally changed Latin America's society and economy. The experts also all assumed, without reservation, a rural Latin America. They, too, were neither incompetents nor fools. But the drop in infant mortality in Latin America and the urbanization of society had barely begun at the time.

In 1972 and 1973, the most experienced labor force analysts in the United States still accepted without question that the participation of women would continue to decline as it had done for many years. When the "baby boomers" came on the labor market in record numbers, they worried (quite unnecessarily, as it turned out) where all the jobs for the young males would be coming from. No one asked where jobs would come from for young females—they were not supposed to need any. Ten years later the labor force participation of American women under fifty stood at 64 per cent, the highest rate ever. And there is little difference in labor force participation in this group between married and unmarried women, or between women with and without children.

These shifts are not only dazzlingly sudden. They are often mysterious and defy explanation. The drop in infant mortality in the Third World can be explained in retrospect. It was caused by a convergence of old technologies: the public-health nurse; placing the latrine below the well; vaccination; the wire screen outside the window; and, of very new technologies, antibiotics and pesticides such as DDT. Yet it was totally unpredictable. And what explains the "baby boom" or the "baby bust"? What explains the sudden rush of American women (and of European women as well, though with a lag of a few years) into the labor force? And what explains the rush into the slums of Latin-American cities?

Demographic shifts in this century may be inherently unpredictable, yet they do have long lead times before impact, and lead times, moreover, which are predictable. It will be five years before newborn babies become kindergarten pupils and need classrooms, playgrounds, and teachers. It will be fifteen years before they become important as customers, and nineteen to twenty years before they join the labor force as adults. Populations in Latin America began to grow quite rapidly as soon as infant mortality began to drop. Still the babies who did not die did not become schoolchildren for five or six years, nor adolescents looking for work for fifteen or sixteen years. And it takes at least ten years—usually fifteen—before any change in educational attainments translates itself into labor force composition and available skills.

What makes demographics such a rewarding opportunity for the entrepreneur is precisely its neglect by decision makers, whether businessmen, public-service staffs, or governmental policymakers. They still cling to the assumption that demographics do not change—or do not change fast. Indeed, they reject even the plainest evidence of demographic changes. Here are some fairly typical examples.

By 1970, it had become crystal clear that the number of children in America's schools was going to be 25 to 30 percent lower than it had been in the 1960s, for ten or fifteen years at least. After all, children entering kindergarten in 1970 have to be alive no later than 1965, and the "baby bust" was well established beyond possibility of rapid reversal by that year. Yet the schools of education in American universities flatly refused to accept this. They considered it a law of nature, it seems, that the number of children of school age must go up year after year. And so they stepped up their efforts to recruit students, causing substantial unemployment for graduates a few years later, severe pressure on teachers' salaries, and massive closings of schools of education.

And here are two examples from my own experience. In 1957, I published a forecast that there would be ten to twelve million college students in the United States twenty-five years later, that is, by the mid-seventies. The figure was derived simply by putting together two demographic events that had already happened: the increase in the number of births and the increase in the percentage of young adults going to college. The forecast was absolutely correct. Yet practically every established university pooh-poohed it. Twenty years later, in 1976, I looked at the age figures and predicted that retirement age in the United States would have to be raised to seventy or eliminated altogether within ten years. The change came even faster: compulsory retirement at any age was abolished in California a year later, in 1977, and retirement before seventy for the rest of the country two years later, in 1978. The demographic figures that made this prediction practically certain were well known and published. Yet most so-called experts—government economists, labor-union economists, business economists, statisticians—dismissed the forecast as utterly absurd. "It will never happen" was the all but unanimous response. The labor unions actually proposed at the time lowering the mandatory retirement age to sixty or below.

This unwillingness, or inability, of the experts to accept demographic realities which do not conform to what they take for granted gives the entrepreneur his opportunity. The lead times are known. The events themselves have already happened. But no one accepts them as reality, let alone as opportunity. Those who defy the conventional wisdom and accept the facts—indeed, those who go actively looking for them—can therefore expect to be left alone for quite a long time. The competitors will accept demographic reality, as a rule, only when it is already about to be replaced by a new demographic change and a new demographic reality.

II

Here are some examples of successful exploitation of demographic changes.

Most of the large American universities dismissed my forecast of 10 to 12 million college students by the 1970s as preposterous. But the entrepreneurial universities took it seriously: Pace University, in New York, was one, and Golden Gate University in San Francisco another. They were just as incredulous at first, but they checked the forecast and found that it was valid, and in fact the only rational prediction. They then organized themselves for the additional student enrollment; the traditional, and especially the "prestige" universities, on the other hand, did nothing. As a result, twenty years later these brash newcomers had the students, and when enrollments decreased nationwide as a result of the "baby bust," they still kept on growing.

One American retailer who accepted the "baby boom" was then a small and undistinguished shoe chain, Melville. In the early 1960s just before the first cohorts of the "baby boom" reached adolescence, Melville directed itself to this new market. It created new and different stores specifically for teenagers. It redesigned its merchandise. It advertised and promoted to the sixteen-and seventeen-year-olds. And it went beyond footwear into clothing for teenagers, both female and male. As a result, Melville became one of the fastest-growing and most profitable retailers in America. Ten years later other retailers caught on and began to cater to teenagers—just as the center of demographic gravity started to shift away from them and toward "young adults," twenty to twenty-five years old. By then Melville was already shifting its own focus to that new dominant age cohort.

The scholars on Latin America whom President Kennedy brought together to advise him on the Alliance for Progress in 1961 did not see Latin America's urbanization. But one business, the American retail chain Sears, Roebuck, had seen it several years earlier—not by poring over statistics but by going out and looking at customers in Mexico City and Lima, Sa~o Paulo and Bogotá. As a result, Sears in the mid-fifties began to build American-type department stores in major Latin-American cities, designed for a new urban middle class which, while not "rich," was part of the money economy and had middle-class aspirations. Sears became the leading retailer in Latin America within a few years.

And here are two examples of exploiting demographics to innovate in building a highly productive labor force. The expansion of New York's Citibank is largely based on its early realization of the movement of young, highly educated and highly ambitious women into the work force. Most large American employers considered these women a "problem" as late as 1980; many still do. Citibank, almost alone among large employers, saw in them an opportunity. It aggressively recruited them during the 1970s, trained them, and sent them out all over the country as lending officers. These ambitious young women very largely made Citibank into the nation's leading, and its first truly "national" bank. At the same time, a few savings and loan associations (not an industry noted for innovation or venturing) realized that older married women who had earlier dropped out of the labor force when their children were small make high-grade employees when brought back as permanent part-time workers. "Everybody knew" that part-timers are "temporary," and that women who have once left the labor force never come back into it; both were perfectly sensible rules in earlier times. But demographics made them obsolete. The willingness to accept this fact—and again such willingness stemmed not from reading statistics but from going out and looking—has given the savings and loan associations an exceptionally loyal, exceptionally productive work force, particularly in California.

The success of Club Mediterranée in the travel and resort business is squarely the result of exploiting demographic changes: the emergence of large numbers of young adults in Europe and the United States who are affluent and educated but only one generation away from working-class origins. Still quite unsure of themselves, still not self-confident as tourists, they are eager to have somebody with the know-how to organize their vacations, their travel, their fun—and yet they are not really comfortable either with their working-class parents or with older, middle-class people. Thus, they are ready-made customers for a new and "exotic" version of the old teenage hangout.

III

Analysis of demographic changes begins with population figures. But absolute population is the least significant number. Age distribution is far more important, for instance. In the 1960s, it was the rapid increase in the number of young people in most developed countries that proved significant (the one notable exception was Great Britain, where the "baby boom" was short-lived). In the 1980s and even more in the 1990s, it will be the drop in the number of young people, the steady increase in the number of early middle-age people (up to forty) and the very rapid increase in the number of old people (seventy and over). What opportunities do these developments offer? What are the values and the expectations, the needs and wants of these various age groups?

The number of traditional college students cannot increase. The most one can hope for is that it will not fall, that the percentage of eighteen-and nineteen-year-olds who stay in school beyond secondary education will increase sufficiently to offset the decline in the total number. But with the increase in the number of people in their mid-thirties and forties who have received a college degree earlier, there are going to be large numbers of highly schooled people who want advanced professional training and retraining, whether as doctors, lawyers, architects, engineers, executives, or teachers. What do these people look for? What do they need? How can they pay? What does the traditional university have to do to attract and satisfy such very different students? And, finally, what are the wants, needs, values of the elderly? Is there indeed any one "older group," or are there rather several, each with different expectations, needs, values, satisfactions?

Particularly important in age distribution—and with the highest predictive value—are changes in the center of population gravity, that is, in the age group which at any given time constitutes both the largest and the fastest-growing age cohort in the population.

At the end of the Eisenhower presidency, in the late fifties, the center of population gravity in the United States was at its highest point in history. But a violent shift within a few years was bound to take place. As a result of the "baby boom," the center of American population gravity was going to drop so sharply by 1965 as to bring it to the lowest point since the early days of the Republic, to around sixteen or seventeen. It was predictable—and indeed predicted by anyone who took demographics seriously and looked at the figures—that there would be a drastic change in mood and values. The "youth rebellion" of the sixties was mainly a shift of the spotlight to what has always been typical adolescent behavior. In earlier days, with the center of population gravity in the late twenties or early thirties, age groups that are notoriously ultra-conservative, adolescent behavior was dismissed as "Boys will be boys" (and "Girls will be girls"). In the sixties it suddenly became the representative behavior.

But when everybody was talking of a "permanent shift in values" or of a "greening of America," the age pendulum had already swung back, and violently so. By 1969, the first effects of the "baby bust" were already discernible, and not only in the statistics. 1974 or 1975 would be the last year in which the sixteen-and seventeen-year-olds would constitute the center of population gravity. After that, the center would rapidly move up: by the early 1980s it would be in the high twenties again. And with this shift would come a change in what would be considered "representative" behavior. The teenagers would, of course, continue to behave like teenagers. But that would again be dismissed as the way teenagers behave rather than as the constitutive values and behavior of society. And so one could predict with near-certainty, for instance (and some of us did predict it), that by the mid-seventies the college campuses would cease to be "activist" and "rebellious," and college students would again be concerned with grades and jobs; but also that the overwhelming majority of the "dropouts" of 1968 would, ten years later, have become the "upward-mobile professionals" concerned with careers, advancement, tax shelters, and stock options.

Segmentation by educational attainment may be equally important; indeed, for some purposes, it may be more important (e.g., selling encyclopedias, continuing professional education, but also vacation travel). Then there is labor force participation and occupational segmentation. Finally there is income distribution, and especially distribution of disposable and discretionary income. What happens, for instance, to the propensity to save in the two-earner family?

Actually, most of the answers are available. They are the stuff of market research. All that is needed is the willingness to ask the questions.

But more than poring over statistics is involved. To be sure, statistics are the starting point. They were what got Melville to ask what opportunities the jump in teenagers offered a fashion retailer, or what got the top management at Sears, Roebuck to look upon Latin America as a potential market. But then the managements of these companies—or the administrators of metropolitan big-city universities such as Pace in New York and Golden Gate in San Francisco—went out into the field to look and listen.

This is literally how Sears, Roebuck decided to go into Latin America. Sears's chairman, Robert E. Wood, read in the early 1950s that Mexico City and São Paulo were expected to outgrow all U.S. cities by the year 1975. This so intrigued him that he went himself to look at the major cities in Latin America. He spent a week in each of them—Mexico City, Guadalajara, Bogotá, Lima, Santiago, Rio, São Paulo—walking around, looking at stores (he was appalled by what he saw), and studying traffic patterns. Then he knew what customers to aim at, what kind of stores to build, where to put the stores, and what merchandise to stock them with.

Similarly, the founders of Club Méditerranée looked at the customers of package tours, talked to them and listened to them, before they built their first vacation resort. And the two young men who turned Melville Shoe from a dowdy, undistinguished shoe chain (one among many) into the fastest-growing popular fashion retailer in America similarly spent weeks and months in shopping centers, looking at customers, listening to them, exploring their values. They studied the way young people shopped, what kind of environment they liked (do teenage boys and girls, for instance, shop in the same place for shoes or do they want to have separate stores?), and what they considered "value" in the merchandise they bought.

Thus, for those genuinely willing to go out into the field, to look and to listen, changing demographics is both a highly productive and a highly dependable innovative opportunity.

CHAPTER 8

Source: Changes in Perception

I

"The Glass Is Half Full"

In mathematics there is no difference between "The glass is half full" and "The glass is half empty." But the meaning of these two statements is totally different, and so are their consequences. If general perception changes from seeing the glass as "half full" to seeing it as "half empty," there are major innovative opportunities.

Here are a few examples of such changes in perception and of the innovative opportunities they opened up—in business, in politics, in education, and elsewhere.

1. All factual evidence shows that the last twenty years, the years since the early 1960s, have been years of unprecedented advance and improvement in the health of Americans. Whether we look at mortality rates for newborn babies or survival rates for the very old, at occurrence of cancers (other than lung cancer) or cure rates for cancer, and so on, all indicators of physical health and functioning have been moving upward at a good clip. And yet the nation is gripped by collective hypochondria. Never before has there been so much concern with health, and so much fear. Suddenly everything seems to cause cancer or degenerative heart disease or premature loss of memory. The glass is clearly "half empty." What we see now

are not the great improvements in health and functioning, but that we are as far away from immortality as ever before and have made no progress toward it. In fact, it can be argued that if there is any real deterioration in American health during the last twenty years it lies precisely in the extreme concern with health and fitness, and the obsession with getting old, with losing fitness, with degenerating into long-term illness or senility. Twenty-five years ago, even minor improvements in the nation's health were seen as major steps forward. Now, even major improvements are barely paid attention to.

Whatever the causes for this change in perception, it has created substantial innovative opportunities. It created, for instance, a market for new health-care magazines: one of them, *American Health*, reached a circulation of a million within two years. It created the opportunity for a substantial number of new and innovative businesses to exploit the fear of traditional foods causing irreparable damage. A firm in Boulder, Colorado, named Celestial Seasonings was started by one of the "flower children" of the late sixties picking herbs in the mountains, packaging them, and peddling them on the street. Fifteen years later, Celestial Seasonings was taking in several hundred million dollars in sales each year and was sold for more than $20 million to a very large food-processing company. And there are highly profitable chains of health-food stores. Jogging equipment has also become big business, and the fastest-growing new business in 1983 in the United States was a company making indoor exercise equipment.

2. Traditionally, the way people feed themselves was very largely a matter of income group and class. Ordinary people "ate"; the rich "dined." This perception has changed within the last twenty years. Now the same people both "eat" and "dine." One trend is toward "feeding," which means getting down the necessary means of sustenance, in the easiest and simplest possible way: convenience foods, TV dinners, McDonald's hamburgers or Kentucky Fried Chicken, and so on. But then the same consumers have also become gourmet cooks. TV programs on gourmet cooking are highly popular and achieve high ratings; gourmet cookbooks have become mass-market best-sellers; whole new chains of gourmet food stores have opened. Finally, traditional supermarkets, while doing 90 percent of their business in foods for "feeding," have opened "gourmet boutiques" which in many cases are far more profitable than their ordinary processed-food business. This new perception is by no means confined to the United States. In West Germany, a young woman physician said to me recently: "Wir essen sechs Tage in der Woche, aber einen Tag wollen wir doch richtig speisen (We feed six days, but one day a week we like to dine)." Not so long ago, "essen" was what ordinary people did seven days a week, and "speisen" what the elite, the rich and the aristocracy, did, seven days a week.

3. If anyone around 1960, in the waning days of the Eisenhower administration and the beginning of the Kennedy presidency, had predicted the gains the American black would make in the next ten or fifteen years, he would have been dismissed as an unrealistic visionary, if not insane. Even predicting half the gains that those ten or fifteen years actually registered for the American black would have been considered hopelessly optimistic. Never in recorded history has there been a greater change in the status of a social group within a shorter time. At the beginning of those years, black participation in higher education beyond high school was around one-fifth that of whites. By the early seventies, it was equal to that of whites and ahead of that of a good many white ethnic groups. The same rate of advance occurred in employment, in incomes, and especially in entrance to professional and managerial occupations. Anyone granted twelve or fifteen years ago an advance look would have considered the "negro problem" in America to be solved, or at least pretty far along the way toward solution.

But what a large part of the American black population actually sees today in the mid-eighties is not that the glass has become "half full" but that it is still "half empty." In fact, frustration, anger, and alienation have increased rather than decreased for a substantial fraction of the American blacks. They do not see the achievements of two-thirds of the blacks who have moved into the middle class, economically and socially, but the failure of the remaining one-third to advance. What they see is not how fast things have been moving, but how much still remains to be done—how slow and how difficult the going still is. The old allies of the American blacks, the white liberals—the labor unions, the Jewish community, or academia—see the advances. They see that the glass has become "half full." This then has led to a basic split between the blacks and the liberal groups which, of course, only makes the blacks feel even more certain that the glass is "half empty."

The white liberal, however, has come to feel that the blacks increasingly are no longer "deprived," no longer entitled to special treatment such as reverse discrimination, no longer in need of special allowances and priority in employment, in promotion, and so on. This became the opportunity for a new kind of black leader, the Reverend Jesse Jackson. Historically, for almost a hundred years—from Booker T. Washington around the turn of the century through Walter White in the New Deal days until Martin Luther King, Jr., during the presidencies of John Kennedy and Lyndon Johnson—a black could become leader of his community only by proving his ability to get the support of white liberals. It was the one way to obtain enough political strength to make significant gains for American blacks. Jesse Jackson saw that the change in perception that now divides American blacks from their old allies and comrades-in-arms, white liberals, is an innovative opportunity to create a totally different kind of black leadership, one based on vocal enmity to the white liberals and even all-out attack on them. In the past, to have sounded as anti-liberal, anti-union, and anti-Jewish as Jackson has done would have been political suicide. Within a few short weeks in 1984, it made Jackson the undisputed leader of the American black community.

4. American feminists today consider the 1930s and 1940s the darkest of dark ages, with women denied any role in society. Factually, nothing could be more absurd. The America of the 1930s and 1940s was dominated by female stars of the first magnitude. There was Eleanor Roosevelt, the first wife of an American President to establish for herself a major role as a conscience, and as the voice of principle and of compassion which no American male in our history has equaled. Her friend, Frances Perkins, was the first woman in an American cabinet as Secretary of Labor, and the strongest, most effective member of President Roosevelt's cabinet altogether. Anna Rosenberg was the first woman to become a senior executive of a very big corporation as personnel vice-president of R. H. Macy, then the country's biggest retailer; and later on, she became Assistant Secretary of Defense for manpower and the "boss" of the generals. There were any number of prominent and strong women as university and college presidents, each a national figure. The leading playwrights, Clare Booth Luce and Lillian Hellman, were both women—and Clare Luce then became a major political figure, a member of Congress from Connecticut, and ambassador to Italy. The most publicized medical advance of the period was the work of a woman. Helen Taussig developed the first successful surgery of the living heart, the "blue baby" operation, which saved countless children all over the world and ushered in the age of cardiac surgery, leading directly to the heart transplant and the by-pass operation. And there was Marian Anderson, the black singer and the first black to enter every American living room through the radio, touching the hearts and consciences of millions of Americans as no black before her had done and none would do again until Martin Luther King, Jr., a quarter century later. The list could be continued indefinitely.

These were very proud women, conscious of their achievements, their prominence, their importance. Yet they did not see themselves as "role models." They saw themselves not as women but as individuals. They did not consider themselves as "representative" but as exceptional.

How the change occurred, and why, I leave to future historians to explain. But when it happened around 1970, these great women leaders became in effect "non-persons" for their feminist successors. Now the woman who is not in the labor force, and not working in an occupation traditionally considered "male," is seen as unrepresentative and as the exception.

This was noted as an opportunity by a few businesses, in particular, Citibank (cf. Chapter 7). It was not seen at all, however, by the very industries in which women had long been accepted as professionals and executives, such as department stores, advertising agencies, magazine or book publishers. These traditional employers of professional and managerial women actually today have fewer women in major positions than they had thirty or forty years ago. Citibank, by contrast, was exceedingly *macho*—which may be one reason why it realized there had been a change. It saw in the new perception women had of themselves a major opportunity to court exceptionally able, exceptionally ambitious, exceptionally striving women; to recruit them; and to hold them. And it could do so without competition from the traditional recruiters of career women. In exploiting a change in perception, innovators, as we have seen, can usually count on having the field to themselves for quite a long time.

5. A much older case, one from the early 1950s, shows a similar exploitation of a change in perception. Around 1950, the American population began to describe itself overwhelmingly as being "middle-class," and to do so regardless, almost, of income or occupation. Clearly, Americans had changed their perception of their own social position. But what did the change mean? One advertising executive, William Benton (later senator from Connecticut), went out and asked people what the words "middle class" meant to them. The results were unambiguous: "middle class" in contrast to "working class" means believing in the ability of one's children to rise through performance in school. Benton thereupon bought up the *Encyclopedia Britannica* company and started peddling the *Encyclopedia*, mostly through high school teachers, to parents whose children were the first generation in the family to attend high school. "If you want to be middle-class," the salesman said in effect, "your child has to have the *Encyclopedia Britannica* to do well in school." Within three years Benton had turned the almost-dying company around. And ten years later the company began to apply exactly the same strategy in Japan for the same reasons and with the same success.

6. Unexpected success or unexpected failure is often an indication of a change in perception and meaning. Chapter 3 told how the phoenix of the Thunderbird rose from the ashes of the Edsel. What the Ford Motor Company found when it searched for an explanation of the failure of the Edsel was a change in perception. The automobile market, which only a few short years earlier had been segmented by income groups, was now seen by the customers as segmented by "lifestyles."

When a change in perception takes place, the facts do not change. Their meaning does. The meaning changes from "The glass is half full" to "The glass is half empty." The meaning changes from seeing oneself as "working-class" and therefore born into one's "station in life," to seeing oneself as "middle-class" and therefore very much in command of one's social position and economic opportunities. This change can come very fast. It probably did not take much longer than a decade for the majority of the American population to change from considering themselves "working-class" to considering themselves "middle-class."

Economics do not necessarily dictate such changes; in fact, they may be irrelevant. In terms of income distribution, Great Britain is a more egalitarian country than the United States. And yet almost 70 percent of the British population still consider themselves "working-class," even though at least two-thirds of the British population are above "working-class" income by economic criteria alone, and close to half are above the "lower middle class" as well. What determines whether the glass is "half full" or "half empty" is mood rather than facts. It results from experiences that might be called "existential." That the American blacks feel "The glass is half empty" has as much to do with unhealed wounds of past centuries as with anything in present American society. That a majority of the English feel themselves to be "working-class" is still largely a legacy of the nineteenth-century chasm between "church" and "chapel." And the American health hypochondria expresses far more American values, such as the worship of youth, than anything in the health statistics.

Whether sociologists or economists can explain the perceptional phenomenon is irrelevant. It remains a fact. Very often it cannot be quantified; or rather, by the time it can be quantified, it is too late to serve as an opportunity for innovation. But it is not exotic or intangible. It is concrete: it can be defined, tested, and above all exploited.

II

The Problem of Timing

Executives and administrators admit the potency of perception-based innovation. But they tend to shy away from it as "not practical." They consider the perception-based innovator as weird or just a crackpot. But there is nothing weird about the *Encyclopedia Britannica*, about the Ford Thunderbird or Celestial Seasonings. Of course, successful innovators in any field tend to be close to the field in which they innovate. But the only thing that sets them apart is their being alert to opportunity.

One of the foremost of today's gourmet magazines was launched by a young man who started out as food editor of an airlines magazine. He became alert to the change in perception when he read in the same issue of a Sunday paper three contradictory stories. The first said that prepared meals such as frozen dinners, TV dinners, and Kentucky Fried Chicken accounted for more than half of all meals consumed in the United States and were expected to account for three-quarters within a few years. The second said that a TV program on gourmet cooking was receiving one of the highest audience ratings. And the third that a gourmet cookbook in its paperback edition, that is, an edition for the masses, had mounted to the top of the best-seller lists. These apparent contradictions made him ask, What's going on here? A year later he started a gourmet magazine quite different from any that had been on the market before.

Citibank became conscious of the opportunity offered by the moving of women into the work force when its college recruiters reported that they could no longer carry out their instructions, which were to hire the best male business school students in finance and marketing. The best students in these fields, they reported, were increasingly women. College recruiters in many other companies, including quite a few banks, told their managements the same story at that time. In response, most of them were urged, "Just try harder to get the top-flight men." At Citibank, top management saw the change as an opportunity and acted on it.

All these examples, however, also show the critical problem in perception-based innovation: timing. If Ford had waited only one year after the fiasco of the Edsel, it might have lost the "lifestyle" market to GM's Pontiac. If Citibank had not been the first one to recruit women MBAs, it would not have become the preferred employer for the best and most ambitious of the young women aiming to make a career in business.

Yet there is nothing more dangerous than to be premature in exploiting a change in perception. In the first place, a good many of what look like changes in perception turn out to be short-lived fads. They are gone within a year or two. And it is not always apparent which is fad and which is true change. The kids playing computer games were a fad. Companies which, like Atari, saw in them a change in perception lasted one or two years—and then became casualties. Their fathers going in for home computers represented a genuine change, however. It is, furthermore, almost impossible to predict what the consequences of such a change in perception will be. One good example are the consequences of the student rebellions in France, Japan, West Germany, and the United States. Everyone in the late 1960s was quite sure that these would have permanent and profound consequences. But what are they? As far as the universities are concerned, the student rebellions seem to have had absolutely no lasting impact. And who would have expected that, fifteen years later, the rebellious students of 1968 would have become the "Yuppies" to whom Senator Hart appealed in the 1984 American primaries, the young, upward-mobile professionals, ultra-materialistic, job conscious, and maneuvering for their next promotion? There are actually far fewer "dropouts" around these days than there used to be—the only difference is that the media pay attention to them. Can the emergence of homosexuals and lesbians into the limelight be explained by the student rebellion? These were certainly not the results the students themselves in 1968, nor any of the observers and pundits of those days, could possibly have predicted.

And yet, timing is of the essence. In exploiting changes in perception, "creative imitation" (described in Chapter 17) does not work. One has to be first. But precisely because it is so uncertain whether a change in perception is a fad or permanent, and what the consequences really are, perception-based innovation has to start small and be very specific.

CHAPTER 9

Source: New Knowledge

Knowledge-based innovation is the "super-star" of entrepreneurship. It gets the publicity. It gets the money. It is what people normally mean when they talk of innovation. Of course, not all knowledge-based innovations are important. Some are truly trivial. But amongst the history-making innovations, knowledge-based innovations rank high. The knowledge, however, is not necessarily scientific or technical. Social innovations based on knowledge can have equal or even greater impact.

Knowledge-based innovation differs from all other innovations in its basic characteristics: time span, casualty rate, predictability, and in the challenges it poses to the entrepreneur. And like most "super-stars," knowledge-based innovation is temperamental, capricious, and hard to manage.

I

The Characteristics of Knowledge-based Innovation

Knowledge-based innovation has the longest lead time of all innovations. There is, first, a long time span between the emergence of new knowledge and its becoming applicable to technology. And then there is another long period before the new technology turns into products, processes, or services in the marketplace.

Between 1907 and 1910, the biochemist Paul Ehrlich developed the theory of chemotherapy, the control of bacterial microorganisms through chemical compounds. He himself developed the first antibacterial drug, Salvarsan, for the control of syphilis. The sulfa drugs which are the application of Ehrlich's chemotherapy to the control of a broad spectrum of bacterial diseases came on the market after 1936, twenty-five years later.

Rudolph Diesel designed the engine which bears his name in 1897. Everyone at once realized that it was a major innovation. Yet for many years there were few practical applications. Then in 1935 an American, Charles Kettering, totally redesigned Diesel's engine, rendering it capable of being used as the propulsion unit in a wide variety of ships, in locomotives, in trucks, buses, and passenger cars.

A number of knowledges came together to make possible the computer. The earliest was the binary theorem, a mathematical theory going back to the seventeenth century that enables all numbers to be expressed by two numbers only: one and zero. It was applied to a calculating machine by Charles Babbage in the first half of the nine-teenth century. In 1890, Hermann Hollerith invented the punchcard, going back to an invention by the early nineteenth-century Frenchman J-M. Jacquard. The punchcard makes it possible to convert numbers into "instructions." In 1906 an American, Lee de Forest, invented the audion tube, and with it created electronics. Then, between 1910 and 1913, Bertrand Russell and Alfred North Whitehead, in their *Principia Mathematica*, created symbolic logic, which enables us to express all logical concepts as numbers. Finally, during World War I, the concepts of programming and feedback were developed, primarily for the purposes of antiaircraft gunnery. By 1918, in other words, all the knowledge needed to develop the computer was available. The first computer became operational in 1946.

A Ford Motor Company manufacturing executive coined the word "automation" in 1951 and described in detail the entire manufacturing process automation would require. "Robotics" and factory automation were widely talked about for twenty-five years, but nothing really happened for a long time. Nissan and Toyota in Japan did not introduce robots into their plants until 1978. In the early eighties, General Electric built an automated locomotive plant in Erie, Pennsylvania. General Motors then began to automate several of its engine and accessory plants. Early in 1985, Volkswagen began to operate its "Hall 54" as an almost completely automated manufacturing installation.

Buckminster Fuller, who called himself a geometer and who was part mathematician and part philosopher, applied the mathematics of topology to the design of what he called the "Dymaxion House," a term he chose because he liked the sound of it. The Dymaxion House combines the greatest possible living space with the smallest possible surface. It therefore has optimal insulation, optimal heating and cooling, and superb acoustics. It also can be built with lightweight materials, requires no foundation and a minimum of suspension, and can still withstand an earthquake or the fiercest gale. Around 1940, Fuller put a Dymaxion House on the campus of a small New England college. And there it stayed. Very few Dymaxion Houses have been built—Americans, it seems, do not like to live in circular homes. But around 1965, Dymaxion structures began to be put up in the Arctic and Antarctic where conventional buildings are impractical, expensive, and difficult to erect. Since then they have increasingly been used for large structures such as auditoriums, concert tents, sports arenas, and so on.

Only major external crises can shorten this lead time. De Forest's audion tube, invented in 1906, would have made radio possible almost immediately, but it would still not have been on the market until the late 1930s or so had not World War I forced governments, and especially the American government, to push the development of wireless transmission of sounds. Field telephones connected by wires were simply too unreliable, and wireless telegraphy was confined to dots and dashes. And so, radio came on the market early in the 1920s, only fifteen years after the emergence of the knowledge on which it is based.

Similarly, penicillin would probably not have been developed until the 1950s or so but for World War II. Alexander Fleming found the bacteria-killing mold, penicillium, in the mid-twenties. Howard Florey, an English biochemist, began to work on it ten years later. But it was World War II that forced the early introduction of penicillin. The need to have a potent drug to fight infections led the British government to push Florey's research: English soldiers were made available to him as guinea pigs wherever they fought. The computer, too, would probably have waited for the discovery of the transistor by Bell Lab physicists in 1947 had not World War II led the American government to push computer research and to invest large resources of men and money in the work.

The long lead time for knowledge-based innovations is by no means confined to science or technology. It applies equally to innovations that are based on nonscientific and nontechnological knowledge.

The comte de Saint-Simon developed the theory of the entrepreneurial bank, the purposeful use of capital to generate economic development, right after the Napoleonic wars. Until then bankers were moneylenders who lent against "security" (e.g., the taxing power of a prince).Saint-Simon's banker was to "invest," that is, to create new wealth-producing capacity. Saint-Simon had extraordinary influence in his time, and a popular cult developed around his memory and his ideas after his death in 1826. Yet it was not until 1852 that two disciples, the brothers Jacob and Isaac Pereire, established the first entrepreneurial bank, the Crédit Mobilier, and with it ushered in what we now call finance capitalism.

Similarly, many of the elements needed for what we now call management were available right after World War I. Indeed, in 1923, Herbert Hoover, soon to be President of the United States, and Thomas Masaryk, founder and president of Czechoslovakia, convened the first International Management Congress in Prague. At the same time a few large companies here and there, especially DuPont and General Motors in the United States, began to reorganize themselves around the new management concepts. In the next decade a few "true believers," especially an Englishman, Lyndall Urwick, the founder of the first management consulting firm which still bears his name, began to write on management. Yet it was not until my *Concept of the Corporation* (1946) and *Practice of Management* (1954) were published that management become a discipline accessible to managers all over the world. Until then each student or practitioner of "management" focused on a separate area; Urwick on organization, others on the management of people, and so on. My books codified it, organized it, systematized it. Within a few years, management became a worldwide force.

Today, we experience a similar lead time in respect to learning theory. The scientific study of learning began around 1890 with Wilhelm Wundt in Germany and William James in the United States. After World War II, two Americans—B. F. Skinner and Jerome Bruner, both at Harvard—developed and tested basic theories of learning, Skinner specializing in behavior and Bruner in cognition. Yet only now is learning theory beginning to become a factor in our schools. Perhaps the time has come for an entrepreneur to start schools based on what we know about learning, rather than on the old wives' tales about it that have been handed down through the ages.

In other words, the lead time for knowledge to become applicable technology and begin to be accepted on the market is between twenty-five and thirty-five years.

This has not changed much throughout recorded history. It is widely believed that scientific discoveries turn much faster in our day than ever before into technology, products, and processes. But this is largely illusion. Around 1250 the Englishman Roger Bacon, a Franciscan monk, showed that refraction defects of the eye could be corrected with eyeglasses. This was incompatible with what everybody then knew: the "infallible" authority of the Middle Ages Galen, the great medical scientist, had "proven conclusively" that it could not be done. Roger Bacon lived and worked on the extreme edges of the civilized world, in the wilds of northern Yorkshire. Yet a mural, painted thirty years later in the Palace of the Popes in Avignon (where it can still be seen), shows elderly cardinals wearing reading glasses; and ten years later, miniatures show elderly courtiers in the Sultan's Palace in Cairo also in glasses. The mill race, which was the first true "automation," was developed to grind grain by the Benedictine monks in northern Europe around the year 1000; within thirty years it had spread all over Europe. Gutenberg's invention of movable type and the woodcut both followed within thirty years of the West's learning of Chinese printing.

The lead time for knowledge to become knowledge-based innovation seems to be inherent in the nature of knowledge. We do not know why. But perhaps it is not pure coincidence that the same lead time applies to new scientific theory. Thomas Kuhn, in his path-breaking book *The Structure of Scientific Revolutions* (1962), showed that it takes about thirty years before a new scientific theory becomes a new paradigm—a new statement that scientists pay attention to and use in their own work.

Convergences

The second characteristic of knowledge-based innovations—and a truly unique one—is that they are almost never based on one factor but on the convergence of several different kinds of knowledge, not all of them scientific or technological.

Few knowledge-based innovations in this century have benefited humanity more than the hybridization of seeds and livestock. It enables the earth to feed a much larger population than anyone would have thought possible fifty years ago. The first successful new seed was hybrid corn. It was produced after twenty years of hard work by Henry C. Wallace, the publisher of a farm newspaper in Iowa, and later U.S. Secretary of Agriculture under Harding and Coolidge—the only holder of this office, perhaps, who deserves to be remembered for anything other than giving away money. Hybrid corn has two knowledge roots. One was the work of the Michigan plant breeder William J. Beal, who around 1880 discovered hybrid vigor. The other was the rediscovery of Mendel's genetics by the Dutch biologist Hugo de Vries. The two men did not know of one another. Their work was totally different both in intent and content. But only by pulling it together could hybrid corn be developed.

The Wright Brothers' airplane also had two knowledge roots. One was the gasoline engine, designed in the mid-1880s to power the first automobiles built by Karl Benz and Gottfried Daimler, respectively. The other one was mathematical: aerodynamics, developed primarily in experiments with gliders. Each was developed quite independently. It was only when the two came together that the airplane became possible.

The computer, as already noted, required the convergence of no less than five different knowledges: a scientific invention, the audion tube; a major mathematical discovery, the binary theorem; a new logic; the design concept of the punchcard; and the concepts of program and feedback. Until all these were available; no computer could have been built. Charles Babbage, the English mathematician, is often called the "father of the computer." What kept Babbage from building a computer, it is argued, was only the unavailability of the proper metals and of electric power at his time. But this is a misunderstanding. Even if Babbage had had the proper materials, he could at best have built the mechanical calculator that we now call a cash register. Without the logic, the design concept of the punchcard, and the concept of program and feedback, none of which Babbage possessed, he could only imagine a computer.

The Brothers Pereire founded the first entrepreneurial bank in 1852. It failed within a few years because they had only one knowledge base and the entrepreneurial bank needs two. They had a theory of creative finance that enabled them to be brilliant venture capitalists. But they lacked the systematic knowledge of banking which was developed at exactly the same time across the Channel by the British, and codified in Walter Bagehot's classic, *Lombard Street*.

After their failure in the early 1860s, three young men independently picked up where the Brothers Pereire had left off, added the knowledge base of banking to the venture capital concept, and succeeded. The first was J. P. Morgan, who had been trained in London but had also carefully studied the Pereires' Crédit Mobilier. He founded the most successful entrepreneurial bank of the nineteenth century in New York in 1865. The second one, across the Rhine, was the young German Georg Siemens, who founded what he called the "Universal Bank," by which he meant a bank that was both a deposit bank on the British model and an entrepreneurial bank on the Pereires' model. And in remote Tokyo, another young man, Shibusawa Eichii, who had been one of the first Japanese to travel to Europe to study banking first-hand, and had spent time both in Paris and in London's Lombard Street, became one of the founders of the modern Japanese economy by establishing a Japanese version of the Universal Bank. Both Siemens's Deutsche Bank and Shibusawa's Daichi Bank are still the largest banks of their respective countries.

The first man to envisage the modern newspaper was an American, James Gordon Bennett, who founded the *New York Herald*. Bennett fully understood the problems: A newspaper had to have enough income to be editorially independent and yet be cheap enough to have mass circulation. Earlier newspapers either got their income by selling their independence and becoming the lackeys and paid propagandists of a political faction—as did most American and practically all European papers of his time. Or, like the great aristocrat of those days, *The Times* of London, they were "written by gentlemen for gentlemen," but so expensive that only a small elite could afford them.

Bennett brilliantly exploited the twin technological knowledge bases on which a modern newspaper rests: the telegraph and high-speed printing. They enabled him to produce a paper at a fraction of the traditional cost. He knew that he needed high-speed typesetting, though it was not invented until after his death. He also saw one of the two nonscientific bases, mass literacy, which made possible mass circulation for a cheap newspaper. But he failed to grasp the fifth.base: mass advertising as the source of the income that makes possible editorial independence. Bennett personally enjoyed a spectacular success; he was the first of the press lords. But his newspaper achieved neither leadership nor financial security. These goals were only attained two decades later, around 1890, by three men who understood and exploited advertising: Joseph Pulitzer, first in St. Louis and then in New York; Adolph Ochs, who took over a moribund *New York Times* and made it into America's leading paper; and William Randolph Hearst, who invented the modern newspaper chain.

The invention of plastics, beginning with Nylon, also rested on the convergence of a number of different new knowledges each emerging around 1910. Organic chemistry, pioneered by the Germans and perfected by Leo Baekeland, a Belgian working in New York, was one; X-Ray diffraction and with it an understanding of the structure of crystals was another; and high-vacuum technology. The final factor was the pressure of World War I shortages, which made the German government willing to invest heavily in polymerization research to obtain a substitute for rubber. It took a further twenty years, though, before Nylon was ready for the market.

Until all the needed knowledges can be provided, knowledge-based innovation is premature and will fail. In most cases, the innovation occurs only when these various factors are already known, already available, already in use someplace. This was the case with the Universal Bank of 1865-75. It was the case with the computer after World War II. Sometimes the innovator can identify the missing pieces and then work at producing them. Joseph Pulitzer, Adolph Ochs, and William Randolph Hearst largely created modern advertising. This then created what we today call media, that is, the merger of information and advertising in "mass communications." The Wright Brothers identified the pieces of knowledge that were missing—mostly mathematics—and then themselves developed them by building a wind tunnel and actually testing mathematical theories. But until all the knowledges needed for a given knowledge-based innovation have come together, the innovation will not take off. It will remain stillborn.

Samuel Langley, for instance, whom his contemporaries expected to become the inventor of the airplane, was a much better trained scientist than the Wright Brothers. As secretary of what was then America's leading scientific institution, the

Smithsonian in Washington, he also had all the nation's scientific resources at his disposal. But even though the gasoline engine had been invented by Langley's time, he preferred to ignore it. He believed in the steam engine. As a result his airplane could fly; but because of the steam engine's weight, it could not carry any load, let alone a pilot. It needed the convergence of mathematics and the gasoline engine to produce the airplane.

Indeed, until all the knowledges converge, the lead time of a knowledge-based innovation usually does not even begin.

II

What Knowledge-based Innovation Requires

Its characteristics give knowledge-based innovation specific requirements. And these requirements differ from those of any other kind of innovation.

1. In the first place, knowledge-based innovation requires careful analysis of all the necessary factors, whether knowledge itself, or social, economic, or perceptual factors. The analysis must identify what factors are not yet available so that the entrepreneur can decide whether these missing factors can be produced—as the Wright Brothers decided in respect to the missing mathematics—or whether the innovation had better be postponed as not yet feasible.

The Wright Brothers exemplify the method at its best. They thought through carefully what knowledge was necessary to build an airplane for manned, motored flight. Next they set about to develop the pieces of knowledge that were needed, taking the available information, testing it first theoretically, then in the wind tunnel, and then in actual flight experiments, until they had the mathematics they needed to construct ailerons, to shape the wings, and so on.

The same analysis is needed for nontechnical knowledge-based innovation. Neither J. P. Morgan nor Georg Siemens published their papers; but Shibusawa in Japan did. And so we know that he based his decision to forsake a brilliant government career and to start a bank on a careful analysis of the knowledge available and the knowledge needed. Similarly, Joseph Pulitzer analyzed carefully the knowledge needed when he launched what became the first modern newspaper, and decided that advertising had to be invented and could be invented.

If I may inject a personal note, my own success as an innovator in the management field was based on a similar analysis in the early 1940s. Many of the required pieces of knowledge were already available: organization theory, for instance, but also quite a bit of knowledge about managing work and worker. My analysis also showed, however, that these pieces were scattered and lodged in half a dozen different disciplines. Then it found which key knowledges were missing: purpose of a business; any knowledge of the work and structure of top management; what we now term "business policy" and "strategy"; objectives; and so on. All of the missing knowledges, I decided, could be produced. But without such analysis, I could never have known what they were or that they were missing.

Failure to make such an analysis is an almost sure-fire prescription for disaster. Either the knowledge-based innovation is not achieved, which is what happened to Samuel Langley. Or the innovator loses the fruits of his innovation and only succeeds in creating an opportunity for somebody else.

Particularly instructive is the failure of the British to reap the harvest from their own knowledge-based innovations.

The British discovered and developed penicillin, but it was the Americans who took it over. The British scientists did a magnificent technical job. They came out with the right substances and the right uses. Yet they failed to identify the ability to manufacture the stuff as a critical knowledge factor. They could have developed the necessary knowledge of fermentation technology; they did not even try. As a result, a small American company, Pfizer, went to work on developing the knowledge of fermentation and became the world's foremost manufacturer of penicillin.

Similarly, the British conceived, designed, and built the first passenger jet plane. But de Havilland, the British company, did not analyze what was needed and therefore did not identify two key factors. One was configuration, that is, the right size with the right payload for the routes on which the jet would give an airline the greatest advantage. The other was equally mundane: how to finance the purchase of such an expensive plane by the airlines. As a result of de Havilland's failure to do the analysis, two American companies, Boeing and Douglas, took over the jet plane. And de Havilland has long since disappeared.

Such analysis would appear to be fairly obvious, yet it is rarely done by the scientific or technical innovator. Scientists and technologists are reluctant to make these analyses precisely because they think they already *know*. This explains why, in so many cases, the great knowledge-based innovations have had a layman rather than a scientist or a technologist for their father, or at least their godfather. The (American) General Electric Company is largely the brainchild of a financial man. He conceived the strategy (described in Chapter 19) that made G.E. the world's leading supplier of large steam turbines and, therewith, the world's leading supplier to electric power producers. Similarly, two laymen, Thomas Watson, Sr., and his son Thomas Watson, Jr., made IBM the leader in computers. At DuPont, the analysis of what was needed to make the knowledge-based innovation of Nylon effective and successful was not done by the chemist who developed the technology, but by business people on the executive committee. And Boeing became the world's leading producer of jet planes under the leadership of marketing people who understood what the airlines and the public needed.

This is not a law of nature, however. Mostly it is a matter of will and self-discipline. There have been plenty of scientists and technologists— Edison is a good example—who forced themselves to think through what their knowledge-based innovation required.

2. The second requirement of knowledge-based innovation is a clear focus on the strategic position. It cannot be introduced tentatively. The fact that the introduction of the innovation creates excitement, and attracts a host of others, means that the innovator has to be right the first time. He is unlikely to get a second chance. In all the other innovations discussed so far, the innovator, once he has been successful with his innovation, can expect to be left alone for quite some time. This is not true of knowledge-based innovation. Here the innovators almost immediately have far more company than they want. They need only stumble once to be overrun.

There are basically only three major focuses for knowledge-based innovation. First, there is the focus Edwin Land took with Polaroid: To develop a *complete system* that would then dominate the field. This is exactly what IBM did in its early years when it chose not to sell computers but to lease them to its customers. It supplied them with such software as was available, with programming, with instruction in computer language for programmers, with instruction in computer use for a customer's executives, and with service. This was also what G.E. did when it established itself as the leader in the knowledge-based innovation of large steam turbines in the early years of this century.

The second clear focus is a *market focus*. Knowledge-based innovation can aim at creating the market for its products. This is what DuPont did with Nylon. It did not "sell" Nylon; it created a consumer market for women's hosiery and women's underwear using Nylon, a market for automobile tires using Nylon, and so on. It then delivered Nylon to the fabricators to make the articles for which DuPont had already created a demand and which, in effect, it had already sold. Similarly, aluminum from the very beginning, right after the invention of the aluminum reduction process by Charles M. Hall in 1888, began to create a market for pots and pans, for rods and other aluminum extrusions. The aluminum company actually went into making these end products and selling them. It created the market which, in turn, discouraged (if it did not keep out altogether) potential competitors.

The third focus is *to occupy a strategic position*, concentrating on a key function (the strategy is discussed in Chapter 18 under Ecological Niches). What position would enable the knowledge innovator to be largely immune to the extreme convolutions of a knowledge-based industry in its early stages? It was thinking this through and deciding to concentrate on mastering the fermentation process that gave Pfizer in the United States the early lead in penicillin it has maintained ever since. Focusing on marketing—on mastery of the requirements of airlines and of the public in respect to configuration and finance—gave Boeing the leadership in passenger planes, which it has held ever since. And despite the turbulence of the computer industry today, a few leading manufacturers of the computer's key component, semiconductors, can maintain their leadership position almost irrespective of the fate of individual computer manufacturers themselves. Intel is one example.

Within the same industry, individual knowledge-based innovators can sometimes choose between these alternatives. Where DuPont, for instance, has chosen to create markets, its closest American competitor, Dow Chemical, tries to occupy a key spot in each market segment. A hundred years ago, J. P. Morgan opted for the key function approach. He established his bank as the conduit for European investment capital in American industry, and furthermore in a capital-short country. At the same time, Georg Siemens in Germany and Shibusawa Eichii in Japan both went for the systems approach.

The power of a clear focus is demonstrated by Edison's success. Edison was not the only one who identified the inventions that had to be made to produce a light bulb. An English physicist, Joseph Swan, did so too. Swan developed his light bulb at exactly the same time as Edison. Technically, Swan's bulb was superior, to the point where Edison bought up the Swan patents and used them in his own light bulb factories. But Edison not only thought through the technical requirements; he thought through his focus. Before he even began the technical work on the glass envelope, the vacuum, the closure, and the glowing fiber, he had already decided on a "system": his light bulb was designed to fit an electric power company for which he had lined up the financing, the rights to string wires to get the power to his light bulb customers, and the distribution system. Swan, the scientist, invented a product; Edison produced an industry. So Edison could sell and install electric power while Swan was still trying to figure out who might be interested in his technical achievement.

The knowledge-based innovator has to decide on a clear focus. Each of the three described here is admittedly very risky. But not to decide on a clear focus, let alone to try to be in between or to attempt more than one focus, is riskier by far. It is likely to prove fatal.

3. Finally, the knowledge-based innovator—and especially the one whose innovation is based on scientific or technological knowledge—needs to learn and to practice entrepreneurial management (see Chapter 15, The New Venture). In fact,

entrepreneurial management is more crucial to knowledge-based innovation than to any other kind. Its risks are high, thus putting a much higher premium on foresight, both financial and managerial, and on being market-focused and market-driven. Yet knowledge-based, and especially high-tech, innovation tends to have little entrepreneurial management. In large measure the high casualty rate of knowledge-based industry is the fault of the knowledge-based, and especially the high-tech, entrepreneurs themselves. They tend to be contemptuous of anything that is not "advanced knowledge," and particularly of anyone who is not a specialist in their own area. They tend to be infatuated with their own technology, often believing that "quality" means what is technically sophisticated rather than what gives value to the user. In this respect they are still, by and large, nineteenth-century inventors rather than twentieth-century entrepreneurs.

In fact, there are enough companies around today to show that the risk in knowledge-based innovation, including high tech, can be substantially reduced if entrepreneurial management is conscientiously applied. Hoffmann-LaRoche, the Swiss pharmaceutical company, is one example; Hewlett-Packard is another, and so is Intel. Precisely because the inherent risks of knowledge-based innovation are so high, entrepreneurial management is both particularly necessary and particularly effective.

III

The Unique Risks

Even when it is based on meticulous analysis, endowed with clear focus, and conscientiously managed, knowledge-based innovation still suffers from unique risks and, worse, an innate unpredictability.

First, by its very nature, it is turbulent.

The combination of the two characteristics of knowledge-based innovations— long lead times and convergences—gives knowledge-based innovations their peculiar rhythm. For a long time, there is awareness of an innovation about to happen—but it does not happen. Then suddenly there is a near-explosion, followed by a few short years of tremendous excitement, tremendous startup activity, tremendous publicity. Five years later comes a "shakeout," which few survive.

In 1856, Werner Siemens in Germany applied the electrical theories Michael Faraday had developed around 1830 (twenty-five years earlier) to the design of the ancestor of the first electrical motor, the first dynamo. It caused a worldwide sensation. From then on, it became certain that there would be an "electrical industry" and that it would be a major one. Dozens of scientists and inventors went to work. But nothing happened for twenty-two years. The knowledge was missing: Maxwell's development of Faraday's theories.

After it had become available, Edison invented the light bulb in 1878 and the race was on. Within the next five years all the major electrical apparatus companies in Europe and America were founded: Siemens in Germany bought up a small electrical apparatus manufacturer, Schuckert. The (German) General Electric Company, AEG, was formed on the basis of Edison's work. In the United States there arose what are now G.E. and Westinghouse; in Switzerland, there was Brown Boveri; in Sweden, ASEA was founded in 1884. But these few are the survivors of a hundred such companies—American, British, French, German, Italian, Spanish, Dutch, Belgian, Swiss, Austrian, Czech, Hungarian, and so on—all eagerly financed by the investors of their time and all expecting to be "billion-dollar companies." It was this upsurge of the electrical apparatus industry that gave rise to the first great science-fiction boom and made Jules Verne and H. G. Wells best-selling authors all over the world. But by 1895-1900, most of these companies had already disappeared, whether out of business, bankrupt, or absorbed by the few survivors.

Around 1910, there were up to two hundred automobile companies in the United-States alone. By the early 1930s, their number had shrunk to twenty, and by 1960 to four.

In the 1920s, literally hundreds of companies were making radio sets and hundreds more were going into radio stations. By 1935, the control of broadcasting had moved into the hands of three "networks" and there were only a dozen manufacturers of radio sets left. Again, there was an explosion in the number of newspapers founded between 1880 and 1900. In fact, newspapers were among the major "growth industries" of the time. Since World War I, the number of newspapers in every major country has been going downhill steadily. And the same is true of banking. After the founders—the Morgans, the Siemenses, the Shibusawas—there was an almost explosive growth of new banks in the United States as well as in Europe. But around 1890, only twenty years later, consolidation set in. Banking firms began to go out of business or to merge. By the end of World War II in every major country only a handful of banks were left that had more than local importance, whether as commercial or private banks.

But each time without exception the survivor has been a company that was started during the early explosive period. After that period is over, entry into the industry is foreclosed for all practical purposes. There is a "window" of a few years during which a new venture must establish itself in any new knowledge-based industry.

It is commonly believed today that that "window" has become narrower. But this is as much a misconception as the common belief that the lead time between the emergence of new knowledge and its conversion into technology, products, and processes has become much shorter.

Within a few years after George Stephenson's "Rocket" had pulled the first train on a commercial railroad in 1830, over a hundred railroad companies were started in England. For ten years railroads were "high-tech" and railroad entrepreneurs "media events." The speculative fever of these years is bitingly satirized in one of Dickens's novels, *Little Dorrit* (published in 1855-57); it was not very different from today's speculative fever in Silicon Valley. But around 1845, the "window" slammed shut. From then on there was no money in England any more for new railroads. Fifty years later, the hundred-or-so English railroad companies of 1845 had shrunk to five or six. And the same rhythm characterized the electrical apparatus industry, the telephone industry, the automobile industry, the chemical industry, household appliances, and consumer electronics. The "window" has never been very wide nor open very long. But there can be little doubt that today the "window" is becoming more and more crowded. The railroad boom of the 1830s was confined to England; later, every country, had its own local boom quite separate from the preceding one in the neighboring country. The electrical apparatus boom already extended across national frontiers, as did the automobile boom twenty-five years later. Yet both were confined to the countries that were industrially developed at the time. The term "industrially developed" encompasses a great deal more territory today, however. It takes in Japan, for instance. It takes in Brazil. It may soon take in China Hong Kong, China Taiwan, and Singapore. Communication today is practically instantaneous, travel easy and fast. And a great many countries have today what only very few small places had a hundred years ago: large cadres of trained people who can immediately go to work in any area of knowledge-based innovation, and especially of science-based or technology-based innovation.

These facts have two important implications.

1. First, science-based and technology-based innovators alike find time working against them. In all innovation based on any other source —the unexpected, incongruities, process need, changes in industry structure, demographics, or changes in perception—time is on the side of the innovator. In any other kind of innovation innovators can reasonably expect to be left alone. If they make a mistake, they are likely to have time to correct it. And there are several moments in time in which they can launch their new venture. Not so in knowledge-based innovation, and especially in those innovations based on scientific and technological knowledge. Here there is only a short time—the "window"— during which entry is possible at all. Here innovators do not get a second chance; they have to be right the first

time. The environment is harsh and unforgiving. And once the "window" closes, the opportunity is gone forever.

In some knowledge-based industries, however, a second "window" does in fact open some twenty to thirty years or so after the first one has shut down. Computers are an example.

The first "window" in computers lasted from 1949 until 1955 or so. During this period, every single electrical apparatus company in the world went into computers—G.E., Westinghouse, and RCA in the United States; the British General Electric Company, Plessey, and Ferranti in Great Britain; Siemens and AEG in Germany; Philips in Holland; and so on. By 1970, every single one of the "biggies" was out of computers, ignominiously. The field was occupied by companies that had either not existed at all in 1949 or had been small and marginal: IBM, of course, and the "Seven Dwarfs," the seven smaller computer companies in the United States; ICL, the remnant of the computer businesses of the General Electric Company, of Plessey, and of Ferranti in Great Britain; some fragments sustained by heavy government subsidies in France; and a total newcomer, Nixdorf, in Germany. The Japanese companies were sustained for a long time through government support.

Then, in the late seventies, a second "window" opened with the invention of micro-chips, which led to word processors, minicomputers, personal computers, and the merging of computer and telephone switchboard.

But the companies that had failed in the first round did not come back in the second one. Even those that survived the first round stayed out of the second, or came in late and reluctantly. Neither Univac nor Control Data, nor Honeywell nor Burroughs, nor Fujitsu nor Hitachi took leadership in minicomputers or personal computers. The one exception was IBM, the undisputed champion of the first round. And this has been the pattern too in earlier knowledge-based innovations.

2. Because the "window" is much more crowded, any one knowledge-based innovator has far less chance of survival.

The number of entrants during the "window" period is likely to be much larger. But the structure of the industries, once they stabilize and mature, seems to have remained remarkably unchanged, at least for a century now. Of course there are great differences in structure between various industries, depending on technology, capital requirements, and ease of entry, on whether the product can be shipped or distributed only locally, and so on. But at any one time any given industry has a typical structure: in any given market there are so many companies altogether, so many big ones, so many medium-sized ones, so many small ones, so many specialists. And increasingly there is only one "market" for any new knowledge-based industry, whether computers or modern banking—the world market.

The number of knowledge-based innovators that will survive when an industry matures and stabilizes is therefore no larger than it has traditionally been. But largely because of the emergence of a world market and of global communications, the number of entrants during the "window" period has greatly increased. When the shakeout comes, the casualty rate is therefore much higher than it used to be. And the shakeout always comes; it is inevitable.

The Shakeout

The "shakeout" sets in as soon as the "window" closes. And the majority of ventures started during the "window" period do not survive the shakeout, as has already been shown for such high-tech industries of yesterday as railroads, electrical apparatus makers, and automobiles. As these lines are being written, the shakeout has begun among micro-processor, minicomputer, and personal computer companies—only five or six years after the "window" opened. Today, there are perhaps a hundred companies in the industry in the United States alone. Ten years hence, by 1995, there are unlikely to be more than a dozen left of any size or significance.

But which ones will survive, which ones will die, and which ones will become permanently crippled—able neither to live nor to die—is unpredictable. In fact, it is futile to speculate. Sheer size may ensure survival. But it does not guarantee success in the shakeout, otherwise Allied Chemical rather than DuPont would today be the world's biggest and most successful chemical company. In 1920, when the "window" opened for the chemical industry in the United States, Allied Chemical looked invincible, if only because it had obtained the German chemical patents which the U.S. government had confiscated during World War I. Seven years later, after the shakeout, Allied Chemical had become a weak also-ran. It has never been able to regain momentum.

No one in 1949 could have predicted that IBM would emerge as the computer giant, let alone that such big, experienced leaders as G.E. or Siemens would fail completely. No one in 1910 or 1914 when automobile stocks were the favorites of the New York Stock Exchange could have predicted that General Motors and Ford would survive and prosper and that such universal favorites as Packard or Hupmobile would disappear. No one in the 1870s and 1880s, the period in which the modern banks were born, could have predicted that Deutsche Bank would swallow up dozens of the old commercial banks of Germany and emerge as the leading bank of the country.

That a certain industry will become important is fairly easy to predict. There is no case on record where an industry that reached the explosive phase, the "window" phase, as I called it, has then failed to become a major industry. The question is,

Which of the specific units in this industry will be its leaders and so survive?

This rhythm—a period of great excitement during which there is also great speculative ferment, followed by a severe "shakeout"—is particularly pronounced in the high-tech industries.

In the first place, such industries are in the limelight and thus attract far more entrants and far more capital than more mundane areas. Also the expectations are much greater. More people have probably become rich building such prosaic businesses as a shoe-polish or a watchmaking company than have become rich through high-tech businesses. Yet no one expects shoe-polish makers to build a "billion-dollar business," nor considers them a failure if all they build is a sound but modest family company. High tech, by contrast, is a "high-low game," in which a middle hand is considered worthless. And this makes high-tech innovation inherently risky.

But also, high tech is not profitable for a very long time. The world's computer industry began in 1947-48. Not until the early 1980s, more than thirty years later, did the industry as a whole reach break-even point. To be sure, a few companies (practically all of them American, by the way) began to make money much earlier. And one, IBM, the leader, began to make a great deal of money earlier still. But across the industry the profits of those few successful computer makers were more than offset by the horrendous losses of the rest; the enormous losses, for instance, which the big international electrical companies took in their abortive attempts to become computer manufacturers.

And exactly the same thing happened in every earlier "high-tech" boom—in the railroad booms of the early nineteenth century, in the electrical apparatus and the automobile booms between 1880 and 1914, in the electric appliance and the radio booms of the 1920s, and so on.

One major reason for this is the need to plow more and more money back into research, technical development, and technical services to stay in the race. High tech does indeed have to run faster and faster in order to stand still.

This is, of course, part of its fascination. But it also means that when the shakeout comes, very few businesses in the industry have the financial resources to outlast even a short storm. This is the reason why high-tech ventures need financial foresight even more than other new ventures, but also the reason why financial foresight is even scarcer among high-tech new ventures than it is among new ventures in general.

There is only one prescription for survival during the shakeout: entrepreneurial management (described in Chapters 12-15). What distinguished Deutsche Bank from the other "hot" financial institutions of its time was that Georg Siemens thought through and built the world's first top management team. What distinguished DuPont from Allied Chemical was that DuPont in the early twenties created the world's first systematic organization structure, the world's first long-range planning, and the world's first system of management information and control. Allied Chemical, by contrast, was run arbitrarily by one brilliant egomaniac. But this is not the whole story. Most of the large companies that failed to survive the more recent computer shakeout—G.E. and Siemens, for instance—are usually considered to have first-rate management. And the Ford Motor Company survived, though only by the skin of its teeth, even though it was grotesquely mismanaged during the shakeout years.

Entrepreneurial management is thus probably a precondition of survival, but not a guarantee thereof. And at the time of the shakeout, only insiders (and perhaps not even they) can really know whether a knowledge-based innovator that has grown rapidly for a few boom years is well managed, as DuPont was, or basically unmanaged, as Allied Chemical was. By the time we do know, it is likely to be too late.

The Receptivity Gamble

To be successful, a knowledge-based innovation has to be "ripe"; there has to be receptivity to it. This risk is inherent in knowledge-based innovation and is indeed a function of its unique power. All other innovations exploit a change that has already occurred. They satisfy a need that already exists. But in knowledge-based innovation, the innovation brings about the change. It aims at creating a want. And no one can tell in advance whether the user is going to be receptive, indifferent, or actively resistant.

There are exceptions, to be sure. Whoever produces a cure for cancer need not worry about "receptivity." But such exceptions are few. In most knowledge-based innovations, receptivity is a gamble. And the odds are unknown, are indeed mysterious. There may be great receptivity, yet no one realizes it. And there may be no receptivity, or even heavy resistance when everyone is quite sure that society is actually eagerly waiting for the innovation.

Stories of the obtuseness of the high and mighty in the face of a knowledge-based innovation abound. Typical is the anecdote which has a king of Prussia predicting the certain failure of that new-fangled contraption, the railroad, because "No one will pay good money to get from Berlin to Potsdam in one hour when he can ride his horse in one day for free." But the king of Prussia was not alone in his misreading of the receptivity to the railroad; the majority of the "experts" of his day inclined to his opinion. And when the computer appeared there was not one single "expert" who could imagine that businesses would ever want such a contraption.

The opposite error is, however, just as common. "Everybody knows" that there is a real need, a real demand, when in reality there is total indifference or resistance. The same authorities who, in 1948, could not imagine that a business would ever want a computer, a few years later, around 1955, predicted that the computer would "revolutionize the schools" within a decade.

The Germans consider Philip Reis rather than Alexander Graham Bell to be the inventor of the telephone. Reis did indeed build an instrument in 1861 that could transmit music and was very close to transmitting speech. But then he gave up, totally discouraged. There was no receptivity for a telephone, no interest in it, no desire for it. "The telegraph is good enough for us," was the prevailing attitude. Yet when Bell, fifteen years later, patented his telephone, there was an immediate enthusiastic response. And nowhere was it greater than in Germany.

The change in receptivity in these fifteen years is not too difficult to explain. Two major wars, the American Civil War and the Franco Prussian War, had shown that the telegraph was by no means "good enough." But the real point is not why receptivity changed. It is that every authority in 1861 enthusiastically predicted overwhelming receptivity when Reis demonstrated his instrument at a scientific meeting. And every authority was wrong.

But, of course, the authorities can also be right, and often are. In 1876-77, for instance, they all knew that there was receptivity for both a light bulb and a telephone—and they were right. Similarly, Edison, in the 1880s, was supported by the expert opinion of his time when he embarked on the invention of the phonograph, and again the experts were right in assuming high receptivity for the new device.

But only hindsight can tell us whether the experts are right or wrong in their assessment of the receptivity for this or that knowledge-based innovation.

Nor do we necessarily perceive, even by hindsight, why a particular knowledge-based innovation has receptivity or fails to find it. No one, for instance, can explain why phonetic spelling has been so strenuously resisted. Everyone agrees that nonphonetic spelling is a major obstacle in learning to read and write, forces schools to devote inordinate time to the reading skill, and is responsible for a disproportionate number of reading disabilities and emotional traumas among children. The knowledge of phonetics is a century old at least. Means to achieve phonetic spelling are available in the two languages where the problem is most acute: any number of phonetic alphabets for English, and the much older, forty-eight-syllable Kana scripts in Japanese. For both countries there are examples next door of a successful shift to a phonetic script. The English have the successful model of German spelling reform of the mid-nineteenth century; the Japanese, the equally successful—and much earlier—phonetic reform of the Korean script. Yet in neither country is there the slightest receptivity for an innovation that, one would say, is badly needed, eminently rational, and proven by example to be safe, fairly easy, and efficacious. Why? Explanations abound, but no one really knows.

There is no way to eliminate the element of risk, no way even to reduce it. Market research does not work—one cannot do market research on something that does not exist. Opinion research is probably not just useless but likely to do damage. At least this is what the experience with "expert opinion" on the receptivity to knowledge-based innovation would indicate.

Yet there is no choice. If we want knowledge-based innovation, we must gamble on receptivity to it.

The risks are highest in innovations based on new knowledge in science and technology. They are particularly high, of course, in innovations in areas that are currently "hot"—personal computers, at the present time, or biotechnology. By contrast, areas that are not in the public eye have far lower risks, if only because there is more time. And in innovations where the knowledge base is not science or technology —social innovations, for instance—the risks are lower still. But high risk is inherent in knowledge-based innovation. It is the price we have to pay for its impact and above all for its capacity to bring about change, not only in products and services but in how we see the world, our place in it, and eventually ourselves.

Yet the risks even of high-tech innovation can be substantially reduced by integrating new knowledge as the source of innovation with one of the other sources defined earlier, the unexpected, incongruities, and especially process need. In these areas receptivity has either already been established or can be tested fairly easily and with good reliability. And in these areas, too, the knowledge or knowledges that have to be produced to complete an innovation can usually be defined with considerable precision. This is the reason why "program research" is becoming so popular. But even program research requires a great deal of system and self-discipline, and has to be organized and purposeful.

The demands on knowledge-based innovators are thus very great. They are also different from those in other areas of innovation. The risks they face are different, too; time, for instance, is not on their side. But if the risks are greater, so are the potential rewards. The other innovators may reap a fortune. The knowledge-based innovator can hope for fame as well.

CHAPTER 10

The Bright Idea

Innovations based on a bright idea probably outnumber all other categories taken together. Seven or eight out of every ten patents belong here, for example. A very large proportion of the new businesses that are described in the books on entrepreneurs and entrepreneurships are built around "bright ideas": the zipper, the ballpoint pen, the aerosol spray can, the tab to open soft drink or beer cans, and many more. And what is called research in many businesses aims at finding and exploiting bright ideas, whether for a new flavor in breakfast cereals or soft drinks, for a better running shoe, or for yet one more nonscorching clothes iron.

Yet bright ideas are the riskiest and least successful source of innovative opportunities. The casualty rate is enormous. No more than one out of every hundred patents for an innovation of this kind earns enough to pay back development costs and patent fees. A far smaller proportion, perhaps as low as one in five hundred, makes any money above its out-of-pocket costs.

And no one knows which ideas for an innovation based on a bright idea have a chance to succeed and which ones are likely to fail. Why did the aerosol can succeed, for instance? And why did a dozen or more similar inventions for the uniform delivery of particles fail dismally? Why does one universal wrench sell and most of the many others disappear? Why did the zipper find acceptance and practically displace buttons, even though it tends to jam? (After all, a jammed zipper on a dress, jacket, or pair of trousers can be quite embarrassing.)

Attempts to improve the predictability of innovations based on bright ideas have not been particularly successful.

Equally unsuccessful have been attempts to identify the personal traits, behavior, or habits that make for a successful innovator. "Successful inventors," an old adage says, "keep on inventing. They play the odds. If they try often enough, they will succeed."

This belief that you'll win if only you keep on trying out bright ideas is, however, no more rational than the popular fallacy that to win the jackpot at Las Vegas one only has to keep on pulling the lever. Alas, the machine is rigged to have the house win 70 percent of the time. The more often you pull, the more often you lose.

There is actually no empirical evidence at all for the belief that persistence pays off in pursuing the "brilliant idea," just as there is no evidence of any "system" to beat the slot machines. Some successful inventors have had only one brilliant idea and then quit: the inventor of the zipper, for instance, or of the ballpoint pen. And there are hundreds of inventors around who have forty patents to their name, and not one winner. Innovators do, of course, improve with practice. But only if they practice the right method, that is, if they base their work on a systematic analysis of the sources of innovative opportunity.

The reasons for both the unpredictability and the high casualty rate are fairly obvious. Bright ideas are vague and elusive. I doubt that anyone except the inventor of the zipper ever thought that buttons or hooks-and-eyes were inadequate to fasten clothing, or that anyone but the inventor of the ballpoint pen could have defined what, if anything, was unsatisfactory about that nineteenth-century invention, the fountain pen. What need was satisfied by the electric toothbrush, one of the market successes of the 1960s? It still has to be hand-held, after all.

And even if the need can be defined, the solution cannot usually be specified. That people sitting in their cars in a traffic jam would like some diversion was perhaps not so difficult to figure out. But why did the small TV set which Sony developed around 1965 to satisfy this need fail in the marketplace, whereas the far more expensive car stereo succeeded? In retrospect, it is easy to answer this. But could it possibly have been answered in prospect?

The entrepreneur is therefore well advised to forgo innovations based on bright ideas, however enticing the success stories. After all, somebody wins a jackpot on the Las Vegas slot machines every week, yet the best any one slot-machine player can do is try not lose more than he or she can afford. Systematic, purposeful entrepreneurs analyze the systematic areas, the seven sources that I've discussed in Chapters 3 through 9.

There is enough in these areas to keep busy any one individual entrepreneur and any one entrepreneurial business or public-service institution. In fact, there is far more than anyone could possibly fully exploit. And in these areas we know how to look, what to look for, and what to do.

All one can do for innovators who go in for bright ideas is to tell them what to do should their innovation, against all odds, be successful. Then the rules for a new venture apply (see Chapter 15). And this is, of course, the reason why so much of the literature on entrepreneurship deals with starting and running the new venture rather than with innovation itself.

And yet an entrepreneurial economy cannot dismiss cavalierly the innovation based on a bright idea. The individual innovation of this kind is not predictable, cannot be organized, cannot be systematized, and fails in the overwhelming majority of cases. Also many, very many, are trivial from the start. There are always more patent applications for new can openers, for new wig stands, and for new belt buckles than for anything else. And in any list of new patents there is always at least one foot warmer than can double as a dish towel. Yet the volume of such bright-idea innovation is so large that the tiny percentage of successes represents a substantial source of new businesses, new jobs, and new performance capacity for the economy.

In the theory and practice of innovation and entrepreneurship, the bright-idea innovation belongs in the appendix. But it should be appreciated and rewarded. It represents qualities that society needs: initiative, ambition, and ingenuity. There is little society can do, perhaps, to promote such innovation. One cannot promote what one does not understand. But at least society should not discourage, penalize, or make difficult such innovations. Seen in this perspective, the recent trend in developed countries, and especially in the United States, to discourage the individual who tries to come up with a bright-idea innovation (by raising patent fees, for instance) and generally to discourage patents as "anticompetitive" is short-sighted and deleterious.

CHAPTER 11

Principles of Innovation

I

All experienced physicians have seen "miracle cures". Patients suffering from terminal illnesses recover suddenly—sometimes spontaneously, sometimes by going to faith healers, by switching to some absurd diet, or by sleeping during the day and being up and about all night. Only a bigot denies that such cures happen and dismisses them as "unscientific." They are real enough. Yet no physician is going to put miracle cures into a textbook or into a course to be taught to medical students. They cannot be replicated, cannot be taught, cannot be learned. They are also extremely rare; the overwhelming majority of terminal cases do die, after all.

Similarly, there are innovations that do not proceed from the sources described in the preceding chapters, innovations that are not developed in any organized, purposeful, systematic manner. There are innovators who are "kissed by the Muses," and whose innovations are the result of a "flash of genius" rather than of hard, organized, purposeful work. But such innovations cannot be replicated. They cannot be taught and they cannot be learned. There is no known way to teach someone how to be a genius. But also, contrary to popular belief in the romance of invention and innovation, "flashes of genius" are uncommonly rare. What is worse, I know of not one such "flash of genius" that turned into an innovation. They all remained brilliant ideas.

The greatest inventive genius in recorded history was surely Leonardo da Vinci. There is a breathtaking idea—submarine or helicopter or automatic forge—on every single page of his notebooks. But not one of these could have been converted into an innovation with the technology and the materials of 1500. Indeed, for none of them would there have been any receptivity in the society and economy of the time.

Every schoolboy knows of James Watt as the "inventor" of the steam engine, which he was not. Historians of technology know that Thomas Newcomen in 1712 built the first steam engine which actually performed useful work: it pumped the water out of an English coal mine. Both men were organized, systematic, purposeful innovators. Watt's steam engine in particular is the very model of an innovation in which newly available knowledge (how to ream a smooth cylinder) and the design of a "missing link" (the condenser) were combined into a process need-based innovation, the receptivity for which had been created by Newcomen's engine (several thousand were by then in use). But the true "inventor" of the combustion engine, and with it of what we call modern technology, was neither Watt nor Newcomen. It was the great Anglo-Irish chemist Robert Boyle, who did so in a "flash of genius." Only Boyle's engine did not work and could not have worked. For Boyle used the explosion of gunpowder to drive the piston, and this so fouled the cylinder that it had to be taken apart and cleaned after each stroke. Boyle's idea enabled first Denis Papin (who had been Boyle's assistant in building the gunpowder engine), then Newcomen, and finally Watt, to develop a working combustion engine. All Boyle, the genius, had was a brilliant idea. It belongs in the history of ideas and not in the history of technology or of innovation.

The purposeful innovation resulting from analysis, system, and hard work is all that can be discussed and presented as the practice of innovation. But this is all that need be presented since it surely covers at least 90 percent of all effective innovations. And the extraordinary performer in innovation, as in every other area, will be effective only if grounded in the discipline and master of it.

What, then, are the principles of innovation, representing the hard core of the discipline? There are a number of "do's"—things that have to be done. There are also a few "dont's"—things that had better not be done. And then there are what I would call "conditions."

II

The Do's

1. Purposeful, systematic innovation begins with the analysis of the

opportunities. It begins with thinking through what I have called the sources of innovative opportunities. In different areas, different sources will have different importance at different times. Demographics, for instance, may be of very little concern to innovators in fundamental industrial processes, to someone looking, say, for the "missing link" in a process such as papermaking, where there is a clear incongruity between economic realities. New knowledge, by the same token, may be of very little relevance to someone innovating a new social instrument to satisfy a need created by changing demographics. But all the sources of innovative opportunity should be systematically analyzed and systematically studied. It is not enough to be alerted to them. The search has to be organized, and must be done on a regular, systematic basis.

2. Innovation is both conceptual and perceptual. The second imperative of innovation is therefore to go out to look, to ask, to listen. This cannot be stressed too often. Successful innovators use both the right side and the left side of their brains. They look at figures, and they look at people. They work out analytically what the innovation has to be to satisfy an opportunity. And then they go out and look at the customers, the users, to see what their expectations, their values, their needs are.

Receptivity can be perceived, as can values. One can perceive that this or that approach will not fit in with the expectations or the habits of the people who have to use it. And then one can ask: "What does this innovation have to reflect so that the people who have to use it will *want* to use it, and see in it *their* opportunity?" Otherwise one runs the risk of having the right innovation in the wrong form—as happened to the leading producer of computer programs for learning in American schools, whose excellent and effective programs were not used by teachers scared stiff of the computer, who perceived the machine as something that, far from being helpful, threatened them.

3. An innovation, to be effective, has to be simple and it has to be focused. It should do only one thing, otherwise, it confuses. If it is not simple, it won't work. Everything new runs into trouble; if complicated, it cannot be repaired or fixed. All effective innovations are breathtakingly simple. Indeed, the greatest praise an innovation can receive is for people to say: "This is obvious. Why didn't I think of it?"

Even the innovation that creates new uses and new markets should be directed toward a specific, clear, designed application. It should be focused on a specific need that it satisfies, on a specific end result that it produces.

4. Effective innovations start small. They are not grandiose. They try to do one specific thing. It may be to enable a moving vehicle to draw electric power while it runs along rails—the innovation that made possible the electric streetcar. Or it may be as elementary as putting the same number of matches into a matchbox

(it used to be fifty), which made possible the automatic filling of matchboxes and gave the Swedish originators of the idea a world monopoly on matches for almost half a century. Grandiose ideas, plans that aim at "revolutionizing an industry,"are unlikely to work.

Innovations had better be capable of being started small, requiring at first little money, few people, and only a small and limited market. Otherwise, there is not enough time to make the adjustments and changes that are almost always needed for an innovation to succeed. Initially innovations rarely are more than "almost right." The necessary changes can be made only if the scale is small and the requirements for people and money fairly modest.

5. But—and this is the final "do"—a successful innovation aims at leadership. It does not aim necessarily at becoming eventually a "big business"; in fact, no one can foretell whether a given innovation will end up as a big business or a modest achievement. But if an innovation does not aim at leadership from the beginning, it is unlikely to be innovative enough, and therefore unlikely to be capable of establishing itself. Strategies (to be discussed in Chapters 16 through 19) vary greatly, from those that aim at dominance in an industry or a market to those that aim at finding and occupying a small "ecological niche" in a process or market. But all entrepreneurial strategies, that is, all strategies aimed at exploiting an innovation, must achieve leadership within a given environment. Otherwise they will simply create an opportunity for the competition.

III

The Dont's

And now the few important "dont's."

1. The first is simply not to try to be clever. Innovations have to be handled by ordinary human beings, and if they are to attain any size and importance at all, by morons or near-morons. Incompetence, after all, is the only thing in abundant and never-failing supply. Anything too clever, whether in design or execution, is almost bound to fail.

2. Don't diversify, don't splinter, don't try to do too many things at once. This is, of course, the corollary to the "do": be focused! Innovations that stray from a core are likely to become diffuse. They remain ideas and do not become innovations. The core does not have to be technology or knowledge. In fact, market knowledge supplies a better core of unity in any enterprise, whether business or

public-service institution, than knowledge or technology do. But there has to be a core of unity to innovative efforts or they are likely to fly apart. An innovation needs the concentrated energy of a unified effort behind it. It also requires that the people who put it into effect understand each other, and this, too, requires a unity, a common core. This, too, is imperiled by diversity and splintering.

3. Finally, don't try to innovate for the future. Innovate for the present! An innovation may have long-range impact; it may not reach its full maturity until twenty years later. The computer, as we have seen, did not really begin to have any sizable impact on the way business was being done until the early 1970s, twenty-five years after the first working models were introduced. But from the first day the computer had some specific current applications, whether scientific calculation, making payroll, or simulation to train pilots to fly airplanes. It is not good enough to be able to say, "In twenty-five years there will be so many very old people that they will need this." One has to be able to say, "There are enough old people around today for this to make a difference to them. Of course, time is with us—in twenty-five years there will be many more." But unless there is an immediate application in the present, an innovation is like the drawings in Leonardo da Vinci's notebook—a "brilliant idea." Very few of us have Leonardo's genius and can expect that our notebooks alone will assure immortality.

The first innovator who fully understood this third caveat was probably Edison. Every other electrical inventor of the time began to work around 1860 or 1865 on what eventually became the light bulb. Edison waited for ten years until the knowledge became available; up to that point, work on the light bulb was "of the future." But when the knowledge became available—when, in other words, a light bulb could become "the present"—Edison organized his tremendous energies and an extraordinarily capable staff and concentrated for a couple of years on that one innovative opportunity.

Innovative opportunities sometimes have long lead times. In pharmaceutical research, ten years of research and development work are by no means uncommon or particularly long. And yet no pharmaceutical company would dream of starting a research project for something which does not, if successful, have immediate application as a drug for health-care needs that already exist.

Three Conditions

Finally, there are three conditions. All three are obvious but often go disregarded.

1. *Innovation is work.* It requires knowledge. It often requires great ingenuity. There are clearly people who are more talented innovators than the rest of us. Also,

innovators rarely work in more than one area. For all his tremendous innovative capacity, Edison worked only in the electrical field. And an innovator in financial areas, Citibank in New York, for instance, is unlikely to embark on innovations in retailing or health care. In innovation as in any other work there is talent, there is ingenuity, there is predisposition. But when all is said and done, innovation becomes hard, focused, purposeful work making very great demands on diligence, on persistence, and on commitment. If these are lacking, no amount of talent, ingenuity, or knowledge will avail.

2. *To succeed, innovators must build on their strengths.* Successful innovators look at opportunities over a wide range. But then they ask, "Which of these opportunities fits *me*, fits *this* company, puts to work what we (or I) are good at and have shown capacity for in performance?" In this respect, of course, innovation is no different from other work. But it may be more important in innovation to build on one's strengths because of the risks of innovation and the resulting premium on knowledge and performance capacity. And in innovation, as in any other venture, there must also be a temperamental "fit." Businesses do not do well in something they do not really respect. No pharmaceutical company—run as it has to be by scientifically minded people who see themselves as "serious"—has done well in anything so "frivolous" as lipsticks or perfumes. Innovators similarly need to be temperamentally attuned to the innovative opportunity. It must be important to them and make sense to them. Otherwise they will not be willing to put in the persistent, hard, frustrating work that successful innovation always requires.

3. And finally, *innovation is an effect in economy and society*, a change in the behavior of customers, of teachers, of farmers, of eye surgeons—of people in general. Or it is a change in a process—that is, in how people work and produce something. Innovation therefore always has to be close to the market, focused on the market, indeed market-driven.

The Conservative Innovator

A year or two ago I attended a university symposium on entrepreneurship at which a number of psychologists spoke. Although their papers disagreed on everything else, they all talked of an "entrepreneurial personality," which was characterized by a "propensity for risk-taking."

A well-known and successful innovator and entrepreneur who had built a process-based innovation into a substantial worldwide business in the space of twenty-five years was then asked to comment. He said: "I find myself baffled by your papers. I think I know as many successful innovators and entrepreneurs as anyone, beginning with myself. I have never come across an 'entrepreneurial personality.' The successful ones I know all have, however, one thing—and only one thing—in common: they are *not* 'risk-takers.' They try to define the risks they have to take and to minimize them as much as possible. Otherwise none of us could have succeeded. As for myself, if I had wanted to be a risk-taker, I would have gone into real estate or commodity trading, or I would have become the professional painter my mother wanted me to be."

This jibes with my own experience. I, too, know a good many successful innovators and entrepreneurs. Not one of them has a "propensity for risk-taking."

The popular picture of innovators—half pop-psychology, half Holly-wood—makes them look like a cross between Superman and the Knights of the Round Table. Alas, most of them in real life are unromantic figures, and much more likely to spend hours on a cash-flow projection than to dash off looking for "risks." Of course innovation is risky. But so is stepping into the car to drive to the supermarket for a loaf of bread. All economic activity is by definition "high-risk." And defending yesterday—that is, not innovating—is far more risky than making tomorrow. The innovators I know are successful to the extent to which they define risks and confine them. They are successful to the extent to which they systematically analyze the sources of innovative opportunity, then pinpoint the opportunity and exploit it. Whether opportunities of small and clearly definable risk, such as exploiting the unexpected or a process need, or opportunities of much greater but still definable risk, as in knowledge-based innovation.

Successful innovators are conservative. They have to be. They are not "risk-focused"; they are "opportunity-focused."

2

THE PRACTICE OF ENTREPRENEURSHIP

INNOVATION AND ENTREPRENEURSHIP
PRACTICE AND PRINCIPLES

The entrepreneurial requires different management from the existing. But like the existing it requires systematic, organized, purposeful management. And while the ground rules are the same for every entrepreneurial organization, the existing business, the public-service institution, and the new venture present different challenges, have different problems, and have to guard against different degenerative tendencies. There is need also for individual entrepreneurs to face up to decisions regarding their own roles and their own commitments.

CHAPTER 12

Entrepreneurial Management

Entrepreneurship is based on the same principles, whether the entrepreneur is an existing large institution or an individual starting his or her new venture singlehanded. It makes little or no difference whether the entrepreneur is a business or a nonbusiness public-service organization, nor even whether the entrepreneur is a governmental or nongovernmental institution. The rules are pretty much the same, the things that work and those that don't are pretty much the same, and so are the kinds of innovation and where to look for them. In every case there is a discipline we might call *Entrepreneurial Management*.

Yet the existing business faces different problems, limitations, and constraints from the solo entrepreneur, and it needs to learn different things. The existing business, to oversimplify, knows how to manage but needs to learn how to be an entrepreneur and how to innovate. The nonbusiness public-service institution, too, faces different problems, has different learning needs, and is prone to making different mistakes. And the new venture needs to learn how to be an entrepreneur and how to innovate, but above all, it needs to learn how to manage.

For each of these three:

- the existing business
- the public-service institution
- the new venture

a specific guide to the practice of entrepreneurship must be developed. What does each have to do? What does each have to watch for? And what had each better avoid doing?

Logically, the discussion might start with the new venture, just as, logically, the study of medicine might start with the embryo and newborn baby. But the medical student starts out by studying the anatomy and pathology of the adult, and the practice of entrepreneurship is likewise best started by discussing the "adult," the existing business and the policies, practices and problems that are pertinent in managing it for entrepreneurship.

Today's businesses, especially the large ones, simply will not survive in this period of rapid change and innovation unless they acquire entrepreneurial competence. In this respect the late twentieth century is totally different from the last great entrepreneurial period in economic history, the fifty or sixty years that came to an end with the outbreak of World War I. There were not many big businesses around in those years, and not even many middle-sized ones. Today, it is not only in the self-interest of the many existing big businesses to learn to manage themselves for entrepreneurship; they have a social responsibility to do so. In sharp contrast to the situation a century ago, rapid destruction of the existing businesses—especially the big ones—by innovation, the "creative destruction" by the innovator, in Joseph Schumpeter's famous phrase, poses a genuine social threat today to employment, to financial stability, to social order, and to governmental responsibility.

Existing businesses will need to change, and change greatly in any event. Within twenty-five years (see Chapter 7) every industrially developed country will see the blue-collar labor force engaged in manufacturing shrink to one-third of what it is now, while manufacturing output should go up three-or four-fold—a development that will parallel the development in agriculture in the industrialized countries during the twenty-five years following World War II. In order to impart stability and leadership in a transition of this magnitude, existing businesses will have to learn how to survive, indeed, how to prosper. And that they can only do if they learn to be successful entrepreneurs.

In many cases, the entrepreneurship needed can only come from existing businesses. Some of the giants of today may well not survive the next twenty-five years. But we now know that the medium-sized business is particularly well positioned to be a successful entrepreneur and innovator, provided only that it organize itself for entrepreneurial management. It is the existing business—and the fair-sized rather than the small one—that has the best capability for entrepreneurial leadership. It has the necessary resources, especially the human resources. It has already acquired managerial competence and built a management team. It has both the opportunity and the responsibility for effective entrepreneurial management.

The same holds true for the public-service institutions, and especially for those discharging nonpolitical functions, whether owned by government and financed by tax money or not; for hospitals, schools, and universities; for the public services of local governments; for community agencies and volunteer organizations such as the Red Cross, the Boy Scouts, and the Girl Scouts; for churches and church-related organizations; but also for professional and trade associations, and many more. A period of rapid change makes obsolete a good many of the old concerns, or at least makes ineffectual a good many of the ways in which they have been addressed. At the same time, such a period creates opportunities for tackling new tasks, for experimentation, and for social innovation.

Above all, there has been a major change in perception and mood in the public domain (cf. Chapter 8). A hundred years ago, the "panic" of 1873 brought to an end the century of *laissez faire* that had begun with Adam Smith's *Wealth of Nations* in 1776. For a hundred years from 1873 on, being "modern," "progressive," or "forward-looking" meant looking to government as the agent of social change and betterment. For better or worse, that period has come to an end in all developed countries. We do not yet know what the next wave of "progressivism" will be. But we do know that anyone who still preaches the "liberal" or "progressive" gospel of 1930—or even of 1960, of the Kennedy and Johnson years—is not a "progressive" but a "reactionary." We do not know whether privatization, [⊖] that is, turning activities back from government to nongovernmental operation (albeit not necessarily to operation by a business enterprise, as most people have interpreted the term) will work or will go very far. But we do know that no non-Communist developed country will move further toward nationalization and governmental control out of hope, expectation, and belief in the traditional promises. It will do so only out of frustration and with a sense of failure. And this is a situation in which public-service institutions have both an opportunity and a responsibility to be entrepreneurial and to innovate.

But precisely because they are public-service institutions, they face specific different obstacles and challenges, and are prone to making different mistakes. Entrepreneurship in the public-service institution thus needs to be discussed separately.

Finally, there is the new venture. This will continue to be a main vehicle for innovation, as it has been in all major entrepreneurial periods and is again today in the new entrepreneurial economy of the United States. There is indeed no lack of would-be entrepreneurs in the United States, no shortage of new ventures.

[⊖] A word that I coined in 1969 in *The Age of Discontinuity* (New York: Harper & Row; London: William Heinemann).

But most of them, especially the high-tech ones, have a great deal to learn about entrepreneurial management and will have to learn it if they are to survive.

The gap between the performance of the average practitioner and that of the leaders in entrepreneurship and innovation is enormous in all three categories. Fortunately, there are enough examples around of the successful practice of entrepreneurship to make possible a systematic presentation of entrepreneurial management that is both practice and theory, both description and prescription.

CHAPTER 13

The Entrepreneurial Business

I

"Big businesses don't innovate," says the conventional wisdom. This sounds plausible enough. True, the new, major innovations of this century did not come out of the old, large businesses of their time. The railroads did not spawn the automobile or the truck; they did not even try. And though the automobile companies did try (Ford and General Motors both pioneered in aviation and aerospace), all of today's large aircraft and aviation companies have evolved out of separate new ventures. Similarly, today's giants of the pharmaceutical industry are, in the main, companies that were small or nonexistent fifty years ago when the first modern drugs were developed. Every one of the giants of the electrical industry—General Electric, Westinghouse, and RCA in the United States; Siemens and Philips on the Continent; Toshiba in Japan —rushed into computers in the 1950s. Not one was successful. The field is dominated by IBM, a company that was barely middle-sized and most definitely not high-tech forty years ago.

And yet the all but universal belief that large businesses do not and cannot innovate is not even a half-truth; rather, it is a misunderstanding.

In the first place, there are plenty of exceptions, plenty of large companies that have done well as entrepreneurs and innovators. In the United States, there is Johnson & Johnson in hygiene and health care, and 3M in highly engineered products for both industrial and consumer markets. Citibank, America's and the world's largest non- governmental financial institution, well over a century old, has been a major innovator in many areas of banking and finance. In Germany, Hoechst—one of the world's largest chemical companies, and more than 125 years old by now—has become a successful innovator in the pharmaceutical industry. In Sweden, ASEA, founded in 1884 and for the last sixty or seventy years a very big company, is a true innovator in both long-distance transmission of electrical power and robotics for factory automation.

To confuse things even more there are quite a few big, older businesses that have succeeded as entrepreneurs and innovators in some fields while failing dismally in others. The (American) General Electric Company failed in computers, but has been a successful innovator in three totally different fields: aircraft engines, engineered inorganic plastics, and medical electronics. RCA also failed in computers but succeeded in color television. Surely things are not quite as simple as the conventional wisdom has it.

Secondly, it is not true that "bigness" is an obstacle to entrepreneurship and innovation. In discussions of entrepreneurship one hears a great deal about the "bureaucracy" of big organizations and of their "conservatism." Both exist, of course, and they are serious impediments to entrepreneurship and innovation—but to all other performance just as much. And yet the record shows unambiguously that among existing enterprises, whether business or public-sector institutions, the small ones are least entrepreneurial and least innovative. Among existing entrepreneurial businesses there are a great many very big ones; the list above could have been enlarged without difficulty to one hundred companies from all over the world, and a list of innovative public-service institutions would also include a good many large ones.

And perhaps the most entrepreneurial business of them all is the large middle-sized one, such as the American company with $500 million in sales in the mid-1980s. ⊖ But *small* existing enterprises would be conspicuously absent from any list of entrepreneurial businesses.

It is not size that is an impediment to entrepreneurship and innovation; it is the existing operation itself, and especially the existing *successful* operation. And it is easier for a big or at least a fair-sized company to surmount this obstacle than it is for a small one. Operating anything—a manufacturing plant, a technology, a product

---

⊖   This has long been suspected. Now, however, conclusive evidence is available in the study of one hundred medium-sized "growth" companies by Richard E. Cavenaugh and Donald K. Clifford, Jr., "Lessons from America's Mid-Sized Growth Companies," *McKinsey Quarterly* (Autumn 1983).

line, a distribution system—requires constant effort and unremitting attention. The one thing that can be guaranteed in any kind of operation is the daily crisis. The daily crisis cannot be postponed, it has to be dealt with right away. And the existing operation demands high priority and deserves it.

The new always looks so small, so puny, so unpromising next to the size and performance of maturity. Anything truly new that looks big is indeed to be distrusted. The odds are heavily against its succeeding. And yet successful innovators, as was argued earlier, start small and, above all, simple.

The claim of so many businesses, "Ten years from now, ninety percent of our revenues will come from products that do not even exist today," is largely boasting. Modifications of existing products, yes; variations, yes; even extensions of existing products into new markets and new end uses—with or without modifications. But the truly new venture tends to have a longer lead time. Successful businesses, businesses that are today in the right markets with the right products or services, are likely ten years hence to get three-quarters of their revenues from products and services that exist today, or from their linear descendants. In fact, if today's products or services do not generate a continuing and large revenue stream, the enterprise will not be able to make the substantial investment in tomorrow that innovation requires.

It thus takes, special effort for the existing business to become entrepreneurial and innovative. The "normal" reaction is to allocate productive resources to the existing business, to the daily crisis, and to getting a little more out of what we already have. The temptation in the existing business is always to feed yesterday and to starve tomorrow.

It is, of course, a deadly temptation. The enterprise that does not innovate inevitably ages and declines. And in a period of rapid change such as the present, an entrepreneurial period, the decline will be fast. Once an enterprise or an industry has started to look back, turning it around is exceedingly difficult, if it can be done at all. But the obstacle to entrepreneurship and innovation which the success of the present business constitutes is a real one. The problem is precisely that the enterprise is so successful, that it is "healthy" rather than degeneratively diseased by bureaucracy, red tape, or complacency.

This is what makes the examples of existing businesses that do manage successfully to innovate so important, and especially the examples of existing large and fair-sized businesses that are also successful entrepreneurs and innovators. These businesses show that the obstacle of success, the obstacle of the existing, *can* be overcome. And it can be overcome in such a way that both the existing and the new, the mature and the infant, benefit and prosper. The large companies. that are successful entrepreneurs and innovators—Johnson & Johnson, Hoechst, ASEA, 3M, or the one hundred middle-sized "growth" companies— clearly know how to do it.

Where the conventional wisdom goes wrong is in its assumption that entrepreneurship and innovation are natural, creative, or spontaneous. If entrepreneurship and innovation do not well up in an organization, something must be stifling them. That only a minority of existing successful businesses are entrepreneurial and innovative is thus seen as conclusive evidence that existing businesses quench the entrepreneurial spirit.

But entrepreneurship is not "natural"; it is not "creative." It is work. Hence, the correct conclusion from the evidence is the opposite of the one commonly reached. That a substantial number of existing businesses, and among them a goodly number of fair-sized, big, and very big ones, succeed as entrepreneurs and innovators indicates that entrepreneurship and innovation can be achieved by any business. But they must be consciously striven for. They can be learned, but it requires effort. Entrepreneurial businesses treat entrepreneurship as a duty. They are disciplined about it ... they work at it ... they practice it.

Specifically, entrepreneurial management requires *policies and practices* in four major areas.

First, the organization must be made receptive to innovation and willing to perceive change as an opportunity rather than a threat. It must be organized to do the hard work of the entrepreneur. Policies and practices are needed to create the entrepreneurial climate.

Second, systematic measurement or at least appraisal of a company's performance as entrepreneur and innovator is mandatory, as well as built-in learning to improve performance.

Third, entrepreneurial management requires specific practices pertaining to organizational structure, to staffing and managing, and to compensation, incentives, and rewards.

Fourth, there are some "dont's": things *not to do* in entrepreneurial management.

II

Entrepreneurial Policies

A Latin poet called the human being "*rerum novarum cupidus* (greedy for new things)." Entrepreneurial management must make each manager of the existing business "*rerum novarum cupidus.* "

"How can we overcome the resistance to innovation in the existing organization?" is a question commonly asked by executives. Even if we knew the answer, it would still be the wrong question. The right one is: "How can we make the organization receptive to innovation, want innovation, reach for it, work for it?" When innovation is perceived by the organization as something that goes against the grain, as swimming against the current, if not as a heroic achievement, there will be no innovation. Innovation must be part and parcel of the ordinary, the norm, if not routine.

This requires specific policies. First, innovation, rather than holding on to what already exists, must be made attractive and beneficial to managers. There must be clear understanding throughout the organization that innovation is the best means to preserve and perpetuate that organization, and that it is the foundation for the individual manager's job security and success.

Second, the importance of the need for innovation and the dimensions of its time frame must be both defined and spelled out.

And finally, there needs to be an innovation plan, with specific objectives laid out.

1. There is only one way to make innovation attractive to managers: a systematic policy of abandoning whatever is outworn, obsolete, no longer productive, as well as the mistakes, failures, and misdirections of effort. Every three years or so, the enterprise must put every single product, process, technology, market, distributive channel, not to mention every single internal staff activity, on trial for its life. It must ask: Would we *now* go into this product, this market, this distributive channel, this technology *today*? If the answer is "No," one does not respond with, "Let's make another study." One asks, "What do we have to do to stop wasting resources on this product, this market, this distributive channel, this staff activity?"

Sometimes abandonment is not the answer, and may not even be possible. But then at least one limits further efforts and makes sure that productive resources of men and money are no longer devoured by yesterday. This is the right thing to do in any event to maintain. the health of the organization: every organism needs to eliminate its waste products or else it poisons itself. It is, however, an absolute necessity, if an enterprise is to be capable of innovation and is to be receptive to it. "Nothing so powerfully concentrates a man's mind as to know that he will be hung on the morning," Dr. Johnson was fond of saying. Nothing so powerfully concentrates a manager's mind on innovation as the knowledge that the present product or service will be abandoned within the foreseeable future.

Innovation requires major effort. It requires hard work on the part of performing, capable people—the scarcest resource in any organization. "Nothing requires more heroic efforts than to keep a corpse from stinking, and yet nothing is quite so futile," is an old medical proverb. In almost any organization I have come across, the best people are engaged in this futile effort; yet all they can hope to accomplish is to delay acceptance of the inevitable a little longer and at great cost.

But if it is known throughout the organization that the dead will be left to bury their dead, then the living will be willing—indeed, eager —to go to work on innovation.

To allow it to innovate, a business has to be able to free its best performers for the challenges of innovation. Equally it has to be able to devote financial resources to innovation. It will not be able to do either unless it organizes itself to slough off alike the successes of the past, the failures, and especially the "near-misses," the things that "should have worked" but didn't. If executives know that it is company policy to abandon, then they will be motivated to look for the new, to encourage entrepreneurship, and will accept the need to become entrepreneurial themselves. This is the first step—a form of organizational hygiene.

2. The second step, the second policy needed to make an existing business "greedy for new things," is to face up to the fact that all existing products, services, markets, distributive channels, processes, technologies, have limited—and usually short—health and life expectancies.

An analysis of the life cycle of existing products, services, and so on has become popular since the 1970s. Some examples are the strategy concepts advocated by the Boston Consulting group; the books on strategy by the Harvard Business School professor Michael Porter; and so-called portfolio management.[⊖]

In the strategies that have been widely advertised these last ten years, especially portfolio management, the findings of such analysis constitute an action program by themselves. This is a misunderstanding and bound to lead to disappointing results, as a good many companies found out when they rushed into such strategies in the late 1970s and early 1980s. The findings should lead to a *diagnosis*. This in turn requires judgment. It requires knowledge of the business, of its products, its markets, its customers, its technologies. It requires experience rather than analysis alone. The idea that bright young people straight from business school and equipped only with sharp analytical tools could crunch out of their computer life-and-death decisions about businesses, products, and markets is pure quackery, to be blunt.

This analysis (in *Managing for Results*, I called it a "Business X-Ray") is intended as a tool to find the right questions rather than a way automatically to

---

⊖ All these approaches have their origin in a book of mine published twenty years ago, *Managing for Results* (New York: Harper & Row, 1964), the first systematic work on business strategy, to my knowledge. This in turn grew out of the Entrepreneurship Seminar I ran in the late fifties at New York University. The analysis presented in *Managing for Results* (Chapters 1—5), with its ranking of all products and services into a small number of categories according to their performance, characteristics, and life expectancies, is still a useful tool for the analysis of product-life and product-health.

come up with the right answers. It is a challenge to all the knowledge that can be found in a given company, and all the experience. It will—and should—provoke dissent. The action that follows from classifying this or that product as "today's breadwinner" is a *risk-taking decision*. And so is what to do with the product that is on the point of becoming "yesterday's breadwinner," or with an "unjustified specialty," or with an "investment in managerial ego. " ⊖

3. The Business X-Ray furnishes the information needed to define how much innovation a given business requires, in what areas, and within what time frame. The best and simplest approach to this was developed by Michael J. Kami as a member of the Entrepreneurship Seminar at the New York University Graduate Business School in the 1950s. Kami first applied his approach to IBM, where he served as head of business planning; and then, in the early 1960s, to Xerox, where he served for several years in a similar capacity.

In this approach a company lists each of its products or services, but also the markets each serves and the distributive channels it uses, in order to estimate their position on the product life cycle. How much longer will this product still grow? How much longer will it still maintain itself in the marketplace? How soon can it be expected to age and decline—and how fast? When will it become obsolescent? This enables the company to estimate where it would be if it confined itself to managing to the best of its ability what already exists. And this then shows the gap between what can be expected realistically, and what a company still needs to do to achieve its objectives, whether in sales, in market standing, or in profitability.

The gap is the minimum that must be filled if the company is not to go downhill. In fact, the gap has to be filled or the company will soon start to die. The entrepreneurial achievement must be large enough to fill the gap, and timely enough to fill it before the old becomes obsolescent.

But innovative efforts do not carry certainty; they have a high probability of failure and an even higher one of delay. A company therefore should have under way at least three times the innovative efforts which, if successful, would fill the gap.

Most executives consider this excessively high. Yet experience has proved that it errs on the low side, if it errs at all. To be sure, some innovative efforts will do better than anyone expects, but others will do much less well. And everything takes longer than we hope or estimate; everything also requires more effort. Finally, the one thing certain about any major innovative effort is that there are going to be last-minute hitches and last-minute delays. To demand innovative efforts which, if everything goes according to plan, yield three times the minimum results needed is

---

⊖ For a definition of these terms, see *Managing for Results*, especially Chapter 4, How Are We Doing?, pp. 51-68.

only elementary precaution.

4. Systematic abandonment; the Business X-Ray of the existing business, its products, its services, its markets, its technologies; and the definition of innovation gap and innovation need—these together enable a company to formulate an *entrepreneurial plan* with objectives for innovation and deadlines.

Such a plan ensures that the innovation budget is adequate. And—the most important result of all—it determines how many people are needed, with what abilities and capacities. Only when people with proven performance capacity have been assigned to a project, supplied with the tools, the money, and the information they need to do the work, and given clear and unambiguous deadlines—only then do we have a plan. Until then, we have "good intentions," and what those are good for, everybody knows.

These are the fundamental policies needed to endow a business with entrepreneurial management; to make a business and its management greedy for new things; to make it perceive innovation as the healthy, normal, necessary course of action. Because it is based on a "Business X-Ray"—that is, on an analysis and diagnosis of the current business, its products, services, and markets—this approach also ensures that the existing business will not be neglected in the search for the new, and that the opportunities inherent in the existing products, services, and markets will not be sacrificed to the fascination with novelty.

The Business X-Ray is a tool for decision making. It enables us, indeed forces us, to allocate resources to results in the existing business. But it also makes it possible for us to determine how much is needed to create the business of tomorrow and its new products, new services, and new markets. It enables us to turn innovative intentions into innovative performance.

To render an existing business entrepreneurial, management must take the lead in making obsolete its own products and services rather than waiting for a competitor to do so. The business must be managed so as to perceive in the new an opportunity rather than a threat. It must be managed to work *today* on the products, services, processes, and technologies that will make a different tomorrow.

III

Entrepreneurial Practices

Entrepreneurship in the existing business also requires managerial practices.

1. First among these, and the simplest, is focusing managerial vision on opportunity. People see what is presented to them; what is not presented tends to be overlooked. And what is presented to most managers are "problems"—especially in the areas where performance falls below expectations—which means that managers tend not to see the opportunities. They are simply not being presented with them.

Management, even in small companies, usually get a report on operating performance once a month. The first page of this report always lists the areas in which performance has fallen below budget, in which there is a "shortfall," in which there is a "problem." At the monthly management meeting, everyone then goes to work on the so-called problems. By the time the meeting adjourns for lunch, the whole morning has been taken up with the discussion of those problems.

Of course, problems have to be paid attention to, taken seriously, and tackled. But if they are the only thing that is being discussed, opportunities will die of neglect. In businesses that want to create receptivity to entrepreneurship, special care is therefore taken that the opportunities are also attended to (cf. Chapter 3 on the unexpected success).

In these companies, the operating report has *two* "first pages": the traditional one lists the problems; the other one lists all the areas in which performance is better than expected, budgeted, or planned for. For, as was stressed earlier, the unexpected success in one's own business is an important symptom of innovative opportunity. If it is not seen as such, the business is altogether unlikely to be entrepreneurial. In fact the business and its managers, in focusing on the "problems," are likely to brush aside the unexpected success as an intrusion on their time and attention. They will say, "Why should we do anything about it? It's going well without our messing around with it." But this only creates an opening for the competitor who is a little more alert and a little less arrogant.

Typically, in companies that are managed for entrepreneurship, there are therefore two meetings on operating results: one to focus on the problems and one to focus on the opportunities.

One medium-sized supplier of health-care products to physicians and hospitals, a company that has gained leadership in a number of new and promising fields, holds an "operations meeting" the second and the last Monday of each month. The first meeting is devoted to problems —to all the things which, in the last month, have done less well than expected or are still doing less well than expected six months later. This meeting does not differ one whit from any other operating meeting. But the second meeting—the one on the last Monday—discusses the areas where the company is doing better than expected: the sales of a given product that have grown faster than projected, or the orders for a new product that are coming in from markets for which it was not designed. The top management of the company (which has grown ten-fold in twenty years) believes that its success is primarily the result of building this opportunity focus into its monthly management meetings. "The opportunities we spot in there," the chief executive officer has said many times, "are not nearly as important as the entrepreneurial attitude which the habit of looking for opportunities creates throughout the entire management group."

2. This company follows a second practice to generate an entrepreneurial spirit throughout its entire management group. Every six months it holds a two-day management meeting for all executives in charge of divisions, markets, and major product lines—a group of about forty or fifty people. The first morning is set aside for reports to the entire group from three or four executives whose units have done exceptionally well as entrepreneurs and innovators during the past year. They are expected to report on what explains their success: "What did we do that turned out to be successful?" "How did we find the opportunity?" "What have we learned, and what entrepreneurial and innovative plans do we have in hand now?"

Again, what actually is reported in these sessions is less important than the impact on attitudes and values. But the operating managers in the company also stress how much they learn in each of these sessions, how many new ideas they get, and how they return back home from these sessions full of plans and eager to try them.

Entrepreneurial companies always look for the people and units that do better and do differently. They single them out, feature them, and constantly ask them: "What are you doing that explains your success?" "What are you doing that the rest of us aren't doing, and what are you *not* doing that the rest of us are?"

3. A third practice, and one that is particularly important in the large company, is a session—informal but scheduled and well prepared—in which a member of the top management group sits down with the junior people from research, engineering, manufacturing, marketing, accounting and so on. The senior opens the session by saying: "I'm not here to make a speech or to tell you anything, I'm here to listen. I want to hear from you what your aspirations are, but above all, where you see opportunities for this company and where you see threats. And what are your ideas for us to try to do new things, develop new products, design new ways of reaching the market? What questions do you have about the company, its policies, its direction ... its position in the industry, in technology, in the marketplace?"

These sessions should not be held too often; they are a substantial time-burden on senior people. No senior executive should therefore be expected to sit down more than three times a year for a long afternoon or evening with a group of perhaps twenty-five or thirty juniors. But the sessions should be maintained systematically. They are an excellent vehicle for upward communications, the best means to enable juniors, and especially professionals, to look up from their narrow specialties and see the whole enterprise. They enable juniors to understand what top management is concerned with, and why. In turn, they give the seniors badly needed insight into the values, vision, and concerns of their younger colleagues. Above all, these sessions are one of the most effective ways to instill entrepreneurial vision throughout the company.

This practice has one built-in requirement. Those who suggest anything new, or even a change in the way things are being done, whether in respect to product or process, to market or service, should be expected to *go to work*. They should be asked to submit, within a reasonable period, a working paper to the presiding senior and to their colleagues in the session, in which they try to develop their idea. What would it look like if converted into reality? What in turn does reality have to look like for the idea to make sense? What are the assumptions regarding customers and markets, and so on. How much work is needed ... how much money and how many people ... and how much time? And what results might be expected?

Again, the yield of entrepreneurial ideas from all this may not be its most important product—though in many organizations the yield has been consistently high. The most valuable achievement may well be entrepreneurial vision, receptivity to innovation, and "greed for new things" throughout the entire organization.

IV

Measuring Innovative Performance

For a business to be receptive to entrepreneurship, innovative performance must be included among the measures by which that business controls itself. Only if we assess the entrepreneurial performance of a business will entrepreneurship become action. Human beings tend to behave as they are expected to.

In the normal assessments of a business, innovative performance is conspicuous by its absence. Yet it is not particularly difficult to build measurement, or at least judgment, of entrepreneurial and innovative performance into the controls of the business.

1. The first step builds into each innovative project feedback from results to expectations. This indicates the quality and reliability of both our innovative plans and our innovative efforts.

Research managers long ago learned to ask at the beginning of any research project: "What results do we expect from this project? When do we expect those results? When do we appraise the progress of the project so that we have control?"

They have also learned to check whether their expectations are borne out by the actual course of events. This shows them whether they are tending to be too optimistic or too pessimistic, whether they expect results too soon or are willing to wait too long, whether they are inclined either to overestimate the impact of a successfully concluded research project or to underestimate it. And this in turn enables them to correct said tendencies, and to identify both the areas in which they do well and the ones in which they tend to do poorly. Such feedback is, of course, needed for all innovative efforts, not merely for technical research and development.

The first aim is to find out what we are doing well, for one can always go ahead and do more of the same, even if we usually do not have the slightest idea why we are doing well in a given area. Next, one finds out the limitations on one's strengths: for instance, a tendency either to underestimate the amount of time needed or to overestimate it; or a tendency to overestimate the amount of research required in a given area while underestimating the resources required for developing the results of research into a product or a process. Or one finds a tendency, very common and very damaging, to slow down marketing or promotion efforts for the new venture just when it is about to take off.

One of the most successful of the world's major banks attributes its achievements to the feedback it builds into all new efforts, whether it is going into a new market such as South Korea, into equipment leasing, or into issuing credit cards. By building feedback from results to expectations for all new endeavors, the bank and its top management have also learned what they can expect from new ventures: How soon a new effort can be expected to produce results and when it should be supported by greater efforts and greater resources.

Such feedback is needed for all innovative efforts, the development and introduction of a new safety program, say, or a new compensation plan. What are the first indications that the new effort is likely to get into trouble and needs to be reconsidered? And what are the indications that enable us to say that this effort, even though it looks as if it were headed for trouble, is actually doing all right, but also that it may take more time than we originally anticipated?

2. The next step is to develop a systematic review of innovative efforts all together. Every few years an entrepreneurial management looks at all the innovative efforts of the business. Which ones should receive more support at this stage and should be pushed? Which ones have opened up new opportunities? Which ones, on the other hand, are not doing what we expected them to do, and what action should we take? Has the time come to abandon them, or, on the contrary, has the time come to redouble our efforts—but with what expectations and what deadline?

The top management people at one of the world's largest and most successful pharmaceutical companies sit down once a year to review its innovative efforts. First, they review every new drug development, asking: "Is this development going in the right direction and at the right speed? Is it leading to something we want to put into our own line, or is it going to be something that won't fit our markets so we'd better license it to another pharmaceutical manufacturer? Or ought we perhaps abandon it?" And then the same people look at all the other innovative efforts, especially in marketing, asking exactly the same questions. Finally, they review, equally carefully, the innovative performance of their major competitors. In terms of its research budget and its total expenditures for innovation, this company ranks only in the middle level. Its record as an innovator and entrepreneur is, however, outstanding.

3. Finally, entrepreneurial management entails judging the company's total innovative performance against the company's innovative objectives, against its performance and standing in the market, and against its performance as a business all together.

Every five years, perhaps, top management sits down with its associates in each major area and asks: "What have you contributed to this company in the past five years that really made a difference? And what do you plan to contribute in the next five years?"

But are not innovative efforts by their nature intangible? How can one measure them?

It is indeed true that there are some areas in which no one can, or should, decide the degree of relative importance. Which is more significant, a breakthrough in basic research, which years later may lead to an effective cure for certain cancers, or a new formulation that enables patients to administer an old but effective medication themselves instead of having to visit a physician or a hospital three times a week? It is impossible to decide. Equally, a company must choose between a new way to service customers, which enables the company to retain an important account it would otherwise have lost, and a new product, which gives the company leadership in markets that, while still small, may within a few years become big and important ones. These are judgments rather than measurements. But they are not arbitrary; they are not even subjective. And they are quite rigorous even though not capable of quantification. Above all, they do what a "measurement" is meant to enable us to do: to take purposeful action based on knowledge rather than on opinion or guesswork.

The most important question for the typical business in this review is probably: Have we gained innovative leadership, or at least maintained it? Leadership does not necessarily equate with size. It means to be accepted as the leader, recognized as the standard-setter; above all, it means having the freedom to lead rather than being obliged to follow. This is the acid test of successful entrepreneurship in the existing business.

V

Structures

Policies, practices, and measurements make possible entrepreneurship and innovation. They remove or reduce possible impediments. They create the proper attitude and provide the proper tools. But innovation is done by people. And people work within a structure.

For the existing business to be capable of innovation, it has to create a structure that allows people to be entrepreneurial. It has to devise relationships that center on entrepreneurship. It has to make sure that its rewards and incentives, its compensation, personnel decisions, and policies, all reward the right entrepreneurial behavior and do not penalize it.

1. This means, first, that the entrepreneurial, the new, has to be organized separately from the old and existing. Whenever we have tried to make an existing unit the carrier of the entrepreneurial project, we have failed. This is particularly true, of course, in the large business, but it is true in medium-sized businesses as well, and even in small businesses.

One reason is that (as said earlier) the existing business always requires time and effort on the part of the people responsible for it, and deserves the priority they give it. The new always looks so puny—so unpromising—next to the reality of the massive, ongoing business. The existing business, after all, has to nourish the struggling innovation. But the "crisis" in today's business has to be attended to as well. The people responsible for an existing business will therefore always be tempted to postpone action on anything new, entrepreneurial, or innovative until it is too late. No matter what has been tried—and we have now been trying every conceivable mechanism for thirty or forty years—existing units have been found to be capable mainly of extending, modifying, and adapting what already is in existence. The new belongs elsewhere.

2. This means also that there has to be a special locus for the new venture within the organization, and it has to be pretty high up. Even though the new project, by virtue of its current size, revenues, and markets, does not rank with existing products, somebody in top management must have the specific assignment to work on tomorrow as an entrepreneur and innovator.

This need not be a full-time job; in the smaller business, it very often cannot be a full-time job. But it needs to be a clearly defined job and one for which somebody with authority and prestige is fully accountable. These people will normally also be responsible for the policies necessary to build entrepreneurship into the existing business, for the abandonment analysis, for the Business X-Ray, and for developing the innovation objectives to plug the gap between what can be expected of the existing products and services and what is needed for survival and growth of the company. They are also normally charged with the systematic analysis of innovative opportunities—the analysis of the innovative opportunities presented in the preceding section of this book, the Practice of Innovation. They should be further charged with responsibility for the analysis of the innovative and entrepreneurial ideas that come up from the organization, for example, in the recommended "informal" session with the juniors.

And innovative efforts, especially those aimed at developing new businesses, products, or services, should normally report directly to this "executive in charge of innovation" rather than to managers further down the hierarchy. They should never report to line managers charged with responsibility for ongoing operations.

This will be considered heresy in most companies, particularly "well-managed" ones. But the new project is an infant and will remain one for the foreseeable future, and infants belong in the nursery. The "adults," that is, the executives in charge of existing businesses or products, will have neither time nor understanding for the infant project. They cannot afford to be bothered.

Disregard of this rule cost a major machine-tool manufacturer its leadership in robotics.

The company had the basic patents on machine tools for automated mass production. It had excellent engineering, an excellent reputation, and first-rate manufacturing. Everyone in the early years of factory automation—around 1975— expected it to emerge as the leader. Ten years later it had dropped out of the race entirely. The company had placed the unit charged with the development of machine tools for automated production three or four levels down in the organization, and had it report to people charged with designing, making, and selling the company's traditional machine-tool lines. These people were supportive; in fact, the work on robotics had been mainly their idea. But they were far too busy defending their traditional lines against a lot of new competitors such as the Japanese, redesigning them to fit new specifications, demonstrating, marketing, financing, and servicing them. Whenever the people in charge of the "infant" went to their bosses for a decision, they were told, "I have no time now, come back next week." Robotics were, after all, only a promise; the existing machine-tool lines produced millions of dollars each year.

Unfortunately, this is a common error.

The best, and perhaps the only, way to avoid killing off the new by sheer neglect is to set up the innovative project from the start as a separate business.

The best known practitioners of this approach are three American companies: Procter & Gamble, the soap, detergent, edible oil, and food producer—a very large and aggressively entrepreneurial company; Johnson & Johnson, the hygiene and health-care supplier; and 3M, a major manufacturer of industrial and consumer products. These three companies differ in the details of practice but essentially all three have the same policy. They set up the new venture as a separate business from the beginning and put a project manager in charge. The project manager remains in charge until the project is either abandoned or has achieved its objective and become a full-fledged business. And until then, the project manager can mobilize all the skills as they are needed—research, manufacturing, finance, marketing—and put them to work on the project team.

A company that engages in more than one innovative effort at a time (and bigger companies usually do) might have all the "infants" report directly to the same member of the top management group. It does not greatly matter that the ventures have different technologies, markets, or product characteristics. They all are new, small, and entrepreneurial. They are all exposed to the same "childhood diseases." The problems from which the entrepreneurial venture suffers, and the decisions it requires, tend to be pretty much the same regardless of technology, of market, or of product line. Somebody has to have time for them, to give them the attention they need, to take the trouble to understand what the problems are, the crucial decisions, the things that really matter in a given innovative effort. And this person has to have sufficient stature in the business to be able to represent the infant project—and to make the decision to stop an effort if it is going nowhere.

3. There is another reason why a new, innovative effort is best set up separately: to keep away from it the burdens it cannot yet carry. Both the investment in a new product line and its returns should, for instance, not be included in the traditional return-on-investment analysis until the product line has been on the market for a number of years. To ask the fledgling development to shoulder the full burdens an existing business imposes on its units is like asking a six-year-old to go on a long hike carrying a sixty-pound pack; neither will get very far. And yet the existing business has requirements with respect to accounting, to personnel policy, to reporting of all kinds, which it cannot easily waive.

The innovative effort and the unit that carries it require different policies, rules, and measurements in many areas. How about the company's pension plan, for instance? Often it makes sense to give people in the innovative unit a participation in future profits rather than to put them into a pension plan when they are producing, as yet, no earnings to supply a pension fund contribution.

The area in which separation of the new, innovative unit from the ongoing business is most important is compensation and rewards of key people. What works best in a going, established business would kill the "infant"—and yet not be adequate compensation for its key people. Indeed, the compensation scheme that is most popular in large businesses, one based on return on assets or on investment, is a near-complete bar to innovation.

I learned this many years ago in a major chemical company. Everybody knew that one of its central divisions had to produce new materials to stay in business. The plans for these materials were there, the scientific work had been done ... but nothing happened. Year after year there was another excuse. Finally, the division's general manager spoke up at a review meeting, "My management group and I are compensated primarily on the basis of return-on-investment. The moment we spend money on developing the new materials, our return will go down by half for at least four years. Even if I am still here in four years time when we should show the first returns on these investments—and I doubt that the company will put up with me that long if profits are that much lower—I'm taking bread out of the mouths of all my associates in the meantime. Is it reasonable to expect us to do this?" The formula was changed and the developmental expenses for the new project were taken out of the return-on-investment figures. Within eighteen months the new materials were on the market. Two years later they had given the division leadership in its field which it has retained to this day. Four years later the division doubled its profits.

In terms of compensation and rewards for innovative efforts, however, it is far easier to define what should not be done than it is to spell out what should. The requirements are conflicting: the new project must not be burdened with a compensation load it cannot carry, yet the people involved must be adequately motivated by rewards appropriate to their efforts.

Specifically, this means that the people in charge of the new project should be kept at a moderate salary. It is, however, quite unrealistic to ask them to work for less money than they received in their old jobs. People put in charge of a new area within an existing business are likely to make good money. They are also the people who could easily move to other jobs, either within or outside the company, in which they would make more money. One therefore has to start out with their existing compensation and benefits.

One method that both 3M and Johnson & Johnson use effectively is to promise that the person who successfully develops a new product, a new market, or a new service and then builds a business on it will become the head of that business: general manager, vice-president, or division president, with the rank, compensation, bonuses, and stock options appropriate to the level. This can be a sizable reward, and yet it does not commit the company to anything except in case of success.

Another method—and which one is preferable will depend largely on the tax laws at the time—is to give the people who take on the new development a share in future profits. The venture might, for instance, be treated as if it were a separate company in which the entrepreneurial managers in charge have a stake, say 25 percent. When the venture reaches maturity, they are bought out at a pre-set formula based on sales and profits.

One thing more is needed: the people who take on the innovating task in an existing business also "venture." It is only fair that their employer share the risk. They should have the option of returning to their old job at their old compensation rate if the innovation fails. They should not be rewarded for failure, but they should certainly not be penalized for trying.

4. As implied in discussing individual compensation, the returns on innovation will be quite different from those of the existing business and will have to be measured differently. To say, "We expect all our businesses to show at least a fifteen percent pre-tax return each year and ten percent annual growth" may make sense for existing businesses and existing products. It makes absolutely no sense for the new project, being at once much too high and much too low.

For a long time (years, in many cases) the new endeavor shows neither profits nor growth. It absorbs resources. But then it should grow very fast for quite a long time and return the money invested in its development at least fifty-fold—if not at a much higher rate—or else the innovation is a failure. An innovation starts small but it should end big. It should result in a new major business rather than in just another "specialty" or a "respectable" addition to the product line.

Only by analyzing a company's own innovative experience, the feedback from its performance on its expectations, can the company determine what the appropriate expectations are for innovations in its industry and its markets. What are the appropriate time spans? And what is the optimal distribution of effort? Should there be a heavy investment of men and money at the beginning, or should the effort at the start be confined to one person, with a helper or two, working alone? When should the effort then be scaled up? And when should "development" become "business," producing large but conventional returns?

These are key questions. The answers to them are not to be found in books. Yet they cannot be answered arbitrarily, by hunch, or by fighting it out. Entrepreneurial companies do know what patterns, rhythms, and time spans pertain to innovations in their specific industry, technology, and market.

The innovative major bank mentioned earlier knows, for instance, that a new subsidiary established in a new country will require investment for at least three years. It should break even in the fourth year, and should have repaid the total investment by the middle of the sixth year. If it still requires investment by the end of the sixth year, it is a disappointment and should probably be shut down.

A new major service—leasing, for example—has a similar though somewhat shorter cycle. Procter & Gamble—or so it looks from the outside—knows that its new products should be on the market and selling two to three years after work on them has begun. They should have established themselves as market leaders eighteen months later. IBM, it seems, figures on a five-year lead time for a new major product before market introduction. Within another year the new product should then start to grow fast. It should attain market leadership and profitability fairly early in its second year on the market, have repaid 'the full investment by the early months of the third year, and peak and level out in its fifth year on the market. By then, a new IBM product should already have begun to make it obsolescent.

The only way, however, to know these things is through the systematic analysis of the performance of the company and of its competitors, that is, by systematic feedback from innovation results to innovation expectations and by regular appraisal of the company's performance as entrepreneur.

And once a company understands what results should and could be expected from its innovative efforts, it can then design the appropriate controls. These will both measure how well units and their managers perform in innovation and determine which innovative efforts to push, which to reconsider, and which to abandon.

5. The final structural requirement for entrepreneurship in the existing business is that a person or a component group should-be held clearly accountable.

In the "middle-sized growth companies" mentioned earlier, this is usually the primary responsibility of the chief executive officer (CEO). In large companies, it probably is more likely a designated and very senior member of the top management group. In smaller businesses, this executive in charge of entrepreneurship and innovation may well carry other responsibilities as well.

The cleanest organizational structure for entrepreneurship, though suitable only in the very large company, is a totally separate innovating operation or development company.

The earliest example of this was set up more than one hundred years ago, in 1872, by Hefner-Alteneck, the first college-trained engineer hired by a manufacturing company anywhere, the German Siemens Company. Hefner started the first "research lab" in industry. Its members were charged with inventing new and different products and processes. But they were also responsible for identifying new and different end uses and new and different markets. And they not only did the technical work; they were responsible for development of the manufacturing process, for the introduction of the new product into the marketplace, and for its profitability.

Fifty years later, in the 1920s, the American DuPont Company independently set up a similar unit and called it a Development Department. This department gathers innovative ideas from all over the company, studies them, thinks them through, analyzes them. Then it proposes to top management which ones should be tackled as major innovative projects. From the beginning, it brings to bear on the innovation all the resources needed: research, development, manufacturing, marketing, finance, and so on. It is in charge until the new product or service has been on the market for a few years.

Whether the responsibility for innovation rests with the chief executive officer, with another member of top management, or with a separate component, whether it is a full-time assignment or part of an executive's responsibilities, it should always be set up and recognized both as a separate responsibility and as a responsibility of top management. And it should always include the systematic and purposeful search for innovative opportunities.

It might be asked, Are all these policies and practices necessary? Don't they interfere with the entrepreneurial spirit and stifle creativity? And cannot a business be entrepreneurial without such policies and practices? The answer is, Perhaps, but neither very successfully nor for very long.

Discussions of entrepreneurship tend to focus on the personalities and attitudes of top management people, and especially of the chief executive. [*] Of course, any top management can damage and stifle entrepreneurship within its company. It's easy enough. All it takes is to say "No" to every new idea and to keep on saying it for a few years— and then make sure that those who came up with the new ideas never get a reward or a promotion and become ex-employees fairly swiftly. It is far less certain, however, that top management personalities and attitudes can by themselves—without the proper policies and practices —create an entrepreneurial business, which is what most of the books on entrepreneurship assert, at least by implication. In the few short-lived cases I know of, the companies were built and still run by the founder. Even then, when it gets to be successful the company soon ceases to be entrepreneurial unless it adopts the policies and practices of entrepreneurial management. The reason why top management personalities and attitudes do not suffice in any but the very young or very small business is, of course, that even a medium-sized enterprise is a pretty large organization. It requires a good many people who know what they are supposed to do, want to do it,

---

[*] The best presentation of this viewpoint is in Rosabeth M. Kanter's *The Change Masters* (New York: Simon & Schuster, 1983).

are motivated toward doing it, and are supplied with both the tools and continuous reaffirmation. Otherwise there is only lip service; entrepreneurship soon becomes confined to the CEO's speeches.

And I know of no business that continued to remain entrepreneurial beyond the founder's departure, unless the founder had built into the organization the policies and practices of entrepreneurial management. If these are lacking, the business becomes timid and backward-looking within a few years at the very latest. And these companies do not even realize, as a rule, that they have lost their essential quality, the one element that had made them stand out, until it is perhaps too late. For this realization one needs a measurement of entrepreneurial performance.

Two companies that were entrepreneurial businesses *par excellence* under their founders' management are good examples: Walt Disney Productions and McDonald's. The respective founders, Walt Disney and Ray Kroc, were men of tremendous imagination and drive, each the very embodiment of creative, entrepreneurial, and innovative thinking. Both built into their companies strong operating day-to-day management. But both kept to themselves the entrepreneurial responsibility within their companies. Both depended on the "entrepreneurial personality" and did not embed the entrepreneurial spirit in specific policies and practices. Within a few years after the death of these men, their companies had become stodgy, backward-looking, timid, and defensive.

Companies that have built entrepreneurial management into their structure—Procter & Gamble, Johnson & Johnson, Marks and Spencer—continue to be innovators and entrepreneurial leaders decade after decade, irrespective of changes in chief executives or economic conditions.

VI

Staffing

How should the existing business staff for entrepreneurship and innovation? Are there such people as "entrepreneurs"? Are they a special breed?

The literature is full of discussions of these questions; full of stories of the "entrepreneurial personality" and of people who will never do anything but innovate. In the light of our experience—and it is considerable —these discussions are pointless. By and large, people who do not feel comfortable as innovators or as entrepreneurs will not volunteer for such jobs; the gross misfits eliminate themselves. The others can learn the practice of innovation. Our experience shows that an executive who has performed in other assignments will do a decent job as an entrepreneur. In successful entrepreneurial businesses, nobody seems to worry whether a given person is likely to do a good job of development or not. People of all kinds of temperaments and backgrounds apparently do equally well. Any young engineer in 3M who comes to top management with an idea that makes sense is expected to take on its development.

Equally, there is no reason to worry where the successful entrepreneur will end up. To be sure, there are some people who only want to work on new projects and never want to run anything. When most English families still had nannies, many did not want to stay after "their" baby got to the stage when it began to walk and talk— in other words, when it was no longer a baby. But many were perfectly content to stay on and did not find it difficult to look after a much older child. The people who do not want to be anything but entrepreneurs are unlikely to be in the employ of an existing business to begin with, and even more unlikely to have been successful in it. And the people who do well as entrepreneurs in an existing business have, as a rule, proved themselves earlier as managers in the same organization. It is thus reasonable to assume that they can both innovate and manage what already exists. There are some people at Procter & Gamble and at 3M who make a career of being project managers and who take on a new project as soon as they have successfully finished an old one. But most people at the higher levels of these companies have made their careers out of "project management," into "product management," into "market management," and finally into a senior company-wide position. And the same is true of Johnson & Johnson and of Citibank.

The best proof that entrepreneurship is a question of behavior, policies, and practices rather than personality is the growing number of older large-company people in the United States who make entrepreneurship their second career. Increasingly, middle-and upper-level executives and senior professionals who have spent their entire working lives in large companies—more often than not with the same employer —take early retirement after twenty-five or thirty years of service when they have reached what they realize is their terminal job. At fifty or fifty-five, these middle-aged people then become entrepreneurs. Some start their own business. Some, especially technical specialists, set up shop as consultants to new and small ventures. Some join a new small company in a senior position. And the great majority are both successful and happy in their new assignment.

Modern Maturity, the magazine of the American Association of Retired Persons, is full of stories of such people, and of advertisements by new small companies looking for them. In a management seminar for chief executive officers that I ran in 1983, there were fifteen such second-career entrepreneurs (fourteen men and one woman) among the forty-eight participants. During a special session for these people, I asked them whether they had been frustrated or stifled while working all those years for big companies, as "entrepreneurial personalities" are supposed to be. They thought the question totally absurd. I then asked whether they had much difficulty changing their roles; they thought this equally absurd. As one of them said—and all the others nodded assent—"Good management is good management, whether you run a $180 million department at General Electric, with its billions of sales as I used to do, or a new, growing diagnostic-instrument innovator with $6 million in sales, as I do now. Of course I do different things and do things differently. But I apply the concepts I learned at G.E. and do exactly the same analysis. The transition was easier, in fact, than when I moved, ten years earlier, from being a bench engineer into my first management job."

Public-service institutions teach the same lesson. Among the most successful innovators in recent American history are two men in higher education, Alexander Schure and Ernest Boyer. Schure started out as a successful inventor in the electronics field, with a good many patents to his name. But in 1955, when he was in his early thirties, he founded the New York Institute of Technology as a private university without support from government, foundation, or big company, and with brand-new ideas regarding the kind of students to be recruited and what they were to be taught as well as how. Thirty years later, his institute has become a leading technical university with four campuses, one of them a medical school, and almost twelve thousand students. Schure still works as a successful electronics inventor. But he has also been for these thirty years the full-time chancellor of his university, and has, by all accounts, built up a professional and effective management team.

In contrast to Schure, Boyer started out as an administrator, first in the University of California system, then in the State University of New York, which with 350,000 student and 64 campuses is the biggest and most bureaucratic of American university systems. By 1970, Boyer, at forty-two, had worked his way to the top and was appointed chancellor. He immediately founded the Empire State College—actually not a college at all but an unconventional solution to one of the oldest and most frustrating failures of American higher education, the degree program for adults who do not have full academic credentials.

Although tried many times, this had never worked before. If these adults were admitted to college programs together with the "regular" younger students, no attention was usually paid to their aims, their needs, and least of all to their experience. They were treated as if they were eighteen years old, got discouraged, and soon dropped out. But if, as was tried repeatedly, they were put into special "continuing education programs," they were likely to be considered a nuisance and shoved aside, with programs staffed by whatever faculty the university could most easily spare. In Boyer's Empire State College, the adults attend regular university courses in one of the colleges or universities of the state university. But first the adult students are assigned a "mentor," usually a member of a nearby state university faculty. The mentor helps them work out their programs and decide whether they need special preparation, and where, conversely, their experience qualifies them for advanced standing and work. And then the mentor acts as broker, negotiating admission, standing, and program for each applicant with the appropriate institution.

All this may sound like common sense—and so it is. Yet it was quite a break with the habits and mores of American academia and was fought hard by the state university establishment. But Boyer persisted. His Empire State College program has now become the first successful program of this kind in American higher education, with more than six thousand students, a negligible dropout rate, and a master's program. Boyer, the arch-innovator, did not cease to be an "administrator." From chancellor of the State University of New York he went on to become, first, President Carter's Commissioner of Education, and then president of the Carnegie Foundation for the Advancement of Teaching—respectively, the most "bureaucratic" and the most "establishment" job in American academia.

These examples do not prove that anyone can excel at being both a bureaucrat and an innovator. Schure and Boyer are surely exceptional people. But their experiences do show that there is no specific "personality" for either task. What is needed is willingness to learn, willingness to work hard and persistently, willingness to exercise self-discipline, willingness to adapt and to apply the right policies and practices. Which is exactly what any enterprise that adopted entrepreneurial management has found out with respect to people and staffing.

To enable the entrepreneurial project to be run successfully, as something new, the structure and organization have to be right; relationships have to be appropriate; and compensation and rewards have to fit. But when all this has been done, the question of who is to run the unit, and what should be done with them when they have succeeded in building up the new project, must be decided on an individual basis for this person or that person, rather than according to this or that psychological theory for none of which there is much empirical evidence.

Staffing decisions in the entrepreneurial business are made like any other decision about people and jobs. Of course, they are risk-taking decisions: decisions about people always are. Of course, they have to be made carefully and conscientiously. And they have to be made the correct way. First, the assignment must be thought through; then one considers a number of people; then one checks carefully their performance records; and finally one checks out each of the candidates with a few people for whom he or she has worked. But all this applies to every decision that puts a person into a job. And in the entrepreneurial company, the batting average in people-decisions is the same for entrepreneurs as it is for other managerial and professional people.

VII

The Dont's

There are some things the entrepreneurial management of an existing business should not do.

1. The most important caveat is not to mix managerial units and entrepreneurial ones. Do not ever put the entrepreneurial into the existing managerial component. Do not make innovation an objective for people charged with running, exploiting, optimizing what already exists.

But it is also inadvisable—in fact, almost a guarantee of failure—for a business to try to become entrepreneurial without changing its basic policies and practices. To be an entrepreneur on the side rarely works.

In the last ten or fifteen years a great many large American companies have tried to go into joint ventures with entrepreneurs. Not one of these attempts has succeeded; the entrepreneurs found themselves stymied by policies, by basic rules, by a "climate" they felt was bureaucratic, stodgy, reactionary. But at the same time their partners, the people from the big company, could not figure out what the entrepreneurs were trying to do and thought them undisciplined, wild, visionary.

By and large, big companies have been successful as entrepreneurs only if they use their own people to build the venture. They have been successful only when they use people whom they understand and who understand them, people whom they trust and who in turn know how to get things done in the existing business; people, in other words, with whom one can work as partners. But this presupposes that the entire company is imbued with the entrepreneurial spirit, that it wants innovation and is reaching out for it, considering it both a necessity and an opportunity. It presupposes that the entire organization has been made "greedy for new things."

2. Innovative efforts that take the existing business out of its own field are rarely successful. Innovation had better not be "diversification." Whatever the benefits of diversification, it does not mix with entrepreneurship and innovation. The new is always sufficiently difficult not to attempt it in an area one does not understand. An existing business innovates where it has expertise, whether

knowledge of market or knowledge of technology. Anything new will predictably get into trouble, and then one has to know the business. Diversification itself rarely works unless it, too, is built on commonality with the existing business, whether commonality of the market or commonality of the technology. Even then, as I have discussed elsewhere, [⊖]diversification has its problems. But if one adds to the difficulties and demands of diversification the difficulties and demands of entrepreneurship, the result is predictable disaster. So one innovates only where one understands.

3. Finally, it is almost always futile to avoid making one's own business entrepreneurial by "buying in," that is, by acquiring small entrepreneurial ventures. Acquisitions rarely work unless the company that does the acquiring is willing and able within a fairly short time to furnish management to the acquisition. The managers that have come with the acquired company rarely stay around very long. If they were owners, they have now become wealthy; if they were professional managers, they are likely to stay around only if given much bigger opportunities in the new, acquiring company. So, within a year or two, the acquirer has to furnish management to run the business that has been bought. This is particularly true when a non-entrepreneurial company buys an entrepreneurial one. The management people in the new acquired venture soon find that they cannot work with the people in their new parent company, and vice versa. I myself know of no case where "buying in" has worked.

A business that wants to be able to innovate, wants to have a chance to succeed and prosper in a time of rapid change, has to build entrepreneurial management into its own system. It has to adopt policies that create throughout the entire organization the desire to innovate and the habits of entrepreneurship and innovation. To be a successful entrepreneur, the existing business, large or small, has to be managed as an entrepreneurial business.

⊖ In *Management: Tasks, Responsibilities, Practices*, especially Chapters 56 and 57.

CHAPTER 14

Entrepreneurship in the Service Institution

I

Public-service institutions such as government agencies, labor unions, churches, universities, and schools, hospitals, community and charitable organizations, professional and trade associations and the like, need to be entrepreneurial and innovative fully as much as any business does. Indeed, they may need it more. The rapid changes in today's society, technology, and economy are simultaneously an even greater threat to them and an even greater opportunity.

Yet public-service institutions find it far more difficult to innovate than even the most "bureaucratic" company. The "existing" seems to be even more of an obstacle. To be sure, every service institution likes to get bigger. In the absence of a profit test, size is the one criterion of success for a service institution, and growth a goal in itself. And then, of course, there is always so much more that needs to be done. But stopping what has "always been done" and doing something new are equally anathema to service institutions, or at least excruciatingly painful to them.

Most innovations in public-service institutions are imposed on them either by outsiders or by catastrophe. The modern university, for instance, was created by a total outsider, the Prussian diplomat Wilhelm von Humboldt. He founded the University of Berlin in 1809 when the traditional university of the seventeenth and eighteenth century had been all but completely destroyed by the French Revolution and the Napoleonic wars. Sixty years later, the modern American university came into being when the country's traditional colleges and universities were dying and could no longer attract students.

Similarly, all basic innovations in the military in this century, whether in structure or in strategy, have followed on ignominious malfunction or crushing defeat: the organization of the American Army and of its strategy by a New York lawyer, Elihu Root, Teddy Roosevelt's Secretary of War, after its disgraceful performance in the Spanish-American War; the reorganization, a few years later, of the British Army and its strategy by Secretary of War Lord Haldane, another civilian, after the equally disgraceful performance of the British in the Boer War; and the rethinking of the German Army's structure and strategy after the defeat of World War I.

And in government, the greatest innovative thinking in recent political history, America's New Deal of 1933-36, was triggered by a Depression so severe as almost to unravel the country's social fabric.

Critics of bureaucracy blame the resistance of public-service institutions to entrepreneurship and innovation on "timid bureaucrats," on time-servers who "have never met a payroll," or on "power-hungry politicians." It is a very old litany—in fact, it was already hoary when Machiavelli chanted it almost five hundred years ago. The only thing that changes is who intones it. At the beginning of this century, it was the slogan of the so-called liberals and now it is the slogan of the so-called neo-conservatives. Alas, things are not that simple, and "better people"—that perennial panacea of reformists—are a mirage. The most entrepreneurial, innovative people behave like the worst time-serving bureaucrat or power-hungry politician six months after they have taken over the management of a public-service institution, particularly if it is a government agency.

The forces that impede entrepreneurship and innovation in a public-service institution are inherent in it, integral to it, inseparable from it. ⊖ The best proof of this are the internal staff services in businesses, which are, in effect, the "public-service institutions" within business corporations. These are typically headed by people who have come out of operations and have proven their capacity to perform in competitive markets. And yet the internal staff services are not notorious as innovators. They are good at building empires—and they always want to do more of the same. They resist abandoning anything they are doing. But they rarely innovate once they have been established.

There are three main reasons why the existing enterprise presents so much

---

⊖   On the public-service institution and its characteristics, see the section on Performance in the Service Institution, Chapters 11-14, in *Management: Tasks, Responsibilities, Practices*.

more of an obstacle to innovation in the public-service institution than it does in the typical business enterprise.

1. First, the public-service institution is based on a "budget" rather than being paid out of its results. It is paid for its efforts and out of funds somebody else has earned, whether the taxpayer, the donors of a charitable organization, or the company for which a personnel department or the marketing services staff work. The more efforts the public service institution engages in, the greater its budget will be. And "success" in the public-service institution is defined by getting a larger budget rather than obtaining results. Any attempt to slough off activities and efforts therefore diminishes the public-service institution. It causes it to lose stature and prestige. Failure cannot be acknowledged. Worse still, the fact that an objective has been attained cannot be admitted.

2. Second, a service institution is dependent on a multitude of constituents. In a business that sells its products on the market, one constituent, the consumer, eventually overrides all the others. A business needs only a very small share of a small market to be successful. Then it can satisfy the other constituents, whether shareholders, workers, the community, and so on. But precisely because public-service institutions—and that includes the staff activities within a business corporation—have no "results" out of which they are being paid, any constituent, no matter how marginal, has in effect a veto power. A public-service institution has to satisfy everyone; certainly, it cannot afford to alienate anyone.

The moment a service institution starts an activity, it acquires a "constituency," which then refuses to have the program abolished or even significantly modified. But anything new is always controversial. This means that it is opposed by existing constituencies without having formed, as yet, a constituency of its own to support it.

3. The most important reason, however, is that public-service institutions exist after all to "do good." This means that they tend to see their mission as a moral absolute rather than as economic and subject to a cost/benefit calculus. Economics always seeks a different allocation of the same resources to obtain a higher yield. Everything economic is therefore relative. In the public-service institution, there is no such thing as a higher yield. If one is "doing good," then there is no "better." Indeed, failure to attain objectives in the quest for a "good" only means that efforts need to be redoubled. The forces of evil must be far more powerful than expected and need to be fought even harder.

For thousands of years the preachers of all sorts of religions have held forth against the "sins of the flesh." Their success has been limited, to say the least. But this is no argument as far as the preachers are concerned. It does not persuade them to devote their considerable talents to pursuits in which results may be more easily attainable. On the contrary, it only proves that their efforts need to be redoubled.

Avoiding the "sins of the flesh" is clearly a "moral good," and thus an absolute, which does not admit of any cost/benefit calculation.

Few public-service institutions define their objectives in such absolute terms. But even company personnel departments and manufacturing service staffs tend to see their mission as "doing good," and therefore as being moral and absolute instead of being economic and relative.

This means that public-service institutions are out to maximize rather than to optimize. "Our mission will not be completed," asserts the head of the Crusade Against Hunger, "as long as there is one child on the earth going to bed hungry." If he were to say, "Our mission will be completed if the largest possible number of children that can be reached through existing distribution channels get enough to eat not to be stunted," he would be booted out of office. But if the goal is maximization, it can never be attained. Indeed, the closer one comes toward attaining one's objective, the more efforts are called for. For, once optimization has been reached (and the optimum in most efforts lies between 75 and 80 percent of theoretical maximum), additional costs go up exponentially while additional results fall off exponentially. The closer a public-service institution comes to attaining its objectives, therefore, the more frustrated it will be and the harder it will work on what it is already doing.

It will, however, behave exactly the same way the less it achieves. Whether it succeeds or fails, the demand to innovate and to do something else will be resented as an attack on its basic commitment, on the very reason for its existence, and on its beliefs and values.

These are serious obstacles to innovation. They explain why, by and large, innovation in public services tends to come from new ventures rather than from existing institutions.

The most extreme example around these days may well be the labor union. It is probably the most successful institution of the century in the developed countries. It has clearly attained its original objectives. There can be no more "more" when the labor share of gross national product in Western developed countries is around 90 percent—and in some countries, such as Holland, close to 100 percent. Yet the labor union is incapable of even thinking about new challenges, new objectives, new contributions. All it can do is repeat the old slogans and fight the old battles. For the "cause of labor" is an absolute good. Clearly, it must not be questioned, let alone redefined.

The university, however, may not be too different from the labor union, and in part for the same reason—a level of growth and success second in this century only to that of the labor union.

Still there are enough exceptions among public-service institutions (although,

I have to admit, not many among government agencies) to show that public-service institutions, even old and big ones, can innovate.

One Roman Catholic archdiocese in the United States, for instance, has brought in lay people to run the diocese, including a married lay woman, the former personnel vice-president of a department store chain, as the general manager. Everything that does not involve dispensing sacraments and ministering to congregations is done by lay professionals and managers. Although there is a shortage of priests throughout the American Catholic Church, this archdiocese has priests to spare and has been able to move forward aggressively to build congregations and expand religious services.

One of the oldest of scientific societies, the American Association for the Advancement of Science, redirected itself between 1960 and 1980 to become a "mass organization" without losing its character as a leader. It totally changed its weekly magazine, *Science*, to become the spokesman for science to public and government, and to be the authoritative reporter on science policy. And it created a scientifically solid yet popular mass circulation magazine for lay readers.

A large hospital on the West Coast recognized, as early as 1965 or so, that health care was changing as a result of its success. Where other large city hospitals tried to fight such trends as those toward hospital chains or freestanding ambulatory treatment centers, this institution has been an innovator and a leader in these developments. Indeed, it was the first to build a freestanding maternity center in which the expectant mother is given a motel room at fairly low cost, yet with all the medical services available should they be needed. It was the first to go into freestanding surgical centers for ambulatory care. But it also started to build its own voluntary hospital chain, in which it offers management contracts to smaller hospitals throughout the region.

Beginning around 1975, the Girl Scouts of the U.S.A., a large organization dating back to the early years of the century with several million young women enrolled, introduced innovations affecting membership, programs, and volunteers— the three basic dimensions of the organization. It began actively to recruit girls from the new urban middle classes, that is, blacks, Asians, Latins; these minorities now account for one-fifth of the members. It recognized that with the movement of women into professions and managerial positions, girls need new programs and role models that stress professional and business careers rather than the traditional careers as homemaker or nurse. The Girl Scouts management people realized that the traditional sources for volunteers to run local activities were drying up because young mothers no longer were sitting at home searching for things to do. But they recognized, too, that the new professional, the new working mother represents an opportunity and that the Girl Scouts have something to offer her; and for any community organization, volunteers are the critical constraint. They therefore set out to make work as a volunteer for the Girl Scouts attractive to the working mother as a good way to have time and fun with her child while also contributing to her child's development. Finally, the Girl Scouts realized that the working mother who does not have enough time for her child represents another opportunity: they started Girl Scouting for preschool children. Thus, the Girl Scouts reversed the downward trend in enrollment of both children and volunteers, while the Boy Scouts—a bigger, older, and infinitely richer organization—is still adrift.

II

Entrepreneurial Policies

These are all American examples, I fully realize. Doubtless, similar examples are to be found in Europe or Japan. But I hope that these cases, despite their limitations, will suffice to demonstrate the entrepreneurial policies needed in the public-service institution to make it capable of innovation.

1. First, the public-service institution needs a clear definition of its mission. What is it trying to do? Why does it exist? It needs to focus on objectives rather than on programs and projects. Programs and projects are means to an end. They should always be considered as temporary and, in fact, short-lived.

2. The public-service institution needs a realistic statement of goals. It should say, "Our job is to assuage famine," rather than, "Our job is to eliminate hunger." It needs something that is genuinely attainable and therefore a commitment to a realistic goal, so that it can say eventually, "Our job is finished."

There are, of course, objectives that can never be attained. To administer justice in any human society is clearly an unending task, one that can never be fully accomplished even to modest standards. But most objectives can and should be phrased in optimal rather than in maximal terms. Then it is possible to say: "We have attained what we were trying to do."

Surely, this should be said with respect to the traditional goals of the schoolmaster: to get everyone to sit in school for long years. This goal has long been attained in developed countries. What does education have to do now, that is, what is the meaning of "education" as against mere schooling?

3. Failure to achieve objectives should be considered an indication that the objective is wrong, or at least defined wrongly. The assumption has then to be that the objective should be economic rather than moral. If an objective has not been

attained after repeated tries, one has to assume that it is the wrong one. It is not rational to consider failure a good reason for trying again and again. The probability of success, as mathematicians have known for three hundred years, diminishes with each successive try; in fact, the probability of success in any succeeding try is never more than one-half the probability of the preceding one. Thus, failure to attain objectives is a *prima facie* reason to question the validity of the objective— the exact opposite of what most public-service institutions believe.

4. Finally, public-service institutions need to build into their policies and practices the constant search for innovative opportunity. They need to view change as an opportunity rather than a threat.

The innovating public-service institutions mentioned in the preceding pages succeeded because they applied these basic rules.

In the years after World War II, the Roman Catholic Church in the United States was confronted for the first time with the rapid emergence of a well-educated Catholic laity. Most Catholic dioceses, and indeed most institutions of the Roman Catholic Church, perceived in this a threat, or at least a problem. With an educated Catholic laity, unquestioned acceptance of bishop and priest could no longer be taken for granted. And yet there was no place for Catholic lay people in the structure and governance of the Church. Similarly, all Roman Catholic dioceses in the United States, beginning around 1965 or 1970, faced a sharp drop in the number of young men entering the priesthood—and perceived this as a major threat. Only one Catholic archdiocese saw both as opportunities. (As a result, it has a different problem. Young priests from all over the United States want to enter it; for in this one archdiocese, the priest gets to do the things he trained for, the things which he entered the priesthood to do.)

All American hospitals, beginning in 1970 or 1975, saw changes coming in the delivery of health care. Most of them organized themselves to fight these changes. Most of them told everybody that "these changes will be catastrophic." Only the one hospital saw in them opportunities.

The American Association for the Advancement of Science saw in the expansion of people with scientific backgrounds and working in scientific pursuits a tremendous opportunity to establish itself as a leader, both within the scientific community and outside.

And the Girl Scouts looked at demographics and said: "How can we convert population trends into new opportunities for us?"

Even in government, innovation is possible if simple rules are obeyed. Here is one example.

Lincoln, Nebraska, 120 years ago, was the first city in the Western world to take into municipal ownership public services such as public transportation, electric power, gas, water, and so on. In the last ten years, under a woman mayor, Helen Boosalis, it has begun to privatize such services as garbage pickup, school transportation, and a host of others. The city provides the money, with private businesses bidding for the contracts; there are substantial savings in cost and even greater improvements in service.

What Helen Boosalis has seen in Lincoln is the opportunity to separate the "provider" of public services, that is, government, and the "supplier." This makes possible both high service standards and the efficiency, reliability, and low cost which competition can provide.

The four rules outlined above constitute the *specific* policies and practices the public-service institution requires if it is to make itself entrepreneurial and capable of innovation. In addition, however, it also needs to adopt those policies and practices that any existing organization requires in order to be entrepreneurial, the policies and practices discussed in the preceding chapter, The Entrepreneurial Business.

III

The Need to Innovate

Why is innovation in the public-service institution so important? Why cannot we leave existing public-service institutions the way they are, and depend for the innovations we need in the public-service sector on new institutions, as historically we have always done?

The answer is that public-service institutions have become too important in developed countries, and too big. The public-service sector, both the governmental one and the nongovernmental but not-for-profit one, has grown faster during this century than the private sector— maybe three to five times as fast. The growth has been especially fast since World War II.

To some extent, this growth has been excessive. Wherever public-service activities can be converted into profit-making enterprises, they should be so converted. This applies not only to the kind of municipal services the city of Lincoln, Nebraska, now "privatizes." The move from non-profit to profit has already gone very far in the American hospital.I expect it to become a stampede in professional and graduate education. To subsidize the highest earners in developed society, the holders of advanced professional degrees, can hardly be justified.

A central economic problem of developed societies during the next twenty or thirty years is surely going to be capital formation; only in Japan is it still adequate for the economy's needs. We therefore can ill afford to have activities conducted as "non-profit," that is, as activities that devour capital rather than form it, if they can be organized as activities that form capital, as activities that make a profit.

But still the great bulk of the activities that are being discharged in and by public-service institutions will remain public-service activities, and will neither disappear nor be transformed. Consequently, they have to be made producing and productive. Public-service institutions will have to learn to be innovators, to manage themselves entrepreneurially. To achieve this, public-service institutions will have to learn to look upon social, technological, economic, and demographic shifts as opportunities in a period of rapid change in all these areas. Otherwise, they will become obstacles. The public-service institutions will increasingly become unable to discharge their mission as they adhere to programs and projects that cannot work in a changed environment, and yet they will not be able or willing to abandon the missions they can no longer discharge. Increasingly, they will come to look the way the feudal barons came to look after they had lost all social function around 1300: as parasites, functionless, with nothing left but the power to obstruct and to exploit. They will become self-righteous while increasingly losing their legitimacy. Clearly, this is already happening to the apparently most powerful among them, the labor union. Yet a society in rapid change, with new challenges, new requirements and opportunities, needs public-service institutions.

The public school in the United States exemplifies both the opportunity and the dangers. Unless it takes the lead in innovation it is unlikely to survive this century, except as a school for the minorities in the slums. For the first time in its history, the United States faces the threat of a class structure in education in which all but the very poor remain outside of the public school system—at least in the cities and suburbs where most of the population lives. And this will squarely be the fault of the public school itself because what is needed to reform the public school is already known (see Chapter 9).

Many other public-service institutions face a similar situation. The knowledge is there. The need to innovate is clear. They now have to learn how to build entrepreneurship and innovation into their own system. Otherwise, they will find themselves superseded by outsiders who will create competing entrepreneurial public-service institutions and so render the existing ones obsolete.

The late nineteenth century and early twentieth century was a period of tremendous creativity and innovation in the public-service field. Social innovation during the seventy-five years until the 1930s was surely as much alive, as productive, and as rapid as technological innovation if not more so. But in these periods the innovation took the form of creating new public-service institutions. Most of the ones we have around now go back no more than sixty or seventy years in their present form and with their present mission. The next twenty or thirty years will be very different. The need for social innovation may be even greater, but it will very largely have to be social innovation within the existing public-service institution. To build entrepreneurial management into the existing public-service institution may thus be the foremost political task of this generation.

CHAPTER 15

The New Venture

For the existing enterprise, whether business or public-service institution, the controlling word in the term "entrepreneurial management" is "entrepreneurial." For the new venture, it is "management." In the existing business, it is the existing that is the main obstacle to entrepreneurship. In the new venture, it is its absence.

The new venture has an idea. It may have a product or a service. It may even have sales, and sometimes quite a substantial volume of them. It surely has costs. And it may have revenues and even profits. What it does not have is a "business," a viable, operating, organized "present" in which people know where they are going, what they are supposed to do, and what the results are or should be. But unless a new venture develops into a new business and makes sure of being "managed," it will not survive no matter how brilliant the entrepreneurial idea, how much money it attracts, how good its products, nor even how great the demand for them.

Refusal to accept these facts destroyed every single venture started by the nineteenth century's greatest inventor, Thomas Edison. Edison's ambition was to be a successful businessman and the head of a big company. He should have succeeded, for he was a superb business planner. He knew exactly how an electric power company had to be set up to exploit his invention of the light bulb. He knew exactly how to get all the money he could possibly need for his ventures. His products were immediate successes and the demand for them practically insatiable. But Edison remained an entrepreneur; or rather, he thought that "managing" meant being the boss. He refused to build a management team. And so every one of his four or five companies collapsed ignominiously once it got to middle size, and was saved only by booting Edison himself out and replacing him with professional management.

Entrepreneurial management in the new venture has four requirements:

It requires, first, a focus on the market.

It requires, second, financial foresight, and especially planning for cash flow and capital needs ahead.

It requires, third, building a top management team long before the new venture actually needs one and long before it can actually afford one.

And finally, it requires of the founding entrepreneur a decision in respect to his or her own role, area of work, and relationships.

I

The Need for Market Focus

A common explanation for the failure of a new venture to live up to its promise or even to survive at all is: "We were doing fine until these other people came and took our market away from us. We don't really understand it. What they offered wasn't so very different from what we had." Or one hears: "We were doing all right, but these other people started selling to customers we'd never even heard of and all of a sudden they had the market."

When a new venture does succeed, more often than not it is in a market other than the one it was originally intended to serve, with products or services not quite those with which it had set out, bought in large part by customers it did not even think of when it started, and used for a host of purposes besides the ones for which the products were first designed. If a new venture does not anticipate this, organizing itself to take advantage of the unexpected and unseen markets; if it is not totally market-focused, if not market-driven, then it will succeed only in creating an opportunity for a competitor.

There are exceptions, to be sure. A product designed for one specific use, especially if scientific or technical, often stays with the market and the end use for which it was designed. But not always. Even a prescription drug designed for a specific ailment and tested for it sometimes ends up being used for some other quite different ailment. One example is a compound that is effectively used in the treatment of stomach ulcers. Or a drug designed primarily for the treatment of human beings may find its major market in veterinary medicine.

Anything genuinely new creates markets that nobody before even imagined. No one knew that he needed an office copier before the first Xerox machine came out around 1960; five years later no business could imagine doing without a copier. When the first jet planes started to fly, the best market research pointed out that there were not even enough passengers for all the transatlantic liners then in service or being built. Five years later the transatlantic jets were carrying fifty to one hundred times as many passengers each year as had ever before crossed the Atlantic.

The innovator has limited vision, in fact, he has tunnel-vision. He sees the area with which he is familiar—to the exclusion of all other areas.

An example is DDT. Designed during World War II to protect American soldiers against tropical insects and parasites, it eventually found its greatest application in agriculture to protect livestock and crops against insects—to the point where it had to be banned for being too effective. Yet not one of the distinguished scientists who designed DDT during World War II envisaged these uses of DDT. Of course they knew that babies die from fly-borne "summer" diarrhea. Of course they knew that livestock and crops are infested by insect parasites. But these things they knew as laymen. As experts, they were concerned with the tropical diseases of humans. It was the ordinary American soldier who then applied DDT to the areas in which he was the "expert," that is, to his home, his cows, his cotton patch.

Similarly, the 3M Company did not see that an adhesive tape it had developed for industry would find myriad uses in the household and in the office—becoming Scotch Tape. 3M had for many years been a supplier of abrasives and adhesives to industry, and moderately successful in industrial markets. It had never even thought of consumer markets. It was pure accident which led the engineer who had designed an industrial product no industrial user wanted to the realization that the stuff might be salable in the consumer market. As the story goes, he took some samples home when the company had already decided to abandon the product. To his surprise, his teenage daughters began to use it to hold their curls overnight. The only unusual thing about this story is that he and his bosses at 3M recognized that they had stumbled upon a new market.

A German chemist developed Novocain as the first local anesthetic in 1905. But he could not get the doctors to use it; they preferred total anesthesia (they only accepted Novocain during World War I). But totally unexpectedly, dentists began to use the stuff. Whereupon—or so the story goes—the chemist began to travel up and down Germany making speeches against Novocain's use in dentistry. He had not designed it for that purpose!

That reaction was somewhat extreme, I admit. Still, entrepreneurs *know* what their innovation is meant to do. And if some other use for it appears, they tend to resent it. They may not actually refuse to serve customers they have not "planned" for, but they are likely to make it clear that these customers are not welcome.

This is what happened with the computer. The company that had the first computer, Univac, knew that its magnificent machine was designed for scientific work. And so it did not even send a salesman out when a business showed interest in it; surely, it argued, these people could not possibly know what a computer was all about. IBM was equally convinced that the computer was an instrument for scientific work: their own computer had been designed specifically for astronomical calculations. But IBM was willing to take orders from businesses and to serve them. Ten years later, around 1960, Univac still had by far the most advanced and best machine. IBM had the computer market.

The textbook prescription for this problem is "market research." But it is the wrong prescription.

One cannot do market research for something genuinely new. One cannot do market research for something that is not yet on the market. Around 1950, Univac's market research concluded that, by the year 2000, about one thousand computers would be sold; the actual figure in 1984 was about one million. And yet this was the most "scientific," careful, rigorous market research ever done. There was only one thing wrong with it: it started out with the assumption, then shared by everyone, that computers were going to be used for advanced scientific work —and for that use, the number is indeed quite limited. Similarly, several companies who turned down the Xerox patents did so on the basis of thorough market research which showed that printers had no use at all for a copier. Nobody had any inkling that businesses, schools, universities, colleges, and a host of private individuals would want to buy a copier.

The new venture therefore needs to start out, with the assumption that its product or service may find customers in markets no one thought of, for uses no one envisaged when the product or service was designed, and that it will be bought by customers outside its field of vision and even unknown to the new venture.

If the new venture does not have such a market focus from the very beginning, all it is likely to create is the market for a competitor. A few years later "those people" will come in and take away "our market," or "those other people" who started "selling to customers we'd never even heard of" all of a sudden will indeed have preempted the market.

To build market focus into a new venture is not in fact particularly difficult. But what is required runs counter to the inclinations of the typical entrepreneur. It requires, first, that the new venture systematically hunt out both the unexpected success and the unexpected failure (cf. Chapter 3). Rather than dismiss the unexpected as an "exception," as entrepreneurs are inclined to do, they need to go out and look at it carefully and as a distinct opportunity.

Shortly after World War II, a small Indian engineering firm bought the license to produce a European-designed bicycle with an auxiliary light engine. It looked like an ideal product for India; yet it never did well. The owner of this small firm noticed, however, that substantial orders came in for the engines alone. At first he wanted to turn down those orders; what could anyone possibly do with such a small engine? It was curiosity alone that made him go to the actual area the orders came from. There he found farmers were taking the engines off the bicycles and using them to power irrigation pumps that hitherto had been hand-operated. This manufacturer is now the world's largest maker of small irrigation pumps, selling them by the millions. His pumps have revolutionized farming all over Southeast Asia.

To be market-driven also requires that the new venture be willing to experiment. If there is any interest in the new venture's product or service on the part of consumers or markets that were not in the original plan, one tries to find somebody in that new and unexpected area who might be willing to test the new product or service and find out what, if any, application it might have. One provides free samples to people in the "improbable" market to see what they can do with it, whether they can use the stuff at all, or what it would have to be like for them to become customers for it. One advertises in the trade papers of the industry whence indications of interest came, and so on.

The DuPont Company never thought of automobile tires as a major application for the new Nylon fiber it had developed. But when one of the Akron tire manufacturers showed interest in trying out Nylon, DuPont set up a plant. A few years later, tires had become Nylon's biggest and most profitable market.

It does not require a great deal of money to find out whether an unexpected interest from an unexpected market is an indication of genuine potential or a fluke. It requires sensitivity and a little systematic work.

Above all, the people who are running a new venture need to spend time outside: in the marketplace, with customers and with their own salesmen, looking and listening. The new venture needs to build in systematic practices to remind itself that a "product" or a "service" is defined by the customer, not by the producer. It needs to work continuously on challenging itself in respect to the utility and value that its products or services contribute to customers.

The greatest danger for the new venture is to "know better" than the customer what the product or service is or should be, how it should be bought, and what it should be used for. Above all, the new venture needs willingness to see the unexpected success as an opportunity rather than as an affront to its expertise. And it needs to accept that elementary axiom of marketing: Businesses are not paid to reform customers. They are paid to satisfy customers.

II

Financial Foresight

Lack of market focus is typically a disease of the "neo-natal," the infant new venture. It is the most serious affliction of the new venture in its early stages—and one that can permanently stunt even those that survive.

The lack of adequate financial focus and of the right financial policies is, by contrast, the greatest threat to the new venture in the next stage of its growth. It is, above all, a threat to the rapidly growing new venture. The more successful a new venture is, the more dangerous the lack of financial foresight.

Suppose that a new venture has successfully launched its product or service and is growing fast. It reports "rapidly increasing profits" and issues rosy forecasts. The stock market then "discovers" the new venture, especially if it is high-tech or in a field otherwise currently fashionable. Predictions abound that the new venture's sales will reach a billion dollars within five years. Eighteen months later, the new venture collapses. It may not go out of existence or go bankrupt. But it is suddenly awash in red ink, lays off 184 of its 275 employees, fires the president, or is sold at a bargain price to a big company. The causes are always the same: lack of cash; inability to raise the capital needed for expansion; and loss of control, with expenses, inventories, and receivables in disarray. These three financial afflictions often hit together at the same time. Yet any one of them by itself endangers the health, if not the life, of the new venture.

Once this financial crisis has erupted, it can be cured only with great difficulty and considerable suffering. But it is eminently preventable.

Entrepreneurs starting new ventures are rarely unmindful of money; on the contrary, they tend to be greedy. They therefore focus on profits. But this is the wrong focus for a new venture, or rather, it comes last rather than first. Cash flow, capital, and controls come much earlier. Without them, the profit figures are fiction—good for twelve to eighteen months, perhaps, after which they evaporate.

Growth has to be fed. In financial terms this means that growth in a new venture demands adding financial resources rather than taking them out. Growth needs more cash and more capital. If the growing new venture shows a "profit" it is a fiction: a bookkeeping entry put in only to balance the accounts. And since taxes are payable on this fiction in most countries, it creates a liability and a cash drain rather than "surplus." The healthier a new venture and the faster it grows, the more financial feeding it requires. The new ventures that are the darlings of the newspapers and the stock market letters, the new ventures that show rapid profit growth and "record profits," are those most likely to run into desperate trouble a couple of years later.

The new venture needs cash flow analysis, cash flow forecasts, and cash management. The fact that America's new ventures of the last few years (with the significant exception of high-tech companies) have been doing so much better than new ventures used to do is largely because the new entrepreneurs in the United States have learned that entrepreneurship demands financial management.

Cash management is fairly easy if there are reliable cash flow forecasts, with "reliable" meaning "worst case" assumptions rather than hopes. There is an old banker's rule of thumb, according to which in forecasting cash income and cash outlays one assumes that bills will have to be paid sixty days earlier than expected and receivables will come in sixty days later. If the forecast is overly conservative, the worst that can happen—it rarely does in a growing new venture—is a temporary cash surplus.

A growing new venture should know twelve months ahead of time how much cash it will need, when, and for what purposes. With a year's lead time, it is almost always possible to finance cash needs. But even if a new venture is doing well, raising cash in a hurry and in a "crisis" is never easy and always prohibitively expensive. Above all, it always sidetracks the key people in the company at the most critical time. For several months they then spend their time and energy running from one financial institution to another and cranking out one set of questionable financial projections after another. In the end, they usually have to mortgage the long-range future of the business to get through a ninety-day cash bind. When they finally are able again to devote time and thought to the business, they have irrevocably missed the major opportunities. For the new venture, almost by definition, is under cash pressure when the opportunities are greatest.

The successful new venture will also outgrow its capital structure. A rule of thumb with a good deal of empirical evidence to support it says that a new venture outgrows its capital base with every increase in sales (or billings) of the order of 40 to 50 percent. After such growth, a new venture also needs a new and different capital structure, as a rule. As the venture grows, private sources of funds, whether from the owners and their families or from outsiders, become inadequate. The company has to find access to much larger pools of money by going "public," by finding a partner or partners among established companies, or by raising money from insurance companies and pension funds. A new venture that had been financed by equity money now needs to shift to long-term debt, or vice versa. As the venture grows, the existing capital structure always becomes the wrong structure and an obstacle.

In some new ventures, capital planning is comparatively easy. When the business consists of uniform and entirely local units—restaurants in a chain, freestanding surgical centers or individual hospitals in different cities, homebuilders with separate operations in a number of different metropolitan areas, specialty stores and the like—each unit can be financed as a separate business. One solution is franchising (which is, in essence, a way to finance rapid expansion). Another is setting up each local unit as a company, with separate and often local investors as "limited" partners. The capital needed for growth and expansion can thus be raised step by step, and the success of the preceding unit furnishes documentation and the incentive for the investors in the succeeding ones. But it only works when: (a) each unit breaks even fairly soon, at most perhaps within two or three years; (b) when the operation can be made routine, so that people of limited managerial competence — the typical franchise holder, or the business manager of a local freestanding surgical center—can do a decent job without much supervision; and (c) when the individual unit itself reaches fairly swiftly the optimum size beyond which it does not require further capital but produces cash surplus to help finance the startup of additional units.

For new ventures other than those capable of being financed as separate units, capital planning is a survival necessity. If a growing new venture plans realistically—and that again means assuming the maximum rather than the minimum need—for its capital requirement and its capital structure three years ahead, it should normally have little difficulty in obtaining the kind of money it needs, when it needs it, and in the form in which it needs it. If it waits until it outgrows its capital base and its capital structure, it is putting its survival—and most assuredly its independence—on the block. At the very least, the founders will find that they have taken all the entrepreneurial risk and worked hard only to make other people the rich owners. From being owners, they will have become employees, with the new investors taking control.

Finally, the new venture needs to plan the financial system it requires to manage growth. Again and again, a growing new venture starts off with an excellent product, excellent standing in its market, and excellent growth prospects. Then suddenly everything goes out of control: receivables, inventory, manufacturing costs, administrative costs, service, distribution, everything. Once one area gets out of control, all of them do. The enterprise has outgrown its control structure. By the time control has been reestablished, markets have been lost, customers have become disgruntled if not hostile, distributors have lost their confidence in the company. Worst of all, employees have lost trust in management, and with good reason.

Fast growth always makes obsolete the existing controls. Again, a growth of 40 to 50 percent in volume seems to be the critical figure.

Once control has been lost, it is hard to recapture. Yet the loss of control can be prevented quite easily. What is needed is first to think through the critical areas in a given enterprise. In one, it may be product quality; in another, service; in a third, receivables and inventory; in a fourth, manufacturing costs. Rarely are there more than four or five critical areas in any given enterprise. (Managerial and administrative overhead should, however, always be included. A disproportionate and fast increase in the percentage of revenues absorbed by managerial and administrative overhead, which means that the enterprise hires managerial and administrative people faster than it actually grows, is usually the first sign that a business is getting out of control, that its management structure and practices are no longer adequate to the task.)

To live up to its growth expectations, a new venture must establish today the controls in these critical areas it will need three years hence. Elaborate controls are not necessary nor does it matter that the figures are only approximate. What matters is that the management of the new venture is aware of these critical areas, is being reminded of them, and can thus act fast if the need arises. Disarray normally does not appear if there is adequate attention to the key areas. Then the new venture will have the controls it needs when it needs them.

Financial foresight does not require a great deal of time. It does require a good deal of thought, however. The technical tools to do the job are easily available; they are spelled out in most texts on managerial accounting. But the work will have to be done by the enterprise itself.

III

Building a Top Management Team

The new venture has successfully established itself in the right market and has then successfully found the financial structure and the financial system it needs. Nonetheless, a few years later it is still prone to run into a serious crisis. Just when it appears to be on the threshold of becoming an "adult"—a successful, established, going concern—it gets into trouble nobody seems to understand. The products are first-rate, the prospects are excellent, and yet the business simply cannot grow.

Neither profitability nor quality, nor any of the other major areas performs.

The reason is always the same: a lack of top management. The business has outgrown being managed by one person, or even two people, and it now needs a management team at the top. If it does not have one already in place at the time, it is very late—in fact, usually too late. The best one can then hope is that the business will survive. But it is likely to be permanently crippled or to suffer scars that will bleed for many years to come. Morale has been shattered and employees throughout the company are disillusioned and cynical. And the people who founded the business and built it almost always end up on the outside, embittered and disenchanted.

The remedy is simple: To build a top management team *before* the venture reaches the point where it must have one. Teams cannot be formed overnight. They require long periods before they can function. Teams are based on mutual trust and mutual understanding, and this takes years to build up. In my experience, three years is about the minimum.

But the small and growing new venture cannot afford a top management team; it cannot sustain half a dozen people with big titles and corresponding salaries. In fact, in the small and growing business, a very small number of people do everything as it comes along. How, then, can one square this circle?

Again, the remedy is relatively simple. But it does require the will on the part of the founders to build a team rather than to keep on running everything themselves. If one or two people at the top believe that they, and they alone, must do everything, then a management crisis a few months, or at the latest, a few years down the road becomes inevitable.

Whenever the objective economic indicators of a new venture— market surveys, for instance, or demographic analysis—indicate that the business may double within three or five years, then it is the duty of the founder or founders to build the management team the new venture will very soon require. This is preventive medicine, so to speak.

First of all the founders, together with other key people in the firm, will have to think through the key activities of their business. What are the specific areas upon which the survival and success of this particular business depend? Most of the areas will be on everyone's list. But if there are divergencies and dissents—and there should be on a question as important as this—they should be taken seriously. Every activity which any member of the group thinks belongs there should go down on the list.

The key activities are not to be found in books. They emerge from analysis of the specific enterprise. Two enterprises that to an outsider appear to be in an identical line of business may well end up defining their key activities quite differently. One, for instance, may put production in the center; the other, customer service. Only two key activities are always present in any organization: there is always the management of people and there is always the management of money. The rest has to be determined by the people within looking at the enterprise and at their own jobs, values, and goals.

The next step is, then, for each member of the group, beginning with the founder, to ask: "What are the activities that *I* am doing well? And what are the activities that each of my key associates in this business is actually doing well?" Again, there is going to be agreement on most of the people and on most of their strengths. But, again, any disagreement should be taken seriously.

Next, one asks: "Which of the key activities should each of us, therefore, take on as his or her first and major responsibility because they fit the individual's strengths? Which individual fits which key activity?"

Then the work on building a team can begin. The founder starts to discipline himself (or herself) not to handle people and their problems, if this is not the key activity that fits him best. Perhaps this individual's key strength is new products and new technology. Perhaps this individual's key activity is operations, manufacturing, physical distribution, service. Or perhaps it is money and finance and someone else had better handle people. But all key activities need to be covered by someone who has proven ability in performance.

There is no rule that says "A chief executive has to be in charge of this or that." Of course a chief executive is the court of last resort and has ultimate accountability. And the chief executive also has to make sure of getting the information necessary to discharge this ultimate accountability. The chief executive's own *work*, however, depends on what the enterprise requires and on who the individual is. As long as the CEO's work program consists of key activities, he or she does a CEO's job. But the CEO also is responsible for making sure that all the other key activities are adequately covered.

Finally, goals and objectives for each area need to be set. Everyone who takes on the primary responsibility for a key activity, whether product development or people, or money, must be asked: "What can this enterprise expect of *you*? What should we hold *you* accountable for? What are *you* trying to accomplish and by what time?" But this is elementary management, of course.

It is prudent to establish the top management team informally at first. There is no need to give people titles in a new and growing venture, nor to make announcements, nor even to pay extra. All this can wait a year or so, until it is clear that the new setup works, and how. In the meantime, all the members of the team have much to learn: their job; how they work together; and what they have to do to enable the CEO and their colleagues to do their jobs. Two or three years later, when the growing venture needs a top management, it has one.

However, should it fail to provide for a top management before it actually needs one, it will lose the capacity to manage itself long before it actually needs a top management team. The founder will have become so overloaded that important tasks will not get done. At this point the company can go one of two ways. The first possibility is that the founder concentrates on the one or two areas that fit his or her abilities and interests. These are key areas indeed, but they are not the only crucial ones, and no one is then left to look after the others. Two years later, important areas have been slighted and the business is in dire straits. The other, worse, possibility is that the founder is conscientious. He knows that people and money are key activities and need to be taken care of. His own abilities and interests, which actually built the business, are in the design and development of new products. But being conscientious, the founder forces himself to take care of people and finance. Since he is not very gifted in either area, he does poorly in both. It also takes him forever to reach decisions or to do any work in these areas, so that he is forced, by lack of time, to neglect what he is really good at and what the company depends on him for, the development of new technology and new products. Three years later the company will have become an empty shell without the products it needs, but also without the management of people and the management of money it needs.

In the first example, it may be possible to save the company. After all, it has the products. But the founder will inevitably be removed by whoever comes in to salvage the company. In the second case, the company usually cannot be saved at all and has to be sold or liquidated.

Long before it has reached the point where it needs the balance of a top management team, the new venture has to create one. Long before the time has come at which management by one person no longer works and becomes mismanagement, that one person also has to start learning how to work with colleagues, has to learn to trust people, yet also how to hold them accountable. The founder has to learn to become the leader of a team rather than a "star" with "helpers."

IV

"Where Can I Contribute?"

Building a top management team may be the single most important step toward entrepreneurial management in the new venture. It is only the first step, however, for the founders themselves, who then have to think through what their own future is to be.

As a new venture develops and grows, the roles and relationships of the original entrepreneurs inexorably change. If the founders refuse to accept this, they will stunt the business and may even destroy it.

Every founder-entrepreneur nods to this and says, "Amen." Everyone has horror stories of other founder-entrepreneurs who did not change as the venture changed, and who then destroyed both the business and themselves. But even among the founders who can accept that they themselves need to do something, few know how to tackle changing their own roles and relationships. They tend to begin by asking: "What do I like to do?" Or at best, "Where do I fit in?" The right question to start with is: "What will the venture need *objectively* by way of management from here on out?" And in a growing new venture, the founder has to ask this question whenever the business (or the public-service institution) grows significantly or changes direction or character, that is, changes its products, services, markets, or the kind of people it needs.

The next question the founder must ask is: "What am I good at? What, of all these needs of the venture, could I supply, and supply with distinction?" Only after having thought through these two questions should a founder then ask: "What do I really want to do, and believe in doing? What am I willing to spend years on, if not the rest of my life? Is this something the venture really needs? Is it a major, essential, indispensable contribution?"

One example is that of the successful American post-World War II metropolitan university, Pace, in New York City. Dr. Edward Mortola built up the institution from nothing in 1947 into New York City's third-largest and fastest-growing university, with 25,000 students and well-regarded graduate schools. In the university's early years he was a radical innovator. But when Pace was still very small (around 1950), Mortola built a strong top management team. All members were given a major, clearly defined responsibility, for which they were expected to take full accountability and give leadership. A few years later, Mortola then decided what his own role was to be and converted himself into a traditional university president, while at the same time building a strong independent board of trustees to advise and support him.

But the questions of what a venture needs, what the strengths of the founder-entrepreneur are, and what he or she wants to do, might be answered quite differently.

Edwin Land, for instance, the man who invented Polaroid glass and the Polaroid camera, ran the company during the first twelve or fifteen years of its life, until the early 1950s. Then it began to grow fast. Land thereupon designed a top management team and put it in place. As for himself, he decided that he was not the right man for the top management job in the company: what he and he alone could contribute was scientific innovation. Accordingly, Land built himself a laboratory and established himself as the company's consulting director for basic research. The company itself, in its day-to-day operations, he left to others to run.

Ray Kroc, the man who conceived and built McDonald's, reached a similar conclusion. He remained president until he died well past age eighty. But he put a top management team in place to run the company and appointed himself the company's "marketing conscience." Until shortly before his death, he visited two or three McDonald's restaurants each week, checking their quality carefully, the level of cleanliness and friendliness. Above all, he looked at the customers, talked to them and listened to them. This enabled the company to make the necessary changes to retain its leadership in the fast-food industry.

Similarly, in a much smaller new venture, a building supply company in the Pacific Northwest of the United States, the young man who built the company decided that his role was not to run the company but to develop its critical resource, the managers who are responsible for its two hundred branches in small towns and suburbs. These managers are in effect running their own local business. They are supported by strong services in headquarters: central buying, quality control, control of credit and receivables, and so on. But the selling is done by each manager, locally and with very little help—maybe one salesman and a couple of truck drivers.

The business depends on the motivation, drive, ability, and enthusiasm of these isolated, fairly unsophisticated individuals. None of them has a college degree and few have even finished high school. So the founder of this company makes it his business to spend twelve to fifteen days each month in the field visiting branch managers, spending half a day with them, discussing their business, their plans, their aspirations. This may well be the only distinction the company has— otherwise, every other building materials wholesaler does the same things. But this performance of the one key activity by the chief executive has enabled the company to grow three to four times as fast as any competitor, even in recession times.

Yet another quite different answer to the same question was given by the three scientists who, together, founded what has become one of the largest and most successful companies in the semiconductor industry. When they asked themselves, "What are the needs of the business?" the answer was that there were three: "One for basic business strategy, one for scientific research and development, and one for the development of people—especially scientific and technical people." They decided which of the three was most suited for each of these assignments, and then divided them according to their strengths. The person who took the human relations and human development job had actually been a prolific scientific innovator and had high standing in scientific circles. But he decided, and his colleagues concurred, that he was superbly fitted for the managerial, the people task, so he took it. "It was not," he once said in a speech, "what I really wanted to do, but it was where I could make the greatest contribution."

These questions may not always lead to such happy endings. They may even lead to the decision to leave the company.

In one of the most successful new financial services ventures in the United States, this is what the founder concluded. He did establish a top management team. He asked what the company needed. He looked at himself and his strengths; and he found no match between the needs of the company and his own abilities, let alone between the needs of the company and the things he wanted to do. "I trained my own successor for about eighteen months, then turned the company over to him and resigned," he said. Since then he has started three new businesses, not one of them in finance, has developed them successfully to medium size, and then quit again. He wants to develop new businesses but does not enjoy running them. He accepts that both the businesses and he are better off divorced from one another.

Other entrepreneurs in this same situation might reach different conclusions. The founder of a well-known medical clinic, a leader in its particular field, faced a similar dilemma. The needs of the institution were for an administrator and money-raiser. His own inclinations were to be a researcher and a clinician. But he realized that he was good at raising money and capable of learning to be the chief executive officer of a fairly large health-care organization. "And so," he says, "I felt it my duty to the venture I had created, and to my associates in it, to suppress my own desires and to take on the job of chief administrator and money-raiser. But I would never have done so had I not known that I had the abilities to do the job, and if my advisors and my board had not all assured me that I had these abilities."

The question, "Where do *I* belong?" needs to be faced up to and thought through by the founder-entrepreneur as soon as the venture shows the first signs of success. But the question can be faced up to much earlier. Indeed, it might be best thought through before the new venture is even started.

This is what Soichiro Honda, the founder and builder of Honda Motor Company in Japan, did when he decided to open a small business in the darkest days after Japan's defeat in World War II. He did not start his venture until he had found the right man to be his partner and to run administration, finance, distribution, marketing, sales, and personnel. For Honda had decided from the outset that he belonged in engineering and production and would not run anything else. This decision made the Honda Motor Company.

There is an earlier and even more instructive example, that of Henry Ford. When Ford decided in 1903 to go into business for himself, he did exactly what

Honda did forty years later: before starting, he found the right man to be his partner and to run the areas where Ford knew he did not belong—administration, finance, distribution, marketing, sales, and personnel. Like Honda, Henry Ford knew that he belonged in engineering and manufacturing and was going to confine himself to these two areas. The man he found, James Couzens, [⊖] contributed as much as Ford to the success of the company. Many of the best known policies and practices of the Ford Motor Company for which Henry Ford is often given credit—the famous $5-a-day wage of 1913, or the pioneering distribution and service policies, for example —were Couzens's ideas and at first resisted by Ford. So effective did Couzens become that Ford grew increasingly jealous of him and forced him out in 1917. The last straw was Couzens's insistence that the Model T was obsolescent and his proposal to use some of the huge profits of the company to start work on a successor.

The Ford Motor Company grew and prospered to the very day of Couzens's resignation. Within a few short months thereafter, as soon as Henry Ford had taken every single top management function into his own hands, forgetting that he had known earlier where he belonged, the Ford Motor Company began its long decline. Henry Ford clung to the Model T for a full ten years, until it had become literally unsalable. And the company's decline was not reversed for thirty years after Couzens's dismissal until, with his grandfather dying, a very young Henry Ford II took over the practically bankrupt business.

The Need for Outside Advice

These last cases point up an important factor for the entrepreneur in the new and growing venture, the need for independent, objective outside advice.

The growing new venture may not need a formal board of directors. Moreover, the typical board of directors very often does not provide the advice and counsel the founder needs. But the founder does need people with whom he can discuss basic decisions and to whom he listens. Such people are rarely to be found within the enterprise. Somebody has to challenge the founder's appraisal of the needs of the venture, and of his own personal strengths. Someone who is not a part of the problem has to ask questions, to review decisions and, above all, to push constantly to have the long-term survival needs of the new venture satisfied by building in the market focus, supplying financial foresight, and creating a functioning top

---

[⊖]   Who later became mayor of Detroit and senator from Michigan, and might well have become President of the United States had he not been born in Canada.

management team. This is the final requirement of entrepreneurial management in the new venture.

The new venture that builds such entrepreneurial management into its policies and practices will become a flourishing large business. [⊖]

In so many new ventures, especially high-tech ventures, the techniques discussed in this chapter are spurned and even despised. The argument is that they constitute "management" and "We are entrepreneurs." But this is not informality; it is irresponsibility. It confuses manners and substance. It is old wisdom that there is no freedom except under the law. Freedom without law is license, which soon degenerates into anarchy, and shortly thereafter into tyranny. It is precisely because the new venture has to maintain and strengthen the entrepreneurial spirit that it needs foresight and discipline. It needs to prepare itself for the demands its own success will make of it. Above all, it needs responsibility —and this, in the last analysis, is what entrepreneurial management supplies to the new venture.

There is much more that could be said about managing the new venture, about financing, staffing, marketing its products, and so on. But these specifics are adequately covered in a number of publications. [⊖] What this chapter has tried to do is to identify and discuss the few fairly simple policies that are crucial to the survival and success of any new venture, whether a business or a public-service institution, whether "high-tech," "low-tech," or "no-tech," whether started by one man or woman or by a group, and whether intended to remain a small business or to become "another IBM."

[⊖] A fine description of this process is to be found in *High-Output Management* (New York: Random House, 1983), by Andrew S. Grove, co-founder and president of Intel, one of the largest manufacturers of semiconductors.

[⊖] For some of these, see the Suggested Readings at the back of this book.

3

ENTREPRENEURIAL STRATEGIES

Just as entrepreneurship requires entrepreneurial management, that is, practices and policies within the enterprise, so it requires practices and policies outside, in the marketplace. It requires entrepreneurial strategies.

CHAPTER 16

"Fustest with the Mostest"

Of late, "strategy in business" ⊖ has become the "in" word, with any number of books written about it. ⊖ However, I have not come across any discussion of entrepreneurial strategies. Yet they are important; they are distinct; and they are different.

There are four specifically entrepreneurial strategies:

1. Being "Fustest with the Mostest";
2. "Hitting Them Where They Ain't";
3. Finding and occupying a specialized "ecological niche";

⊖ The 1952 edition of the *Concise Oxford Dictionary* still defined strategy as: "Generalship; the art of war; management of an army or armies in a campaign." Alfred D. Chandler, Jr., first applied the term to the conduct of a business in 1962 in his pioneering *Strategy and Structure* (Cambridge, Mass.: M.I.T. Press), which studied the evolution of management in the big corporation. But shortly thereafter, in 1963, when I wrote the first analysis of business strategy, the publisher and I found that the word could not be used in the title without risk of serious misunderstanding. Booksellers, magazine editors, and senior business executives all assured us that "strategy" for them meant the conduct of military or election campaigns. The book discussed most that is now considered "strategy." It uses the word in the text. But the title we chose was *Managing for Results*.

⊖ Of which I have found Michael Porter's *Competitive Strategies* (New York: Free Press, 1980) the most useful.

4. Changing the economic characteristics of a product, a market, or an industry.

These four strategies are not mutually exclusive. One and the same entrepreneur often combines two, sometimes even elements of three, in one strategy. They are also not always sharply differentiated; the same strategy might, for instance, be classified as "Hitting Them Where They Ain't" or as "Finding and occupying a specialized 'ecological niche.'" Still, each of these four has its prerequisites. Each fits certain kinds of innovation and does not fit others. Each requires specific behavior on the part of the entrepreneur. Finally, each has its own limitations and carries its own risks.

I

Being "Fustest with the Mostest"

Being "Fustest with the Mostest" was how a Confederate cavalry general in America's Civil War explained consistently winning his battles. In this strategy the entrepreneur aims at leadership, if not at dominance of a new market or a new industry. Being "Fustest with the Mostest" does not necessarily aim at creating a big business right away, though often this is indeed the aim. But it aims from the start at a permanent leadership position.

Being "Fustest with the Mostest" is the approach that many people consider the entrepreneurial strategy *par excellence*. Indeed, if one were to go by the popular books on entrepreneurs, [⊖] one would conclude that being "Fustest with the Mostest" is the only entrepreneurial strategy—and a good many entrepreneurs, especially the high-tech ones, seem to be of the same opinion.

They are wrong, however. To be sure, a good many entrepreneurs have indeed chosen this strategy. Yet being "Fustest with the Mostest" is not even the dominant entrepreneurial strategy, let alone the one with the lowest risk or the highest success ratio. On the contrary, of all entrepreneurial strategies it is the greatest gamble. And it is unforgiving, making no allowances for mistakes and permitting no second chance.

But if successful, being "Fustest with the Mostest" is highly rewarding.

Here are some examples to show what this strategy consists of and what it requires.

Hoffmann-LaRoche of Basel, Switzerland, has for many years been the world's largest and in all probability its most profitable pharmaceutical company.

[⊖] E.g., George Gilder's *The Spirit of Enterprise* (New York: Simon & Schuster, 1984), perhaps the most readable recent example of the genre.

But its origins were quite humble: until the mid-1920s, Hoffmann-LaRoche was a small and struggling manufacturing chemist, making a few textile dyes. It was totally overshadowed by the huge German dye-stuff makers and two or three much bigger chemical firms in its own country. Then it gambled on the newly discovered vitamins at a time when the scientific world still could not quite accept that such substances existed. It acquired the vitamin patents—nobody else wanted them. It hired the discoverers away from Zürich University at several times the salaries they could hope to get as professors, salaries even industry had never paid before. And it invested all the money it had and all it could borrow in manufacturing and marketing these new substances.

Sixty years later, long after all vitamin patents have expired, Hoffmann-LaRoche has nearly half the world's vitamin market, now amounting to billions of dollars a year. The company followed the same strategy twice more: in the 1930s, when it went into the new sulfa drugs even though most scientists of the time "knew" that systemic drugs could not be effective against infections; and twenty years later, in the mid-fifties, when it went into the muscle-relaxing tranquilizers, Librium and Valium—at that time considered equally heretical and incompatible with what "every scientist knew."

DuPont followed the same strategy. When it came up with Nylon, the first truly synthetic fiber, after fifteen years of hard, frustrating research, DuPont at once mounted massive efforts, built huge plants, went into mass advertising—the company had never before had consumer products to advertise—and created the industry we now call plastics.

These are "big-company" stories, it will be said. But Hoffmann-LaRoche was not a big company when it started. And here are some more recent examples of companies that started from nothing with a strategy of getting there "Fustest with the Mostest."

The word processor is not much of a "scientific" invention. It hooks up three existing instruments: a typewriter, a display screen, and a fairly elementary computer. But this combination of existing elements has resulted in a genuine innovation that is radically changing office work. Dr. An Wang was a lone entrepreneur when he conceived of the combination some time in the mid-fifties. He had no track record as an entrepreneur and a minimum of financial backing. Yet he clearly aimed from the beginning at creating a new industry and at changing office work—and Wang Laboratories has, of course, become a very big company.

Similarly, the two young engineers who started the Apple computer in the proverbial garage, without financial backers or previous business experience, aimed from the beginning at creating an industry and dominating it.

Not every "Fustest with the Mostest" strategy needs to aim at creating a big business, though it must always aim at creating a business that dominates its market. The 3M Company in St. Paul, Minnesota, does not —as a matter of deliberate policy, it seems—attempt an innovation that might result in a big business by itself. Nor does Johnson & Johnson, the health-care and hygiene producer. Both companies are among the most fertile and most successful innovators. Both look for innovations that will lead to medium-sized rather than to giant enterprises, which are, however, dominant in their markets.

Being "Fustest with the Mostest" is not confined to businesses. It is also available to public-service institutions. When Wilhclm von Humboldt founded the University of Berlin in 1809—an event mentioned before in this book—he clearly aimed at being "Fustest with the Mostest." Prussia had just been defeated by Napoleon and had barely escaped total dismemberment. It was bankrupt, politically, militarily, and, above all, financially. It looked very much the way Germany was to look after Hitler's defeat in 1945. Yet Humboldt went out to build the largest university the Western world had ever seen or heard of—three to four times as large as anything then in existence. He went out to hire the leading scholars in every single discipline, beginning with the foremost philosopher of the time, Georg W. F. Hegel. And he paid his professors up to ten times as much as professors had ever been paid before, at a period when first-class scholars were going begging since the Napoleonic wars had forced many old and famous universities to disband.

A hundred years later, in the early years of this century, two surgeons in Rochester, an obscure Minnesota town far from population centers or medical schools, decided to establish a medical center based on totally new—and totally heretical—concepts of medical practice, and especially on building teams in which outstanding specialists would work together under a coordinating team leader. Frederick William Taylor, the so-called father of scientific management, had never met the Mayo Brothers. But in his well-known testimony before the Congress in 1911, he called the Mayo Clinic the "only complete and successful scientific management" he knew. These unknown provincial surgeons aimed from the beginning at dominance of the field, at attracting outstanding practitioners in every branch of medicine and the most gifted of the younger men, and at attracting also patients able and willing to pay what were then outrageous fees.

And twenty-five years later, the strategy of being "Fustest with the Mostest" was used by the March of Dimes to organize research into infantile paralysis (polio). Instead of aiming at gathering new knowledge step by step, as all earlier medical research had done, the March of Dimes aimed from the beginning at total victory over a completely mysterious disease. No one before had ever organized a "research lab without walls," in which a large number of scientists in a multitude of research institutions were commissioned to work on specific stages of a planned and managed research program. The March of Dimes established the pattern on which the United States, a little later, organized the first great research projects of World War II: the atom bomb, the radar lab, the proximity fuse, and then another fifteen years later, "Putting a Man on the Moon"—all innovative efforts using the "Fustest with the Mostest" strategy.

These examples show, first, that being "Fustest with the Mostest" requires an ambitious aim; otherwise it is bound to fail. It always aims at creating a new industry or a new market. At the least, as in the case of the Mayo Clinic or the March of Dimes, being "Fustest with the Mostest" aims at creating a quite different and highly unconventional process. The DuPonts surely did not say to themselves in the mid-twenties when they brought in Carothers: "We will establish the plastics industry" (indeed, the term was rarely used until the 1950s). But enough of the internal DuPont documents of the time have been published to show that the top management people did aim at creating a new industry. They were far from convinced that Carothers and his research would succeed. But they knew that they would have founded something big and brand new in the event of success, and something that would go far beyond a single product or even beyond a single major product line. Dr. Wang did not coin the term "the Office of the Future," as far as I know. But in his first advertisements, he announced a new office environment and new concepts of office work. Both the DuPonts and Wang from the beginning clearly aimed at dominating the industry they hoped they would succeed in creating.

The best example of what is implied in the strategy of being "Fustest with the Mostest" is not a business case but Humboldt's University of Berlin. Humboldt was actually not a bit interested in a university, as such. It was for him the means to create a new and different *political* order, which would be neither the absolute monarchy of the eighteenth century nor the democracy of the French Revolution in which the bourgeoisie ruled. Rather, it would be a balanced system, in which a totally apolitical professional civil service and an equally apolitical professional officer corps, recruited and promoted strictly by merit, would be autonomous in their very narrow spheres. These people—today we would call them technocrats— would have limited tasks and would be under the strict supervision of an independent professional judiciary. But within these limits they would be the masters. There would then be two spheres of individual freedom for the bourgeoisie, a moral and cultural one, and an economic one.

Humboldt had presented this concept earlier in book form. ⊖ After the total defeat of the Prussian monarchy by Napoleon in 1806, the collapse paralyzed all

⊖ Under the title *The Limits on the Effectiveness of Government (Die Grenzen der Wirksamkeit des Staates)*, one of the very few original books on political philosophy ever written by a German.

the forces that would otherwise have stopped Humboldt—the king, the aristocracy, the military. He ran with the opportunity and founded the University of Berlin as the main carrier of his political concepts, with brilliant success. The University of Berlin did indeed create the peculiar political structure the Germans in the nineteenth century called the "*Rechtsstaat*" (the Lawful State), in which an autonomous and self-governing elite of civil servants and general staff officers was in full control of the political and military sphere; an autonomous and self-governing elite of educated people ("*die Gebildeten Staende*") organized around self-governing universities provided a "liberal" cultural sphere; and in which there was an autonomous and largely unrestricted economy. This structure first gave Prussia the moral and cultural, and soon thereafter the political and economic ascendancy in Germany. Both leadership in Europe and admiration outside of it followed in short order, especially on the part of the British and the Americans for whom the Germans, until 1890 or so, were the cultural and intellectual models. All this was exactly what Humboldt in the hour of darkest defeat and total despair had envisaged and aimed at. Indeed, he spelled out his aims clearly in the prospectus and the charter of his university.

Perhaps because "Fustest with the Mostest" must aim at creating something truly new, something truly different, nonexperts and outsiders seem to do as well as the experts, in fact, often better. Hoffmann- LaRoche, for instance, did not owe its strategy to chemists, but to a musician who had married the granddaughter of the company's founder and needed more money to support his orchestra than the company then provided through its meager dividends. To this day the company has never been managed by chemists, but always by financial men who have made their career in a major Swiss bank. Wilhelm von Humboldt himself was a diplomat with no earlier ties to academia or experience in it. The DuPont top management people were businessmen rather than chemists and researchers. And while the Brothers Mayo were well-trained surgeons, they were totally outside the medical establishment of the time and isolated from it.

Of course, there are also the true "insiders," Dr. Wang or the people at 3M or the young computer engineers who designed the Apple computer. But when it comes to being "Fustest with the Mostest," the outsider may have an advantage. He does not know what everybody within the field knows, and therefore does not know what cannot be done.

II

The strategy of being "Fustest with the Mostest" has to hit right on target or it misses altogether. Or, to vary the metaphor, being "Fustest with the Mostest" is very much like a moon shot: a deviation of a fraction of a minute of the arc and the missile disappears into outer space. And once launched, the "Fustest with the Mostest" strategy is difficult to adjust or to correct.

To use this strategy, in other words, requires thought and careful analysis. The entrepreneur of so much of the popular literature or of Hollywood movies, the person who suddenly has a "brilliant idea" and rushes off to put it into effect, is not going to succeed with it. In fact, for this strategy to succeed at all, the innovation must be based on a careful and deliberate attempt to exploit one of the major opportunities for innovation that were discussed in Chapters 3 to 9.

There is, for instance, no better example of exploiting a *change in perception* than Humboldt's University of Berlin. The French Revolution with its Terror, followed by Napoleon's ruthless wars of conquest, had left the educated bourgeoisie disillusioned with politics; and yet they also quite clearly would have rejected any attempt to move the clock back and return to the absolute monarchy of the eighteenth century, let alone to feudalism. They needed a "liberal" but apolitical sphere, coupled with an apolitical government based on the same principles of law and education in which they themselves believed. And all of them at the time were followers of Adam Smith, whose *Wealth of Nations* was probably the most widely read and most highly respected political book of the period. It was this which Humboldt's political structure exploited and which his plan for the University of Berlin translated into institutional reality.

Wang's word processor brilliantly exploited a process need. By the 1970s the fear of the computer that had been rampant in offices only a little while earlier was beginning to be replaced by the question, "And what will the computer do for *me*?" By that time, office workers had become familiar with the computer in such activities as making payroll or controlling inventories; they also by that time had acquired office copiers so that the paperload in every office was going up very sharply. Wang's word processor then addressed itself to the one remaining nonautomated chore, a chore every office worker hated: rewriting letters, speeches, reports, manuscripts to embody minor changes, and having to do so again and again.

Hoffmann-LaRoche, in picking the vitamins in the early twenties, exploited new knowledge. The musician who laid down its strategy understood the "structure of scientific revolutions" a full thirty years before a philosopher, Thomas Kuhn, wrote the celebrated book by that title. He understood that a new basic theorem in science, even though buttressed by enough evidence to make it impossible to reject, will still not be accepted by a majority of scientists should it conflict with basic theorems they have grown up with and hold as articles of faith. They pay no attention to it for a long time, until the old "paradigm," the old basic theory, becomes totally untenable. And during that time those who accept the new theorem and run with it have the field all to themselves.

Only with such a base in careful analysis can the strategy of being "Fustest with the Mostest" possibly succeed.

Even then, it requires extreme concentration of effort. There has to be one clear-cut goal and all efforts have to be focused on it. And when this effort begins to produce results, the innovator has to be ready to mobilize resources massively. As soon as DuPont had a usable synthetic fiber—long before the market had begun to respond to it—the company built large factories and bombarded both textile manufacturers and the general public with advertisements, trial presentations, and samples.

Then, after the innovation has become a successful business, the work really begins. Then the strategy of "Fustest with the Mostest" demands substantial and continuing efforts to retain a leadership position; otherwise, all one has done is create a market for a competitor. The innovator has to run even harder now that he has leadership than he ran before and to continue his innovative efforts on a very large scale. The research budget must be higher *after* the innovation has successfully been accomplished than it was before. New uses have to be found; new customers must be identified, and persuaded to try the new materials. Above all, the entrepreneur who has succeeded in being "Fustest with the Mostest" has to make his product or his process obsolete before a competitor can do it. Work on the successor to the successful product or process has to start immediately, with the same concentration of effort and the same investment of resources that led to the initial success.

Finally, the entrepreneur who has attained leadership by being "Fustest with the Mostest" has to be the one who systematically cuts the price of his own product or process. To keep prices high simply holds an umbrella over potential competitors and encourages them (on this, see the next chapter, "Hit Them Where They Ain't").

This was established by the longest-lived private monopoly in economic history, the Dynamite Cartel, founded by Alfred Nobel after his invention of dynamite. The Dynamite Cartel maintained a worldwide monopoly until World War I and even beyond, long after the Nobel patents had expired. It did this by cutting price every time demand rose by 10 to 20 percent. By that time, the companies in the cartel had fully depreciated the investment they had had to make to get the additional production. This made it unattractive for any potential competitor to build new dynamite factories, while the cartel itself maintained its profitability. It is no accident that DuPont has consistently followed this policy in the United States, for the DuPont Company was the American member of the Dynamite Cartel. But

Wang has done the same with respect to the word processor, Apple with respect to its computers, and 3M with respect to all its products.

III

These are all success stories. They do *not* show how risky the strategy of being "Fustest with the Mostest" actually is. The failures disappeared. Yet we know that for everyone who succeeds with this strategy, many more fail. There is only one chance with the "Fustest with the Mostest" strategy. If it does not work right away, it is a total failure.

Everyone knows the old Swiss story of Wilhelm Tell the archer, whom the tyrant promised to pardon if he succeeded in shooting an apple off his son's head on the first try. If he failed, he would either kill the child or be killed himself. This is exactly the situation of the entrepreneur in the "Fustest with the Mostest" strategy. There can be no "almost-success" or "near-miss."There is only success or failure.

Even the successes may be perceived only by hindsight. At least we know that in two of the examples failure was very close; a combination of luck and chance saved them.

Nylon only succeeded because of a fluke. There was no market for a synthetic fiber in the mid-thirties. It was far too expensive to compete with cotton and rayon, the cheap fibers of the time, and was actually even more expensive than silk, the luxury fiber which the Japanese in the severe depression of the late thirties had to sell for whatever price they could get. What saved Nylon was the outbreak of World War II, which stopped Japanese silk exports. By the time the Japanese could start up their silk industry again, around 1950 or so, Nylon was firmly entrenched, with its cost and price down to a fraction of what both had been in the late thirties. The story of 3M's best known product, Scotch Tape, was told earlier. Again, but for pure accident, Scotch Tape would have been a failure.

The strategy of being "Fustest with the Mostest" is indeed so risky that an entire major strategy—the one that will be discussed in the next chapter under the heading Creative Imitation—is based on the assumption that being "Fustest with the Mostest" will fail far more often than it can possibly succeed. It will fail because the will is lacking. It will fail because efforts are inadequate. It will fail because, despite successful innovation, not enough resources are deployed, are available, or are being put to work to exploit success, and so on. While the strategy is indeed highly rewarding when successful, it is much too risky and much too difficult to be used for anything but major innovations, for creating a new political order as Humboldt successfully did, or a whole new field of therapy as Hoffmann-

LaRoche did with the vitamins, or a new approach to medical diagnosis and practice as the Mayo Brothers set out to do. In effect, it fits a fairly small minority of innovations. It requires profound analysis and a genuine understanding of the sources of innovation and of their dynamics. It requires an extreme concentration of effort and substantial resources. In most cases alternative strategies are available and preferable—not primarily because they carry less risk, but because for most innovations the opportunity is not great enough to justify the cost, the effort, and the investment of resources required for the "Fustest with the Mostest" strategy.

CHAPTER 17

"Hit Them Where They Ain't"

Two completely different entrepreneurial strategies were summed up by another battle-winning Confederate general in America's Civil War, who said: "Hit Them Where They Ain't." They might be called creative imitation and entrepreneurial judo, respectively.

I

Creative Imitation

Creative imitation[⊖] is clearly a contradiction in terms. What is creative must surely be original. And if there is one thing imitation is not, it is "original." Yet the term fits. It describes a strategy that is "imitation" in its substance. What the entrepreneur does is something somebody else has already done. But it is "creative" because the entrepreneur applying the strategy of "creative imitation" understands what the innovation represents better than the people who made it and who innovated.

⊖ The term was coined by Theodore Levitt of the Harvard Business School.

The foremost practitioner of this strategy and the most brilliant one is IBM. But it is also very largely the strategy that Procter & Gamble has been using to obtain and maintain leadership in the soap, detergent, and toiletries markets. And the Japanese Hattori Company, whose Seiko watches have become the world's leader, also owes its domination of the market to creative imitation.

In the early thirties IBM built a high-speed calculating machine to do calculations for the astronomers at New York's Columbia University. A few years later it built a machine that was already designed as a computer—again, to do astronomical calculations, this time at Harvard. And by the end of World War II , IBM had built a real computer —the first one, by the way, that had the features of the true computer: a "memory" and the capacity to be "programmed." And yet there are good reasons why the history books pay scant attention to IBM as a computer innovator. For as soon as it had finished its advanced 1945 computer—the first computer to be shown to a lay public in its showroom in midtown New York, where it drew immense crowds—IBM abandoned its own design and switched to the design of its rival, the ENIAC developed at the University of Pennsylvania. The ENIAC was far better suited to business applications such as payroll, only its designers did not see this. IBM structured the ENIAC so that it could be manufactured and serviced and could do mundane "numbers crunching." When IBM's version of the ENIAC came out in 1953, it at once set the standard for commercial, multipurpose, mainframe computers.

This is the strategy of "creative imitation." It waits until somebody else has established the new, but only "approximately." Then it goes to work. And within a short time it comes out with what the new really should be to satisfy the customer, to do the work customers want and pay for. The creative imitation has then set the standard and takes over the market.

IBM practiced creative imitation again with the personal computer. The idea was Apple's. As described earlier (in Chapter 3), everybody at IBM "knew" that a small, freestanding computer was a mistake—uneconomical, far from optimal, and expensive. And yet it succeeded. IBM immediately went to work to design a machine that would become the standard in the personal computer field and dominate or at least lead the entire field. The result was the PC. Within two years it had taken over from Apple leadership in the personal computer field, becoming the fastest-selling brand and the standard in the field.

Procter & Gamble acts very much the same way in the market for detergents, soaps, toiletries, and processed foods.

When semiconductors became available, everyone in the watch industry knew that they could be used to power a watch much more accurately, much more reliably, and much more cheaply than traditional watch movements. The Swiss soon brought out a quartz-powered digital watch. But they had so much investment in traditional watchmaking that they decided on a gradual introduction of quartz-powered digital watches over a long period of time, during which these new timepieces would remain expensive luxuries.

Meanwhile, the Hattori Company in Japan had long been making conventional watches for the Japanese market. It saw the opportunity and went in for creative imitation, developing the quartz-powered digital watch as the standard timepiece. By the time the Swiss had woken up, it was too late. Seiko watches had become the world's bestsellers, with the Swiss almost pushed out of the market.

Like being "Fustest with the Mostest," creative imitation is a strategy aimed at market or industry leadership, if not at market or industry dominance. But it is much less risky. By the time the creative imitator moves, the market has been established and the new venture has been accepted. Indeed, there is usually more demand for it than the original innovator can easily supply. The market segmentations are known or at least knowable. By then, too, market research can find out what customers buy, how they buy, what constitutes value for them, and so on. Most of the uncertainties that abound when the first innovator appears have been dispelled or can at least be analyzed and studied. No one has to explain any more what a personal computer or a digital watch are and what they can do.

Of course, the original innovator may do it right the first rime, thus closing the door to creative imitation. There is the risk of an innovator bringing out and doing the right job with vitamins as Hoffmann-LaRoche did, or with Nylon as did DuPont, or as Wang did with the word processor. But the number of entrepreneurs engaging in creative imitation, and their substantial success, indicates that perhaps the risk of the first innovator's preempting the market by getting it right is not an overwhelming one.

Another good example of creative imitation is Tylenol, the "nonaspirin aspirin." This case shows more clearly than any other I know what the strategy consists of, what its requirements are, and how it works.

Acetaminophen (the substance that is sold under the Tylenol brand name in the U.S.) had been used for many years as a painkiller, but until recently it was available in the United States only by prescription. Until recently also, aspirin, the much older pain-killing substance, was considered perfectly safe and had the pain-relief market to itself. Acetaminophen is a less potent drug than aspirin. It is effective as a painkiller but has no anti-inflammatory effect and also no effect on blood coagulation. Because of this it is free from the side effects, especially gastric upsets and stomach bleeding, which aspirin can cause, particularly if used in large doses and over long periods of time for an illness like arthritis.

When acetaminophen became available without prescription, the first brand on the market was presented and promoted as a drug for those who suffered side effects from aspirin. It was eminently successful, indeed, far more successful than its makers had anticipated. But it was this very success that created the opportunity for creative imitation. Johnson & Johnson realized that there was a market for a drug that *replaced* aspirin as the painkiller of choice, with aspirin confined to the fairly small market where anti-inflammatory and blood coagulation effects were needed. From the start Tylenol was promoted as the safe, *universal* painkiller. Within a year or two it had the market.

Creative imitation, these cases show, does not exploit the failure of the pioneers as failure is commonly understood. On the contrary, the pioneer must be successful. The Apple computer was a great success story, and so was the acetaminophen brand that Tylenol ultimately pushed out of market leadership. But the original innovators failed to understand their success. The makers of the Apple were product- focused rather than user-focused, and therefore offered additional hardware where the user needed programs and software. In the Tylenol case, the original innovators failed to realize what their own success meant.

The creative innovator exploits the success of others. Creative imitation is not "innovation" in the sense in which the term is most commonly understood. The creative imitator does not invent a product or service; he perfects and positions it. In the form in which it has been introduced, it lacks something. It may be additional product features. It may be segmentation of product or services so that slightly different versions fit slightly different markets. It might be proper positioning of the product in the market. Or creative imitation supplies something that is still lacking.

The creative imitator looks at products or services from the viewpoint of the customer. IBM's personal computer is practically indistinguishable from the Apple in its technical features, but IBM from the beginning offered the customer programs and software. Apple maintained traditional computer distribution through specialty stores. IBM—in a radical break with its own traditions—developed all kinds of distribution channels, specialty stores, major retailers like Sears, Roebuck, its own retail stores, and so on. It made it easy for the consumer to buy and it made it easy for the consumer to use the product. These, rather than hardware features, were the "innovations" that gave IBM the personal computer market.

All told, creative imitation starts out with markets rather than with products, and with customers rather than with producers. It is both market-focused and market-driven.

These cases show what the strategy of creative imitation requires:

It requires a rapidly growing market. Creative imitators do not succeed by taking away customers from the pioneers who have first introduced a new product or service; they serve markets the pioneers have created but do not adequately service. Creative imitation satisfies a demand that already exists rather than creating one.

The strategy has its own risks, and they are considerable. Creative imitators are easily tempted to splinter their efforts in the attempt to hedge their bets. Another danger is to misread the trend and imitate creatively what then turns out not to be the winning development in the marketplace.

IBM, the world's foremost creative imitator, exemplifies these dangers. It has successfully imitated every major development in the office- automation field. As a result, it has the leading product in every single area. But because they originated in imitation, the products are so diverse and so little compatible with one another that it is all but impossible to build an integrated, automated office out of IBM building blocks. It is thus still doubtful that IBM can maintain leadership in the automated office and provide the integrated system for it. Yet this is where the main market of the future is going to be in all probability. And this risk, *the risk of being too clever*, is inherent in the creative imitation strategy.

Creative imitation is likely to work most effectively in high-tech areas for one simple reason: high-tech innovators are least likely to be market-focused, and most likely to be technology-and product-focused. They therefore tend to misunderstand their own success and to fail to exploit and supply the demand they have created. But as acetaminophen and the Seiko watch show, they are by no means the only ones to do so.

Because creative imitation aims at market dominance, it is best suited to a major product, process, or service: the personal computer, the worldwide watch market, or a market as large as that for pain relief. But the strategy requires less of a market than being "Fustest with the Mostest." It carries less risk. By the time creative imitators go to work, the market has already been identified and the demand has already been created. What it lacks in risk, however, creative imitation makes up for in its requirements for alertness, for flexibility, for willingness to accept the verdict of the market, and above all, for hard work and massive efforts.

II

Entrepreneurial Judo

In 1947, Bell Laboratories invented the transistor. It was at once realized that the transistor was going to replace the vacuum tube, especially in consumer electronics such as the radio and the brand-new television set. Everybody knew this; but nobody did anything about it. The leading manufacturers—at that time they were all Americans— began to study the transistor and to make plans for conversion to the transistor "sometime around 1970." Till then, they proclaimed, the transistor "would not be ready." Sony was practically unknown outside of Japan and was not even in consumer electronics at the time. But Akio Morita, Sony's president, read about the transistor in the newspapers. As a result, he went to the United States and bought a license for the new transistor from Bell Labs for a ridiculous sum, all of $25,000. Two years later, Sony brought out the first portable transistor radio, which weighed less than one-fifth of comparable vacuum tube radios on the market, and cost less than one-third. Three years later, Sony had the market for cheap radios in the United States; and five years later, the Japanese had captured the radio market all over the world.

Of course, this is a classic case of the rejection of the unexpected success. The Americans rejected the transistor because it was "not invented here," that is, not invented by the electrical and electronic leaders, RCA and G.E. It is a typical example of pride in doing things the hard way. The Americans were so proud of the wonderful radios of those days, the great Super Heterodyne sets that were such marvels of craftsmanship. Compared to them, they thought silicon chips low grade, if not indeed beneath their dignity.

But Sony's success is not the real story. How do we explain that the Japanese repeated this same strategy again and again, and always with success, always surprising the Americans? They repeated it with television sets and digital watches and hand-held calculators. They repeated it with copiers when they moved in and took away a large share of the market from the original inventor, the Xerox Company. The Japanese, in other words, have been successful again and again in practicing "entrepreneurial judo" against the Americans.

But so did MCI and Sprint when they used the Bell Telephone System's (AT&T) own pricing to take away from the Bell System a very large part of the long-distance business (see Chapter 6). So did ROLM when it used Bell System's policies against it to take away a large part of the private branch exchange (PBX) market. And so did Citibank when it started a consumer bank in Germany, the *Familienbank* (Family Bank), which within a few short years came to dominate German consumer finance.

The German banks knew that ordinary consumers had obtained purchasing power and had become desirable clients. They went through the motions of offering consumers banking services. But they really did not want them. Consumers, they felt, were beneath the dignity of a major bank, with its business customers and its rich investment clients. If consumers needed an account at all, they should have it with the postal savings bank. Whatever their advertisements said to the contrary, the banks made it abundantly clear when consumers came into the august offices of the local branch that they had little use for them.

This was the opening Citibank exploited when it founded its German *Familienbank*, which catered to none but individual consumers, designed the services consumers needed, and made it easy for consumers to do business with a bank. Despite the tremendous strength of the German banks and their pervasive presence in a country where there is a branch of a major bank on the corner of every downtown street, Citibank's *Familienbank* attained dominance in the German consumer banking business within five years or so.

All these newcomers—the Japanese, MCI, ROLM, Citibank—practiced "entrepreneurial judo." Of the entrepreneurial strategies, especially the strategies aimed at obtaining leadership and dominance in an industry or a market, entrepreneurial judo is by all odds the least risky and the most likely to succeed.

Every policeman knows that a habitual criminal will always commit his crime the same way—whether it is cracking a safe or entering a building he wants to loot. He leaves behind a "signature," which is as individual and as distinct as a fingerprint. And he will not change that signature even though it leads to his being caught time and again.

But it is not only the criminal who is set in his habits. All of us are. And so are businesses and industries. The habit will be persisted in even though it leads again and again to loss of leadership and loss of market. The American manufacturers persisted in the habits that enabled the Japanese to take over their market again and again.

If the criminal is caught, he rarely accepts that his habit has betrayed him. On the contrary, he will find all kinds of excuses—and continue the habit that led to his being captured. Similarly, businesses that are being betrayed by their habits will not admit it and will find all kinds of excuses. The American electronics manufacturers, for instance, attribute the Japanese successes to "low labor costs" in Japan. Yet the few American manufacturers that have faced up to reality, for example, RCA and Magnavox in television sets, are able to turn out in the United States products at prices competitive with those of the Japanese, and competitive also in quality, despite their paying American wages and union benefits. The German banks uniformly explain the success of Citibank's *Familienbank* by its taking risks they themselves would not touch. But *Familienbank* has lower credit losses with consumer loans than the German banks, and its lending requirements are as strict as those of the Germans. The German banks know this, of course. Yet they keep on explaining away their failure and *Familienbank's* success. This is typical. And it explains why the same strategy—the same entrepreneurial judo—can be used over and over again.

There are in particular five fairly common bad habits that enable newcomers to use entrepreneurial judo and to catapult themselves into a leadership position in an industry against the entrenched, established companies.

1. The first is what American slang calls "NIH" ("Not Invented Here"), the arrogance that leads a company or an industry to believe that something new cannot be any good unless they themselves thought of it. And so the new invention is spurned, as was the transistor by the American electronics manufacturers.

2. The second is the tendency to "cream" a market, that is, to get the high-profit part of it.

This is basically what Xerox did and what made it an easy target for the Japanese imitators of its copying machines. Xerox focused its strategy on the big users, the buyers of large numbers of machines or of expensive, high-performance machines. It did not reject the others; but it did not go after them. In particular, it did not see fit to give them service. In the end it was dissatisfaction with the service—or rather, with the lack of service—Xerox provided for its smaller customers that made them receptive to competitors' machines.

"Creaming" is a violation of elementary managerial and economic precepts. It is always punished by loss of market.

Xerox was resting on its laurels. They were indeed substantial and well earned, but no business ever gets paid for what it did in the past. "Creaming" attempts to get paid for past contributions. Once a business gets into that habit, it is likely to continue in it and thus continue to be vulnerable to entrepreneurial judo.

3. Even more debilitating is the third bad habit: the belief in "quality." "Quality" in a product or service is not what the supplier puts in. It is what the customer gets out and is willing to pay for. A product is not "quality" because it is hard to make and costs a lot of money, as manufacturers typically believe. That is incompetence. Customers pay only for what is of use to them and gives them value. Nothing else constitutes "quality."

The American electronics manufacturers in the 1950s believed that their products with all those wonderful vacuum tubes were "quality" because they had put in thirty years of effort making radio sets more complicated, bigger, and more expensive. They considered the product to be "quality" because it needed a great deal of skill to turn out, whereas a transistor radio is simple and can be made by unskilled labor on the assembly line. But in consumer terms, the transistor radio is clearly far superior "quality." It weighs much less so that it can be taken on a trip to the beach or to a picnic. It rarely goes wrong; there are no tubes to replace. It costs a great deal less. And in range and fidelity it very soon surpassed even the most magnificent Super Heterodyne with sixteen vacuum tubes, one of which always burned out just when needed.

4. Closely related to both "creaming" and "quality" is the fourth bad habit, the delusion of the "premium" price. A "premium" price is always an invitation to the competitor.

For two hundred years, since the time of J. B. Say in France and of David Ricardo in England in the early years of the nineteenth century, economists have known that the only way to get a higher profit margin, except through a monopoly, is through lower costs. The attempt to achieve a higher profit margin through a higher price is always self-defeating. It holds an umbrella over the competitor. What looks like higher profits for the established leader is in effect a subsidy to the newcomer who, in a very few years, will unseat the leader and claim the throne for himself. "Premium" prices, instead of being an occasion for joy—and a reason for a higher stock price or a higher price/earnings multiple—should always be considered a threat and dangerous vulnerability.

Yet the delusion of higher profits to be achieved through "premium" prices is almost universal, even though it always opens the door to entrepreneurial judo.

5. Finally, there is a fifth bad habit that is typical of established businesses and leads to their downfall—Xerox is a good example. They maximize rather than optimize. As the market grows and develops, they try to satisfy every single user through the same product or service.

A new analytical instrument to test chemical reaction is being introduced, for instance. At first its market is quite limited, let's say to industrial laboratories. But then university laboratories, research institutes, and hospitals all begin to buy the instrument, but each wants something slightly different. And so the manufacturer puts in one feature to satisfy this customer, then another one to satisfy that customer, and so on, until what started out as a simple instrument has become complicated. The manufacturer has maximized what the instrument can do. As a result, the instrument no longer satisfies anyone. For, by trying to satisfy everybody, one always ends up satisfying nobody. The instrument also has become expensive, as well as being hard to use and hard to maintain. But the manufacturer is proud of the instrument; indeed, his full-page advertisement lists sixty-four different things it can do.

This manufacturer will almost certainly become the victim of entrepreneurial judo. What he thinks is his very strength will be turned against him. The newcomer will come in with an instrument designed to satisfy one of the markets, the hospital, for instance. It will not contain a single feature the hospital people do not need, and do not need every day. But everything the hospital needs will be there and with higher performance capacity than the multipurpose instrument can possibly offer. The same manufacturer will then bring out a model for the research laboratory, for the government laboratory, for industry —and in no time at all the newcomer will have taken away the markets with instruments that are specifically designed for their users, instruments that optimize rather than maximize.

Similarly, when the Japanese came in with their copiers in competition with Xerox, they designed machines that fitted specific groups of users—for example, the small office, whether. that of the dentist, the doctor, or the school principal. They did not try to match the features of which the Xerox people themselves were the proudest, such as the speed of the machine or the clarity of the copy. They gave the small office what the small office needed most, a simple machine at a low cost. And once they had established themselves in that market, they then moved in on the other markets, each with a product designed to serve optimally a specific market segment.

Sony similarly first moved into the low end of the radio market, the market for cheap portables with limited range. Once it had established itself there, it moved in on the other market segments.

Entrepreneurial judo aims first at securing a beachhead, and one which the established leaders either do not defend at all or defend only halfheartedly—the way the Germans did not counterattack when Citibank established its *Familienbank*. Once that beachhead has been secured, that is, once the newcomers have an adequate market and an adequate revenue stream, they then move on to the rest of the "beach" and finally to the whole "island." In each case, they repeat the strategy. They design a product or a service which is specific to a given market segment and optimal for it. And the established leaders hardly ever beat them to this game. Hardly ever do the established leaders manage to change their own behavior before the newcomers have taken over the leadership and acquired dominance.

There are three situations in which the entrepreneurial judo strategy is likely to be particularly successful.

The first is the common situation in which the established leaders refuse to act on the unexpected, whether success or failure, and either overlook it altogether or try to brush it aside. This is what Sony exploited.

The second situation is the Xerox situation. A new technology emerges and grows fast. But the innovators who have brought to the market the new technology (or the new service) behave like the classical "monopolists": they use their leadership position to "cream" the market and to get "premium" prices. They either do not know or refuse to acknowledge what has been amply proven: that a leadership position, let alone any kind of monopoly, can only be maintained if the leader behaves as a "benevolent monopolist" (the term is Joseph Schumpeter's).

A benevolent monopolist cuts his prices before a competitor can cut them. And he makes his product obsolete and introduces new product before a competitor can do so. There are enough examples of this around to prove the validity of the thesis. It is the way in which the DuPont Company has acted for many years and in which the American Bell Telephone System (AT&T) used to act before it was overcome by the inflationary problems of the 1970s. But if the leader uses his leadership position to raise prices or to raise profit margins except by lowering his cost, he sets himself up to be knocked down by anyone who uses entrepreneurial judo against him.

Similarly, the leader in a rapidly growing new market or new technology who tries to maximize rather than to optimize will soon make himself vulnerable to entrepreneurial judo.

Finally, entrepreneurial judo works as a strategy when market or industry structure changes fast—which is the *Familienbank* story. As Germany became prosperous in the fifties and sixties, ordinary people became customers for financial services beyond the traditional savings account or the traditional mortgage. But the German banks stuck to their old markets.

Entrepreneurial judo is always market-focused and market-driven. The starting point may be technology, as it was when Akio Morita traveled to the United States from a Japan that had barely emerged from the destruction of World War II to acquire a transistor license. Morita looked at the market segment which the existing technology satisfied the least, simply because of the weight and fragility of vacuum tubes: the market for portables. He then designed the right radio for that market, a market of young people with little money but also fairly simple demands with respect to range of the instrument and to quality of sound, a market, in other words, that the old technology simply could not adequately serve.

Similarly, the long-distance discounters in the United States who saw the opportunity to buy from the Bell Telephone System wholesale and to resell retail, designed a service first for the fairly modest number of substantial businesses that were too small to build their own long-distance system but large enough to have heavy long-distance bills. Only after they had secured a substantial share of that market did they move out and try to go after both the very big and the small users.

To use the entrepreneurial judo strategy, one starts out with an analysis of the industry, the producers and the suppliers, their habits, especially their bad habits, and their policies. But then one looks at the markets and tries to pinpoint the place where an alternative strategy would meet with the greatest success and the least resistance.

Entrepreneurial judo requires some degree of genuine innovation. It is, as a rule, not good enough to offer the same product or the same service at lower cost. There has to be something that distinguishes it from what already exists.

When the ROLM Company offered a private branch exchange—a switchboard for business and office users—in competition with AT&T, it built in additional features designed around a small computer. These were not high-tech, let alone new inventions. Indeed, AT&T itself had designed similar features. But AT&T did not push them—and ROLM did. Similarly, when Citibank went into Germany with the *Familienbank*, it put in some innovative services which German banks as a rule did not offer to small depositors, such as travelers checks or tax advice.

It is not enough, in other words, for the newcomer simply to do as good a job as the established leader at a lower cost or with better service. The newcomers have to make themselves distinct.

Like being "Fustest with the Mostest" and creative imitation, entrepreneurial judo aims at obtaining leadership position and eventually dominance. But it does not do so by competing with the leaders—or at least not where the leaders are aware of competitive challenge or worried about it. Entrepreneurial judo "Hits Them Where They Ain't."

CHAPTER 18

Ecological Niches

The entrepreneurial strategies discussed so far, being "Fustest with the Mostest," creative imitation, and entrepreneurial judo, all aim at market or industry leadership, if not at dominance. The "ecological niche" strategy aims at control. The strategies discussed earlier aim at positioning an enterprise in a large market or a major industry. The ecological niche strategy aims at obtaining a practical monopoly in a small area. The first three strategies are competitive strategies. The ecological niche strategy aims at making its successful practitioners immune to competition and unlikely to be challenged. Successful practitioners of "Fustest with the Mostest," creative imitation, and entrepreneurial judo become big companies, highly visible if not household words. Successful practitioners of the ecological niche take the cash and let the credit go. They wallow in their anonymity. Indeed, in the most successful of the ecological niche strategies, the whole point is to be so inconspicuous, despite the product's being essential to a process, that no one is likely to try to compete.

There are three distinct niche strategies, each with its own requirements, its own limitations, and its own risks:

- the toll-gate strategy;
- the specialty skill strategy; and
- the specialty market strategy.

I

The Toll-gate Strategy

Earlier, in Chapter 4, I discussed the strategy of the Alcon Company, which developed an enzyme to eliminate the one feature of the standard surgical operation for senile cataracts that went counter to the rhythm and the logic of the process. Once this enzyme had been developed and patented, it had a "toll-gate" position. No eye surgeon would do without it. No matter what Alcon charged for the teaspoonful of enzyme that was needed for each cataract operation, the cost was insignificant in relation to the total cost of the operation. I doubt that any eye surgeon or any hospital ever even inquired what the stuff cost. The total market for this particular preparation was so small—maybe $50 million dollars a year worldwide—that it clearly would not have been worth anybody's while to try to develop a competing product. There would not have been one additional cataract operation in the world just because this particular enzyme had become cheaper. All that potential competitors could possibly do, therefore, would have been to knock down the price for everybody, without deriving much benefit for themselves.

A very similar toll-gate position has been occupied for many years by a medium-sized company which, fifty or sixty years ago, developed a blowout protector for oil wells. The cost of drilling an oil well may run into many millions. One blowout will destroy the entire well and everything that has been invested in it. The blowout protector, which safeguards the well while being drilled, is thus cheap insurance, no matter what its price. Again, the total market is so limited as to make it unattractive for any would-be competitor. Lowering the price of blowout protectors, which constitute maybe 1 percent of the total cost of a deep well, could not possibly stimulate anyone to drill more wells. Competition could only degrade the price without increasing the demand.

Another example of a toll-gate strategy is Dewey & Almy—now a division of W. R. Grace. This company developed a compound to seal tin cans in the 1930s. The seal is an essential ingredient of the can: if a can goes bad, it can cause catastrophic damage. One death from one case of botulism in a can can easily destroy a food packer. A can-sealing compound that offers protection against spoilage is therefore cheap at any price. And yet the cost of sealing—a fraction of a cent at best—is so insignificant to both the cost of the total can and the risk of spoilage that nobody is much concerned about it. What matters is performance, not cost. Again, the total market, while larger than that for enzymes in cataract operations or for blowout protectors, is still a limited one. And lowering the price for can-sealing compound is quite unlikely to increase the demand by a single can.

The toll-gate position is thus in many ways the most desirable position a company can occupy. But it has stringent requirements. The product has to be essential to a process. The risk of not using it—the risk of losing an eye, losing an oil well, or spoilage in a tin can—must be infinitely greater than the cost of the product. The market must be so limited that whoever occupies it first preempts it. It must be a true "ecological niche" which one species fills completely, and which at the same time is small and discreet enough not to attract rivals.

Such toll-gate positions are not easily found. Normally they occur only in an incongruity situation (cf. Chapter 4). The incongruity, as in the case of Alcon's enzyme, might be an incongruity in the rhythm or the logic of a process. Or, as in the case of the blowout protector or the can-sealing compound, it might be an incongruity between economic realities—between the cost of malfunction and the cost of adequate protection.

The toll-gate position also has severe limitations and serious risks. It is basically a static position. Once the ecological niche has been occupied, there is unlikely to be much growth. There is nothing the company that occupies the toll-gate position can do to increase its business or to control it. No matter how good its product or how cheap, the demand is dependent upon the demand for the process or product to which the toll-gate product furnishes an ingredient.

This may not be too important for Alcon. Cataracts can be assumed to be impervious to economic fluctuations, whether boom or depression. But the company making blowout protectors had to invest enormous amounts of money in new plants when oil drilling skyrocketed in 1973, and again after the 1979 petroleum panic. It suspected that the boom could not last; yet it had to make the investments even though it was reasonably sure it could never earn them back. Not to have done so would have meant losing its market irretrievably. Equally, it was powerless when, a few years later, the oil boom collapsed and oil drilling shrank by 80 percent within twelve months, and with it orders for oil-drilling equipment.

Once the toll-gate strategy has attained its objective, the company is "mature." It can only grow as fast as its end users grow. But it can go down fast. It can become obsolete almost overnight if someone finds a different way of satisfying the same end use. Dewey & Almy, for instance, has no defense against the replacement of tin cans by other container materials such as glass, paper, or plastics, or by other methods of preserving food such as freezing and irradiation.

And the toll-gate strategist must never exploit his monopoly. He must not become what the Germans call a *Raubritter* (the English "robber baron" does not mean quite the same thing) who robbed and raped the hapless travelers as they passed through the mountain defiles and river gorges atop of which perched his castle. He must not abuse his monopoly to exploit, to extort, to maltreat his customers. If he does, the users will put another supplier into business, or they will switch to less effective substitutes which they can then control.

The right strategy is the one Dewey & Almy has successfully pursued for more than forty years now. It offers its users, especially those in the Third World, extensive technical service, teaches their people, and designs new and better canning and can-sealing machinery for them to use with the Dewey & Almy sealing compounds. Yet it also constantly upgrades the compounds.

The toll-gate position might be impregnable—or nearly so. But it can only control within a narrow radius. Alcon tried to overcome this limitation by diversifying into all kinds of consumer products for the eye: artificial tears, contact lens fluids, anti-allergic eyedrops, and so on. This was successful insofar as it made the company attractive to one of the leading consumer goods multinationals, the Swiss Nestlé Company, which bought out Alcon for a very substantial sum. To the best of my knowledge, Alcon is the only toll-gate company of this kind that succeeded in establishing itself in markets outside its original position and with products that were different in their economic characteristics. But whether this diversification into highly competitive consumer markets of which the company knew very little was profitable, is not known.

II

The Specialty Skill

Everybody knows the major automobile nameplates. But few people know the names of the companies that supply the electrical and lighting systems for these cars, and yet there are far fewer such systems than there are automobile nameplates: in the United States, the Delco group of GM; in Germany, Robert Bosch; in Great Britain, Lucas; and so on. Practically no one outside of the automobile industry knows that one firm, A. O. Smith of Milwaukee, has for decades been making every single frame used in an American passenger car, nor that for decades another firm, Bendix, has made every single set of automotive brakes used by the American automobile industry.

By now these are all old and well-established firms, of course, but only because the automobile is itself an old industry. These companies established their controlling position when the industry was in its infancy, well before World War I. Robert Bosch, for instance, was a contemporary and friend of the two German auto pioneers, Carl Benz and Gottfried Daimler, and started his firm in the 1880s.

But once these companies had attained their controlling position in their specialty skill niche, they retained it. Unlike the toll-gate companies, theirs is a fairly large niche, yet it is still unique. It was obtained by developing high skill at a very early time. A. O. Smith developed what today would be called "automation" in making automobile frames during and shortly after World War I. The electrical system which Bosch in Germany designed for Mercedes staff cars around 1911 was so far advanced that it was put into general use even in luxury automobiles only after World War I. Delco in Dayton, Ohio, developed the self-starter before becoming a part of General Motors, that is, before 1914. Such specialized skills put these companies so far ahead in their field that it was hardly worth anybody's while to try to challenge them. They had become the "standard."

Specialty skill niches are by no means confined to manufacturing. Within the last ten years a few private trading firms, most of them in Vienna, Austria, have built a similar niche in what used to be called "barter" and is now called "counter-trade": taking goods from a developing importing country, Bulgarian tobacco or Brazilian-made irrigation pumps, in payment for locomotives, machinery, or pharmaceuticals exported by a company in a developed country. And much earlier, an enterprising German attained such a hold on one specialty skill niche that guidebooks for tourists are still called by his name, "Baedeker."

As these cases show, timing is of the essence in establishing a specialty skill niche. It has to be done at the very beginning of a new industry, a new custom, a new market, a new trend. Karl Baedeker published his first guidebook in 1828, as soon as the first steamships on the Rhine opened tourist travel to the middle classes. He then had the field virtually to himself until World War I made German books unacceptable in Western countries. The counter-traders of Vienna started around 1960, when such trade was still the rare exception, largely confined to the smaller countries of the Soviet Bloc (which explains why they are concentrated in Austria). Ten years later, when hard currencies had become scarce all through the Third World, they had honed their skills and become the "specialists."

To attain a specialty niche always requires something new, something added, something that is genuine innovation. There were guidebooks for travelers before Baedeker, but they confined themselves to the cultural scene—churches, sights, and so on. For practical details— the hotels, the tariff of the horse-drawn cabs, the distances, and the proper amount to tip—the traveling English milord relied on a professional, the courier. But the middle class had no courier, and that was Baedeker's opportunity. Once he had learned what information the traveler needed, how to get at it and to present it (the format he established is still the one many guidebooks follow), it would not have paid anyone to duplicate Baedeker's investment and build a competing organization.

In the early stages of a major new development, the specialty skill niche offers an exceptional opportunity. Examples abound. For many, many years there were only two companies in the United States making airplane propellers, for instance. Both had been started before World War I.

A specialty skill niche is rarely found by accident. In every single case, it results from a systematic survey of innovative opportunities. In every single case, the entrepreneur looks for the place where a specialty skill can be developed and can give a new enterprise a unique controlling position. Robert Bosch spent years studying the new automotive field to position his new company where it could immediately establish itself as the leader. Hamilton Propeller, for many years the leading airplane propeller manufacturer in the United States, was the result of a systematic search by its founder in the early days of powered flight. Baedeker made several attempts to start a service for the tourist before he decided on the guidebook that then bore his name and made him famous.

The first point, therefore, is that in the early stages of a new industry, a new market, or a new major trend, there is the opportunity to search systematically for the specialty skill opportunity—and then there is usually time to develop a unique skill.

The second point is that the specialty skill niche does require a skill that is both unique and different. The early automobile pioneers were, without exception, mechanics. They knew a great deal about machinery, about metals and about engines. But electricity was alien to them. It required theoretical knowledge which they neither possessed nor knew how to acquire. There were other publishers in Baedeker's time, but a guidebook that required on-the-spot gathering of an enormous amount of detailed information, constant inspection, and a staff of traveling auditors was not within their purview. "Counter-trade" is neither trading nor banking.

The business that establishes itself in a specialty skill niche is therefore unlikely to be threatened by its customers or by its suppliers. Neither of them really wants to get into something that is so alien in skill and in temperament.

Thirdly, a business occupying a specialty skill niche must constantly work on improving its own skill. It has to stay ahead. Indeed, it has to make itself constantly obsolete. The automobile companies in the early days used to complain that Delco in Dayton, and Bosch in Stuttgart, were pushing them. They turned out lighting systems that were far ahead of the ordinary automobile, ahead of what the automobile manufacturers of the times thought the customer needed, wanted, or could pay for, ahead very often of what the automobile manufacturer knew how to assemble.

While the specialty skill niche has unique advantages, it also has severe limitations. One is that it inflicts tunnel-vision on its occupants. In order to maintain themselves in their controlling position, they have to learn to look neither right nor left, but directly ahead at their narrow area, their specialized field. Airplane electronics were not too different from automobile electronics in the early stages. Yet the automobile electricians —Delco, Bosch, and Lucas—are not leaders in airplane electronics. They did not even see the field and made no attempt to get into it.

A second, serious limitation is that the occupant of a specialty skill niche is usually dependent on somebody else to bring his product or service to market. It becomes a component. The strength of the automobile electrical firms is that the customer does not know that they exist. But this is of course also their weakness. If the British automobile industry goes down, so does Lucas. A.O.Smith prospered making automotive frames until the energy crisis. Then American automobile manufacturers began to switch to cars without frames. These cars are substantially more expensive than cars with frames, but they weigh less and therefore burn less fuel. A.O.Smith could do nothing to reverse the adverse trend.

Finally, the greatest danger to the specialty niche manufacturer is for the specialty to cease being a specialty and to become universal.

The niche that the Viennese counter-traders now occupy was occupied in the 1920s and 1930s by foreign exchange traders who were mostly Swiss. Bankers of those days, having grown up before World War I, still believed that currencies ought to be stable. And when currencies became unstable, when there were blocked currencies around, currencies with different exchange rates for different purposes, and other such monstrosities, the bankers did not even want to handle the business. They were only too happy to let the specialists in Switzerland do what they thought was a dirty job. So a fairly small number of Swiss foreign exchange traders occupied a highly profitable specialty skill niche. After World War □, with the tremendous expansion of world trade, foreign exchange trading became routine. By now every bank, at least in the major money centers, has its own foreign exchange traders.

The specialty skill niche, like all ecological niches, is therefore limited—in scope as well as in time. Species that occupy such a niche, biology teaches, do not easily adapt to even small changes in the external environment. And this is true, too, of the entrepreneurial skill species. But within these limitations, the specialty skill niche is a highly advantageous position. In a rapidly expanding new technology, industry, or market, it is perhaps the most advantageous strategy. Very few of the automobile makers of 1920 are still around; every single one of the electrical and lighting systems makers is. Once attained and properly maintained, the specialty skill niche protects against competition, precisely because no automobile buyer knows or cares who makes the headlights or the brakes. No automobile buyer is therefore likely to shop around for either. Once the name "Baedeker" had become synonymous with tourist guidebooks, there was little danger that anybody else would try to muscle in, at least not until the market changed drastically. In a new technology, a new industry, or a new market, the specialty skill strategy offers an optimal ratio between opportunity and risk of failure.

III

The Specialty Market

The major difference between the specialty skill niche and the specialty market niche is that the former is built around a product or service and the latter around specialized knowledge of a market. Otherwise, they are similar.

Two medium-sized companies, one in northern England and one in Denmark, supply the great majority of the automated baking ovens for cookies and crackers bought in the world. For many decades, two companies—the two earliest travel agents, Thomas Cook in Europe and American Express in the United States—had a practical monopoly on travelers checks.

There is, I am told, nothing very difficult or particularly technical about baking ovens. There are literally dozens of companies around that could make them just as well as those two firms in England and Denmark. But these two know the market: they know every single major baker, and every single major baker knows them. The market is just not big enough or attractive enough to try to compete with these two, as long as they remain satisfactory. Similarly, travelers checks were a backwater until the post-World War II period of mass travel. They were highly profitable since the issuer, whether Cook or American Express, has the use of the money and keeps the interest earned on it until the purchaser cashes the check—sometimes months after the checks were purchased. But the market was not large enough to tempt anyone else. Furthermore, travelers checks required a worldwide organization, which Cook and American Express had to maintain anyhow to service their travel customers, and which nobody else in those days had any reason to build.

The specialty market is found by looking at a new development with the question, What opportunities are there in this that would give us a unique niche, and what do we have to do to fill it ahead of everybody else? The travelers check is no great "invention." It is basically nothing more than a letter of credit, and that has been around for hundreds of years. What was new was that travelers checks were offered—at first to the customers of Cook and American Express, and then to the general public—in standard denominations. And they could be cashed wherever Cook or American Express had an office or an agent. That made them uniquely attractive to the tourist who did not want to carry a great deal of cash and did not have the established banking connections to make them eligible for a letter of credit.

There was nothing particularly advanced in the early baking ovens, nor is there any high technology in the baking ovens installed today. What the two leading firms did was to realize that the act of baking cookies and crackers was moving out of the home and into the factory. They then studied what commercial bakers needed so that they could manufacture the product their own customers, grocers and supermarkets, could in turn sell and the housewife would buy. The baking ovens were not based on engineering but on market research; the engineering would have been available to anyone.

The specialty market niche has the same requirements as the specialty skill niche: systematic analysis of a new trend, industry, or market; a specific innovative contribution, if only a "twist" like the one that converted the traditional letter of credit into the modern travelers check; and continuous work to improve the product and especially the service, so that leadership, once obtained, will be retained.

And it has the same limitations. The greatest threat to the specialty market position is success. The greatest threat is when the specialty market becomes a mass market.

Travelers checks have now become a commodity and highly competitive because travel has become a mass market.

So have perfumes. A French firm, Coty, created the modern perfume industry. It realized that World War I had changed the attitude toward cosmetics. Whereas before the war only "fast women" used cosmetics—or dared admit to their use—cosmetics had become accepted and respectable. By the mid-twenties Coty had established itself in what was almost a monopoly position on both sides of the Atlantic. Until 1929 the cosmetics market was a "specialty market," a market of the upper middle class. But then during the Depression it exploded into a genuine mass market. It also split into two segments: a prestige segment, with high prices, specialty distribution, and specialty packaging; and popular-priced, mass brands sold in every outlet including the supermarket, the variety store, and the drugstore. Within a few short years, the specialty market dominated by Coty had disappeared. But Coty could not make up its mind whether to try to become one of the mass marketers in cosmetics or one of the luxury producers. It tried to stay in a market that no longer existed, and has been drifting ever since.

CHAPTER 19

Changing Values and Characteristics

In the entrepreneurial strategies discussed so far, the aim is to introduce an innovation. In the entrepreneurial strategy discussed in this chapter, the strategy itself is the innovation. The product or service it carries may well have been around a long time—in our first example, the postal service, it was almost two thousand years old. But the strategy converts this old, established product or service into something new. It changes its utility, its value, its economic characteristics. While physically there is no change, economically there is something different and new.

All the strategies to be discussed in this chapter have one thing in common. They create a customer—and that is the ultimate purpose of a business, indeed, of economic activity. [⊖] But they do so in four different ways:

- by creating utility;
- by pricing;
- by adaptation to the customer's social and economic reality;
- by delivering what represents true value to the customer.

[⊖] As was first said more than thirty years ago in my *The Practice of Management* (New York: Harper & Row, 1954).

I

Creating Customer Utility

English schoolboys used to be taught that Rowland Hill "invented" the postal service in 1836. That is nonsense, of course. The Rome of the Caesars had an excellent service, with fast couriers carrying mail on regular schedules to the furthest corners of the Empire. A thousand years later, in 1521, the German emperor Charles V, in true Renaissance fashion, went back to Classical Rome and gave a monopoly on carrying mail in the imperial domains to the princely family of Thurn and Taxis. Their generous campaign contributions had enabled him to bribe enough German Electors to win the imperial crown—and the princes of Thurn and Taxis still provided the postal service in many parts of Germany as late as 1866, as stamp collectors know. By the middle of the seventeenth century, every European country had organized a postal service on the German model and so had, a hundred years later, the American colonies. Indeed, all the great letter-writers of the Western tradition, from Cicero to Madame de Sévigné, Lord Chesterfield, and Voltaire, wrote and posted their letters long before Rowland Hill "invented" the postal service.

Yet Hill did indeed create what we would now call "mail." He contributed no new technology and not one new "thing," nothing that could conceivably have been patented. But mail had always been paid for by the addressee, with the fee computed according to distance and weight. This made it both expensive and slow. Every letter had to be brought to a post office to be weighed. Hill proposed that postage should be uniform within Great Britain regardless of distance; that it be prepaid; and that the fee be paid by affixing the kind of stamp that had been used for many years to pay other fees and taxes. Overnight, mail became easy and convenient; indeed, letters could now be dropped into a collection box. Immediately, also, mail became absurdly cheap. The letter that had earlier cost a shilling or more—and a shilling was as much as a craftsman earned in a day—now cost only a penny. The volume was no longer limited. In short, "mail" was born.

Hill created utility. He asked. What do the customers *need* for a postal service to be truly a service to them? This is always the first question in the entrepreneurial strategy of changing utility, values, and economic characteristics. In fact, the reduction in the cost of mailing a letter, although 80 percent or more, was secondary. The main effect was to make using the mails convenient for everybody and available to everybody. Letters no longer had to be confined to "epistles." The tailor could now use the mail to send a bill. The resulting explosion in volume, which doubled in the first four years and quadrupled again in the next ten, then brought the cost down to where mailing a letter cost practically nothing for long years.

Price is usually almost irrelevant in the strategy of creating utility. The strategy works by enabling customers to do what serves *their purpose*. It works because it asks: What is truly a "service," truly a "utility" to the customer?

Every American bride wants to get one set of "good china." A whole set is, however, far too expensive a present, and the people giving her a wedding present do not know what pattern the bride wants or what pieces she already has. So they end up giving something else. The demand was there, in other words, but the utility was lacking. A medium-sized dinnerware manufacturer, the Lenox China Company, saw this as an innovative opportunity. Lenox adapted an old idea, the "bridal register," so that it only "registers" Lenox china. The bride-to-be then picks one merchant whom she tells what pattern of Lenox china she wants, and to whom she refers potential donors of wedding gifts. The merchant then asks the donor: "How much do you want to spend?" and explains: "That will get you two coffee cups with saucers." Or the merchant can say, "She already has all the coffee cups; what she needs now is dessert plates." The result is a happy bride, a happy wedding-gift donor, and a very happy Lenox China Company.

Again, there is no high technology here, nothing patentable, nothing but a focus on the needs of the customer. Yet the bridal register, for all its simplicity— or perhaps because of it—has made Lenox the favorite "good china" manufacturer and one of the most rapidly growing of medium-sized American manufacturing companies.

Creating utility enables people to satisfy their wants and their needs *in their own way*. The tailor could not send the bill to his customer through the mails if it first took three hours to get the letter accepted by a postal clerk and if the addressee then had to pay a large sum— perhaps even as much as the bill itself. Rowland Hill did not add anything to the service. It was performed by the same postal clerks using the same mail coaches and the same letter carriers. And yet Rowland Hill's postal service was a totally different "service.". It served a different function.

II

Pricing

For many years, the best known American face in the world was that of King Gillette, which graced the wrapper of every Gillette razor blade sold anyplace in the world. And millions of men all over the world used a Gillette razor blade every morning.

King Gillette did not invent the safety razor; dozens of them were patented in the closing decades of the nineteenth century. Until 1860 or 1870, only a very small number of men, the aristocracy and a few professionals and merchants, had to take care of their facial hair, and they could well afford a barber. Then, suddenly, large numbers of men, tradesmen, shopkeepers, clerks, had to look "respectable." Few of them could handle a straight razor or felt comfortable with so dangerous a tool, but visits to the barber were expensive, and worse, time-consuming. Many inventors designed a "do-it-yourself" safety razor, yet none could sell it. A visit to the barber cost ten cents and the cheapest safety razor cost five dollars—an enormous sum in those days when a dollar a day was a good wage.

Gillette's safety razor was no better than many others, and it was a good deal more expensive to produce. But Gillette did not "sell" the razor. He practically gave it away by pricing it at fifty-five cents retail or twenty cents wholesale, not much more than one-fifth of its manufacturing cost. But he designed it so that it could use only his patented blades. These cost him less than one cent apiece to make: he sold them for five cents. And since the blades could be used six or seven times, they delivered a shave at less than one cent apiece—or at less than one-tenth the cost of a visit to a barber.

What Gillette did was to price what the customer buys, namely, the shave, rather than what the manufacturer sells. In the end, the captive Gillette customer may have paid more than he would have paid had he bought a competitor's safety razor for five dollars, and then bought the competitor's blades selling at one cent or two. Gillette's customers surely knew this; customers are more intelligent than either advertising agencies or Ralph Nader believe. But Gillette's pricing made sense to them. They were paying for what they bought, that is, for a shave, rather than for a "thing." And the shave they got from the Gillette razor and the Gillette razor blade was much more pleasant than any shave they could have given themselves with that dangerous weapon, the straight-edge razor, and far cheaper than they could have gotten at the neighborhood barber's.

One reason why the patents on a copying machine ended up at a small, obscure company in Rochester, New York, then known as the Haloid Company, rather than at one of the big printing-machine manufacturers, was that none of the large established manufacturers saw any possibility of selling a copying machine. Their calculations showed that such a machine would have to sell for at least $4,000. Nobody was going to pay such a sum for a copying machine when carbon paper cost practically nothing. Also, of course, to spend $4,000 on a machine meant a capital-appropriations request, which had to go all the way up to the board of directors accompanied by a calculation showing the return on investment, both of which seemed unimaginable for a gadget to help the secretary. The Haloid Company—the present Xerox—did a good deal of technical work to design the final machine. But its major contribution was in pricing. It did not sell the machine; it sold what the machine produced, copies. At five or ten cents a copy, there is no need for a capital-appropriations .request. This is "petty cash," which the secretary can disburse without going upstairs. Pricing, the Xerox machine at five cents a copy was the true innovation.

Most suppliers, including public-service institutions, never think of pricing as a strategy. Yet pricing enables the customer to pay for what he buys—a shave, a copy of a document—rather than for what the supplier makes. What is being paid in the end is, of course, the same amount. But how it is being paid is structured to the needs and the realities of the consumer. It is structured in accordance with what the consumer actually buys. And it charges for what represents "value" to the customer rather than what represents "cost" to the supplier.

III

The Customer's Reality

The worldwide leadership of the American General Electric Company (G.E.) in large steam turbines is based on G.E.'s having thought through, in the years before World War I , what its customers' realities were. Steam turbines, unlike the piston-driven steam engines which they replaced in the generation of electric power, are complex, requiring a high degree of engineering in their design, and skill in building and fitting them. This the individual electric power company simply cannot supply. It buys a major steam turbine maybe every five or ten years when it builds a new power station. Yet the skill has to be kept in being all the time. The manufacturer, therefore, has to set up and maintain a massive consulting organization.

But, as G.E. soon found out, the customer cannot pay for consulting services. Under American law, the state public utility commissions would have to allow such an expenditure. In the opinion of the commissions, however, the companies should have been able to do this work themselves. G.E. also found that it could not add to the price of the steam turbine the cost of the consulting services which its customers needed. Again, the public utility commissions would not have accepted it. But while a steam turbine has a very long life, it needs a new set of blades fairly often, maybe every five to seven years, and these blades have to come from the maker of the original turbine. G.E. built up the world's foremost consulting engineering organization on electric power stations—though it was careful not to call this consulting engineering but "apparatus sales"—for which it did not charge. Its steam turbines were no more expensive than those of its competitors. But it put the added cost of the consulting organization plus a substantial profit into the price it charged for replacement blades. Within ten years all the other manufacturers of steam turbines had caught on and switched to the same system. But by then G.E. had world market leadership.

Much earlier, during the 1840s, a similar design of product and process to fit customer realities led to the invention of installment buying. Cyrus McCormick was one of many Americans who built a harvesting machine—the need was obvious. And he found, as had the other inventors of similar machines, that he could not sell his product. The farmer did not have the purchasing power. That the machine would earn back what it cost within two or three seasons, everybody knew and accepted, but there was no banker then who would have lent the American farmer the money to buy a machine. McCormick offered installments, to be paid out of the savings the harvester produced over the ensuing three years. The farmer could now afford to buy the machine— and he did so.

Manufacturers are wont to talk of the "irrational customer" (as do economists, psychologists, and moralists). But there are no "irrational customers." As an old saying has it, "There are only lazy manufacturers." The customer has to be assumed to be rational. His or her reality, however, is usually quite different from that of the manufacturer. The rules and regulations of public utility commissions may appear to make no sense and be purely arbitrary. For the power companies that have to operate under them, they are realities nonetheless. The American farmer may have been a better credit risk than American bankers of 1840 thought. But it was a fact that American banks of that period did not advance money to farmers to purchase equipment. The innovative strategy consists in accepting that these realities are not extraneous to the product, but *are*, in fact, the product as far as the customer is concerned. Whatever customers buy has to fit their realities, or it is of no use to them.

IV

Delivering Value to the Customer

The last of these innovative strategies delivers what is "value" to the customer rather than what is "product" to the manufacturer. It is actually only one step beyond the strategy of accepting the customer's reality as part of the product and part of what the customer buys and pays for.

A medium-sized company in America's Midwest supplies more than half of all the special lubricant needed for very large earth-moving and hauling machines: the bulldozers and draglines used by contractors building highways; the heavy equipment used to remove the overlay from strip mines; the heavy trucks used to haul coal out of coal mines; and so on. This company is in competition with some of the largest oil companies, which can mobilize whole battalions of lubrication specialists. It competes by not selling lubricating oil at all. Instead, it sells what is, in effect, insurance. What is "value" to the contractor is not lubrication: it is operating the equipment. Every hour the contractor loses because this or that piece of heavy equipment cannot operate costs him infinitely more than he spends on lubricants during an entire year. In all these activities there is a heavy penalty for contractors who miss their deadlines—and they can only get the contract by calculating the deadline as finely as possible and racing against the clock. What the Midwestern lubricant maker does is to offer contractors an analysis of the maintenance needs of their equipment. Then it offers them a maintenance program with an annual subscription price, and guarantees the subscribers that their heavy equipment will not be shut down for more than a given number of hours per year because of lubrication problems. Needless to say, the program always prescribes the manufacturer's lubricant. But this is not what contractors buy. They are buying trouble-free operations, which are extremely valuable to them.

The final example—one that might be called "moving from product to system"—is that of Herman Miller, the American furniture maker in Zeeland, Michigan. The company first became well known as the manufacturer of one of the early modern designs, the Eames chair. Then, when every other manufacturer began to turn out designer chairs, Herman Miller moved into making and selling whole offices and work stations for hospitals, both with considerable success. Finally, when the "office of the future" began to come in, Herman Miller founded a Facilities Management Institute that does not even sell furniture or equipment, but advises companies on office layout and equipment needed for the best work flow, high productivity, high employee morale, all at low cost. What Herman Miller is doing is *defining* "value" for the customer. It is telling the customer, "You may pay for furniture, but you are buying work, morale, productivity. And this is what you should therefore be paying for."

These examples are likely to be considered obvious. Surely, anybody applying a little intelligence would have come up with these and similar strategies? But the father of systematic economics, David Ricardo, is believed to have said once,

"Profits are not made by differential cleverness, but by differential stupidity." The strategies work, not because they are clever, but because most suppliers—of goods as well as of services, businesses as well as public-service institutions—do not think. They work precisely because they are so "obvious." Why, then, are they so rare? For, as these examples show, anyone who asks the question, "What does the customer really buy?" will win the race. In fact, it is not even a race since nobody else is running. What explains this?

One reason is the economists and their concept of "value." Every economics book points out that customers do not buy a "product," but what the product does for them. And then, every economics book promptly drops consideration of everything except the "price" for the product, a "price" defined as what the customer pays to take possession or ownership of a thing or a service. What the product does for the customer is never mentioned again. Unfortunately, suppliers, whether of products or of services, tend to follow the economists.

It is meaningful to say that "product A costs X dollars." It is meaningful to say that "we have to get Y dollars for the product to cover our own costs of production and have enough left over to cover the cost of capital, and thereby to show an adequate profit." But it makes no sense at all to conclude, "... and therefore the customer has to pay the lump sum of Y dollars in cash for each piece of product A he buys." Rather, the argument should go as follows: "What the customer pays for each piece of the product has to work out as Y dollars *for us*. But how the customer pays depends on what makes the most sense to him. It depends on what the product does for the customer. It depends on what fits his reality. It depends on what the customer sees as 'value.'"

Price in itself is not "pricing," and it is not "value." It was this insight that gave King Gillette a virtual monopoly on the shaving market for almost forty years; it also enabled the tiny Haloid Company to become the multibillion-dollar Xerox Company in ten years, and it gave General Electric world leadership in steam turbines. In every single case, these companies became exceedingly profitable. But they earned their profitability. They were paid for giving their customers satisfaction, for giving their customers what the customers wanted to buy, in other words, for giving their customers their money's worth.

"But this is nothing but elementary marketing," most readers will protest, and they are right. It is *nothing* but elementary marketing. To start out with the customer's utility, with what the customer buys, with what the realities of the customer are and what the customer's values are—this is what marketing is all about. But why, after forty years of preaching Marketing, teaching Marketing, professing Marketing, so few suppliers are willing to follow, I cannot explain. The fact remains that so far, anyone who is willing to use marketing as the basis for strategy is likely to acquire leadership in an industry or a market fast and almost without risk.

Entrepreneurial strategies are as important as purposeful innovation and entrepreneurial management. Together, the three make up *innovation and entrepreneurship*.

The available strategies are reasonably clear, and there are only a few of them. But it is far less easy to be specific about entrepreneurial strategies than it is about purposeful innovation and entrepreneurial management. We know what the areas are in which innovative opportunities are to be found and how they are to be analyzed. There are correct policies and practices and wrong policies and practices to make an existing business or public-service institution capable of entrepreneurship; right things to do and wrong things to do in a new venture. But the entrepreneurial strategy that fits a certain innovation is a high- risk decision. Some entrepreneurial strategies are better fits in a given situation, for example, the strategy that I called entrepreneurial judo, which is the strategy of choice where the leading businesses in an industry persist year in and year out in the same habits of arrogance and false superiority. We can describe the typical advantages and the typical limitations of certain entrepreneurial strategies.

Above all, we know that an entrepreneurial strategy has more chance of success the more it starts out with the users—their utilities, their values, their realities. An innovation is a change in market or society. It produces a greater yield for the user, greater wealth-producing capacity for society, higher value or greater satisfaction. The test of an innovation is always what it does for the user. Hence, entrepreneurship always needs to be market-focused, indeed, market-driven.

Still, entrepreneurial strategy remains the decision-making area of entrepreneurship and therefore the risk-taking one. It is by no means hunch or gamble. But it also is not precisely science. Rather, it is judgment.

The Entrepreneurial Society

I

"Every generation needs a new revolution," was Thomas Jefferson's conclusion toward the end of his long life. His contemporary, Goethe, the great German poet, though an arch-conservative, voiced the same sentiment when he sang in his old age:

Vernunft wird Unsinn
Wohltat, Plage. [⊖]

Both Jefferson and Goethe were expressing their generation's disenchantment with the legacy of Enlightenment and French Revolution. But they might just as well have reflected on our present-day legacy, 150 years later, of that great shining promise, the Welfare State, begun in Imperial Germany for the truly indigent and disabled, which has now become "everybody's entitlement" and an increasing burden on those who produce. Institutions, systems, policies eventually outlive themselves, as do products, processes, and services. They do it when they accomplish their objectives and they do it when they fail to accomplish their objectives. The mechanisms may still tick. But the assumptions on which they were designed have become invalid—as, for example, have the demographic assumptions on which health-care plans and retirement schemes were designed in all developed

---

⊖   Reason becomes nonsense, /Boons afflictions.

countries over the last hundred years. Then, indeed, reason becomes nonsense and boons afflictions.

Yet "revolutions," as we have learned since Jefferson's days, are not the remedy. They cannot be predicted, directed, or controlled. They bring to power the wrong people. Worst of all, their results—predictably —are the exact opposite of their promises. Only a few years after Jefferson's death in 1826, that great anatomist of government and politics, Alexis de Tocqueville, pointed out that revolutions do not demolish the prisons of the old regime, they enlarge them. The most lasting legacy of the French Revolution, Tocqueville proved, was the tightening of the very fetters of pre-Revolutionary France: the subjection of the whole country to an uncontrolled and uncontrollable bureaucracy, and the centralization in Paris of all political, intellectual, artistic, and economic life. The main consequences of the Russian Revolution were new serfdom for the tillers of the land, an omnipotent secret police, and a rigid, corrupt, stifling bureaucracy—the very features of the czarist regime against which Russian liberals and revolutionaries had protested most loudly and with most justification.

Indeed, we now know that "revolution" is a delusion, the pervasive delusion of the nineteenth century, but today perhaps the most discredited of its myths. We now know that,"revolution" is not achievement and the new dawn. It results from senile decay, from the bankruptcy of ideas and institutions, from failure of self-renewal.

And yet we also know that theories, values, and all the artifacts of human minds and human hands do age and rigidify, becoming obsolete, becoming "afflictions."

Innovation and entrepreneurship are thus needed in society as much as in the economy, in public-service institutions as much as in businesses. It is precisely because innovation and entrepreneurship are not "root and branch" but "one step at a time," a product here, a policy there, a public service yonder; because they are not planned but focused on this opportunity and that need; because they are tentative and will disappear if they do not produce the expected and needed results; because, in other words, they are pragmatic rather than dogmatic and modest rather than grandiose—that they promise to keep any society, economy, industry, public service, or business flexible and self-renewing. They achieve what Jefferson hoped to achieve through revolution in every generation, and they do so without bloodshed, civil war, or concentration camps, without economic catastrophe, but with purpose, with direction, and under control.

What we need is an entrepreneurial society in which innovation and entrepreneurship are normal, steady, and continuous. Just as management has become the specific organ of all contemporary institutions, and the integrating organ of our society of organizations, so innovation and entrepreneurship have to become an integral life-sustaining activity in our organizations, our economy, our society.

This requires of executives in all institutions that they make innovation and entrepreneurship a normal, ongoing, everyday activity, a practice in their own work and in that of their organization. To provide concepts and tools for this task is the purpose of this book.

II

What Will Not Work

The first priority in talking about the public policies and governmental measures needed in the entrepreneurial society is to define what will not work— especially as the policies that will not work are so popular today.

"Planning" as the term is commonly understood is actually incompatible with an entrepreneurial society and economy. Innovation does indeed need to be purposeful and entrepreneurship has to be managed. But innovation, almost by definition, has to be decentralized, *ad hoc*, autonomous, specific, and micro-economic. It had better start small, tentative, flexible. Indeed, the opportunities for innovation are found, on the whole, only way down and close to events. They are not to be found in the massive aggregates with which the planner deals of necessity, but in the deviations therefrom—in the unexpected, in the incongruity, in the difference between "The glass is half full" and "The glass is half empty," in the weak link in a process. By the time the deviation becomes "statistically significant" and thereby visible to the planner, it is too late. Innovative opportunities do not come with the tempest but with the rustling of the breeze.

It is popular today, especially in Europe, to believe that a country can have "high-tech entrepreneurship" by itself. France, West Germany, even England are basing national policies on this premise. But it is a delusion. Indeed, a policy that promotes high tech and high tech alone—and that otherwise is as hostile to entrepreneurship as France, West Germany, and even England still are—will not even produce high tech. All it can come up with is another expensive flop, another supersonic *Concorde*; a little *gloire*, oceans of red ink, but neither jobs nor technological leadership.

High tech in the first place—and this is, of course, one of the major premises of this book—is only one area of innovation and entrepreneurship. The great bulk of innovations lies in other areas. But also, a high-tech policy will run into political obstacles that will defeat it in short order. In terms of job creation, high tech is the maker of tomorrow rather than the maker of today. As we saw initially (in the Introduction), "high tech" in the United States created no more jobs in the period 1970-85 than "smokestack" lost: about five to six million. *All* the additional jobs in the American economy during that period—a total of 35 million—were created by new ventures that were not "high-tech" but "middle-tech," "low-tech," or "no-tech." The European countries, however, will be under increasing pressure to find additional jobs for a growing work force. And if then the focus in innovation and entrepreneurship is high-tech, the demand that governments abandon the high-tech policies which sacrifice the needs of today—the bolstering of the ailing industrial giants—to the uncertain promise of a high-tech future will become irresistible. In France this has been the issue over which the Communists pulled out of President Mitterand's cabinet in 1984, and the left wing of Mitterand's own Socialist Party is also increasingly unhappy and restless.

Above all, to have "high-tech" entrepreneurship alone without its being embedded in a broad entrepreneurial economy of "no-tech," "low-tech," and "middle-tech," is like having a mountaintop without the mountain. Even high-tech people in such a situation will not take jobs in new, risky, high-tech ventures. They will prefer the security of a job in the large, established, "safe" company or in a government agency. Of course, high-tech ventures need a great many people who are not themselves high-tech: accountants, salespeople, managers, and so on. In an economy that spurns entrepreneurship and innovation except for that tiny extravaganza, the "glamorous high-tech venture," those people will keep on looking for jobs and career opportunities where society and economy (i.e., their classmates, their parents, and their teachers) encourage them to look: in the large, "safe," established institution. Neither will distributors be willing to take on the products of the new venture, nor investors be willing to back it.

But the other innovative ventures are also needed to supply the capital that high tech requires. Knowledge-based innovation, and in particular high-tech innovation, has the longest lead time between investment and profitability. The world's computer industry did not break even until the late seventies, that is, after thirty loss years. To be sure, IBM made very good money quite early. And one after another of the "Seven Dwarfs," the smaller American computer makers, moved into the black during the late sixties. But these profits were offset several times over by the tremendous losses of all the others, and especially of the big old companies who failed totally in computers: General Electric, Westinghouse, ITT, and RCA in America; the (British) General Electric Company, Ferranti, and Plessey in Great Britain; Thomson- Houston in France; Siemens and Telefunken in Germany; Philips in Holland; and many others. History is repeating itself now in minicomputers and personal computers: it will be many years before the industry worldwide moves into the black. And the same thing is happening in biotechnology. This was also the pattern a hundred years ago in the electrical apparatus industry of the 1880s, for instance, or in the automobile industry of 1900 or 1910.

And during this long gestation period, non-high-tech ventures have to produce the profits to offset the losses of high tech and provide the needed capital.

The French are right, of course: economic and political strength these days requires a high-tech position, whether in information technology, in biology, or in automation. The French surely have the scientific and technical capacity. And yet it is most unlikely (I am tempted to say impossible) for any country to be innovative and entrepreneurial in high tech without having an entrepreneurial economy. High tech is indeed the leading edge, but there cannot be an edge without a knife. There cannot be a viable high-tech sector by itself any more than there can be a healthy brain in a dead body. There must be an economy full of innovators and entrepreneurs, with entrepreneurial vision and entrepreneurial values, with access to venture capital, and filled with entrepreneurial vigor.

III

The Social Innovations Needed

There are two areas in which an entrepreneurial society requires substantial social innovation.

1. The first is a policy to take care of redundant workers. The numbers are not large. But blue-collar workers in "smokestack industries" are concentrated in a very few places; three-quarters of all American automobile workers live in twenty counties, for instance. They are therefore highly visible, and they are highly organized. More important, they are ill equipped to place themselves, to redirect themselves, to move. They have neither education nor skill nor social competence — and above all not much self-confidence. They never applied for a job throughout their life; when they were ready to go to work, a relative already working in the automobile plant introduced them to the supervisor. Or the parish priest gave them a letter to one of his parishioners who was already working in the mill. And the "smokestack" workers in Great Britain—or the Welsh coal miners—are no different, nor are the blue-collar workers in Germany's Ruhr, in Lorraine, or in the Belgian Borinage. These workers are the one group in developed societies that have not experienced in this century a tremendous growth in education and horizon. In

respect to competence, experience, skill, and schooling they are pretty much where the unskilled laborer of 1900 was. The one thing that has happened to them is an explosive rise in their incomes —on balance they are the highest-paid group in industrial society if wages and benefits are added together—and in political power as well. They therefore do not have enough capacity, whether as individuals or as a group, to help themselves, but more than enough power to oppose, to veto, to impede. Unless society takes care of placing them—if only in lower-paying jobs— they must become a purely negative force.

The problem is soluble if an economy becomes entrepreneurial. For then the new businesses of the entrepreneurial economy create new jobs, as has been happening in the United States during the last ten years (which explains why the massive unemployment in the old "smokestack industries" has caused so little political trouble so far in the United States and has not even triggered a massive protectionist reaction). But even if an entrepreneurial economy creates the new jobs, there is need for organized efforts to train and place the redundant former "smokestack" workers—they cannot do it by themselves. Otherwise redundant "smokestack" labor will increasingly oppose anything new, including even the means of their own salvation. The "mini-mill" offers jobs to redundant steel workers. The automated automobile plant is the most appropriate work place for displaced automobile workers. And yet both the "mini-mill" and automation in the car factory are bitterly fought by the present workers—even though they know that their own jobs will not last. Unless we can make innovation an opportunity for redundant workers in the "smokestack" industries their feeling of impotence, their fears, their sense of being caught will lead them to resist all innovation—as is already the case in Great Britain (or in the U.S. Postal Service). The job has been done before—by the Mitsui *Zaibatsu* of Japan in the sharp Japanese Depression after the Russo- Japanese war of 1906, by the Swedes after World War II in the deliberate policy which converted a country of subsistence farmers and forest workers into an industrialized and highly prosperous nation. And the numbers are, as already said, not very large—especially as we need not concern ourselves overmuch with the one-third of the group that is fifty-five years old and older and has available adequate early-retirement provisions, and with another third that is under thirty years of age and capable of moving and of placing themselves. But the policy to train and place the remaining one-third—a small but hard core—of displaced "smokestack" workers has yet to be worked out.

2. The other social innovation needed is both more radical and more difficult and unprecedented: to organize the systematic abandonment of outworn social policies and obsolete public-service institutions. This was not a problem in the last great entrepreneurial era; a hundred years ago there were few such policies and

institutions. Now we have them in abundance. But by now we also know that few if any are for ever. Few of them even perform more than a fairly short time.

One of the fundamental changes in world view and perception of the last twenty years—a truly monumental turn—is the realization that governmental policies and agencies are of human rather than of divine origin, and that therefore the one thing certain about them is that they will become obsolete fairly fast. Yet politics is still based on the age-old assumption that whatever government does is grounded in the nature of human society and therefore "forever." As a result there is no political mechanism so far to slough off the old, the outworn, the no-longer-productive in government.

Or rather what we have is not working yet. In the United States there has lately been a rash of "sunset laws," which prescribe that a governmental agency or a public law lapse after a certain period of time unless specifically re-enacted. These laws have not worked, however— in part because there are no objective criteria as to when an agency or a law becomes dysfunctional; in part because there is so far no organized process of abandonment; but perhaps mostly because we have not yet learned to develop new or alternative methods for achieving what an ineffectual law or agency was originally supposed to achieve. To develop both the principles and the process for making "sunset laws" meaningful and effective is one of the important social innovations ahead of us—and one that needs to be made soon. Our societies are ready for it.

IV

The New Tasks

These two social policies needed are, however, only examples. Underlying them is the need for a massive reorientation in policies and attitudes, and above all, in priorities. We need to encourage habits of flexibility, of continuous learning, and of acceptance of change as normal and as opportunity—for institutions as well as for individuals.

Tax policy is one area—important both for its impact on behavior and as a symbol of society's values and priorities. In developed countries, sloughing off yesterday is at present severely penalized by the tax system. In the United States, for instance, the tax collector treats monies realized by selling or liquidating a business or a product line as income. Actually the amounts are, of course, repayments of capital. But under the present tax system the company pays corporation income tax on them. And if it distributes the proceeds to its shareholders, they pay full personal income tax on them as if they were ordinary "dividends"— that is, distribution of "profits." As a result businesses prefer not to abandon the old, the obsolescent, the no-longer-productive; they'd rather hang on to it and keep on pouring money into it. Worse still, they then assign their most capable people to "defending" the outworn in a massive misallocation of the scarcest and most valuable resource—the human resource that needs to be allocated to making tomorrow, if the company is to have a tomorrow. And when the company then finally liquidates or sells the old, obsolescent, no-longer-productive business or product line, it does not distribute the proceeds to the shareholders and does not therefore return them to the capital market where they become available for investment in innovative entrepreneurial opportunities. Rather the company keeps these funds and commonly invests them in its old, traditional, declining business or products—that is, into those parts of its operations and activities for which it could not easily raise money on the capital market—again resulting in a massive misallocation of scarce resources.

What is needed in an entrepreneurial society is a tax system that encourages moving capital from yesterday into tomorrow rather than one that, like our present one, prevents and penalizes it.

But we also should be able in and through the tax system to assuage the most pressing financial problem of the new and growing business: cash shortage. One way might be acceptance of economic reality: during the first five or six years of the life of a new, and particularly of a growing, business, "profits" are an accounting fiction. During these years the costs of staying in business are always—and almost by definition— larger for a new venture than the surplus from yesterday's operations (that is, the excess of current income over yesterday's costs). This means in effect that a new and growing venture always has to invest every penny of operating surplus to stay alive; usually, especially if growing fast, it has to invest a good deal more than it can possibly hope to produce as "current surplus" (that is, as "profit") in its current accounts. For the first few years of its life the new and growing venture —whether standing by itself or part of an existing enterprise— should therefore be exempt from income taxes, for the same reason for which we do not expect a small and rapidly growing child to produce a "surplus" that supports a grown-up. And taxes are the means by which a producer supports somebody else— namely, a nonproducer. By the way, exempting the new venture from taxation until it has "grown up" would almost certainly in the end produce a substantially higher tax yield.

If this, however, is deemed too "radical," the new venture should at least be able to postpone paying taxes on the so-called profits of its infant years. It should be able to retain the cash until it is past the period of acute cash-flow pressure, and to do so without penalty or interest charges.

All together, an entrepreneurial society and economy require tax policies that encourage the formation of capital.

Surely one "secret" of the Japanese is their officially encouraged "tax evasion" on capital formation. Legally a Japanese adult is allowed *one* medium-sized savings account the interest on which is tax-exempt. Actually Japan has five times as many such accounts as there are people in the country, children and minors included. This is, of course, a "scandal" against which newspapers and politicians rail regularly. But the Japanese are very careful not to *do* anything to "stop the abuse." As a result they have the world's highest rate of capital formation. This may be considered too circuitous a way to escape the dilemma of modern society: the conflict between the need for capital formation at a high rate and the popular condemnation of interest and dividends as "unearned income" and "capitalist," if not as sinful and wicked. But one way or another any country that wants to remain competitive in an entrepreneurial era will have to develop tax policies which do what the Japanese do by means of semi-official hypocrisy: encourage capital formation.

Just as important as tax and fiscal policies that encourage entrepreneurship— or at least do not penalize it—is protection of the new venture against the growing burden of governmental regulations, restrictions, reports, and paperwork. My own prescription, though I have no illusion of its ever being accepted, would be to allow the new venture, whether an independent enterprise or part of an existing one, to charge the government for the costs of regulations, reports, and paperwork that exceed a certain proportion (say 5 percent) of the new venture's gross revenues. This would be particularly helpful to new ventures in the public-service sector— for example, a freestanding clinic for ambulatory surgery. In developed countries public-service institutions are even more heavily burdened by governmental red tape, and even more loaded down with doing chores for the government than are businesses. And they are even less able, as a rule, to shoulder the burden whether in money or in people.

Such a policy, by the way, would be the best—perhaps the only— remedy for that dangerous and insidious disease of developed countries: the steady growth in the invisible cost of government. It is a real cost in money and, even more, in capable people, their time, and their efforts. The cost is invisible, however, since it does not show in govern- mental budgets but is hidden in the accounts of the physician whose nurse spends half her time filling out governmental forms and reports, in the budget of the university where sixteen high-level administrators work on "compliance" with governmental mandates and regulations, or in the profit-and-loss statement of the small business nineteen of whose 275 employees, while being paid by the company, actually work as tax collectors for the government, deducting taxes and Social Security contributions from the pay of their fellow workers, collecting tax-identification numbers of suppliers and customers and reporting them to the government, or, as in Europe, collecting value-added-tax (VAT). And these invisible governmental overheads are totally unproductive. Does anyone, for instance, believe that tax accountants contribute to national wealth or to productivity, and altogether add to society's wellbeing, whether material, physical or spiritual? And yet in every developed country government mandates misallocation of a steadily growing portion of our scarcest resource, able, diligent, trained people, to such essentially sterile pursuits.

It may be too much to hope that we can arrest—let alone excise— the cancer of government's invisible costs. But at least we should be able to protect the new entrepreneurial venture against it.

We need to learn to ask in respect to any proposed new governmental policy or measure: Does it further society's ability to innovate? Does it promote social and economic flexibility? Or does it impede and penalize innovation and entrepreneurship? To be sure, impact on society's ability to innovate cannot and should not be the determining, let alone the sole criterion. But it needs to be taken into consideration before a new policy or a new measure is enacted—and today it is not taken into account in any country (except perhaps in Japan) or by any policy maker.

V

The Individual in Entrepreneurial Society

In an entrepreneurial society individuals face a tremendous challenge, a challenge they need to exploit as an opportunity: the need for continuous learning and relearning.

In traditional society it could be assumed—and was assumed—that learning came to an end with adolescence or, at the latest, with adulthood. What one had not learned by age twenty-one or so, one would never learn. But also what one had learned by age twenty-one or so one would apply, unchanged, the rest of one's life. On these assumptions traditional apprenticeship was based, traditional crafts, traditional professions, but also the traditional systems of education and the schools. Crafts, professions, systems of education, and schools are still, by and large, based on these assumptions. There were, of course, always exceptions, some groups that practiced continuous learning and relearning: the great artists and the great scholars, Zen monks, mystics, the Jesuits. But these exceptions were so few that they could safely be ignored.

In an entrepreneurial society, however, these "exceptions" become the exemplars. The correct assumption in an entrepreneurial society is that individuals will have to learn new things well after they have become adults—and maybe more than once. The correct assumption is that what individuals have learned by age twenty-one will begin to become obsolete five to ten years later and will have to be replaced— or at least refurbished—by new learning, new skills, new knowledge.

One implication of this is that individuals will increasingly have to take responsibility for their own continuous learning and relearning, for their own self-development and for their own careers. They can no longer assume that what they have learned as children and youngsters will be the "foundation" for the rest of their lives. It will be the "launching pad"—the place to take off from rather than the place to build on and to rest on. They can no longer assume that they "enter upon a career" which then proceeds along a pre-determined, well-mapped and well-lighted "career path" to a known destination—what the American military calls "progressing in grade." The assumption from now on has to be that individuals on their own will have to find, determine, and develop a number of "careers" during their working lives.

And the more highly schooled the individuals, the more entrepreneurial their careers and the more demanding their learning challenges. The carpenter can still assume, perhaps, that the skills he acquired as apprentice and journeyman will serve him forty years later. Physicians, engineers, metallurgists, chemists, accountants, lawyers, teachers, managers had better assume that the skills, knowledges, and tools they will have to master and apply fifteen years hence are going to be different and new. Indeed they better assume that fifteen years hence they will be doing new and quite different things, will have new and different goals and, indeed, in many cases, different "careers." And only they themselves can take responsibility for the necessary learning and relearning, and for directing themselves. Tradition, convention, and "corporate policy" will be a hindrance rather than a help.

This also means that an entrepreneurial society challenges habits and assumptions of schooling and learning. The educational systems the world over are in the main extensions of what Europe developed in the seventeenth-century. There have been substantial additions and modifications. But the basic architectural plan on which our schools and universities are built goes back three hundred years and more. Now new, in some cases radically new, thinking and new, in some cases radically new, approaches are required, and on all levels. Using computers in preschool may turn out to be a passing fad. But four-year-olds exposed to television expect, demand, and respond to very different pedagogy than four-year-olds did fifty years ago. Young people headed for a "profession"—that is, four-fifths of today's college students—do need a "liberal education." But that clearly means something quite different from the nineteenth-century version of the seventeenth-century curriculum that passed for a "liberal education" in the English-speaking world or for *"Allgemeine Bildung"* in Germany. If this challenge is not faced up to, we risk losing the fundamental concept of a "liberal education" altogether and will descend into the purely vocational, purely specialized, which would endanger the educational foundation of the community and, in the end, community itself. But also educators will have to accept that schooling is not for the young only and that the greatest challenge—but also the greatest opportunity—for the school is the continuing relearning of already highly schooled adults.

So far we have no educational theory for these tasks. So far we have no one who does what, in the seventeenth century, the great Czech educational reformer Johann Comenius did or what the Jesuit educators did when they developed what to this day is the "modern" school and the "modern" university. But in the United States, at least, practice is far ahead of theory. To me the most positive development in the last twenty years, and the most encouraging one, is the ferment of educational experimentation in the United States—a happy by-product of the absence of a "Ministry of Education"—in respect to the continuing learning and relearning of adults, and especially of highly schooled professionals. Without a "master plan," without "educational philosophy," and, indeed, without much support from the educational establishment, the continuing education and professional development of already highly educated and highly achieving adults has become the true "growth industry" in the United States in the last twenty years.

The emergence of the entrepreneurial society may be a major turning point in history.

A hundred years ago, the worldwide panic of 1873 terminated the Century of Laissez-Faire that had begun with the publication of Adam Smith's *The Wealth of Nations* in 1776. In the Panic of 1873 the modern welfare state was born. A hundred years later it had run its course, almost everyone now knows. It may survive despite the demographic challenges of an aging population and a shrinking birthrate. But it will survive only if the entrepreneurial economy succeeds in greatly raising productivities. We may even still make a few minor additions to the welfare edifice, put on a room here or a new benefit there. But the welfare state is past rather than future—as even the old liberals now know.

Will its successor be the Entrepreneurial Society?

Suggested Readings

Most of the literature on entrepreneurship is anecdotal and of the "Look, Ma, no hands" variety. The best of that genre may be the book by George Gilder: *The Spirit of Enterprise* (New York: Simon & Schuster, 1984). It consists mainly of stories of individuals who have founded new businesses; there is little discussion of what one can learn from their example. The book limits itself to new small businesses and omits discussion of entrepreneurship in both the existing business and the public-service institution. But at least Gilder does not make the mistake of confining entrepreneurship to high tech.

Far more useful to the entrepreneur—and to those who want to understand entrepreneurship—are the studies by Karl H. Vesper of the University of Washington in Seattle, Washington, especially his *New Venture Strategy* (Englewood Cliffs, N.J.: Prentice-Hall, 1980), and his annual publication, *Frontiers of Entrepreneurship Research* (Babson Park, Mass.: Babson College). Vesper, too, confines himself to the new and especially to the small business. But within these limits, his stimulating works are full of insights and practical wisdom.

The Center for Entrepreneurial Management (83 Spring Street, New York, N.Y. 10012), founded and directed by Joseph R. Mancuso, focuses entirely on "How to Do It" in the small business, as does Mancuso's well-known text *How to Start, Finance and Manage Your Own Small Business* (Englewood Cliffs, N.J.: Prentice-Hall, 1978).

Entrepreneurial management in the existing and especially in the large business is the subject of two very different books that complement each other. Andrew S. Grove, one of the founders and now the president of Intel Corporation, discusses the policies and practices needed to maintain entrepreneurship in the business that has grown fast and to large size in his *High-Output Management* (New

York: Random House, 1983). Rosabeth M. Kanter, an organizational psychologist at Yale University, discusses the attitudes and behavior of corporate leaders in entrepreneurial companies in her book *The Change Masters* (New York: Simon & Schuster, 1983). By far the most penetrating discussion of entrepreneurship in existing businesses is the almost inaccessible article by two members of the consulting firm of McKinsey & Company, Richard E. Cavenaugh and Donald K. Clifford, Jr.: "Lessons from America's Mid-Sized Growth Companies," *McKinsey Quarterly* (Autumn 1983). Publication of a book by the same authors, based on the article and the study on which it reports, is expected in 1985 or 1986.

Of the many books on strategy, the most useful may be Michael Porter's *Competitive Strategies* (New York: Free Press, 1980).

In my own earlier works, entrepreneurship and entrepreneurial management are discussed in *Managing for Results* (New York: Harper & Row, 1964), especially Chapters 1-5, and in *Management. Tasks, Responsibilities, Practices* (New York: Harper & Row, 1973), Chapters 11-14 (The Service Institution) and Chapters 53-61 (Strategies and Structures).

樊登　樊登读书创办人

《创新与企业家精神》是樊登读书在 2017 年解读的一本书。关于企业创新、创业，管理学大师、现代管理学之父德鲁克早在 30 多年前，就提出了许多洞见。真正的智慧不会因岁月褪色，穿越时光，反而熠熠生辉，这就是经典的魅力。

冯仑　御风集团董事长，万通集团创始人

《创新与企业家精神》中讲到了很多优秀的企业家，当今中国也拥有着一批"爱折腾"的企业家，他们通过创新改变世界，把世界变得更加美好。创业需要承担很多责任和风险，德鲁克先生在书中提到的方法和原则，给企业家提供了一个很好的"做强做大""做精做久"的参考。非常推荐大家进行阅读。

刘润　中国知名商业顾问，润米咨询创始人，微软前战略合作总监

如果世界一成不变，后起者哪有机会？不确定性、不连续性，是一切机会的源头。可是，怎么抓住机会？唯有去创新，去做一成不变的世界的统治者没有做到，甚至没有做过的事情。德鲁克在这本书里，系统性地阐述了 7 种创新机会源、4 种方法，以及能够大胆创新的人（也就是"企业家"）的核心特征。这本书是真正的经典，值得每一位在路上的创业者，仔细阅读。

刘永好　新希望集团董事长

传统企业实现转型的关键是需要通过"组织再造＋数字化转型"实现

创新，从而全面提升企业竞争力，进而迈向新商业文明。《创新与企业家精神》不仅谈到了产品创新，还涉及管理的创新、企业文化的创新、员工意识的转变，这其实就是组织再造的过程。德鲁克的这本经典作品给传统企业甚至互联网企业都会带来启发。愿创新意识和企业家精神在中国企业家群体里常见常新。

秦朔　人文财经观察家，秦朔朋友圈、中国商业文明研究中心发起人

德鲁克的《创新与企业家精神》，不仅深刻阐述了企业家精神的重要性，而且把企业家精神延伸到整个社会的范畴。创新不仅是企业家的灵魂，也是社会生生不息向前发展的动力。

滕斌圣　长江商学院副院长、战略学教授

能常读常新的书不多，即为经典。彼得·德鲁克先生著作等身，本书为其代表之一。经典如陈年普洱，浮华尽去，细品沁人心脾。创新难以总结，但德鲁克的深刻不靠时髦概念，而用贴切故事，条分缕析，揭示贯穿的脉络，令人惊奇。

田涛　著名管理学家，华为公司国际咨询委员会顾问，浙江大学睿华创新管理研究所联席所长

当全社会都在为企业家精神的匮乏和创新困顿而焦虑时，管理学者和企业家不妨一群人围坐一起，打开德鲁克的《创新与企业家精神》，放声朗读，激情讨论，理性辩论，然后付诸行动。德翁眼中的企业家精神不是被神化了的非侠即雄，他认知中的"创新"亦非遥不可及的"镜中之花"。"管理是一种信仰"，始于信，终于行；企业家精神则始于无处不在的创新，终于资源收益率的改变和提升。

向松祚　五卷本《新经济学》作者

德鲁克对创新和企业家精神的研究不局限于企业家个体，也不局限于营利性企业，而是扩展到包括大学和宗教组织等非营利性机构。他试图深入回答的一个基本问题是：为什么一些机构具有令人惊叹的创新活力；而许多企业和非营利机构却毫无创新活力？拙著《新经济学》第四卷和第五卷从另外一个视角深入讨论了德鲁克所提出的重大课题。《创新与企业家精神》是常读常新的经典名著，值得所有企业家、政府官员、管理学者和经济学者仔细品读、认真思考、努力实践。

徐少春 金蝶国际软件集团有限公司、董事会主席兼首席执行官

彼得·德鲁克先生是现代管理学的珠峰，也一直是我学习和研究管理的启蒙大师。《创新与企业家精神》告诉我，管理者不应该仅仅解决问题，而更应该专注于寻找创新机会，这让我获益匪浅。

杨斌 清华大学经济管理学院领导力研究中心主任

企业家精神，绝非企业家专属。德鲁克的这本书，思想性强，毫不过时。工商业的人应该读一读，工商业之外的人更应该读一读，并对理解和推动各种各类的创新，对促进大批创新人才的脱颖而出，反躬自省，身体力行。

张瑞敏 海尔集团董事局主席、首席执行官

德鲁克是永恒的，因他对问题的真知灼见会让你回味无穷，终身受益。初读本书时，一句"企业家精神就是视变化为常规"激励我在 30 多年的市场变幻中不懈地打造海尔品牌。

今天，书中的"成功的企业家"不是"专注于风险"而是"专注于机会"又让我抓住互联网的机遇，以"人单合一"的模式让每个员工都拥有企业家精神。

赵曙明 南京大学资深教授、商学院名誉院长、行知书院院长、博士生导师、德鲁克论坛创始人

创新是这个时代最鲜明的特征，人们对创新的重要性深信不疑，同时也赋予了创新种种神秘的色彩。管理学大师德鲁克在《创新与企业家精神》这本书里面，根据一些创新、创业案例，首次将创新与企业家精神视为所有企业和机构有组织、有目的、有系统的工作，并归纳总结了 7 个创新机会源，从而为我们揭开了创新的神秘面纱。至于如何创新，在这本书里你会找到答案。

推荐阅读

欧洲管理经典 全套精装

欧 洲 最 有 影 响 的 管 理 大 师
（奥） 弗雷德蒙德·马利克 著

ISBN: 978-7-111-56451-5　　　ISBN: 978-7-111-56616-8　　　ISBN: 978-7-111-58389-9

转变：应对复杂新世界的思维方式

作者：应秋月 ISBN: 978-7-111-56451-5定价：40.00元

在这个巨变的时代，不学会转变，错将是你的常态，
这个世界将会残酷惩罚不转变的人。

管理：技艺之精髓

ISBN: 978-7-111-59327-0 定价：59.00元

帮助管理者和普通员工更加专业、更有成效地完成
其职业生涯中各种极具挑战性的任务。

公司策略与公司治理：如何进行自我管理

ISBN: 978-7-111-59322-5 定价：59.00元

公司治理的工具箱，
帮助企业创建自我管理的良好生态系统。

正确的公司治理:发挥公司监事会的效率应对复杂情况

ISBN: 978-7-111-59321-8 定价：59.00元

基于30年的实践与研究，指导企业避免短期行为，
打造后劲十足的健康企业。

战略：应对复杂新世界的导航仪

ISBN: 978-7-111-56616-8 定价：60.00元

制定和实施战略的系统工具，
有效帮助组织明确发展方向。

管理成就生活（原书第2版）

ISBN: 978-7-111-58389-9 定价：69.00元

写给那些希望做好管理的人、希望提升绩效的人、
希望过上高品质的生活的人。不管处在什么职位，
人人都要讲管理，出效率，过好生活。

读者交流QQ群：84565875

彼得·德鲁克全集

序号	书名	要点提示
1	工业人的未来 The Future of Industrial Man	工业社会三部曲之一，帮助读者理解工业社会的基本单元——企业及其管理的全貌
2	公司的概念 Concept of the Corporation	工业社会三部曲之一揭示组织如何运行，它所面临的挑战、问题和遵循的基本原理
3	新社会 The New Society：The Anatomy of Industrial Order	工业社会三部曲之一，堪称一部预言，书中揭示的趋势在短短10几年间变成了现实，体现了德鲁克在管理、社会、政治、历史和心理方面的高度智慧
4	管理的实践 The Practice of Management	德鲁克因为这本书开创了管理"学科"，奠定了现代管理学之父的地位
5	已经发生的未来 Landmarks of Tomorrow：A Report on the New "Post-Modern" World	论述了"后现代"新世界的思想转变，阐述了世界面临的四个现实性挑战，关注人类存在的精神实质
6	为成果而管理 Managing for Results	探讨企业为创造经济绩效和经济成果，必须完成的经济任务
7	卓有成效的管理者 The Effective Executive	彼得·德鲁克最为畅销的一本书，谈个人管理,包含了目标管理与时间管理等决定个人是否能卓有成效的关键问题
8 ☆	不连续的时代 The Age of Discontinuity	应对社会巨变的行动纲领，德鲁克洞察未来的巅峰之作
9 ☆	面向未来的管理者 Preparing Tomorrow's Business Leaders Today	德鲁克编辑的文集，探讨商业系统和商学院五十年的结构变化，以及成为未来的商业领袖需要做哪些准备
10 ☆	技术与管理 Technology，Management and Society	从技术及其历史说起，探讨从事工作之人的问题，旨在启发人们如何努力使自己变得卓有成效
11 ☆	人与商业 Men，Ideas，and Politics	侧重商业与社会，把握根本性的商业变革、思想与行为之间的关系，在结构复杂的组织中发挥领导力
12	管理：使命、责任、实践（实践篇） Management:Tasks,Responsibilities,Practices	
13	管理：使命、责任、实践（使命篇） Management:Tasks,Responsibilities,Practices	为管理者提供一套指引管理者实践的条理化"认知体系"
14	管理：使命、责任、实践（责任篇） Management:Tasks,Responsibilities,Practices	
15	养老金革命 The Pension Fund Revolution	探讨人口老龄化社会下，养老金革命给美国经济带来的影响
16	人与绩效：德鲁克论管理精华 People and Performance: The Best of Peter Drucker on Management	广义文化背景中，管理复杂而又不断变化的维度与任务，提出了诸多开创性意见
17 ☆	认识管理 An Introductory View of Management	德鲁克写给步入管理殿堂者的通识入门书
18	德鲁克经典管理案例解析（纪念版） Management Cases(Revised Edition)	提出管理中10个经典场景，将管理原理应用于实践

彼得·德鲁克全集

序号	书名	要点提示
19	旁观者：管理大师德鲁克回忆录 Adventures of a Bystander	德鲁克回忆录
20	动荡时代的管理 Managing in Turbulent Times	在动荡的商业环境中，高管理层、中级管理层和一线主管应该做什么
21 ☆	迈向经济新纪元 Toward the Next Economics and Other Essays	社会动态变化及其对企业等组织机构的影响
22 ☆	时代变局中的管理者 The Changing World of the Executive	管理者的角色内涵的变化、他们的任务和使命、面临的问题和机遇以及他们的发展趋势
23	最后的完美世界 The Last of All Possible Worlds	德鲁克生平仅著两部小说之一
24	行善的诱惑 The Temptation to Do Good	德鲁克生平仅著两部小说之一
25	创新与企业家精神 Innovation and Entrepreneurship:Practice and Principles	探讨创新的原则，使创新成为提升绩效的利器
26	管理前沿 The Frontiers of Management	德鲁克对未来企业成功经营策略和方法的预测
27	管理新现实 The New Realities	理解世界政治、政府、经济、信息技术和商业的必读之作
28	非营利组织的管理 Managing the Non-Profit Organization	探讨非营利组织如何实现社会价值
29	管理未来 Managing for the Future:The 1990s and Beyond	解决经理人身边的经济、人、管理、组织等企业内外的具体问题
30 ☆	生态愿景 The Ecological Vision	对个人与社会关系的探讨，对经济、技术、艺术的审视等
31 ☆	知识社会 Post-Capitalist Society	探索与分析了我们如何从一个基于资本、土地和劳动力的社会，转向一个以知识作为主要资源、以组织作为核心结构的社会
32	巨变时代的管理 Managing in a Time of Great Change	德鲁克探讨变革时代的管理与管理者、组织面临的变革与挑战、世界区域经济的力量和趋势分析、政府及社会管理的洞见
33	德鲁克看中国与日本：德鲁克对话"日本商业圣手"中内功 Drucker on Asia	明确指出了自由市场和自由企业，中日两国等所面临的挑战，个人、企业的应对方法
34	德鲁克论管理 Peter Drucker on the Profession of Management	德鲁克发表于《哈佛商业评论》的文章精心编纂，聚焦管理问题的"答案之书"
35	21世纪的管理挑战 Management Challenges for the 21st Century	德鲁克从6大方面深刻分析管理者和知识工作者个人正面临的挑战
36	德鲁克管理思想精要 The Essential Drucker	从德鲁克60年管理工作经历和作品中精心挑选、编写而成，德鲁克管理思想的精髓
37	下一个社会的管理 Managing in the Next Society	探讨管理者如何利用这些人口因素与信息革命的巨变，知识工作者的崛起等变化，将之转变成企业的机会
38	功能社会：德鲁克自选集 A Functioning society	汇集了德鲁克在社区、社会和政治结构领域的观点
39 ☆	德鲁克演讲实录 The Drucker Lectures	德鲁克60年经典演讲集锦，感悟大师思想的发展历程
40	管理(原书修订版) Management(Revised Edition)	融入了德鲁克于1974～2005年间有关管理的著述
41	卓有成效管理者的实践（纪念版） The Effective Executive in Action	一本教你做正确的事，继而实现卓有成效的日志笔记本式作品

注：序号有标记的书是新增引进翻译出版的作品